JOHN

THE NIV
APPLICATION
COMMENTARY

From biblical text . . . to contemporary life

THE NIV APPLICATION COMMENTARY SERIES

EDITORIAL BOARD

General Editor
Terry Muck

Consulting Editors
New Testament

Eugene Peterson   *Scot McKnight*

Marianne Meye Thompson   *Klyne Snodgrass*

Zondervan Editorial Advisors

Stanley N. Gundry
Vice President and Editor-in-Chief

Jack Kuhatschek   *Verlyn Verbrugge*
Senior Acquisitions Editor   Senior Editor

JOHN

THE NIV APPLICATION COMMENTARY

From biblical text . . . to contemporary life

GARY M. BURGE

ZONDERVAN.com/
AUTHORTRACKER
follow your favorite authors

 **ZONDERVAN®**

The NIV Application Commentary: John
Copyright © 2000 by Gary M. Burge

Requests for information should be addressed to:

Zondervan, *Grand Rapids, Michigan 49530*

Library of Congress Cataloging-in-Publication Data

Burge, Gary M., 1952–
    John / Gary M. Burge.
        p. cm.—(The NIV application commentary)
    Includes bibliographical references and indexes.
    ISBN-10: 0-310-49750-7
    ISBN-13: 978-0-310-49750-9
    1. Bible. N.T. John—Commentaries. I. Title. II. Series.
BS2615.3.B79 2000
226.5'077 — dc21   00-033383

This edition printed on acid-free paper.

Printed in the United States of America

10 11 12 13 14 15 • 20 19 18 17 16 15 14

To my daughters

Ashley and Grace

Contents

The NIV Application Commentary Series

When complete, the NIV Application Commentary
will include the following volumes:

Old Testament Volumes

Genesis, John H. Walton
Exodus, Peter Enns
Leviticus/Numbers, Roy Gane
Deuteronomy, Daniel I. Block
Joshua, Robert L. Hubbard Jr.
Judges/Ruth, K. Lawson Younger
1-2 Samuel, Bill T. Arnold
1-2 Kings, Gus Konkel
1-2 Chronicles, Andrew E. Hill
Ezra/Nehemiah, Douglas J. Green
Esther, Karen H. Jobes
Job, Dennis R. Magary
Psalms Volume 1, Gerald H. Wilson
Psalms Volume 2, Jamie A. Grant
Proverbs, Paul Koptak
Ecclesiastes/Song of Songs, Iain Provan
Isaiah, John N. Oswalt
Jeremiah/Lamentations, J. Andrew Dearman
Ezekiel, Iain M. Duguid
Daniel, Tremper Longman III
Hosea/Amos/Micah, Gary V. Smith
Jonah/Nahum/Habakkuk/Zephaniah,
    James Bruckner
Joel/Obadiah/Malachi, David W. Baker
Haggai/Zechariah, Mark J. Boda

New Testament Volumes

Matthew, Michael J. Wilkins
Mark, David E. Garland
Luke, Darrell L. Bock
John, Gary M. Burge
Acts, Ajith Fernando
Romans, Douglas J. Moo
1 Corinthians, Craig Blomberg
2 Corinthians, Scott Hafemann
Galatians, Scot McKnight
Ephesians, Klyne Snodgrass
Philippians, Frank Thielman
Colossians/Philemon, David E. Garland
1-2 Thessalonians, Michael W. Holmes
1-2 Timothy/Titus, Walter L. Liefeld
Hebrews, George H. Guthrie
James, David P. Nystrom
1 Peter, Scot McKnight
2 Peter/Jude, Douglas J. Moo
Letters of John, Gary M. Burge
Revelation, Craig S. Keener

To see which titles are available,
visit our web site at http://www.zondervan.com

NIV Application Commentary
Series Introduction

THE NIV APPLICATION COMMENTARY SERIES is unique. Most commentaries help us make the journey from our world back to the world of the Bible. They enable us to cross the barriers of time, culture, language, and geography that separate us from the biblical world. Yet they only offer a one-way ticket to the past and assume that we can somehow make the return journey on our own. Once they have explained the *original meaning* of a book or passage, these commentaries give us little or no help in exploring its *contemporary significance*. The information they offer is valuable, but the job is only half done.

Recently, a few commentaries have included some contemporary application as *one* of their goals. Yet that application is often sketchy or moralistic, and some volumes sound more like printed sermons than commentaries.

The primary goal of the NIV Application Commentary Series is to help you with the difficult but vital task of bringing an ancient message into a modern context. The series not only focuses on application as a finished product but also helps you think through the *process* of moving from the original meaning of a passage to its contemporary significance. These are commentaries, not popular expositions. They are works of reference, not devotional literature.

The format of the series is designed to achieve the goals of the series. Each passage is treated in three sections: *Original Meaning, Bridging Contexts,* and *Contemporary Significance.*

THIS SECTION HELPS you understand the meaning of the biblical text in its original context. All of the elements of traditional exegesis—in concise form—are discussed here. These include the historical, literary, and cultural context of the passage. The authors discuss matters related to grammar and syntax and the meaning of biblical words.[1] They also seek to explore the main ideas of the passage and how the biblical author develops those ideas.

---

1. Please note that in general, when the authors discuss words in the original biblical languages, the series uses a general rather than a scholarly method of transliteration.

After reading this section, you will understand the problems, questions, and concerns of the *original audience* and how the biblical author addressed those issues. This understanding is foundational to any legitimate application of the text today.

THIS SECTION BUILDS a bridge between the world of the Bible and the world of today, between the original context and the contemporary context, by focusing on both the timely and timeless aspects of the text.

God's Word is *timely*. The authors of Scripture spoke to specific situations, problems, and questions. The author of Joshua encouraged the faith of his original readers by narrating the destruction of Jericho, a seemingly impregnable city, at the hands of an angry warrior God (Josh. 6). Paul warned the Galatians about the consequences of circumcision and the dangers of trying to be justified by law (Gal. 5:2–5). The author of Hebrews tried to convince his readers that Christ is superior to Moses, the Aaronic priests, and the Old Testament sacrifices. John urged his readers to "test the spirits" of those who taught a form of incipient Gnosticism (1 John 4:1–6). In each of these cases, the timely nature of Scripture enables us to hear God's Word in situations that were *concrete* rather than abstract.

Yet the timely nature of Scripture also creates problems. Our situations, difficulties, and questions are not always directly related to those faced by the people in the Bible. Therefore, God's word to them does not always seem relevant to us. For example, when was the last time someone urged you to be circumcised, claiming that it was a necessary part of justification? How many people today care whether Christ is superior to the Aaronic priests? And how can a "test" designed to expose incipient Gnosticism be of any value in a modern culture?

Fortunately, Scripture is not only timely but *timeless*. Just as God spoke to the original audience, so he still speaks to us through the pages of Scripture. Because we share a common humanity with the people of the Bible, we discover a *universal dimension* in the problems they faced and the solutions God gave them. The timeless nature of Scripture enables it to speak with power in every time and in every culture.

Those who fail to recognize that Scripture is both timely and timeless run into a host of problems. For example, those who are intimidated by timely books such as Hebrews, Galatians, or Deuteronomy might avoid reading them because they seem meaningless today. At the other extreme, those who are convinced of the timeless nature of Scripture, but who fail to discern its timely element, may "wax eloquent" about the Melchizedekian priesthood to a sleeping congregation, or worse still, try to apply the holy wars of the Old Testament in a physical way to God's enemies today.

The purpose of this section, therefore, is to help you discern what is timeless in the timely pages of the Bible—and what is not. For example, how do the holy wars of the Old Testament relate to the spiritual warfare of the New? If Paul's primary concern is not circumcision (as he tells us in Gal. 5:6), what *is* he concerned about? If discussions about the Aaronic priesthood or Melchizedek seem irrelevant today, what is of abiding value in these passages? If people try to "test the spirits" today with a test designed for a specific first-century heresy, what other biblical test might be more appropriate?

Yet this section does not merely uncover that which is timeless in a passage but also helps you to see *how* it is uncovered. The authors of the commentaries seek to take what is implicit in the text and make it explicit, to take a process that normally is intuitive and explain it in a logical, orderly fashion. How do we know that circumcision is not Paul's primary concern? What clues in the text or its context help us realize that Paul's real concern is at a deeper level?

Of course, those passages in which the historical distance between us and the original readers is greatest require a longer treatment. Conversely, those passages in which the historical distance is smaller or seemingly nonexistent require less attention.

One final clarification. Because this section prepares the way for discussing the contemporary significance of the passage, there is not always a sharp distinction or a clear break between this section and the one that follows. Yet when both sections are read together, you should have a strong sense of moving from the world of the Bible to the world of today.

THIS SECTION ALLOWS the biblical message to speak with as much power today as it did when it was first written. How can you apply what you learned about Jerusalem, Ephesus, or Corinth to our present-day needs in Chicago, Los Angeles, or London? How can you take a message originally spoken in Greek, Hebrew, and Aramaic and communicate it clearly in our own language? How can you take the eternal truths originally spoken in a different time and culture and apply them to the similar-yet-different needs of our culture?

In order to achieve these goals, this section gives you help in several key areas.

(1) It helps you identify contemporary situations, problems, or questions that are truly comparable to those faced by the original audience. Because

contemporary situations are seldom identical to those faced by the original audience, you must seek situations that are analogous if your applications are to be relevant.

(2) This section explores a variety of contexts in which the passage might be applied today. You will look at personal applications, but you will also be encouraged to think beyond private concerns to the society and culture at large.

(3) This section will alert you to any problems or difficulties you might encounter in seeking to apply the passage. And if there are several legitimate ways to apply a passage (areas in which Christians disagree), the author will bring these to your attention and help you think through the issues involved.

In seeking to achieve these goals, the contributors to this series attempt to avoid two extremes. They avoid making such specific applications that the commentary might quickly become dated. They also avoid discussing the significance of the passage in such a general way that it fails to engage contemporary life and culture.

Above all, contributors to this series have made a diligent effort not to sound moralistic or preachy. The NIV Application Commentary Series does not seek to provide ready-made sermon materials but rather tools, ideas, and insights that will help you communicate God's Word with power. If we help you to achieve that goal, then we have fulfilled the purpose for this series.

The Editors

General Editor's Preface

IN SOME WAYS John's Gospel functions as both a gospel and a letter. As a gospel it tells the story of Jesus, of his role as revealer of God the Father and provider of redemption to all humanity. As a letter it encouraged first-century Christians in the life they had chosen (and it encourages us today), showing how life in Christ differed from Judaism and Gnosticism. It corrected some followers of John the Baptist who didn't quite get who the Baptizer was in relation to Jesus. As Gary Burge shows in this fine commentary, the Gospel of John narrates the life of Jesus and teaches what that life meant to those who knew him or had heard about him.

This dual purpose lends itself particularly well to one of the principle emphases of the book of John—Christology. Christology is the doctrine that studies the person and work of Christ. Needless to say, "Christology" was not a "doctrine" in John's day. Jesus had come among them. He had done signs that revealed God's plan of redemption to them in public settings around Galilee and Jerusalem. He taught those who chose to follow him, and they were with him when he encountered resistance and was crucified. He was raised from the dead. Yet in spite of the miraculous signs, pointed teachings, and resurrection (the raw data out of which Christology was shaped), it took hundreds of years for the church to come to some agreement about Jesus' incarnation—his humanity and divinity. The Gospel of John is in many ways the first reflection on his incarnated nature.

Little wonder, then, that the Gospel of John has been used to support the misplaced emphases that such a difficult teaching can fall prey to—and that it is still used to support mistaken impressions of who Jesus was. The present book is valuable today because in talking about who Jesus was, it resonates so clearly with spiritual needs common to our twenty-first century world.

For example, one of those needs is to be assured that Jesus was indeed the Son of God. Our faith rests on it. Although some suggest that we could better identify with a purely human Jesus, such a teaching would result in a much different religion—call it Jesusianity—that would do little to meet our needs for God. True, Christ's divinity can be overemphasized if it ignores his humanity. Some early Christians did precisely that, saying that Christ was only divine and that his fleshly body was an illusion. That position (often called adoptionism), however, overlooks a second, balancing teaching in John regarding Christ's humanity. We need a human Jesus with whom to identify. But such a Jesus can only help us if he also has the power of God as part of his make-up. Jesus Christ needs to be both human and divine.

Jesus' power to help us comes through another teaching of the book, the power of the Holy Spirit. The author makes clear that Jesus was filled with Holy Spirit power and that when he left the earth, the power of that Holy Spirit remained with us, accessible to us all to enable us to reach out to God.

An adequate Christology needs all of these elements today: a human Christ to redeem us, a divine Christ to reveal God's nature, and a powerful, Spirit-filled Christ to help us lead holy lives. The Gospel/letter of John provides all three—and it does so in a mysterious, literate way that beguiles and reveals as it pulls us deeper and deeper into the mystery of who God is.

Arguably the best-known passage in this book is the prologue, the first eighteen verses of John 1, where the author invites us to join in a poetic witness of intellectual praise to who Jesus was. The prologue tells us that Jesus was God, the *logos* or "Word [that] was with God, and the Word was God. He was with God in the beginning." But the Word was more than God: "The Word became flesh and made his dwelling among us."

That's a summation of Christology. It tells us who Jesus was. It is the distinctive teaching of our faith, and the world has never needed it more than now. The Gospel of John tells us the story.

Terry C. Muck

Author's Preface

THE GOSPEL OF JOHN has always been the "beloved Gospel" of the church. Every pastor knows that a series of sermons from John—or an adult education course on John—will be greeted with enthusiasm. I have asked audiences to tell me their favorite verses from the Gospels, and they will always recite a dozen or more from John's Gospel. "For God so loved the world. . . ." "I am the resurrection and the life. . . ." "In my Father's house are many rooms. . . ." John *is* the beloved Gospel because John probes the depth of Christ's character with a simplicity and majesty that cannot be forgotten. This is why, perhaps, this Gospel gained a reputation (thanks to Clement of Alexandria) for being the "spiritual Gospel." And why medieval scribes symbolized the Gospel with an eagle. Profundity is matched with clarity in a manner not found elsewhere in the New Testament. When the earliest theological councils in the fourth and fifth centuries worked to define Christian beliefs about the Trinity and the Incarnation, it was John's Gospel that gave critical guidance.

My initial interest in the writings of John came almost twenty years ago when I began a doctoral program in Scotland under the mentorship of Prof. I. Howard Marshall. I now realize that my present instincts for the wedding of history and theology in this Gospel were shaped under Dr. Marshall's wise leadership. I will always be in his debt. That early study on John's view of the Spirit (published in 1987) launched a fascination with the Gospel that has not ended. A variety of articles, a seminary primer on John (1992, 1998[2]), and a commentary on John's three letters in the present NIV Application Commentary series (1996) have each permitted me to pursue these interests further. The present commentary is written for the pastor/teacher laboring in the church. I have always kept in mind the man or woman who works week after week feeding the flock of Christ from pulpit and lectern. If this book brings some gift of insight or inspiration, I will be deeply gratified.

While every commentary should provide solid exegesis to get at John's original meaning, this series posed a new challenge. Each chapter explains how John's ancient text can be "bridged" to the present modern context. Then specific examples are given that show how these passages can be applied in preaching and teaching. Most commentaries give cursory attention to modern application, but in this series writers have been challenged not only to show examples of application but to explain the interpretive (or hermeneutical) method at work. This task was the most difficult—and the most exhilarating aspect of writing. Like never before, I became aware of the power and relevance of this Gospel for our present age.

It remains to thank many who have rendered remarkable support over the course of two years of writing. Marianne Meye Thompson and Terry Muck read the manuscript with great care, providing countless corrections and advice. They improved the commentary immeasurably. At Zondervan Publishing Jack Kuhatschek wins the award for the most patient editor. And Verlyn Verbrugge's expert editorial skill has helped the manuscript on every page. Finally, special thanks are due to Ashley Burge, who compiled the Scripture index with care and accuracy—a difficult task indeed.

Much of my research was completed during a sabbatical in 1998, when I worked at Tyndale Library in Cambridge, England. To be surrounded by one of Europe's best theological libraries with its tremendously helpful staff has to be every writer's dream. Special thanks belong to Tyndale's administrative staff: Bruce Winter (Warden), Fiona Craig, Denise Jillions, and Bruce Longenecker; to Lyn Winter, for her cheerful hospitality and advice about British cooking and ironmongers; and in the library to David Instone Brewer and Kirsty Corrigall, who were never too busy to help track down obscure articles or rabbinic texts. Above all, I owe my greatest debt to my wife, Carol, whose unending support has always sustained and encouraged me.

Most of my students know that J. B. Lightfoot will always remain one of my personal heroes. Born in 1828, Lightfoot's gifts of intellect were quickly recognized at Trinity College, Cambridge, where he was tutored in classics by B. F. Westcott. From 1859 till 1879 he taught at Cambridge, defending the historicity of the New Testament against "new" historical criticism coming from Tübingen, Germany.[1] In 1879 Lightfoot became Bishop of Durham, which meant leaving the academy and ministering in the church. From 1879 till his death in 1889 he lived at Auckland Castle and over the years discipled eighty-six young men who lived at the castle with him and became "sons of Auckland"—or perhaps more accurately, sons of "the Bishop."[2]

John's Gospel was deeply important to Lightfoot. He recognized its theological value for the theology of the church and defended its historicity when many other voices gave John limited serious attention. But above all, John's Gospel fed this great scholar's soul. Lightfoot summed up its value in a lecture given in 1871, and his words are a fitting reminder of the treasure this Gospel offers to any who study it:

---

1. To this day, the postgraduate New Testament seminar at Cambridge University meets in the "Lightfoot Room," under an imposing portrait of the scholar.
2. See G. R. Eden and F. C. MacDonald, ed., *Lightfoot of Durham Memories and Appreciations* (Cambridge: Cambridge Univ. Press, 1932) The motto of the fellowship was ἀνδρίζεσθε κραταιοῦσθε ("be courageous, be strong"), taken from 1 Cor. 16:13.

I believe from my heart that the truth which [St. John's] Gospel more especially enshrines—the truth that Jesus Christ is the very Word incarnate, the manifestation of the Father to mankind—is the one lesson which duly apprehended will do more than all our feeble efforts to purify and elevate human life here by imparting to it hope and light and strength; the one study which alone can fitly prepare us for a joyful immortality hereafter.[3]

Gary M. Burge
Epiphany, 2000
Wheaton, Illinois

---

3. J. B. Lightfoot, *Biblical Essays* (London: MacMillan, 1893), 44.

Abbreviations

AB	Anchor Bible
ABD	*Anchor Bible Dictionary*
ABR	*Australian Biblical Review*
ASV	American Standard Version
b.	*Babylonian Talmud*
BA	*Biblical Archaeologist*
BAR	*Biblical Archaeology Review*
BAGD	Bauer, Arndt, Gingrich, Danker, *A Greek-English Lexicon of the New Testament*
BBC	Broadman Bible Commentaries
BDF	Blass, Debrunner, Funk, *A Greek Grammar of the New Testament*
Bib	*Biblica*
BBR	*Bulletin for Biblical Research*
BSac	*Bibliotheca sacra*
BSC	The Bible Speaks Today
BTB	*Biblical Theology Bulletin*
BZ	*Biblische Zeitschrift*
CBQ	*Catholic Biblical Quarterly*
EBC	Expositor's Bible Commentary
EGNT	Expositor's Greek New Testament
ETL	*Ephemerides theologicae lovanienses*
EvQ	*Evangelical Quarterly*
ExpTim	*Expository Times*
IBS	*Irish Biblical Studies*
IEJ	*Israel Exploration Journal*
IRM	*International Review of Missions*
ISBE	*International Standard Bible Encyclopedia*
ICC	International Critical Commentary
Int	*Interpretation*
IVPNTC	InterVarsity Press New Testament Commentary
KJV	King James Version
JBL	*Journal of Biblical Literature*
JETS	*Journal of the Evangelical Theological Society*
JQR	*Jewish Quarterly Review*
JSNT	*Journal for the Study of the New Testament*

Abbreviations

JSNTSup	Journal for the Study of the New Testament Supplement Series
JTS	*Journal of Theological Studies*
LXX	The Septuagint (Greek translation of the Old Testament)
m.	*Mishnah*
NAC	New American Commentary
NCS	New Century Series
NEB	New English Bible
NIBC	New International Biblical Commentary
NICNT	New International Commentary on the New Testament
NIV	New International Version
NIVAC	NIV Application Commentary
NovT	*Novum Testamentum*
NRSV	New Revised Standard Version
NLT	New Living Translation
NTS	*New Testament Studies*
RB	*Revue biblique*
REB	Revised English Bible
RSV	Revised Standard Version
SBLDS	Society of Biblical Literature Dissertation Series
SJT	*Scottish Journal of Theology*
SVTQ	*St. Vladimir's Theological Quarterly*
TDNT	*Theological Dictionary of the New Testament*
TLZ	*Theologische Literaturzeitung*
TNTC	Tyndale New Testament Commentaries
TR	*Theological Review*
TS	*Theological Studies*
TT	*Theology Today*
UBS	United Bible Societies
VE	*Vox Evangelica*
WBC	Word Biblical Commentary
ZNW	*Zeitschrift für die neutestamentliche Wissenschaft*

Introduction

IMAGINE A SCENE in the renowned city of ancient Ephesus. Ships heavy with cargo ply the Aegean Sea bringing commercial goods from as far away as Rome. Marble quays protrude into the water waiting to receive the ships' cargo and passengers while wagons filled with products from eastern provinces such as Galatia, Cappadocia, and Bithynia stand idle, waiting for their trip west. Ephesus thrives on its celebrated status. Visitors can see any number of famous temples dedicated to the Greek gods. Some consider the Temple of Artemis one of the wonders of the ancient world. Ephesus' great theater, built into the shoulder of Mount Pion, seats twenty-five thousand guests. From the harbor travelers walk into the city along a column-lined road over thirty feet wide, which reminds them of the grandeur of the city they are about to enter.[1]

And yet on this day, few visitors see the small circle of Greeks gathered at a graveside beyond the columned thoroughfare. They are no different than the usual citizens of the city, with the exception that a few seem to have the characteristic dress and head coverings of Jews. They are poor; one can see this at once. But together they are burying a person of such significance, of such importance, that his marble tomb suggests a costliness far beyond the reach of any one person in the circle. These are Christians. And they have come to bury their beloved pastor and leader, John.[2]

Christianity had begun in this cosmopolitan city through the efforts of the apostle Paul in about A.D. 52 (see Acts 18). It was anchored within the large, influential Jewish community there,[3] and its earliest leadership consisted of Priscilla and Aquila (whom Paul left behind on his earliest trip, 18:19), Paul himself (who spent more than two years there later in his ministry, 19:10; 20:3), and Timothy (1 Tim. 1:3). However, the community also enjoyed a large group of Greeks with no Jewish heritage, who became influential as well. Paul's letter to the Ephesians and his two letters to Timothy give a glimpse

---

1. Ephesus today is a city of impressive ruins, located in western Turkey. Although its seaport today is completely silted up (the sea is now ten kilometers away), in antiquity it was a major thoroughfare connecting commerce traffic between Greece and Asia Minor.

2. Firm traditions from the early centuries of the church indicate that John was buried in Ephesus. According to the fourth-century historian Eusebius and the theologian Irenaeus, John had made his home in Ephesus. A generation after John, Ignatius of Antioch could write of the faithfulness and strength of the Ephesian church (*Eph.* 8–9).

3. Josephus, *Ant.* 14.225ff; 14.262–63.

of what life must have been like. These were average citizens of the city, people like any today, with names such as Epaenetus, Mary, Andronicus, Junia, Ampliatus, Urbanus, Stachys, Apelles, Aristobulus, Herodion, Narcissus, Asyncritus, Phlegon, Hermes, Patrobas, Hermas, Philologus, Julia, Nereus, Rufus, and Olympas.[4]

John too became a leader. Ephesus may have been his base of ministry if he had jurisdiction over the seven leading churches of Asia (Rev. 1–3). He no doubt traveled to places such as Pergamum, Sardis, and Thyatira. For these churches, John was the historian and theologian who brought to them the story of Jesus. He was a valued eyewitness to the life of Jesus (John 19:35), the source of their many stories from faraway Galilee and Judea. He could write with authority:

> That which was from the beginning, which we have heard, which we have seen with our eyes, which we have looked at and our hands have touched—this we proclaim concerning the Word of life. The life appeared; we have seen it and testify to it, and we proclaim to you the eternal life, which was with the Father and has appeared to us. We proclaim to you what we have seen and heard, so that you also may have fellowship with us. And our fellowship is with the Father and with his Son, Jesus Christ. (1 John 1:1–3)

John had been there. He had heard and seen and touched the Word of life himself. He was the one who told about Nicodemus and rebirth, who described Jesus' miracle at Cana and many other episodes in his life. Other stories were circulating about Jesus, but John had his own recollection, his own insights into the thoughts of Jesus. Surely, they thought, John was Jesus' beloved disciple. In the final years of John's life, he knew that he would not be with his followers forever, so he began to organize his stories into writing, providing an early edition of his beloved "Fourth Gospel."

John also stood by the church in times of terrible persecution and conflict. When it seemed as if the fledgling community's struggle with the prestigious synagogue community would overwhelm them, John stood fast, holding to a courageous witness to Jesus Christ. When struggles later came to the church, struggles of internal controversy and conflict, John again was the community's strength. Writing letters to encourage and exhort (see 1–3 John), he became known as the heroic pastor-theologian of Asia Minor, a spiritual giant whose Gospel would be known as "the spir-

---

4. These names are taken from Romans 16. Some scholars believe that the numerous names listed in this final chapter of Romans actually refer to Ephesian Christians, not Roman. According to this theory, another copy of this letter left for Ephesus as well as Rome.

itual Gospel." When later medieval scribes copied this Gospel into sacred collections of scriptures, this gift of the Beloved Disciple would be decorated with an eagle—a majestic eagle—to indicate the heights attained by the Gospel's thought.

The Fourth Gospel Today

TODAY, THE FOURTH Gospel is the legacy of John's ministry—and it is no less beloved today than it was in the earliest years among his disciples. Few books of the Bible have influenced the life and thought of Christendom as has the Gospel of John. Its profundity and literary energy have always been noted. Here Christians have discovered a portrait of Christ that has been deeply satisfying. We are intrigued to witness how John joins intimacy of expression with penetrating insight. Scholars have poured so much energy into unraveling the Gospel's many enigmas that the flood of academic articles and books published regularly shows no sign of abating. The Gospel seems to evade our grasp and as a result has become an inexhaustable subject of interest.

In the New Testament there is a considerable body of literature traditionally attributed to John: a Gospel, three letters, and the book of Revelation. In addition there are extrabiblical writings that make some claim on his name: The legendary Acts of John was written almost two hundred years later and provides a fictional biography of the apostle. The *Syriac History of John* shows the apostle to be a magic-working evangelist. Gnostic sources[5] such as the Gospel of Philip show fragments of Johannine-style sayings while others provide accounts of his contact with Jesus, his mission, and his martyrdom.[6] But while this apocryphal literature may be set aside with ease, the significance of the biblical Johannine material has aroused considerable academic debate.

The Early Period

IN THE EARLY church, the Fourth Gospel was given the highest place of honor. Since it was thought to originate with the apostle (the Beloved Disciple)

---

5. Gnostic and Gnosticism (from the Gk word *ginosko*, to know) refer to a complex religious movement which, in its Christian form, came into clear prominence by the second century A.D. Sects quickly formed, following prominent leaders whose teaching directly opposed that of the orthodox church.

6. E. Hennecke, *The New Testament Apocrypha*, 2 vols. (Philadelphia: Westminster, 1963, 1964); many of these texts are now available on the World Wide Web at http://www.noncanonical.org.

who was one of the closest to Jesus, it was esteemed as the most valuable Gospel. John offered a depth of insight that was unparalleled in the Synoptics. But unfortunately even the heretics loved it. A second-century gnostic writer in Egypt penned the Gospel of Truth, which shows surprising Johannine parallels. Even the earliest commentaries on John were gnostic (see Heracleon, a disciple of Valentinus). Themes in the Gospel were so popular that one charismatic leader (Montanus) claimed he was the coming Paraclete or Comforter described in John 14–16! Because of this gnostic interest, many orthodox leaders were reluctant to promote the Gospel; in fact, they were openly opposed to it. But on the whole where it was accepted, John was deeply revered.[7]

Early fathers such as Irenaeus (c. A.D. 175) also learned that John's incarnational theology was an important resource against the sort of heresies being spawned in Christian-gnostic circles. Later in the fourth century, when the Arians were depicting Jesus as fully subordinate to the Father—a creature along with us—Athanasius and the leaders of Nicea looked to the Fourth Gospel's incarnational theology and doctrine of Christ as an uncompromising affirmation of Jesus' divinity.[8]

Medieval Christendom gave the Gospel this same respect. From Augustine to Aquinas, John provided the portrait of a Jesus who directly revealed the Father. Mysticism and sacramentalism likewise found in John the language and symbolic images they enjoyed. Therefore commentaries from this period abound.

Until the eighteenth century, the Fourth Gospel was held to be the most accurate and valuable Gospel of all. But with the rise of technical biblical criticism, John's prominence went into eclipse. Critics noted its differences with the Synoptic Gospels (Matthew, Mark, and Luke). Lengthy discourses had replaced parables and pithy sayings. John's language and theology seemed to indicate that here the story of Jesus had been refashioned for the Greek world. The result was that the Fourth Gospel was no longer viewed as contributing reliably to the history of Jesus' life. Its early apostolic origin was regarded with grave doubt.

---

7. See M. Hengel, *The Johannine Question* (London: SCM, 1989), 1–23.

8. M. Wiles, *The Spiritual Gospel. The Interpretation of the Fourth Gospel in the Early Church* (Cambridge: Cambridge Univ Press, 1960); R. Schnackenburg, *John*, 1:193–210; J. N. D. Kelly, *Early Christian Doctrines* (London: A. & C. Black, 1977), 52–79, 223–51; see the thorough though now-dated bibliography of E. Malatesta, *St John's Gospel, 1920–1965* (Rome. Pontifical Institute, 1967), 157–171, "John in the History of Exegesis." For an appreciation of John's incarnational theology, see E. Harrison, "A Study of John 1·14," in R. Guelich, ed., *Unity and Diversity in New Testament Theology* (Grand Rapids· Eerdmans, 1978), 23–36; M. M. Thompson, *The Humanity of Jesus in the Fourth Gospel* (Philadelphia: Fortress, 1988).

A New Look on John

TODAY SCHOLARS HOLD a tremendous variety of opinions concerning John's Gospel. Textual, grammatical, historical, and theological issues are constantly being weighed. There are few "agreed" results. This alone should caution us when yet another interpretative theory is ushered into view. But at least one trend can be charted in this mass of literature. Since the 1950s a fresh appreciation for John has almost become universal. J. A. T. Robinson of Cambridge University has even dubbed it "a new look" altogether. While John does diverge from the Synoptic Gospels, still, its independent narratives are to be valued. For instance, only John records Jesus' dialogue with Nicodemus, but this single witness in no way implies that the story never happened.

More important, John's cultural orientation is now viewed as heavily dependent on the Palestinian Judaism of Jesus' day. John's thought world, in other words, does not have to be Greek. For example, important Jewish scrolls discovered near Israel's Dead Sea (Qumran) have proven that Judaism in Jesus' day was using language similar to that of the Fourth Gospel. Even archaeological finds have substantiated some of the specific narratives of the Gospel that formerly had weathered heavy criticism (such as the pool with five porticoes in John 5:2).

This "new look" has reopened a number of old questions. If John's frame of reference is Jewish, then the Gospel's date may be early. And if it is early, it may have originated with the circle of apostles—even John son of Zebedee. Now the possibility of apostolic authority behind the Gospel is a legitimate defensible alternative. Johannine study has indeed come full circle.

Above all, this new outlook on John demands that the exegete seriously use the Old Testament and all available Jewish materials. No longer will it do to interpret, say, the miracle at Cana (2:1–11) in terms of the Hellenistic god Dionysus, who also supposedly changed water into wine. On the contrary, John's primary reference is to Jesus' messianic announcement (using Old Testament and synoptic imagery). This will be the approach used in our commentary. The message of the Fourth Gospel is clothed with allusions and metaphors that spring from first-century Judaism. Granted, this Judaism was complex and well-acquainted with Greek influences, but still, the Gospel's text is elucidated best when seen as firmly rooted in the Old Testament and Palestinian Judaism.

Authorship

THE FOURTH GOSPEL provides no explicit internal evidence concerning its author. "John" is nowhere identified as such. But this silence is not unusual and is a feature found in the Synoptics as well. The Fourth Gospel may, however, provide us with clues concealed in the enigmatic figure of the "Beloved Disciple" (NIV, "the disciple whom Jesus loved"). This title occurs in five passages (13:23; 19:26; 20:2; 21:7, 20). John 21:24 describes the Beloved Disciple (cf. 21:20) as the "disciple who testifies to these things and who wrote them down." Therefore the origin of the Gospel must in some way be connected to this person. The Gospel of John may be a record of his eyewitness account of Jesus' life.

But who is this disciple? (1) Initially, some have suggested that he is an idealized literary figure: the ideal Christian disciple. To a degree this is true (he is faithful and intimate in his knowledge of Jesus). But this hardly excludes the possibility of a genuine historical person.

(2) Lazarus has sometimes been nominated. Lazarus is the only figure of whom it is said that Jesus loved him (11:3, 36). Further, the Beloved Disciple texts occur only after Lazarus is introduced in chapter 11. But this solution is unlikely. Why would Lazarus's name be mentioned in chapters 11–12 but then left shrouded in subsequent accounts?

(3) A man named John Mark was a part of the early church (Acts 12:12), and he was associated with Peter. This may explain the rivalry between Peter and our disciple in John (cf. 20:2–8; 21:7–14). Furthermore, if Mark was related to the Levite Barnabas (Col. 4:10), this may also explain how the Beloved Disciple knows the high priest in 18:15. Nevertheless, there is a strong patristic tradition that Mark authored the Second Gospel; besides, the Beloved Disciple was certainly one of the twelve apostles (13:23), and John Mark was not.

(4) The most recent suggestion points to Thomas as the Beloved Disciple. Throughout the Gospel Thomas is presented as a person of leadership (11:16). His story with Jesus even concludes the Gospel (assuming that chapter 20 originally ended the book) and parallels the resurrection story of the apostles. Above all, Thomas asks to see the wound in Jesus' side, and the Beloved Disciple was the only one who would have known about this (19:35). Added to this is evidence for a "school or community of Thomas" with its own literature (*Gospel of Thomas, Acts of Thomas, Infancy Gospel of Thomas*, etc.) and its interest in the Fourth Gospel.[9]

(5) The best solution is the traditional one: John son of Zebedee (Mark 3:17; Acts 1:13). This man was one of the Twelve and along with James and Peter formed an inner circle around Jesus. This is the origin of his eyewitness

---

9. See J. H. Charlesworth, *The Beloved Disciple. Whose Witness Validates the Gospel of John?* (Valley Forge, Pa.: Trinity, 1995). This is a thorough study of authorship (437 pages!) covering most of the options. Charlesworth argues at length for Thomas as author. See also S. M. Schneiders, "'Because of the Woman's Testimony . . . ' Reexamining the Issue of Authorship in the Fourth Gospel," *NTS* 44 (1998): 513–35.

testimony and penetrating insight. In the Synoptics John appears with Peter more than with any other, and in Acts they are companions in Jerusalem (Acts 3–4) as well as in Samaria (8:14). This dovetails with the Peter/John connection in the Fourth Gospel. Raymond Brown has offered a novel theory to buttress this.[10] He suggests evidence that John and Jesus may have been cousins (through their mothers). This would explain why Jesus entrusts Mary to John (19:25)—a natural family relation (she may have been John's aunt)—and John was known by the high priest through Mary's priestly relatives (18:15–16; cf. Luke 1:5, 36).

Patristic evidence seems to confirm this conclusion. Irenaeus, writing at about A.D. 200, says that the Beloved Disciple was John, the disciple of Jesus, and that John originated the Gospel at Ephesus. Irenaeus even writes that when he himself was young, he knew another teacher, Polycarp, Bishop of Smyrna (c. A.D. 69–155), who claimed to have been tutored by John. The church historian Eusebius (c. A.D. 300) records this John/Polycarp/Irenaeus connection in the same way. Further, Polycrates, Bishop of Ephesus (A.D. 189–198), refers to John's association with the Gospel in his letter to Victor the Bishop of Rome. It is also confirmed by Clement of Alexandria (c. A.D. 200) and the Latin Muratorian Canon (A.D. 180–200).

Criticisms of this conclusion are commonplace, and we would do well to consider the most important ones. (1) Earlier in the 1900s critics regularly pointed to John's inaccuracies on geographical details. This, it was affirmed, could hardly come from an eyewitness writer. But subsequent historical and archaeological study have, if anything, shown John's reliability.

(2) Could a fisherman-turned-apostle have penned a work of such subtlety and insight? Could a Galilean such as this be acquainted with Greek thought? Of course. Recent study of Palestinian Judaism has shown a remarkable degree of Greek cultural penetration at all levels of society. While the New Testament does affirm that John the apostle was a "commoner" (Acts 4:13), we still are unwise to predict what John could or could not accomplish. Furthermore, this criticism fails to consider that the *final* edition of the Gospel may have been edited by John's disciples, an amanuensis (professional scribe), or John's community.

(3) Finally, some lodge the complaint that this Gospel was not readily accepted in the early church. This is true. But we have to reckon with two facts. (a) Our evidence for John's neglect is not as weighty as it seems. Important early writers may not quote John or allude to him, but to note what a

---

10. R. Brown, *Commentary on John*, 2 vols. [1966, 1970] l:xcvii; 2:905–6. Brown changed his mind in 1979 and abandoned the view that the Beloved Disciple was John son of Zebedee, one of the Twelve. See his *The Community of the Beloved Disciple* (New York: Paulist, 1979), 33–34.

patristic writer fails to say is an argument from silence. (b) John found wide acceptance in heretical, gnositic circles. This has been confirmed recently by the gnostic documents found at Nag Hammadi, where in *The Gospel of Truth* Johannine themes abound. The unorthodox on the fringes of the Greek church embraced John and provided the earliest widely known commentaries (Valentinus, Heracleon). Therefore the church was cautious in its use of the gospel because of its dangerous abuse elsewhere.

Date and Origin

ALL THAT WE have been saying about the new appreciation for the Jewishness of the Fourth Gospel and the fact that John son of Zebedee stands behind the Gospel's authority infers some conclusion about its date. The sources of John must be early and have their roots in first-generation Christianity. But fixing a certain date for the publication of the Gospel is difficult because objective data is slim. The latest possible date is A.D. 125. Not only do patristic references, allusions in apocryphal gospels (*Gospel of Peter*), and Nag Hammadi point to this, but recently in Egypt two papyrus fragments of John (Rylands Papyrus 457 and Egerton Papyrus 2) have been dated to the first half of the second century. Allowing time for John to circulate, we may wish to say that John could not have been completed long after 110.

The earliest possible date for the Gospel is more difficult. If John knows and employs the Synoptics (and this is disputed), then A.D. 70 or 80 is appropriate. In John 9:22, 12:42, and 16:2 we read about Jewish believers being excommunicated from the synagogues. In A.D. 85 the rabbis of Palestine instituted such expulsions for Christians (Rabbi Gamaliel II). Therefore we find a remarkable consensus of scholarly opinion that John was published somewhere between A.D. 80 and 100. Irenaeus says that the apostle lived to a great age—until the reign of Trajan (A.D. 98–117). And Jerome, writing much later (ca. 375), argued that John died "in the 68th year" after Jesus' death: hence, about A.D. 98.

Nevertheless, an earlier date may be within reach. Current research has challenged John's "dependence" on the Synoptics (esp. Mark and Luke). If anything, John may know pre-Synoptic traditions. Above all, the way in which John describes the topography of Jerusalem, his knowledge of the geographical and political divisions in Judaism, and his use of metaphors all point to a date approximating that of the Synoptic writers. The great watershed date of A.D. 70 (when Jerusalem was destroyed by Rome) is critical: John presupposes a Judaism before this war. And with his critical disposition toward the temple (2:13ff.; 4:21ff.) and severe conflicts with Jewish leadership (cf. chs. 5, 8, 10), we are surprised to find no mention of this catastrophic event. To paraphrase C. H. Dodd, much in John is "barely intelligible" outside of the context of pre–70 Judaism.

To sum up, the traditions about Jesus that John preserves most likely stem from the earliest apostolic period—perhaps A.D. 60–65. But the final edition of the Gospel may have been published later. John and/or his disciples may have edited the work, making additions and sharpening its message for later Christianity (see more on this below). Tradition tells us that the place of writing was Ephesus, and no decisive reasons have been raised against it. There may even be biblical support for it. The Fourth Gospel entertains a polemic aimed at followers of John the Baptist (see 1:19–28, 35–42; 3:22–36; 10:40–42). Elsewhere in the book of Acts we learn about Paul's encountering followers of John the Baptist with deficient beliefs. Surprisingly, they too are located in Ephesus.

John's Theological Interests

THE INTERPRETATION OF any Biblical book is strengthened when we understand the deeper motives and concerns that have led the author to write. John's vigor and concentration reveal a remarkable intensity of purpose. It is as if a powerful truth had broken upon him and he was compelled to express it. To a greater extent than the Synoptics, each section of the Fourth Gospel contributes to a central theme: the appearance of the Son of God in human history. John explores two facets of this appearing: its revelation and its redemption.

Revelation and Redemption

"THE LIGHT SHINES in the darkness, but the darkness has not understood it" (1:5). Dualistic language describes this remarkable invasion of the world by God. Offending every modern sensibility, John writes that in Christ we behold the glory of God—even though he appeared in flesh. But this offense is an ancient one, too. The darkness assails the light but cannot vanquish it. The world is in permanent enmity with the Son. But even though Jesus is persecuted, tried, and crucified, John still affirms that the light is not extinguished.

But the gift of Christ is not simply his revelation of the Father (14:9). John's second message concerns redemption. "In him was life, and that life was the light of all people" (1:4). There is hope for us in the world. The message of history's invasion is also a message of sacrifice and redemption. Those who embrace this revelation, who identify with the light and have faith, will gain eternal life. The life of the Son is poured out in sacrifice, thereby creating the community of the redeemed (17:6ff., 20–26). They bear Christ's Spirit, which sustains them because the hatred once extended toward the Son is now extended to them (15:12ff.).

Thus John's purpose in writing is to explain this revelation and redemption and to explicate its possibilities. In 20:31 the author makes clear this aim: "But these are written that you may believe that Jesus is the Christ, the Son of God, and that by believing you may have life in his name." Here all of our major themes converge: belief, acknowledgment of Jesus' sonship, and the promise of life.

But even here the mystery of John confronts us. A textual variant (see comments on 20:30–31) in the word "believe" (*pisteuēte* [pres. subjunctive] vs. *pisteusēte* [aorist subjunctive]) places the meaning of the verse in doubt. One reading implies that John is evangelistic (the aorist: "that you may come to believe"); the other implies encouragement (the present: "that you may continue believing"). This latter reading has the best manuscript support and more helpfully explains the character of John. It is written for Christians who, already knowing the rudiments of Christ's life and Christian truth, now wish to go further. Not only is there an uncompromising maturity of thought in this Gospel, but also its narratives imply that it was written to address certain practical circumstances in the church. Some would say that John is engaged in a polemic: asserting Christian truth amidst unsympathetic forces. Yet John's purpose also includes the clarification of Christian doctrines at an early stage of church development.

Jewish Concerns

THE CONFLICT BETWEEN Jesus and the Pharisees that we meet in the Synoptics is given marked attention in John. A brief reading of 8:31–59 or 10:19–39 makes it clear. There is a sustained attack on the religious position of Judaism. For instance, "the Jews" virtually becomes a technical term in John (used seventy times) for those who reject Jesus. In 9:22, for example, the parents of the blind man (who are Jewish) fear "the Jews." But this is not all. The messiahship of Jesus and his relationship to the festivals and institutions of Judaism are both emphasized.

What does this mean? Each Gospel was written not only to record the history of Jesus, but also to address particular circumstances in the life of its first readers. This saying or story was recorded and not that one for a reason. Here the Christians of John's church may have needed encouragement because of persecution and hostilities. John buttresses Christian claims against Jewish unbelief. The historic fact of Jewish unbelief in Jesus' day is joined with Jewish opposition in John's day.

Christian Concerns

AT THE TIME the Gospel was published, the early Christian church had grown and diversified considerably. Therefore it comes as no surprise to find that

John has included historic materials relevant to Christian needs in his generation. It would be a mistake, however, to think that any of these needs became the controlling force in John's literary design. On the contrary, they serve as subthemes that run through the Gospel and clarify John's situation. Scholars have identified an incredible list of topics, but we will note in passing only five prominent motifs:

The significance of John the Baptist. Did the Baptist have followers (perhaps even a sect) who failed or refused to follow Jesus? Luke 3:15 and Acts 19:1–7 imply this while later writings confirm it.[11] The Fourth Gospel takes pains to affirm that the Baptist was not the Messiah (1:20; 3:28), that he was not the light (1:8–9), and that Jesus is superior (1:30; 3:29–30; 10:41). We even witness disciples of John the Baptist becoming Jesus' first converts (1:35–42). Matthew, Mark, and Luke have no parallel motif.

The place of sacramentalism. John has a "sacramental" view of history inasmuch as the incarnation of Christ for him means the genuine appearance of God in history. Worship can affirm such genuine appearances when worship symbols (baptism, the Lord's Supper) take on the real properties of that which they depict. Hence they are called "sacraments." Scholars have identified a unique Johannine interest in the sacraments of Christian worship, but there is little agreement over John's intention. Some note an absence of interest (e.g., the Lord's Supper is omitted) while others see allusions everywhere (baptism: chs. 3, 5, 9; Eucharist: chs. 2, 6; both: 19:34). It seems best to conclude that John's principal message about each (found in 3:1–21 and 6:52–65) is corrective: Without the Spirit these expressions of worship become powerless rituals void of their original purpose.

Christology. The second-century church father, Irenaeus, wrote that the Gospel of John was penned to refute the gnostic heretic Cerinthus. While this is not likely, nevertheless, Irenaeus correctly observed that John's presentation of Christ was carefully considered. Questions about Jesus' nature, origin, and relation to the Father are examined in a fashion unparalleled by the Synoptics. For instance, John affirms the oneness of Jesus and the Father (10:30; 14:9–10), their distinction from each other (14:28; 17:1–5), and their unity of purpose (5:17–18; 8:42). It comes as no surprise that in the formation of Trinitarian doctrine, John played a notable role (cf. Tertullian, *Against Praxeas*). This was particularly true at the council of Nicea (325), when Arius denied the eternal nature of the Son. In later Arian debates, Athanasius was heavily dependent on the Fourth Gospel and found in the Johannine prologue's title "Logos" a most serviceable tool depicting the person of Christ.[12]

---

11. See the Latin Pseudo-Clementine, *Recognitions*.
12. See his *On the Incarnation of the Word of God.*

John asserts the divinity for Christ. If anyone were inclined toward adoptionism (i.e., that Jesus was a divinely inspired man), this Gospel gives an unrelenting argument to the contrary. On the other hand, the Greek world was comfortable with divinities and, if anything, hesitated to affirm Jesus' full humanity (Docetism). John contends that Jesus is truly human, truly of "flesh" (1:14; cf. 20:27). The brilliance and abiding value of this Gospel is that it embraces both positions. Jesus was eternally divine and fully incarnate—fully God and fully man.

But scholars have been quick to point out that this "balanced Christology" seems artificial. If one removes the prologue (1:1–18), the balance is tipped and, in the words of some, John becomes a "naive docetist."[13] But this seems unfairly harsh.[14] One solution has been to view John having stages of development. That is, the prologue may have been added to the Gospel at a later stage, when the letters of John were published. The battle cry of 1 John is certainly against Docetism (1 John 4:1–3), and if the high Christology of the Fourth Gospel had been fueling heretical docetic beliefs, then the addition of the hymn would give the needed balance.

Nevertheless, it is vital to say that the humanity of Christ is intrinsic to the whole of the gospel of John. "John portrays Jesus in a two-fold light without reflection or speculation. He is equal to God; he is indeed God in the flesh; yet he is fully human."[15] This affirmation alone has given John an inestimable value to the church and its creeds.

The Holy Spirit. John provides us with a wealth of information concerning the Spirit and in many cases places unique emphases on theological features of the Spirit that are not found in the Synoptic Gospels. His treatment moves in two directions. (1) Christologically, John underscores how the Spirit is an integral feature of Jesus' experience of God. During Jesus' baptism, for instance, John narrates the story but adds that the Spirit *remained* on Jesus (1:32–33), underscoring the permanence of God's indwelling in him. Jesus stands out from John the Baptist because God has given him the Spirit *without measure* (3:34). The Spirit is described metaphorically as a source of living water (4:10), which later we learn is a source flowing from within Jesus himself (7:37–39). In fact, the release of the Spirit is dependent on Jesus' death (7:39), and he remarks in the Upper Room, "It is for your good that I am going away. Unless I go away, the Counselor will not come to you" (16:7). As we will see in the com-

---

13. E. Käsemann, *The Testament of Jesus* (Philadelphia: Fortress, 1968).

14. L. Morris, "The Jesus of St. John," *Unity and Diversity in New Testament Theology: Essays in Honor of George E. Ladd* (Grand Rapids: Eerdmans, 1978), 37–53; also M. M. Thompson, *The Humanity of Jesus in the Fourth Gospel* (Philadelphia: Fortress, 1988).

15. G. E. Ladd, *A Theology of the New Testament* (Grand Rapids: Eerdmans, 1974), 252.

---

mentary, this imagery that joins Spirit and Christ may be at work in the cross when Jesus is wounded and water (along with blood) flows from him (19:34).

(2) John also talks about the promise of the Spirit for believers. He alone provides us with the Nicodemus dialogue, in which Jesus challenges the rabbi to be born again (3:1–10). This is a work not of intellectual or moral conversion, but of supernatural activity. The same is true for the Samaritan woman, a character who stands theologically and socially opposite Nicodemus. The living water she seeks (4:15) is later defined as the Spirit (7:37–38), and Jesus takes advantage of Samaria's cultural rift with Judaism to talk about true worship that engages the Spirit (4:24). More hints of the Spirit abound in the Gospel (see 6:63); they culminate in Jesus' lengthy farewell discourse (chs. 14–16), where the Spirit is described and promised for all believers. Unlike the Synoptics, John even records Jesus' giving the Spirit to his disciples on Easter Sunday as a final gift that hallmarks his departure (20:22).

All of this is to say that for John's outlook, the Holy Spirit is no incidental feature of Jesus' life and identity, nor is the Spirit an optional dimension to Christian discipleship. To be united with Jesus is to experience his Spirit, which is set free for the world at the cross.[16]

Our future hope: eschatology. Many of the early Christians longed for the second coming of Christ and anticipated an imminent end to history. This explains the cherished sayings of Jesus about his second coming in the Synoptics (see Matt. 24; Mark 13; Luke 21). How did they cope when this hope was frustrated (cf. 2 Peter 3:1–12)? John does not record anything like Jesus' Synoptic eschatological discourses. He still maintains the future hope (John 5:25ff.; 1 John 2:28) but introduces a fresh emphasis: The longed-for presence of Jesus is mediated to us now in the Spirit. In the Upper Room Jesus' announcement of the Spirit takes on eschatological tones (see John 14:18–23). That is, in one vital way that we often overlook, Jesus has come back and is with us already in the Spirit. In technical terms, John emphasizes a realized eschatology in contrast to the apocalyptic hope of the Synoptics.

---

16. See the studies of G. Johnston, *The Spirit-Paraclete in the Gospel of John* (Cambridge: Cambridge Univ. Press, 1970); G. Burge, *The Anointed Community: The Holy Spirit in the Johannine Tradition* (Grand Rapids: Eerdmans, 1987) (see esp. bibliography, 225–54); J. Breck, *Spirit of Truth: The Holy Spirit in the Johannine Tradition*, 2 vols. (Crestwood: St. Vladimir's, 1991, vol. 2 forthcoming); S. Smalley, "The Paraclete: Pneumatology in the Johannine Gospel and Apocalypse," in R. A. Culpepper and C. Black, eds., *Exploring the Gospel of John (in Honor of D. M. Smith)* (Louisville: Westminster/J. Knox, 1996), 289–300; a popular treatment is found in F. G. Carver, *When Jesus Said Good-Bye: John's Witness to the Holy Spirit* (Kansas City: Beacon Hill, 1996).

How John's Gospel Was Built

EXEGESIS MUST BEGIN with a thorough knowledge of the text *as we have it*. It will not do to study a passage in isolation from its context. Nor will it do to neglect the wider theological framework of John and think that we can accurately discern the meaning of a particular narrative. This is an *ancient* text, a story that is almost two thousand years removed from us. It bears no copyright, no editorial history; we don't even possess an original first edition. Scribes hand-copied this Gospel for centuries—some of whom were scrupulous and scholarly; others were, frankly, sloppy. Therefore, what is the shape or condition of this story as it now sits in our hands? *What is the literary phenomenon of the Fourth Gospel?*

The literary phenomenon of the text of John is nothing less than a daunting mystery. In fact, there is a voluminous scholarly literature that has tried just to solve this Johannine mystery.[17] This is perhaps why Raymond Brown once remarked that Johannine scholars often enjoy detective stories in their leisure time.

We have a couple of assignments as we open up this task. First, can we learn something about how this Gospel was built? Does it betray any sources? What if the Fourth Gospel is really made up of a variety of editorial layers; perhaps collections of stories about Jesus and his miracles were combined with lengthy accounts of his teachings. If this is true and based on good evidence, then we will learn a great deal more about our text. Second, we need to stand back and look at the Gospel as a whole. In its present canonical form,[18] can we discern a logic and symmetry that is useful? Does the Fourth Gospel possess an organizational structure that explains its unity and theological message?

Literary Layers in John

THE PUZZLE OF John's literary history was the first critical issue recognized in the Gospel. As early as the second century, Tatian's *Diatessaron* rearranged

---

17. Surveys of this literature are stunning in that they show the tremendous energy applied to the Fourth Gospel Note these important works: E. Malatesta, *St. John's Gospel 1920–1965* (Rome: Pontifical Biblical Institute, 1967), G. VanBelle, *Johannine Bibliography 1966–1985. A Cumulative Bibliography on the Fourth Gospel* (Leuven. Leuven Univ. Press, 1988); R. Kysar, *The Fourth Evangelist and His Gospel* (Minneapolis: Augsburg, 1975); J. Ashton, ed , *The Interpretation of John* (Philadelphia: Fortress, 1986); and G. Sloyan, *What Are They Saying About John?* (New York· Paulist, 1991). For a current survey of European research, see K. Scholtissek, "Johannine Studies: A Survey of Recent Research with Special Regard to German Contributions," *Currents in Research Biblical Studies* 6 (1998): 227–59

18 The term *canonical* refers to the received literary form accepted in the church.

---

major portions of John to fit the synoptics. But the process of textual dislocation must have been widespread. The Sinaitic Syriac version found in 1892 at St. Catherine's monastery in the Sinai desert of Egypt rearranged John 18 (the order of the Caiaphas/Annas interrogation) in order to "improve" the narrative.

What we seem to have are internal clues—perhaps we might label them literary seams—that betray a history of composition in this Gospel. Unfortunately the solution to this problem is unlike that in the Synoptics, where multiple traditions can be compared. For instance, if Matthew and Luke used Mark, their patterns of dependence and divergence can be analyzed. Some of course have argued that John may have known the outline of Mark or a few of Luke's sections, but few would dare suggest direct literary dependence on the order of, say, Matthew's use of Mark. On the contrary, John's sources have left only subtle traces of their history.

Since John's sources are not "given away," scholars have developed techniques to unravel the Gospel's mysteries.[19] (1) We might look for *stylistic evidences*, where additional editorial hands are suspected. We could note, for instance, how *logos* ("word") is employed in chapter 1 and then drops away. The same is true of crucial words like *pleroma* ("fullness") and *charis* ("grace"). But the best studies have rejected this tool. Careful linguistic work has fatally weakened source theories based on style and convinced us that the same hand was at work from chapters 1–21.[20] For instance, note how an important word like *dynamis* ("power") is consistently omitted in John and replaced with a so-called "Johannine vocabulary" for miracles: *ergon* ("work") and *semeion* ("sign").

(2) We might look for *ideological tendencies*, in which rival points of view are in the text. John has witnessed a good deal of attention here as well. When any author adopts a source, he or she may exhibit disagreements with it even if on an unconscious level. Where these disagreements are discernable, the source and the editor may be distinguished. Rudolf Bultmann was the expert at this sort of detective work. He catalogued numerous tendencies, such as interest in the Beloved Disciple, works versus signs, and eschatology. Note how in 3:26 and in 4:1 traditional narratives tell us that Jesus was providing water baptism. And then much to our surprise in 4:2 the story is corrected

---

19. See R. Fortna, *The Gospel of Signs· A Reconstruction of the Narrative Source Underlying the Fourth Gospel* (Cambridge: Cambridge Univ. Press, 1970), 1–22. More recently, R. Fortna, *The Fourth Gospel and Its Predecessors· From Narrative Source to Present Gospel* (Philadelphia: Fortress, 1988).

20. E. Schweizer, *Ego Emi. Die religionsgeschichtliche Herkunft und theologische Bedeutung der johanneischen Bildreden, Zugleich ein Beitrag zur Quellenfragan des vierten Evangeliums* (Gottingen: Vandenhoeck, 1938, 1965²); E. Ruckstuhl, *Die literarische Einheit des Johannesevangeliums: Der gegenwärtige Stand der einschlägigen Forschungen* (Freiburg: St. Paul, 1951).

to say that Jesus really did not baptize—only his followers did. Bultmann urges that this is evidence of disagreement between an author and his source.

But scholars have been equally critical of this approach too. D. Moody Smith and Robert Fortna question our ability to discern ideological strata.[21] The themes in John are too subtle, too nuanced—and besides, any author may write employing a number of inner tensions. To assign one view to a more primitive level and another view to a redactor or editor simply lacks an objective basis.

(3) A third tool is more promising: *contextual evidence.* Contextual evidence is that which shows some irregularity in the text, some narrative rift. It comes in a variety of forms. (a) There is *textual evidence,* where ancient manuscripts show discrepancies in the tradition. One Greek manuscript may record a paragraph or sentence one way while another offers a different version. This is so, for example, in Mark's longer ending (see Mark 16:9–20). But it is sadly infrequent in John. The story of the adulteress (7:53–8:11) comes quickly to mind, but seldom do textual discrepancies bear a major significance for the interpretation of the Fourth Gospel (cf. 1:13, 18, 41; 3:34; 6:69; 14:3).[22]

(b) A second contextual tool is to locate and study the *parenthetical remarks* of the narrator/editor. These are comments that interrupt the story in order to assist the reader, which imply that the author is using materials, sources, or traditions his readers may not understand. These are frequent in John. For instance, in John 1:41 we are taught that the Aramaic name "Cephas" means Peter (Gk. *petros*). In 19:31 we are told that the Jewish Sabbath is a (lit.) "high day." In 4:9 Jewish/Samaritan tensions are footnoted ("Jews do not associate with Samaritans").

Occasionally John explains some awkwardness in the logic of the text. For example, in 2:9 the steward of the wedding party may not have known the origin of the wine, but the narrator reminds us that the servants were genuine witnesses to the miracle. The same "reader helps" can be found in 4:2, where we are reminded that Jesus did not baptize anyone. But usually the narrator just assists the story as in 6:1, when he says that the Sea of Galilee and the Sea of Tiberius are one and the same. This is where the source critic sits up. If John's reader understood "Sea of Tiberius" and if John wrote the entire narrative without sources, why did he not use this phrase in the first place?

---

21. D. Moody Smith, *The Composition and Order of the Fourth Gospel Bultmann's Literary Theory* (New Haven: Yale Univ. Press, 1965); R. Fortna, *The Gospel of Signs,* and *The Fourth Gospel and Its Predecessors.*

22. For a study of the text of John, see V. Salmon, *The Fourth Gospel. A History of the Text* (Collegeville: Liturgical, 1976); commentaries on the Greek text of John (esp. that of C K. Barrett, 1978[2]) generally point out specific text problems.

(c) The third contextual tool is where we identify what I label *literary seams* in the text. These are instances where the chronological, topical, or dramatic flow of the narrative appears disjointed. John's Gospel abounds with these in a way that is completely different from the Synoptics.

These phenomena are so common that they have even received a technical name. In 1907 Edward Schwartz coined the term *aporia* for these "difficulties."[23] Today this term has been taken up by Robert Fortna and Howard Teeple.[24] In English the earliest work on this problem followed Schwartz by three years and can be found in Warburton Lewis, *Disarrangements in the Fourth Gospel*.[25] A quick look at just a few of these will make the point:

- First take note of John's prologue (1:1–18) with its distinctive idiom and poetic style. Without it the Gospel would begin at 1:19 with John the Baptist and parallel the traditional Synoptic starting point. What is the origin of this poem? Who wrote it? What is its relation to the body of the Gospel?
- Note how John uses the term *sign* (Gk. *semeion*) for Jesus' miracles. In 2:11 and 4:54 these are numbered (the first and second "signs"), but the numbering system is not maintained. Besides, many have asked how 4:54 can be the second sign when 2:23 says that Jesus had done multiple signs earlier in Jerusalem.
- In 3:22 the text says that Jesus "went out into the Judean countryside." The problem is that he had been in Judea all along since he had attended a Passover Feast in Jerusalem (2:23–3:21).
- One of the most fascinating puzzles is the sequence of John 5 and 6. The present order makes Jesus move abruptly from Samaria to Galilee to Jerusalem back to Galilee again and back once more to Jerusalem— all without transitions. In chapter 5, for example, Jesus has been engaged in a debate in Jerusalem. Now look at 6:1 (lit.): "After this Jesus went to the other side of the Sea of Galilee." Many scholars would like to reverse the order of chapters 5 and 6.[26]

---

23. From the Greek *aporia* (a difficult passing; cf. *aporeo*, "to be at a loss"), which described either an impassable maritime strait or, in debate, a difficulty in logic. See E. Schwartz, "Aporien im vierten Evangelium," in *Nachrichten von der königlichen Gesellschaft der Wissenschaften zu Gottingen* (1907), 342–72; (1908), 115–88, 497–650.

24. R. Fortna, *The Fourth Gospel and Its Predecessors*; H. Teeple, *The Literary Origin of the Gospel of John* (Evanston: Religion and Ethics Institute, 1974).

25. Warburton Lewis, *Disarrangements in the Fourth Gospel* (Cambridge: Cambridge Univ. Press, 1910).

26. Compare this with what we gain just by transposing chapters 5 and 6 (the new chapter sequence: John 3, 4, 6, 5, 7). (1) John 6:1 makes chronological sense because Jesus finishes a miracle in Galilee at the close of ch. 4. Jesus then moves from the west bank of

- Consider the pericope of the adulteress (7:53–8:11), which, although it interrupts the Tabernacles discourse, still has theological links with it. Here is the one case where manuscript evidence is significant. This is probably a floating Gospel episode that entered John (and Luke) late.[27]
- Another *aporia* could be noted at 11:2. Here Mary of Bethany is introduced as the woman who "anointed the Lord with ointment and wiped his feet with her hair." The only problem is that this anointing does not take place until the next chapter (ch. 12).
- In 14:31 it appears that Jesus has completed his Upper Room discourse and implies that his arrest is at hand: "I will not speak with you much longer, for the prince of this world is coming" (14:30). Then he says, "Come, now; let us leave" (14:31). The striking thing is that Jesus *does* have much to say—eighty-six verses or so!—before the coming of Judas. Should 14:31 be followed by 18:1? If you read the story in this sequence, you will be surprised by the ease with which the narrative flows.
- Another *aporia* is found at 16:5: "Yet none of you asks me, 'Where are you going.'" On the contrary, just the opposite is the case, since in 13:36 Peter has asked the identical question and in 14:5 Thomas has done the same. This has inspired a host of rearrangement theories that try to place 16:5 before 13:36.
- A final *aporia* is linked to the foregoing: What do we make of John 21? The closing verses of chapter 20 seem to end the Gospel. A whole host of technical questions follow. Did the same author who wrote chapters 1–20 write this one? Stylistically it is the same—even 21:14 employs a numbering system for the resurrection episodes that presupposes all of those in chapter 20. Equally important, the rivalry between Peter and John found in John 13 and 20 is replayed again in chapter 21, when Jesus is sighted on the shore. Nevertheless, a careful editor could have shaped the chapter to the style and format of

---

the sea to the east bank. (2) Likewise, 7:1 currently follows chapter 6 only with difficulty: "After this, Jesus went around in Galilee; purposely staying away from Judea because the Jews there were waiting to take his life " This concern for death should be preceded immediately by chapter 5, where in Judea the Jews elect to kill him. (3) What is the "one miracle" in 7:21 for which Jesus is persecuted? As 7:23 explains, this is the healing of the lame man in chapter 5. (4) There are numerous theological links between chs. 4 and 6 (water of life/bread of life; sign theology; doing the work of God, etc.), which ch. 5 interrupts. (5) Finally, this harmonizes John's chronology with that of Mark, where events in Galilee are climaxed by the great feeding and then the scene shifts to Judea. The new arrangement gathers up the Galilee stories into a unit (chs. 4, 6) before Jesus works in Judea (chs. 5, 7–11).

27. G. M. Burge, "John 7:53–8:11: The Woman Caught in Adultery," *JETS* 27 (1984): 141–48.

chapters 1–20. The most fascinating section is in the final two verses (21:24–25). Amazingly, here editors or writers different from the Beloved Disciple betray their identity, "This is the disciple . . . who wrote [these things] down. *We* know that *his* testimony is true." Who is the "we" in this verse? Is this firsthand evidence of John's disciples who assisted him in editing the Gospel?

To sum up, this literary evidence simply means that when John was writing his Gospel, he used sources. For me, sources point to the antiquity of the Johannine tradition. Some scholars take the unnecessary step of weighing these sources to locate those that are more historically reliable. But most see this as evidence that deliberate editorial selecting of stories and arranging went on in the earliest period. Few believe that the Beloved Disciple wrote his Gospel at one sitting from front to back. Instead it developed over a period of time. It is likely that the Fourth Gospel underwent a series of stages of composition, and the literary seams are examples of where the stages came together. Much like a house that has undergone numerous expansions and additions, identifying the seams helps to reconstruct the intentions of the original builders.

A Proposed Reconstruction

MANY SCHOLARS HAVE tried to outline the stages of building that make up the Gospel, but there is little agreement. A conservative reconstruction of this process might look like this:

- **Stage one.** A basic collection of teachings from Jesus circulated among the earliest Christians. Many of these were collected by John, memorized or written down, and used in his personal ministry.
- **Stage two.** An early community formed (possibly from the followers of John the Baptist, see chs. 1–4), living in strong tension with its neighboring Jewish community.[28] This explains the frequent argument in the Gospel against "the Jews" and the Gospel's use of Jewish cultural and theological materials. It also explains the Gospel's dualism and its repeated warnings about "the world." The Gospel's stories were shaped by the church's life and needs as it struggled for existence in its community.
- **Stage three.** As the community grew and consolidated its identity, an early draft of the Gospel was penned, based on John's memoirs of

---

28. Here I follow the patristic tradition and suggest the community was in or near Ephesus. Note that the Johannine community is keenly interested in the Baptist community (witness the polemic in 1:6–9, 19–28, 3:22–36; and 10:40–42). Note also that in Acts 19:1–8 Paul encounters followers of John the Baptist who did not follow Jesus; *this takes place in Ephesus.*

Jesus' life. This "pre-gospel" possibly began with the story of John the Baptist (1:19) and ended with chapter 20:31.

- **Stage four.** Suddenly the community found itself struggling internally, wrestling with early gnostic heresies and inner divisions. John wrote his three letters (1, 2, 3 John) and at the same time the prologue to his Gospel (John 1:1–18), which was attached to the Gospel as an explicit affirmation of John's incarnational Christology. It is an eloquent and powerful overture to more subtle affirmations elsewhere in the Gospel.
- **Stage five.** Following John's death, his disciples reverently gathered up his final stories of the resurrection (ch. 21) and paid tribute to the lasting importance of John's eyewitness testimony (19:35; 21:24). As they edited the Gospel story itself, they generously gave John the title "Beloved Disciple," recognizing his intimacy with Jesus and the depth of his teaching. They also gave the Gospel its final arrangement, splicing in stories where appropriate and putting the finishing touches on John's treasured memoirs.[29]

Literary Structure

AN EXCELLENT EXERCISE is to photocopy the Fourth Gospel and make a paste-up of the text.[30] This enables us to see the Gospel in its entirety and note connections between units of text. John 11 (the raising of Lazarus) can now easily be compared with John 20 (the raising of Jesus). Thematic shifts can also be marked with ease.[31] For example, the abrupt shifts between John 5 and 6 are now evident.

---

29. Possibly at this time the story of the woman caught in adultery entered the narrative of John 7 and 8. Critical scholars suggest a severe editing at this time that adjusted the Gospel's eschatology (5:19ff.) and sacramentalism (6:52–59). For some scholars, the writing of the letters and the prologue come from a period after John's death. The "elder" of the letters is a trusted disciple of John who assumes leadership in the community. Nevertheless, many other scholars have disagreed with this reconstruction (e.g., Morris, Carson), urging convincingly that the Gospel's composition did develop in stages, that the Evangelist was involved with the final edition of the Gospel, and that the Gospel did not undergo a theological "editing."

30. This is best done by photocopying a small devotional text with fine print, cutting apart the columns of text, and then pasting them in sequence on a large sheet of paper. The whole Gospel can now be viewed on a couple of sheets.

31. An interesting first exercise is to highlight (with a colored pen) every reference to a Jewish festival in the Gospel. You will find references to Sabbath, Passover, Tabernacles, and Rededication/Hannukah. Now note what stories are adjacent to these references. Is there a connection? Now use two different colors to highlight texts whose setting is in Judah and other texts whose setting is in Galilee. Do these exercises show a pattern?

If we scan the entire Gospel, we at once can see some natural divisions. All along, however, keep in mind that the chapter divisions in the Gospel are artificial. *We want to locate any natural literary divisions.* It seems that Jesus is at work in public from chapters 1–12, showing signs and teaching to diverse public audiences. Then from chapters 13–17 he is in private speaking to his followers, almost saying "Farewell" to them. Finally, the story ends with a detailed Passion/resurrection account.

Let's look at the transitions between these units carefully. Chapter 12 seems to be a clear climax to the public ministry: It ends with a "summing up" of Jesus' efforts, a cry of despair concerning disbelief, and a final reaffirmation of the divine origins of Jesus' words. John 13:1 switches the scene to Passover, remarks that Jesus is now departing from the world, and narrows the stage to those who have followed him. Chapter 17 ends a lengthy prayer, and another geographical shift (the Kidron Valley) moves us to yet another scene: Jesus' arrest, trial, and death. *Lengthy discourses give way to dramatic narrative.*

Scholars have been quick to note these divisions and label them. Chapters 1–12 are called the "Book of Signs" since they record Jesus' numerous revelatory miracles. Chapters 13–21 (uniting the Upper Room and Passion sections) are called the "Book of Glory," since on the cross Jesus is glorified (13:31).

The Book of Signs (John 1–12). Now look closer at the first section, the Book of Signs. Note how the hymn at the beginning is almost an overture, a curtain-raiser to the drama that really begins at 1:19. This is followed by a unit centered on John the Baptist and his disciples (and their earliest contacts with Jesus). Then the story moves quickly from scene to scene: a miracle at Cana, cleansing the temple, Nicodemus, and so on.

Try sorting these units by theme, noting major narrative shifts. At once it becomes clear that these sections are *topically arranged.* From chapters 2–4 Jesus is working miracles on institutions in Judaism; from chapters 5–10 he is making appearances at a series of Jewish festivals (note how each festival is actually named in each section). In each of these—institutions and festivals—he is replacing some Jewish symbol with abundance, messianic abundance (water ➤ living water; manna ➤ living bread, etc.). We might venture an outline such as this:

    A. The Prologue (1:1–18)
    B. Jesus and the Baptist (1:19–51)
    C. Jesus and the Jewish Institutions (2:1–4:54)[32]
      1. At Cana: Purification Vessels (2:1–12)
      2. In Jerusalem: The Temple (2:13–25)

---

32. In each case, the significant element in the Jewish institution is identified for us and Jesus is seen replacing it with his own presence.

Note how many of the literary units are shown by *internal* indicators of each division. Episodes in Cana (miracles, each of which are numbered) frame the section on Jewish institutions. The festival section clearly refers to each respective festival, exploits a major symbol in the festival (Sabbath/work, Passover/bread, Tabernacles/water and light, Rededication/Jesus' consecration), and generally offers a discourse expanding the meaning of the symbols (see 6:15–35 as a comment on Passover). The final reference to John the Baptist (10:40–42) refers back to the beginning of the entire sequence of signs (1:19ff.), making another closing frame and reiterating the value of Jesus' signs. Finally, the closing two chapters serve as a sobering warning of what is to come.

---

33. Compare this unit with John 1 19–51. Many scholars think that both sections originated from a similar setting.

34. As in the previous section, here the festival is mentioned and its primary symbols are described for us. Jesus is then shown replacing the symbol or demonstrating his own authority over the meaning of the festival. For example, at Tabernacles, when the temple was sponsoring water and light ceremonies, Jesus stands in the temple and announces that he is "living water" and "the light of the world."

35. This unit has been studied at great length and is no doubt foreign to this setting in John. Manuscript traditions are divided on its authenticity. See my "John 7:53–8:11: The Woman Caught in Adultery" and the numerous references to studies listed there.

36. A careful comparison of this section and the passion story (chs. 19–20) shows remarkable parallels.

What conclusions can we draw from this? Suddenly it appears that the Fourth Gospel may be topically arranged (at least in chs. 1–12), even though the units or stories themselves have a clear historical and chronological character. John is telling us more about Jesus' messianic impact on Judaism than he is about the sequence of events in Jesus' ministry. The episodes are not arranged by any accident. The final edition of John that we possess has a careful, intentional organization.

The Book of Glory (John 13–21). Much the same can be argued for the Book of Glory (chs. 13–21). In this major section Jesus turns in private to his disciples during his final Passover. Remarkably, all nine chapters center on just a few days of Jesus' life. He teaches them privately about servanthood, washes their feet, explains the coming Holy Spirit in terms of personal revelation and persecution, and prays at length for his followers and their disciples. Chapter 18 opens the story of the trial and death of Jesus. As an extended narrative, it reads much like the Synoptics, moving quickly from scene to scene without the characteristic Johannine discourses. The cross is followed by a detailed resurrection account, in which Jesus anoints his followers with the Spirit. Finally, chapter 21 is likely an addition that adds resurrection stories in Galilee and Jesus' lengthy discussion with Peter.

A. The Passover Meal (13:1–30)
   1. The Footwashing (13:1–20)
   2. The Betrayal of Judas (13:21–30)
B. The Farewell Discourse (13:31–17:26)
   1. Jesus' Departure and Provision (13:31–14:31)
   2. The True Vine (15:1–17)
   3. The Disciples and the World (15:18–16:33)
     a. The Enmity of the World (15:18–16:4a)
     b. Further Work of the Spirit (16:4b–33)
   4. The Priestly Prayer of Jesus (17:1–26)
C. The Suffering and Death of Jesus (18:1–19:42)
   1. Arrest and Interrogation (18:1–19:16)
     a. Arrest (18:1–11)
     b. The Jewish Trial (18:12–27)
     c. The Roman Trial (18:28–19:16)
   2. Crucifixion and Burial (19:17–42)
D. The Resurrection (20:1–29)
E. Epilogue (21:1–25)
   1. The Miracle of 153 Fish (21:1–14)
   2. Jesus and Peter (21:15–23)
   3. Editorial Appendix (21:24–25)

The Book of Glory is dominated by the events of the Upper Room and the Passion account. From chapters 13–17 Jesus is center stage, preparing his disciples for his death. Chapter 18, on the other hand, is a different sort of story. It seems that the account of Jesus' trial and death was firmly established in early Christianity, perhaps by oral tradition. John 18–19 has more parallels with the Synoptic Gospels than any other section. This is why C. H. Dodd began with the Passion narrative of John when he probed the Fourth Gospel's historical worth.[37] He concluded, however, that while the Gospel echoes the Synoptics, its divergences were such that it probably recorded an ancient and authentic strain of the oral tradition about Jesus' death.

But what at first sight appears to be a smooth narrative shows up on closer inspection to be a story assembled in much the same way as the Book of Signs. Jesus' farewell (13:31–17:26), for instance, reads like a patchwork of teachings. We have already noted how 16:5 and the question of "going" follows 13:36 with difficulty. Commentators often point out the many parallels between chapters 14 and 16, suggesting that we may have two renditions of similar materials. Nevertheless the final editing of this Gospel combined these sources of tradition, organized them here, and worked to give a coherent presentation of Jesus' final days.

---

37. C. H. Dodd, *Historical Tradition in the Fourth Gospel* (Cambridge: Cambridge Univ. Press, 1963), 21–151; F. F. Bruce, "The Trial of Jesus in the Fourth Gospel," *Gospel Perspectives I: Studies of History and Tradition in the Four Gospels,* R. T. France and D. Wenham, eds. (Sheffield: JSOT, 1980), 1:7–20; D. Carson, "Historical Tradition in the Fourth Gospel. After Dodd, What?" *Gospel Perspectives II. Studies of History and Tradition in the Four Gospels,* R. T. France and D. Wenham, eds. (Sheffield: JSOT, 1981), 2:83–145.

The Structure of John's Gospel

A full diagram of the Fourth Gospel can be structured as follows:

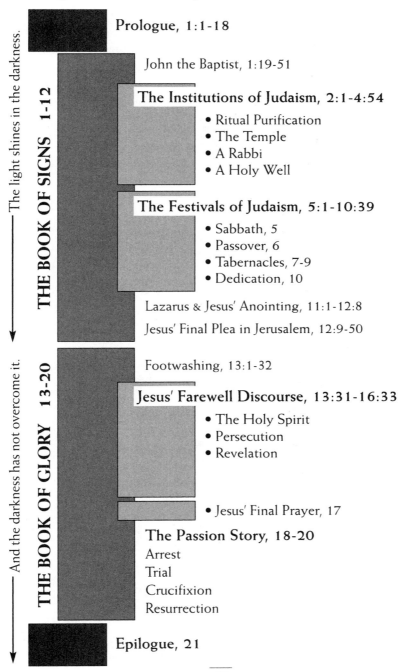

The light shines in the darkness.

Prologue, 1:1-18

John the Baptist, 1:19-51

THE BOOK OF SIGNS 1-12

The Institutions of Judaism, 2:1-4:54
- Ritual Purification
- The Temple
- A Rabbi
- A Holy Well

The Festivals of Judaism, 5:1-10:39
- Sabbath, 5
- Passover, 6
- Tabernacles, 7-9
- Dedication, 10

Lazarus & Jesus' Anointing, 11:1-12:8

Jesus' Final Plea in Jerusalem, 12:9-50

And the darkness has not overcome it.

THE BOOK OF GLORY 13-20

Footwashing, 13:1-32

Jesus' Farewell Discourse, 13:31-16:33
- The Holy Spirit
- Persecution
- Revelation

- Jesus' Final Prayer, 17

The Passion Story, 18-20
Arrest
Trial
Crucifixion
Resurrection

Epilogue, 21

Bibliography

Commentaries

Barclay, W. *The Gospel of John*. 2 vols. Edinburgh: St. Andrew's, 1956.

Barrett, C .K. *The Gospel According to St. John*. Philadelphia: Westminster, 1955, 1978.

Beasley-Murray, G. R. *John*. WBC. Waco, Tex.: Word, 1987.

Bernard, J. H. *The Gospel of John*. 2 vols. ICC. Edinburgh: T. & T. Clark, 1928.

Blank, J. *The Gospel According to John*. New York: Crossroads, 1981.

Boice, J. *The Gospel of John*. Grand Rapids: Zondervan, 1979.

Borchert, G. L. *John 1–11*. NAC. Nashville: Broadman, 1996.

Brodie, T. L. *The Gospel of John: A Literary and Theological Commentary*. New York: Oxford Univ. Press, 1993.

Brown, R. E. *The Gospel According to John*. 2 vols. AB. New York: Doubleday, 1966, 1970.

Bruce, F. F. *The Gospel of John*. Grand Rapids: Eerdmans, 1983.

Bultmann, R. *The Gospel According to John*. Philadelphia: Westminster, 1964, 1971.

Calvin, J. *The Gospel According to St. John*. 2 vols. Trans. T. H. L. Parker. Grand Rapids: Eerdmans, 1959, 1961.

Carson, D. A. *The Gospel According to John*. Grand Rapids: Eerdmans, 1991.

Comfort, P. *I Am the Way: A Spiritual Journey Through the Gospel of John* Grand Rapids: Baker, 1994.

Dodd, C. H. *The Interpretation of the Fourth Gospel*. Cambridge: Cambridge Univ. Press, 1953.

Dodds, M. *The Gospel According to St. John*. EGNT. Grand Rapids: Eerdmans, 1976.

Fenton, J. C. *The Gospel According to St. John*. Oxford: Clarendon, 1970.

Filson, F. *The Gospel of St. John*. Atlanta: John Knox, 1963.

Grayston, K. *The Gospel of John*. Narrative Commentaries. Philadelphia: Trinity Press, 1990.

Haenchen, E. *A Commentary on the Gospel of John*. 2 vols. Hermeneia. Philadelphia: Fortress, 1984.

Hendriksen, W. *The Gospel of John*. 2 vols. Grand Rapids: Baker, 1954.

Hoskyns, E., and F. N. Davey. *The Fourth Gospel*. London: Faber & Faber, 1947.

Howard, W. F. *Saint John: Introduction and Exegesis*. The Interpreter's Bible, vol. 8. Nashville: Abingdon, 1952.

Hull, W. E. *John*. BBC. Nashville: Broadman, 1970.

Hunter, A. M. *The Gospel According to John*. Cambridge: Cambridge Univ. Press, 1965.

Kealy, S. P. *That You May Believe: The Gospel According to St. John*. Middlegreen, Slough: St. Paul Pub., 1978.

Kysar, R. *John*. Augsburg Series. Minneapolis: Augsburg, 1986.

_____. *John's Story of Jesus*. Philadelphia: Fortress, 1984.

Lightfoot, R. H. *St. John's Gospel*. Oxford: Oxford Univ. Press, 1960.

Lindars, B. *The Gospel of John*. NCS. London: Oliphants, 1972.

MacGregor, G. H. C. *The Gospel of John*. London: Hodder, 1928.

MacRae, G. W. *Invitation to John*. New York: Doubleday, 1978.

Marsh, J. *Saint John*. Penguin Series. Philadelphia: Westminster, 1968.

McPolin, J. *John*. Dublin: Veritas Pub., 1979.

Michaela, J. R. *John*. NIBC. Peabody, Mass.: Hendrickson, 1984, 1989.

Milne, B. *The Message of John*. BST. Downers Grove: Intervarsity, 1993.

Morris, L. *The Gospel According to St. John*. NICNT. Grand Rapids: Eerdmans, 1995².

Newbigin, L. *The Light Has Come: An Exposition of the Fourth Gospel*. Grand Rapids: Eerdmans, 1982.

Plummer, A. *The Gospel According to St. John*. Cambridge: Cambridge Univ. Press, 1891.

Richardson, A. *The Gospel According to St. John*. London: SCM, 1959.

Ridderbos, H. *The Gospel of John*. Grand Rapids: Eerdmans, 1997.

Sanders, J. N., and B. A. Mastin. *A Commentary on the Gospel According to St. John*. HNTC. London: A. & C. Black, 1968.

Schnackenburg, R. *The Gospel According to St. John*. 3 vols. New York: Seabury, 1968, 1980, 1982.

Sloyan, G. *John*. Interpretation. Atlanta: John Knox, 1988.

Smith, D. M. *John*. Philadelphia: Fortress, 1976.

Strachan, R. H. *The Fourth Gospel*. London: SCM, 1941.

Tasker, R. B. G. *John*. TNTC. Grand Rapids: Eerdmans, 1960.

Temple, Wm. *Readings in St. John's Gospel*. London: MacMillan, 1945.

Tenney, M. *John: The Gospel of Belief*. Grand Rapids: Eerdmans, 1948.

Tenney, M. *The Gospel of John*. EBC 9. Grand Rapids: Zondervan, 1981.

Westcott, B. F. *The Gospel According to St. John: The Greek Text with Intro. and Notes*. 2 vols. London: J. Murray, 1908.

_____. *The Gospel According to John*. Grand Rapids: Eerdmans, 1973 (orig. 1881).

Whitacre, R. A. *John*. IVPNTC. Downers Grove: InterVarsity, 1999.

Witherington, B. *John's Wisdom*. Louisville: Westminster/John Knox, 1995.

Special Studies

Ashton, J., ed. *The Interpretation of John.* Minneapolis: Fortress, 1986.

Ashton, J. *Understanding the Fourth Gospel.* Oxford: Clarendon, 1991.

Barrett, C. K. *Essays on John.* Philadelphia: Westminster, 1982.

_____. *The Gospel of John and Judaism.* London: SPCK, 1975.

Burge, G. M. *The Anointed Community: The Holy Spirit in the Johannine Tradition.* Grand Rapids: Eerdmans, 1987.

_____. *Interpreting the Gospel of John.* Grand Rapids: Baker, 1992.

Culpepper, R. A. and C. C. Black, eds. *Exploring the Gospel of John.* Louisville: Westminster, 1996.

Dodd, C. H. *Historical Tradition in the Fourth Gospel.* Cambridge: Cambridge Univ. Press, 1963.

_____. *The Interpretation of the Fourth Gospel.* Cambridge: Cambridge Univ. Press, 1953.

Ellis, E. E. *The World of St. John.* Grand Rapids: Eerdmans, 1984.

Harvey, A. E. *Jesus on Trial: A Study in the Fourth Gospel.* London: SPCK, 1976.

Hunter, A. M. *According to John: The New Look on the Fourth Gospel.* Philadelphia: Westminster, 1968.

Kysar, R. *The Fourth Evangelist and His Gospel: An Examination of Contemporary Scholarship.* Minneapolis: Augsburg, 1975.

Painter, J. *The Quest for the Messiah: The History, Literature and Theology of the Johannine Community.* Nashville: Abingdon, 1993[2].

Robinson, J. A. T. *The Priority of John.* Grand Rapids: Eerdmans, 1986.

Smalley, S. *John: Evangelist and Interpreter.* New York: Thomas Nelson, 1978.

Smith, D. M. *Johannine Christianity: Essays on Its Setting, Sources and Theology.* Columbia: Univ. of South Carolina Press, 1984.

Smith, D. M. *John Among the Gospels: The Relationship in Twentieth Century Research.* Minneapolis: Fortress, 1992.

Smith, D. M. *The Theology of the Gospel of John.* Cambridge: Cambridge Univ. Press, 1995.

Thompson, M. M. *The Humanity of Jesus in the Fourth Gospel.* Philadelphia: Fortress, 1988.

Vanderlip, D. G. *Christianity According to John.* Philadelphia: Westminster, 1979.

Wiles, M. F. *The Spiritual Gospel: The Interpretation of the Fourth Gospel in the Early Church.* Cambridge: Cambridge Univ. Press, 1960.

Using the Internet

Today a great deal of bibliographic information is available on the Internet. The following sites are useful resources for research and study.

Bibliography

(1) **The New Testament Gateway.** http://www.bham.ac.uk/theology/ goodacre/links.htm. This outstanding site is organized by Dr. Mark Goodacre at the Univ. of Birmingham (England). Goodacre identifies both Web links and book and article references to every conceivable subject in New Testament studies.

(2) **The Wabash Center Guide to Internet Resources for Teaching and Learning in Theology and Religion.** http://www.wabashcenter. wabash.edu/Internet/front.htm. Originally organized by a librarian at Regent College, Vancouver, and funded by the Lilly Endowment, this site lists links to bibliography, publications, electronic texts and journals, and courses found on the web. In addition, it covers all fields of religious studies.

(3) **Resource Pages for Biblical Studies.** http://www.hivolda.no/asf/kkf/ rel-stud.html. Maintained by Dr. Torrey Seland at Volda College, Volda, Norway, this site is fast becoming a popular resource for research. Subjects are organized around five pages: (1) biblical texts published on the World Wide Web; (2) biblical studies published electronically; (3) aspects of the Mediterranean world; (4) biblical studies and computer technology; (5) Philo of Alexandria.

(4) **The Argus Clearinghouse.** http://www.clearinghouse.net/. This Michigan site organizes and evaluates web indexing sites. Look under "arts and humanities," then "philosophy and religion," etc.

(5) **Jesus of Nazareth in the Early Christian Gospels.** http://www. earlygospels.net/. This outstanding site by Andrew Bernhard gives all links to ancient Gospels (from Synoptic Gospels to Thomas) now available on the web.

(6) **A Synopsis of the Gospels.** http://www.princeton.edu/~jwm/synopsis/ met-syni.htm. This Princeton University site (published by Princeton's Religion Department) permits you to look at John's Gospel in parallel with the other three Synoptic Gospels as well as the Gospel of Thomas.

(7) Two sites offer dedicated bibliographical research on John's Gospel: (a) http://www.uscsu.sc.edu/~johnlitr/ (A. Gagne, Univ. of Southern Carolina, Sumter); (b) http://private.fuller.edu/~talarm/iss4/iss4s1.html (James McGrath, Durham, England).

John 1:1–18

IN THE BEGINNING was the Word, and the Word was with God, and the Word was God. ²He was with God in the beginning.

³Through him all things were made; without him nothing was made that has been made. ⁴In him was life, and that life was the light of men. ⁵The light shines in the darkness, but the darkness has not understood it.

⁶There came a man who was sent from God; his name was John. ⁷He came as a witness to testify concerning that light, so that through him all men might believe. ⁸He himself was not the light; he came only as a witness to the light. ⁹The true light that gives light to every man was coming into the world.

¹⁰He was in the world, and though the world was made through him, the world did not recognize him. ¹¹He came to that which was his own, but his own did not receive him. ¹²Yet to all who received him, to those who believed in his name, he gave the right to become children of God—¹³children born not of natural descent, nor of human decision or a husband's will, but born of God.

¹⁴The Word became flesh and made his dwelling among us. We have seen his glory, the glory of the One and Only, who came from the Father, full of grace and truth.

¹⁵John testifies concerning him. He cries out, saying, "This was he of whom I said, 'He who comes after me has surpassed me because he was before me.'" ¹⁶From the fullness of his grace we have all received one blessing after another. ¹⁷For the law was given through Moses; grace and truth came through Jesus Christ. ¹⁸No one has ever seen God, but God the One and Only, who is at the Father's side, has made him known.

ONE REASON WHY the Gospel of John was symbolized in the ancient church by the eagle is the lofty heights attained by its prologue. With skill and delicacy, John handles issues of profound importance. It comes as no surprise that this prologue has been foundational to the classic Christian formulation of the doctrine of Christ. Here divinity and humanity, preexistence and incarnation, revelation and sacrifice are each discussed by John with deceptive simplicity.

This prologue may well have been an ancient Christian hymn. We know of other hymns extant especially in Paul's writing, and here too there is an artful flowing of language and theology.[1] In the medieval church the prologue was so venerated that it was sometimes worn in an amulet around the neck to ward off disease and evil spirits. The Roman church read it over the sick and newly baptized. It was even the final prayer of the Roman mass.

Many scholars have attempted to give some literary form to the hymn, and it is impossible here to survey their results.[2] I have found a satisfying structure that combines a number of scholarly insights and breaks down the prologue into four theologically distinguishable *strophes*. In Greek literature a strophe was a turn (as in dance) or a choral poem or lyric used with dance. In poetry we might call it a stanza. Here John offers four artful "turnings," which give us separate glimpses of the Word and his relation to God and the world.

This prologue is also an overture to the story of the rest of Gospel. Themes mentioned here will be picked up later and given fuller development: the preexistence of Christ (1:1; 17:5), divine light entering the world (1:4, 9; 8:12; 9:5), the opposition of light and darkness (1:5; 3:19), the visibility of glory (1:14; 12:41), Jesus as the *only* Son (1:14, 18; 3:16), divine birth (1:12–13; 3:1ff.), and the place of John the Baptist in Jesus' work (1:7, 15; 1:19, 30).[3] More precisely, 1:11–12 reflect the layout or the emphasis of the Gospel's entire structure: "He came to that which was his own, but his own did not receive him. Yet to all who received him, to those who believed in his name, he gave the right to become children of God." The first half of the Gospel (chs. 1–12, the Book of Signs) describes the rejection of Jesus by Judaism, "his own people." The second half of the book (chs. 13–21, the Book of Glory) describes the "flock of Jesus," those who have embraced his messiahship and followed him.

In its earliest edition, John's Gospel may have begun at 1:19 with the story of John the Baptist.[4] This hymn was presumably later added by John

---

1. Other New Testament hymns are found in Eph. 5:19; Phil. 2:5–11; Col. 1:15–20; 3:15.

2. Rearrangement theories are often criticized since there is so little consensus. See the number of theories outlined in Brown, *John*, 1:22ff. Some have found chiasm (inverted parallelisms) here: see A. Culpepper, "The Pivot of John's Prologue," *NTS* 27 (1980–81): 1–31; J. Staley, "The Structure of John's Prologue: Its Implications for the Gospel's Narrative Structure," *CBQ* 48 (1986): 241–63.

3. For a more complete list, see D. A. Carson, *The Gospel According to John*, 111.

4. This is a commonplace reconstruction of the literary history of the Fourth Gospel found in most technical commentaries (see Brown, Barrett, Smalley, Schnackenburg, Morris).

about the same time he wrote his letters (cf. the opening verses of 1 John and the Gospel) to serve as a literary preface or prologue. In order to knit this section to his Gospel, John added material from the story of John the Baptist (1:6–8, 15) as well as his own personal commentary on the hymn (1:13, 17–18). Of course, any reconstruction such as this is speculative; but when examined closely, it enhances our understanding of the theological message of the prologue.[5]

The First Strophe

In the beginning was the Word,
And the Word was with God,
And the Word was God.
He was in the beginning with God.

The Second Strophe

All things came into being through him,
and without him not one thing came into being.
What has come into being in him was life,
and the life was the light of all people.
The light shines in the darkness,
and the darkness has not overcome it.

[There was a man sent from God, whose name was John. He came as a witness to testify to the light, so that all might believe through him. He himself was not the light, but he came to testify to the light.]

The Third Strophe

The true light, which enlightens everyone, was coming into the world.
He was in the world, and the world came into being through him;
yet the world did not know him.
He came to what was his own people,
and his own people did not accept him.
But to all who received him, who believed on his name,
he gave the power to become children of God.

[Who were {who was} born, not of blood or of the will of the flesh or of the will of man, but of God.]

The Fourth Strophe

And the Word became flesh and dwelt
among us, full of grace and truth.

---

5. In the following structure, I am using my own translation

And we have seen his glory,
the glory as of a father's only son.

[John testified to him and cried out, "This is he of whom I said, 'He who comes after me ranks ahead of me because he was before me.'"]

From his fullness
we have all received grace upon grace.

[The law indeed was given through Moses; grace and truth came through Jesus Christ. No one has ever seen God. It is {God} the only Son, who is close to the Father's bosom, who has made him known.]

The First Strophe: The Logos and God (1:1–2)

THE FIRST VERSES of John's Gospel are a triumph of Christian theology. John begins by establishing the preeminence of the Word existing before the creation of the world. The initial allusion to Genesis 1 cannot be missed (John 1:1). This is a Gospel that will record the re-creation of men and women, the giving of life in darkness where there is no hope. This parallels the thought of Genesis 1, in which God breathes life into the nostrils of Adam and provides new possibilities for the world.

John begins by introducing Jesus as "the Word" (*logos*) and is building here on much contemporary Jewish thought, where the word of God took on personal creative attributes (Gen. 1; Ps. 33:6, 9).[6] In the New Testament period it was personified (Wisd. Sol. 7:24; 18:15–16) and known by some as the immanent power of God creatively at work in the world (Philo). John identifies this Word as Jesus Christ. As such John can attribute to him various divine functions, such as creation (John 1:3, 10) and giving of life (1:4, 14, 16).

But John goes further. He is ready to infer some personal identity between the Logos and God. "And the Word *was* God" (1:1). John often employs similar Greek verbs in order to develop a contrast of themes. The Greek words *ginomai* (to become) and *eimi* (to be) have similar nuances, but John frequently uses them together to make a point. For instance, in 8:58 Jesus says (lit.), "Before Abraham was [*ginomai*], I am [*eimi*]." The first verb suggests "coming *into* being," such as Abraham's birth; the second implies ongoing existence. Thus in 1:6 John writes, "There *came* [*ginomai*] a man sent from God." In 1:1 John carefully writes, "In the beginning *was* the Word"—"the Word *was* with God"—"the Word *was* God." In each case he uses *eimi*. John

---

6. Some scholars are convinced that the best contextual setting for *logos* is Hellenistic. While it is true that Hellenism had deeply influenced Jewish thought by the first century, the commentary will make clear that John's frame of reference is primarily indebted to traditional Jewish religious concepts.

is making an absolute affirmation about the eternal existence of the Word. It did not come into being nor was there ever a time when "the Word was not."[7] Whatever we can say about God, we can and must say about the Word.

But who is this Word? "The Word was *God*." Attempts to detract from this literal translation for grammatical reasons (e.g., "the word was a god [or divine]") run aground when we consider the number of other times when such a divine ascription is made for Jesus. For example, Jesus employs the divine Old Testament title "I Am" (8:24, 28, 58, etc.), he is "one with God" (10:30), and he is even addressed by Thomas in the Gospel's final scene as "my Lord and my God" (20:28).

Some have argued that because *theos* (God) does not have a definite article, the better translation would be, "The word was divine," thereby limiting any absolute claim for the Logos. But this cannot be the case. Greek has another common word for divine (*theios*), and in other passages, John omits the article but does not imply a change in meaning.[8] In Greek the word order is even reversed ("and *God* was the Word"), emphasizing not that the Word contains the entirety of the Godhead, but that the divinity possessed by God is also possessed by this Word.

This is John's overture to Christology and the beginnings of his Trinitarian thought. Indeed, "John intends that the whole of his gospel shall be read in the light of this verse. The deeds and words of Jesus are the deeds and words of God."[9] This is the theme that will be echoed throughout the Gospel. We will be introduced to Jesus time and time again, and in each case we will be forced to picture Jesus with increasingly profound images. He is the greatest of all people; he is the Messiah of Jewish expectation; but more (this is John's unique message), he is the Son of God, the divine messenger from the Father. Any reading of the Fourth Gospel that omits this supreme and ultimate claim for Jesus misses its central affirmation.

The Second Strophe: The Logos and Creation (1:3–8)

ONCE JOHN HAS identified the Logos with God, he continues to mark the relation of this Logos to the world. As God's creative agent, he was responsible for the creation of the world. John's language here is careful and specific: The Logos was not one preeminent creation that went on to create others. In fact, the Logos was never created. *Nothing* came into being without

---

7. These are the words of Arius, a fourth-century theologian who questioned the eternal existence of the Logos. Arian theology was deemed heretical in A.D. 325 at the Council of Nicea.

8. John 1.49; 8:39; 17·17; cf. Rom. 14:17; Rev. 1:20.

9. Barrett, *John*, 156.

him (v. 3).[10] This is another parallel with the thought world of Genesis. In Genesis 1 we are introduced to the God of Israel, Creator of the universe. Now we learn more. The creative capacity of God was Logos. Therefore John stresses not merely that who God is, the Logos is (Strophe One), but that what God does, the Logos does. Therefore in the Gospel, what Jesus does is divine activity. When he heals or speaks—when he gives eternal life (v. 4)—this is God at work, just as God worked at the foundation of the world.

The entry of the Logos into the world (his incarnation) is described as light shining in the darkness (v. 5). Even though John the Baptist's testimony was clear (vv. 6–9), still, Jesus experiences rejection (vv. 10–11). But there is more. The darkness is hostile. There is enmity. The NIV translates 1:5 that the world cannot *understand* the Word, following the traditional KJV reading. But the verb used here has a double significance: to grasp with the mind and so to comprehend; and to grasp with the hand and so to overcome or destroy. Both ideas are at work in John, but the second meaning seems foremost here.[11]

John suggests that the darkness cannot defeat or overcome the Word. This theme gives us some hint of the struggle between light and darkness that will sound throughout the Gospel. The opposition to Jesus will be severe. The world that the Logos enters and God loves is a place of remarkable unbelief. Those opposed to him will try to defeat this Word. But they will fail. John is thinking of the cross—the place of attempted defeat. But as this Gospel will show, the cross is not a place of defeat, but of glory. Jesus overcomes the world (16:33; cf. 12:31; 14:30).

I have set apart verses 6–9 to distinguish them from the prologue itself. This section (as well as v. 15) may come from materials John has added into the prologue in order to weave it into the body of the Gospel. In fact, these tie in nicely with the story that begins at 1:19.[12] John emphasizes the true nature of the Baptist's ministry and shows how he came as a witness to Jesus; this theme is clear in the other "Baptist" sections of the Gospel (1:19–34; 3:22–36; 10:40–42). What does the writer say? John the Baptist was *not* the Messiah (1:20) or the light. Instead, he came as a witness to tell the truth about what was happening in the world.

---

10. John makes this completely clear· *Everything* (Gk. *panta*) came to be through him.

11. The Gk. *katalambano* is in the active voice in Greek here. In nine of its fifteen New Testament uses, it means to seize with hostile intent. In Mark 9:18 a demon "seizes" a man. In John 12:35 Jesus says to walk in the light lest the darkness "overtake" you. John also uses it in 8:3–4 (the woman is "caught" in adultery), and a variant of 6:17 reads that the darkness had not yet "overtaken" people. When the word appears in the middle voice, it generally means "comprehend" (see Acts 4:13; 10:34; 25·25; Eph. 3:18).

12. We might even speculate that the Gospel originally began at 1:6 with these short verses, then continued with 1:19. It was only later that the prologue was added (both before and after 1:6–9).

This is the first time we see the word group for "witness" (Gk. *martyreo, martys, martyria*) in the Gospel. This group is important because it communicates what happens as the Word enters the world.[13] As if in a courtroom, evidence and witnesses will come forward to verify the truth of Jesus' case. John the Baptist is the first of these "literary" witnesses. We will see this more completely in 1:19ff., where the Baptist (as forerunner to Jesus) speaks directly to Judaism's leadership about the identity of Jesus. But here we have a foreshadowing, a hint, that John (and others like him) will enter the Johannine stage providing insight into the meaning of Jesus (5:31–37, 39; 8:18; 10:25; 15:27; 19:35; 1 John 5:6–11). Essential to John's mission is a denial of his own significance: "He was not the light." This will reappear in a triple denial in John 1:19–24, suggesting that John's main role is simply to glorify and identify Jesus.

The Third Strophe: The Logos and Revelation (1:9–13)

JOHN THE BAPTIST was bearing witness not to an abstraction or a hope, but to a reality. The "true light" was coming. "Coming into the world" is difficult. It can modify either "everyone" (i.e., the true light enlightens everyone who comes into the world) or "light" (i.e., the true light, which enlightens everyone, was coming into the world).[14] Because the entry of the Word into the world is such a frequent thought for John, the latter reading is the better interpretation (cf. 1:10; 3:17, 19, etc.).[15]

However, the virtue of this divine entry is in how it reaches all people, particularly those hostile to God. In John's vocabulary, the "world" (Gk. *kosmos*) is an important theological term, appearing seventy-eight times in this Gospel alone. In some cases it bears a positive connotation (e.g., 3:16: "God so loves the world"). Other times it is neutral (e.g., 8:26, where Jesus says, "What I have heard from him [God] I tell the world"). But for the most part, references to *kosmos* are decidedly negative. The world is not the created order of things; it is not the natural environment per se. It is the sphere of creation that lives in rebellion (1:10; 7:7; 14:17, 22, 27, 30; 15:18–19; 16:8, 20, 33; 17:6, 9, 14, 25). Thus when we read about Jesus' appearance in the world, God's love for the world (3:16), or Jesus' salvation of the world (4:42), such passages are not ringing endorsements of the world, but testimonies to the character of God and his love.[16]

---

13. The word group appears in the Johannine literature 64 times (47 in this Gospel).

14. The NIV places the first option in the margin. The grammar can fit either exegesis.

15. The Gk. phrase "into the world" occurs 14 times in John and almost always refers to Jesus.

16. Carson, *John*, 123.

But if the world is hostile—and here we anticipate the rejection described in 1:10—how can it enlighten *everyone*? Does the arrival of this true light illumine every heart? Perhaps John is thinking of the accessibility of everyone to this one source of illumination. Or is this the distribution of the knowledge of God (general revelation) that makes all people responsible, as Paul argues in Romans 1?[17] Another option is to think of the primary meaning of the verb *photizo*: to light up, expose, bring to light. What is at stake here is how the objective revelation of the Word works: The light invades the darkness, shining on every person and exposing them for who they are. No one is exempt, and in the course of this Gospel the divine revelation divides the audience: Some flee because their deeds are evil (3:19—20), while some receive the revelation because their deeds are true (3:21). Either way, the light shines on everyone, forcing a distinction (8:12; 9:39—41).

Despite the presence of the Logos in the world (1:10a), despite his creative work making the world (1:10b) and leaving the marks of general revelation, still, the world failed to recognize him. "He came to that which was his own [neut. pl., *his own place or home*], but his own [now masc. pl., *his own people*] did not receive him." The focus of revelation has been Judaism, the spiritual birthplace of the Messiah. And the great irony of this Gospel's story is that *even here*, where readiness and receptivity should have been keen, there was only rejection. Similar to Luke's description of Bethlehem's homes, there was no room. Similar to the parable of the vineyard owner and his renters, the residents repudiated his visit (Mark 12:1—12). Therefore John has made a startling claim. Even though the focus of revelation has been in Israel, the natural home for the truth of God, the Word has come for the entire world, not merely Judaism.

John indicates, however, that the light has its followers; Jesus has his disciples (1:12—13). Even though his own people—adherents to Judaism— spurned his message, those who did receive him obtained power to become God's children. Verses 12—13 anticipate the story of Nicodemus (3:1—21), in which this rebirth is explored.

Verse 13 poses an interesting challenge. Some manuscripts supply a singular verb in verse 13a: "who *was* born, not of blood . . . ," implying that the subject here is Jesus. That is, Jesus was born uniquely through the will of God. Most translations, however, retain the plural, so that verse 13 echoes the thought of verse 12. Those who follow the Word, who believe and obtain divine power, will share in divine birth. This is John's understanding of conversion: Deliberate faith joined with divine transformation. A careful reading of 1 John shows that "child of God," "rebirth," and "born of God" were commonplace names describing Johannine discipleship (1 John 3:2, 9; 4:4,

---

17. So J. Calvin, *John 1—10* (Calvin's New Testament Commentaries; Grand Rapids: Eerdmans, 1961), 15

7, 12–13). In other words, there will be a powerful transformation of those who embrace this light, who align themselves with the light instead of the darkness, who cling to the Messiah instead of the world.

The Fourth Strophe: The Logos and Incarnation (1:14–18)

THE PROLOGUE'S FINALE is found in verses 14–18. John sums up in fresh language what has already been said. Now the abstract thought of light and darkness gives way to concrete Old Testament images.

John 1:14 is one of the most important verses in the Bible. The Word did not just appear to be human; *the Word became flesh.* This assertion stunned the Greek mind for whom the separation of the divine spirit and the mundane world (flesh, *sarx*) was an axiom of belief. But the second phrase is equally stunning for the Jew. This Word dwelt (*skenoo*) among us and revealed his glory (*doxa*). This verb for dwelling is employed in the Greek Old Testament for the tabernacle of God. In other words, Christ is the locus of God's dwelling with Israel *as he had dwelt with them in the tabernacle in the desert* (Ex. 25:8–9; Zech. 2:10). Hence the glory of God, once restricted to the tabernacle (Ex. 40:34), is now visible in Christ (John 1:14b).

But two things must be noted. (1) This experience of glory is concrete. It is not a mystical vision and an inward illumination. The glory of God took up tangible form and was touched (20:20–29; 1 John 1:1ff.). (2) This glory was not merely a display of power. For John the deepest irony is how glory is to be found in suffering and humiliation, for in this Gospel, the cross of Christ is again and again described as Jesus' *glorification* (John 12:23–24; 13:31). His signs and miracles showed his glory, to be sure (2:11; 11:4), but it is in the cross that the mysterious, unfathomable glory of God is to be found.

It is curious that the word "grace," so common in the rest of the New Testament, is virtually unused by John and appears only here in the prologue (four times) and then disappears. Following the common understanding of the New Testament, John likely has in mind the generous work of God in sending his Son, which results in our salvation. Grace is found in God's coming and working *despite* the hostility and rejection of the world. Grace is not merely an attribute of God. It is known when someone enjoys his goodness. It is the recipient who knows grace, not the theologian who has studied it. Thus in 1:16 John emphasizes our experience and reception of this grace as its chief merit.

The more important word for John, however, is "truth."[18] Most simply it is the opposite of falsehood; but John sees truth as penetrating far deeper.

---

18. "Truth" appears 25 times in this Gospel and 20 times in the letters. The entire word group based on "truth" (true, truthful, etc.) appears 55 times in the Gospel.

Truth is the self-disclosure that alone comes from God; truth is not just what is right, but what is divine *and this is right*. Thus Jesus can describe himself as the truth (14:6) and likewise say that the Holy Spirit is the Spirit of truth (15:26; 16:13). Therefore the incarnation of Christ (1:14a) silences the fraudulent voices of the world whose truth claims are inimical to God.

John the Baptist's cry as a witness to Jesus (1:15; see comments on 1:6–7) repeats his role as witness. Even though Jesus comes after John chronologically, this does not give John priority. These words pick up on the theme in all of the Baptist texts, where John's secondary status is underscored. However, here we find the reason why Jesus is superior: As in 1:1, his eternal pre-existence surpasses John the Baptist's status in every way. Jesus does not have a relative superiority, but an absolute superiority.

Throughout this Gospel, it is clear that the apostle John and his community are struggling with the counterclaims of the Jewish synagogue. As in John 9, the healed blind man must decide if he is a follower of Moses or a follower of Jesus. One (apparently) cannot be both (9:28)—or at least that is how John's opponents are putting it.[19] John makes clear here that Moses did indeed play an unparalleled role: He provided the first five books of the Bible, the Torah, which John here calls "the law" (1:17). These are not being discredited, for surely grace and truth came through Moses too. John does not intend to show that the grace of Christ stands at odds with the revelation of Moses. The law likewise contains the grace of God and is an earlier display of it.[20]

But what is at stake here is the exhaustive character of the Christian revelation. It is interesting that in Exodus 33:18 Moses' request to see God is denied (33:20; cf. Deut. 4:12); but Jesus has come to us from the very heart of the Father (John 1:18). Indeed, he has seen the Father—and no one else has.[21] This goes beyond Moses and every other claimant for the truth in the world. Hebrews 3:1–6 carries this same thought: The Son's revelation cannot by definition have any rivals.[22]

The NIV indicates an interesting variation in 1:18: "No one has ever seen God, but *God* the One and Only, who is at the Father's side, has made him known." Some manuscripts insert "Son" for "God,"[23] but the NIV's more diffi-

---

19. See also 5:39, 46; 6.32; 8:32ff.

20. R. Edwards, "χαϋριν ἀντὶ χάριτος (Jn 1:16). Grace and the Law in the Johannine Prologue," JSNT 32 (1988): 3–15, see also Brown, *John*, comments on 1:16; Carson, *John*, 131–34.

21. John's Greek word order makes is emphatic: *"God no one has seen."*

22. Even though in Ex. 33·11 the Lord spoke to Moses "face to face," this is metaphorical since in 33·17–23 Moses must be protected from seeing God's face, which would surely destroy him (33:20).

23. "Only Son" is a common Johannine expression (see 3.16, 18; 1 John 4:9).

cult, explicit affirmation of Christ's divinity is likely original. John 1:18 then joins 1:1 as the closing frame of the prologue, offering a summary statement about the divine origin and exhaustive knowledge of the Son. Christ's revelation is unique for ontological reasons: It is his identity, his being, the essence of who he is that makes his words God's words. Indeed, Christ is fully God, who in his incarnation is revealing *himself* to the world.[24]

THESE VERSES OF Scripture are perhaps some of the most important words ever penned. As I work to appropriate their meaning into my own generation, I must be alert to the major theological themes that John has woven into them. The prologue to John's Gospel is densely packed with ringing affirmations about Jesus Christ, God's relation to the world, and the character of humanity. Each of these not only had incisive things to say to John's generation, but likewise to ours. The three themes I have listed here will unfold in the narrative of the Gospel and here can serve as an outline to what is to come.

The identity of the Son of God. In early Christian reflection, the catalyst for thinking about the identity and mission of Christ (Christology) was no doubt the resurrection. Jesus had been vindicated and the truth of his claims was assured, because God had delivered him from the grave. The fact of the resurrection and the failure of the cross to defeat Jesus becomes the center of New Testament preaching throughout Acts. Peter's Pentecost speech finds its critical junction at the point where Jesus is described as rescued from the grave: "'He was not abandoned to the grave, nor did his body see decay'" (Acts 2:31). It is the present reality of Christ, his lordship, and his presence in the church that fuel the church's mission and confidence.

This emphasis is evident in Paul's letters, which manifest virtually no interest in Jesus' earthly life. Paul writes with passion about the present, empowering lordship of Christ, who is a life-giving Spirit (1 Cor. 15:45) and who is sovereign over the church (Col. 1:18). He describes the future when Jesus in glory will return to the world to redeem his church (1Thess. 5:2).

But it was not long before reflection migrated into the early years of Jesus' life. The earliest narratives written focused on the Passion story and provided an answer to the pressing question: Why was Jesus crucified?[25] And if

---

24. The Greek verb "made him known" (*exegeomai*), from which we obtain the term *exegesis*, was often used in pagan religions for the revelation of divine secrets.
25. The close parallels among the four Gospels in their Passion stories reflect the uniform explanation given in the early church.

he exhibited power over the grave, surely this power was evident during his ministry. Thus, the Gospels explore other questions: What was the character of God's presence with Jesus on earth?[26] How do we explain his messianic role in Judaism?[27] The work of Mark, Matthew, and Luke began to answer these questions, but there was one more line of inquiry that pressed Christological reflection a step further: Did Jesus have a preexistence? Matthew and Luke's nativity stories open this discussion directly, but it was left to John to give a full theological explanation.

The prologue is the most complete, indeed, the most explicit study of Christ's preexistence in the New Testament. The significance of Jesus is not merely in his ability to be a powerful worker of mighty deeds. Nor is it in his wisdom as a great teacher. Rather, Jesus is God-become-flesh. That is, the phenomenon of Jesus Christ is a phenomenon unlike anything the world has witnessed before. He is God-in-descent, God stepping into the context of humanity. In more technical terms, Jesus has an *ontological* divinity.[28] His being, his essence, his very nature is one with God. This is to be compared with an *ethical* divinity, in which Jesus is valued or aligned with God—as evidenced in what he does. This may at first seem obvious to those who have been nurtured in the Christian environment, but today it simply cannot be assumed that men and women truly understand the Christological implications of John's incarnational theology.

Springing from this doctrine of the high divinity of Jesus—a divinity anchored to preexistence—comes a host of theological themes that I must press home when I apply this text. John's understanding of *revelation* lifts Jesus' words above those of a prophet and any human being. The voice of Jesus becomes the voice of God. It is for this reason that Jesus can tell Philip that seeing him is equivalent to seeing the Father (14:9). This is also why Thomas, at the close of the Gospel, can give Jesus the high acclaim, "My Lord and my God" (20:28). In a similar fashion, John's understanding of *redemption* now becomes a divine work that parallels Paul's words in 2 Corinthians 5:19: "God was reconciling the world to *himself* in Christ." Redemption is thus no divinely inspired human event that sets out to placate God. Redemption is God himself at work in the world, achieving his own goals for repairing the consequences of sin and bringing humanity back into relationship with himself.

---

26. Here the accounts of Jesus' baptism and his many miracles and exorcisms helped explain who he was.

27. Here the many messianic prophesies and links to Judaism were woven into the Gospel record.

28. Ontology comes from the Greek verb "to be" (in its participial form). It refers to essence or being.

To sum up, therefore, Jesus must be explained in terms of his unique origin and mission, and this explanation must be forged with a clear understanding of his unity with the Father. To compromise this delicate theme in the Fourth Gospel is to jeopardize John's portrayal of Jesus throughout the Gospel.

The nature of the world. High on John's theological agenda is his interest in explaining the rejection of Jesus by Judaism and the world—a rejection leading to the cross. For John this does not mean that Jesus failed in any way; rather, it uncovers the character of the world (a place of darkness) and discloses how the world reacts whenever it is penetrated by the light. John's worldview is strictly dualistic: The forces of light and darkness, good and evil, God and Satan are arrayed against one another to such a degree that there can be no compromise. No intermingling. No association.

John's theology of the world is his vehicle for explaining Jesus' rejection by Judaism (1:11), the failure of most to understand the things of God (1:10), and the hostility of the world in general when the things of God are brought to the fore (1:5). John writes, "Light has come into the world, but [people] loved darkness instead of light because their deeds were evil" (3:19). In short, *darkness* is a theological description that betrays the world's commitments and confusions. For this reason Nicodemus, who can barely understand Jesus, comes "at night" (3:2). And after Judas betrays Jesus, he departs the Upper Room into the night (13:30). These are literary devices John employs to tell us about the environment in which these two men live and work: "But those who walk at night stumble, because the light is not in them" (11:10 NRSV).

The world, then, is not a neutral place, a place of open inquiry and curiosity about God. As I bring this passage into the modern world, I need to keep John's cosmology, his theology of the world, foremost in my thinking. The world is opposed to the light. Yet despite the world's hopeless and hostile condition, still, God loves the world and has entered it in order to save it (3:16—17). *The world* is thus a *theological* term for humanity set against God. "God so loved the world" is not about God's love for nature, but God's love for those arrayed against him.

The possibilities for humanity. John's third message is his theology of hope. The desperate condition of humanity is set against the goodness of God and his overtures toward the world in Christ. This alone, this supernatural intervention, is the only possibility for men and women today. The darkness of the world cannot defeat the Word (1:5) because the Word created the world and understands everything that has gone into it (1:3). In 2:24—25 Jesus is celebrated by many who witnessed his signs at Passover, but then John provides a remarkable commentary about Jesus' savvy understanding of this shallow popularity: He understood all people and understood what was in each one of them.

This is the hope to which John clings: Despite the fallenness and corruption of humanity—a corruption at the very heart of things, despite the hostility of humanity to God—nevertheless God empowers men and women to be transformed and become his children (1:12). This is hope: that despite the darkness, One Light shined and this Light worked to illumine others. Despite the darkness, the glory of God radiated in the world (1:14b), displaying the grace and truth of the Father (1:14a).

This is an essentially modern message because we live in a culture that is looking for hope. For some, hope has been anchored in human systems and possibilities. For younger generations, there often seems to be no hope, and as they look at their world, they feel despair. The key here is that I must proclaim a Christological eschatology, an ultimate and final message that is anchored in the possibilities brought about through God in Christ, or else I have betrayed the very essence of what God has done in the Incarnation.

VOICES. THE WORLD in which we live is looking for a diagnosis of its condition and its possibilities for renewal. There are countless voices providing messages that promise to alleviate the struggle of life or the questions that trouble us. We hear political and economic voices, arguing that if we reallocate or reorganize or restructure, we will build the sort of world where equity and charity win the day. Other voices are more deeply personal, arguing that the problem is not sociological but human—the human soul is in need of repair or renewal—and if we provide the right education or therapy or vision of our neighbor, then all will be made right. These voices, these messages, are secular, and they can be heard in pulpits every Sunday. These prophets of our day offer services that are deeply needed and useful, but their voices cannot replace The Voice that John 1:1–18 introduces.

The prologue to John is not about a message that offers hope, but about The Message that is the only hope. It is not about an idea, but a person. *The Word became flesh* tells us that God is intent on communicating with us not about mere concepts; he is intent on communicating about himself. *The Word became flesh* tells us that The Message is accessible and not hidden away for mystics and scholars but was lived in the world and was touched and heard by many. *The Word became flesh* tells us that the man Jesus was no mere mortal. He was not an inspired carpenter or a model human. Jesus was God himself—taking on the clothing of humanity, embracing it fully and eternally, walking in it, speaking through it, and delivering the reality of God to the world in a manner never done before. This prologue tells us that something definitive has happened in time, something objective and absolute. A marker has been placed in human history, and all humanity is now being called to mark time and progress by that post.

Three strands. The prologue provides a theological template, weaving together three strands of thinking that, when taken together, form the essential fabric of the Christian message. Each message is tied to the other two, and together they comprise the core of our faith that men and women, even young children, should have as essential spiritual equipment. These commitments should be reflexes, beliefs so deeply ingrained that we cannot view the world in any other way except through them.

(1) *Definitive Christology.* The scandal that must never be compromised is the nature of Christ and his relation to the Father. Jesus is not one savior among the world's many saviors, nor is he one good man among many men. Jesus is God-in-flesh. Or as the theologians of Nicea framed it, Christ and the Father share the same essence or being. There never was a time when the Son did not exist.

This basic scandal—this unyielding affirmation about Jesus Christ—is constantly at issue in discussions concerning the truth of Christianity and the validity of alternative religions and philosophical systems.[29] But more fundamentally, this notion challenges a major shift in the way the modern world views reality.

This came home to me recently when I read Lesslie Newbigin's *Foolishness to the Greeks: The Gospel and Western Culture.*[30] Newbigin was a career missionary in India, who returned to his home in England after spending forty years in central Asia. But when he returned, he discovered that the culture he was reentering was as alien to the gospel as anything he witnessed in India. During his career he was accustomed to studying culture in order to understand the intellectual structures of a society and how he might communicate cross-culturally. But when he returned home, he discovered that if he was going to speak of the gospel at all in Western Europe, this communication too had to be cross-cultural. To his modern listeners, the gospel sounded like foolishness—much as Paul experienced among the Greeks in Corinth (cf. 1 Cor. 1:23).

In brief, Western society had emptied modern life of the ability to see the world *theocentrically*. God had been dismissed from his role of running the external world, thanks to the advent of science, and God's last domain—the inner world—had been taken over by psychology. While the notion of

---

29. See here D. Okholm and T. Phillips, eds., *More Than One Way? Four Views on Salvation in a Pluralistic World* (Grand Rapids: Zondervan, 1995).

30. Grand Rapids: Eerdmans, 1986.

an ambiguous God may still have a place, so Newbigin argues, the idea of a personal, self-revealing God has become incomprehensible to many. This means that we cannot simply announce that God has become human in Christ; rather, we must lay bare the fundamental structures of modern thought that have invalidated this idea in the first place. We must uncover today's *pagan cosmology*.[31]

History is not simply buffeted by the forces of social change. The cosmos is not merely explained by cause and effect. God is the architect of history, who delights in making himself known and who enters our reality through word and miracle, showing his glory and power. And what we claim he has done in Jesus Christ fits excellently into any *theological cosmology*: Christ is God once more at work, disclosing himself to his creation. Christ is God reaching into the realm of men and women; he takes *their form* in order to give exhaustive and certain revelation of who he is.

This theme will reappear as we continue to examine the balance of John's Gospel. Jesus is God's intervention in the world, and as the gospel story unfolds, his audiences will intuit that here there is something—someone— greater than Moses. Someone who antedates Abraham. Someone whose history goes back to the beginning of time.

(2) *Complete rejection.* The great irony of Christian theology is that the very medicine that can cure the human condition is rejected. People love the darkness rather than the light because their deeds are evil (3:19). It is naive to think that the world is eagerly waiting for some disclosure from heaven. Such a disclosure is welcome if it comes in the world's terms, if it is a message that affirms the systems of the world, upholding the personal aggrandizement of power and the prowess of human capacity. But if it names the darkness for what it is, if it describes sin for what it does, if it identifies unbelief in its many sophisticated forms, then the Word will experience sheer antagonism. If the Creator of the world now calls for dominion as its Creator and Lord, the world will have no part.

Christian theology affirms that humanity is in a state from which there is no freedom. Sin is not a series of bad choices, but a state of being from which bad choices continually come. This means that humanity's moral, intellectual, even aesthetic capacities are fallen and poised to move away from the presence of the Light. This is true for the world that is steeped in darkness as well as it is true for those who have a religious disposition: "He came to ... his own, but his *own [people]* did not receive him" (1:10, italics added). No one is exempt from this dilemma.

---

31. The same case has been made by D F. Wells, *God in the Wasteland The Reality of Truth in a World of Fading Dreams* (Grand Rapids: Eerdmans, 1994)

John understands that we do not live in a nice world that God desires to make nicer. We live rather in a world that repudiates the Truth and replaces it with fashionable truths. The Truth of God must excise from the human soul the condition that has been honed since Adam and Eve. Humanity must be reborn.

(3) *Absolute transformation.* There is only one hope, and it is God in Christ. In this incarnation God has exhibited the glory and grace that is native to his selfhood; and through this incarnation, humankind can regain the glory and grace it once had when it was created. The natural eye cannot see the glory of God since it is dimmed by sin. Instead, it is necessary for God to work, to self-disclose, to send his Son, who alone has exposed God's heart (1:18).

When God takes this initiative, new possibilities are born. Divine power is released into the broken world and its broken lives so that new life is possible. The theological key that the world finds so foreign lies here: Transformation and hope cannot be the fruit of some human endeavor. Only God can take the initiative, and men and women must see, receive, and believe the work he desires to do. And when they do, they are reborn to become God's children.

The pitfall of the pagan world is to find hope in its own canons of thought and behavior. But history has proven the futility of this dream. The pitfall of the religious person is to think that human spiritual proclivities can bring God into reality through religious devotion and practice. John says that God takes the initiative, for God becomes flesh. God discloses himself. God enters our world bearing truth and grace in order to transform whoever will receive him. Transformation is not an inspired human work; it is a divine work through and through.

I am reminded at every turn how the world is aware that it needs transformation, that it is incomplete and in need of repair. The self-help books in bookstores and the late-night info-mercials bear eloquent testimony to the deficiencies sensed by the world's citizenry. One late-night commercial is by the hypnotist Marshall Snyder, who promises to deliver "Prosperity, Passion, and Power" to any who purchase his tapes (three easy installments of $39.95). These three promises unveil the world's admission that all is not well, but they also unveil the emptiness of the world's solution.

John 1:19-51

NOW THIS WAS John's testimony when the Jews of Jerusalem sent priests and Levites to ask him who he was. ²⁰He did not fail to confess, but confessed freely, "I am not the Christ. "

²¹They asked him, "Then who are you? Are you Elijah?"

He said, "I am not."

"Are you the Prophet?"

He answered, "No."

²²Finally they said, "Who are you? Give us an answer to take back to those who sent us. What do you say about yourself?"

²³John replied in the words of Isaiah the prophet, "I am the voice of one calling in the desert, 'Make straight the way for the Lord.'"

²⁴Now some Pharisees who had been sent ²⁵questioned him, "Why then do you baptize if you are not the Christ, nor Elijah, nor the Prophet?"

²⁶"I baptize with water," John replied, "but among you stands one you do not know. ²⁷He is the one who comes after me, the thongs of whose sandals I am not worthy to untie."

²⁸This all happened at Bethany on the other side of the Jordan, where John was baptizing.

²⁹The next day John saw Jesus coming toward him and said, "Look, the Lamb of God, who takes away the sin of the world! ³⁰This is the one I meant when I said, 'A man who comes after me has surpassed me because he was before me.' ³¹I myself did not know him, but the reason I came baptizing with water was that he might be revealed to Israel."

³²Then John gave this testimony: "I saw the Spirit come down from heaven as a dove and remain on him. ³³I would not have known him, except that the one who sent me to baptize with water told me, 'The man on whom you see the Spirit come down and remain is he who will baptize with the Holy Spirit.' ³⁴I have seen and I testify that this is the Son of God."

³⁵The next day John was there again with two of his disciples. ³⁶When he saw Jesus passing by, he said, "Look, the Lamb of God!"

³⁷When the two disciples heard him say this, they followed Jesus. ³⁸Turning around, Jesus saw them following and asked, "What do you want?"

They said, "Rabbi" (which means Teacher), "where are you staying?"

[39]"Come," he replied, "and you will see."

So they went and saw where he was staying, and spent that day with him. It was about the tenth hour.

[40]Andrew, Simon Peter's brother, was one of the two who heard what John had said and who had followed Jesus. [41]The first thing Andrew did was to find his brother Simon and tell him, "We have found the Messiah" (that is, the Christ). [42]And he brought him to Jesus.

Jesus looked at him and said, "You are Simon son of John. You will be called Cephas" (which, when translated, is Peter).

[43]The next day Jesus decided to leave for Galilee. Finding Philip, he said to him, "Follow me."

[44]Philip, like Andrew and Peter, was from the town of Bethsaida. [45]Philip found Nathanael and told him, "We have found the one Moses wrote about in the Law, and about whom the prophets also wrote—Jesus of Nazareth, the son of Joseph."

[46]"Nazareth! Can anything good come from there?" Nathanael asked.

"Come and see," said Philip.

[47]When Jesus saw Nathanael approaching, he said of him, "Here is a true Israelite, in whom there is nothing false."

[48]"How do you know me?" Nathanael asked.

Jesus answered, "I saw you while you were still under the fig tree before Philip called you."

[49]Then Nathanael declared, "Rabbi, you are the Son of God; you are the King of Israel."

[50]Jesus said, "You believe because I told you I saw you under the fig tree. You shall see greater things than that." [51]He then added, "I tell you the truth, you shall see heaven open, and the angels of God ascending and descending on the Son of Man."

Original Meaning

THE BALANCE OF chapter 1 moves us into the narrative world of this Gospel. But it is important to keep in mind that we have already been introduced to John the Baptist in the prologue. He was Jesus' forerunner—a witness to the coming of the Messiah, Jesus (1:6ff.). And he understood clearly that Jesus was superior, that Jesus was replacing John's baptizing ministry with his own (1:15, 33).[1] The evangelist gives minimal attention to the identity and ministry of John the Baptist compared with the Synoptics (cf. Matt 3:1–6; Mark 1:2–6; Luke 1:1–24, 57–80; 3:1–13). Instead, his chief interest is the role the Baptist plays identifying and exalting Jesus.

Verses 19–50 enjoy an interesting unity. The section can be divided into four paragraphs, each marking a successive day ("the next day," 1:29, 35, 43). In each section we learn something about who Jesus is and what he will accomplish; but more, we learn something about discipleship and what it means to be his witness. There is even a geographical outline. An interesting structure looks like this:

A. One Disciple in Perea [Bethany Across the Jordan] (1:19–34) [Days 1–2]
   1. John the Baptist's Self-Denial (1:19–28) [Day 1]
      • The Baptist bears no witness to himself.
   2. John the Baptist Tells Who Jesus Is (1:29–34) [Day 2]
      • The Baptist bears witness to Jesus.
B. Two Disciples in Judea (1:35–42) [Day 3]
      • Andrew and Peter become disciples and model true discipleship.
C. Two Disciples in Galilee (1:43–51) [Day 4]
      • Philip and Nathanael become disciples and model true discipleship.

This structure at once makes clear that the author's purpose in these verses is the nature of discipleship and what it means to meet, know, and follow Jesus. In each case, disciples are invited to have a personal contact with Jesus and to recognize who he truly is. This is a recurring theme in the Gospel: experiencing Jesus and having a correct understanding of his person. John's literary technique is to tell a story and then exploit that story for some theological purpose: to identify Jesus for us as readers or to help us see what is transpiring in the minds of Jesus' interrogators.

John the Baptist's Self-Denial (1:19–28)

THE AUTHOR IS not narrating the events of John the Baptist and Jesus. He is telling someone else's story. This entire account is the "testimony" of John the

---

1. I suggested above that it is likely in an early draft of the Gospel (before the addition of the prologue) these verses (1:6ff., 15) were attached to 1:19 and served as the introduction to the Gospel. Some commentators prefer to include them in the present section. See B. Witherington, *John's Wisdom: A Commentary on the Fourth Gospel* (Louisville: Westminster/John Knox, 1995), 60–75.

Baptist ("this was John's testimony," v. 19), as if we were in a judicial setting and the evidence for and against Jesus was being set before us as readers.[2] The story reads as if the Baptist were telling this in retrospect and John the author is letting the Baptist now have the spotlight.

John's baptizing activity at the Jordan River attracted a great deal of attention, leading many people from Jerusalem and the surrounding regions of Judea to come out to him either to be baptized or to inquire about his work (Matt. 3:5). One such delegation was sent by "the Jews" to interrogate the Baptist (John 1:19). The term *the Jews* (Gk. *Ioudaios*) appears seventy-one times in this Gospel and generally represents the Jewish leadership in Jerusalem (particularly the temple) who are hostile to Jesus. Some have even argued that *Ioudaios* refers to "Judeans" who are hostile to Jesus and his Galilean movement. It clearly cannot refer to all Judaism, for in chapter 9 the parents of the man born blind are Jewish, and we read that they "were afraid of the Jews" (9:22). "The Jews" in this Gospel has a specialized usage stemming from John's own world, a world in which synagogue and church were struggling (see the Introduction).[3]

The delegation coming to John consists of "priests and Levites," so that what we have here is an interrogation by emissaries from "official Judaism," from the temple and its interests. John the Baptist was an odd phenomenon and needed investigating. Three names are at stake and together each of them probe John's intentions vis-à-vis Israel: Does John see himself as an eschatological figure in some way calling Israel to justice? Is he putting the nation on notice because God is about to intervene?

(1) John first denies that he is "the Christ." "Christ" is a Greek translation of the Hebrew word for "Messiah." Throughout the late Old Testament period and especially in intertestamental Judaism hope in a coming Messiah was widespread. This would be "the Lord's anointed," someone filled with God's power and Spirit who would work some saving miracle on behalf of God's people. Judaism frequently thought about Moses as perhaps the ideal messianic model. Not only did he give the people spiritual leadership, but he also provided political redemption from Egypt. It is no accident that in the days of Greek and Roman oppression (a period of over three hundred years), the term *Messiah* (or *Christ*) was filled with political connotations. John the Baptist declares firmly he is not the Messiah.

---

2. An important book that explores the judicial themes of John is A. E Harvey, *Jesus on Trial* (London: SPCK, 1976).

3. Some scholars, particularly Jewish theologians, have concluded that John's frequent use of "the Jews" contributed to Christian anti-Semitism over the centuries. John was Jewish and when this messianic Jew found himself in conflict with his fellow citizens, this intramural rhetoric was born.

(2) Malachi 4:5 taught that the Old Testament prophet Elijah would precede the coming Messiah. If John were not the Messiah, perhaps then he was Elijah. Because Elijah had been taken from the earth without dying (2 Kings 2:11), Jewish speculation proposed that he was mysteriously alive and would return at the end of time (cf. Mark 8:28). John says clearly he is not Elijah (John 1:21). One difficulty with this message is that in Matthew 11:14 Jesus says that John is "Elijah who was to come." The solution is that John was fulfilling the forerunner's *role* of Elijah, as Luke explains: "He will go on before the Lord, in the spirit and power of Elijah" (Luke 1:17). John, on the other hand, denies that he is Elijah who has returned to the earth.[4]

(3) "The Prophet" is likely a reference to Deuteronomy 18:15–19, where a prophet "like Moses" would return to Israel sometime in the future. This led to enormous Jewish speculation concerning who this prophet would be and in some cases led to a conflation with the image of the Messiah. Other Jews distinguished the Messiah and the Prophet (see John 7:40; 1 Macc. 4:46; *T. Ben.* 9:2) and understood that he would be simply a forerunner. Qumran, for instance, looked for an eschatological "prophet" who would accompany the Messiah (1QS 9). John's answer is succinct: No.

Following this series of denials John now identifies who he is. He is "a voice" and quotes Isaiah 40:3 in order to identify his role in Jesus' mission. He does not elevate himself as having a stature of importance and never identifies his own name. He is a tool in God's hand, pointing to Another on the horizon. It is interesting that Isaiah 40:3 was also used by the Dead Sea Community (Qumran) as one of their chief passages to identify who they were. They were building a community, preparing a place in the desert, for the arrival of the Messiah. John's message said that the dawn of the messianic era was at hand and virtually no waiting was needed.[5]

Judaism knew about ritual washings for ceremonial cleansing. But baptism was generally reserved for Gentiles who had converted to Judaism. It was a total cleansing that marked a threshold crossed. John, however, was calling *Jews* to be baptized (1:26), and of course this prompted the question, "What is the threshold? What is the new order that would change us as Jews?" The promise on the horizon is not a new religion but a person (1:26–27). John describes him as so great that by comparison, he (though a prophet) will be

---

4. Another possibility is that John did not know he was Elijah or at least did not accept the title. That is, in the Synoptics Jesus gives him a title he preferred to reject. "The Baptist humbly rejects the exalted title, but Jesus, on the contrary, bestows it on him" (C. F. D Moule, *The Phenomenon of the New Testament* [London: SCM, 1967], 70, cited by L. Morris, *John*, 119n.18).

5. Many scholars have drawn a connection between John the Baptist and the community of Qumran. Not only were they both in the desert with a critical message of Judaism (based on Isa. 40), but each also employed water baptism as a regular means of cleansing.

less than a slave. Untying a sandal thong was a chore never done by disciples for their teacher. Rather, it was a chore reserved for slaves. John says he is unworthy even to do the work of a slave for this One who is coming. This is the measure of Jesus' greatness.

The location of Bethany "on the other side of the Jordan" has always been a puzzle. This is not the village just east of Jerusalem (home of Lazarus, Mary, and Martha, cf. John 11). The patristic father Origen visited the area in the third century looking for the site and identified it as the village "Betharaba," which inspired numerous manuscript variants. But this is surely wrong. This Bethany is in Perea, the region east of the Jordan River, but its location is now lost.

John the Baptist Bears Witness to Jesus (1:29–34)

THE EPISODE ON "the next day" is a continuation of John the Baptist's testimony to Jesus (see 1:34). While previously John could only hint at the coming of Christ, now he identifies Christ plainly. Note how confidently the Baptist can speak of his knowledge of Jesus (1:33). The point here is that John can be compared with the questioners from Jerusalem who do not know about God and likely will not understand the things of Jesus. Borchert is correct when he says that "John's knowledge of the coming one was not *innate knowledge* (1:31–33). It was knowledge that had come to him through revelation—when the Spirit descended on Jesus" (1:32).[6] This is John's theology of revelation at work. True knowledge of God is beyond human reach: It is a gift of divine disclosure. John has a number of opportunities to speak directly of the identity and purpose of Jesus.

(1) Jesus is identified as "the Lamb of God, who takes away the sin of the world" (v. 29). Every interpreter finds this phrase to be difficult because the words "Lamb of God," while commonplace in Christian vocabulary, do not appear elsewhere in the New Testament except here and 1:36. The crux is understanding what "Lamb" (Gk. *amnos*) means. Some suggest that it refers to the Passover sacrifice, which could be a lamb (although this was not necessary). However, this animal was not termed *amnos* in Greek-speaking Judaism but rather "the *pascha.*" Since John is keenly interested in seeing Jesus as a Passover victim (see 19:31–36), it would not be unnatural for him to use this concept and language for Jesus.[7]

Other suggestions include the sacrificial lamb of Isaiah 53:7 or even the lamb of Genesis 22:8 (provided to Abraham in order to preserve Isaac). John

---

6. G. Borchert, *John*, 1:137.

7. Others have argued that the Passover sacrifice did not remove sin. But this is disputed, and many hold that virtually all Jewish sacrifices had some salvific dimension.

may have been thinking of the triumphant eschatological Lamb of Revelation 5. Another possibility is that John is thinking about the daily temple sacrifices, in which a lamb was offered both morning and evening (Ex. 29:38–46). But this is uncertain. It is at least clear that for the Palestinian Jew, all lamb sacrifices were memorials of deliverance (esp. Isaac's deliverance), forgiveness of sin, and messianic salvation.[8] It would *not* be impossible for John to have the Passover lamb in mind in the present context.

The chief thing to keep in mind is that here we see Jesus as a gift provided *by God* to take away sin. As a lamb he becomes a sacrificial animal whose death "carries away" a condition that is prohibited in the presence of God. Since this Gospel highlights the festivals of Judaism, and in particular the Passover, it is not unreasonable to see Passover imagery here as well.

In 1:30 John describes Jesus as one who was "before [him]." This statement repeats an almost identical phrase in 1:15, which declares the importance of Jesus to be not in what he does but in who he is. This is one of many Christological affirmations in the Gospel that associate Jesus clearly with God.

(2) John's second testimony on this day occurs in 1:32–33. Rather than narrating the story of Jesus' baptism (as in the Synoptics), the Fourth Gospel simply invites John the Baptist to describe what he witnessed that day in the Jordan. Here his testimony is remarkable. John does not emphasize the voice from heaven or the baptism in the river, as do the Synoptics. Instead, three times he refers to the coming of the Spirit on Christ. The Old Testament expected the messianic era to be a day of renewal when the Spirit would not only transform Israel (Isa. 32:15; Ezek. 36:26–27; 37:14; *Jub.* 1:23) but would rest mightily on the Messiah himself (Isa. 11:2; 42:1; *T. Jud.* 24:1–3).

The appearance of the Spirit was common in the Old Testament, but it appeared mainly among designated leaders (such as a king, judge, or prophet) and remained only for the duration of their God-appointed work. John the Baptist's comment is telling: The Spirit descended and *remained* on him. This is a permanent anointing; this is an anointing unlike anything witnessed before in Judaism; this is the messianic anointing. Moreover, this Jesus is not merely anointed himself with the Spirit at his baptism, but he will baptize others in the Holy Spirit as well. Indeed, John has witnessed the dawning of the messianic era.

(3) The final testimony given by John the Baptist in this day appears in 1:34: "I have seen and I testify that this is the Son of God." Important ancient manuscripts, however, replace "Son of God" (NIV, NRSV) with "chosen of God" (NEB).[9] I am convinced that "chosen of God" is correct. John will affirm

---

8. G. Vermes, *Scripture and Tradition in Judaism* (Leiden: Brill, 1961), 193–227.

9. Variant witnesses are more numerous for "Son," but "chosen" is represented by many strong manuscript families, including Sinaiticus. Some readings conflate the readings with "chosen Son." See any textual apparatus for complete witnesses.

Jesus' title as Son later in 1:49. But here "chosen" is a more difficult reading, which scribes likely changed to the more familiar "Son." Further, "chosen" likely comes from Isaiah 42:1, which emphasizes the Spirit-anointing of the Messiah and uses this title for him: "Here is my servant, whom I uphold, my *chosen one* in whom I delight; I will put my *Spirit* on him, and he will bring justice to the nations." This goes to the heart of John's testimony about Jesus: This Messiah is known by his unique anointing, his unparalleled identity in the Spirit of God.

John the Baptist has completed his personal witness. In humility he has deflected glory and interest away from himself and drawn attention to Jesus, describing powerfully who he is and what he will do. It is not in this Gospel's interest to record Jesus' temptations as we have them in Matthew 4 and Luke 4. This chapter is about testimonies, about men who meet Jesus, who recognize they will be changed forever, and who discover the true identity of Jesus.

Peter and Andrew in Judea (1:35–42)

JOHN THE BAPTIST continues his role as witness by speaking to yet another audience. On the third day of this sequence he speaks to his own followers, directing them to follow Jesus instead of himself. On one level, the story serves to show that disciples who followed the Baptist must shift their allegiance to Jesus. On another level, the story provides a template for discipleship generally—now in Judea (1:35–42), later in Galilee (1:43–51).

In verse 37 we learn that two disciples hear John testify to Jesus. One is Andrew, Simon Peter's brother (v. 43). Andrew finds his brother and brings him to Jesus. But that leaves unanswered the identity of the other disciple in verse 37. In the Synoptic Gospels the earliest converts to Jesus are Andrew, Peter, James, and *John* (cf. Mark 1:16–20). It is no accident that this unnamed disciple in verse 37 may be our first hidden reference to the apostle John, likely the person behind the mysterious title "Beloved Disciple" used elsewhere in the Gospel. But note the close connection between the followers of the Baptist and the followers of Jesus: Many who later become Jesus' disciples originally worked in the Baptist's ministry.

The language of 1:38 is explicit language of discipleship. These two disciples follow Jesus, and when asked about their interests by him ("What do you want?") they ask where he is staying (or remaining). "Come . . . and you will see," he replies. This language is consciously designed to describe discipleship: to "follow" (Gk. *akoulotheo*), to "come and see," and to "stay, remain" (Gk. *meno*) each describe aspects of discipleship. It is interesting to see that the same pattern of discipleship is played out with Philip and Nathanael in the following section.[10] As we explore the wider meaning of this disciple-ship (see Bridging Contexts section), we will examine these words with some care.

We are told that these events occur "about the tenth hour," probably about 4:00 P.M. today.[11] This is not only one more indication that John is providing an eyewitness account (cf. 4:6, 52; 18:28; 19:14), but it sig-nals something of Jesus' intention. This is the end of the day and may refer to the fact that here Jesus has invited them to spend the *entire* day with him. This visit becomes a teaching session, in which Jesus discloses not only his messianic identity, but likewise his mastery over these new followers.

Each time we meet Andrew in the Gospel he is bringing someone to Jesus (6:8; 12:22).[12] When Andrew finds his brother, Peter, and brings him to Jesus, Peter's name is changed to "Cephas."[13] Cephas comes from the Aramaic word *Kephas*, which means "rock." Peter likewise means "rock" (Gk. *petros*), and John is the only Gospel writer to tell us about Jesus' original Aramaic play on words. Neither *Petros* in Greek nor *Kephas* in Aramaic are usual names but are actually nicknames (like the American "Rocky"), which often point to some feature of a person's character.

In Jewish culture naming is a significant event.[14] Names unveil some-thing of the character of the person (e.g., Jacob means "he clutches" [his brother's heel], Gen. 25:26), and renaming indicates something of the authority of one person over another (as God renames Abram, Gen. 17:5). Jesus is here asserting his authority over Peter and telling him that he is a different man, a man who is about to acquire the character of his true name, a name he has likely forgotten. It is striking that "rock" is not the image that comes through the portrait of Peter. Peter is impulsive and in the end will deny Jesus. But despite Peter's frailty, this name signals Jesus' vision for what Peter will become.

---

10. For some scholars, the reference to coming, seeing, and remaining refers directly to Jewish wisdom. In the Wisdom of Solomon, we are instructed to pursue a romance with Wis-dom (Gk. *sophia*, a fem. noun), to discover her, to meet her, and to remain with her (cf. Prov. 8; Sir. 51). Witherington (*John's Wisdom*) believes that here John is presenting Jesus as both a sage and the Wisdom sages sought.

11. Even though Jews counted their days from sundown to sundown, they still seem to have adopted the habit of marking the hour of the day from sunrise, following a Roman custom.

12. Morris, *John*, 140.

13. This event occurs in the Synoptics later on in Jesus' ministry, when Peter confesses Jesus' identity at Caesarea Philippi (Matt. 16:13–20).

14. *The New Bible Dictionary* (3d ed., 1996), 810, gives numerous excellent examples of naming in biblical culture and shows how names could signal an event, a status, even a transformation.

Philip and Nathanael in Galilee (1:43–51)

JESUS' DECISION TO move to Galilee (about a hundred miles north) was not as abrupt as the story suggests. John is building the theater for his Gospel and is eager to bring out representative characters. We are moving from one snapshot to the next, from one frame to another, meeting now more characters on John's stage.

The north shore of the Sea of Galilee hosted a number of fishing villages (Bethsaida means "house of fishing"), and Jesus based his Galilean ministry among them. Bethsaida (likely Bethsaida Junias) was east of the Jordan River's northern inlet into the sea and was nearby Capernaum (found just west of the Jordan's inlet). Peter and Andrew were from Bethsaida (1:44) but had moved to Capernaum (Mark 1:21, 29). The Gospels indicate that Jesus did numerous miracles in these villages and because of their failure to respond, they would suffer terrible judgment (Matt. 11:20–24). Nevertheless they were important places because they resided on the main highway (the *Via Maris* or Way of the Sea) that brought traffic from the coastal hills of Judea to the northern regions of the country.

Philip and Nathanael were from Bethsaida. Philip had a Greek name (meaning "horse lover") that was popular in Hellenistic Judaism. His brother's Hebrew name (Nathanael, meaning "gift from God") shows the mingling of cultures that must have been common in this area. Philip appears only rarely in the Gospels: He is in the Synoptic list of apostles (Mark 3:18; Acts 1:13), and in the Fourth Gospel he expresses concern at the miraculous feeding (John 6:7) and is later approached by Greeks in Jerusalem who want to see Jesus (12:21–22). It is also Philip who tells Jesus in the final evening with him that he should just show them the Father and they will be happy (14:8–9). Nathanael is not listed among the apostles; this has led to speculation that perhaps he should be identified as Matthew or even Bartholomew. In all three Synoptic stories Batholomew is listed with Philip (Matt. 10:3).[15] But we cannot be sure. Jesus had many other disciples—seventy in Luke 10—who worked alongside the Twelve; Nathanael may have been one of them.

In any case, when Nathanael hears about Jesus as a man who fulfills the messianic predictions of Moses, his response is curious: "Nazareth! Can anything good come from there?" (1:46). Nathanael was from Cana, another village north of Nazareth (21:2), and it is likely that his comment tells us something about the rivalry of the regional Galilean villages. Nazareth did not have a bad reputation in Jesus' day, but neither did it have a famous reputation. It was a small south Galilee mountain village, a fraction of the size

---

15. Bartholomew is not actually a personal name. It means "son [*bar*] of Tolmai," as Simon bar Jonah is Simon, son of Jonah (bar is Aramaic for "son").

of the modern Arab Christian city. Nathanael is expressing the cynicism of a man who has not met the compelling evidence that will win his life. Besides, Galilee had already seen a number of men come forward who had made some claim to messiahship. Nathanael will have none of it.[16] Philip's challenge is appropriate: evidence becomes convincing when it is appropriated personally. "Come and see" is the refrain heard the previous day in Judea (1:39) and now becomes Nathanael's challenge.

Jesus describes Nathanael as "a true Israelite, in whom there is nothing false [*dolos*: no guile, RSV; no deceit, NRSV]." This word occurs eleven times in the New Testament and conveys the meaning of trickery or cunning. This is the concept behind the description of Jacob when he steals his brother's birthright (Gen. 27:35). Jesus sees in Nathanael a good man, an honest man. And much to Nathanael's surprise, Jesus refers to seeing him "under the fig tree" at an earlier time. Was this a time of prayer and meditation? Study?[17] Fig trees with their ample shade were used thus in antiquity. But the main point is that Nathanael knows exactly what Jesus is talking about; Jesus has a capacity for knowing that which is more than human. That is, he *knows* Nathanael before Nathanael knows him. Nathanael has witnessed a miracle, and from it decides to make a remarkable step of faith.

At once Nathanael, who now has experienced Jesus for himself, addresses him with a litany of titles: "Rabbi! ... Son of God ... King of Israel." "Rabbi" is a title of respect for a Jewish teacher (1:38). "Son of God" is an unexpected recognition of Jesus' deity that was used with tremendous reserve in the Old Testament. "King of Israel" is used elsewhere at the triumphal entry (12:13) and when Jesus is on the cross (Matt. 27:42); here it is no doubt an expression of Jesus' identity as the Messiah. Together these three names complete the portrait of John that has been building throughout this chapter. Nathanael is the perfect Israelite, the man in whom God finds favor, the man who recognizes the things of God instinctively and immediately. It is such a man who recognizes the true identity of Jesus.

Throughout the description of Nathanael we have heard echoes of Jacob, a man who was deceitful and yet who became the instrument of God's redemptive efforts in history. Indeed, Jacob became the great patriarch of Israel, whose sons formed Israel's twelve tribes. And his name changes so that Jacob is called "Israel." Nathanael is as unlike the old Jacob-deceit as he is like the ideal Israel that God envisions.

Yet this chapter has one more surprise. John 1:51 introduces Jesus' first use of the *"amen, amen"* formula (obscured in the NIV's "I tell you the truth"). Literally

---

16. Josephus, *Ant.* 20.5; Acts 5:36–37.
17. These are images commonly associated with fig trees in Judaism (see 1 Kings 4:25; Mic. 4.4; Zech. 3:10).

Jesus says, "Truly [*amen*], truly [*amen*] I say to you...." In the Synoptic Gospels *amen* occurs only once when the expression is used, but it is characteristically doubled throughout the Fourth Gospel (used twenty-five times). The word is a Hebrew or Aramaic idiom that implies certainty or confirmation and generally was appended to corporate prayers (1 Cor. 14:16; cf. Ps. 41:13). Jesus uses it to *introduce* sayings that for him are solemn or significant; no genuine parallels from Judaism have been found. This is Jesus' unique Aramaic teaching style, embedded in the Greek Gospel story.

While one might think that Jesus is still talking with Nathanael in 1:51, the verb changes from the singular to the plural, "*You* will see...." Jesus is making a pronouncement to all of his disciples—and to his readers too—that culminates all that has been revealed about him these four days. Drawing again on the Jacob imagery, Jesus describes angels ascending and descending on the Son of Man as the heavens open. This image springs from Jacob's life. In Genesis 28 when Jacob is en route from Beersheba to Haran, he stops in Bethel and sleeps. "He had a dream in which he saw a stairway resting on the earth, with its top reaching to heaven, and the angels of God were ascending and descending on it" (28:12). The dream is so overpowering that Jacob is awed (28:16–19):

> When Jacob awoke from his sleep, he thought, "Surely the LORD is in this place, and I was not aware of it." He was afraid and said, "How awesome is this place! This is none other than the house of God; this is the gate of heaven." ... He called that place Bethel.

In Hebrew, Bethel means "house of God," and Jesus is indicating that this is precisely who he is. The vision of Jacob described the locus of revelation, the point of connection between heaven and earth. Jesus is this place. Jesus incarnates the dream of Jacob, and Nathanael is going to see it himself. It is interesting that Nathanael is from Cana; immediately following this promise Jesus moves to Cana and works his first sign (John 2:1–11).

John 1:51 also introduces us for the first time to the curious phrase "Son of Man." This phrase was used as a literal translation of the Aramaic and was not commonly used in Greek. It is curious because Jesus employs it frequently in the Gospels as his preferred self-description. The Fourth Gospel records its use thirteen times, while the Synoptics use it sixty-nine times. It is absent in Paul and only appears on the lips of Stephen in Acts 7:56.

While "Son of Man" is likely a Hebrew self-ascription meaning "I," it must have carried other connotations. In Daniel 7:13–14 it appears as the title of a heavenly personage who is given ultimate authority by God. Jesus likely picks up this term and uses it extensively in order to avoid titles such as Messiah, Son of David, and King of Israel, which were loaded with political ideas. With it he can forge his own identity that is sufficiently ambiguous (to avoid the fantasies of Judaism messianic hopes) and which conveys overtones of divinity and authority.

IT WOULD BE EASY with a section like this to become overwhelmed with the numerous details of history and theology that the passage presents. There is the interrogation of John the Baptist with its many questions about formal Jewish titles. There is the baptism of Jesus and its theological meaning. There are also the four men—Andrew and Peter, Philip and Nathanael—and the key that their stories hold as we unlock the meaning of the passage.

A testimony on two levels. Foremost in my thinking, however, is that this passage is offered to us as a *testimony*: "This was John's testimony [*martyria*] . . . " (1:19). It will not do to immediately open the Synoptic Gospels and try to harmonize the conversion of the earliest followers of Jesus found there. John is painting a portrait—his own portrait—and it must be read in its own terms. This is a story offered to us in order to persuade and teach about the nature of conversion and discipleship. In fact, these episodes encapsulate what John is doing throughout his Gospel, providing a compelling story that weaves characters in and out who will convince and persuade. Thus as a story, it is not constructed in a haphazard fashion. This story has been honed by the evangelist in order for us to see its unifying themes.

We watch John the Baptist enter the stage and deliver his lines about Jesus (1:19–34); then four disciples have the same opportunity, first in Judea and then in Galilee (1:35–51). This is not to deny that there is an historical element in these narratives. It is simply to say that history is being used in the service of literature and theology. John has selectively built his Gospel from materials in the early church's record in order to provide *us* with a portrait of Jesus and discipleship. In this manner it would not be entirely wrong to see the sudden shift to plural verbs in 1:51 as directed to us: "You shall see heaven open. . . . " We as readers will see the wonder of the Son of God if we continue with the story that John is about to unfold.

John is therefore writing on two levels. Historically, he is trying to describe the pivotal events of the life of Jesus Christ so that through this record, we will have an accurate reconstruction of what transpired. But in addition, he is writing fully conscious that he has a readership. The story promotes interactions not simply among its characters but also between its script and its readers. John is aware that we are reading him, and he crafts his story so that we *as readers* will find a progression of ideas unfolding before our eyes.

John occasionally lets us know that we understand more than his characters do, giving us ironic humor or a sense of impending doom. We are given insights that sometimes the characters do not even have, and this gives us a *point of view* inaccessible to John's historical characters.

Names of Jesus. As a testimony, two concepts stand out as compelling, timeless features of the story. John wants us to have an experience similar to that portrayed by these five men. He wants us to become disciples whose growth in knowledge and devotion is inspired by these stories. John is claiming that discipleship has two essential elements: Disciples must know who Jesus is, and they must have a personal experience that completely reorients who they are.

One of the striking features of this story is that people who become disciples of Jesus know what to call him. Within the story there is a litany of titles that could almost serve as an index to the New Testament list of names for Jesus:

- Messiah (vv. 20, 41)
- the Prophet (v. 21)
- Jesus (v. 29)
- Lamb of God (v. 29, 36)
- one who baptizes with the Spirit (v. 33)
- chosen [Son] of God (v. 34)
- rabbi/teacher (vv. 38, 49)
- Christ/anointed one (v. 41)
- son of Joseph (v. 45)
- Nazarene (v. 45)
- Son of God (v. 49)
- King of Israel (v. 49)
- Son of Man (v. 51)

No other chapter in the New Testament provides a comprehensive list like this. On the historical level it is surprising that here, this early in Jesus' ministry, followers have an accurate appraisal of who he is. I expect they did not understand the full implications of what they were saying since Jesus had not yet worked any of his signs. John makes this clear in the next chapter, "After he was raised from the dead, his disciples recalled what he had said. Then they believed the Scripture and the words that Jesus had spoken" (2:22). It was not until after Easter that the full implications of Jesus came rushing home to his followers.

But the more important thing to see here is the literary effect this has on us as readers. Here in the first dramatic scene we have been exposed to the *Christological content* of discipleship. As we read the story, we are witnessing what inquirers need to know in order to become true disciples. Being a follower of Jesus does not mean thoughtlessly following a person named Jesus. It does not mean having an experience that is void of theological content. Discipleship is a necessary commitment to content as well as conversion; it is a form of persuasion that includes both the heart and the mind. Thus, when John the Baptist completes his series of self-denials on Day One (vv. 19–28), his second scene on Day Two finds him identifying Jesus accurately for his disciples and the world.

Furthermore, we must realize that Jesus is not merely the sum total of the titles given here. These descriptors unveil something of Jesus' activity among us and his identity with the Father. The baptismal narrative is trying to tell us something Christological: Jesus is uniquely filled with the Holy Spirit, and this is a feature of his messianic identity. He is the one to whom we must look for our own baptism in the Spirit (1:33). Jesus as "Lamb" means that he will be a sacrifice offered to the Father for the sins of the world. He is the one to whom we must look for redemption and forgiveness. Jesus as "King" refers to his rulership, his dominance over Israel as Messiah. John will use this title sixteen times in the ongoing story to underscore the majesty of Jesus' role.

These names add an anticipatory element to our reading. We are eager to watch them unfold as the story unfolds, as they are picked up again and again and their meaning is enriched. Like the table of contents in a book, this list of names forces us to look ahead at how this remarkable person named Jesus will be explained in the following twenty chapters.

The characters and discipleship. The second dramatic feature of the story turns on the characters themselves. We are told little about them. There is no detailed history about families or homes. We are not even told about their occupations or how it happened that Peter and Andrew were working for John the Baptist. The central focus of the story is about their contact with Jesus.

Initially John the Baptist becomes a template for conversion and discipleship as he offers a sustained series of denials about who he is. No doubt on a historical level, this is an attempt to speak to followers of John the Baptist in the first century who need to recognize that their devotion to the Baptist now needs to shift to Jesus.[18] But more broadly, John becomes a template for Christian discipleship generally. Affirmation of contact with Jesus leads to self-denial.

The most important imagery comes with the two stories that follow. In Judea Jesus meets Andrew, who follows Jesus personally. In Galilee Jesus

---

18. In the Introduction we discussed how followers of John the Baptist formed a sect that promoted him to a divine or at least messianic status.

meets Philip, who, like Andrew, follows him. Then Andrew goes to Peter—and Philip goes to Nathanael—and makes the same challenge: "Come and see" (1:39, 46). Peter and Nathanael will not know the truth about Jesus until they have had their *own* personal experience. In fact, Nathanael is cynical until his encounter takes place. This is a conversion template for John. Throughout the Gospel many people will be challenged to "come and see." Conversion is not about knowledge alone; it is about coming yourself and appropriating a relationship with Jesus personally.

In each case the experience of discipleship carries one more dimension. John the Baptist, Andrew, and Philip each bring others to Jesus quite intentionally. Converts make new converts. They speak what they know about Jesus and they bring other people along so that they too will "come and see."

Finally, John is aware that the process of discipleship and conversion are not matters left in human hands. Nathanael must "come and see," but Jesus has "seen" him already. "I saw you while you were still under the fig tree before Philip called you" (1:48). These are remarkable words that point to Jesus' supernatural knowledge, but also to God's sovereign awareness of those who will accept the light. God sees us before we see him. God will "come and see" before we ever think about discipleship. God makes his overture before we consider making our own. This too is a central Johannine theme and is the anchor of the disciple's assurance.

LOVE FOR GOD and knowledge about God. I once asked a youth minister about the goal of his ministry. "When my students graduate," he commented, "they will learn to love God." What he was saying is that in the end, a heartfelt piety was the aim of his ministry, and I could tell that his efforts working among high school students made this goal evident. Ministry was centered on activities that would bind the youth together into a community of personal prayer and support. The students that graduated from this ministry did love God.

Wheaton College (where I teach) enjoys a student body that is passionately committed to God. There is no doubt that they "love God" and have come from evangelical churches whose ministries are similar to the one I just described. And yet in recent years we have been experimenting with an interesting test to determine the *depth* of these students' knowledge about what they believe concerning the Bible, theological thought, and the history of the church.

We have been shocked at what we learned. Students from strong, conservative churches were sending us some of their best Christian eighteen-year-old students who did not know who came first, Abraham or Moses.

They were not sure if Barnabas was in the Old Testament or the New Testament. When asked to put a list of *major* biblical books in proper order (such as Exodus, Psalms, Isaiah, Matthew, Romans), they failed miserably. When asked if Paul believed in the resurrection of the body, most said "No." Here were young Christians for whom personal piety ran deep, but for whom a coherent, intelligent grasp of the Bible was beyond their reach. Recently one of my students told me that she was sure Jesus was baptized in the Dead Sea of Israel. Another thought that Paul was one of the twelve apostles. These were not weak students; rather, these were *excellent* students with an articulate and passionate commitment to Christ.[19]

When the test moved to matters of theology and church history, it became clear that these students were not sure what to do with names like Augustine, Luther, or Wesley. Keep in mind that we were not testing arcane matters of historical theology. We were seeing if the gigantic heroes of the faith were even recognized. We wondered whether some of the most important decisions about life and belief were a part of their theological equipment. Could they explain Christian belief from the ground up—beginning with our commitment to one God (monotheism) and leading on to an orthodox Christology? We looked at fundamental matters of Christology, salvation, the doctrine of Scripture; in most cases, students seemed singularly incapable of formulating a coherent doctrinal basis for their identity as Christians. *Nevertheless they did "love God."*

This discovery sobered many of us and renewed our commitment to curricular goals that go far beyond mere piety. Students are coming to us who understand the "Christian walk," but who do not understand "Christian thought." Their lives have been baptized, but seemingly, their minds have not. They have devoted their hearts to following the Lord, but they have not mastered the bare essentials of Christian history and theology, much less Biblical theology and history.

Many mainline denominations have been wrestling for some time with the question of the ordination of homosexuals. Recently I attended a major discussion in my own denomination led by some of our elected ordained leaders.[20] I was amazed as I watched the presentation unfold. The foremost virtue, we were told, was loving God and loving our neighbor, and since homosexuals were our neighbors, we should not only love them but ordain them to the ministry. Of course, love is a virtue—but so is a well-reasoned theo-

---

19. See G. M. Burge, "The Greatest Story Never Read: Recovering Biblical Literacy in the Church," *Christianity Today* 43 (Aug., 1999), 45–50. The earliest tests began with a colleague of mine, Dr. Dennis Okholm.

20. I am ordained in the Presbyterian Church, U.S.A.

logical anthropology and a well-reasoned use of the Scriptures. Here is my point: Piety without theology was winning the day. Loving God became a spiritual mantra while there was no room for obeying him or listening for the more complex nuances of his expectations in the human enterprise. In other words, there was no compelling theological framework from which our leadership could answer the question: Should I ordain the homosexual? The point here is not homosexuality, but that the theological toolshed of these leaders' ministerial vocation was empty.

John's theology in this chapter stands against such emptiness. On the one hand, we are called to be like John the Baptist, Andrew, Peter, Nathanael, and Philip—people who have a personal experience of Christ, who "come and see," who do not simply have a scholastic understanding of the Christian faith, but who remain where he is and are transformed by being with him. In other words, these are people who have an experiential dimension to faith, whose heart is engaged, and who "love God" and enjoy a depth of piety and devotion.

But more is called for. John the Baptist is not only experiencing personal self-effacement and an overwhelming desire to glorify Jesus, he can also give a correct theological explanation of who Jesus is. There is a theological substratum beneath his commitment. The same is true of the four men who follow in the story.

John 1:19–51 is a theological model for what it means to follow Christ. It forms a secondary, subsidiary introduction to the entire Gospel (following the prologue [1:1–14]). As a model, it urges that personal piety ("loving God") must be wed to theological sophistication ("knowing God"). Christian faith is not merely commitment but content as well. Interrogators can come and press their questions with force and power, but like John the Baptist, the disciple must give unflinching answers. When asked, "Who are you?" (1:19), the disciple knows *exactly* what to say. Men and women can come and meet Jesus, but in the end, they acquire an increasingly informed understanding of who Jesus is (e.g., Jesus, Rabbi, Messiah, Son of God). And when they have wed their piety with theological insight, they go to others and evangelize them. They challenge others to have an experience and to understand the truth.

This twin emphasis on personal piety and theological sophistication is desperately needed in the church today. Like the students in our college test sample, our pews are filled with men and women whose love for God is strong and yet whose understanding of the content of the faith is diminishing. They cannot explain it, and when intellectually challenged, they struggle to defend it. I once asked a mature adult believer why Jesus was called the "Lamb of God" and was told, "Because Jesus is gentle and nice." How enthralled he was when I explained the sacrificial connotations of the term.

What is the explanation for this? Is it generous assumptions about the abilities of our laity? Is it the lack of academic stamina among our pastoral leadership? Is it preaching that promotes personal experience and well-being instead of hard-won exegetical insights? Is it the therapeutic intellectual environment of our day that validates only those things anchored to the inner life? Honed theological expertise is as valuable as personal spiritual experience. It is the anchor that will keep Philip and Andrew committed with their minds as well as their hearts.

John 2:1–25

O N THE THIRD day a wedding took place at Cana in Galilee. Jesus' mother was there, ²and Jesus and his disciples had also been invited to the wedding. ³When the wine was gone, Jesus' mother said to him, "They have no more wine."

⁴"Dear woman, why do you involve me?" Jesus replied. "My time has not yet come."

⁵His mother said to the servants, "Do whatever he tells you."

⁶Nearby stood six stone water jars, the kind used by the Jews for ceremonial washing, each holding from twenty to thirty gallons.

⁷Jesus said to the servants, "Fill the jars with water"; so they filled them to the brim.

⁸Then he told them, "Now draw some out and take it to the master of the banquet."

They did so, ⁹and the master of the banquet tasted the water that had been turned into wine. He did not realize where it had come from, though the servants who had drawn the water knew. Then he called the bridegroom aside ¹⁰and said, "Everyone brings out the choice wine first and then the cheaper wine after the guests have had too much to drink; but you have saved the best till now."

¹¹This, the first of his miraculous signs, Jesus performed at Cana in Galilee. He thus revealed his glory, and his disciples put their faith in him.

¹² After this he went down to Capernaum with his mother and brothers and his disciples. There they stayed for a few days.

¹³When it was almost time for the Jewish Passover, Jesus went up to Jerusalem. ¹⁴In the temple courts he found men selling cattle, sheep and doves, and others sitting at tables exchanging money. ¹⁵So he made a whip out of cords, and drove all from the temple area, both sheep and cattle; he scattered the coins of the money changers and overturned their tables. ¹⁶To those who sold doves he said, "Get these out of here! How dare you turn my Father's house into a market!"

¹⁷His disciples remembered that it is written: "Zeal for your house will consume me."

¹⁸Then the Jews demanded of him, "What miraculous sign can you show us to prove your authority to do all this?"

¹⁹Jesus answered them, "Destroy this temple, and I will raise it again in three days."

²⁰The Jews replied, "It has taken forty-six years to build this temple, and you are going to raise it in three days?" ²¹But the temple he had spoken of was his body. ²²After he was raised from the dead, his disciples recalled what he had said. Then they believed the Scripture and the words that Jesus had spoken.

²³Now while he was in Jerusalem at the Passover Feast, many people saw the miraculous signs he was doing and believed in his name. ²⁴But Jesus would not entrust himself to them, for he knew all men. ²⁵He did not need man's testimony about man, for he knew what was in a man.

IN THE INTRODUCTION I suggested that knowing the structure of the Fourth Gospel helps us to understand the literary and theological profile of Jesus that John is building. For instance, we saw that the book is divided into two main parts: the Book of Signs (chs. 1–12), where Jesus works public "signs" conveying to Judaism the nature of his identity; and the Book of Glory (chs. 13–21), where Jesus interprets the "hour of glorification," namely, his departure through the cross. Some scholars see this division anticipated in 1:9. The Book of Signs describes how the light shines in the darkness (1:9a), while the Book of Glory tells how the darkness attempts and fails to overcome it (1:9b).

Within these sections, however, John has introduced further subdivisions in each half of his Gospel that organize his thought and allow him to analyze particular features of Jesus' messiahship. The key here is to see that while John is using historical material, he is organizing this material topically (or theologically) in order to give an interpretative presentation of Jesus. The backdrop of each presentation is cultural and religious themes from Judaism.

John 2 opens one such section for us. Within the Book of Signs, John concentrates on both the festivals and institutions of Judaism, using them as interpretative vehicles that give clearer insight into Jesus' personhood. While not all scholars would organize chapters 1–12 this way, it is fully defensible as an effective means of viewing this section of John.[1] Throughout the section, we watch Jesus appearing at important events in Judaism, exploiting symbols that are associated with these events (in order to make his own identity clear), providing something in abundance that the event promises, and generally being misunderstood along the way.

For instance, Jesus appears at a Passover in John 6 (a festival commemorating the miraculous departure from Egypt and the food miracle of manna), feeds his Galilean audience miraculously with an abundance of food, announces that he is living bread—a food that surpasses anything in the Jewish tradition—and meets with incomprehension not only among the crowds but also among his disciples. When Jesus talks with Nicodemus in John 3, the same thing happens: Jesus is now the Teacher who instructs the rabbi, offering not simply wisdom but utter transformation. In both instances Jesus is misunderstood, which opens the way for irony and humor: At the Passover, the crowds wonder how they can "eat" Jesus (6:52), and Nicodemus wonders how he can reenter his mother's womb and be reborn (3:4).

Many of the units that make up the Book of Signs will follow this four-part literary organization; recognizing them as each episode unfolds will add meaning and delight as we study them. A brief outline of the episodes helps to make clear John's literary agenda:

Institutions in Judaism (**chs. 2–4**)
- A wedding in Cana (2:1–12)
- The temple in Jerusalem (2:13–25)
- A rabbi in Jerusalem (3:1–21)
- A well in Samaria (4:1–42)

Festivals in Judaism (**chs. 5–10**)
- Sabbath (5:1–47)
- Passover (6:1–71)
- Tabernacles (7:1–9:41)
- Hanukkah (10:1–39)[2]

Far from being an exhaustive list, John has selected a number of representative settings in which Jesus' appearance bears some symbolic theological

---

1. Many scholars argue for the divisions I am explaining here. Among them, see R. Brown, *The Gospel of John*, 2 vols. (New York: Doubleday, 1966–71).

2. Following the festival section in the Book of Signs, it only remains for John to provide a parabolic episode about life, death, and resurrection, namely, the story of Lazarus, which mirrors the fate of Jesus (ch. 11) and after which Jesus' death is planned (11:45ff.). Finally, we see in chapter 12 Jesus' preparation for death through the anointing of Mary, the plot to kill Lazarus and, by extension, Jesus (12:9ff.), Jesus' final entry to Jerusalem (12:12ff.), and his final public plea (12·27ff.).

meaning for Judaism.[3] The story of Cana, therefore, is far more than a story about a wedding and some wine. It is a story that carries remarkable symbolism for Jews and their Messiah. Moreover, it is a story that makes a sweeping commentary on the world into which Jesus is coming. "They have no wine" is not simply a comment by Mary about the panic of the wedding's host. It is a theological statement about the Judaism that is now meeting its Messiah in his very first miracle. Technically, it is about messianic replacement and abundance. In fact, John's entire section—from Cana to Cana (2:1–4:54)—recalls Jesus' Synoptic saying about new wine and old wineskins (Mark 2:22), or Paul's words in 2 Corinthians 5:17, "The old has gone; the new has come!" Jesus is about to demonstrate the obsolescence of Judaism's religious forms.

The Cana Story (2:1–12)

FROM THE REGION around the north shore of the Sea of Galilee (Capernaum and Bethsaida), the scene now shifts to the hills in the west, to a small village north of Nazareth called Cana.[4] Jesus and his disciples appear at a wedding, and when asked, he performs his first "sign," changing water into wine. Earlier we learned that Nathanael was from Cana, and the village's proximity from Nazareth makes it natural for members of Jesus' family to be there as well.

A number of exegetical questions have always surrounded the story. What is the relationship of Mary (Jesus' mother) to the wedding? Why does she feel responsible for the lack of wine? Why does Jesus seem to treat his mother so abruptly? Others have wondered if this text is here to legitimize either Christian use of wine or the institution of marriage. At center is how much John intends us to see the story symbolically. In 2:1 he mentions "the third day." For some, it is an innocent and simple chronological reference to Jesus' progress through Galilee. For others, the "third day" suggests an inevitable reference by John to the coming "third day" of the resurrection.[5] Still others count from the beginning of chapter 1 and find seven days (Cana occurs three days after the Nathanael story, day 4) and thus John is reporting a week of activities, much like God's week of creative work in Genesis. But these conclusions are far from certain.

---

3. Note that there are some episodes in the narrative that serve other purposes as well. John adds a long section correcting the followers of John the Baptist (3:22ff.) and ends the section on Institutions with a closing frame in Cana with the official's son (4:46–54).

4. This is about four miles northeast of Nazareth. Today there is a Palestinian Christian village called Kfar Kanna, where rival churches claim the spot of the miracle. Some scholars believe instead that the site is Khirbet Kana, an archaeological site about nine miles north of Nazareth in North Galilee

5. Borchert, *John*, 1:153.

In the village culture of Palestine, weddings were important events, announced well in advance and recognized by the entire village. In some respects, they were *the chief celebrations* enjoyed in the year and thus provided the imagery for messianic celebration and joy as well (see below). When Jews reflected on what heaven or the arrival of the Messiah would be like, they thought about banquets, and the wedding banquet was the foremost model that came to mind.

Following a public betrothal that was far more permanent than a modern engagement, the family announced the wedding date, and elaborate preparations were made for a ceremony that could last for as long as a week (Judg. 14:12). The parable of the wise and foolish maidens (Matt. 25:1) supplies a useful backdrop for the nighttime procession of the groom, who would walk with his friends to the bride's home, collect her, and then lead a procession back to his home, where celebrations would begin.

Gift-giving was carefully considered, not as a simple gesture of goodwill, but as a means of bringing honor on the couple and their families.[6] In fact, legal ramifications followed when appropriate custom was not followed because it implied public shame on the couple. This gives us an interesting insight into the concern of the servants when the feast suddenly runs out of wine (2:2). This is not merely an embarrassing situation; it is a dishonoring crisis for the host. Since these festivals could go on for days, it is no surprise that such a calamity might happen.

Mary's statement in verse 3 ("They have no more wine") prompts Jesus to respond in an unexpected way, "Woman, why do you involve me?" The English tone of this seems harsh, but it is simply formal—Jesus uses the same form of address ("woman") for the woman of Samaria (4:21), the woman caught in adultery (8:10), his mother at the cross (19:26), and Mary Magdalene at the tomb (20:15). Nevertheless, it is unusual for him to address his mother this way when other titles would be preferred. In some sense, Mary is presuming on her relationship with him as her son (Luke 2:51), yet Jesus is redefining this: He cannot act under her authority but must instead follow the course that has been determined for him by God.[7]

Jesus' response is not rude, simply inflexible. "Why do you involve me" is literally, "What do we have in common," or as a paraphrase, "How can this matter that concerns you be of mutual interest to us?" Jesus' orientation for activity is elsewhere: "My time has not yet come." The NIV's "time"

---

6. See J. D. M. Derrett, *Law in the New Testament* (London: Dartman, Longman, and Todd, 1970), 228–46 (reprint of "Water into Wine," *BZ* 7 [1963]: 80–97).

7. Some have suggested that Mary is asking Jesus to work a miracle here. However, since this is Jesus' first miracle, no such expectation is reasonable. She wants him merely to take some responsibility for finding a solution to the wedding's problem.

obscures the important Greek word "hour" [*hora*] used throughout this Gospel to look forward to Jesus' important work on the cross (5:28; 7:30; 12:23; 13:1). Mary's request for activity is thus given an ironic spin inasmuch as Jesus will act on behalf not simply of this wedding, but of the entire world. His death on the cross will provide far more than wine.

Nevertheless Jesus indicates that he will act since his mother directs the servants to obey him (2:4). The story gives us an important clue as to its meaning when we discover that six stone jars will now be the source of the new wine. These are not merely jars for holding water. The note that they are stone is a signal that they are for Jewish purification washings (see Mark 7:1–4). Clay jars could become ritually contaminated and have to be destroyed (Lev. 11:33); but stone jars, according to rabbinic law, could not. Because this is a large feast, the six jars hold considerable volume, each with a capacity for over twenty gallons. Since Jesus has the stewards fill them to the brim, his miracle is about to produce over 120 gallons of wine.

The stewards are then told to take some of the water-now-become-wine and bring it to the head steward. Many think that this person cannot possibly be a servant because he can summon the bridegroom. He may simply be a trusted friend, an honored friend of the family who is playing the role of banquet host. Either way, the head steward makes a pronouncement with telling significance: Common sense teaches that in most banquets, the best wine is served first; then, when the guests have drunk their fill, the cheaper wine can be served (2:10).

It is unwarranted to speculate about the degree of intoxication implied by the saying. It simply observes that when palates are more sensitive, superior wine will be more fully enjoyed (and cheaper wine more quickly noticed). But Jesus is delivering something to the banquet quite unexpected. It is superior to anything the banquet has witnessed. John's emphasis, therefore, is on the quality of this wine and its timing; things served before this wine are inferior.

John offers a summary comment about the episode in 2:11–12. Rather than using the Synoptic term for miracle (Gk. *dynamis*), John consistently refers to Jesus' mighty works as "signs" (Gk. *semeion*). A miracle underscores power and is generally received with awe (cf. Mark 6:2: "Many who heard him were amazed. 'Where did this man get these things?... What's this wisdom that has been given him, that he even does miracles!'"). A sign is revelatory, disclosing something from God, something hidden before. The signs are not merely acts of power and might, they unveil that God is at work in Jesus and indeed is present in him. Thus John remarks that through this sign Jesus reveals his "glory." This is an essential affirmation for John, and it moves to the center of what he affirms about Jesus. Jesus is not merely a man; he is more, he conveys the presence of God in the world (1:14), and since he radiates the presence of God, he appropriately shows forth God's glory.

Following the wedding, Jesus departs with his followers and his family, returning to Capernaum (2:12). Capernaum is "below" Cana (he goes "down") in the sense that Cana is located in the mountains of upper Galilee while Capernaum is a coastal town on the northwest shore of the Sea of Galilee. John does not make clear the reason for the trip since we are told earlier that Jesus is from Nazareth (1:45). However, the Synoptic picture helps make clear that throughout his public ministry, Capernaum was the base of Jesus' work. Matthew even refers to it as "his [Jesus'] own town" (Matt. 9:1). As a small village on the main north-south highway through Galilee, Capernaum enjoyed wide recognition and easy access to travelers.

That Jesus is accompanied by his "brothers and his disciples" has led to a wide variety of interpretations. The most natural view is to say that Joseph and Mary had more children following Jesus' birth. This is often the plain meaning in the Synoptics (Mark 6:3, "Isn't this the carpenter? Isn't this Mary's son and the brother of James, Joseph, Judas and Simon?") and fits well here.[8] However, when the perpetual virginity of Mary became an affirmation in the second century, other views of verses like this came into use: These were either Joseph's children by previous marriage or Jesus' cousins. Protestants generally believe that Jesus had genuine siblings (cf. John 7:1–8).[9]

The Temple Story (2:13–25)

IT IS VITAL to keep the story of Cana in mind when we turn to Jesus' cleansing of the temple in 2:13–22. The literary and theological themes we saw in 2:1–12 occur here as well. In the first section, Jesus was in a home attending a wedding party; because of a crisis concerning wine, he worked a miracle on Jewish purification vessels. Now Jesus comes to Jerusalem for a major festival in the city. He enters the temple (a place of sacrificial purification) and likewise does a symbolic work demonstrating that it too will experience replacement and fulfillment (just as the stone water vessels in Cana were filled with new wine). Jesus is a temple himself (v. 21), whose destruction and resurrection will make the reconstruction of this Jerusalem temple pale by comparison (v. 20). As in 1:35ff, Cana and Jerusalem, representing activity in the north and south (Galilee and Judea), are placed in literary and theological juxtaposition.

---

8 Matt. 1 25 (Joseph "had no union with her [Mary] until she gave birth to a son") suggests the birth of more children.

9. It is important to note that John does use "brother" (*adelphos*) for his disciples (see 20.17; 21:23).

One historical footnote is in order. While there are a limited number of places that John and the Synoptics overlap (chs. 1–5 have virtually none), this story of the temple cleansing finds a parallel in the other Gospels (Matt. 21:12–13; Mark 11:15–17; Luke 19:45–46). There are a number of differences both of vocabulary and theme between John and the Synoptics: John alone mentions oxen, sheep, the whip of chord, and the command to depart. The Synoptics provide a Scripture citation (Isa. 56:7; Jer. 7:11). The most important difference has to do with time. The Synoptics place the temple cleansing at the end of the ministry of Jesus while John introduces it at the beginning. For the Synoptics, this event acts as a catalyst to galvanize the temple's opposition to Jesus. John has the episode launching his public ministry in Judea; what becomes the chief aggravating reason for Jesus' capture is the raising of Lazarus (11:1–57; 12:9–11).

This question of chronology has led to a lively debate among scholars who assess the historical worth of these narratives. Are John and the Synoptics recording the same story? Scholars who conclude that there was only one temple cleansing usually maintain that John's sequencing is incorrect and the Synoptic account is accurate. They argue, for instance, that anyone who would have tried such a thing would surely have been pursued and arrested, as the Synoptics tell us. In addition, critical scholars are generally reluctant to admit the historicity of "doubles" (similar sayings or stories), seeing in them rather evidence of how Christian theology evolved and expanded.

But conservative writers such as L. Morris have made an eloquent defense for another point of view.[10] Why, Morris asks, should we assume that there was only one cleansing? Pointing out numerous differences between the two cleansings, he suggests that the best reconstruction would have Jesus cleansing the temple twice. When Jesus' repeats the act at the end of his ministry, the authorities are ready for him. The problem here is that there are also several parallels between the Synoptics and John (e.g., Passover, money-changers, Jesus' authority). In addition, one element in the Johannine version is *presupposed* in the Synoptic trial: In 2:19 Jesus refers to the destruction of the temple, but nowhere does this subject appear in the Synoptics. Note Mark 14:58: "We heard him say, 'I will destroy this man-made temple and in three days will build another, not made by man'"; *a basis for this comment occurs only in John.*

For a complete account of what actually happened, we do well to read both versions together. I suggest that John has recorded his own version of one cleansing and while it is an historical record, he has moved it chrono-

---

10. Morris, *John*, 167–68; Carson, *John*, 176–78.

logically for theological reasons. There is no doubt that all four evangelists felt free to place sayings and stories from Jesus' life in settings that suited their literary purposes. Using uncompromised historical material, John is creating a theological portrait of Jesus' display of signs in the context of Judaism. Jesus is the fulfillment and replacement of Judaism's festivals and institutions. And the temple is high on his list as a place that soon (through his death) will no longer serve the purposes of God.

Jesus' arrival at Passover (2:13) signals his commitment to the festivals of Judaism. John's Gospel mentions three Passovers (2:13; 6:4; 11:55),[11] which is often the basis of measuring the duration of Jesus' three-year ministry. Passover was an annual festival celebrated each spring that retold the story of Israel's departure from Egypt.[12] Israelite families were spared when the angel of death "passed over" the homes that had been marked by the sacrifice of a lamb (Ex. 12). In his anguish, Pharaoh released the Israelites, who fled to Mount Sinai through the desert. Over the centuries Passover had become a pilgrimage festival in which Jewish families were expected to travel to Jerusalem and participate in sacrifice, a symbolic meal, and reflective study of Israel's salvation.

Since pilgrims would need approved animals for sacrifice, a considerable business grew in the city at this time of year. Some evidence suggests that Caiaphas had a dispute with the Sanhedrin over whether it was permissible to sell animals in the courts of the temple.[13] Apparently Caiaphas had won out, even though this meant that the temple was transformed from a house of worship into a place of commerce. In addition, Jewish men (over twenty) were required to pay a half-shekel annual tax at the temple. Jesus had no objection to this since we have a record that he paid the tax himself (Matt. 17:24–27). The presence of moneychangers met a legal requirement that all donations be made in special coinage (as stipulated in the oral law, later penned as the *Mishnah*). This rule was not to avoid pagan images on foreign coins but to ensure the quality and purity of the money coming into the treasury. Moneychangers exchanged currencies and retained some profit for themselves, but there is no evidence of corruption.

Jesus' frustration does not stem from supposed wholesale greed or graft, but from the fact that these transactions are happening in the temple at all:

---

11. Some scholars believe 5:1 is also a Passover

12. Passover occurs during the first full moon following the spring equinox, on the 14th day of the lunar month of Nisan. It is followed by the week-long Festival of Unleavened Bread (Nisan 15–22).

13. The animal selling to which Jesus objects took place in the *hieron* (2:14). This is to be distinguished from the inner sanctuary or *naos*. The *hieron* included the outer courts surrounding the sanctuary, particularly the massive Court of the Gentiles.

"Get these out of here! How dare you turn my Father's house into a market!" (2:16) is a prophetic command to return the temple to its intended use: worship, prayer, instruction, and pious sacrifice. The original language of John contains a fine play on words that is missed in the English: "Take these things away! Stop making my Father's *house* a *house* of trade." Jesus is attacking the financial machinery of the festival system, which certainly would put him at odds with Caiaphas and the temple leadership.

When his disciples witness this shocking spectacle (2:17), they recall Psalm 69:9, "Zeal for your house consumes me." Theologically this is John's way of indicating two things. (1) Jesus is acting out of his relationship with the Father. As Messiah and God's Son, he is driven to defend and promote God's interests in the world. When he sees the human ruin of God's house, he is overwhelmed with a desire to act. The cleansing or challenging of the temple is a frequent Old Testament theme in which complete renewal of Israel in the Day of the Lord is linked with the renewal of the temple (Isa. 56:7; Jer. 7:11; Zech. 14:21; Mal. 3:1).

(2) John often uses the Old Testament at the major junctures of Jesus' life. Even though he does not cite the Old Testament frequently (compared, e.g., with Matthew), still the Scriptures are there in the background, defining Jesus' activity at every important turn. He is working out the purposes of God—purposes he knows have already been outlined in God's Word.

The ensuing conversation in the temple is unique to John (2:18–22). When confronted with his actions, his critics demand that he show some sign to demonstrate his authority to cause such upheaval. Curiously, Jesus does not refer to the deficiencies of the temple, but instead refers to his *own* destruction and resurrection: "Destroy this temple, and I will raise it again in three days." As is typical in so many of the Johannine narratives (e.g., 3:3ff.; 4:10ff.; 6:41ff.; 11:11ff.; 14:7ff.), Jesus' audience misunderstands him and thinks he is referring (ironically) to the Jerusalem temple.

In 20 B.C. Herod the Great began a massive rebuilding program at the temple in order to placate his Jewish subjects, who despised him as an outsider (Herod was Idumean). He intended this new temple to rival that of Solomon. In order to assure purity, a thousand priests were trained as stone cutters and architects. A total of 18,000 men worked full time until it was finished in A.D. 64.[14] Some stones weighed as much as seventy tons and can be seen today in the walls holding up the temple mount.

That Jesus would destroy such an edifice—now underway for forty-six years—and rebuild it in three days seemed ludicrous (2:20). Anyone who could do such a thing could certainly make a claim over the temple's opera-

---

14. Sadly, six years later (in A.D. 70) the Jerusalem temple was destroyed by the Roman army.

tion! But such a word is not as strange as we might think. In Judaism in this period, many spiritual leaders expected that a new temple would be built and that the present temple in Jerusalem would be replaced. In Ezekiel 40–46, for instance, details of this new temple are given in detail. At the Dead Sea community of Qumran, the hope and plans for a new temple were a part of that community's belief. The Jews of Qumran were severely critical of Herod's temple project. Even after the Roman destruction of the temple in A.D. 70, Jews continued to retain a hope in the coming of the Messiah, who would bring a newly built temple. In synagogues in the late first century, Jews confessed the "Eighteen Benedictions," of which the fourteenth looks forward to the new temple and Messiah.

But Jesus' deeper meaning referred to his body, which would serve the same function as the temple, even replacing it. The confusion that appears at Jesus' trial (Mark 14:58) concerning Jesus' warning of the destruction of the temple and his promise to build a new temple in three days have been taken up today by modern scholars who find here a genuine threat by Jesus against the temple authorities. This, they claim, is what galvanized anger against him.

But Jesus' teachings in the Fourth Gospel regularly use cryptic statements that have double meaning (similar in some respects to his parables in the Synoptics). And explanations are often given that clear up such misunderstandings (7:5; 11:13; 12:6). Thus in this case, Jesus is predicting his death and resurrection, which will create a new covenant with God and make the services of the Jerusalem temple obsolete.[15] In his conversation with the Samaritan woman, Jesus says plainly that the hour is coming when true worship will not take place in Jerusalem (at the temple) or in Samaria, but it will happen "in spirit and in truth" (4:24). This is a revolution. There is a messianic work now in the world that will utterly change how worship and sacrifice are understood.

During this Passover many are intrigued with Jesus, for many "believed" (lit., came to belief). But we should not make too much of this, for the basis of their faith was signs. When Jesus made a demonstration of power and authority, they conceded belief. But throughout the Gospel, faith predicated on God's showing evidence of himself is criticized (4:48). While such faith is better than no faith (6:26), it is not the deepest faith possible (20:29).[16]

John provides a telling wordplay in 2:24. The same Greek word translated "believe" in verse 23 appears in verse 24: Even though some of these people *believed* in him ... Jesus would not *believe* in them.[17] The reason given is not that

---

15. The "body" to which Jesus refers is his own body, not the church, even though Paul commonly uses the body as a metaphor for the church (Rom. 12:5; 1 Cor. 12:12).

16. Morris, *John*, 181.

17. The NIV uses the verb "entrust" for *pisteuo* in 2:24.

he knew all of them (i.e., those in the temple), but that he was cognizant of all people. John is making a statement here about Jesus and humanity generally. Jesus understood about all of humanity and its capacity for deception and duplicity. No one needed to explain it to him (2:24a). In 1:48 Nathanael is surprised that Jesus knew him without having met him. This section ends on the same note, but now John is making a sweeping theological affirmation about Jesus and divine knowledge. God alone knows the hearts of men and women—and now Jesus has this same capacity.

The text of John 2 assumes that we will keep on reading directly into 3:1. "He [Jesus] did not need man's testimony about man [*anthropos*], for he knew what was in man [*anthropo*]. Now there was a man [*anthropos*] of the Pharisees named Nicodemus . . . " (2:25–3:1). The Greek noun *anthropos* (which can refer to a male or to people in general) threads its way through the paragraph and links chapters 2 and 3. Nicodemus will now demonstrate for us what such people in Jerusalem can really understand about Jesus and God's new work in him.

THE CANA STORY. Interpreters of the Cana story can easily misuse it to emphasize all the wrong things. For instance, this is not an account designed to show how Jesus sanctifies a particular marriage or the office of marriage itself. Ministerial marriage manuals often use the Cana story for a sentimental glimpse of what it would be like for Jesus to attend a wedding. Among evangelicals concern is sometimes raised that the story might be used to promote the consumption of wine or alcoholic beverages. One thing is clear: In this story, the wedding party did not serve grape juice. Rather, Jesus and the wedding host served genuine wine here—wine in abundance. Wine was the normal beverage at meals in the Greco-Roman world. Generally it was so strong that it was diluted with water to improve the taste.

Jesus did not abstain from wine or party festivities; he was not antisocial. When asked why he and his disciples did not fast, his response was that his presence should inspire celebration, not asceticism (Mark 2:18–20). Harsh critics pointed their fingers at his habit of attending parties saying, "Here is a glutton and a drunkard, a friend of tax collectors and 'sinners'" (Matt. 11:19). This does not necessarily mean, however, that Jesus became drunk. Today there may be various good reasons for abstaining from alcoholic beverages, but this passage cannot be called to service such a point of view.

Yet these are secondary questions to what John is hoping we will see as readers. Jesus' miracle in historic Cana is less important than the implications of Jesus' arrival now in the theological setting of Judaism. Historically, John is making a firm statement that Judaism is to see and hear: The Messiah has arrived and the messianic banquet (portrayed as a wedding feast) has begun. It is appropriate that Jesus reveals his glory first here at the wedding. In the literature of Judaism, the "wedding banquet" was pregnant with meaning.

Moreover, John gives us numerous clues that the story should be viewed symbolically. The wedding scene, the huge volume of wine, and the reference to stone jars all suggest a second level of meaning. The Messiah has not just appeared in Judaism amidst its festivities, he has come to fulfill and indeed upend what he finds there. We must keep in mind the Johannine themes of messianic replacement and abundance. Judaism's vessels of purification are now being filled with new things. Or more important, the wine that has been served already is exhausted and Jesus' new wine is replacing it. "You have saved the best [wine] till now" is thus a theological statement about Jesus and the relative merits of the religious environment he has come to fulfill.

Finally, John makes an important connection between the sign (the miracle of water into wine) and belief. 'This, the first of his miraculous signs, Jesus performed in Cana of Galilee. He thus revealed his glory, and his disciples put their faith in him" (2:11). This invites a series of questions about faith and miracles. As I noted above, John is careful not to call these events miracles. He prefers the word "sign" (e.g., 2:23; 4:54; 6:2, 14, 26; 7:31; 9:16; 10:41). This is because the act of power in itself is less important to John than what the act says about Jesus.

The capacity to work miracles was not unique to Jesus. Even prophets like Elijah could do mighty deeds. Indeed in Jesus' day there were other miracle-working mystics who made similar claims. John wants us to see beyond this event, to see the sign as a means to an end, not an end in itself. The story prompts us not simply to promote Jesus' power and somehow prove that because he has this power, he is who he claims. The story invites us to ask penetrating questions about this person, and when we glimpse his glory (2:11a), we will discover faith.

To sum up, as I look at this passage and bring its meaning into my own world, I can distill a series of three ideas that bring the meaning of the story to life: the significance of Jesus in God's historical plan of salvation, the significance of Jesus for religious renewal, and the relation of "signs and glory" to the believer's life of faith.

The temple story. We dare not miss the importance of what Jesus has done in Jerusalem. When we begin to realize the significance and the grandeur of the Jerusalem temple in Jesus' day, we will begin to feel the magnitude of what he tried to do. The temple was the organizing center of Jewish life in the first century. It was the center of government (brokered at this time by Roman authority), judicial law, religious life, and taxation. It set the moral, religious, and political tone of the country. When Judas Maccabeus decided to defeat the Greeks in the second century B.C., he knew he needed to capture the temple first in order to win popular Jewish support. When the Romans occupied the land in 63 B.C. under the conquest of Pompey, they recognized immediately the need for a fortress in Jerusalem next to the temple, and at once began fortifying the Antonia Fortress on the temple's northwest corner. This is the site where Pilate's soldiers "prepared" Jesus for crucifixion.

When the Zealots stood against Rome in A.D. 66, once again the temple became their fortress and standard, the rallying point for Judaism's fight for survival. The temple was the basis of Jewish religious and national pride. When we add to this Herod's rebuilding program that lasted over eighty years, it is no wonder that when the Galilean disciples of Jesus arrive in Jerusalem, they exclaim about the wonder of the place. "Look, Teacher! What massive stones! What magnificent buildings!" (Mark 13:1). The Jerusalem temple dazzled visitors. When the Roman Titus's troops stormed the temple in A.D. 70, he was so amazed at the splendor of the place that he tried to preserve it from looting and destruction. But his soldiers, having fought a vicious, lengthy battle for the city, discovered its riches, and the temple was doomed. Burned to the ground in A.D. 70, it has never been rebuilt.[18]

Therefore Jesus' activity was not merely upsetting, it was outrageous. He was in the center of the public square, and he made a public protest.

We have to be careful not to make too much of the violence of this scene, however. I have seen pictures of Jesus brandishing a terrible black whip, eyes glaring, tables flying, people running, animals yelping. The Jewish law stipulated that weapons could not be brought into the temple, and a whip was classified as a weapon. Temple police (particularly at festival time) were charged with keeping public order. Hence Jesus probably did not bring a formal whip into the temple, but instead improvised something with straw or rushes used for animal bedding. If he had brought in anything else, I expect he would have been arrested.

Nevertheless the scene is dramatic, provocative, and upsetting. Furniture was broken; animals went running; coins flew from their scales. Jesus makes a disturbance and acts out the core of his prophetic message. But it is not the power of the whip that makes his message succeed. It is his moral power; the truth of what he says strikes to the heart of these people's consciences. It is interesting that in the concluding conversation, no one argues with Jesus about what he has done. No one objects, saying that such activity is inappropriate. Instead, they ask about the basis of his doing it. In other words,

---

18. This explains the passions of modern Israel to occupy Jerusalem and the Temple Mount today. Among some zealous Jews, the dream of rebuilding the temple is still alive.

many likely know that Jesus is right and that the temple has turned into a noisy market. Its services have been compromised. They sense too something of God's divine and righteous anger at work in Jesus, something of God's impatience with a people who have misused the sanctity of his house.

The passage bears down on my century with the following question: What do I do with Jesus' civil disobedience? Does this become a license for our disobedience at the center of our places of living?

A second subject centers on the Christological message of the narrative. On a historical level, Jesus is confronting the chief religious institution of his day. Implicit in his ironic, closing statement is that something will be destroyed (the temple? his body?) and something again will be raised in three days. Jesus is pointing out the deficits of the institution of the temple; he is confronting its misdirection and its brokenness, and in the process (as happens throughout the Gospel) he indicates that the real activity of God, the real temple, is Jesus Christ himself. In other words, the focal point of Jewish religious affections must be replaced by someone new. And that replacement will undergo a violent and miraculous death and rebirth.

The troubling connection with my world is the extent to which our religious institutions are doing the same thing as the Jerusalem temple. Put more directly, if Jesus were to arrive at a church in my city, would he build a whip out of pew rope or would he praise God for what is happening there? This passage invites speculation about religious institutions generally (like the story in Cana invites reflection about personal religious preoccupations). Left on the historical level, it simply becomes one more story about Jesus and his struggles and conflicts with Judaism. But when I examine the timeless meaning of this story, I see here the struggle between God's desire to be worshiped and the religious institutions humans frequently build and edify in order to facilitate that worship. The two are not always the same. Religious institutions sometimes pursue financial interests or social agendas when all they are designed to do is facilitate our relationship with God and set us loose in the world to change it.

A WEDDING IN CANA. From the earliest days, the Eastern Church has kept January 6 as the festival of Epiphany. On this day, the nativity of Jesus, the coming of the wise men, Jesus' baptism, and the miracle of Cana are all remembered.[19] It is significant that Cana is included

---

19. By the fourth century (A.D. 336) the Western church, led by Rome, began celebrating the nativity of Jesus on December 25. The West designated January 6 for the coming of the Magi.

in this list. In some sense, the church fathers were reflecting the idea that something happened at Cana that parallels what occurred both in Bethlehem and in the Jordan River. Christ's glory—his true identity—was unveiled for humanity to see. The revelation of glory is precisely what happened at Cana. Jesus was just one more visitor at a wedding until he was called upon to act. In that activity, his disciples saw something they had not seen before.

There is a practical side to this story that we can easily miss, thanks to our zeal to collect some spiritual truth from the passage. Jesus stepped into a wedding of good friends and fixed a simple problem. They were out of wine and the crisis could prove socially tragic unless a remedy was found. It is easy for us to spiritualize the work of Christ today and conclude that he is only in the business of saving souls and renewing lives. But is he really interested in the commonplace events of my life? Is he really interested in the simple conundrums of everyday living? The Cana story says "yes." We can invite Christ into dilemmas that seem embarrassingly inconsequential—dilemmas that seem ridiculously practical—and ask him to help.

There is also an important theological message that this story is telling us, which I must approach on two levels. (1) John is telling us something about Judaism and history. The arrival of the Messiah means that something unparalleled is happening in the world. Jesus' public display of glory here is a definitive event against which no other event can compare. Nothing in Judaism is like it because here the "glory" of God has suddenly become visible in human form. John has in mind the Shekinah glory that resided first in the tabernacle and then in the temple of Jerusalem (Ex. 24:16; 40:35; 1 Kings 8:11). Now that radiant divine presence is resident in Christ. Recall John 1:14: "And the Word became flesh and made his dwelling among us. We have seen his glory, the glory of the One and Only, who came from the Father, full of grace and truth" (cf. 8:54; 11:4; 17:5). Jesus Christ is a man, and yet no mere man can bear this glory. Hence Jesus Christ is also divine, God's Son, who has united with humanity in perfect union.

(2) But if this is the case, if indeed God is at work in the world in unprecedented ways, then his appearance among us ultimately alters the value of all religious ritual expressions. This is a message that John will give in many of his stories about Jesus. Here the focus is on Jewish rituals of purification, the six stone jars.[20] These are being filled with new contents, producing an abundance of wine. This wine recalls the many prophetic words about the Day of the Lord, when God's arrival and blessings are seen particularly in an abundance of wine in the land (Hos. 2:22; Amos 9:13—14). Therefore these vessels

---

20. For some interpreters, the number six is symbolic. Since in Judaism seven is the number of perfection, six (which falls short) is the number of imperfection.

of purification cannot be put to their former use. The Messiah has touched them and made them obsolete for purification. Religious instruments that had been treasured in the traditions of many generations must undergo severe rethinking.

This is an idea that must be brought into my contemporary world. We have created a world of religious vessels no less traditional than the ones described in Cana. We have created rituals and customs that have everything to do with religious habits but may have little to do with God. In some fashion I have to be willing to permit Jesus to step into my world and affect a dramatic critique of these things I cherish and defend. The Cana story says: God has arrived and Christ desires an immediacy, an intimacy with us that will not be impeded by ritual forms that no longer bring life.

Perhaps this is what we mean in the Reformed tradition when we speak of the church as always reforming itself. Renewal must be joined with an ever-vigilant spirit that looks for religious forms that serve as God's proxy. I must courageously look at my personal Christian tradition, the church I attend, and the habits of my own spiritual life and examine each of them. Jesus was bringing a renewal to Cana and to Judaism that would forever change everything they did. He no doubt desires to do the same with us.

One Easter I traveled to Jerusalem with my then fourteen-year-old daughter in order to lead a conference in Bethlehem for Palestinian and messianic-Jewish pastors. I planned the trip so that the two of us could be in Jerusalem on Easter morning. Many pilgrims were in the city, as were reporters and their video cameras, looking for some way or some place that would make the day meaningful. I walked with Ashley through the Damascus gate and into the markets, winding our way through the Christian Quarter to the Church of the Holy Sepulcher, the place of Jesus' tomb, and, of course, the place of his resurrection. This site (as the Byzantines and the Crusaders and virtually every other pilgrim believes) is one of the most sacred sites in the world.

As we stood looking at the tomb, watching the veneration of crowds of people kissing stone and observing Greek and Coptic religious rites, I could not help but wonder what this tomb has become. Resurrection meant that this tomb lost whatever significance it ever enjoyed. This tomb points elsewhere, beyond death to life. Something tragic and fossilized has happened in Christian rituals that kiss stone in order to embrace a living Lord.[21]

The moment seemed fascinating and historic to be sure, but it also seemed sad. People were taking pictures and looking for souvenirs amidst a cacophony

---

21. Of course I am taking into account the very different forms of worship and veneration practiced among Eastern Christians. My point here is not the form of their worship, but its object or focus.

of incense and noise. We then walked to a place beneath the church, into a cave where the ancient bedrock from the first century has not been chiseled away. Together we put our hands on the bedrock, the "living stone" (as some like to call it). Even though the church around us wasn't here on Easter, I said, this rock was. It was a witness to an earthquake, a tremor, that shook back one closed tomb (Matt. 28:2). And this bedrock shook too. Easter was about power and life, resurrection, and earthquakes, not about the remembrance of death and the pious rituals of people.

This is the message of Cana. Jesus has come to transform what we do religiously, what we do from habit. He is raised from the tomb—and we build a church there and build our rituals. Instead, he wants us to see him as Mary saw him in the garden and to have our religious preconceptions changed.

Finally, the Cana story forces us to probe the relation of faith and miracle. The disciples saw the sign and believed in him. Does this mean that experiencing the miraculous can be an avenue to faith? To be sure, many people (and demons, for that matter) saw Jesus' miracles and were convinced of his power but did not believe in him. Thus, simply experiencing divine power does not necessarily lead someone to faith. In fact, someone who says, "Just show me a miracle and then I'll believe," is likely telling us that they are not ready to embrace Christ in faith.[22]

In addition, many interpreters would have us remember Jesus' closing words to Thomas, "Blessed are those who have not seen [Jesus' signs or miracles or the resurrection] and yet have believed" (20:29). Is Jesus critiquing "miracle-faith"? Jesus' exhortation refers to Thomas's unwillingness to believe until he had seen the resurrected Christ, evidence that subsequent believers are not able to see. Note especially 6:26, where Jesus comments after he has fed the five thousand, who then pursue him eagerly: "You are looking for me, not because you saw miraculous signs but because you ate the loaves and had your fill" (6:26). The chief problem with faith anchored to the miraculous is that miracles become an end in themselves. People begin to seek bread rather than the Bread of Life. They see a miracle but not a sign. When miracles no longer bear their revelatory power, when Christ is no longer glorified and experienced through the work, Jesus has little use for them.

Having sounded a firm caution, still, evangelicals need to note that Jesus did provide signs. He worked wonders and through these displayed his glory. Miraculous signs may become a powerful means to discover or strengthen faith, and we should not be reluctant to use them. For some in our rational, cause-and-effect scientific world this avenue for discovering God seems remote. But the world is not necessarily built the way we Westerners think.

---

22. B. Witherington, *John's Wisdom*, 82

Christy Wilson has been a professor of evangelism and missions at Gordon Conwell Seminary for many years. Born to missionary parents in Iran, he spent twenty-two years in Afghanistan as a missionary/teacher. Recently I have been reading his book, *More to be Desired Than Gold*, which is a catalogue of stories (175 pages of them) from his missionary work.[23] In these chapters Wilson describes in story after story how God is at work providing miraculous signs to Muslim people and how through these God draws men and women to faith in Christ. The stories make riveting, compelling reading, and they force us in the West to ask, "Is not God interested in displaying his glory here today in the same manner?" I think he is.

Disruptions in Jerusalem. The cleansing of the temple is a troubling and important story. If left on the historical level, it is easy to stereotype the temple as corrupt (which is not entirely true) and to see Jesus as rebuking its players (which is only half the story). Much more is going on here. The closer I come to applying the story and the closer I come to seeing the courage and daring of Jesus' act, the less comfortable I begin to feel.

Recently I had a conversation at church concerning Promise Keepers, the men's ministry that was popular in the 1990s. Following a number of years of successful city ministries around the United States, Promise Keepers decided (in 1997) to call Christian men to come to Washington, D.C., in order to pray for the government and provide a witness to those in power. I had not attended any of the Promise Keeper events, but many of my friends had participated, and this particular trip to Washington intrigued me. "Maybe I'll come along," I announced to a small group of men at the coffee hour. If nothing else, I thought, it was a movement that I needed to understand.

But then I heard a surprise from a conservative church leader. "The problem with going to Washington is that it makes Promise Keepers look political, and that could compromise its efforts." I was surprised because a number of my friends seemed to agree. A praise celebration in Chicago with 60,000 men? Yes. A march on Washington? No. In some fashion, the two spheres—politics and spirituality—are not supposed to mix.

But this is what Jesus did. He came to the center of Jewish life, and he was outrageous. It was a center where in that day politics, religion, and law were virtually inseparable. He made a harsh judgment on what motivated the people who lived at that center. Of course, I am aware that there are significant differences today and that I cannot move simply from Jerusalem to Washington. Our society has intentionally separated church and state, and their domains appear completely distinct. Yet it is not so simple. For one thing, secular society does indeed promote an innocuous sort of religion that is a brew

23. South Hamilton, Mass.: Gordon Conwell Seminary, 1994.

of patriotism, self-sacrifice, tolerance, and openness. Any visit to Washington's National Cathedral will at once show how a country can baptize its national interests in religious rhetoric. "Aren't churches supposed to promote good things like this?" argue the priests of that temple.

I am always intrigued to listen to worship services around the Fourth of July or to listen as Army R.O.T.C. officers lead prayer in our college chapel near Veteran's Day. Isn't patriotism a religious duty (they imply)? One year at graduation our college faculty enjoyed sounding the alarm when the audience sang the national anthem, and the color guard holding the flags dipped the Christian flag noticeably so that the American flag was prominent. A little thing, to be sure, but sometimes symbols are important.

Moreover, the communities, states, and nations in which we live can shape the religious ethos of our day (is it supportive? hostile?) and determine the exercise of religious values. In my community, Prison Fellowship and its local supporters wanted to minister to converted, released convicts who needed a new start. They wanted to rent a home for six Christian men. Local Christians fully backed the program. Immediately the city government went into action making new laws to stop it. "It will hurt property values," a neighbor wrote in the local paper. Should Christians be outrageous at City Hall?

But I am also called to be a participant in my society: to respect it, yes, but also to be a witness for God's interests. To be salt and light. To be a light on a hill that cannot be missed. I need to be an agent for change that not only speaks the gospel to my world, but which also is angered by the things that anger God. I need to be a saboteur who promotes kingdom values whenever and wherever I can. If it means being outrageous as Jesus was outrageous, as Martin Luther King Jr. was outrageous, as Promise Keepers is outrageous, so be it.

I cannot fear the public arena or the specter of political entanglements if I am zealously pursuing God's passions in the world. When my society (or government) does something that is wrong, such as promoting an unjust war, an unjust economic policy, or discriminatory practices, or something that penalizes the church for pursuing its mission, I have to be willing to move to action. The prophetic voice is directed not only to believers but to the powers of the state as well.

This is why, I think, a passage such as this makes us uncomfortable. Evangelical Christianity is not often outrageous. We speak with boldness in the pulpit and narthex, but rarely envision ourselves speaking with boldness on the Washington Mall.[24] Yet Jesus went to Washington. He was outrageous.

---

24 Anti-abortion efforts today represent some of the most important attempts by evangelicals to be politically active. But even here, the principle of civil disobedience is debated among evangelical leaders.

Jesus and Christians are at odds with the world. His kingdom is at odds with the kingdoms of this world. As Stanley Hauerwas and William Willimon have written, the world has learned to enable Christians to share power without being a problem for the powerful.[25] And when the church begins to overstep its boundaries and to afflict discomfort on the comfortable and powerful, there is conflict.

Some interpreters will be unhappy with this application. For them, Jesus becomes the quintessential spiritual reformer, and "secular" politics (if there was such in the first century) was not his sphere of activity. He comes to God's house of worship and expresses utter disdain for the activities he finds there. In the Synoptic account, before Jesus enters the temple, he finds and curses a fig tree, a prophetic symbol of God's judgment on that temple that was bearing no fruit. In this respect, the passage forces us to reflect on our religious institutions and the extent to which they serve interests that would earn Jesus' outrageous rebuke.

But it is still an uncomfortable passage, because to a large degree, the church is a human institution (as well as a spiritual one) that is not free from the shortcomings of human society. The church is a fallen institution, filled with sinners, which aspires to goodness but which sometimes succumbs to programs and agendas that have little to do with the kingdom of God. Now if this is true, then it stands to reason that petty financial or social interests may drive the church's life just as the temple of Jerusalem was driven in the first century. Religious politics may be the order of the day in congregations or denominational headquarters. Leadership may succumb to pressures to be modern and contemporary. Or leaders may succumb to pressures to defend empty tradition and habit. In a word, religious institutions only reflect the wholeness known by their architects. And in many cases, the brokenness of those builders is considerable.

John 2:13–25 asks that I look with some care at the life of my own religious house. It asks me to imagine what would happen if Jesus were to come for a visit. Would he be outraged by battles between choirs and contemporary worship teams? With struggles over plans to build or not to build? Would he question words spoken that have lost meaning, or words that take their meaning from the pundits of the secular arena? Is there a chance that he would interrupt things?

John 2:23–25 assures us that Jesus knows entirely what is going on inside of us and our churches. Thus, we cannot rest comfortably thinking that his ire was reserved for the Jewish temple or for the liberals next door but not for us. I can't help but think about John's letters to the seven churches in

---

25. S. Hauerwas and W. Willimon, *Resident Aliens* (Nashville: Abingdon, 1989), 27.

Revelation 1–3. Here we have congregations that were founded by apostolic leadership and enjoyed many strengths. Yet John's letters, inspired by the vision and voice of Jesus, provide a seriousness and severity no different than what we have here in John 2.

John expects that at the end of chapter 2, we will pause and reflect on both this story in Jerusalem and the story of Cana. In each episode, similar themes challenge us, and we are invited to contrast them. Cana is in the north (Galilee); Jerusalem is in the south (Judea).[26] Cana offered stone jars (for purification) and now Jesus has challenged a stone temple (for sacrifice). Cana was out of wine and the temple was likewise filled with the wrong thing. Jesus' solution in each case is to provide an alternative: He will be the giver of new wine and will become a new temple. In each case, we are given the suggestion that the event to watch is "the hour" (2:4, 21) in which Jesus will die and return to life. However, Galilee and Jerusalem offer different responses to Jesus' work: In Galilee Jesus finds receptivity and faith; but in Judea, while some believe (2:22), Jesus is suspicious.

Throughout this Gospel, Galilee and Jerusalem play out as virtual metaphors of response. Through them we are challenged to reflect on how we will respond too, should Jesus visit a wedding or a temple today.

---

26. Recall how the Jerusalem/Galilee comparison was at work in chapter 1.

John 3:1–36

OW THERE WAS a man of the Pharisees named Nicodemus, a member of the Jewish ruling council. [2]He came
to Jesus at night and said, "Rabbi, we know you are a
teacher who has come from God. For no one could perform
the miraculous signs you are doing if God were not with him."

[3]In reply Jesus declared, "I tell you the truth, no one can
see the kingdom of God unless he is born again. "

[4]"How can a man be born when he is old?" Nicodemus
asked. "Surely he cannot enter a second time into his mother's
womb to be born!"

[5]Jesus answered, "I tell you the truth, no one can enter the
kingdom of God unless he is born of water and the Spirit.
[6]Flesh gives birth to flesh, but the Spirit gives birth to spirit.
[7]You should not be surprised at my saying, 'You must be born
again.' [8]The wind blows wherever it pleases. You hear its
sound, but you cannot tell where it comes from or where it is
going. So it is with everyone born of the Spirit."

[9]"How can this be?" Nicodemus asked.

[10]"You are Israel's teacher," said Jesus, "and do you not
understand these things? [11]I tell you the truth, we speak of
what we know, and we testify to what we have seen, but still
you people do not accept our testimony. [12]I have spoken to
you of earthly things and you do not believe; how then will
you believe if I speak of heavenly things? [13]No one has ever
gone into heaven except the one who came from heaven—the
Son of Man. [14]Just as Moses lifted up the snake in the desert,
so the Son of Man must be lifted up, [15]that everyone who
believes in him may have eternal life.

[16]"For God so loved the world that he gave his one and only
Son, that whoever believes in him shall not perish but have
eternal life. [17]For God did not send his Son into the world to
condemn the world, but to save the world through him. [18]Who-
ever believes in him is not condemned, but whoever does not
believe stands condemned already because he has not believed
in the name of God's one and only Son. [19]This is the verdict:
Light has come into the world, but men loved darkness instead
of light because their deeds were evil. [20]Everyone who does evil

hates the light, and will not come into the light for fear that his deeds will be exposed. ²¹But whoever lives by the truth comes into the light, so that it may be seen plainly that what he has done has been done through God."

²²After this, Jesus and his disciples went out into the Judean countryside, where he spent some time with them, and baptized. ²³Now John also was baptizing at Aenon near Salim, because there was plenty of water, and people were constantly coming to be baptized. ²⁴(This was before John was put in prison.) ²⁵An argument developed between some of John's disciples and a certain Jew over the matter of ceremonial washing. ²⁶They came to John and said to him, "Rabbi, that man who was with you on the other side of the Jordan—the one you testified about—well, he is baptizing, and everyone is going to him."

²⁷To this John replied, "A man can receive only what is given him from heaven. ²⁸You yourselves can testify that I said, 'I am not the Christ but am sent ahead of him.' ²⁹The bride belongs to the bridegroom. The friend who attends the bridegroom waits and listens for him, and is full of joy when he hears the bridegroom's voice. That joy is mine, and it is now complete. ³⁰He must become greater; I must become less.

³¹"The one who comes from above is above all; the one who is from the earth belongs to the earth, and speaks as one from the earth. The one who comes from heaven is above all. ³²He testifies to what he has seen and heard, but no one accepts his testimony. ³³The man who has accepted it has certified that God is truthful. ³⁴For the one whom God has sent speaks the words of God, for God gives the Spirit without limit. ³⁵The Father loves the Son and has placed everything in his hands. ³⁶Whoever believes in the Son has eternal life, but whoever rejects the Son will not see life, for God's wrath remains on him.

JOHN HAS DESCRIBED the wonder of Jesus through signs worked both in Cana and in Jerusalem (chapter 2). Both deeds—the one miraculous, the other a prophetic sign—unveiled the glory of Christ and demonstrated how the coming of the Messiah not only replaces, but overwhelms the traditional institutions of Judaism. He offers something new and abundant and makes an absolute call on those who would follow him. Jewish ritual vessels and the Jewish temple, both instruments of religious cleansing, now find a replacement in Christ. But in order for this replacement to be complete, we must await "the [hour]" (2:4), the time when "the temple . . . [of] his body" will be torn down and rebuilt (2:19). In other words, Jesus' glorification on the cross will be the turning point in which Judaism discovers its dissolution and renewal.

Jesus and Nicodemus (3:1–21)

JOHN GOES ON to give us another glimpse of Jesus and his mission. John 1:4 told us that "in him was life, and that life was the light of [human beings]." Jesus does not merely replace religious institutions, he comes to give life, hope, and renewal to people. Notice how 2:25 anticipates the section before us. While he was in Jerusalem, Jesus knew that many people were watching him. But he did not entrust himself to any of them, for he knew the inner character of people. The Greek sets up the present story nicely (lit.): "for he knew what was in a *man* [Gk. *anthropos*]. Now there was a *man* [Gk. *anthropos*] of the Pharisees named Nicodemus . . . " (2:25–3:1).

In other words, Nicodemus steps forward not as a random observer of Jesus, but as a representative of those in Jerusalem who had witnessed the work of Jesus in chapter 2. Moreover, he represents an institution within Judaism: the rabbis or teachers of the law.[1] These were men who specialized in knowing the law, who led in synagogue worship and instruction, and who served as spiritual guides. The Synoptics record many struggles with these people; this is Jesus' first encounter in the Gospel of John.

The story of Nicodemus, therefore, is another story in which Jesus continues to reverse the prominence of institutions in Judaism—to replace them, to show their incompleteness in light of his arrival, to supplant their function with his own life and work. It also begins a series of stories in which Jesus converses with the very people he knows so well (2:24): a Samaritan woman (4:1–26), a Gentile official (4:43–53), and a crippled man at Bethsaida (5:1–15).

But the Nicodemus story also serves as a twin with the Samaritan woman story that follows in chapter 4 (just as Cana is a twin story to the temple cleansing in chapter 2). Nicodemus is a Jew, a man, and a member of the higher social strata of Jewish society; in chapter 4 we meet a Samaritan, a woman, and someone from the lower social strata. Nicodemus could boast in his righteousness; the Samaritan woman stands as a sinner. The irony of

---

1. Some have wondered if it is likely that a Jewish leader would approach Jesus after he had just "cleansed" the temple. However, the Pharisees had limited involvement in the temple, which was chiefly the domain of Sadducean interest and control.

the comparison is the relative success that Jesus discovers with each. Those whom one would think are least ready to understand and accept Jesus (i.e., the woman) embrace him, while the theologian who comes at night (Nicodemus) offers Jesus nothing but questions. As we saw in chapter 2, in Jerusalem Jesus finds limited interest and faith; when he travels away from Jerusalem (to Galilee and Samaria), surprising results occur.

Some scholars have argued at length that Nicodemus represents more than a historical figure in Jesus' day, that he represents a symbolic member of John's immediate audience, a Jew who either holds a deficient faith based on signs or a Jew who is a "secret believer," someone who fears the synagogue more than he or she loves Christ. This group may even be described in 12:42: "Many even among the leaders believed in him [Jesus]. But because of the Pharisees they would not confess their faith for fear they would be put out of the synagogue."[2]

John, however, is clear in his own mind when he distinguishes the era of Jesus and the era of his church (see 2:22). Thus it is inappropriate to see Nicodemus as simply a literary foil. Nevertheless, John's historical reporting of these episodes is not simplistic. He writes to convert, so that his reader will grow in faith (20:31). Inasmuch as *every* episode is designed to speak to John's audience using the uniqueness of a historical figure (the educated, the outcast, the poor, the wealthy), this is true of John 3. Nicodemus's encounter with Jesus is a drama describing one night in Jerusalem as well as any possible night anywhere.

We should also note that John now employs a literary structure that we will see throughout his Gospel: the *discourse*. No doubt Jesus and Nicodemus talked long into the night and not the merely two or three minutes it takes to read this chapter. Therefore John has built an artificial story structure that represents the essence of their conversation. In Johannine discourses throughout this Gospel, questions are posed to Jesus in order to transport the story onto a higher plane of discussion. The questioner is often blissfully— and ironically—ignorant of what is being asked of him or her, and this leads to dramatic misunderstandings.

Note how Nicodemus steps onto the stage three times to make inquiries (3:1, 4, 9) and each of these questions permit Jesus a fuller explanation of his views. Note also how Nicodemus uses ironic misunderstanding, "Surely [a man] cannot enter a second time into his mother's womb to be born!" (3:4). The notion in this and so many other discourses is that unless some deficit is met (generally faith or the Spirit), deeper penetration into the words of Jesus is impossible.

---

2. This is the view promoted by J. L. Martyn, *History and Theology in the Fourth Gospel* (2d ed.; Nashville: Abingdon, 1979).

John 3 is also organized with a simple literary pattern. In 3:1–15 a dialogue represents the conversation between Jesus and Nicodemus. John 3:16–22 has always posed a problem for translators since it is impossible to know where the citation from Jesus ends (since Greek has no quotation marks). It is likely that 3:16 begins another section of commentary provided by the evangelist, which leads us more deeply into the meaning of the preceding dialogue. Then, in 3:22–36 the same pattern follows: An initial dialogue (this time centering on John the Baptist, 3:22–30) is followed by more commentary (3:31–36), which leads us into insights that compare the respective roles of Jesus and the Baptist.[3] Therefore John has given us two dialogues, each of which concludes with theological remarks that uncover the meaning of what has gone before.

The name of "Nicodemus" (3:1) is attested among Jews of the era although it is Greek. There is evidence, for instance, of a Jewish leader named Nicodemus (Naqdimon ben Gorion) who survived the war of A.D. 70; some have taken the unlikely position that the two men are the same. The chief problem is that such an identification would make the character of John 3 very young whereas the passage indicates that he is a member of the Sanhedrin as well as a distinguished teacher.[4] Nicodemus appears twice more in the Fourth Gospel as a defender of Jesus' interests: first at the feast of Tabernacles (7:50–52) and later at Jesus' burial with Joseph of Arimathea (19:39). In each case he blends a mix of curiosity, courage, and timidity.

We know that Nicodemus was a member of the Sanhedrin ("the Jewish ruling council") and that he was a Pharisee. Since the Pharisees had a limited stake in the temple operations, it would not have concerned him (possibly even amused him) that Jesus had just upset the markets in the temple courts. Still, if he was politically savvy, he may have seen this act of Jesus as politically explosive and dangerous.

We also know he was a rabbi (3:1, 10), a teacher no doubt of some fame. In 3:10 Jesus refers to him as (lit.) "*the* teacher [not *a* teacher] of Israel." This at least must refer to his distinguished reputation in Jerusalem. When this rabbi comes to Jesus at night (3:2), it may simply refer to his desire for privacy stemming from fear. He might worry that the temple authorities, whom Jesus has just challenged, might see him as a collaborator.

But "night" is also likely a theological symbol (used frequently by John) that expresses Nicodemus's spiritual relation to the truth. John often refers

---

3. Some scholars have argued that 3:31–36 has been displaced and should appear between vv. 12 and 13. Although this makes the passage easy to understand, there is no manuscript for it and this would interrupt the present symmetry of the chapter.

4. If Nicodemus was, say, seventy years old in A.D. 70, that would make him 25–30 in the present scene. But this is an unusually young age for a Sanhedrin leader.

---

to darkness as the realm of evil, untruth, and unbelief (e.g., 9:4; 11:10). The only other actor who appears at night is Judas Iscariot, who departs into the night to betray Jesus (13:30). Nicodemus is a man of the darkness while Jesus is the light (1:4, 8). John's subsequent commentary (3:19ff.) says this plainly: Jesus is light that has come into the world, but men and women prefer darkness. In this case, however, Nicodemus has made a serious choice: He has stepped into the light to make inquiries.

Nicodemus's first question (3:2) shows admirable respect. He acknowledges Jesus as a teacher (despite Jesus' lack of credentials, 7:15) and is willing to give him the benefit of the doubt: His activities must come from God and his efforts must have some divine endorsement. This is an "opener" launched by one theologian to another. Nicodemus wants to engage Jesus theologically, to launch a discussion. His use of plurals (*"we* know") even suggests he represents a group. Is he an emissary from somewhere? An inquirer assigned to return with a report?

Jesus' response is unexpected (3:3). Instead of joining Nicodemus by engaging his question, he forces the rabbi to move to another level of inquiry. Jesus is not interested in the divine authentication of signs but in the reality of someone's relationship with God. Nicodemus has to keep up; he has to choose to follow Jesus' lead or retreat back into the dark. Two terms require definition. (1) Although the Old Testament does not use the phrase *kingdom of God* in full, still, the notion of God's sovereign, kingly rule is implicit throughout the Jewish Scriptures (Ps. 103:19). The Scriptures also predicted a final kingdom that was coming at the end of time, a kingdom of grand dimensions supervised by a descendent of David (Isa. 9:1–7; Zech. 9:9–10) or Isaiah's Servant of the Lord (Isa. 42:1–9; 49:1–26). Judaism taught that this was to be a future kingdom and that all Jews who faithfully kept the law would be admitted to it freely.[5]

(2) Jesus, however, says that there is a new prerequisite to see or enter this kingdom. "No one can see the kingdom of God unless he is born *again* [Gk. *anothen*]." *Anothen* can either mean "again" or "from above," and it is clear from the other Johannine uses that the local sense ("from above") is John's usual meaning (3:31; 19:11, 23). But since Nicodemus sees it one way and Jesus means it another, John has provided us here with one of the first misunderstandings in his Gospel. In order to enter the kingdom, in order to understand divine revelations such as this, one must have an experience that transports beyond the mere observation of "signs." Divine signs are ambiguous without divine aid.

---

5. "Kingdom of heaven" and "kingdom of God" represent the most frequent themes in Jesus' Synoptic teachings, occurring over ninety times in separate contexts.

The notion of divine birth would have made sense to someone with a Hellenistic background (and later Hellenistic readers of John would have recognized it easily) since divine regeneration was a frequent idea there. But if we keep the historicity of the episode intact, we have to ask what a Jew of Nicodemus's background would have understood. True, Judaism was thoroughly Hellenized in this era and Nicodemus would have understood the language of non-Jewish faiths, much like we understand the language of Muslims and Jews. Proselytes in Judaism were often called newly born children.[6] But the language Jesus uses would have seemed unusual to Nicodemus. Jesus is driving at something comprehensive, a complete renewal of the whole person. As Calvin commented, "by the word 'born again' he means not the amendment of a part but the renewal of the whole nature. Hence it follows that there is nothing in us that is not defective."[7]

Nicodemus's second question (3:4) is either wistful ("Can human nature *really* be changed? Can we really start over?") or cynical ("And I should return to my mother's womb? I don't think so.").[8] Above all it shows that Nicodemus is outside the kingdom and that he cannot penetrate its deeper truths. Thus Jesus must explain more fully (3:5–8). Divine birth is now explained as birth "of water and the Spirit."

This critical phrase has given interpreters genuine difficulty. (1) Some have argued that when Jesus refers to water, he is thinking about literal birth. Water, then, refers to human birth or birth from flesh (3:6), which must be followed later by spiritual rebirth. The chief problem here is that this culture did not refer to natural birth as birth "by water" (although we may do so today, thinking of water as either amniotic fluid or semen).[9]

(2) Following this line of thought, some have unified "water and Spirit" and created a metaphor. Some ancient sources show that water could refer to male semen and in religious literature could be a metaphor for divine birth or "spiritual seed." But this is obscure, and one cannot help but wonder if Nicodemus would understand it.

(3) Another set of options views water as baptism. For critical scholars, John is referring to Christian baptism that is accompanied by spiritual regeneration. Certainly as John wrote this passage, knowing that his readership would have this background, he was not unaware that this understanding would result. Thus a secondary meaning such as this is likely. But certainly Nicodemus could not be expected to know this, and such a view makes John

---

6. See references in Morris, *John*, 190; Carson, *John*, 189–93.

7. As cited in Barrett, *John*, 206.

8. The grammatical form of the question betrays its disbelief: "Certainly a person cannot reenter. . . can he?"

9. Ancients might refer to natural birth as "birth by blood."

a terrible storyteller since in 3:10 Jesus upbraids the rabbi for not understanding.[10] Thus, a more likely view is to see this as a reference to John the Baptist's baptism, which the Gospel has already introduced in the narrative. Nicodemus (by this reading) must submit to the baptism of repentance offered by the Baptist at the Jordan. Following this he can experience the Spirit and transformation.

(4) Another option suggests that "water and Spirit" form a unified concept to express the eschatological renewal promised in the Old Testament. The prophets in particular described a coming era when the transforming Spirit of God would be poured out generously on all people (Isa. 32:15–20; Joel 2:28). Sometimes this renewal is described metaphorically as water. Note Isaiah 44:3: "For I will pour *water* on the thirsty land, and streams on the dry ground; I will pour my *Spirit* on your offspring, and my blessing on your descendants." Note how *water* and *Spirit* are easily joined as the life-giving gifts of God. This figurative pair appears again and again in the Old Testament, and no doubt Ezekiel 36:25–27 is the most important eschatological image of all. Here Israel's heart will be transformed:

> I will sprinkle clean water on you, and you will be clean; I will cleanse you from all your impurities and from all your idols. I will give you a new heart and put a new spirit in you; I will remove from you your heart of stone and give you a heart of flesh. And I will put my Spirit in you and move you to follow my decrees and be careful to keep my laws.

In other words, Jesus is here pointing to the dawning of a new eschatological era. John the Baptist has inaugurated this era, and submission to his message—his water baptism, which is the precursor for Christian baptism—is expected. Jesus now is the baptizer "in Spirit" (1:33), who will complete the dawning of this time. But above all, Nicodemus must understand that this era will be an era when the Spirit of God moves among humanity. Jesus compares this with the "wind," another Greek wordplay, since *pneuma* can mean either "spirit" or "wind" (3:8). Its origin and movements are mysterious, and they cannot be contained by the human religious systems Jesus has already challenged.

Nicodemus's third and final question is rhetorical in the narrative. "How can this be?" likely disguises a thoroughgoing and lengthy inquiry by the rabbi, whose religious categories have now been upended. He is baffled. He is disturbed. His commitment to the Torah and obedience, to prayer and sacrifice, and his understanding of election, responsibility, and privilege have all been challenged. He should have no problem understanding that the

---

10. Carson, *John*, 192.

Spirit of God can transform; but he is a man standing on the frontier, looking at a new country and wondering how such momentous events will unfold.

For the third (and final) time Jesus begins his answer with (lit.) "Truly, truly I say to you," as if to underscore the importance of what he is about to say (3:3, 5, 11).[11] The irony of his response is that he refers to Nicodemus as a rabbi (3:10), just as Nicodemus had referred to Jesus (3:2), but now we see that this teacher does not know the answers. Jesus is the only "true rabbi" who can explain the deeper mysteries of God.

But the problem is far deeper. It is not simply with this teacher; rather, there is a general problem with the religious world of first-century Judaism (just as at the close of ch. 2 there is a problem with humanity). The "we" in 3:11 likely refers to Jesus and his followers, who are witnesses to the signs of the kingdom. They have all seen this new kingdom and can bear witness to it. The problem rests on a refusal by many (pl. "you" in 3:11b, 12) to receive this testimony and believe. It is not really a problem of knowledge (3:10). The signs and Scriptures are accessible here on earth, and if these cannot be understood and believed, it is not possible for profound heavenly things to be believed. People who stumble on the elemental teachings of Jesus cannot hope to grasp the deeper realities.

Jesus is unique among all others to disclose these heavenly truths because he is the only one among humankind who has truly entered heaven's realms (3:13). Human teachers do not have access to this sort of revelation. He alone brings a capacity for disclosure that exceeds both human imagination and wisdom. But just as Jesus descended with this knowledge, making him the unparalleled rabbi, so too Jesus must return (3:14).

Jesus then refers to a story from Numbers 21, in which Moses built a serpent of bronze and elevated it among the Israelites so that whoever gazed on it would be healed from the snakes that bit them in the desert. In the same manner, Jesus says, he must be "lifted up" in order to become the source of eternal life for all who believe. The Greek *hypsoo* (lift up) is an important Johannine verb to describe Jesus' "ascent" or "lifting up" to the cross (3:14; 8:28; 12:32, 34). Luke uses this same verb in Acts for Jesus' ascension/exaltation (Acts 2:33; 5:31). John has in mind that the cross will not simply be a place of sacrifice and suffering, but a place of departure, of return, when Jesus resumes his life with the Father (17:1–19). Jesus *ascends* to the cross. As we will see later in this Gospel, the cross will actually be a place of glorification.

Many scholars agree that 3:16–21 provides reflections or meditations written by John. This means that (contra the NIV) the quotation marks should end

---

11. This is a unique preface in John In the Synoptics Jesus prefaces his words with a single "truly" (*amen*). In John a double *amen* is used for added emphasis (see comment on 1:51).

at 3:15, where Jesus uses his characteristic title "Son of Man." Note that in 3:16 Jesus' death is described as past (God *gave* his one and only Son), and much of the language of these verses is distinctly Johannine.[12] With verse 16 we are reading John's commentary on the importance of Jesus' words to Nicodemus.

The statement that God loves *the world* is surprising on two counts (3:16). (1) Judaism rarely (or never) spoke of God's loving the world outside of Israel. God desires to reach this world through Israel, his child. It is a uniquely Christian idea to say that God's love extends beyond the limits of race and nation. (2) John tells his readers elsewhere that they are not to love the world (1 John 2:15–17) because it is a place of disbelief and hostility (cf. John 15:18–19; 16:8). Carson comments effectively, "There is no contradiction between this prohibition and the fact that God does love it [the world]. Christians are not to love the world with the selfish love of participation; God loves the world with the selfless, costly love of redemption."[13]

This helpful insight gives a clue to what John means by "the world." In John's writings "world" (Gk. *kosmos*) is not a reference to the natural world of trees, animals, and plants—a world defended by the Sierra Club and Greenpeace.[14] For John *kosmos* (used seventy-eight times in this Gospel, twenty-four times in his letters) is the realm *of humanity* arrayed in opposition to God (1:9; 7:7). Thus Jesus enters this world in his incarnation, knowing that hostility will result and that sacrifice will be needed in order to redeem the world (1:29; 3:17; 6:51). This dimension of the Son's work must be underscored: The Son did not come to the world to save a select few (those chosen, those privileged); rather, he came to save *the world*, namely, the all-encompassing circle of men and women who inhabit this planet, people who embrace darkness habitually (3:19–21).

In this respect, the entry of the Son into the darkness of this world is an act of judgment (3:19; cf. 9:39) inasmuch as divine light has penetrated and unveiled the darkness for what it is. Jesus has not come to condemn the world (3:17) but to reveal and save, to provide a way of escape for those shuttered in the darkness. His coming does not bring a "verdict" (NIV), but a process by which judgment is active on those who witness his coming. Those who see this light and recognize the tragedy of their own situation have one responsibility: to believe (3:16, 18).

---

12. The phrase "one and only" (*monogenes*) is a word used exclusively by John and not by Jesus (1:14, 18; 1 John 4:9). The phrases "believe in the name" (3:18) and "live by the truth" (3:21) likewise never occur in speeches of Jesus.

13. Carson, *John*, 205.

14. Some Christian environmentalists have mistakenly used 3:16 as a defense of Christian commitment to nature. God indeed calls us to be caring custodians of nature, but this is not the intent of John's words here.

Yet it is not so simple. The affections of people in the world are corrupt; their desires are fallen; they are not eager to be redeemed. They "love darkness instead of light"; in fact, they "hate" the light. This is strong language, which uncovers something of the seriousness of the moral struggle between God and the world. Evil and darkness do not ignore the light; they wage war against it, trying to bring it down. But despite these efforts, the darkness cannot vanquish the light (1:9). The darkness launches a battle that brings about its own defeat.

By contrast, those who love the coming of the light, who look on and trust the "upraised," crucified Son, who believe in Jesus and "live by the truth" (3:21), these people not only enjoy eternal life (3:16, 18) but they come to the light and yearn for its truth. John does not have in mind here people in the world who already have the goodness of God at work in their hearts and whom the light reveals. John is describing what happens when those in the world make a choice to believe; they are transformed into children of God (1:12; 11:52; 1 John 3:10), experiencing the power of the Spirit (3:5–6) and living the truth (3:21). Such people live righteously because God is at work in them (3:21b), not because they have a native desire to be godly.

Jesus and John the Baptist (3:22–36)

WHILE THE FIRST half of chapter 3 examined the discussion of Nicodemus and Jesus, now John the Baptist comes on stage. Just as Nicodemus must be born "from above" (3:3), so now the Baptist becomes a witness to Jesus as one who is "from above" (3:31). Jesus has descended from heaven (3:12–13), bringing heavenly gifts of the Spirit and rebirth; he is a messenger who reveals what he has seen and heard in heaven's precincts (3:31–32). Just as Nicodemus represents Jewish leadership in Jerusalem, John the Baptist is a Jewish prophet. Both men are from "the earth" while Jesus is "from above."

Some scholars see this section (along with the narratives devoted to the Baptist in ch. 1) as serving a need in the congregation to whom this Gospel is addressed. In the introduction I mentioned that the Gospel of John may have been written with an eye not simply to evangelism, but to address issues that troubled the Christian church as well. The portrait of Jesus, the stories selected from historical archives, and the sayings preserved in the stories all serve to meet needs relevant to John's readers.[15]

---

15. This is not to deny the historicity of the Gospel narrative. Rather, the process by which historical episodes were preserved, selected, and arranged in the Gospel was influenced by the life and needs of the early church. Stories about Jesus that were important were preserved. But the immediate question is, important to whom? The Gospels represent the cherished stories of Jesus preserved in the earliest church.

Acts 19:1—7 tells us that there were people in Ephesus who were followers of John the Baptist but who did not believe in Jesus. Later postapostolic evidence even suggests that such communities continued to exist a few generations later, which elevated John the Baptist and rejected Jesus' messiahship. If such a polemic existed in the communities that first read the Fourth Gospel, 3:22—36 becomes a potent corrective. John the Baptist becomes a premier witness to Jesus, dispelling rumors of a rivalry and urging his followers to believe in him. The Baptist devalues his own status—as the friend (3:29) compared with the bridegroom—and says explicitly, "He must become greater; I must become less" (3:30). But even though the passage may have an interest in a polemic with "the Baptist sect," this should not undermine a historical reading of these verses. We have evidence in the earliest days of disciples who are willing to champion John the Baptist and give lukewarm interest in Jesus.

John 3:22—36 mirrors 3:1—21 in one respect. The narrative running from 3:22—30 likely ends with the finality of the Baptist's personal devaluation. As the evangelist followed 3:1—15 with commentary (3:16—21), so he follows the Baptist narrative of 3:22—30 with further commentary (3:31—36). This means that chapter 3 is built with two halves, each containing structurally similar features. As the evangelist weaves the chapter together, he concentrates on similar theological themes and literary symmetries to make it a unified whole.[16]

Following his conversation with Nicodemus, Jesus and his followers move into the regions east of Jerusalem, where he conducts a ministry much like that of John the Baptist (3:22). This is an interesting note since it is our only record that Jesus had a baptizing ministry. But we must remain clear that at this point Jesus is conducting a baptism of repentance, no doubt like that of John, since, as 7:37—39 says, the Spirit (a feature of *Christian* baptism) has not yet been given. However, John goes on to make clear that Jesus' disciples, not Jesus himself, baptized people (4:2). Imagine the sort of elitism that could have developed in the ancient church between those baptized by Jesus and those baptized by anyone else.

At this time (3:23) the Baptist is working at Aenon near Salim—a transliterated Semitic phrase meaning "the springs" (*aenon*), which were near a place named for "peace" (Heb. *shalom*; Arabic, *salam*). The location of this is disputed. The least likely suggestion is just north of the Dead Sea. A second possibility is south of the ancient city Beth Shan (New Testament Scythopolis) in the Jordan Valley. A third is near Samaria, where the note about springs

---

16. Some scholars (such as R. Brown) suggest that 3:22—36 is a displaced narrative that records one of Jesus' earliest encounters with John, perhaps following the baptism. This would explain the awkwardness.

would make sense since Jesus would not then be using the Jordan River. Nevertheless, there are many springs around the region of Beth Shan also and thus the location is uncertain.

The editorial note of 3:24 suggests that John the evangelist presupposes the Synoptic story.[17] John's arrest is only recorded in the Synoptics (Matt. 14:1–12; Mark 1:14; 6:14–29; Luke 3:19–20), and from that account we get the impression that once John is taken captive, Jesus begins his aggressive ministry in Galilee. But this is an unwarranted conclusion. The Fourth Gospel makes it plain that Jesus and the Baptist worked simultaneously for some time before Jesus moved north.

But this does not mean that John and the Synoptics are at odds. The first three Gospels imply that Jesus moves to Galilee because in some fashion he might be in jeopardy in light of John the Baptist's arrest (Matt. 4:12). If Jesus had not been recognized as yet publicly, why would he worry about an association with the Baptist? The Fourth Gospel completes the picture. Jesus and the Baptist worked together, and when the one was arrested, the other had to move north out of the region.

The dispute described in 3:25–26 is the root of the problem that the Baptist's subsequent speech (3:27–30) will address. We cannot know the name of the "certain Jew" of verse 25, nor can we be certain about the nature of the argument between him and the Baptist's followers. John 3:26 suggests that it was about baptism and if we are right, then someone in Jewish leadership may be debating the theological correctness of ceremonial purity and how it relates to John's baptism. Baptism such as this was commonplace for converted Gentiles entering Judaism since it represented a spiritual threshold the convert was crossing. Ceremonial washings were also common among Jews who cleansed themselves for service or prayer. But baptism *for Jews* did not make sense. Was this a ceremonial cleansing? Was it a threshold? Certainly these questions stand behind the interrogation of John reported at the beginning of all four Gospels.

But the key here is that Jesus' baptism is drawn into the debate (3:26). If the argument is about ceremonial effectiveness and legitimacy, the critique from Judaism is less important than the threat posed by Jesus' newfound popularity. This verse indicates that the Baptist had followers who knew about the events surrounding Jesus' baptism, who knew John's testimony concerning him, and likely knew Jesus by name. But curiously, they do not refer to Jesus personally ("that man who was with you") and they harbor considerable

---

17. John 3:24 joins a number of other passages in John (11:2) that imply John assumes his reader knows the stories told in the Gospel of Mark. See R. Bauckham, "John for Readers of Mark," in R. Bauckham, ed., *The Gospels for All Christians: Rethinking the Gospel Audiences* (Grand Rapids/Edinburgh: Eerdmans/T. & T. Clark, 1998), 147–71.

envy for Jesus' fame ("everyone is going to him."). They seem disgruntled, unhappy that Jesus is becoming a celebrated leader.

The Baptist's rejoinder (3:27–30) corrects the rivalry. God has provided the successes and increases enjoyed by Jesus. It is not that John is now receiving a lesser role (though this is true), but that Jesus is "receiving" more followers (cf. 3:26), and he has "received" these from heaven. Such growth should not be criticized. Above all, John affirms (as he did in ch. 1) that he is not the Christ (3:28) but his forerunner. Drawing on wedding imagery, John compares himself with a "friend who attends the bridegroom." The groom alone has the bride, and the friend rejoices. Jesus frequently used such analogies (Mark 2:19–20), and later in the New Testament, the bride is described as the church (see Rev. 18:2; 19:7; 21:2, 9; 22:17).[18]

But this is not the present text's interest and should not be allegorized. John 3:28–29 serves simply to emphasize what is stated forcefully in 3:29: "He must become greater; I must become less." John the Baptist, despite the affections of his followers, must always play a secondary role. Now with the advent of Jesus' appearance and ministry, John's followers must discover a new allegiance to Jesus. This allegiance is precisely what John was encouraging in 1:35–42 when he identified Jesus and urged his disciples to follow Jesus.

The final paragraph of chapter 3 has often been viewed as a puzzle. Do the quotation marks continue through to verse 36 (NIV) or to they end at verse 31? Some scholars have noted the many links between it and the Nicodemus dialogue in 3:1–21 and have argued that it fits that section better. Some have even gone so far as to say that 3:31–36 should follow 3:21 as a fitting conclusion to the Nicodemus section.[19] Yet this paragraph also sums up the differences between the Baptist and Jesus as well as uses the theological framework outlined in 3:1–21. In this respect, 3:31–36 is likely a meditation or theological epilogue written by the evangelist to highlight the differences between John and Jesus, using language established at the beginning of the chapter.

Jesus is superior because of his heavenly origins (3:31). He is "from above" (*anothen*, the same word that appeared in 3:3 [NIV, "again"]). This status must be carefully compared to anyone who comes "from the earth." Human teaching cannot be compared with divine revelation, where the courier brings a message from God. But even when the heavenly message is delivered (3:32),

---

18. This is important because some critical scholars have criticized the historical nature of these verses based on John's reference to the bride and the groom for Jesus and his followers.

19. The following themes appear in both sections: from above, comes from heaven, speaks from the earth, bearing witness to what is seen and heard, not receiving testimony, gift of the Spirit, receiving the Son, and having eternal life.

the world is still a place of darkness and will not receive the testimony of what this courier, this Son, has witnessed (cf. 3:11). Truth, then, is something that *descends*, not something discovered through human labor. It is foreign. It comes from outside and thus runs the risk of rejection.

The two Greek verbs at the center of 3:33 are in the aorist tense ("the man who *has accepted* it *has certified* that God is truthful," italics added). This describes men and women who have made a firm decision once and for all. They have acknowledged Jesus, accepted him and his witness, and made a theological deduction about God. In other words, to affirm the central ideas about Jesus is to commit oneself to a larger theological complex of ideas. To affirm the divine sonship of Jesus drives one immediately to affirmations about God and revelation and truth. John's imagery is graphic. In antiquity wax seals were used to give authentication and ownership to letters and possessions. Even illiterate people could recognize the official seals of important persons. Hence, to embrace Jesus is to set a seal, to confirm, and to defend an entire constellation of beliefs central to Christian faith and God.

What is at stake here is the nature of Jesus and his authority (3:34–36). God's love for the Son is so complete that *nothing* is beyond the Son's reach; anything belonging to God has been placed in the Son's hands. The Father has provided the Son with the words he speaks ("What he has seen and heard," 3:32). The Father has commissioned the Son to come to us.

Above all, the Father has provided the Son with the Holy Spirit (3:34). Even though the subject of the final clause in 3:34 is ambiguous (lit., "for he gives the Spirit without limit") and some have speculated that the verse describes how the Son gives the Spirit to believers, it seems clear that these verses are about what God has given to Jesus, equipping him for his mission in the world. This verse does not refer to Jesus' giving the Spirit to us, but to God's giving the Spirit to his Son, underscoring the remarkable interconnectedness of Father and Son once more.

Jesus bears a divine nature and carries God's authority. Earlier John the Baptist testified, "I saw the Spirit come down from heaven as a dove and remain on him" (1:32). Therefore, the gift of life and Spirit that the Son will distribute (1:33; 3:3, 36) comes from the gift of life and Spirit that the Son already enjoys. It is a gift that comes "from above," now resident in the Son's life—a gift that will be distributed once the Son of God is glorified (7:37–39).

In 3:36b John then looks at salvation from the other point of view. Those who reject the Son will not see life; instead, God's wrath rests on them. This verse does not indicate that God is angry in light of their rejection of him. Rather, it means that the world of darkness and unbelief stands under the judgment of God (Rom. 1:18ff.), and those who refuse the light, who reject Jesus, remain in the darkness and thus continue to live under divine judgment.

JESUS AND NICODEMUS. Few passages in the Fourth Gospel have enjoyed the sort of attention awarded to 3:1–21. John 3:16 is arguably the most memorized Scripture verse in the entire Bible. And few verses are used more often in evangelism than Jesus' words about rebirth. One of Chuck Colson's best-selling books is even titled *Born Again*.[20] Without seeing the index, we can predict that John 3 figured largely into his outline for the book.

But John has more to say to us here than to describe God's love and the matter of our conversion. This passage has theological nuances that bear genuine relevance to a modern audience. As I claimed earlier, the conversation with Nicodemus is a model conversation, a paradigm if you will, of Jesus bringing the light of God to one who is captive in darkness. Nicodemus is not a literary foil per se (he was a true historical figure), but his evening with Jesus supplies John with raw materials from which he can build a model conversation. If John were asked, "What would Jesus say to someone in the darkness, someone with religious ambitions?" John would likely supply this narrative and say, Nicodemus was a man—and he is everyone.

(1) Note the profile of Nicodemus: He is one of the people Jesus would not trust (2:24) because he knew them so well. Morris infers from the passage that Nicodemus was a man who loved the truth, was timid about its expression, but in the end stood in Jesus' defense when his disciples fled.[21] This may be true, but we can also say that Nicodemus portrays a character whose life has not been completely penetrated by Christ, who asks questions but does not become a disciple, who listens but does not believe. Glimmers of courage surface in chapter 7—and certainly the choice to assist in Jesus' burial was courageous—but in the end, Nicodemus does not become a model disciple. Disciples confess Jesus' identity, remain with him, and tell others (cf. the disciples of chs. 1 and 4). Nicodemus' story exhibits none of these features.

Above all, Nicodemus comes from "Jerusalem" instead of Galilee.[22] He is a theological insider. He is adept at spiritual things and is famous for his skill at teaching. On the historical plane, I have argued that John is signaling to us something about messianic replacement and abundance: Jesus is the rabbi or teacher who brings heavenly wisdom (3:13) while the average rabbi cannot understand the deeper things of God (3:10). Jesus is *the* Rabbi who makes all other teachers schooled in Judaism redundant. In fact, one wonders if his

---

20. See, e g., the twentieth anniversary edition: Grand Rapids· Revell/Baker, 1996.
21. Morris, *John*, 186
22. Recall John's symbolic use of geography (see above)

theological skill becomes an impediment to Nicodemus's ability to become a disciple.

Is there a comment here about *our capacity* to genuinely accept Jesus? Should Nicodemus serve as a mirror for some of us to see ourselves? John's emphasis on Christology hardly makes him anti-intellectual. But in some fashion, I cannot avoid wondering if John would have us reflect on the relation between religious ambition and sophistication and our ability to see and hear a personal Jesus today.

(2) In these verses John has given careful attention to the work of Christ. Of course, John mentions the saving work of Christ on the cross (3:14), but he has far more to say. Initially John has an interest in how Christ's work extends to those in darkness even though he is "the light." He speaks to Nicodemus *at night*. That is, Jesus must step into darkness itself in order to redeem those captive to it. This notion reminds me of Jesus' saying in Mark 2:17: "It is not the healthy who need a doctor, but the sick. I have come to call not the righteous, but sinners." God is not demanding some moral or religious preparation from us that makes us interesting and acceptable to him. On the contrary, his mission is to enter the darkness and find us.

This strikes me as a terribly important theme. In the Synoptics, Jesus tells stories about shepherds looking for lost sheep. In John, Jesus uses the abstract dualistic metaphor of light and darkness, and in chapter 3 he is the light looking in darkness for men and women who will become children of God.

Another feature of Jesus' work has to do with revelation. Jesus is not simply another human teacher who outdoes one of Jerusalem's leading rabbis. Jesus is not simply a superior human expositor of Scripture who in debate can outrun any rival. Jesus is a *divine* teacher and revealer of God. We saw this already in 1:18: "No one has ever seen God, but God the One and Only, who is at the Father's side, has made him known." The importance of Jesus is not found simply in what he says but in where he comes from. Therefore there is an *ontological* dimension to Christology in John that is essential. Jesus has descended from heaven (3:13). This notion offers a remarkable appeal to my century: Christology makes an absolute claim, an outrageous claim, to religious truth. No other source can rival what is being claimed here for Jesus. He provides access to God that is unlike any other religious founder.

(3) John's most obvious contribution has to do with human transformation and its possibilities. Of course when Jesus challenges Nicodemus that he must be "born again/from above," he is making a fundamental statement about theological anthropology. That is, humanity is broken beyond all repair. God's work in the world is not a question of fixing the part, but rebuilding the whole. It is described comprehensively as nothing short of another birth. The significance of this new birth gains weight theologically as soon

as we develop our doctrine of the comprehensiveness of human fallenness and sin. As Augustine once taught, the problem with humanity is not that we sin, but that we are in a *state of sin* that needs a comprehensive solution. Nicodemus, then, and everyone in Jerusalem (2:23)—as well as everyone in the world (2:25)—lives with this infirmity. Its ramifications bear unusual importance for modern society.

The transformation offered to Nicodemus also opens the question of the nature of true religion. That is, religion is not necessarily a matter of personal knowledge or ethical behavior. Nor is it fidelity to religious traditions, no matter how virtuously they evoke higher ethical, religious behavior among us. Jesus is claiming that true spirituality is *not* discovering some latent capacity within the human soul and fanning it to flame. It is *not* uncovering a moral consciousness that is hidden by sedimentary layers of civilization's corruptions. Nor is it inspiring aesthetic qualities that promote society in its finest form. It is *not* a "horizontal" experience that takes up the materials available around us in the world.

Rather, Jesus claims, true religion is "vertical." It has to do not with the human spirit, but with God's Spirit. It is a foreign invasion, sabotage of the first order. True religion unites humanity with God's powerful Spirit, who overwhelms, transforms, and *converts* (in the full meaning of the word) its subject. Our role in this transformation is belief (3:16, 18), and yet it is a belief that is aided by God's work within us since we live in the darkness and have our spiritual capacities handicapped by sin. As I convey this concept to my world, I need to search for creative metaphors, clever images that bring the full impact of this idea home.

Jesus and John the Baptist. This is one of the least celebrated sections of this Gospel, overshadowed no doubt by the dramatic and well-known dialogue with Nicodemus. Historically it gives us some information we do not find elsewhere in the New Testament. We learn, for instance, that John the Baptist had a committed circle of disciples and that some of them struggled with the decision to shift their commitments from John to Jesus. We also learn that Jesus and John enjoyed a simultaneous period of ministry in Judea.

The Synoptic picture of Jesus has him beginning a Galilean ministry following his baptism and temptation; it provides no information about this early period. But in Mark 6:14–29 we are left wondering why Herod Antipas (who murdered John the Baptist) would conclude that John and Jesus were linked in the popular imagination unless they had been together at some previous time. Seeing Jesus some cried, "John the Baptist has been raised from the dead" (Mark 6:14). Herod even believed it (6:16). This connection is explained by John 3:22–36. Jesus and John knew each other well. They worked together. Their disciples knew each other. And in the turmoil of John's arrest and death, some of those disciples were deeply conflicted about their commitments.

These insights bring a peculiar but human dimension to the early ministries of Jesus, John, and their followers. Even the disciples of Jesus were not as generous as we might think. At one point in Galilee they discover someone working in Jesus' name, and they eagerly report it to him, "Master ... we saw a man driving out demons in your name and we tried to stop him, because he is not one of us" (Luke 9:49). Jesus refuses to act and gives them a gentle rebuke. The same thing happened in the early churches founded by Paul. At Corinth Christians were quarreling about allegiances to Paul, Apollos, and Cephas/Peter (1 Cor. 1:10–17). Perhaps we need to set aside the fantasy that the earliest Christians worked easily with each other and did not form human loyalties that got in the way.

(1) John the evangelist certainly finds a universal lesson in this story—a lesson no less pertinent for us today. The followers of John the Baptist were not able to see that their affection for and devotion to the prophet made them unable to follow Jesus. I am sure that they would not oppose Jesus, for that would have put them at odds with their master. Nor did they deny that Jesus was in some respect unique, fulfilling the work of God in the world. But what explains John's firm reminder in 3:28, "You yourselves can testify that I said, 'I am not the Christ ... '"? Are some claiming that perhaps John *is* the Christ? Are they unwilling to let John "become less" so that Jesus might be glorified? Has their investment in John become so all-consuming that they have promoted him to a place John would never accept himself? These are important questions and need to be explored today if we create commitments and investments that may impede genuine devotion to Jesus.

(2) A second lesson is imbedded in John's unqualified affirmation of Jesus. The theological uniqueness of Christ is not centered on the effectiveness or persuasiveness of his ministry. It is not that Jesus provides wisdom or insight that resonates with us and is confirmed by us. Theological certainty is not awarded by earthly degrees. Simply put, Jesus is "from above." He bears God's Spirit without limit (3:34). He bears revelation that is utterly different from anything in the world, a revelation that comes directly from God the Father.

Two things result from this realization. (a) It should come as no surprise that the world cannot understand or recognize this revelation (3:32). The world is steeped in darkness, blinded by its own fallenness, and without God's Word, it is a helpless, pitiful, lifeless thing (3:36). As this Gospel unfolds, we will hear a great deal more about the incapacities of this darkened world, its anger toward the light, and its desire to destroy those who respond to God's light.

(b) John is making a statement about authority. If it is true that this is revelation "from above," revelation from God, then Christian revelation is not on a par with any other religious system in the world. Noble attempts to domesticate Jesus by making him one more sage along with many other religious teachers fall short here. The Christian theological affirmation is that in Christ something unparalleled has been disclosed, something the world has never seen. The implications of this affirmation fan out like ripples in a pond: Our understanding of salvation, Scripture, and revelation (among others) is permanently affected.

(3) Finally, John began the chapter with the Nicodemus story and now ends by making us wonder about the fate not only of Nicodemus, but also of John's followers. Nicodemus is pointed to "water and Spirit" as a means of renewal. The followers of John the Baptist are locked in debate about ceremonial washing. Both parties need to discover that the only one who can truly transform and cleanse is Jesus because he bears the eschatological Spirit from God.

This challenge is ours as well. Will we "certify" (3:33) and affirm the truth of what God is doing? Will we step out of the darkness, out of the world, out of death, and place our seal on the truth of what Jesus says and who he is? The first half of the chapter (3:1–21) pointed to an *experience* that is necessary for entry into the kingdom of God—a powerful, transforming encounter with the Holy Spirit. The second half of the chapter (3:22–36) now underscores a *commitment of belief*, a challenge to embrace the true identity, origin, and mission of Jesus. This is not simply a commitment to some small truth, but to an idea of Truth, a system of understanding reality, God, and ourselves.

THE CONVERSION OF NICODEMUS. The longer I am in the church, the more I am in need of conversion stories. That is, fresh stories of conversion remind me of the nature of the world (from which I am increasingly isolated, as my circle of professional and personal friends are increasingly Christian). These stories also remind me of the power of God (about which I can become increasingly blasé). Of course there are moments when I have a glimpse of the darkness. And there are other moments when I see the radiance of the Light, and suddenly I inherit the dualistic up/down, right/wrong, dark/light worldview that John would have me possess. Conversion stories help me understand the drama of sentences like 3:20–21: "Everyone who does evil hates the light, and will not come into the light for fear that his deeds will be exposed. But whoever lives by the truth comes into the light, so that it may be seen plainly that what he has done has been done through God."

Living with new converts who have been recently transformed by God's Spirit is like living on a political frontier and receiving and welcoming refugees from a terrible war. In Chicago I often meet recent arrivals from the civil war in Bosnia. They have stories to tell. In fact, they cannot keep from telling these stories nor can they keep from expressing their heartfelt gratitude for their rescue and salvation. To convey the decision that faced Nicodemus and the prospect for his renewal, I have to tell stories that describe what would have happened if Nicodemus had been "born again/from above."

On a recent trip to Israel I rented a car with one of my daughters and drove south through the desert to the port city of Eilat. Our aim was to see the desert in its springtime glory, visit the copper mines of Timna, and go snorkeling in the Gulf of Aqaba's coral reefs. On our first evening I contacted a messianic Jewish fellowship that I knew had a large, successful ministry in Eilat. Following dinner (at our first kosher Burger King restaurant),[23] we drove to a nearby neighborhood and found a large home whose living room had been designed as a worship center.

Following the usual greetings and introductions we sat transfixed in a room packed with Russians, Chinese, Rumanians, and Americans (all with a Jewish heritage—except the Chinese). Following a time of worship, a gifted teacher gave an evangelistic message based on the thieves on the cross: one who asked for mercy, another who refused. As the teacher spoke in English, translators around the room converted his words into Russian, Chinese, and Rumanian. When the translators came to an impasse, they lapsed into Hebrew with the teacher in order to straighten out his meaning. The international flavor of the scene was fascinating.

I wondered where these people had come from. The Rumanians and Russians had come to Israel as Jewish refugees, leaving lands with historic records of persecution. They could tell stories of the collapse of the Russian economy and the rise of corruption, as well as the frightening threat of renewed racism and anti-Semitism. Few of them were piously orthodox, and Judaism was chiefly their ticket to get out of Russia, a chance to discover a new start. The Chinese were laborers building the many high-rise hotels found throughout the city. Over the years hundreds of them had become Christians (thanks to these messianic congregations) and had taken their faith back to China. And the word had spread. Laborers were coming and discovering Christ every week. The irony of God's plan stunned me. Who would guess that the desert streets of Eilat would be at the forefront of Chinese evangelism?

---

23. What distinguishes a *kosher* Burger King? No milk products (hence, no cheeseburgers, shakes, or ice cream made with milk)!

My attention was drawn to a particularly upset young woman of eighteen or nineteen, who had just left Russia to join her young fiancé in Eilat. She still wore the traditional clothes of the Russian countryside while he now sported jeans and a T-shirt. She had left everything behind: family, home, tradition, language, security, and job. Her world had been overturned. For the first time, in the confusion of her personal storm, she was hearing the gospel. Her fiancé had become a Christian weeks earlier, and now he wanted this young woman to discover the same. She wept through the entire Bible study.

Nicodemus was challenged to think about the frontier between what is above and what is below, between the darkness and the light. This Russian woman was learning the same. Her new world in Israel came with something unexpected: It now was offering her a new birth. We left thinking about the preciousness of the events we had just witnessed.

The drama of belief, of choosing to come to the light, is a drama that must remain before me so that as a Christian I can understand where I stand and where an unbeliever must move in order to enter the light. In some churches, pastors regularly tell stories of such conversions. One of my favorite books is *Conversions*, which describes the stories of famous conversions (Augustine, Muggeridge, Tolstoy, Spurgeon, Wesley, etc.).[24] Some pastors let people tell their own stories regularly in worship in order to reinforce the idea that Christianity is not something that you follow as much as it is a power that transforms.

There is also a provocative secondary message here, which has to do with cultural and intellectual bondage. Nicodemus was entrenched in his career, locked into the status quo of Jerusalem's mainstream; he was so invested in it that he had to have a clandestine meeting with Jesus. The young Russian woman of Eilat had lost her career and was experiencing acute personal and cultural dislocation. As a result her world—her life—was open. There is an important lesson in this, namely, that there is a link between spiritual receptivity and the degree to which we are "settled" into a system of life and belief. The greater our comfort, the less our chances to receive a new word, a transforming word from God. This is probably the reason why as people age, the possibility of their conversion tends to decrease.

Our arena of comfort also has to do with the scope of our religious knowledge. Nicodemus was a man skilled in religious rhetoric. He knew the Word of God and had no doubt built his own "systematic theology" that explained God, his world, and his relation to both. His problem was not a lack of knowledge; in fact, his great knowledge in some fashion may have anesthetized him from true spiritual conversion. Religious knowledge can become

---

24. H. T Kerr and J M. Mulder, *Conversions* (Grand Rapids: Eerdmans, 1983).

a shield, a defense with which we protect ourselves from the very God we claim to know. It is like visiting a Pentecostal worship service with a theologian or a sociologist. They can always explain what is going on without reference to genuine divine power.

When I am leading a group of students or adults through the Holy Land, I occasionally listen in as other Israeli guides take their groups through biblical sites. On one occasion I happened to get to know a remarkable Jewish man named Moshe, who was thoroughly versed in the religious history of his country. At Capernaum he could provide a brilliant five-century history of the site, and he could tell virtually every story and teaching that Jesus told in that lakeside village. I was intrigued. I once asked him, "Since you know more about Jesus than most Christians, what do you think about the truth of his words?" Surely, I reasoned, I was not the first American Christian to ask him that question. "Jesus' words are interesting, but I'm a Jew and that's where I'm comfortable."

Moshe's problem was not a question of knowledge. He (along with hundreds of licensed Jewish tour guides in Israel) possesses more knowledge about Jesus than the average pastor. Such guides are like Nicodemus inasmuch as they are professional observers who can talk about Jesus but have not experienced him, who can give accurate lectures but who have not had a transforming spiritual experience, who know all about wine but have not tasted it.[25]

But is John 3 a message that only pertains to the non-Christian? To be sure, the invitation to believe in Jesus and to be born of water and Spirit is an invitation to Christian discipleship. But Nicodemus was a man steeped in religious tradition; he knew how to teach and defend it. I firmly believe that there are men and women in the church today who have not really heard the Nicodemus story. They have grown up in their tradition, they have taught it and defended it, but it has become a tame and predictable thing. One of the problems that comes with discussions of transformation and the power of the Spirit is how some people with longstanding spiritual interest, personal experience, or theological degrees will respond to stories like John 3. They can be skeptical. Or they may have determined a way to theologize their way around the mystical gift offered to Nicodemus. Jesus is talking about mystical experiences and spiritual power. One can harness this Spirit no more than one can harness the wind.

Each year I require beginning theology students to read an old book written by Helmut Thielicke, *A Little Exercise for Young Theologians*.[26] The good

---

25. This is one reason, for instance, that I always work with Christian guides in Israel (messianic Jewish or Palestinian) because they may understand at a completely different level the Christian pilgrim's desire to "worship in spirit and in truth" (cf. 4:24).

26. Helmut Thielicke, *A Little Exercise for Young Theologians* (Grand Rapids: Eerdmans, 1962).

fortune of this assignment is that I have to read the book as well every year. The slim volume consists of a series of sermons delivered to seminary students in Hamburg, Germany, where for many years Thielicke was a famous and popular professor and pastor. This is a book full of wisdom and warnings. Above all it describes a "diabolical theology" that can infect the most well-intentioned, passionate, Christian leader. It is possible, Thielicke argues, to get one's theology right but to get one's relationship with God all wrong. There is a pathology to theological education—a spiritual disease, he calls it—that can distance us from God. Nicodemus was a theologian. I am a theologian. Mature Christians are theologians. We must always be on the alert to see if we are linked to the spiritually unpredictable Holy Spirit of God.

A final contemporary note has to do with the work of Christ and Christology. I mentioned above that it is essential for us to communicate something of the salvific and revelatory work of Christ to our Christian audiences. Today's intellectual climate is offended by the absolute claim of religious truth, but a faithful rendering of New Testament Christology demands this. This theme will continue to come up throughout the Gospel of John, but at this juncture John has said something important that we must pause and note.

Many Christians today think about the work of Christ with an unfortunate, ill-informed understanding of God and Christ. I see this again and again both in classes I teach and in the church. The imaginative picture used by many to express the work of Christ is that Jesus has died in order to placate an angry God, whereas the cross expresses the love of Christ for us and his work appeases God's threatening wrath. This makes God an opponent and an adversary while Jesus is our ally.

But this is not what John says in 3:16. "God so loved the world. . . ." The work of Christ is *God* at work, *God* saving the world, *God* extending himself into the condition of our humanity and bringing about reconciliation. The center of this error is a deficient view of the Trinity or, more precisely, a deficient understanding of what the church's earliest theologians were trying to express at the Council of Nicea (A.D. 325). Christ was not created—there was no time in history when he "was not"—and so he enjoys an eternal existence precisely like God. Further, he shares the very essence or being of God (the Council of Nicea used the word *homoousios* to express this concept). Why is this important? Because it means that God himself is on our side. God himself is at work on our behalf. He did not send a messenger (Jesus) to do the dirty work. God himself came to the cross and suffered in order to bring his beloved creation back to himself.[27]

---

27. I suspect that many Christians today unwittingly adopted an "Arian" view of Christ's person and work, which is the very reason the Council of Nicea was called

This understanding is expressed repeatedly by Paul. In 2 Corinthians 5:18–19 he describes the goodness of God in rescuing us and remarks: "All this is from God, who reconciled us to himself through Christ and gave us the ministry of reconciliation: that God was reconciling the world to himself in Christ, not counting men's sins against them. And he has committed to us the message of reconciliation." Or again, in the words of Colossians 1:19–20: "For God was pleased to have all his fullness dwell in [Christ], and through him to reconcile to himself all things, whether things on earth or things in heaven, by making peace through his blood, shed on the cross." The cross is thus God's work. Jesus Christ came to earth not in order to change God's mind, but to express God's mind.

I remember the first time I explained this in a theology class and literally witnessed a couple of students weep. They claimed it was a revolution in their thinking since it meant that heaven no longer harbored an adversary. Now when I speak about the cross, I never fail to reinforce the important conclusions of a sound Trinitarian theology.

John the Baptist and charismatic leadership. The impulse to follow a charismatic religious leader is with us today as much as it was with the first disciples in the first century. We have simply replaced those ancient names (e.g., Apollos, Paul, John, Peter) with contemporary names of spiritual heroism and theological insight. It is not as if we are less committed to God because we elevate these leaders. All of this is taking place indeed in a spiritual context! It is simply that these leaders' view of the religious life, their formulation of community and conviction, and their ability to captivate our imaginations and emotions make them models worthy of a following. In some cases these are nationally known names, men and women whose writing and speaking become the model against which a pastor's sermons and skills are compared. In other cases, these are local leaders, people who have found great influence in the parish and who truly have a "following."

The easiest thing to do at this point is to compare such modern leaders with John the Baptist in John 3 and point out that the problem is not necessarily with their contributions, but with their followers, who have a personal interest in elevating them to levels that the leaders would not accept for themselves. John the Baptist was doing exactly what God had gifted and called him to do; contemporary leaders are often doing the same. But their followers exploit the leader's stature as a means of leveraging their own power or position in the kingdom of God.

It does not take the average pastor much imagination to recall times when laypersons have argued, "But John Stott sees it differently." Or, "The pastor of the Vineyard Fellowship is really in touch with God." These pastors and theologians are not in error. But in some cases their admirers employ their names in order to discredit those whom God has called into local leadership. By pointing to their hero John, the Baptist's followers could effectively eliminate their obligation to shift their efforts to Jesus and support his work for the kingdom.

My local community recently provided me with a perfect example. I know a charismatic, influential teacher who joined a growing local church, gained a strong following, and then after two years found himself at odds with the pastoral leadership. He left, discrediting the church's leadership as he departed. This month I learned that over a hundred people are "leaving" with him and that now he is going to launch his own church. All of this behavior is disguised in religious language; but in this case, this leader needs to take a lesson from John the Baptist: He must become less while Jesus becomes greater. Make no mistake, of course; he would quickly say that Jesus is "increasing" thanks to his independent, groundbreaking work. Perhaps this is the root of the problem: Religious allegiances are so deceptive they trick those who cherish them dearly.

John 3:22—36 is all about the fragmentation that results in the kingdom of God when Jesus is made to compete with human vessels in this world. No one will admit that they are competing with Jesus. No one will say that they are impeding the kingdom's growth. Words like envy, jealousy, and rivalry are never admitted. But just as the Baptist's followers were interested in making him into an institution, so too the Christian church can become a human institution built on the foundation of human enterprise and personality.

At the core of the Baptist's argument against his followers' views is an understanding of Jesus that sets him apart from every other human being. Jesus Christ is superior to any other person on earth. He has "come from above," he has been sent by God, and God has given him the Spirit without limit. The Baptist cannot rival these credentials. Therefore every form of human wisdom, every form of religious expression, must be seen as secondary to the revelation that we possess in Jesus Christ. Indeed, every charismatic teacher and every gifted leader must decrease so that Jesus alone is seen as preeminent.

Last month I was flying home alone from the Middle East on the Israeli airline, El Al. My seat companion for eleven hours was an articulate orthodox Jewish woman whose husband was completing a Ph.D. in psychology at Northwestern University in Chicago. She was headed back to Chicago to join him. She asked what I did for a living almost before the pilot pulled up the wheels above Tel Aviv. By the time we were over Greece, we had locked into a dense theological discussion about Jesus and his relationship with Jewish religious thinkers through the ages. I knew better than to begin a debate about Jesus' messianic credentials; this was a theme that the synagogues in

Israel speak about regularly. Instead, I framed the "question of Jesus" around the nature of rabbinic authority. I could see she was intrigued.

Jesus was not, I argued, simply about the fulfillment of prophecy. I agreed to set that subject aside (whereupon she noticeably relaxed). With the theologies of Nicea and Chalcedon as my targets, I argued that Jesus was a mystery, a self-revelation of God that had not happened before in human history. Jesus was more than a rabbi, even more than a prophet. To her objection that my Christology was idolatry, violating the second commandment, I reached for an analogy that fit her frame of reference. God can occupy holy space, I argued, and this is what defined the sanctity of the Most Holy Place in the temple, where stone and wood took on properties that were beyond human touch and comprehension but which nevertheless retained their original form in the world.[28] What if God did this same thing in human flesh? What if God disclosed himself dramatically, descending from heaven, assuming the form of humanity in order to communicate with us and deliver us? If God was in Christ like this, I urged, then we have an utterly new model of revelation surpassing anything found in Moses' words in Torah or in the ongoing insights of *Mishnah* and *Talmud*.

I recall that at this moment she raised her finger to make us pause. "And here is precisely where Judaism and Christianity truly take separate paths," she noted. I agreed. As the hours flew by, we discussed the importance of finding common ground where the synagogue and church might meet. Monotheism, ethics, justice—these were all common themes. But she knew now with certainty that there is a pivotal theological issue that will forever keep us apart. I cannot say that Jesus was just a rabbi or sage or prophet. Jesus was not like John the Baptist. Jesus is God in descent. Jesus is God incarnate. This is the starting point of every Christology—not the wisdom of Jesus, his perfection, or his fulfillment of prophecy.

It is this starting point that John the Baptist is driving home to his followers. "The one who comes from above is above all; the one who is from the earth belongs to the earth, and speaks as one from the earth" (3:31). Jesus is above all. His words are above every human word. When we speak about Jesus today, the same theme must resonate from every pulpit and lectern. Jesus is God in descent. Jesus is important and glorified not because his teaching is winsome, but because has come from the very heart of the Father. Indeed, he and the Father are one.

---

28. Another approach to this line of thinking for orthodox Jews is to compare Jesus (the incarnate Word) with the sanctity of the Torah (the written Word). Each have been manifested on earth in physical form. Of course, the analogy breaks down (as the theologians of Chalcedon would remind us), but at least it is a starting point for dialogue

John 4:1-54

THE PHARISEES HEARD that Jesus was gaining and baptizing more disciples than John, ²although in fact it was not Jesus who baptized, but his disciples. ³When the Lord learned of this, he left Judea and went back once more to Galilee.

⁴Now he had to go through Samaria. ⁵So he came to a town in Samaria called Sychar, near the plot of ground Jacob had given to his son Joseph. ⁶Jacob's well was there, and Jesus, tired as he was from the journey, sat down by the well. It was about the sixth hour.

⁷When a Samaritan woman came to draw water, Jesus said to her, "Will you give me a drink?" ⁸(His disciples had gone into the town to buy food.)

⁹The Samaritan woman said to him, "You are a Jew and I am a Samaritan woman. How can you ask me for a drink?" (For Jews do not associate with Samaritans.)

¹⁰Jesus answered her, "If you knew the gift of God and who it is that asks you for a drink, you would have asked him and he would have given you living water."

¹¹"Sir," the woman said, "you have nothing to draw with and the well is deep. Where can you get this living water? ¹²Are you greater than our father Jacob, who gave us the well and drank from it himself, as did also his sons and his flocks and herds?"

¹³Jesus answered, "Everyone who drinks this water will be thirsty again, ¹⁴but whoever drinks the water I give him will never thirst. Indeed, the water I give him will become in him a spring of water welling up to eternal life."

¹⁵The woman said to him, "Sir, give me this water so that I won't get thirsty and have to keep coming here to draw water."

¹⁶He told her, "Go, call your husband and come back."

¹⁷"I have no husband," she replied.

Jesus said to her, "You are right when you say you have no husband. ¹⁸The fact is, you have had five husbands, and the man you now have is not your husband. What you have just said is quite true."

¹⁹"Sir," the woman said, "I can see that you are a prophet. ²⁰Our fathers worshiped on this mountain, but you Jews claim that the place where we must worship is in Jerusalem."

²¹Jesus declared, "Believe me, woman, a time is coming when you will worship the Father neither on this mountain nor in Jerusalem. ²²You Samaritans worship what you do not know; we worship what we do know, for salvation is from the Jews. ²³Yet a time is coming and has now come when the true worshipers will worship the Father in spirit and truth, for they are the kind of worshipers the Father seeks. ²⁴God is spirit, and his worshipers must worship in spirit and in truth."

²⁵The woman said, "I know that Messiah" (called Christ) "is coming. When he comes, he will explain everything to us."

²⁶Then Jesus declared, "I who speak to you am he."

²⁷Just then his disciples returned and were surprised to find him talking with a woman. But no one asked, "What do you want?" or "Why are you talking with her?"

²⁸Then, leaving her water jar, the woman went back to the town and said to the people, ²⁹"Come, see a man who told me everything I ever did. Could this be the Christ?" ³⁰They came out of the town and made their way toward him.

³¹Meanwhile his disciples urged him, "Rabbi, eat something."

³²But he said to them, "I have food to eat that you know nothing about."

³³Then his disciples said to each other, "Could someone have brought him food?"

³⁴"My food," said Jesus, "is to do the will of him who sent me and to finish his work. ³⁵Do you not say, 'Four months more and then the harvest'? I tell you, open your eyes and look at the fields! They are ripe for harvest. ³⁶Even now the reaper draws his wages, even now he harvests the crop for eternal life, so that the sower and the reaper may be glad together. ³⁷Thus the saying 'One sows and another reaps' is true. ³⁸I sent you to reap what you have not worked for. Others have done the hard work, and you have reaped the benefits of their labor."

³⁹Many of the Samaritans from that town believed in him because of the woman's testimony, "He told me everything I ever did." ⁴⁰So when the Samaritans came to him, they urged him to stay with them, and he stayed two days. ⁴¹And because of his words many more became believers.

⁴²They said to the woman, "We no longer believe just because of what you said; now we have heard for ourselves, and we know that this man really is the Savior of the world."

⁴³After the two days he left for Galilee. ⁴⁴(Now Jesus himself had pointed out that a prophet has no honor in his own country.) ⁴⁵When he arrived in Galilee, the Galileans welcomed him. They had seen all that he had done in Jerusalem at the Passover Feast, for they also had been there.

⁴⁶Once more he visited Cana in Galilee, where he had turned the water into wine. And there was a certain royal official whose son lay sick at Capernaum. ⁴⁷When this man heard that Jesus had arrived in Galilee from Judea, he went to him and begged him to come and heal his son, who was close to death.

⁴⁸"Unless you people see miraculous signs and wonders," Jesus told him, "you will never believe."

⁴⁹The royal official said, "Sir, come down before my child dies."

⁵⁰Jesus replied, "You may go. Your son will live."

The man took Jesus at his word and departed. ⁵¹While he was still on the way, his servants met him with the news that his boy was living. ⁵²When he inquired as to the time when his son got better, they said to him, "The fever left him yesterday at the seventh hour."

⁵³Then the father realized that this was the exact time at which Jesus had said to him, "Your son will live." So he and all his household believed.

⁵⁴This was the second miraculous sign that Jesus performed, having come from Judea to Galilee.

Original Meaning

THE LENGTHY AND IMPORTANT story about Jesus' interaction with a Samaritan woman continues the form begun in chapter 3, where Jesus speaks with particular people who bear so many features of the world of first-century Palestine. The dialogue with Nicodemus makes perfect sense—a Jerusalem rabbi and leader interviews a seemingly outrageous teacher from Galilee—but here in chapter 4 we have a story that amuses as much as it surprises.

Jesus and the Samaritan Woman (4:1–26)

THIS NEW CHARACTER is a woman—a Samaritan woman, no less—and a person of questionable moral character. As we will note below, in this culture it was highly irregular for a man with Jesus' profile to speak with anyone possessing such features. He is male, single, religious, and Jewish, and clearly defined social boundaries ought to keep him from speaking with a woman in such a private setting.

But here is the irony in the story. As Nicodemus's character fell silent in chapter 3, leaving us to wonder what would become of this religious Jewish leader, suddenly we see that this irreligious woman takes the unexpected step: She acknowledges Jesus' lordship, remains "in the light," and exhibits some of the signs of discipleship we learned in chapter 1. She runs and tells others, bringing them to Jesus, and as a result many come to believe (4:39). It is no accident that the story of Nicodemus takes place "at night" and this episode occurs at about noon (4:6). Light and darkness are such prominent Johannine motifs that their presence in the narrative signals important theological meanings.[1]

But there is another level of interest in the story linking it to what has gone before. I have argued that we are reading a series of probings in which Jesus' messianic presence overwhelms some feature or institution of Judaism. In chapter 2 Jesus revealed his glory as he refilled Jewish purification pots, and then went to the temple indicating that it would be refilled or replaced with his own life. In chapter 3 Jesus challenges Judaism's teaching office, asking how it is that a rabbi like Nicodemus could not understand basic things about God. Now Jesus moves to the periphery of Judaism, to Samaria, and here he not only meets a woman, but he demonstrates that his gift surpasses any gift that can be found in a deeply historic, potentially superstitious well. Jacob's well is no match for Jesus' well. One of the challenges set before the woman is for her to unravel the mystery of Jesus' words as he replaces the very well she reveres. He has water she has never seen, and she must discern how to get it.

John 4:1–3 provides the setting. It is not surprising that the Pharisees take an interest in Jesus (4:1) since they have already investigated the work of the Baptist (1:19, 24). It would take little searching to discover that many of Jesus' followers had come from the ranks of the Baptist (1:35–37). Later, when Jesus arrives in Galilee, inquiries by Herod Antipas firmly identify Jesus with the Baptist as well (Mark 6:14–16).

Since the Synoptics describe Jesus' public ministry beginning in Galilee (along with the call of the disciples, Mark 1:14–20), some critical scholars

---

1. M. Pazadan, "Nicodemus and the Samaritan Woman: Contrasting Models of Discipleship," *BTB* 17 (1987): 145–48.

are reluctant to accept John's account of an earlier Judean ministry. That Jesus' work had already begun and that his fame was spreading and his circle of disciples growing at this point is unrecorded elsewhere. But this early Judean popularity is suggested in the Synoptics from another vantage. It is not until John is arrested in Perea (across the Jordan) that Jesus moves to Galilee (Mark 1:14). Jesus likely had reason to fear his own arrest (hence his move north) *because of* his association with the now-imprisoned John. Jesus no doubt works at length with his new disciples, having them continue their baptizing work (4:1–2); then in Galilee as the ranks of his followers grows, he calls a select number to full-time ministry.

This crisis in Judea may also explain Jesus' decision to travel north through Samaria (4:4). This route was *not* the usual way for a Jew to travel between Judea and Galilee. It was faster, but not preferred by most religious Jews.[2] Travelers would generally go east to Jericho[3] and then travel north, skirting the hills of Judea and Samaria just west of the Jordan River. When Mount Gilboa came into view, they came to the city of Scythopolis (Old Testament Beth Shan) and turned west into the Jezreel Valley, whose open, well-watered plains guided them into the Galilee interior. The route through Samaria was easier, but it forced the traveler to enter this region of mountains inhabited by people with whom rivalry and strife had an ancient history.

The apostasy of the Old Testament northern kingdom of Israel (finally based in the city of Samaria) was well known. When the Assyrians conquered and exiled the northern kingdom in 722 B.C., they repopulated the region with people from throughout their empire (2 Kings 17:23–24). Remnants of the defeated Israelite kingdom now mixed with Persians and other conquered peoples. The paganism known to Jeroboam now was mixed with countless other practices, making the religious impurity of the land infamous (2 Kings 17:25ff.).

In time, the monotheism of Judaism prevailed, but it suffered important modifications. The Samaritans rejected the writings of the Prophets (including the histories [1–2 Samuel, 1–2 Kings, 1–2 Chronicles]) and wisdom literature (Proverbs, Psalms, etc.) because of these writings' emphasis on Judea and David's line centered on Jerusalem. Their Scriptures were limited to the Pentateuch (Genesis through Deuteronomy), and their worship was centered on a new temple on Mount Gerizim, towering above ancient Shechem,

---

2. However, Josephus reports that Galileans did travel through Samaria en route to Jerusalem for the annual feasts (*Ant.* 20.118). But Josephus does not give convincing evidence that the Samaritan route was commonplace for religiously conservative Jews.

3. The route through Jericho explains the many stories of Jesus that take place in the city, e.g., Bartimaeus (Mark 10:46) and Zacchaeus (Luke 19:2). This is the return route used by Jesus as he comes to Jerusalem in his Passion.

while Jerusalem was rejected as a place of pilgrimage. Following the Babylonian exile when Zerubbabel led the rebuilding of the temple, Samaritan help was adamantly refused (Ezra 4:2–3), which fueled more conflict. When Alexander the Great and later Greek generals controlled Palestine (beginning about 330 B.C.), they made Samaria an important base, knowing that here they could find sympathetic, anti-Jewish allies. When the Jews had their opportunity (128 B.C.) they attacked Samaria, destroyed Shechem, and burned the Samaritan temple on Mount Gerizim.

By Jesus' day, a smoldering tension existed between the regions of Judea and Samaria. Partly based on race and religion, it echoed many centuries of terrible political fights.[4] Therefore when we read that Jesus, in passing through the region, meets a "Samaritan woman," the story does not mean that she is a resident of the city of Samaria, but that she is from the region of Samaria. She is a woman bearing the history, language, religion, and attitudes of people on the far margin of Judaism. A first-century reader would barely expect Jesus and the woman to acknowledge each other's presence, much less speak.[5]

The location of Sychar (4:5) is problematic since no ancient literature refers to it. Sychar may be the modern Arab village of ʿAskar, although scholars are divided since ʿAskar is an early medieval town.[6] Jacob did indeed purchase land in the vicinity, naming it "Shechem" (from the Heb. word for "shoulder," the shoulder of a hill, Gen. 33:19), and he gave some of it to Joseph (48:22). Even though we have no account of Jacob's digging a well, it is not unlikely and today an ancient well is accessible adjacent to Shechem (Arab Balata). It is probably best to conclude that Sychar refers then to Shechem and that the well nearby (visited by many pilgrims) is the historic well.[7] One of the wonderful things about sites like this in the Middle East is that bedrock wells from antiquity do not change their location over time.

In John 4:6 the Greek word for "well" actually refers to a "spring" (Gk. *pege*), that is, a free-flowing water source or fountain (such as Jerusalem's Gihon Spring). By contrast, a well, properly speaking (Gk. *phrear*, 4:11–12), is dug by hand. Rather than an ironic comparison with Jesus' "spring" (4:10), this is

---

4. While Mark and Matthew record no stories from Samaria, Luke shows Jesus' interest in Samaria with various stories (Luke 9:52; 10:53; 17 11). This history also adds power to the parable of the good Samaritan (who becomes a hero) and, in Acts, to the decision of Philip and the apostles to extend ministry to the region (Acts 8).

5. J. Kopas, "Jesus and Women in John's Gospel," *TT* 41 (1984): 201–5.

6. The name experienced "corruption" through the centuries, much like ancient Neapolis (the new Roman city built at Shechem) today has become modern Arab *Nablus*. Biblical Shechem is not to be identified with modern Nablus, although it is nearby.

7. Today the remains of a 4th century cruciform church are visible beneath the ruins of a crusader sanctuary which placed the well in its crypt. In 1914 reconstruction of the crusader church was begun but never finished.

likely a commonplace description of a dug well that has tapped a free-flowing spring (which the hundred-foot well does today). In the first century, the well would have had a short perimeter wall around its mouth (preventing people, animals, and debris from falling in), a stone lid (see Gen. 29:2), a stone trough nearby for animals to be watered, and perhaps a tripod for attaching a rope/container for drawing water.[8]

Jesus arrives at the well, sits on the wall at its edge to relieve his fatigue, and presents an unavoidable obstacle to a woman who has come to get water. His fatigue is an interesting note. Throughout this Gospel, John emphasizes the divinity of Jesus in the strongest terms. But here he easily and comfortably shows an incidental human feature: Jesus is tired. John's Christology does not emphasize one dimension of Jesus at the expense of the other.

It is the sixth hour, that is, noon.[9] Two notes are helpful. (1) In this culture water collection was a responsibility of women.[10] In a world that isolated women socially, the task was not entirely burdensome but became an opportunity for women to meet and talk. Therefore wells became the one locale where women could be either avoided or met. When Abraham's servant returned north to Haran looking for a wife for Isaac, he found the local well (Gen. 24) and met Rebekah there. Likewise Moses fled to Midian and at a well met the daughters of Jethro (Ex. 2:15–16), one of whom became his wife (Zipporah). This motif is so prominent, some scholars have suggested John 4 may be influenced by ancient betrothal scenes in which (symbolically) Jesus calls a woman without proper marriage to a new, redeeming relationship with him.[11]

(2) Historically, water-drawing took place either in the early morning or at dusk in order to avoid the Mediterranean heat. While mid-afternoon work like this was not unknown, the scene reminds us of this woman's social isolation. She draws water when other women are absent. Later, of course, we learn the reason for her isolation (4:18): She has doomed her reputation and broken the morals of her community. This makes Jesus' overture and conversation all the more remarkable. He is crossing many boundaries. In this world men rarely speak to women in public, even if they are married to them. Single men *never* speak to or touch women at any time.

Above all, a rabbi (as Jesus is known) would observe these ideals scrupulously. This explains the woman's surprise in 4:9: She is not merely a Samar-

---

8. R. Bull, "An Archaeological Context for Understanding John 4," *BA* 38 (1975): 54–59.

9. The Jewish custom was to count the hours from sunrise. Romans (like us) would count the hours from midnight and noon.

10. This explains why in Mark 14:13 Jesus can use a *man* carrying water as a signal for his disciples to locate the room of his final Passover.

11. The story of Hagar (Gen. 16:7) invites further comparison, where the angel of the Lord meets the destitute woman at a desert spring of water.

itan, but a Samaritan *woman*.[12] This also explains the disciples' astonishment in 4:27 when they return to him after purchasing some food (cf. 4:8). Their minds are racing with thoughts they dare not express: "What is going on here? Why this irregular conversation?" The surprising thing is not that Jesus would ask her for help with a drink; rather, it is that he would ask her *anything*.[13]

The conversation between Jesus and the woman is a delightful, dramatic play. As a classic Johannine discourse, questions are asked that will bring Jesus' listener from earthly thoughts (well water) to heavenly realities (living water). Raymond Brown has convincingly outlined how the passage provides two scenes in which earthly and heavenly realities are addressed. In 4:7–15 Jesus explores the meaning of living water; in 4:16–26 Jesus discusses the sinful life of the woman and talks about true worship. In each case, conversations begin with mundane, earthly subjects (wells, husbands), and Jesus presses the woman to examine what these earthly things really mean for her. Woven through these sections are two questions, two challenges launched by Jesus in 4:10: Will this woman comprehend the gift of God and its giver? Will she ask for a drink? We are left in suspense, wondering if the woman will have the courage to ask Jesus to be her water source and will identify him accurately for who he is.

As with Nicodemus, earthly questioners cannot understand heavenly things. They stumble over misunderstandings, which lead to humorous, ironic double meanings. As a resident of Shechem, the woman knows the location of every water source. But here Jesus says something unexpected: He is able to provide "living water" (4:10b). "Living water" refers to water that flows as in a spring, river, or stream, that is, *moving* water. Other water stood still, and one could find it in a well, cistern,[14] or pond. Living water was precious and valued and, according to rabbinic law, was the only water that could be used in ritual washings to make pure unclean worshipers.[15] Everyone knew that Shechem had no rivers or streams. Even Jacob had to dig a

---

12. The parenthetical comment in 4:9b ("For Jews do not associate with Samaritans.") is most likely a comment by John as narrator and should not be viewed as a part of the woman's statement.

13 Today in the outlaying villages of the Arab Middle East, these values are still at work. I have mistakenly addressed women in remote Palestinian villages (not far from ancient Shechem), to my own and the woman's embarrassment and the shock of the village men.

14. A cistern is an underground reservoir or cavity generally dug into the soft limestone and lined with plaster. Rainwater is directed into the cistern's small opening and a lid keeps out light thereby keeping algae from growing. Villages throughout Palestine still use cistern systems today. Some were small for a household. Masada's 12 cisterns on its western slope held 1.5 million cubic feet of water.

15. A good example of this is found at Qumran where numerous ritual baths are fed by the requisite amounts of "running water" caught from the mountain valley just west of the site.

well in order to water his flocks here (4:12). How could a Jewish outsider, someone who barely knew the terrain, offer water that no one else had found? *There is no living water in Shechem.*

But the woman stumbles on the metaphor and misunderstands. She is curious about the possibility of a nearby stream or spring (4:11b), but Jesus wants her to look beyond, to the spiritual significance of what this water means. This is water that eliminates thirst (4:13), a water that leads to eternal life (4:14). It is no surprise that in this arid country, something so precious as running water would take on symbolic meaning. Living water is life nourished by God. Jeremiah rebukes Israel saying, "My people have committed two sins: They have forsaken me, the spring of living water, and have dug their own cisterns, broken cisterns that cannot hold water" (Jer. 2:13). God is the source of spiritual renewal, and other avenues simply must be rejected.

Isaiah uses this imagery when he exhorts all in Israel who are thirsty to come to the waters supplied by God (Isa. 55:1). At the end of time, when God's blessings deluge the land, Ezekiel and Zechariah foresee such living water literally flowing out of Jerusalem's temple, entering the Dead Sea in the east and the Mediterranean Sea in the west (Ezek. 47:1–12; Zech. 14:8). However, rabbinic interpreters in Jesus' day understood this to be a prophetic symbol of the Holy Spirit that would renew and cleanse the earth in the last days (Ezek. 36:25–27).[16]

Jesus is talking about a new life that is available through the Spirit of God (4:14). Water has become a symbol of this new reality since the beginning of the book (1:31; 2:7; 3:5) and later will be defined as the Holy Spirit (7:37–39). Christ himself is the source of precious living water, which can transform even this woman in her isolation. It is the "gift" (*dorea*) of God—a word that later Christians associated with the Holy Spirit (Acts 2:38; 8:20; 10:45; 11:17; Heb. 6:4).

But Jesus takes this promise a step further. It is not simply an experience that changes our "state" (such as a "state of salvation"), but it is a dynamic experience that makes a life as living as the water itself. The water (or Spirit) will transform a life into a well that "wells up" (Gk. *allomai*, 4:14). In the LXX, this word is used of the Holy Spirit that "leaps" on great leaders such as Samson, Saul, and David. Jesus' image is dramatic: The woman in search of a well discovers that the Spirit could transform her life into a well that does not require reaching and dipping, but which roils and gurgles with water until it spills over its rim.

The woman is clearly intrigued but incredulous. But in 4:15 she makes a request that fulfills one of Jesus' earlier two challenges from 4:10, "Sir, give

---

16. Even at the desert community of Qumran, water was associated with the Spirit of God (1QS 4:21).

me this water." Yet her perception of what she is asking is flawed. She is still seeking literal water (as Nicodemus questioned a literal rebirth [3:4] and as the Galileans will ask for bread [6:34]). She is still thinking about earthly things—about water for her jar, not living water for her soul.

The woman has requested water, but she does not understand the gift, nor does she know the identity of the giver. The second round of questions (4:16–26) now must pursue this second theme of Jesus' identity and fulfill Jesus' second challenge of 4:10. No doubt Jesus' request that she summon her husband was a shock (4:16). Her response that she has no husband (4:17) may have been true were she divorced or a widow. But Jesus knows it is untrue. Unveiling his divine capacity (cf. Nathanael, 1:49), he reminds her that she has had five husbands, and her current lover is either a sixth husband or a man to whom she is not married.[17]

This number should not be allegorized but taken at its most simple level.[18] Either way, she has sinned, and the reputation that has dogged her incessantly now has surfaced again. But Jesus is not simply judging her. She rightly sees that this uncovers his abilities as a messenger from God and recoils, looking for a way to deflect the moral probings of this stranger. Despite what she says in 4:19–20, she continues to "remain in the light," for she continues to speak with Jesus and not walk away.

The Samaritans did not believe that there were prophets such as Amos and Isaiah in the biblical period. Since they embraced only the Pentateuch, they understood the expectation of Deuteronomy 18:18, which said a great prophet would follow Moses ("I will raise up for them a prophet like you from among their brothers; I will put my words in his mouth, and he will tell them everything I command him"). But this was to be the messianic figure of the final day. Therefore in referring to Jesus as a prophet (*the* prophet?), the woman unwittingly has opened the subject of messianism for Jesus. This is a common Johannine technique, in which characters operating on an earthly plane not only fail to understand spiritual things, but occasionally use language that bears a meaning more profound than they realize (cf. 10:50; 18:37, 39; 19:19–22).

---

17. In the first century Jewish women could not divorce their husbands (this was strictly a man's prerogative), but they could petition a court to urge their husbands to release them. Five divorces was highly irregular. Rabbis considered two, perhaps three divorces the limit for a woman (see Morris, *John*, 234n.41).

18. Some scholars have suggested that the five husbands represent the divinities of the Samaritans brought from foreign lands (2 Kings 17:24). However, while there were five nations, in fact there were seven deities brought to Samaria (17:30–31). J. D. M. Derrett once suggested that the five husbands represented the "five senses" known to Jews and Greeks ("The Samaritan Woman's Pitcher," *Downside Review* 102 (1984): 252–61). Most exegetes find such speculation farfetched.

In 4:20 the woman launches what she hopes will be her most potent salvo. To free herself from the shame of her past (and present) in the eyes of this prophet, to deflect any more of his questions, she refers to the historic religious division between Jews and Samaritans. Both groups understood that God had commanded a place be set aside for worship, where his name might be known (Deut. 12:5), but they had serious disagreements about its location. King David decided to select Jerusalem, and after he acquired land and brought the tabernacle there, his son Solomon built God's temple. Even after its destruction, the site was continuously rebuilt.

The Samaritans rejected this tradition (when they rejected the later Old Testament books). In the Pentateuch the first place where Abraham built an altar was at Shechem beneath Mount Gerizim. This same mountain was also the destination of the Israelites when they entered Canaan under Joshua's command (Deut. 11:29; 27:12; Josh. 8:33) so that the law and its blessings could be read aloud.[19] Thus, given their historical commitments, it made sense that this mountain was deemed to be the place chosen by God. Even following the destruction of the Samaritan temple in the second century B.C., priests continued to sacrifice and worship there.

Jesus is therefore being invited to enter this historical-religious quagmire and give comment. The woman's reference to "our fathers" does not point to recent history, but to antiquity when Abraham (Gen. 12:7) and Jacob (33:20) revered this area. This mountain, the woman avers, has historic religious importance, validated not merely by her people but by the patriarchs. Yet the "you" in John 4:20b is emphatic, referring not to Jesus, but to the Jewish nation he represents.[20] "Your people worship in Jerusalem and our people worship here; therefore, we have little in common" paraphrases nicely the woman's intention.[21] But once again Jesus deflects her appeal to racial division (as he did in 4:9) and supplies a sharp commentary on worship (4:21–24). (On Jesus' formal use of "woman" as a word of respectful address in 4:21, see comment on 2:4.)

(1) Jesus comments on the inadequacy of Samaritan worship (4:22). Unlike anywhere else in the New Testament, he aligns himself with the

---

19. An adjacent mountain to the north, Mount Ebal, was the site from which the curses of the law were read. The Hebrew Old Testament says that an altar should be built on Mount Ebal. The Samaritan version of the Pentateuch, however, significantly changed this reference in Deut. 27:4 to Mount Gerizim. Today a small, little-known group of Samaritans in Israel continue to revere the mountain and offer sacrifices there.

20. The NIV "you Jews" (which does not appear in the Gk.) is a paraphrase serving this emphasis.

21. R. Bull, "Archaeological Footnote to 'Our Father Worshipped on this Mountain,' John 4:20," *NTS* 23 (1977): 460–62.

traditions of Judaism: "We [emphatic] worship what we do know, for salvation is from the Jews." Jesus is a Jew. The Messiah was to be a Jew. Therefore Judaism is the trajectory of religious history through which God has been at work. This is an uncompromising remark about the deficiencies of Samaritan beliefs. "You [pl., emphatic] . . . worship what you do not know" is directed to her tradition and world.

(2) Jesus indicates that the debate between Gerizim and Jerusalem is only marginally important anyway since both places will soon be obsolete (4:21). In 2:19–22 we already heard a hint of this when Jesus mentioned destroying "this temple" and John immediately explained that Jesus was referring to the temple of "his body." Thus Jesus' body (the locale of God's presence, 1:14) and the temple share similar fates, or at least interpret one another. The NIV obscures an important word here when Jesus says, "The hour [*hora*; NIV time] is coming. . . ." We met the theological use of this word initially in 2:4 and learned that it refers to "the hour" of Jesus' glorification (in John, his death and resurrection). Hence a cataclysmic change will occur *in worship* when Jesus comes to the cross, offering himself as sacrifice.

(3) Finally, Jesus defines carefully what is coming and what is even now dawning on earth (4:23–24). Worship in "spirit and truth" (v. 23) is the key phrase that controls what Jesus means and is no doubt tied to Jesus' affirmation that "God is spirit" (v. 24). This is not merely a commonplace explanation about the incorporeality of God. Jesus is not speaking about metaphysics. Rather, he is describing something of the dynamic and life-giving character of God. As in 3:8, this God cannot be apprehended, but his effects cannot be denied. Just as "God is love" or "God is light," so "God is spirit."

These describe the ways God reveals himself to and impacts men and women in our world.[22] Therefore "worship in spirit" does not refer to "the human spirit."[23] It is worship that is dynamically animated by God's Holy Spirit. But it is more. One preposition governs "spirit and truth" in 4:23–24 (which the NIV shows incorrectly). Such worship "in spirit and truth" means that we do not have a catalogue of two features here, but one inseparable concept. This is worship empowered by God but also informed by the revelation of God and provided to humans by the One who is the truth, Jesus Christ (14:6). Later Jesus will refer to this Spirit as "the Spirit of truth" (14:17; 15:26). This is worship not tied to holy places but impacted by a holy Person, who through his cross will inaugurate the era in which the Holy Spirit will change everything.

---

22. Carson, *John*, 225.
23. *Contra*, Morris, *John*, 239, and many others.

The woman's final statement to Jesus (4:26) again tries to deflect his clarification. The Samaritans did believe in the coming of the Messiah, based on Deuteronomy 18:18, and understood that this person would explain everything to them. But the woman implies that both she and Jesus will have to wait. "When *he* comes" disguises the Greek emphatic pronoun, meaning that to this woman, Jesus does not qualify to be this Messiah, but that such spiritual explanations are on the horizon for them. But unwittingly, she has used the very words that best describe Jesus. With simple dignity, Jesus accepts the titles for himself (4:26). This now completes the second challenge of 4:10. The woman has rightly identified Jesus (cf. 4:29b).

The Greek phrase of 4:26 (lit., "I am—who speaks to you") holds a term that is peculiar to the Fourth Gospel and will recur with some frequency: "I am" (Gk. *ego eimi*). This expression may be a mere self-identification (so the NIV, NRSV, etc.) but the pronoun "he" in "I who speak to you am *he*" does not exist in the Greek sentence. The phrase is emphatic and unusual. As we will see later (8:58), it is not always just a term of self-identification that bears a predicate (e.g., "I am the bread of life," 6:48). It is also the divine name of God uttered on Mount Sinai to Moses (see Ex. 3:14). When this term (Heb. *Yahweh*) was translated into Greek, it became *ego eimi* ("I am"), and throughout John we will see Jesus' absolute use of this phrase without a predicate to disclose more of his divine identity.

The Food of Jesus (4:27–42)

THE COMPLETION OF the second challenge from 4:10 closes this frame of the discourse. Jesus' disciples, who had left to get food (4:8), now return and express normal amazement that he is talking with a woman, much less a Samaritan (4:27). Of course they are likely thinking about the prohibitions lived in tradition and written in law that forbade a man to talk casually with a woman (see above). But they may also have been intrigued that Jesus would engage a woman *theologically*. The rabbis taught that theological education, that is, instruction in the law, was for men alone. To teach women or girls not only was a waste of time, but a profaning of sacred things. Jesus disregards such custom and here is talking to a singularly *irreligious* woman about matters of utmost spiritual profundity.

Much has been made of the woman leaving her jar behind (4:28) in order to report to her neighbors. For some, this is an irresistible opportunity for allegory (her former life? the law?), but it must be resisted. Perhaps she is leaving the jar for Jesus to drink. Perhaps she does not want to carry it home when she intends soon to return. Most likely her zeal to share her discovery made her leave behind anything that would hinder her. Morris prefers a mild symbolism: "She abandoned the bringing of water for the bringing of men."[24]

This is the heart of John's meaning. One sign of discipleship is the testimony given to others—words that eagerly spill out because of the preciousness of discovery. "Come, see"(4:29) is a Johannine phrase of invitation (1:39, 46). Potential converts do not need mere information about Jesus—note that the woman is even tentative about Jesus' identity as the Christ (4:29); they need only to come and have their own experience with him.

In the woman's absence, the disciples urge Jesus to eat. Suddenly we find ourselves in a mini-discourse bearing all the features already seen in chapter 4. Jesus' claim to possess food (4:32) baffles them since their assignment was to acquire food. Could someone (the woman?) have given him food (4:34)? But they are thinking of earthly things, and their misunderstanding enables Jesus to press their thinking to another level. Obeying the Father is Jesus' more deeply satisfying task. The Father has given the Son work to do (5:30; 6:38; 7:18; 8:50; 9:4; 10:37–38; 12:49–50) and his mission is to see it to completion. In his final prayer Jesus will say, "I have brought you glory on earth by completing the work you gave me to do" (17:4). When Jesus says "It is finished" on the cross, it is not merely his life expiring, but a gratifying expression of the climax of his life of obedience.

In 4:35 Jesus reminds his disciples of a farming proverb in order to point them to their present obedience. Scholars have wondered about the origin of this saying (it is not attested anywhere) and its meaning (grain harvests take more than four months to ripen). Further, what harvests are "white" (NIV "ripe") when harvested? Endless speculation about Jewish and Samaritan festival origins seems futile; instead, we are likely hearing a village proverb shared orally (of which the Middle East seems to have no end of supply).

Jesus is thinking about the span of time between planting and harvest when the grain is growing but not mature, when the fields are full but not ready for cutting. The farmer relaxes and enjoys the promise of plenty. But Jesus abruptly changes the image. The fields are *now* ready for gathering! He has planted the seed (at the well) and now the harvest (of Samaritans) is coming in. As he thinks about white harvests, some wonder if he is reflecting on the approaching Samaritans (4:40, dressed in white?), who will become a crop for eternal life (4:36). Jesus is in the world, God has invaded the field with seed, and it is bearing fruit already.

Jesus reaches for another agricultural metaphor in 4:37–38 as he explains what he expects of his disciples. In farming (as in so many other labors) significant labor precedes harvest. Sometimes those who do the preparatory work are not the same as those who harvest. But what does Jesus mean by

24. Morris, *John*, 243n.68.

"others [who] have done the hard work"?[25] This is possibly John the Baptist or Jesus himself, who has prepared the way for the coming church. Either way it is an important theological statement since it defines Christian mission in terms of what has gone on before, what God has been doing in advance of our efforts. Christian labor is never a solitary effort, divorced from the labor of God. Christians are called to go where God has already "done the hard work" and in this place reap the harvest.

In 4:39 the Samaritans reenter the scene and the harvest is at hand. Their faith (they "believed in him") is based on the woman's testimony, which underscores the value of human witness to the work of God (17:20). Evangelism is a cooperative effort, in which the preparatory work of God joins with our witness to what he has done and is doing in the world. Jesus and his followers agree to remain two days (4:40), which confirms the Samaritans' conviction that Jesus is indeed the long-awaited Messiah.[26] Their stay there brought even more successes since many more came to faith. It is likely this groundwork that contributes to the later efforts of Philip in Acts 8 when he comes to Samaria following Stephen's martyrdom. The Samaritans eagerly receive Philip, confess their faith, are baptized, and receive the Holy Spirit.

The narrative's final statement (4:42) is an important summary of the fruit of the woman's labor. The Samaritans evidence what every believer must have—a faith that is not secondary or dependent on someone else. *Rather, they have come and seen and experienced Christ for themselves.* This personal experiential feature is a constant concern for John. Potential converts must not only have their beliefs in order, but they must also be able to testify to a personal experience ("He told me everything I ever did!" 4:39b). But there is one more intriguing aspect of the Samaritans' testimony. They refer to Jesus as "the Savior of the world." This is an unusual phrase, which occurs in only one other place in the New Testament (1 John 4:14). But it parallels 3:17 in thought: "God did not send the Son into the world to condemn the world, but to save the world through him."

The "world" points to the far horizon of paganism and disbelief beyond Jewish and Samaritan cultural frontiers. God's work in Christ is not limited to Israel (or even Samaria). This is a first glimpse of the universal mission of Jesus, to reach those outside the boundaries of Judaism. In a similar way Jesus remarks in 10:16 that he has *"other* sheep that are not of this sheep pen. I must bring them also" (italics added). The harvest of Jesus is barely what the disciples can imagine.

25. Critical scholars for whom the historical horizon has minimal interest have seen evidence here of those, such as Philip (Acts 8), who went to Samaria to evangelize.
26. Note that the Greek verb *meno* (to stay, remain) is also a sign of discipleship (cf. 1:38–39).

Jesus Returns to Cana (4:43–54)

JESUS LEAVES SAMARIA after his two-day stay (4:40, 43) and continues north, crossing the Jezreel Valley and entering the region of Galilee. This small story brings us full circle from where Jesus began his public ministry, namely, in Cana. In fact, the story provides a closing "frame" to the section of the Gospel that outlines Jesus and four institutions of Judaism (purification, temple, rabbi, a well). As I mentioned in the Introduction, the original edition of the Fourth Gospel did not have chapter divisions and so literary markers invite us to note the progress of the story. Each Cana miracle is even numbered for our convenience (2:11; 4:54).

- Jesus works a miracle in Cana (his *first* sign, 2:11)
- Jesus and the Jerusalem temple
- Jesus and a Jerusalem rabbi
- Jesus and a Samaritan woman
- Jesus works a miracle in Cana (his *second* sign, 4:54)

This numbering clears up questions that readers often have for 4:54 and the sequencing of signs. This is not the second sign Jesus did since Jesus had done other signs (2:23). Even the language of the text betrays its purpose: (lit.) "This he did [as] a second sign." This is now the second sign Jesus is working in Galilee, matching the first one at the Cana wedding.[27]

The parenthetical comment in 4:44 has given commentators endless problems, and Carson notes no fewer than ten solutions.[28] The problem is simple: Jesus says prophets have no honor in their own country. However if Galilee is his country, it is a peculiar statement because in 4:55 the Galileans welcome him, and we have nothing in John like Luke's story of the rejection at Nazareth (Luke 4). Some (Westcott, Hoskyns) make Judea "his country," thereby explaining the ultimate rejection there in Jerusalem. But this interpretation fails when we remember how often John (and the Synoptics) refer to Nazareth as Jesus' home (1:45–46; 18:5, 7; 19:19; cf. 7:41 ["Galilee"]). Matthew, Mark, and Luke all refer to this saying following Jesus' visit to Nazareth (Matt. 13:57; Mark 6:4; Luke 4:24).

Carson effectively suggests that we should think of "Israel" as his country. The comparison in 4:44 is not between Judea and Galilee, but between

---

27. Scholars interested in the sources behind the Fourth Gospel have used 4:54 as evidence for a "Signs Source" behind the Gospel. That is, John had access to a narrative of miracles or signs that he has woven into a "source" containing longer discourses. However, such a theory is not necessary. The remainder of Jesus' signs are not numbered, and the reason for the numbering here is to refer us back to the first sign in Cana.

28. Carson, *John*, 235; Carson refers to an article of his in *JBL* 97 (1978): 424n.50.

Samaria (which he has just left) and the Jewish regions of the country. In Samaria Jesus has just enjoyed an overwhelming success. At best, his audiences in Jerusalem were cautious; in 2:18, 20 the Jews challenged him there. The Galileans in the present story welcome him not because he might be the Messiah (cf. the Samaritans, 4:29, 41) but because they have witnessed his activity in Jerusalem (4:45b), which likely refers to his cleansing of the temple. Their interest in Jesus, therefore, refers to his role in opposition to the temple authorities. Even Jesus' rebuke in 4:48 is in the plural, showing that he is speaking of everyone in Galilee ("'Unless you people see miraculous signs and wonders,' Jesus told him, 'you will never believe'").

In other words, John is writing with genuine irony in 4:45 when he talks about the Galileans' welcome. As the next section in Galilee makes clear, they do not understand him; in fact, they readily misrepresent his aims (6:15), and some of his disciples even fall away (6:66).[29] As a Jew, Jesus is commenting on his home culture, Judaism, which cannot provide one of its own prophets with honor.

When Jesus visits Cana, he is approached by a man from Capernaum (4:46) whose son is desperately ill and about to die. He was an important man ("a royal official") since he likely worked for Herod Antipas in Galilee. The man asks Jesus persistently[30] if he will come down to Capernaum to heal his son (4:47, 49). Since Cana is in the hills of Galilee and Capernaum is by the sea, "coming down" is a note of accuracy embedded in the story. The two villages were about twenty miles apart, separated by hills. Jesus heals the boy at a distance instead of traveling to Capernaum (4:50). Later, as the man returns home, his servants meet him with news of the healing (4:52) that occurred precisely when Jesus uttered his words of healing (4:53).[31]

On two other occasions Jesus heals from a distance: the healing of the centurion's slave (Matt. 8:5–13; Luke 7:2–10) and the healing of the Phoenician woman's daughter (Matt. 15:21–28; Mark 7:24–30). These stories invite comparisons with the Johannine story since there are parallels (even verbal parallels), particularly with the story of the centurion's slave. For some scholars, John's story (set in Cana) and the centurion story (set in Capernaum) describe the same event. But this seems unlikely. In the Synoptics we read

---

29. Carson, *John*, 236–37.

30. The Gk "begged him" is imperfect, suggesting continuous action

31. The "seventh hour" poses some unnecessary difficulty for interpreters. By Jewish custom, the seventh hour would be about 1:00 P.M. But if this was the time of healing, why did the man postpone his return home till the next day (4:52b)? He could have returned home the same day. The idea that we should read "Roman time" here (7:00 P.M.) for the healing fails when we see that John never uses this form. But the man's business in Cana or the demands to socialize in this culture as a gesture of thankfulness can explain his travel plans.

about a Gentile soldier who has a slave that is paralyzed. Jewish elders plead with Jesus in Capernaum (because the Gentile had built the Capernaum synagogue), but the soldier insists that Jesus not come to his home. In the end, the soldier's faith is praised ("I tell you, I have not found such great faith even in Israel," Jesus remarks in Luke 7:9). By contrast, our story is set in Cana with a hapless father who begs Jesus to enter his home far away. He pleads alone for his son who has a fever and is never praised by Jesus. In the end, these stories are anchored in two important personalities—a famous military officer and a Herodian bureaucrat—and have more differences than similarities.[32]

Even though the official and his family believe in Jesus (4:53), the critical sentence in the story is 4:48: "'Unless you people see miraculous signs and wonders,' Jesus told him, 'you will never believe.'" The attitude of the Galileans is the issue here. As noted at 2:11, the word "sign" describes a revelatory unveiling of God that may be worked through a miracle. When John links "sign" with "wonder" (Gk. *teras*), he is describing a different phenomenon. The Galileans want Jesus to *prove himself* with an act of power. The same attitude surfaces in Galilee in 6:30 after Jesus feeds the five thousand. In this case, the Galileans miss the *revelatory sign* Jesus has given and press him to do something spectacular so that they can believe. Jesus' point is sharp: They simply want miracles, but they do not want to see what God is really doing among them (6:26).

The NIV softens the language of the exchange between Jesus and the official. "Come down [an imperative], for my little child dies" (4:49, lit. trans.) is matched by Jesus' equally abrupt response, "Go [also an imperative], for 'your son' lives." Despite the man's later belief, he still views Jesus as a miracle worker who may be commanded to come and go. The royal official has given an order; Jesus now does the same.

JESUS AND THE **Samaritan woman.** It is not the task of the exegete to unfold the psychological or social profile of this woman (or most of the characters in John). This has been done at length in the church, making the woman in her isolation, sin, and openness the center of the story's interest. Much imaginative preaching has succeeded to dramatize the story along these lines, but it misrepresents John's intention. Evangelicals have been guilty of this, but the same is true of other exegetes.

---

32. The verbal parallels may be accounted for by the process by which "form stories" of healing were remembered in the early Christian tradition. Separate stories may begin to share words when pious recorders and repeaters know both stories well.

On some occasions writers have emphasized the nameless, faceless character of the woman and tried to uncover a tendency in the Scripture to marginalize not just this woman but every woman. But this too is far from John's mind. He is not writing about how women are marginalized and how Jesus has come to rescue them. Nor is he inviting us to probe the inner world of this woman. She remains in the background so that John's Christological focus can stay solidly in the foreground. Nicodemus receives a name because he becomes an ongoing player in the story, speaking up for Jesus in the Sanhedrin and assisting in his burial (7:50; 19:39). This woman becomes a temporary player on the Johannine stage in order to model to us an appropriate response to Christ. She clings to her tradition as a religious cover to dodge this discerning rabbi.

Characters such as this woman are mirrors in which to view Jesus from another angle.[33] The best that can be said is that Nicodemus is a closed religious character and the woman is an open irreligious character—and each demonstrates different levels of receptivity to Jesus and his message. Nicodemus launches questions; the woman is looking for Jesus' answers.

To be sure, this woman is a person of courage, a person who has lost all hope and who is socially isolated, living on the periphery of society. We know from many Synoptic accounts that Jesus is keenly interested in such people. Note again Mark 2:17: "It is not the healthy who need a doctor, but the sick. I have not come to call the righteous, but sinners." In fact, his commitment to such people was a regular source of criticism for him (Luke 15:1–2). But our task is to locate and develop what is central to the passage, what is pressing on John's mind as he explores this conversation in Samaria for us.[34]

(1) *Jesus and religion.* The leading message of the story is about Jesus and his relation to religion. On one level we can speak about Jesus and his impact on historic first-century Judaism. As we witnessed in all of the institutions of Judaism that Jesus confronts (ritual purity at Cana, the Jerusalem temple, Nicodemus), he overwhelms and replaces abundantly those things that the institutions offered. Jesus fills water vessels with wine, astonishing a party; he challenges the temple, suggesting that he himself will replace what it offers; he instructs a Jewish teacher in the deeper things of God. Now he comes to a traditional well associated with one of Israel's greatest heroes, Jacob, and he offers what Jacob never could: living water (interpreted as the Holy Spirit) that turns people into life-giving wells (4:14). Jesus even challenges the sanctity and significance of Mount Gerizim and Jerusalem, holy places to Samar-

---

33. Ridderbos, *John*, 152.

34. For an excellent survey of how this chapter has been exegeted, see C. Blomberg, "The Globalization of Biblical Interpretation: A Test Case—John 3–4," *BBR* 5 (1995): 1–16.

itans and Jews. "Neither on this mountain nor in Jerusalem" (4:21) are shocking words to anyone who has any investment in history and tradition.

On another level we can also say that John views the advent of Jesus in history as upending the way that men and women should embrace the religious traditions in which they may take refuge. The Samaritan woman provides a classic case study of someone who, when challenged to assess the reality of her spirituality, immediately tosses up the barrier and says, as it were, "But look, I am a Samaritan and we have our own way of doing things" (cf. 4:20). Jesus will not permit his presence to be invalidated by human claims to culture, history, or tradition. If Jesus—the Rabbi, Messiah, Son of God—can question the religious significance of Jerusalem (4:21), what else could stand in his way? The woman's argument for Mount Gerizim does not stand a chance (especially in light of its dubious historical moorings). But likewise, John would insist, those items that we have turned into sacred mountains do not stand a chance either. This is a troubling and fruitful theme that John 4 invites us to explore.

(2) *The Samaritan woman and religion.* There is likewise much to learn from the profile of this woman. The key here is not so much her background (except that she is marginalized from Judaism as a Samaritan and isolated from the community of women) as it is her attitude to Jesus. John invites us to step into her shoes, to marvel at Jesus' interest, and to examine the themes he raises. We should take careful note that Jesus even speaks to her at all. No self-respecting rabbi in the first century would have spoken to a woman in this setting. But Jesus delights in breaking traditional cultural barriers that separate people. He takes a risk. He reaches out. He speaks. And, John would have us reflect, if Jesus is willing to speak to her, who won't he speak to in the first century or today?

No doubt as readers we anticipate the climax in 4:17, "I have no husband." Watching the conversation unfold is like watching someone unwrap a box in which is hidden a lively spring. When Jesus inquires about her marital status, the spring is loosed and we wonder what will happen next. Here we have a potential disciple who has hidden a profound sin in her life. Perhaps it is a way of life that must be addressed. But Jesus recognizes that there is no going forward, no reaching the living water, until this hidden thing is exposed and cleansed. But in the end I admire this woman. Throughout the conversation with Jesus she must choose whether to remain in the light with Jesus or walk away. In some respects, she dramatizes what we learned in 3:20, "Everyone who does evil hates the light and will not come to the light for fear that his deeds will be exposed." The light has exposed her, but she chooses to remain, and it must have been a decision of remarkable courage and will.

But as a potential disciple, what should be expected of this woman? Since chapter 1, we have watched men and woman come forward, listen to Jesus, and respond. As this Gospel unfolds, we will see more. But here in this story we have the development of a profile, a template perhaps, of what it means to become a disciple. Note once again Jesus' challenge in 4:10. Converts must know how to identify the gift and its giver and converts must ask for a drink.

I see two dimensions to conversion here, one cognitive and one experiential. (a) The woman must be able to identify correctly who Jesus is. In theological terms, there is a doctrinal expectation. Content matters. To have a spirituality (no matter how profound) that is not based on the truth should not be trusted. "God is spirit, and his worshipers must worship in spirit and in truth" (4:24). (b) There is an experiential hope. To have correct theology, to be doctrinally sound and orthodox, but to have never tasted the water or to have never felt the Holy Spirit is to miss a vital component of discipleship. For John, the "head" and the "heart" must both be engaged.

But there is also a necessary corollary. The motif of misunderstanding at work in the discourse implies that men and women who do not believe, who have not experienced the Holy Spirit, who do not know the living water—such people are incapable of understanding the deep things of God. Jesus tries to elevate understanding but fails because his subjects constantly view things from an earthly vantage. What does this mean for our understanding of revelation? When we read the Scriptures, for instance, does the Spirit supply some facility to the Christian that is inaccessible to others? Is belief a necessary prerequisite for understanding?

Now if we return as readers to the passage with this profile of confession and experience in mind, we see some amazing new things because John wants us as readers to have a relationship with Jesus just as it may have happened for the woman. Note as the story unfolds how there is a remarkable display of titles for Jesus (exactly as we saw in 1:35–51). The woman and the story mature in their perception of Jesus:

- Jesus (4:6)
- Jew (4:9)
- Sir (Lord)[35] (4:11, 15, 19)
- Prophet (4:19)
- Messiah (4:25)
- Christ (4:25, 29)
- I am[36] (4:26)

---

35. Most likely used as a title of respect

36. As we suggested in the notes, this may be an incidental self-description, using *ego eimi*. Nevertheless, in a list of Christological titles it may imply some link to the divine use given elsewhere in the Gospel

- Rabbi (4:31)
- Savior of the world (4:42)

Such a list is not accidental. As readers we cannot overlook how titles of respect evolve into titles of belief. In other words, the story's language models for us the demand for intelligent belief, for identifying Jesus properly and fully.

The woman offers one final model of discipleship, namely, her desire to bear witness to what she now believes and has experienced. I find this decision on her part to be courageous and heroic as well. She is living on the margin of her community. This is a society where life is lived in public, where secrets are always brought into the public forum. And this woman is a sinner. Nevertheless, she takes a tremendous risk, returning to her town and telling the townsfolk about religion as one who has flaunted its precepts for years. The striking part is that they listen to her and respond. In some fashion the story is telling us that when people who are irreligious meet God, their words have a potency that surpasses those of the pious.

(3) *The life and mission of the church.* Even though this story is set in the first century, its attention to harvests (4:34–38), the role of the disciples, and Jesus' comments on worship each suggest that the life and mission of the church are a theme here. Writing in the mid-first century, John understood fully the significance of Jesus' traveling through Samaria. When Philip had evangelized Samaria (Acts 8:5), John was one of the apostles sent there with Peter to facilitate the coming of the Spirit. Therefore this story was important to him, and we cannot help but wonder whether, when John went to Samaria, he met some of these same people.[37]

This means that the story before us did indeed have meaning for the later church inasmuch as mission to Samaria was a part of the church's vision. This story spoke volumes to where the church should go and what it could expect when it got there. No doubt sayings such as 4:38 were treasured: "I sent you to reap what you have not worked for. Others have done the hard work, and you have reaped the benefits of their labor." Here we have a theological comment about the nature of evangelism and God's participation with us.

Moreover, Jesus' mission to Samaria presented a challenge to communities for whom travel beyond their cultural frontiers was difficult. John's account asks a probing question: If Jesus could go to Samaria, where are there "new Samarias" for the church today? If the John 4/Acts 8 parallel is helpful, then when we find these places, we will likely discover that Jesus has been there already.

---

37. Some critical scholars have seen in John 4 a description of the birth of Samaritan Christianity decades later (quite removed from the historic ministry of Jesus). See O. Cullmann, *The Johannine Circle* (Philadelphia: Westminster, 1975).

John 4 also offers an unavoidable critique about worship and tradition. On the historical plane, it is easy for us to understand how the historic sites of Gerizim and Jerusalem have changed their importance in light of Jesus' death and resurrection. Here Jesus is announcing a new immediacy with God that will not be mediated through place, but rather through the Spirit. Juxtaposed to the Spirit is no doubt the tradition that the Samaritan woman and every first-century Jew was willing to defend. But today similar questions can be asked. What traditions of place, form, or ritual do we defend that suddenly find themselves at odds with the work of the Holy Spirit? Do humans (Christian and non-Christian alike) have a tendency to create religious traditions as a part of the architecture of their lives? Does tradition have limited value? Are Jesus' work and the work of the Spirit at odds with such traditions?

Jesus returns to Cana. The healing of the royal official's son at its most basic level is a story of compassion. Sons were of unique value to families in first-century Jewish culture.[38] Fathers never referred to the number of their "children." They would always describe how many sons and daughters they had, with emphasis on the former. In fact, the father in our story uses a Greek term of endearment to describe his "little boy" (4:49). The phrase tells us that this is not merely one of the man's "sons." This is a child, a little boy whose illness has torn his father's heart. Perhaps this is the man's firstborn son, in which case there is a great deal at stake. Firstborn sons carried the heritage of the family: property, name, and responsibility for women. Jesus understands these emotions and values, and he acts with compassion and speed.

Therefore I can look at this story and rightly see a message about Jesus' interest in meeting the needs of the suffering. But John offers a few unique twists. We have become accustomed to reading about Jesus' care for the poor in many Gospel stories. But here we see Jesus interacting with a man of some means, a man of power, a man who is linked to politics, much like Nicodemus was linked to religion. Even though this man at first insists and then orders Jesus to do what he wants, Jesus complies. What are some avenues of exploration for us? No doubt we should reflect on the healing work of Jesus, but also on his compassion when people misunderstand his purposes and even when they may wish to exploit him.

One of the curious themes in the Fourth Gospel is the "absence of Jesus."[39] On more than one occasion, Jesus chooses not to be where he is expected.

---

38. B. Malina, *Windows on the World of Jesus* (Louisville: Westminster/John Knox, 1993), 72–87.

39. R. Sloan, "The Absence of Jesus," in R Sloan and M. Parsons, eds., *Perspectives on John. Method and Interpretation in the Fourth Gospel* (Lewiston: Edwin Mellen, 1993), 208–12, cited in G. L. Borchert, *John*, 220.

Sometimes Jesus is sought by officials (9:12) or crowds (7:11) who cannot find him. Nathanael is perplexed (1:48) because Jesus can see things when he is not there. Jesus suddenly appears across the Sea of Galilee when the crowds are looking for him elsewhere (6:22ff.). Jesus must explain that not only is his origin a mystery but his destination will be unexpected (7:28–29, 33–36; 8:21). When he is expected in Bethany for the ailing Lazarus, he chooses to be absent (11:21). And of course, when the women look for him at his tomb, he is absent as well (20:1–2).

What does all of this mean? Why is it unnecessary for Jesus to travel to Capernaum to heal this young boy? At the very least this lends a dimension of mystery to Jesus' movements and activity. Jesus is not confined to place. His capacity, his knowledge, and his interest go beyond human imagination and ability. His power makes his movements and his actions indecipherable to those who do not have faith.

Finally, John is supplying a theologically sophisticated comment here about faith based on signs. This aspect of the story is likely one of the central reasons why the apostle included it in his Gospel. God's desire to disclose himself in the natural world results in revelatory "signs." When this display involves acts of power, miracles result. Such self-disclosure by God should lead men and women to faith so that they see the dramatic penetration of God in the world and praise and worship him. But here is the problem. Those who witness these signs and who are captive to the darkness of this world will only see deeds of power, not divine deeds of revelation. John therefore is asking us to reflect on the relation among signs and miracles and faith.

Or more broadly, John is opening up the question of the relation of history to revelation and whether God discloses himself historically—and if he does, how it can be beneficial. Can humans witness anything from God, given the nature of the world? The Galileans were seeking signs, but this Gospel gives a critique of faith based merely on signs and announces a blessing on those who believe without having seen (signs) at all (20:29). Nevertheless, Jesus came to offer such "signs," and he provided them generously (12:37; 20:30). The question for us is related to this: What can we expect from God? Can we expect signs and wonders? What pitfalls await those seeking such things?

THE BRIDGING CONTEXTS section shows that there are many themes in John 4 that must be pressed into service in today's contemporary church. This is not simply a story about a woman who meets the Lord, discovers her sin, and then begins a walk of faith in light of her discovery. It is more. Far more.

Jesus and the world. Where is Samaria today? I am not referring to the geographical location of hills a few miles north of Jerusalem. I am thinking about Samaria as a metaphor that represents a major political and cultural boundary that stands between the church and a needy people. Jesus has crossed such a boundary and so should we. At the end of the story, he is described as "Savior of *the world*"—a remarkable title coming from a society that was as ethnically and culturally divided as ours. We must think about those social, economic, and political boundaries that circumscribe the church's activity, and we must cross them.

Witherington perceptively identifies the tendency today among Christians to concentrate on those audiences that will be most receptive to their message.

> The suggestion is that one should target certain *kinds* of people to recruit for one's church, because they can be more easily assimilated into the preexisting mix of one's congregation for the very good reason that they are so much like the congregation in race, ethnic origins, socioeconomic status, education, and the like.[40]

This has led to selective activity that avoids "Samaria," making Sunday morning one of the most segregated times of our week. We talk about going to Samaria, we study the possibilities, but we rarely get there. Commentator G. Campbell Morgan once asked what would have happened if Jesus invited his followers to study the prospect of going to Samaria.

> If those disciples had been appointed as a commission of inquiry as to the possibilities of Christian enterprise in Samaria I know exactly the resolution they would have passed. The resolution would have been: Samaria undoubtedly needs our Master's message, but it is not ready for it. There must be first ploughing, then sowing, and then waiting. It is needy, but it is not ready.[41]

John 4 challenges us to take a risk, to examine the margins of our world and cross them. I am impressed that a trip to Samaria meant nothing short of "risk" for Jesus. It meant leaving the usually traveled highway that was well known and comfortable. It meant traveling without the usual companions. And when Jesus went into Samaria as an outsider, risk was joined to cost. As any traveler knows, prices change when the retailer hears your accent.

But there is another intriguing aspect. A comparison of the woman with Nicodemus shows how far she is from the "acceptable standards" of Jewish

---

40. Witherington, *John*, 124.
41. G. C. Morgan (1951), as cited by Morris, *John*, 247n.84

society. Yet unlike Nicodemus, she responds in a way that no doubt delights Jesus. Unfettered by the theological questions that followed Nicodemus like a shadow, this woman in her simplicity gets it right. She knows a prophet when she meets one and concludes that he may well be the Messiah. And she is willing to tell her friends. Those to whom the Gospel is truly "new" news, who live on the far periphery of religion, sometimes see the meaning of God's Word with a simple and refreshing clarity.

I recently had a conversation with a friend who has worked at a car rental agency since his release from prison. As a young believer, he sees the commands of Jesus simply and obeys them. When I talk with graduate students about those same commands, we suddenly find ourselves enmeshed in all sorts of theological debates.

There are also many insights here concerning evangelism. The woman's comment, "I have no husband," reminds me of the phrase in Judges, "Israel had no king" (Judg. 17:6; 18:1; 19:1; 21:25). In fact, this woman has a list of husbands, just as the Israelites had decided to be their own kings. Each one needs one King, one Husband. As Jesus' conversation with the woman unfolds, he will not let himself get sidetracked by secondary issues but continues to press home his interest in her personal life. Her ethnicity, religious history, and gender may not become barriers. *She needs living water.*

In evangelism the same situation often arises. Muslims will make a last ditch appeal to Muhammad and centuries of mosque/church rivalry. They may even ask about the state of Israel, another minefield of troubles. "What do you think of gays in the church?" is always a conversation stopper when you suspect that the question bears some relevance to the person's identity and life. "But don't evangelicals really put down women?" is another statement designed to give pause. These sentences and hundreds of others like them are attempts to deflect the real issue at hand. Jesus will have none of it. In John 4:10 we learn his double agenda: Do you know the Christ? And will you drink his living water?

Not every evangelical is comfortable with Jesus' evangelistic strategy here. Indeed, he challenges the woman's presuppositions, exhibits care in her life and background, and gently uncovers her sin. We like these approaches. But it is not until Jesus utters a word of prophecy that suddenly the woman's eyes are opened in a new way. *Jesus exhibits the power of the Spirit at work for her and thereby models the power of the Spirit that may some day be within her.*

We may quickly say that this prophetic word was simply a feature of Jesus' sonship. But I am sure John would disagree. Jesus affirms that our abilities will imitate his. "I tell you the truth, anyone who has faith in me will do what I have been doing. He will do even greater things than these, because I am going to the Father" (14:12). Jesus is explaining that the endowment of the Spirit given to the disciples following his glorification will equip them in a way similar to his. Even the letters of John indicate that prophecy was a gift that was active in John's churches (1 John 4:1). But what does this mean for evangelism? Is a convincing testimony simply about a coherent presentation of belief or a persuasive presentation of the facts? It must be more. Those outside the kingdom deserve to see signs; they deserve to see the Holy Spirit in us before they will step closer to faith themselves.

I believe that John is also telling us something about the incapacity of this woman—or any other person, for that matter—to grasp the things of God by themselves. This is the meaning of the misunderstandings in the discourse. *She does not understand what Jesus is talking about.* She cannot. Jesus is bringing a divine revelation to darkness. We live in darkness. Our senses, our morals, our instincts, and our intellect are all fallen beyond our ability to repair them. In fact, God's effort in the Incarnation is an attempt to penetrate this darkness in his Son, Jesus Christ. Moreover, the Holy Spirit is his effort to penetrate our hearts so that we can believe and understand. John repeats this theme in one of his later letters: "This is the one who came by water and blood—Jesus Christ. He did not come by water only, but by water and blood. And it is the *Spirit* who testifies, because the Spirit is the truth" (1 John 5:6, italics added).

When Jesus asked his disciples who he was at Caesarea Philippi, all but Peter answered incorrectly. Then Jesus remarks, "Blessed are you, Simon son of Jonah, for this was not revealed to you by man, but by my Father in heaven" (Matt. 16:17). Spiritual discernment is entirely a work of God, initiated by God and directed by him. Thus Jesus says, "Others have done the hard work" (John 4:38), meaning that harvesters (evangelists) can be assured God has gone before them.

Calvin stressed this point with powerful clarity (see his *Institutes*, 2.2.18–21). He compared human reason to a man walking through a field in the dark of night. We are like travelers "who in a momentary lightning flash see far and wide, but the sight vanishes so swiftly that [they are] plunged again into the darkness of the night before [they] can even take a step."[42] God illumines us sufficiently for us to know that there are villages and mountains on the horizon, but we cannot make a map or find our way successfully. Spiritual transformation is thus an act of grace that enables us to understand the things we yearn to know.[43]

---

42. J. Calvin, *The Institutes of the Christian Religion*, trans J T. McNeill (Philadelphia: Westminster, 1960), 1:277 [2.2 18].

43. The inability of the world to grasp the things of God is also discussed by Paul in 1 Cor 1–3

Jesus, tradition, and "place." Both Jews and Samaritans had their sacred mountains. Mount Gerizim and Mount Zion (Jerusalem) both held a sacred history that anchored the religious identities of their people. They provided a means for each group to consolidate itself, to identify itself over against others, to gain religious prestige, and to enjoy assurance that "on *this* mountain" God is rightly worshiped and heard. In the story these mountains not only come up for criticism by Jesus (4:21), but they become a way for the woman to deflect Jesus' word to her. She appeals to her tradition and hopes that her position will keep Jesus at bay.

Such mountains are enclaves of refuge where religion can be embraced, but likewise where God *might* be avoided. Religious mountains can have as much to do with the Truth as a well in Shechem has to do with the living Water offered by God. One of the deepest memories I have comes from my upbringing in a Christian tradition that is as old as the sixteenth century. From childhood I grew up in the Swedish Lutheran community that had its roots in Chicago. I say "Swedish" because as *everyone* seemed to know, the German Lutherans simply did not have a corner on the truth. Through Sunday School, worship services (where I was an acolyte), and confirmation, I learned to be proud of this tradition. I memorized the liturgies and Luther's Shorter Catechism. My Catholic friends wore fashionable "St. Christopher" medallions and I dutifully wore a chain inscribed on one side with Lutheran symbols (heart and cross) and on the other the words, "I am a Lutheran." It did not occur to me that it could have said, "I am a Christian." Lutheran was a subset of Christian—a superior subset.

This identity worked fine until at my university I met a graduate student in chemistry who led a Bible study sponsored by Calvary Chapel (Costa Mesa, California). It was 1972, the Jesus Movement was just underway, and the beach ministries of Calvary Chapel were being born. Anyone can guess what I said when pressed about my faith: "I am a Lutheran." Luther was my hero. I even possessed my grandfather's catechism texts from Europe to prove it in case my medallion was insufficient. But then he asked irritating questions about Jesus and the Bible ("What about Luther and the Catechism?") and probed whether it was possible to be religious without being Christian.[44] Jesus is not interested in Samaritan identities any more than he is interested in Lutheran credentials. The questions remain the same: Have you discovered living water? And do you know who supplies it?

Tradition is not the evil some evangelicals would think, however. Tradition can give needed perspective and depth, which today I seek and value. However,

---

44. Those were heady days of youth when discernment seemed to be hard won. Today I look back with continuing appreciation for that Lutheran tradition that laid the bedrock of my theology, and I thank God for one bold, bearded disciple who would not be dissuaded by religious rhetoric.

religious tradition can become a badge that is more important than our faith itself. Do evangelicals possess such traditions, such places of identity that have little to do with God? I can think of coalitions, institutions, churches, colleges— even special interests—that become so important to evangelicals that these items define what it means to be spiritual. We become impenetrable to the work of God but nevertheless remain thoroughly religious.

Tradition receives its most poignant critique from Jesus and its most lively debates today when the subject of worship is raised. "Neither on this mountain nor in Jerusalem" has its historical moorings, but imagine what it meant for subsequent Christians wrestling with competing worship traditions. When early Christians from Antioch met with Christians from Rome, were there struggles? What would 4:24 have meant to them? "God is spirit, and those who worship him must worship in spirit and truth."

In countless churches today congregations struggle with the nature of worship and the perceived forms that are traditional and "holy." I have witnessed this in two congregations. Younger people want something "contemporary" while older folks (who don't realize that their liturgies began in the 1940s or 1950s) defend traditional forms. "Spirit and truth" ought to be an exhortation aimed at both parties. Neither synthesizers nor eighteenth-century hymns guarantee genuine worship that engages the Spirit of God.

Finally, the story of the Samaritan woman places a question mark over another reflex so common among us. When Jesus challenges the sanctity of Gerizim, I can recognize this as a correction to erroneous Samaritan thinking. But when he questions the ongoing validity of Jerusalem as a *locale* of worship and reverence (4:21), something different has happened. "Neither on this mountain nor in Jerusalem" addresses something profound about how our architects build religion. Because our faith is historically anchored (and not gnostic), "place" becomes important as does "time." Questions of *when* and *where* are vital to theological discourse. The problem comes when these places become ends in themselves, when they are protected and revered in unholy ways, when they no longer point to the God who was there, but instead point to the place where he acted.

Of course, this propensity has been with us for a long time. I am not thinking here about religiously historic places such as Dallas, Colorado Springs, or Wheaton (or any host of names); I am thinking quite literally about Jerusalem in the Middle East. It does not take long for a visitor in Israel to get a sense of holy places, and the defense of these places has led to terrible examples of violence and bloodshed. The Crusades are one severe example. But even recently outside Bethlehem, Rachel's tomb is a place where Jews have decided they must pray, and the violence there became so acute that Israeli authorities have now built a twelve-foot wall around it to cordon off the worshipers. Passersby cannot even see the tomb from the road anymore.

Evangelical Christians today have had an unholy relation to Jerusalem and the land of Israel. They have adopted a "Holy Land Theology," in which the defense of "place" has become a religious duty. So-called embassies, federations, and foundations have organized evangelical money and clout in order to defend political interests in the region. What is most distressing is that as evangelicals have defended this "place," they have forgotten that they have Arab brothers and sisters in Christ (135,000 of them) who often suffer because of these politics.[45]

Christians may well speak to issues of peace and justice in the Middle East, but when mountains are defended in the name of God and people are sacrificed, something is amiss. "Neither on this mountain nor in Jerusalem" is Jesus' critique of "place." God is spirit (4:24), which at the very least means he is not tied to "place," but transcends all such things.

Jesus, miracles, and faith. I have a friend (whom I will call Anthony) who claims to have a secret library hidden under his bed. He is a mainline minister whose reputation and prestige are likely the envy of many of his colleagues. Anthony pastors a "tall steeple" church and has even had experience as a college and seminary professor. When someone visits his office, they can see the appropriately displayed volumes of Luther, Calvin, and Barth mixed with the best in contemporary theology and exegesis. But then there is this hidden library, which, he swears, would be his undoing if anyone found out.

This library is about miraculous healing and exorcism. Some of these books bear titles that amaze and entertain; many are from publishers no one has ever seen before. They have breathtaking cover art. Not only does Anthony read these things but he has taken a step further, attending meetings where the "full gospel" can be heard *and experienced.* His sermons exhibit genuine sophistication, eloquence, and rigorous theological orthodoxy. He is a homiletic marvel. But his secret library seems never to penetrate these sermons.

I have often wondered about the value of these paperback theologies to Anthony. One time he gave me a glimpse into their unexpected secrets. Their miraculous stories provided certainty amidst his many questions— assurance that God was real and powerful when orthodox rationality and logic did not satisfy his heart. Once he said that *if* these things were true, just imagine how it would revolutionize the church. "If?" He had tome upon tome claiming that they were absolutely true. He had even tasted some of their powerful promises himself.

---

45. My own interest in this subject led me to write *Who Are God's People in the Middle East?* (Grand Rapids: Zondervan, 1993).

Anthony had concluded that the miraculous sign was the ultimate validation of God's reality. He assumed that if he had sufficient exposure to these things—if the church had sufficient exposure—the demons of doubt and sin and disbelief would vanish. But as most Pentecostal ministers (for whom this sort of thing is their stock and trade) admit, it isn't so easy. Miraculous signs do not automatically lead to faith, nor do they vanquish the darkness that haunts us.

John 4:43–54 opens a question that it does not entirely answer, namely, what are the advantages and disadvantages of a faith based on miraculous signs? Jesus' surprising rebuke in 4:48, "Unless you people see miraculous signs and wonders ... you will never believe," suggests that the evidence sought by the Galileans did not meet with Jesus' favor. While in Jerusalem, Jesus had the same feeling about the Jews who believed because he could work a sign (2:23–25). Later, when he was in Galilee, the crowd pursued him not because of his sonship, but because of his miracle: "not because you saw miraculous signs but because you ate the loaves and had your fill" (6:26). The crowds saw a miraculous supply of bread, but they did not necessarily see who gave the bread (the Bread of Life!) or what it really meant.

For John, a sign is a divine revelation that leads to an enlightened faith in God. But most who live in this world can only experience the surface apprehension of power. For each of us burdened by human frailty, God must help. This is where my friend Anthony's theological fantasy is fundamentally flawed. It suggests that if the church or the world sees more miracles, only then will it embrace true faith.

During my first semester in seminary a professor told me a remarkable story from his early years as a pastor. A young woman had become critically ill and her prognosis was grim; she would likely die within the year. Her family had a nominal "Easter and Christmas Eve" commitment to the church, so the discussions in the hospital between this young pastor and this family always plowed new ground. The woman challenged him: If Jesus healed in the Bible, he should be able to heal me today. If not, what use was he? So she prayed. The pastor prayed. The whole family prayed—and pleaded and begged and bargained. If God would only show mercy, the family urged, they would completely recommit themselves and come to church every Sunday. This earnest young pastor prayed with all his heart. He refused to join the ranks of those who said, "If it is thy will." It was God's will that she be healed, he concluded.

Then to his amazement, God healed her—completely. And with the physicians shaking their heads, she was sent home from the hospital. Next Sunday, the entire family was there in the front pew, dressed and sparkling. The young woman gave her testimony, praising God for his goodness. The following Sunday, the family was there again. In four weeks, it was only the woman and her husband. And after that, attendance was sporadic until they dropped into their previous pattern. Before long, the woman rationalized the entire incident. She had experienced the most dramatic sign God could give her: healing, bathed in prayer and surrounded by the church. But after only two months, its power dimmed to nothing.

This is not to say that miraculous signs have no place in the ministry of the church. They do. But John 4:43–54 suggests to us that they have a limited scope and usefulness. E. Schweizer once wrote, "The false component here does not consist in that he [the royal official] is not at all interested in Jesus himself, only in something to be obtained through him."[46] This is where the story finds its deepest meaning. Miracles were a natural part of Jesus' ministry and led people to faith (10:38). But Jesus is more than this, and he expects more. He looks for men and women not only to believe in his ability to work a miracle, but especially to believe in him. Merely witnessing or experiencing a miracle does not mean that one has experienced a gift from God; rather, it is faith itself that permits someone to participate in the miracle he grants; it is faith that turns these miracles into "divine signs."[47]

The royal official sought a miracle. Jesus placed himself between the request and the healing, so that the man had to act in faith and walk home without the thing he wanted. He had to decide if he would trust Jesus, not simply bring him and his reputation to Capernaum. The young woman had sought a miracle but did not seek Jesus who stood behind it. And once she had it, she could dispense with God. Anthony's library is simply a fantasy because it promotes the possibility that a miracle or power encounter will solidify faith and spark renewal. It will not.

The root problem is our fallen capacity to receive and accept things from God. We will accept gifts that benefit us directly, that heal us or profit us; but a divine revelation, a divine sign, discloses who we are and who God really is. Divine signs, like light, are painful since they disclose everything hidden in the dark (3:19). I often recall the astounding story of Jesus in Luke 16:19–31, the rich man and Lazarus. When the tormented rich man asks that his brothers be warned about the doom awaiting them, the conversation between hell and heaven ends with a comment by Abraham: Even if a person on earth is given every sign, even if someone were to come back from the dead, they would not believe. The human capacity to seek after God and to identify him and worship him is entirely broken. It was as true in Galilee as it is today.

---

46 E. Schweizer, as cited in H. Ridderbos, *John*, 175n.218
47. Ridderbos, *John*, 177

John 5:1-47

S OME TIME LATER, Jesus went up to Jerusalem for a feast
of the Jews. ²Now there is in Jerusalem near the Sheep
Gate a pool, which in Aramaic is called Bethesda and
which is surrounded by five covered colonnades. ³Here a
great number of disabled people used to lie—the blind, the
lame, the paralyzed. ⁵One who was there had been an invalid
for thirty-eight years. ⁶When Jesus saw him lying there and
learned that he had been in this condition for a long time, he
asked him, "Do you want to get well?"

⁷"Sir," the invalid replied, "I have no one to help me into
the pool when the water is stirred. While I am trying to get in,
someone else goes down ahead of me."

⁸Then Jesus said to him, "Get up! Pick up your mat and
walk." ⁹At once the man was cured; he picked up his mat and
walked.

The day on which this took place was a Sabbath, ¹⁰and so
the Jews said to the man who had been healed, "It is the Sabbath; the law forbids you to carry your mat."

¹¹But he replied, "The man who made me well said to me,
'Pick up your mat and walk.'"

¹²So they asked him, "Who is this fellow who told you to
pick it up and walk?"

¹³The man who was healed had no idea who it was, for
Jesus had slipped away into the crowd that was there.

¹⁴Later Jesus found him at the temple and said to him, "See,
you are well again. Stop sinning or something worse may happen to you." ¹⁵The man went away and told the Jews that it
was Jesus who had made him well.

¹⁶So, because Jesus was doing these things on the Sabbath,
the Jews persecuted him. ¹⁷Jesus said to them, "My Father is
always at his work to this very day, and I, too, am working."
¹⁸For this reason the Jews tried all the harder to kill him; not
only was he breaking the Sabbath, but he was even calling
God his own Father, making himself equal with God.

¹⁹Jesus gave them this answer: "I tell you the truth, the Son
can do nothing by himself; he can do only what he sees his
Father doing, because whatever the Father does the Son also

does. ²⁰For the Father loves the Son and shows him all he does. Yes, to your amazement he will show him even greater things than these. ²¹For just as the Father raises the dead and gives them life, even so the Son gives life to whom he is pleased to give it. ²²Moreover, the Father judges no one, but has entrusted all judgment to the Son, ²³that all may honor the Son just as they honor the Father. He who does not honor the Son does not honor the Father, who sent him.

²⁴ "I tell you the truth, whoever hears my word and believes him who sent me has eternal life and will not be condemned; he has crossed over from death to life. ²⁵I tell you the truth, a time is coming and has now come when the dead will hear the voice of the Son of God and those who hear will live. ²⁶For as the Father has life in himself, so he has granted the Son to have life in himself. ²⁷And he has given him authority to judge because he is the Son of Man.

²⁸"Do not be amazed at this, for a time is coming when all who are in their graves will hear his voice ²⁹and come out— those who have done good will rise to live, and those who have done evil will rise to be condemned. ³⁰By myself I can do nothing; I judge only as I hear, and my judgment is just, for I seek not to please myself but him who sent me.

³¹"If I testify about myself, my testimony is not valid. ³²There is another who testifies in my favor, and I know that his testimony about me is valid.

³³"You have sent to John and he has testified to the truth. ³⁴Not that I accept human testimony; but I mention it that you may be saved. ³⁵John was a lamp that burned and gave light, and you chose for a time to enjoy his light.

³⁶"I have testimony weightier than that of John. For the very work that the Father has given me to finish, and which I am doing, testifies that the Father has sent me. ³⁷And the Father who sent me has himself testified concerning me. You have never heard his voice nor seen his form, ³⁸nor does his word dwell in you, for you do not believe the one he sent. ³⁹You diligently study the Scriptures because you think that by them you possess eternal life. These are the Scriptures that testify about me, ⁴⁰yet you refuse to come to me to have life.

⁴¹"I do not accept praise from men, ⁴²but I know you. I know that you do not have the love of God in your hearts. ⁴³I have come in my Father's name, and you do not accept me;

but if someone else comes in his own name, you will accept him. ⁴⁴How can you believe if you accept praise from one another, yet make no effort to obtain the praise that comes from the only God?

⁴⁵"But do not think I will accuse you before the Father. Your accuser is Moses, on whom your hopes are set. ⁴⁶If you believed Moses, you would believe me, for he wrote about me. ⁴⁷But since you do not believe what he wrote, how are you going to believe what I say?"

COMMENTATORS CANNOT AGREE on how John 5–11 should be organized, but there is a general consensus that chapter 5 opens a new section separate from chapters 1–4. John is no longer comparing Jesus with institutions of Jewish piety and history (chs. 2–4) but with some of the major festivals of Judaism. These chapters refer specifically to festivals such as Passover and Tabernacles. Jesus makes an appearance in the Jewish festivities and exploits some imagery, which lends deeper understanding of who he is. Our goal as exegetes must be uncovering the religious and cultural patterns understood by John and his original audience in order to gain a clearer picture of Jesus' activities.

Some refer to these chapters as John's "festival cycle." Once this pattern is recognized, new insight is possible on otherwise difficult paragraphs. In my outline (see Introduction) I have suggested that one effective way to organize the section is to group the four major festivals together, leaving the Lazarus story to one side (as foreshadowing of death and resurrection).[1] An outline of the festivals makes John's structure clear.

- **The Sabbath Festival** in Jerusalem (ch. 5)
- **The Passover Festival** in Galilee (ch. 6)
- **The Tabernacles Festival** in Jerusalem (chs. 7–8)
- Case Study: A Blind Man and "Light" (ch. 9)
- **The Hanukkah Festival** in Jerusalem (ch. 10)[2]

---

1. This follows R. Brown's organization of the chapters Some scholars (Carson, Sloyan) divide chs. 5–10 into subunits (chs. 5–7, 8–10), but this interrupts John's treatment of Tabernacles. Others (Beasley-Murray, Morris) are not persuaded that there is a structural pattern here at all.

2. Other scholars include in this list ch. 11, in which Jesus moves toward Jerusalem to raise Lazarus during another Passover (11:55) But this Passover is not in the festival cycle. It belongs to the Passion story, in which Jesus is crucified.

One cannot overestimate the importance of such festivals in first-century Judaism. Leviticus 23 offers a list of these festivals and stresses their importance. The cycle of festivals was old (Purim and Hanukkah were the newest, but centuries-old in Jesus' day) and the liturgies of the temple and the responsibilities of Jewish families well established. Three times each year Jewish families were expected to travel to Jerusalem for worship (Passover in spring, Pentecost seven weeks later, Tabernacles in autumn), thanking God for the harvest of crop and herd and remembering great episodes from Israel's history.[3]

The Sabbath was the only weekly festival, observed in homes and synagogues in Israel's villages. But in some respects, the Sabbath set the tone for what it meant to have a period of time set aside for reverence and devotion for any festival. The first day of Passover (according to Lev. 23:7) was to be "a sacred assembly" in which no work could be done. The onset of festivals mimicked the observance of Sabbath. This means that Sabbath set the pace, outlining the pattern of Jewish devotion for what was to follow.[4]

Some scholars have argued strenuously that John 5 is a troubling chapter in that it does not refer to its festival directly and is out of place sequentially. Note how Jesus is in Galilee at the end of chapter 4, then he moves to Jerusalem in chapter 5, and unexpectedly in 6:1 he goes "to the other side of the Sea of Galilee." If chapters 5 and 6 are reversed, so the argument runs, John's stories about Galilee are gathered together (4:46–54; 6:1–71) and his Jerusalem stories come together as well (5:1–47, followed by 7:1ff.). The new chapter order would be John 1, 2, 3, 4, 6, 5, 7, 8, etc.

While this solves some problems, it fails to see the intrinsic value of the Sabbath of chapter 5 as heading an all-important festival list. John's literary efforts are not haphazard. If anything, a careful study of this Gospel shows that sequence and image are never accidental, but quite sophisticated. The festival here is the Sabbath (see 5:9), and the argument that flows from it is based on rabbinic expectations for behavior and piety on the Sabbath. But above all, John (and Jesus) has a "Sabbath understanding" of the festivals that we will see surface repeatedly in the festival cycle. Festivals were made by God to bring good gifts to his people, not to legislate and control behavior. This outlook will unfold particularly in chapter 5, and like so many Synoptic conflict stories, Jesus' understanding of the Sabbath gets him into considerable trouble.

Chapter 5 not only opens the festival cycle, but it also introduces a theme that will weave its way throughout the Gospel. John's Gospel places Jesus on trial not simply at the end of his life (as in the Synoptics), but rather

---

3. It is uncertain, however, if such compliance was universal.
4. Borchert, *John*, 230.

continually.[5] Jesus' arrival in the world forces men and women to take stock of his coming, to examine and decide the truth of his mission and word. In this sense, Jesus is "in the dock" or on trial in every episode. In fact, one of the ways John introduces the miracles of Jesus is to offer them as "evidence," as if Jesus were on trial.

But there is an ironic twist here because in the end, it is not Jesus who is on trial; the world is on trial. Even though Jesus is clear that he is not judging the world (8:15; 12:47), still, the entry of the light into the world exposes the darkness and judges it for what it is. "This is the verdict: Light has come into the world, but men loved darkness instead of light because their deeds were evil" (3:19).

Judicial settings appear in John with surprising frequency. Jesus is examined by Nicodemus, the woman, and the Jewish leaders (chs. 6, 8, and 9). Jesus must produce witnesses for his case (John the Baptist, God, followers, healed men in chs. 5 and 9), and he produces evidence that may substantiate his claims (particularly his works, cf. 5:36; "The very work that the Father has given me to finish, and which I am doing, testifies that the Father has sent me"; cf. also 10:25, 37–38; 14:11; 15:24). Above all, in the final scenes of the Gospel, Jesus appears before Pilate and the high priest in a climactic judicial sequence in which he is found innocent (18:38) but nevertheless is killed.

This judicial background is important because it sets the stage for the meaning of John 5. This chapter is not simply about a Sabbath day when Jesus heals a man and then is accused of breaking the law. Mark 3:1–6 provides that sort of story. This chapter is a template of accusation and response, of prosecution and defense. A simple outline of the chapter makes this clear:

The Crime (5:1–15)
- A man at Bethesda is healed on the Sabbath
- The man is interrogated
- The criminal [Jesus] is identified

The Decision to Prosecute (5:16–18)
- First basis: Jesus violates the Sabbath
- Second basis: Jesus is making divine claims

Jesus Goes to Trial (5:19–47)
- Jesus describes his "criminal" work
- Jesus brings witnesses in his defense
- Jesus prosecutes his opponents
- Jesus identifies their crimes
- Jesus challenges their ability to appeal

---

5. The most accessible presentation of this theme is A. E. Harvey, *Jesus on Trial. A Study in the Fourth Gospel* (London: SPCK, 1976).

John 5 therefore is a trial—perhaps it is "the trial" of Jesus played out for us. This episode serves a literary role for John that exceeds its particular setting in Jesus' historic life, showing us the kind of accusation and rejection Jesus experienced, his defense, and above all, the genuine spiritual jeopardy his opponents are in.[6]

The Crime (5:1–15)

THE STORY OPENS with Jesus coming to Jerusalem during a feast (which is Sabbath, 5:9) and arriving at a gate in the city's northeast wall called the Sheep Gate.[7] It is interesting that this northeast section of the walled city has continued to sponsor a sheep market one day per week just outside St. Stephen's Gate. The NIV refers to the name of a pool there called in Aramaic "Bethesda," but this has posed innumerable problems for the translator. Greek texts offer many alternatives for the site: Bethzatha, Bethsaida, Belzetha, and Bethesda; some suggest a new word, "Bethseta," which means "house of sheep."

The manuscript tradition is so divided it is clear that later scribes, who did not know the place, easily made errors and postulated corrections. Bethsaida, for instance, is likely a confusion with the city in Galilee. However in Qumran we have located a reference to *"Beth 'esda"* [in its dual form, *beth 'esdatayin*], which means "house of flowing." Bethesda is the Greek transliteration of it. John refers to the word (lit.) as Hebrew, but throughout his Gospel he regularly means "Aramaic," the familiar language of Jesus (19:13, 17, 20; 20:16). In Jewish literature, the words are interchangeable. Today this pool, complete with five porches, is located adjacent to the Church of St. Anne inside Jerusalem's Old City.

We learn in the story that many people viewed the pool as a healing sanctuary (5:3). Such places were not uncommon in antiquity, and once a site was identified as a sanctuary of healing, the tradition was impossible to stop. Excavations at the site show that after the New Testament era, the pools continued to be used as an Asclepion (a healing sanctuary[8]), which confirms the tradition. One explanation for the crowd at the pool has slipped into the

---

6. Luke does the same thing with a "rejection template" in his description of Jesus' rejection at the Nazareth synagogue (Luke 4:16–30).

7. This is the NIV solution to a notorious Greek difficulty. Literally the text says that in Jerusalem "there is a pool called [Bethzatha] by the sheep ___." "Sheep" is an adjective, and either it can modify "pool" or one can supply a word such as "gate" (NRSV, NIV, REB) or "market" (KJV). It may well be that John is pointing not to a gate, but to a "sheep pool," taking the phrase together (as did every ancient translation and commentary).

8. This is from the Greek god of healing, Asclepius. After a healing, offerings were left behind that symbolized that part of the body healed (arm, leg, finger, etc.). A dramatic collection of healing tributes is available at the Corinth Asclepion museum.

text (5:3b–4), which most of the manuscripts of John leave out (cf. the NIV); it was likely inserted to explain the "stirring of the waters" in 5:7. The people understood that occasionally an angel would descend and stir the water of the pool, and the first one to touch the water would be healed. The man Jesus meets had been ill for thirty-eight years (in 5:8–9 John indicates he was paraplegic, having lost the ability to use his legs). This area was likely a regular place for him to spend the day. Here he could beg from people coming to the pool and take his chances at being healed.

Jesus takes the initiative with the man (as he generally does in the Gospel) with words whose meaning likely goes beyond the mere miracle at hand: "Do you want to get well?" (5:6). These same words could have been used metaphorically for Nicodemus and the Samaritan woman. The man, of course, does not recognize Jesus and cannot understand his healing powers. The man then appeals to his dilemma: As a paraplegic, he cannot outrace the others getting into the pool for healing (5:7). But Jesus ignores both the superstition surrounding the pool and the man's complaint. The Greek tenses of his commands in 5:8 unveil his interest: Pick up your bed (an aorist imperative, a single event), get yourself up and start walking (present imperatives, continuous events). The healing is immediate. The man makes no testimony of who Jesus is and provides no orthodox confession; he simply obeys and is healed.

The importance of the story comes to us in 5:9b. It is the Sabbath when Jesus heals the man, and immediately the story takes an abrupt and unsettling turn. Jerusalem had always been a place of religious zeal (as it is today), and now a self-appointed enforcer of Sabbath law upbraids the man (5:10). The Jews protected the Sabbath and held it aloft as a vital symbol of Jewish culture and religion.[9] The oral laws of Judaism at this time (reflected in the *Mishnah*) outlined thirty-nine categories of things that were forbidden on Sabbath, and carrying something such as a bed from one place to another was prohibited (*Shabbath* 7:2).

The man does not know Jesus. He simply points to his own healing, and no doubt with joy that matched his inquisitors' zeal, he says that a man with the authority to heal told him to do this. Any reader of the story can sympathize with him. The man's life has been transformed! The joy of new life obliterates the legalism he now must debate. It is only later when Jesus meets him in the temple (5:14–15) that the man identifies Jesus to the authorities.

---

9. The same is true today. In sections of Jerusalem if you drive your car through certain neighborhoods, you run the risk of being stoned. A major debate in recent years has been whether Jerusalem should permit films to be shown on Friday evenings, the beginning of Sabbath. A few months ago I took a picture on the Sabbath near the Temple Mount and was immediately confronted by a passerby who wanted to enforce the same law. "Pushing the shutter button is work," he yelled as he grabbed my camera lens.

The story has taken an ominous turn. For the first time in the Gospel, Jesus' opponents show themselves in all their hostility. Their question shifts rapidly from the error of the healed man to the identity of the healer who has incited this breach of law: "Who is this fellow?" (5:12). Jesus has slipped away (5:13b), as was his pattern following miracles (cf. 6:15). In 5:16–18 these opponents will summarize their complaint against Jesus.

When Jesus meets the former paraplegic in the temple, there is an important exchange that requires explanation (5:14). We can surmise that the man has gone to the temple to offer praise to God for his healing (cf. Luke 17:14) or perhaps to confirm his healing with priests. When Jesus sees him, he says two things. "See, you are [lit., have become] well" is no doubt a recognition that his cure was not short-lived, as many supposed cures were. But then Jesus remarks, "Stop sinning or something worse may happen to you."

Is Jesus making some link between sin and physical ills? Interpreters have struggled with the meaning of this verse. No doubt Jesus' exhortation must be connected to his warning here. The man's sin and his condition are linked. Scripture indicates that some tragedies may be the result of specific sins (1 Cor. 11:30), and this may be why Jesus has chosen the man for healing. There were two levels at which God needed to work in him (cf. Mark 2:1–12). But those with an infirmity have not *necessarily* sinned, and those who sin do not necessarily endure suffering as a consequence. Luke 13:1–5 and John 9:3 provide Jesus' correction of that sort of thinking. Suffering is *not* an index of a person's sin. But having said that, specific suffering may still come from specific sins. The most natural reading of the verse suggests that Jesus is pointing the man to repentance because in his case there is such a link.

The Decision to Prosecute (5:16–18)

WE DARE NOT miss the pivotal importance of these three verses. These are John's own comments explaining the nature of Jesus' persecution. John tells us about Jesus' opponents and assesses the reason for their fury. In 5:18 he anticipates the conclusion of the story with a shocking disclosure: His opponents want to kill Jesus (cf. 7:1). The Jewish leadership has located two crimes that are major offenses deserving the death penalty. If we keep John's fascinating "trial motif" in mind, these verses contain the "legal complaint" that the Jewish authorities held against Jesus.

(1) The Greek of 5:16 says that the persecution is tied not simply to this offense (healing the paraplegic), but to Jesus' habit of doing such things on the Sabbath. This parallels the Synoptic picture of Sabbath violations that brought significant conflict. Jesus was viewed as indifferent to divine Sabbath law as mediated through Jewish tradition, and observers to such violations were obligated to punish the offender (Num. 15:32–36). It is interesting

that John uses a technical term for "persecute" in 5:16 (Gk. *dioko*, a word used in Greek literature for a legal prosecution). Thus John is telling us that Jesus is not simply being persecuted, but that his prosecution, his trial, is already underway. His prosecutors have now leveled their charge against him.

(2) The second charge against Jesus has to do with blasphemy. Jesus' defense of his Sabbath activity is given in 5:17 (lit.): "My Father is still working, and I also am working." The offense is not anchored in Jesus' claim to have a unique relationship with God, such as calling God "my Father" (cf. 10:33). This is secondary. The offense is anchored to the nature of Jesus' self-defense in light of Sabbath charges. The rabbis enforced the prohibition against work on the Sabbath but agreed that in some fashion, God himself continues working. For instance, God sustains the universe *every* day. Moreover, God continues to exert his prerogative over life and death since people die and children are born on the Sabbath.[10] Jesus' claim fits precisely here: He is God's Son, and as such, if God (who made the Sabbath) can continue to work positively while commanding rest, and if Jesus' works are the works of God, then Jesus' works on the Sabbath are defensible. Jesus is assuming divine prerogatives (5:19).

This is a dangerous defense to make. Can it be proven? If the defense is true, a breathtaking claim is being set before Judaism. If it is false, a serious crime has been committed. Jesus is claiming equality with God (5:18), a claim that will reappear throughout the course of the Gospel. But we must be clear about Jesus' claim. Borchert writes, "What Jesus, as the One and Only Son of God (1:14, 18), claimed was to be sent by God, on a mission for God, doing the works of God, obedient to God, and bringing glory to God. That is not the role of one who displaces God but one who is a representative or emissary of God."[11] As God's divine agent, Jesus has the right and the ability to do what God does.

Therefore John interprets the persecution and eventual death of Jesus as leading from Jesus' divine claims about himself. In the present instance, the cultural and religious interests of the Sabbath have provided a platform for these claims to be set out boldly.

Jesus Goes to Trial (5:19–40)

THE DISCOURSE THAT follows is the third in the Gospel and presents us with claims unlike anything we have thus far heard. Jesus makes explicit claims to

---

10. C. H. Dodd, *Interpretation of the Fourth Gospel*, 321–28. God's work in matters of life and death became the basis of arguing that life-saving efforts were acceptable on Sabbath. This basis was also relevant to the subject of war on the Sabbath, particularly if the alternative was pious death.

11. Borchert, *John*, 236.

his divinity inasmuch as he associates himself directly with God. His defense here has three distinct elements: (1) Jesus describes his work as sheltered under the same divine prerogatives as when God "works" on the Sabbath. In saying this Jesus is virtually making a divine claim for himself. (2) Since Jesus is on trial, he brings forward witnesses who can verify this divine authority in him. (3) Jesus turns the tables on his opponents and moves from defense to prosecution, describing the root problem of his opponents.

(1) **Jesus and God (5:19–30).** Scholars frequently explain that the form of Jesus' response in this discourse is thoroughly rabbinic. Not only does it assume an understanding of the Sabbath and its laws, but its form of reasoning is somewhat foreign to our Western styles today. Jesus begins formally "giving them an answer." His speech begins with (lit.) "truly, truly I say to you" (see comment on 1:51). It reminds us of the antiquity and authenticity of these Johannine discourses and how we need to unpack them carefully.

The central motif in the discourse is the relation of a father and a son as it would be viewed in this culture through the trade or skill the son was learning. We can think of Jesus growing up with Joseph in the carpentry shop, obediently learning skills and later imitating them. In a similar manner, Jesus is connected to the Father. His activity is never independent or self-initiated but always dependent, deriving its purpose from his Father's will. In this model we have to remember that there is no reciprocal relationship. "The Father initiates, sends, commands, commissions, grants; the Son responds, obeys, performs his Father's will, receives authority."[12] Moreover, the Son does not simply draw inspiration from the Father, but imitates him tirelessly and successfully. What makes this possible? John 5:20–23 provides three answers (anchored to three Gk. *gar* [for] clauses).

The most important affirmation is that the Father loves the Son.[13] The Greek present tense suggests an ongoing, continuous affection here, which leads to complete disclosure of the deeper mysteries of the Father (5:20). It is the same thought we find in 1:18, which describes the intimacy enjoyed between the Father and the Son's revelation of the Father to the world. Thus Jesus is unique inasmuch as he has seen and heard things no one else has.

This love spills into two tasks entrusted to the Son that belong exclusively to the Father. Jesus is sovereign over life (5:21) and judgment (5:22). That God alone has power over life and can raise people from death is no surprise (Deut. 32:39; 1 Sam. 2:6). That Jesus can do it too sets him apart in Judaism (cf. Elijah and Elisha). But this giving of life has also to do with judgment (5:22). In the theology of this Gospel, judgment is not an event left for the

---

12. Carson, *John*, 251.
13. This is the only place where John uses *phileo* for the Father's love of the Son.

end of time. Judgment and the gift of life happen now, in this world. And since Jesus is in this world, since he is the One through whom light and life are mediated, he becomes the catalyst of divine judgment. Those who love darkness find themselves under judgment already (3:19). Whoever believes in the Son has life already (3:36).

This makes Jesus God's premier agent in the world (5:24b). In antiquity, being an "agent" referred to a role in which authority and power were delegated to do a task. If a king wanted to negotiate peace or the price of cereal crops from a distance, he would assign an agent to represent himself fully. The agent's words were binding both on his audience and on the king who sent him. Therefore the agent had to be completely trustworthy. This is the imagery Jesus has in mind. As 5:23 makes explicit, whoever wishes to honor the Father must likewise honor the Son who represents him. And whoever dishonors the Son offends the Father whose presence stands behind him.[14]

The repetition in 5:24 of (lit.) "truly, truly I say to you" signals a natural break in Jesus' answer. Now that the groundwork has been laid (God loves Jesus and has delegated to him ultimate divine authority), Jesus expands and interprets what life and judgment really mean (5:24–30). To hear the words of Jesus (i.e., to accept his entire presence and message) is to believe God (who sent him). God's word and Jesus' word are one and the same, and so to embrace one is to embrace the other (5:24).

This decision has *present* consequences: Eternal life begins immediately and condemnation and death disappear. But Jesus' work as life-giver and judge (in both cases, again, implementing God's work, 5:30) also go into the future (5:25, 28–29). Jesus will be God's instrument on the great Day of Judgment. To reinforce this theme, Jesus calls himself "God's Son" (5:25), one of only three times he does so in this gospel (10:36; 11:4; cf. 19:7).

The key in these verses is to see that Jesus is expanding his divine claim. His authority over the Sabbath leads now to authority over eternal life. His rabbinic logic argues "from the lesser to the greater." If it is true that his identity as God's Son permits him to assume authority on the Sabbath, then he can assume divine authority elsewhere. All of the tasks listed in 5:24–30 are tasks firmly established in the Old Testament as works of God. Life is a gift from God (Gen. 2:7; Ps. 16:11); judgment is a work of God (Gen. 18:25; Judg. 11:27). Because of *who* he is, Jesus can do what God does. Note how in 5:31 Jesus no longer speaks of this abstractly but rather speaks in the first person, using the personal "I" numerous times. This is emphatic speech. Jesus does not want his claim obscured.

---

14. This image of "agency" explains the numerous times the Gospel refers to Jesus as the one "sent" by God. The "sent one" becomes virtually a Christological title in the Gospel.

(2) **Witnesses for Jesus' case (5:31—40).** John 5:31 is crucial in Jesus' trial. In Old Testament law, more than one witness was needed in order to condemn someone (Deut. 17:6). This idea was expanded in judicial settings to say that more than one person was needed to confirm someone's testimony (*Mishnah, Ketuboth* 2:9). In 5:31 Jesus is not saying that any self-testimony he gives is false, but rather that its validity is inadmissible unless it is confirmed by other witnesses. Jesus' claims are extraordinary. But if he is the only one making them, they will carry little weight with his audience. But if the claims are corroborated, they stand.

Jesus therefore identifies five witnesses whose words and deeds buttress his claims. (a) The first witness is God, even though 5:32 does not say so explicitly (though cf. 5:37). The thought is not necessarily that God provides an audible voice of testimony, unless John has in mind the baptism of Jesus (1:32—34; cf. 12:28). Rather, here Jesus may be pointing to the inward presence of God that gives him confidence about his mission (17:1—6). God's word and power are within Jesus, he has been sent by the Father, and these data point to the truth of who he is.

(b) The next witness is John the Baptist (5:33—35). John preceded Jesus, identified him, worked with him, and directed his followers to become Jesus' disciples. Although his ministry was enjoyed (or indulged) for a time, in the end, it was rejected.

(c) Jesus points to his own works (5:36), which demand some explanation. These are not simply powerful miracles, but signs, culminating in the great works of the cross and resurrection. These point not merely to Jesus' identity but to the Father, who alone can enable such things.

(d) Jesus adds the Scriptures to his list of witnesses (5:39—40). First-century Judaism was zealous in its study of the Scriptures. Yet, Jesus says, his contemporaries do not see the central message about Jesus and how he fulfills the Scripture. Luke shows a fascinating story about such use of the Scriptures in Luke 24 when Jesus comes to Emmaus. There he opens "Moses and all the Prophets" to these two disciples (Luke 24:27), who understand for the first time.

(e) The final witness is contained in the next element of Jesus' defense. It is Moses (5:46—47), who is represented in Scripture, but his words about the Messiah are unequivocal (Deut. 18:15). Moses is the "patron saint" of Judaism, the defender of its people, an advocate on their behalf before God (see Moses' farewell, Deut. 33). But, Jesus remarks, even Moses' words have gone ignored.

(3) **Jesus prosecutes his opponents (5:41—47).** A remarkable and unexpected feature of the discourse is the way in which Jesus finishes by attacking his opponents. In fact, he prosecutes them during his own trial! This was

not unusual in Jewish courts. Unlike today, defendants did not simply prove their innocence and thus end the trial. Jewish trials worked to uncover the truth, and accusers who made false claims in court could find themselves placed in the defense and subject to serious jeopardy. Punishments they had hoped to inflict on their opponent now could turn back on them.

Jesus understands this. Thus as his "trial" is played out in this chapter, he turns the tables and moves from defense to prosecution. The final impact of his defense in 5:31–40 leaves the impression that Jesus' hearers bear some responsibility for what God has done. If they cannot see the Father's work in their midst, if they cannot understand a sign when they see it, if they repudiated John the Baptist and read the Bible with closed hearts, something must be profoundly wrong. The irony runs deeper still since these people do indeed measure the validity of human witnesses (5:43) and seek eagerly the affirmation and recognition that come from human quarters. If the problem were intellectual, an explanation would do. But it lies deeper. Jesus' opponents are spiritually ill. Their disbelief is deliberate and the diagnosis severe: They do not have the love of God in their hearts (5:42). They love the religious life, but they have forgotten how to love God.

Jesus' final reference to Moses in 5:45–47 points not only to Moses' role as a witness (cf. above), but also to his role as judge. Judaism took great pride in Moses and his work in setting the Jewish faith on its present course. Identity with him was important (cf. esp. chs. 8–10). It was a religious badge of security. But if Moses is possessed and not obeyed, if Judaism is exploited as a mark of identity instead of a path to God, the very tenets of the Bible, the very words of Moses, will come back to haunt and to judge. To possess the Bible and to know the Scriptures but to not know God is to be in *the* most precarious place of all.

THIS IS A LONG and complex chapter, and one can get bogged down in the details of its debate and the intricacies of Jesus' argument. Interpreters have often been tempted to allegorize the story in order to find some relevance for present generations. For instance, Augustine and many others have looked at the pool with five porches at Bethesda as a symbol of the Torah, the five books of Moses.[15] The man, as it were, is trying to be cured in Judaism, but Jesus must redirect him another way. Patristic interpreters such as Tertullian and Chrysostom thought that the water of

---

15. "These five porches signified the law which bears the sick but does not heal them, discovers them but does not cure them" (Augustine, as cited by Hoskyns, *John*, 264).

the pool represented baptism, which, when stirred by heavenly beings, could heal. Similarly, the thirty-eight years of illness reminds some of Israel's thirty-eight years of desert wandering in the Old Testament. Jesus has come to bring the man to the Promised Land.

But such allegorizing is unnecessary and likely inappropriate. There once was an era when archaeology could not find any such pool in Jerusalem, and the Fourth Gospel was severely criticized as not representing historic Judaism. Then in the twentieth century a pair of twin pools was discovered in the northeast section of Jerusalem (inside St. Stephen's Gate, at St. Anne's Church).[16] The "five porches" resulted from an expansion of a pool that had been under heavy demand. Bethesda was fed by aqueducts, and each side had steps leading to the water and porches and platforms for people coming for water. When the pool was expanded, instead of making the original pool larger, an adjacent pool was dug, separated from the first by a wall and steps. This "double pool" then had "five" porches, with one porch separating the two main pools.

A time of trial and conflict. John 5 is a story about trial and conflict. The paraplegic in the story plays a role smaller than that of the woman in chapter 4. Once he identifies Jesus, he exits the stage, only to make way for the opponents of Jesus to accuse him and for Jesus to provide his defense. Thus, the story becomes a model for us to explain something about Jesus— why he died and how he should be defended.

But more than this, this story also should tell us something about our lives before the world. John's Gospel is clear that no disciple will be exempt from persecution if he or she is following the Lord. In the Upper Room Jesus warns, "Remember the words I spoke to you: 'No servant is greater than his master.' If they persecuted me, they will persecute you also" (15:20). This verse tells any would-be disciple that the account recorded in chapter 5 may well be the story of their own lives.

Why is this trial motif displayed in chapter 5 so interesting to John? Why does he take the time to weave it so carefully into the fabric of his Gospel, suggesting, as it were, that Jesus spent his whole life on trial? The answer is simple: John himself and his congregations are experiencing this sort of examination and trial as well. A gospel that speaks of Jesus' life in this way will greatly encourage people living under serious threats.

Paul does the same thing in 1 Thessalonians 2. He understands that these Greek Christians have suffered greatly for their faith. Thus he encourages them, saying that they are not only now walking in the steps of the earliest

---

16. J. Jeremias, *The Rediscovery of Bethesda* (Louisville, Ky.: Southern Baptist Theol. Seminary, 1966).

church of Judea (2:14), but in the very steps of Jesus when they suffer (1 Thess. 2:15). John has the same pastoral interest, but he is bringing this encouragement by putting in high relief this one dimension of Jesus' life.

The church in John's day is being questioned about the validity of Jesus. They are being forced to produce evidence of their convictions and offer the names of witnesses to validate their beliefs. We get a glimpse of this in a number of ways. John's view of the "world" is consistently negative, as if it were a place of hostility and conflict. The opponents of these Johannine Christians are likely Jewish leaders in a rival "synagogue," since the Johannine church is likely viewed as a "Christian synagogue." This explains the many uses of "Jews" in a derisive way. The language of conflict known so well in the Johannine church is appearing in the Gospel itself. John 9 later will become a test case of a man whom Jesus heals and who then experiences interrogation and excommunication. Any Johannine Christian who reads this story will be relieved to learn that he or she is not alone, that people healed by Jesus have experienced the same thing.

Or consider the theology of 15:18–25. Jesus begins by saying, "If the world hates you, keep in mind that it hated me first." These are potent words to Jesus' apostles. But they are also precious words to John's followers, who are being hated as well. Imagine a sermon in the first century based on this passage, directed to the same people reading 1 John! This is a community under siege, a community that knows suffering and conflict. This is a community that needs to be reminded that Jesus walked the same path. Therefore one theme that deserves exploration centers on the nature of persecution and the Christological center that must be protected.

There is another level of meaning in this "trial motif." John is aware that he is not simply recording a story for the sake of an archive; rather, he is writing for us. He is conscious that his reader is being exposed to Jesus on every page and therefore we too are caught up in this trial. We are seeing the evidence for and against Jesus. As we read, we too must come to a verdict. Will we believe or will we condemn? Just as the Fourth Gospel shows people coming into contact with Jesus and either believing or denying him, so too we must make the same decision.

The character of Jesus' opponents. This brings us to the most serious level of reflection for this chapter. At some point we must reflect on the description of the character of Jesus' opponents at the end of chapter 5. It is far too simplistic to say that these paragraphs outline what is wrong with "Judaism." A simplistic reading of John 5 has led too many Christians to be critical of Judaism and Jews. *Being Jewish is not the problem.* Jesus was Jewish as were his early followers. Jesus' opponents consist of Jews who have turned their otherwise excellent faith into something deadening, soul-destroying. John invites us to reflect on the spiritual malady that brings darkness and death to those interrogating Jesus throughout this Gospel.

But today I cannot help but wonder if we have not recreated this same context in our own religious settings. Is Jesus not still on trial today? A quick answer points an evangelistic finger to the world and its unbelief. But I ask: Are there no religious contexts in the church where Jesus is on trial? No religious systems that are so well-defined, so comfortable, so safe that Jesus himself would have difficulty being accepted? Is there no one in our churches who has "lost the love for God" in his or her heart, but nevertheless remains consistently and vigorously religious?

MINISTRY TO THE SUFFERING. A couple of years ago, Dr. Dwight Peterson spoke at a meeting of professional biblical scholars about the episodes where Jesus heals paraplegics.[17] I say "paraplegics" because in the contemporary idiom, we have to see the healed man as among us. No one uses "paralytic" today for people in a wheelchair. The lecturer had many good ideas, but one feature of his presentation stood out: *He himself was in a wheelchair*, he too was a paraplegic. Even though I recognize that the thrust of John 5 is aimed at disclosing to us the Christological identity of Jesus, this scholar reminded us that we have to recognize *the person* whom Jesus touches in these stories.

Peterson spoke at length about things we rarely consider. The challenges of a paraplegic in the twenty-first century (which are considerable) pale by comparison with a person in the first century. Problems of mobility and livelihood and social isolation just begin the list. Consider the problem of personal hygiene (which Peterson described graphically). Paraplegics frequently do not have bowel and bladder control. Taking these issues together, we can build a portrait of this man's life: People moved him from place to place unless he crawled; most of his income came from begging or from the charity of friends and family; and if he did not have bladder or bowel control, his hygiene problem would have been enormous. People stayed away from him. His hands (used for mobility) were rough and torn from the streets. I have seen these people in rural Egypt, where they live a step below the poorest of the poor. Their life is agony.

Among the many at Bethesda looking for healing that day, Jesus selects a man who is a particularly difficult "case." He does not reach out to those

---

17. This occurred at the Society of Biblical Literature Convention in New Orleans, Louisiana (November 1996). Dr. Peterson now teaches at Eastern College in Pennsylvania.

who are spiritually on the margin but socially "safe." Instead, he reaches out to someone whose suffering and isolation are beyond measure. I cannot help but think about the ministry of Mother Teresa and her Sisters of Charity in this regard. She is now deceased, but since her death in September 1997, story upon story have swept over us telling us how she touched, embraced, loved, and inspired the poorest in Calcutta's streets. She told her sisters, "Let the poor eat you up." Their neediness looks so overwhelming, but this is exactly the place Jesus likes to go.

What implications does this have for where the church "goes" today? What social risks does John 5 insist that we take? The same theme could be sounded from John 4 and, together with this chapter, a convicting message of vision for ministry could be articulated.

Spiritual heroism. A second theme centers on the identity of Jesus as it springs from the debate of the passage. Jesus is claiming a remarkable authority here. There is an ethical dimension to his claim. He claims he can break the law. Of course, we rightly say that first-century society had distorted the intent of God's law and Jesus correctly refocuses it. But there is something else that is interesting here. Does this mean that societal laws that distort or twist God's law deserve to be broken? John 5 may be an indirect argument for civil disobedience that makes many of us uncomfortable. Rabbinic law was the law of the land; it was the glue that held society together. Yet Jesus challenges it.

Of course we cannot claim to have the authority of Jesus, but here Jesus models something that we, bearing the name and Spirit of Jesus, ought to consider. Are there areas of modern life that need to be violated in the name of God so that God's person and justice can be seen by everyone? When I think of past examples of this, such as the Abolitionist Movement to end slavery, I am comfortable and show open support for their heroism. But rarely do I have the courage to recreate the spiritual heroism demanded today. What would it take for evangelicals to break the law in the name of God in the present century?

The identity of Jesus. Jesus' remarkable claims in this chapter lead us to a line of thinking that has to do not with ethics but with theology proper. Too often Jesus is described in the church or in the world as simply a nice man. Some may call him a charismatic teacher, and some may elevate him to a dispenser of religious wisdom or a prophet. One scholar sees him as a "peasant rebel" offering a "brokerless kingdom of God" to the world. Some prefer to see in him a model of the spiritual life. The trouble with these descriptions is that they omit a key ingredient to the New Testament's message about Jesus.

Jesus Christ makes *ultimate* claims for himself in the Gospels. Nowhere is this more obvious than in John 5. It is not simply that Jesus is doing the

Father's business that makes him unique; it is that Jesus has a relationship with the Father that goes beyond anything humanity has seen before. John reaches for language to express this (sonship, agency), but in the end he is uncompromising. In one of the climaxes of Jesus' farewell, Jesus remarks to Philip, "Anyone who has seen me has seen the Father" (14:9). This unflinching affirmation reminds me of C. S. Lewis's words penned so long ago:

> I am trying here to prevent anyone saying the really foolish things that people often say about Him: "I am ready to accept Jesus as a great moral teacher, but I don't accept His claim to be God." That is the one thing we must not say. A man who was merely a man and said the sort of things Jesus said would not be a great moral teacher. He would either be a lunatic—on a level with the man who says he is a poached egg—or else he would be the Devil of Hell. You must make your choice. Either this man was, and is, the Son of God: or else a madman or something worse. You can shut Him up for a fool, you can spit at Him and kill Him as a demon; or you can fall at His feet and call Him Lord and God. But let us not come with any patronising nonsense about His being a great human teacher.[18]

But to make an absolute claim about Jesus is to invite precisely the thing that John 5 describes: persecution. A strong witness to Jesus as Lewis describes it *necessarily* offends. This is as true today as it has ever been. We live in a world of pluralism and tolerance that exerts enormous pressure on us to refine away the distinctives of our faith that might offend. We will hear: It is fine to make Jesus one way to God, but do not make him The Way. It is fine to affirm Jesus as one version of the truth, but make no claim that he is The Truth against which all other truths must be weighed.

In my academic community, the Jewish/Christian dialogue is predicated on the notion that together we will find religious commonalities that do not offend the other party. To speak otherwise is to "blaspheme" the process of interfaith discourse (cf. John 5:18). In the university marketplace of ideas, Christian religious belief is generally held suspect because most assume that lurking beneath the surface is an absolute argument for truth that wants to upend secular systems of thought and faith. They are right.

In a pluralistic society it is a truism that absolute claims to religious truth will lead to certain conflict. More precisely, the "higher" my claims for Christ—that is, the more I affirm his divinity, his exclusive relationship with God—the more separation and alienation I will feel. It is foolish to think I can have it otherwise. Jesus was judged as a blasphemer, the incriminating

---

18. C. S. Lewis, *Mere Christianity* (New York: MacMillan, 1952), 41.

designation of someone who trampled on pure religious truth. Jesus was crucified for the strength of his disclosure about himself. But the same is true of Jesus' followers as well as the church of John that cherished (and lived out) this chapter.

John 5 poses a terrible question for me: Am I willing to be labeled as a blasphemer to the religious canons of my day when my hour comes? Is my church equipped to do this? Are we ready to be judged and expelled, to experience social shame and public damning *in the name of religion* because we are holding on to an absolute faith in Jesus, the Son of God? As Hoskyns says, we will be charged with religious "egotism."[19]

Spiritual sickness. The final matter that must attend us concerns the spiritual sickness of Jesus' opponents. It is an uncomfortable theme to preach, but it is as necessary for a pastor to discuss it as it is for a physician to mention the prospects for cancer in a patient. It will not go away if we simply deny its existence. Every believer is susceptible to it. I suggest that men and women in religious leadership (like the opponents in John 5)—pastors, priests, teachers, Sunday School leaders, professors, elders, deacons—are uniquely vulnerable.

As noted above, it is incorrect simply to use 5:39–47 as a criticism of Judaism. First-century Judaism had countless people whose hearts were truly open to God. The same is true today. Jesus is describing the perversion of religion that can no longer hear God's voice. Jesus' inquisitors represent the "religious establishment" for whom the vigorous preservation of religious tradition counts more highly than the spontaneity and openness of faith. These people know their Scriptures and use them to defend all of the wrong things.

Karl Barth provides a harrowing description of this sickness in his famous 1919 commentary on Romans (see his remarks on Rom. 2). Barth thinks about people who live in a wilderness alongside a canal. The canal was there to bring them water and life, and it was with great effort and cost that the project was built for their place in time. Great sacrifices were made, and many died as the canal was cut through mountain and desert. But the great irony is that the canal has become dry, and while its walls still convey evidence of the coursing of water, there is nothing there that can give life to anyone. Nevertheless, the people continue to service it, to defend it, to name their children after its architects and engineers; but it is only an historic thing. A canal meant to convey something—water and life—now has become static, an end instead of a means. Something for the museum. People tell stories about it instead of drink from it. The older ones treasure the stories most; the younger ones have to be initiated deliberately; but each generation seems to lose a fraction of the

---

19. Hoskyns, *John*, 274.

true vision of the canal as time goes on. And no one has a memory of what water in the canal really looks like.

Barth's warning to the Swiss and German church following World War I is a word we should heed today. The possibility always exists that my life, my church, my tradition, my denomination, even my Bible will become relics of religious curiosity instead of living instruments of God. Men and women will be ordained, earn Ph.D.s, and launch magazines, publishing houses, colleges, and seminaries with solid evangelical commitments, and it will *all* be for nothing. Empty canals. There are specialists who can cite Scripture and verse, who can measure orthodoxy with exacting precision, who can identify the religious speck in someone's eye from a great distance, but in whom love for God does not exist (5:42).

On a national level I have seen evangelicals unsheathe their religious swords over arcane doctrinal matters ("But this is a slippery slope!" "But this is where liberalism begins!" "This is an agenda that must be exorcised!"). On a local level I have seen older church members viciously lash out because "the contemporary service" isn't to their liking or they perceive that their power and influence are diminishing. All of it, John 5 suggests, is empty religion, religion that seeks its own glory. In the end, it is religion that would condemn and crucify Jesus as a *religious* duty.

John 6:1-71

SOME TIME AFTER this, Jesus crossed to the far shore of the Sea of Galilee (that is, the Sea of Tiberias), ²and a great crowd of people followed him because they saw the miraculous signs he had performed on the sick. ³Then Jesus went up on a mountainside and sat down with his disciples. ⁴The Jewish Passover Feast was near.

⁵When Jesus looked up and saw a great crowd coming toward him, he said to Philip, "Where shall we buy bread for these people to eat?" ⁶He asked this only to test him, for he already had in mind what he was going to do.

⁷Philip answered him, "Eight months' wages would not buy enough bread for each one to have a bite!"

⁸Another of his disciples, Andrew, Simon Peter's brother, spoke up, ⁹"Here is a boy with five small barley loaves and two small fish, but how far will they go among so many?"

¹⁰Jesus said, "Have the people sit down." There was plenty of grass in that place, and the men sat down, about five thousand of them. ¹¹Jesus then took the loaves, gave thanks, and distributed to those who were seated as much as they wanted. He did the same with the fish.

¹²When they had all had enough to eat, he said to his disciples, "Gather the pieces that are left over. Let nothing be wasted." ¹³So they gathered them and filled twelve baskets with the pieces of the five barley loaves left over by those who had eaten.

¹⁴After the people saw the miraculous sign that Jesus did, they began to say, "Surely this is the Prophet who is to come into the world." ¹⁵Jesus, knowing that they intended to come and make him king by force, withdrew again to a mountain by himself.

¹⁶When evening came, his disciples went down to the lake, ¹⁷where they got into a boat and set off across the lake for Capernaum. By now it was dark, and Jesus had not yet joined them. ¹⁸A strong wind was blowing and the waters grew rough. ¹⁹When they had rowed three or three and a half miles, they saw Jesus approaching the boat, walking on the water; and they were terrified. ²⁰But he said to them, "It is I; don't be

afraid." ²¹Then they were willing to take him into the boat, and immediately the boat reached the shore where they were heading.

²²The next day the crowd that had stayed on the opposite shore of the lake realized that only one boat had been there, and that Jesus had not entered it with his disciples, but that they had gone away alone. ²³Then some boats from Tiberias landed near the place where the people had eaten the bread after the Lord had given thanks. ²⁴Once the crowd realized that neither Jesus nor his disciples were there, they got into the boats and went to Capernaum in search of Jesus.

²⁵When they found him on the other side of the lake, they asked him, "Rabbi, when did you get here?"

²⁶Jesus answered, "I tell you the truth, you are looking for me, not because you saw miraculous signs but because you ate the loaves and had your fill. ²⁷Do not work for food that spoils, but for food that endures to eternal life, which the Son of Man will give you. On him God the Father has placed his seal of approval."

²⁸Then they asked him, "What must we do to do the works God requires?"

²⁹Jesus answered, "The work of God is this: to believe in the one he has sent."

³⁰So they asked him, "What miraculous sign then will you give that we may see it and believe you? What will you do? ³¹Our forefathers ate the manna in the desert; as it is written: 'He gave them bread from heaven to eat.'"

³²Jesus said to them, "I tell you the truth, it is not Moses who has given you the bread from heaven, but it is my Father who gives you the true bread from heaven. ³³For the bread of God is he who comes down from heaven and gives life to the world."

³⁴"Sir," they said, "from now on give us this bread."

³⁵Then Jesus declared, "I am the bread of life. He who comes to me will never go hungry, and he who believes in me will never be thirsty. ³⁶But as I told you, you have seen me and still you do not believe. ³⁷All that the Father gives me will come to me, and whoever comes to me I will never drive away. ³⁸For I have come down from heaven not to do my will but to do the will of him who sent me. ³⁹And this is the will of him who sent me, that I shall lose none of all that he has given

me, but raise them up at the last day. ⁴⁰For my Father's will is that everyone who looks to the Son and believes in him shall have eternal life, and I will raise him up at the last day."

⁴¹At this the Jews began to grumble about him because he said, "I am the bread that came down from heaven." ⁴²They said, "Is this not Jesus, the son of Joseph, whose father and mother we know? How can he now say, 'I came down from heaven'?"

⁴³"Stop grumbling among yourselves," Jesus answered. ⁴⁴"No one can come to me unless the Father who sent me draws him, and I will raise him up at the last day. ⁴⁵It is written in the Prophets: 'They will all be taught by God.' Everyone who listens to the Father and learns from him comes to me. ⁴⁶No one has seen the Father except the one who is from God; only he has seen the Father. ⁴⁷I tell you the truth, he who believes has everlasting life. ⁴⁸I am the bread of life. ⁴⁹Your forefathers ate the manna in the desert, yet they died. ⁵⁰But here is the bread that comes down from heaven, which a man may eat and not die. ⁵¹I am the living bread that came down from heaven. If anyone eats of this bread, he will live forever. This bread is my flesh, which I will give for the life of the world."

⁵²Then the Jews began to argue sharply among themselves, "How can this man give us his flesh to eat?"

⁵³Jesus said to them, "I tell you the truth, unless you eat the flesh of the Son of Man and drink his blood, you have no life in you. ⁵⁴Whoever eats my flesh and drinks my blood has eternal life, and I will raise him up at the last day. ⁵⁵For my flesh is real food and my blood is real drink. ⁵⁶Whoever eats my flesh and drinks my blood remains in me, and I in him. ⁵⁷Just as the living Father sent me and I live because of the Father, so the one who feeds on me will live because of me. ⁵⁸This is the bread that came down from heaven. Your forefathers ate manna and died, but he who feeds on this bread will live forever." ⁵⁹He said this while teaching in the synagogue in Capernaum.

⁶⁰On hearing it, many of his disciples said, "This is a hard teaching. Who can accept it?"

⁶¹Aware that his disciples were grumbling about this, Jesus said to them, "Does this offend you? ⁶²What if you see the Son of Man ascend to where he was before! ⁶³The Spirit gives life; the flesh counts for nothing. The words I have spoken to

you are spirit and they are life. ⁶⁴Yet there are some of you who do not believe." For Jesus had known from the beginning which of them did not believe and who would betray him. ⁶⁵He went on to say, "This is why I told you that no one can come to me unless the Father has enabled him."

⁶⁶From this time many of his disciples turned back and no longer followed him.

⁶⁷"You do not want to leave too, do you?" Jesus asked the Twelve.

⁶⁸Simon Peter answered him, "Lord, to whom shall we go? You have the words of eternal life. ⁶⁹We believe and know that you are the Holy One of God."

⁷⁰Then Jesus replied, "Have I not chosen you, the Twelve? Yet one of you is a devil!" ⁷¹(He meant Judas, the son of Simon Iscariot, who, though one of the Twelve, was later to betray him.)

JOHN 6 CONTINUES the sequence of festivals introduced in chapter 5 (where I outlined the festival sequence in this Gospel). In this case the festival is Passover (6:3), and John expects that we will understand the many stories and themes associated with the feast (whose story can be found in Ex. 1–17).

The Feeding of the Five Thousand (6:1–15)

JESUS HAS RETURNED to Galilee from Jerusalem in the springtime, and the season of Passover is approaching.[1] This is John's second reference to Passover (2:13, 23), which gives us some sense that Jesus observed the requirement of Judaism to recognize and celebrate these feasts. The setting of the story is the Sea of Galilee, which John clarifies for those readers who may not know Israel, calling it also the Sea of Tiberias.[2] Tiberias was a new city on the west shore of the sea, founded in about A.D. 26 by Herod Antipas (the regional ruler of Galilee and son of Herod the Great).[3]

---

1. In ch. 5 I mentioned the difficulty of 6:1 in the sequence of events given in chs. 5–6 and showed why some scholars believe that chs. 5 and 6 should be reversed. If this is so, the events in Cana in ch. 4 are followed by these further events in Galilee

2. In the Old Testament this is the Sea of Kinnereth (Num. 34:11; Josh 12:3). Kinnereth means "harp" in Hebrew, since the lake is approximately the shape of the ancient instrument.

3 Josephus, *Ant* 18.36.

The Sea of Galilee lies in a vast inland basin 650 feet below sea level; it is thirteen miles long and six miles wide (from its widest point, near Magdala). It is fed by the Jordan River system that begins in the far north at Mount Hermon. The sea is surrounded by hills and mountains that reach an elevation of 2,000 feet in the west and over 4,000 feet in the east. At its northwest corner is a fertile plain called the Gennesaret (which occasionally also gives the lake its name, Luke 5:1). East-west valleys pull cool Mediterranean air from the west every afternoon, which collides with the heated desert air of the basin, creating strong winds and frequent storms that swirl over the sea at the base of the eastern cliffs. This is the background of the "storm" miracle of Jesus (6:16–21).

The sea was surrounded by numerous fishing villages, whose harbors have been discovered in the last twenty-five years as the water level has dropped. Villages such as Capernaum, Bethsaida, Magdala, Chorazin, Tiberias, and many others enjoyed a flourishing fishing industry, particularly in the northern half of the lake, where freshwater springs attract numerous fish (near modern Tabgha[4]). This explains Jesus' ministry in these villages, his use of fishing as an illustration, and his recruitment of fishermen as followers. But we must also keep in mind that this is a poor society. Galilee was a peasant agrarian society, where farmers were taxed heavily and frequently lost their land to a wealthier elite, who ruled either through the Herodian dynasty or who collected tax revenue for Rome. Jesus' interest in these people and his sympathy for their needs inspired widespread support for his message.

Jesus is in the region teaching his disciples (6:3; sitting down was common among rabbis, Mark 4:1; 9:35), but even though he is in the western hills, his reputation as a healer (already won in Cana, Capernaum, and elsewhere) brings great crowds to him. Jesus' compassion leads him to provide food— miraculous food—for all five thousand people. Through this miracle and the following discussion with the people, he hopes to unveil more of his identity, as he did in Jerusalem (ch. 5). After the feeding, Jesus puts his followers on a boat (rejoining them later at sea), and in Capernaum he engages the crowds and his disciples in an intense theological explanation of the meaning of the miraculous sign.

We need to pause and underscore some of the motifs that were well known in the Passover story, motifs that every Jew understood fully as shaping the background to Jesus' deeds in Galilee. Among Moses' many miracles in Egypt, two stand out as particularly remarkable: (1) his departure through the sea (Ex. 14), and (2) his miraculous feeding of the people with manna for forty years in the desert (Ex. 16:35; Ps. 78:24). These were potent symbols

---

4. An Arabic form of the Greek Heptapegon, which means "seven springs."

of God's preservation of his people: rescuing them from harm and sustaining them in a desert.

In John 6, Jesus appears at Passover, repeating many of these themes. The people are a multitude not unlike those in the desert; Jesus feeds them with "heavenly" bread; and following the feeding, when the disciples are on the sea, Jesus comes to them walking on water. Moreover, the question of Jesus in 6:5 ("Where shall we buy bread for these people to eat?") echoes that of Moses in Num. 11:13, "Where can I get meat for all these people?" In fact, Numbers 11 provides numerous parallels to the present story.[5]

Verses in Numbers 11	Content of Numbers 11	Parallel in John 6
11:1	people grumbling	6:41, 43
11:7–9	description of the manna	6:31
11:13	"Give us meat to eat"	6:51ff.
11:22	"Would they have enough if all the fish [Gk. *opsos* LXX] in the sea [Gk. *synago*] were caught for them?"	6:9 (*opsarion*, fish), 12 (*synago*, gather)

These parallels offer some intriguing conclusions. This Passover story of Jesus makes direct connections with prominent Old Testament motifs that tumble over one another in rapid succession. They provide a growing impression that in some fashion the hero of Passover, Moses, has now been superceded by Jesus, who not only provides "bread from heaven" but is himself "the bread of life" (6:35).

This feeding miracle must have had widespread fame and was locked into the collective memory of early Christianity as a key event in Jesus' life. The Synoptics record the feeding of the five thousand (Matt. 14:13–21; Mark 6:35–44; Luke 9:10–17) as well as another feeding of four thousand (Matt. 15:32–38; Mark 8:1–9). John's account is so close to that of Mark 6 that some believe John is using either Mark's story or the same source as Mark.[6] Nevertheless, John provides insights no other Gospel possesses. Jesus not only wants to provide food, but he wishes to test the developing faith of Philip (John 6:5; cf. 1:44; 12:21–22). Philip's response indicates that he does not yet grasp Jesus' miraculous ability. He exclaims that "eight months' wages" for a common laborer would not provide enough to feed that crowd (6:7). As in 4:31ff., food and incomprehension come together for the disciples.

5. Brown, *John*, 1:233.
6. C. K. Barrett, *John*, 271, believes that John is using elements from both Mark 6 and 8 in his story.

But Andrew, Peter's brother, locates a young boy (*paidarion*) who can possibly help.[7] This boy is carrying five barley loaves and two salted fish. Only John mentions that the bread is barley, which is a signal of the poverty of this crowd. Barley was considered the bread of the poor and this lad has five pieces of it—much like five round loaves of today's pita bread. Luke 11:5 implies that three such pieces might make a meal for one person. These details are important because in 2 Kings 4:42−44 is another Old Testament miracle, where Elisha feeds a hundred men with twenty barley loaves and is assisted by a *paidarion* or young servant. As with the twelve baskets left after Jesus' miracle,[8] Elisha had baskets of food left over.

What is happening here? These images and motifs from the Old Testament suggest that Jesus is fulfilling and recreating images from Israel's sacred past. He is a figure who harks back to great historic figures (Moses and Elisha) who knew God's power intimately. Unlike the Synoptic Gospels, Jesus alone distributes the bread and the fish (6:11), although we can assume with Mark that Jesus needed assistance with so many eager and hungry people (Mark 6:41). John's point is to underscore that Jesus is the provider of food, the source of life for these people (as thus far we have seen him be the source of rebirth, living water, and healing).

The crowd interprets Jesus' miracle as messianic. *He has just recreated the miracle of Moses!* To identify him as "the Prophet who is to come into the world" (6:14) is no doubt a reference to Deuteronomy 18:15−19, which prophesies that a prophet like Moses will some day return; this was viewed in Judaism as a messianic promise. The Jews at the Dead Sea community of Qumran expected a prophet to come in their messianic vision (1QS 9:10−11; 4QTest 5−8). For many, Moses had become the image of the ideal Messiah, unifying images of king and prophet.

Most disturbing is what happens next. Mark concludes the feeding miracle with a cryptic ending, "Immediately Jesus made his disciples get into the boat and go on ahead of him to Bethsaida, while he dismissed the crowd. After leaving them, he went up on a mountainside to pray" (Mark 6:45−46). The impression we get is that Jesus is fleeing the scene and urging his disciples to do the same. Bethsaida was in the political region of Philip (on the eastern side of the Jordan inlet to the sea), so he is removing them from the grasp of Herod Antipas.

It is not until we read John 6:15 that we get the full picture. "Jesus, knowing that they intended to come and make him king *by force*, withdrew again

---

7. The Gk. word *paidarion* can represent either a young boy (cf. Gen 37.30 LXX, where it describes Joseph at age seventeen) or a servant (cf. Ruth 2:5−6).

8 Some scholars wonder if this is John's first reference to the twelve apostles: one basket for each to collect scraps (cf. 6.67, 70)

to a mountain by himself" (italics added). This reflects a crass misunderstanding by the crowd. The verb used here (*harpazo*) means "to seize." In Matthew 11:12 it describes what violent people will do to the kingdom, in 12:29 how one must "tie up" a strong man before his property can be plundered, and in 13:19 how Satan will "snatch away" what is sown in a convert's heart. Here in John, the crowd wants to *force* Jesus to define his mission and work politically, to become a king who will rival the Herodians or the Romans. Jesus wants no part of such a kingship. He will not be tempted by "the kingdoms of this world" (Matt. 4:8).[9] Thus he must flee and must push his disciples out to sea in order to preserve himself and his work from the political ambitions of the crowd.

Jesus Walks on the Water (6:16–24)

WHILE JESUS LEAVES for the mountains of upper Galilee (near Mount Meron?), the disciples set sail, heading for the lake's northeast shore. After rowing three or four miles, a storm catches them in the middle of the lake. As noted above, such east/west winds are common on this sea, and fishermen watched for them carefully. Their fear of the rough water, however, was surpassed by their terror at seeing Jesus walking to them on the water (6:19). Again, we have another motif from the Old Testament—a water miracle—that reminds us of the moment when Moses led Israel through the water (Ex. 13–15). Psalm 77 describes this moment in Israel's life and explains that it was in fact God who led them.

> The waters saw you, O God,
> > the waters saw you and writhed;
> > the very depths were convulsed. . . .
> Your path led through the sea,
> > your way through the mighty waters,
> > though your footprints were not seen.
> You led your people like a flock
> > by the hand of Moses and Aaron. (Ps. 77:16, 19–20)

When Jesus arrives at the boat, he identifies himself with a term that was sure to evoke further images of the Exodus story: "It is I" (Gk. *ego eimi*). As in 4:26 (see comments), this may be a mere form of self-identification.[10] But it

---

9. Ridderbos, *John*, 216. This theme appears in the temptation account of Jesus. In Mark 6 the feeding miracle is attached to Herod Antipas's severe worry about the growing popularity of Jesus. With 5,000 men gathered in his region, he likely worried about political insurrection.

10. So Barrett, *John*, 281; cf. Mark 6:50.

may imply more. The verb to be (*eimi*) possesses no predicate here and thus reflects God's divine name given to Moses on Mount Sinai (Ex. 3:14).[11] Even Jesus' call not to fear echoes Moses' response on the mountain when he learned God's name and saw the burning bush: "At this, Moses hid his face, because he was afraid to look at God" (Ex. 3:6). Jesus approaches and even though he is now providing an awesome and overwhelming presentation of his powers, they need not fear.

While Mark says that Jesus stilled the storm when he entered the boat (Mark 6:51), John 6:21 almost implies that they barely were able to get him into the boat when they reached their destination. Many interpreters suspect that here we have yet another miracle as Jesus leads his disciples to their port. Barrett thinks that Psalm 107 may provide the background imagery for this scene. This psalm describes the terror of mariners caught in a storm being heaved by waves and suffering the disorienting confusion of fear and physical nausea.

> For he spoke and stirred up a tempest
>> that lifted high the waves.
> They mounted up to the heavens and went down to the depths;
>> in their peril their courage melted away.
> They reeled and staggered like drunken men;
>> they were at their wits' end.
> Then they cried out to the LORD in their trouble,
>> and he brought them out of their distress.
> He stilled the storm to a whisper;
>> the waves of the sea were hushed.
> They were glad when it grew calm,
>> and he guided them to their desired haven. (Ps. 107:25–30)

Again, Jesus is fulfilling the role of God—feeding, protecting, rescuing, and guiding his followers despite the natural calamities that surround them.

Questions surface the next day when the crowd discovers that although Jesus did not accompany the men on the boat, he nevertheless arrived with them at their destination (John 6:22–23). More boats arrive at the site of the feeding from nearby Tiberias, and when Jesus is not found, the people, charged with excitement, travel to Capernaum to see if he can be located.[12]

---

11. In the Hebrew Old Testament God's name (Yahweh) is based on the verb "to be." The LXX translated this as *ego eimi* ("I am") in Ex. 3.

12. The locations of these places can be imagined if one thinks of the Sea of Galilee like as a clock. The feeding miracle (according to tradition) occurred at "10:00 P.M." on the clock (on the northwest shore, Gennesaret, Mark 6:53; cf Matt. 14:34) Tiberius is located at "9:00 P.M." while Capernaum is on the north shore (about "11:00 P.M."). The crowd from Tiberius stops at the site of the miracle, then continues to Capernaum.

Their arrival in the village of Capernaum introduces Jesus' major "Bread of Life Discourse" (6:25–58), in which he defines carefully his relation to the miracle and its deeper meaning. In 6:22–34 he speaks directly to those who witnessed his miracle the day before. Then in Capernaum others who have not seen the miracle join the audience; they too ask for a sign (6:30–31). It is easier to understand the discourse if we see it in three parts (6:25–34, 35–50, 51–58) with a concluding episode that shows the difficulty Jesus' followers had with the teaching.

Bread from Heaven (6:25–34)

THE FULL FORCE of Jesus' sermon comes alive if we keep in mind certain details. Jesus is in the Capernaum synagogue (6:59), and it is Passover. At this time the Jewish community has been studying the Scriptures that pertain to the departure from Egypt (through the sea) and the flight into the desert. Following an initial question about how Jesus arrived here (6:25)—and it is not at all unlikely that we should see this as a two-level question, one material (he came by boat) and another spiritual (he came from heaven, 6:33; cf. 7:28)—discussion then turns to the central event, Jesus' feeding miracle and its meaning.

Some scholars have effectively shown how Jesus' words serve as a commentary on "he gave them bread from heaven to eat" (6:31). What was this Passover bread? Where did it really come from? Will it return? The quote from 6:31 is possibly from Psalm 78:24 (but has affinities with Ex. 16:4, 15). The complex of ideas involved a fascination with the manna miracle. Judaism understood that there was a storehouse or "treasury" of manna in heaven that had been opened to feed the people during the era of Moses. The Israelites had been fed with "bread from heaven." This treasury would be reopened with the coming of the Messiah: "The treasury of manna shall again descend from on high, and they will eat of it in those years" (2 Bar. 29:8). This would be a messianic second exodus, in which blessedness would rain down from on high.[13] An early Jewish commentary on Exodus 16:4 says, "As the first redeemer caused manna to descend . . . so will the *latter redeemer* cause manna to descend" (*Midrash Rabbah Eccles.* 1:9).

As Jesus teaches in the synagogue, he desires to lift his hearers above a material understanding of his miracle. He argues that their efforts should be focused not on the loaves and fish, but on the greater food that lasts forever (6:26–27). Initially it is not the gift that is important, but the Giver (Jesus, the Son of Man), on whom God has set his seal (6:27). This mark on Jesus

---

13. Numerous references to Jewish literature are found in Brown, *John*, 1:265; and Morris, *John*, 321n.88.

likely alludes to the Spirit, which we learned in 1:32ff. and 3:34 rests on Jesus powerfully, endorsing his ministry. To "work" as God would have it begins with believing in Jesus (6:28–29).

But the synagogue audience offers a challenge. If it is true that in the days of Moses the treasury of manna was opened, and if it is true that Jesus is making some messianic claim, then what sort of sign can Jesus give to validate his word? Can he reopen the treasury (6:30–31)? Is he claiming that he has recreated the messianic miracle of Moses?

Jesus' interpretation of the manna follows rabbinic lines perfectly. First, the true source of the manna was not Moses but God. *It is God who sends bread.* Furthermore, the manna story goes beyond mere bread; it is a spiritual metaphor for how God feeds us his word. Deuteronomy 8:3 may well have entered Jesus' debate: "[God] humbled you, causing you to hunger and then feeding you with manna, which neither you nor your fathers had known, to teach you that man does not live on bread alone but on every word that comes from the mouth of the LORD."[14]

If God is truly the source of true heavenly bread and if Jesus has been sent by God, the shocking turn in 6:33 should come as no surprise. The bread of God is *a person* ("he who comes down from heaven"), a person who gives life to the world. With a stroke of genius, Jesus has done precisely what he has done throughout the Gospel: He exploits some feature of Jewish belief and ritual and reinterprets it to refer to himself. He is the manna from God's treasury for which Israel has been waiting. *He has been sent by God as manna descended in the desert.*

The response of the crowd in 6:34 forms a climax in precisely the same way as did the response of the woman in 4:15. She had been looking for water and Jesus reinterpreted it as a spiritual gift. When Jesus described his gift, she remarked, "'Sir, give me this water so that I won't get thirsty and have to keep coming here to draw water.'" The crowd in Capernaum now say the same thing. "'Sir,' they said, 'from now on give us this bread.'" Bread and water—two potent symbols of God's wisdom and blessing in Judaism—are now distributed by Jesus, the true gift from God.

"I Am the Bread of Life" (6:35–50)

JESUS NOW PRESSES the logic of his case to the next level: "I am the bread" of Passover, the heavenly manna, the contents of God's divine treasury. Jesus is "living bread," as once before he offered "living water." This famous saying ("I am the bread of life") heads the list of what we call the "I-am sayings" in

---

14. The spiritualizing of manna was a common theme in Judaism (see Wisd. Sol. 16:20, 26; Neh. 9:20). Philo turns the manna into a metaphor for wisdom.

John. We have already noted those places so far where Jesus uses "I am" without a predicate, implying some absolute use that echoes God's name in Exodus. But there are seven places in the Gospel where Jesus provides a clear predicate noun to describe himself, and they take on features that sound like solemn pronouncements.

- I am the bread of life (6:35; cf. 41, 48, 51)
- I am the light of the world (8:12; cf. 18, 23)
- I am the gate for the sheep (10:7, 9)
- I am the good shepherd (10:11, 14)
- I am the resurrection and the life (11:25)
- I am the way and the truth and the life (14:6)
- I am the true vine (15:1, 5)

In each of these sayings Jesus is taking a motif from Judaism (often in the context of a miracle or major festival discourse) and reinterpreting it for himself. He now supplies that which Judaism sought in its activities and stories. As the people yearned for the heavenly bread and as the rabbis reinterpreted this bread to mean the wisdom or life-sustaining presence of God, so now Jesus is that precious gift (cf. 6:48, 51). As in chapter 4 Jesus' water banishes thirst, so now Jesus' bread banishes hunger (6:35b).

With remarkable candor, Jesus announces his disappointment with the crowd. This has happened before in Galilee (cf., e.g., 4:46–54). On Jesus' second visit to Capernaum he experiences the same thing. The crowd is either twisting Jesus' mission (6:15) or demanding more evidence (6:30), but they are not willing to come to Jesus and confess their thirst (6:35). In 6:36 Jesus says that their first step must be belief, but they refuse to take it. Such belief is not a leap into the darkness, for they have had the opportunity to see ("you have seen me"). Hence their decision is a willful refusal to act on what God has set before them.

Throughout 6:37–40 Jesus speaks confidently about the success of his work and the fulfillment of his mission. The confusion of the crowd in Capernaum and the refusal of some to believe will not frustrate him. He is not worried, for the success of his efforts depends entirely on the Father, who is at work in him. Indeed Jesus' entire mission is to conform his life to the will of the Father (6:38). It is God who has sent him (6:39) and who has gone before him, sovereignly calling people to come to him (6:37, 44). The darkness of the world is so severe that God alone must penetrate it in order to free people to see Jesus clearly. The people are in darkness; later we will see some of Jesus' disciples in the same state (6:59–66), including Judas Iscariot (6:70–71).

The determinism of these verses is sometimes softened by 6:37b: "Whoever comes to me I will never drive away." But it is a mistake to view this as a promise that points to Jesus' reception of anyone who comes to him confessing belief. The verb here is "cast out" (Gk. *ekballo*), and it refers regularly to something that is already "in" (see 2:15; 9:35; 12:31). Therefore the idea is not about Jesus' welcoming people, but about Jesus' keeping people whom the Father has given into his care. John 6:37b is about the protecting, nurturing capacity of Jesus. This interpretation is confirmed by 6:38: Jesus will not lose a single one of those who have come to him (cf. 10:1–18).

This theme of the sovereignty of God is important throughout the Fourth Gospel and will return at some length in 12:37–43. But it occurs regularly in incidental places, such as 10:29 ("My Father, who has given them to me, is greater than all; no one can snatch them out of my Father's hand") and Jesus' prayer in chapter 17 (vv. 2, 4, 6, 9, etc.). John affirms with ease both God's sovereign control and the responsibility of individuals. Note the balance found in 6:40: The Father's will is that everyone will look upon the Son, believe, and have life eternal. But the stress here is that God's will cannot be frustrated despite the darkness of the world, which cannot defeat him (1:5). Above all, those who have come into Jesus and believe will never be lost. The one exception is Judas Iscariot, whom Jesus did choose to be among the Twelve (see 6:70–71).

The sayings that began at 6:35 serve the larger program of the Bread of Life Discourse because they place in abstract what Jesus has been saying parabolically all along. God is the supplier of divine bread, and whoever eats of it will live forever. The identity of this "bread of life" is actually Jesus, just as the object of faith now should be Jesus (6:35, 40).

But this is the great turning point that the synagogue audience cannot bear.[15] It is one thing to say that we should have faith in God and be fed by him, but it is quite another for Jesus to say that he is the source of that meal, the object of believing vision. The "grumbling" described in 6:41, 43 (and 51) is reminiscent of the "murmuring" of the Israelites against Moses in the desert,[16] and it completes yet one more Passover theme. But this time there is a Johannine literary twist. The crowd misunderstands Jesus just as people and crowds have misunderstood him in most of the discourses since chapter 2. Unenlightened vision sees merely a man, the son of Jewish parents (6:42) coming from a commonplace Jewish family. That Jesus and his family were well known in Capernaum may even suggest that they were living there (2:12).

---

15. John refers to these people as "the Jews," and we are probably to understand that these are Jewish leaders in the synagogue. "The Jews" is a common rubric throughout the Gospel for this leadership, which eventually condemns and crucifies Jesus.

16. The Gk. word *gongyzo* is used throughout the desert story in the LXX (Ex. 17:3; Num. 11:1; 14:27, 29; etc.). In the Gk. text of John 6:41, grumbling is placed first in the sentence for emphasis.

After Jesus' firm exhortation to stop grumbling (6:43), it is interesting that he does not defend himself against their complaint ("How can he now say, 'I came down from heaven'?") but instead returns to the problem of their spiritual receptivity. The idea of Jesus' divine origin and descent (supplied to us as readers in ch. 1) is impossible for the crowd unless God in some fashion illumines them. John 6:44 parallels 6:37 (emphasizing God's sovereignty) but now is followed by an explanation of what this "drawing" means. John 6:45 echoes Isaiah 54:13 (or Jer. 31:33–34), where the prophet foresees a rebuilt Jerusalem (following the Exile) where intimacy with God will be regained. Jesus looks at this prophesy and sees its relevance. God must move the inner heart of a person before he or she can see the things of God. And this takes place on God's initiative (cf. 5:37).

From this point, Jesus repeats the major themes found in the introduction to the discourse: 6:48 matches 6:35; 6:49–50 match 6:31–33. All of this is reinforcement because in the final clause of 6:50 Jesus introduces a deeper nuance on the bread motif. This bread that reminds us of Moses, this bread that is now disclosed as Jesus Christ himself—this bread must be *consumed* (as, of course, any bread must be). Jesus stretches the bread analogy by announcing, "But here is the bread that comes down from heaven, which a man may eat and not die." When Jesus disclosed the identity as this heavenly bread (himself), it scandalized his audience (6:41). Now he will scandalize them again, for this bread must be eaten (6:50). This "eating" uses the Greek aorist tense: It is a singular event, a decision to believe and appropriate the gift of eternal life.

The Flesh and Blood of the Son of Man (6:51–58)

THE FIRST TWO thoughts of 6:51 repeat what we have already seen: Jesus is the living bread that came down (aorist tense), referring to his incarnation, and one must eat this bread (aorist tense), referring to the decisive moment when one believes. But it is in the third sentence of the verse where Jesus makes a pivotal statement, "This bread is my flesh, which I will give for the life of the world." When Jesus refers to his "flesh" (Gk. *sarx*), we are at once reminded of 1:14, where *sarx* was used to describe the comprehensive life of the Son.[17]

But *sarx* is a surprising, even graphic word that runs deeper than 1:14, and it will become the unifying thread of this portion of the discourse.[18] *Jesus is flesh offered in sacrifice.* The gift of this bread, this flesh, will come with his

---

17. For some scholars, flesh refers to the eucharistic language, "This is my body." While this imagery may be secondary, it does not truly become a part of John's literary imagery until 6:53ff.

18. Of John's twelve uses of *sarx*, seven occur here in 6:51–63.

death. The second half of this sentence tells us that this flesh will be given for the life of the world. Jesus is giving *himself*. The word "for" (Gk. *hyper*) occurs regularly in sacrificial contexts in this Gospel (John 10:11, 15; 11:51–52; 15:13; 17:19; 18:14) and means here that the gift of Jesus is nothing other than a sacrifice, a blood sacrifice, a temple sacrifice, that will benefit the world. This thought parallels 1:29, 36, where Jesus was described as the "Lamb of God," referring once more to a sacrificial victim.[19]

If Jesus' audience was amazed that he miraculously fed the multitudes, they were startled when he described himself as the heavenly bread from God. Now they are aghast as he makes the next step. Earthly bread—heavenly bread—Jesus as bread—Jesus as bread to eat—Jesus as sacrifice. It is all too much, and so their grumbling turns to argument (6:52).[20] Once again, the traditional form of the Johannine discourse comes into play and the crowd *misunderstands* what Jesus is saying: "How can this man give us his flesh to eat?" Of course, Jesus is not proposing religious cannibalism. Earthly symbols must be converted into spiritual truths. How, then, are we to understand this life-giving meal? What deeper spiritual truth needs to be uncovered?

Jesus' answer in 6:53–58 has proven difficult for almost every commentator. When Jesus refers to "eating my flesh and drinking my blood," he uses imagery that steps far beyond Passover. In fact, it is almost incomprehensible from within a Jewish theological framework. Some writers, such as Brown, follow a long line of patristic and medieval commentators (as well as many modern writers) who think that these words refer to the Eucharist. Carson believes that a secondary reference to the Eucharist is inevitable.[21]

Two issues compel this result: (1) Drinking blood was looked on as forbidden in Old Testament law (Gen. 9:4; Lev. 3:17; Deut. 12:23), and to eat someone's flesh refers to hostility toward them (Ps. 27:2; Zech. 11:9). The only Judeo-Christian setting where such words make good sense is the Christian Eucharist. (2) It is significant that John does *not* record the words of institution later in the Upper Room Discourse. When we look at his language here (beginning in 6:51), it echoes Luke's language at the supper: "This is my body given for you" (Luke 22:19).[22]

---

19. We need to emphasize this theme in the Gospel since many critical scholars have frequently argued that John does not view salvation as tied to Christ's sacrificial death. John 6:51c gives evidence that is almost impossible to refute.

20. The Gk. word *machomai*, translated "argue" in NIV, refers in Acts 7:26 to fighting (cf. 1 Tim. 2:24; Jas. 4:2).

21. Brown, *John*, 1:284–85; Carson, *John*, 295–99.

22. Brown even suggests that the section may be a displaced teaching that originated in the setting of the Lord's Supper but has been moved to chapter 6 for its thematic unity with Passover and heavenly bread.

But writers such as Morris are firm in their rejection of this interpretation. "This is the section of the discourse that is claimed most confidently to refer to the Holy Communion. The language of eating the flesh and drinking the blood is said to be explicable only, or at least naturally, in terms of the sacrament. But is this so? Surely not!"[23] Morris is quick to point out that the Johannine saying refers to eating flesh while the Synoptic (and Pauline) sayings always refer to "body" ("This is my body given for you").[24] For Morris, the language is symbolic of the assimilation of God's revelation and wisdom.

Certainly as Jesus speaks these words, their graphic and shocking character stun the audience. Regardless of their theological meaning, they are graphic, compelling, and confusing. This eating and drinking give eternal life (6:53, 54, 57, 58) and form the basis of the interior, intimate experience one may have with Christ (6:56). Nothing in Old Testament history compares, not even the experience with Moses and manna (6:59). Other religious bread does not address mortality; only this bread, this flesh and blood, this sacrifice, can give eternal life.

Some Disciples Fall Away (6:59–71)

IF JESUS' REVELATION that he himself was bread made the crowds grumble (6:41), this new revelation offends Jesus' own disciples (6:61).[25] For them this is not simply a difficult teaching (6:60) but is something unacceptable, a disclosure beyond their comprehension. It recalls the great turning point in the Synoptic Gospels, where Jesus' true identity is unveiled at Caesarea Philippi (Peter: "You are the Christ," Mark 8:29), immediately after which Jesus discloses his coming sacrificial death. In Mark, the Twelve can barely comprehend it. They try to talk Jesus out of it, and then they wrestle with their fate in light of it. The same is true here in John 6. This difficult teaching sifts Jesus' followers: Some of them fall away and refuse to follow him any longer (6:66) while one other disciple likely finds in this a catalyst for his own personal rebellion and betrayal (6:70–71).

These are the deeper things of Jesus, and only with divine help can anyone comprehend them. Therefore Jesus points to yet one more feature of this coming hour. If his death brings offense, what of his ascension (6:62)? If the first idea of death was scandalous, this further idea will be even harder. An earlier mention of "ascending" (3:13) used the metaphor of "lifting up" in a

---

23. Morris, *John*, 333.

24. Brown responds that since Jesus spoke in Aramaic and there is no word for "body" in Aramaic as we think of it, Jesus likely said "flesh."

25. John likely means here the wider group of followers, not simply the Twelve.

clever literary pun: The Son of Man will be "lifted up" to the cross, and the Son of Man will be "lifted up" into heaven. For John, Jesus' movement toward the cross (his glorification) is also his movement "heavenward," returning to the glory he enjoyed from the beginning (17:5). This *full* glorification is thus the complete picture of Jesus' death (cross, resurrection, ascension) that the disciples must now understand. Not only will he die, but he will return to heaven. It is through this complete work of Christ that life can be given to the world.

There is an important gift, however, a vital endowment, that will be a part of this life-giving work. The "flesh" that is of no avail in 6:63 recalls the literal flesh of 6:53 (cf. 3:6). Jesus clarifies that taking his words literally ("eat my flesh; drink my blood") is not the point. If eucharistic symbolism is at work, it is not a mechanical sacramentalism that Jesus has in mind, for the life-giving gift is the Holy Spirit. This thought parallels Jesus' message to Nicodemus and the woman of Samaria: What they need cannot be found in the material things of this world. They require new birth, living water. Moreover, Jesus is giving a signal that here in the course of his glorification, when the Son of Man ascends, a gift will be provided that will facilitate belief and give life. Jesus will say this explicitly at the Feast of Tabernacles (7:37–39) and later give its fulfillment in 20:22.

With some of his following now collapsing, Jesus turns to the Twelve to inquire if they wish to depart as well (6:67). This is clearly a turning point for Jesus. The mystery of his person and work has now been laid out in full. For Peter this difficult exchange provides an opportunity to give a courageous confession: "Lord, to whom shall we go? You have the words of life. We believe and know that you are the Holy One of God." In the Synoptics, this title "Holy One" appears only among demons (Mark 1:24; Luke 4:34). But it is a potent and unusual title—one used throughout the Old Testament (thirty times in Isaiah) for God ("the Holy One of Israel"), who defends his people and redeems them (Isa. 41:14; 43:14–15).

Jesus recognizes the confession not simply as a tribute to Peter's courage but also as evidence of God's supernatural movement in his life (cf. Matt. 16:17, "Blessed are you, Simon son of Jonah, for this was not revealed to you by man, but by my Father in heaven"). These deeper things cannot be embraced by anyone, only by those whom God has enabled (John 6:65) and called (6:70). This is a profound and important thought for John, and one we will meet again and again in his Gospel. God's entry into the world in Christ is not the only act of grace; God must also empower men and women to see it and embrace it. Humanity cannot defeat the darkness that holds it in its grip; only God possesses this sort of power.

UNLIKE MANY COMMENTATORS, I have chosen to keep this lengthy chapter unified because of the many connecting themes that knit together its paragraphs. John has written this chapter (and the others) with a literary mastery that should not be missed. To read, for instance, the feeding of the five thousand in isolation from the closing theological debate in Capernaum is to miss the sweeping interpretation Jesus gives to the miracle. Or to forget that the entire chapter is included under John's heading of "Passover" is to miss its many nuances to Passover and its many symbols embedded in the story, as I have pointed out above.

Encouragement and warning. Throughout the story, we are presented with the idea of sustenance, material and spiritual. As with the other miracle stories, the discussion moves from the obvious (bread on a hillside), to the symbolic ("I am the bread of life!"), to the spiritually mystical ("You must eat my flesh and drink my blood!"). Each step of the way misunderstanding and incomprehension trail the discussions. The attitude of the crowds depicts the passion that fuels such a quest for food—whether common or spiritual food—and how important it is to see what it means to be "fed by God." But once the discovery is made, once the crowds determine that Jesus is a supplier of this food, once they grasp the potential and power of religion when it is in their hands, they move to exploit it to their own ends. They come to "make him king by force."

Thus, we are encouraged and warned simultaneously. We are encouraged to come and feed at the meal served by Jesus, to learn ultimately that the bread he offers is more than bread; it is life itself hidden in his sacrificed life. But we are also warned, because misapprehension and confusion can overtake us and we may unwittingly find ourselves grasping after religious things (bread, a religious king, sacraments) that in themselves are misdirected. As 6:63 says it, "The flesh counts for nothing." The chapter begins with Jesus testing his disciples about food: Would they understand the implications of his presence here, his capacities, his goals? The passage then ends with some disciples grumbling in offense, others falling away, and Judas making plans for betrayal. There is a deep revelation of Christ at work here that divides the audience.

A glimpse of God. The first elementary episodes of revelation should be seen as twin pictures of what it means to obtain a glimpse of God and not understand it. The feeding miracle (6:1–15) can be viewed as a commonplace act of compassion by Jesus—and indeed it was. The crowds are hungry, they need food, and as we have seen in other times, Jesus responds to people's needs. This alone is a subject worthy of our attention in the twenty-first century.

But John wants to show us something more than the mere satisfaction of hunger. He wants us to look beyond the obvious fulfillment of Passover motifs that the feeding supplies. The climax of the story is unsettling and perverse: The crowd fits Jesus into their religious categories ("This is the prophet!") and decide that *they* can control, promote, and fashion something religiously constructive out of this event. They want Jesus for their own ends; they want to pursue a political agenda (revolution? social upheaval? dissent?), and Jesus must flee. In the end the picture is penetratingly clear: They have no clue what they have just witnessed. In their arrogance they wish to exploit it like a marketing company exploits a new household invention.

The second elementary episode (6:16–21) takes us to the lake, where we once again see Jesus' compassion, this time for his disciples. They are working against the waves, trying to cross the lake as Jesus had ordered. Jesus comes to help, and once again we see his heartfelt concern for his friends. But John wants to take us further again. Like the crowd, the disciples do not understand what they see. But to their credit, they are afraid. They know an epiphany when they see it even though they cannot comprehend it completely. It is beyond their grasp and all they can do is remain with Jesus, hoping to gain clearer sight as things progress.

Together these two episodes provide an intriguing bridge to bring this chapter to us today. They provoke questions about religious apprehension and the wrong use of spiritual things. They also describe how disciples should act when their ignorance is no different than that of the crowd, and how disciples should act with appropriate reverence when they see divine things at work. To their credit, the crowd goes in pursuit of Jesus, and it seems that in the end they give up their agenda of the previous day and now ask for the same thing the Samaritan woman found herself requesting: nourishment, spiritual nourishment (6:34). Have they been humbled? Have they redefined what they want from Jesus?

The subsequent Capernaum discourse (6:22–59) supplies one of the most open and candid discussions by Jesus concerning his identity and mission. Passover images tumble over one another again as Jesus increases the complexity and difficulty of ideas: He is the bread of life that descends, bread that must be consumed, bread that will be given in sacrificed flesh. The meaning of this leaves everyone in shock. Religious questions (6:25) turn to grumbling (6:41), which in turn leads to sharp argument (6:52). In the end even his closest followers admit that the sayings are hard (6:60), and soon some begin falling away in disbelief. Mixed into these responses are assurances from Jesus that only God can supply the sort of faith and vision that will enable a person to grasp such things. "Everyone who listens to the Father and learns from him comes to me" (6:45). Jesus knows who will believe (6:64) and knows as well that it is God who is sovereignly at work, opening hearts and eyes to see these deeper things.

Surely John wants us to reflect on our human capacity for comprehending the true meaning of what has happened when God was at work in Christ. These things are beyond our reach, and at best we are called to do no less than Peter: stand where there is life despite its utter incomprehensibility. "To whom shall we go?" he asks (6:68). Eternal life can be found nowhere else but here in Jesus.

This is yet another theme to be brought into our century. If it is God who alone gives divine insight into the meaning of his Son ("No one can come to me unless the Father has enabled him," 6:65), what does this mean for the average Christian experience? If distortion and fear accompany our best efforts to understand the deeper things of God, what is the human role in evangelism or teaching in the mission of the church? If God unlocks the human heart, how do I participate, how do I encourage this divine work? John raises tantalizing questions in this story, but does not provide obvious answers.

Fed by God. To summarize, the unifying subject of the chapter turns on one idea: *What does it mean to be fed by God?* We are reminded of material feedings (Jesus with the five thousand, Moses with his multitudes at Passover) but then exhorted that these feedings have nothing to do with the deeper things of life. The Israelites still died in the desert; Jesus' hillside gathering will still go hungry the next day. The same is true today. The pursuit of bread—spiritual or otherwise—is a universal compulsion of human civilization. It often takes wrong turns. But for those who are most intuitive, who sense the deeper realities of life and possess a more profound vision, they understand that this pursuit must engage religious interests. The human spirit cannot be denied in the quest for life, for meaningful life today.

Thus the question remains: How am I fed by God? How can I find bread that lasts forever? How can I discover transcendence or spiritual nurture? How can I discover God in a way that will not diminish before my next meal? The obvious answer is that we should find this in Jesus. But it is not so easy. People twist and distort religion, manipulating it to their own ends. Religious forms are developed and promoted (sacramental forms?); still, these do not reach the desired goal. Even Christians reach a point of exhaustion when the traditional forms of religious experience become tired.

In the end, being fed by God is beyond our natural comprehension. It is utterly mysterious and will evoke feelings of fear and confusion and in some cases anger. These are divine things, heavenly realities that lie beyond our abilities. We should not complain or grumble about them. It is God alone who can supply divine insight. Our task is simply to stand and receive, to engage, to be open to the work of the Spirit as he permits us glimpses into realities too deep for us.

Therefore we watch. For some, this critique of religion and engagement of everything that religion was meant to be are too much to bear. For some—particularly the purveyors of religious traditions—this demolition and rebuilding are unacceptable. Some flee. Others argue. Still others join Judas and plot to destroy that which would threaten them.

Consequently the chief themes I need to take from this text could be organized around four headings: (1) The pursuit of bread: What are the perceived needs of society and the attempts to satisfy hunger? (2) The religious pursuit of bread: How is religion employed in this pursuit? How have the things of Jesus been distorted in this quest? (3) Being fed by God: What does God desire for us? Are religious forms such as the Eucharist impediments to a deeper experience with him? What is God's role in the pursuit of bread? (4) Rebellion: What are the predictable reactions of many who find this revelation intolerable? What sinful reflexes are at work among those who grumble and work to stop God's work to feed his people?

 WHEN BRENDA ENTERED my office, I had no idea that she would stay for an hour and bare her soul. Before she was born, her father was converted in part through the writings of Francis Schafer. He went to Dallas Seminary in the 1970s but found himself to be at odds with the school because midway through his M.Div. program he began speaking in tongues.[26] He was permitted to graduate only if he did not make this experience well known. The family migrated to charismatic communities and finally settled in the Assemblies of God.

Brenda was nurtured on evangelistic sermons and an open display of charismatic gifts. But the family also missed the rigor of Schafer's intellectualism that had been reinforced at Dallas. They migrated again back into the mainstream of evangelicalism and reached a spiritual cul-de-sac. Cavalier criticisms of their secret charismatic spiritual history were heard regularly; evangelistic hymns and hard-hitting, soul-winning sermons replaced prophesy and healings. Despair and cynicism settled over the family like a damp fog. Today her father rarely goes to church.

Brenda wept when she told me that now, as a young woman, all of it seemed hollow to her: the sermons, the Bible, the Lord's Supper—all of it. Even speaking in tongues (which she did less and less) seemed artificial. She desired to be

---

26. The rigidity of seminaries (Dallas and many others) to the charismatic renewal of the 1970s is well known. Today the spiritual climate and openness in these places is completely different.

fed by God, but her deepest fear was that nothing could reach her heart, nothing could penetrate her cynicism. *She had seen it all.* And she had watched Christian leaders with bravado use their own style of religion to defeat their competitors in the Christian marketplace of ideas. She had watched the healers, the revival preachers, the moral majority, and almost every other religious configuration. *Now she was tired.* She simply wanted to be with God, to find out if there was any way to be fed once more, to see if there was any new dance that she had not already seen. She was hungry, but had reached that level of despair in which a person doubts the existence of food.

Two weeks later, Brenda entered a nearby Catholic monastery as a temporary guest. She returned radiant and transformed.

The pursuit of bread. The needs of the crowd in Galilee were obvious. In some way they represent the needs of humanity from the beginning of time. We need the things necessary for survival ("Give us this day our *daily bread*"). And if those needs go unmet, if hunger goes ignored, then the pursuit of any higher virtue (religious or otherwise) collapses. This is why Jesus rightly makes sure that the crowd is fed. It is ethically responsible to care for the body before nurturing the soul.

This is the outlook that fuels ministries such as Venture Middle East.[27] This ministry is a behind-the-scenes evangelical work that parallels the efforts of giants such as World Vision. Its president, Leonard Rodgers, carries aid for the physical needs of people into areas that are dangerous, where the gospel has barely penetrated and where World Vision with its high profile cannot enter.

As the founder of Youth For Christ in Lebanon, Len went on to direct the ministries for World Vision in the Middle East. But then he decided to take a plunge into ministry "behind the lines." He is building wheelchair factories today on the doorstep of Afghanistan in Muslim countries that have overwhelming needs. Muslim amputees from land mines build chairs and use them and, in their joy, hear that Len follows Jesus. His "family-to-family" support program links American families with poverty-stricken Christian families in Arab countries where persecution and devastation are commonplace. Funneling money through Arab pastors, Venture Middle East has helped countless people. In the aftermath of the Gulf War, he has carried millions of dollars of medical supplies by truck to the people of Iraq, impoverished by a United Nations embargo.[28] This is bread. This is the Galilean

27. Venture Middle East is located at P.O. Box 15313, Seattle, Washington, 98115–0313. Phone: 1–800–421–2159. On the internet, they can be visited at http://logos.ghn.org/vme.

28. At the time of this writing (1999) the United Nations estimates that 6,500 children are dying monthly in Iraq because of starvation from the United Nations imposed embargo. Fully 27 percent of the children of southern Iraq are malnourished. Since the *end* of the Gulf War, the United Nations estimates that 500,000 children have died.

bread distributed by Jesus, and it calls for the church to pursue similar ministries of care and relief.

If bread is what we need to survive in order to feel well and wholesome, the pursuit of bread becomes complicated when people determine that their needs include things unnecessary for true life. It would be as if the crowd asked Jesus for an ice cream break. Would he serve this too? Christians in the West are familiar with this theme, but we have difficulty diagnosing it in ourselves. Living in a consumer society fueled by sophisticated advertising and relative affluence, we have been given the means and the motivation to pursue countless forms of bread. If I simply possess this car or that cologne, my self-image will be healed and my sense of safety and well-being renewed. Once we possess these things, of course, their seductive appeal evaporates, and we move on to new targets of gratification.

Christians are not exempt from the seductions of the material culture around us. We define the "bread" we need with lives of remarkable indulgence. One Christian minister came to head a significant evangelical ministry recently and enjoyed a salary package that included a $125,000 annual paycheck, a custom-built home, a luxury car, a private parking space, and a renovated office suite. It was breathtaking. But remarkably—this is the real point—few in the ministry questioned it because the notion of "comfort and success" had permeated the corporate culture of the organization. The quest for bread had become twisted beyond recognition.

This explains the crowd's initial zeal when Jesus supplies such bread miraculously. On one level, it was the right thing to feed them. But on another level it is as if the Sony Corporation had pulled up to the local high school and began distributing an endless supply of stereo equipment. The men in suits would be awarded messianic status. And in a short length of time, the scene might become ugly. The abundance of the miracle overwhelmed everybody.

The religious pursuit of bread. But more thoughtful persons down through the ages have always argued that the material things of life do not provide the secret to true happiness. Even among those people who embrace an utterly pagan worldview, deep spiritual instincts lead them to explore everything from meditation to philosophy. For the average person, the pursuit of religion is an inevitable dimension of their pursuit of life.

The crowd in Galilee put a religious spin on the miracle of Jesus: "This is the prophet who is to come into the world." When they relocated him on shore at Capernaum, they peppered him with questions about their own religious heritage with Moses and how Jesus fit in. In the end the people wanted to see a religious figure here, not simply a supplier of bread.

When the human instinct for religion is unleashed, it rarely reaches its true goal. One evening recently I returned home from watching the film *Seven Years in Tibet* (starring Brad Pitt), only to find a full review of the movie announced on the cover of *Time*. The magazine's interest was not simply in this movie, but in the increasing interest in Buddhism in America. Writers cleverly demonstrated how Buddhist language has been spilling into the American vernacular and how New Age interests are now intersecting with ancient Asian religious systems. The message was clear: Americans are as religious as ever, and now they are seeking "religious bread" wherever they can find it, particularly in Asia.

There is another way we can look at the crowd's attempt to "take Jesus by force" (6:15). They come to kidnap him, to promote him as a hero, to make him a *religious figure* in their own image and serve their agenda. When Christians pursue "spiritual bread," they likewise are tempted to make Jesus serve their religious agenda. When this happens, Jesus is "taken by force" in the church. He is exploited and manipulated, forged into a "poster boy" for this campaign or that venture. In the present story, the agenda is purely political: The people want a king and Jesus will do just fine. If this prophet can overthrow Rome's domination of Israel, with the crowd's help Jesus just may be successful.

Conservatives have often criticized the violent use of Jesus among more liberal Christians who wish to baptize their politics with his image. Conservatives point to forms of "liberation theology" that work to emancipate women or minorities or the poor. These social concerns are good and legitimate, but as this work progresses, it seems as if the emphases of Jesus fall to the background and political agendas of social justice take center stage.

In some cases, the complaint is accurate. I was flying home recently from a conference accompanied by a theology professor from the University of Chicago. He was deeply involved in the National Council of Churches and the World Council of Churches. Over two hours he explained to me the history of these two organizations and how they built an ecumenical consensus by eliminating potentially divisive doctrinal statements. In the end, all that remained in these groups was a commitment to social justice without any undergirding commitment to uniquely Christian theology. Jesus' name remained on the flag, but his words were strictly edited.

But conservatives have likewise tried to take Jesus by force. Since the 1970s evangelicals have discovered a new political consciousness. To their delight, they have power and respect in arenas where once they were excluded. Ralph Reed, for instance, has given stature to evangelicals in Washington unlike few in the past. We are now a powerful *electoral* force. But evangelicals have taken "Jesus by force" as well. We identify social platforms, national security interests, and moral crusades, and we baptize them in the name of Jesus. Many of us have difficulty being critical of these agendas since for the most part we agree with them. Isn't Jesus against socialism? Doesn't he abhor Saddam Hussein? Wouldn't Jesus endorse free market capitalism?[29] Would he not take a hard line against Islam? Isn't he against the gay lobby? Wouldn't he march on Washington against abortion?

Before we know it, we are carrying a flag with a cross, singing crusader songs, and laying siege to secular Jerusalems throughout our society. One important ministry in Colorado Springs understands the sort of power that can be harnessed when 3.5 million religious radio listeners suddenly are told to send letters to Congress. Washington insiders remark that in a matter of days the capitol is flooded with mail. Nervous leaders find themselves consulting Christians in Colorado to learn Jesus' view on sex ethics or the family or religious freedom. That's power. Raw power—particularly when the budget of this organization exceeds that of the largest Protestant denomination in the United States (the Southern Baptist Church).

To test the union of religion and politics among evangelicals, one simply has to contradict a thoroughly endorsed theme. When a magazine like *Sojourners* or a speaker like Tony Compolo dares to challenge the assured political conclusions of the church, it is interesting to see what happens. The merits of the case are not debated; rather, one's fidelity to Jesus is placed in question because Jesus supports the item under debate.

I had an interesting experience with this type of mentality in the early 1990s. I wrote a book entitled *Who Are God's People in the Middle East? What Christians Are Not Being Told About Israel and the Palestinians.*[30] In it I openly questioned whether the church was right in giving unquestioned political support to Israel, given Israel's notorious record of human rights abuses and theft of Palestinian land. Jews who wrote to me helpfully debated the shortcomings of my arguments. But evangelicals who wrote (and there were many) instead questioned how someone could claim to follow Jesus, believe in the Bible, teach at Wheaton College, and still hold these views. Jesus was on the side of Israel, not the Palestinians. Thus, in their eyes, this set me against Jesus, for of course he is politically a hawk when it comes to Middle East politics.[31]

---

29. A major cathedral in Los Angeles is today building a monument and museum to "the Christian heroes of Capitalism." Future archaeologists will some day uncover it and describe it as the perfect symbol of the American economic secularization of religion.

30. Grand Rapids: Zondervan, 1993.

31. A sustained argument for this type of politicized Christian Zionism among evangelicals can be found in H. W. House, ed., *Israel, the Land and the People An Evangelical Affirmation of God's Promises* (Grand Rapids: Kregel, 1998). An academic critique can be found in P. W. L. Walker, *Jesus and the Holy City: New Testament Perspectives on Jerusalem* (Grand Rapids: Eerdmans, 1996).

When Jesus is taken by force to serve as a pawn in our religiously sanctioned political program, we are no different than the crowds in Galilee.

Being fed by God. I need to come back to Brenda and her quest for God. She was tired of Christian politics and revivals and was cynical of religious forms that no longer captured her imagination. She had witnessed people taking Jesus by force. She was identifying hollow façades and was worried that there was no mystery, no presence, no possibility of discovering anything beyond her own being. Even the Bible had lost its power. God's voice had been silenced by religion.

When Brenda approached the monastery, she was apprehensive. She had called ahead and they said there was room; but she had never seen a nun up close, nor had she genuinely penetrated this foreign Catholic world. The grounds were beautiful, large, and private, with many places for contemplation. The buildings were old but good. A sister answered her knock at the door, but she didn't wear the expected black and white habit. It was her face that said everything. Brenda was among people who knew God, who knew what she needed, and who knew how to nurture her. She was taken to her simple room and told she could stay "as long as you need to." She asked about costs and was told no money was required.

In the silence and simplicity and beauty of that place, Brenda's soul was restored. Fellow pilgrims (priests and sisters) who had walked the road of faith far longer than Brenda spoke to her gently about their discoveries of knowing God. And they loved her. The clutter of her religious history began to dissipate. She began to hear God's voice speaking words of affection and assurance. She realized how many religious habits she had acquired when she only needed a pure and pristine walk with Jesus. He was the bread of life. Her earlier life was filled to the brim with religious bread in abundance, but there had been little life in it.

All Christian traditions, Protestant as well as Catholic, provide forms and traditions that are designed to feed us, to nurture us. Refugees from Catholic parishes have appeared on many Protestant doorsteps, just as Brenda entered the monastery. Being fed by God is so simple that in a world congested with busyness, it has become hard to understand. Like the pursuit of joy, the more we run after it with strategies and plans, the more it seems to flee. It is not gained by ministry accomplishments, righteous efforts, or the intellectual mastery of the Bible. Being fed by God requires a conversion of thinking, a discovery that God is eager to give life and renewal to anyone who can listen in simplicity and piety.

I think, for instance, of the life of Cardinal Joseph Bernardin of Chicago, who died November 14, 1996. His book, *The Gift of Peace*, completed just before his death, is a testimony to the simplicity of a life lived in utter dependence on

God. "Giving up and trust" were the themes of his life, and in his story there is a profound renunciation of things superficially religious and an embrace of everything divine.[32] When he died, Christians throughout Chicago (Catholic and Protestant) knew that a great life was passing.

John does not provide simplistic answers to the question of the divine life. But he does make one comment. While religious forms might be useful, they dare not replace the immediacy of a personal relationship with Jesus Christ. Most commentators agree that John is at least making a veiled allusion to the sacrament of the Lord's Supper in chapter 6. Yet curiously, his treatment of it is similar to his veiled allusion to baptism in chapter 3, which he makes and then moves on, providing a critique that is anchored in an understanding of the Spirit. In John 3 references to "birth by water" drop away, and we learn that it is only the Spirit that gives renewal. In John 6, Jesus finally remarks that "the Spirit gives life; the flesh counts for nothing" (6:63). The sacrament itself is simply a vehicle to communicate divine life to the worshiper. It is used rightly when Christ is identified and the Spirit is experienced in all his glory and power.

The consumption of Jesus described so explicitly in 6:52—58 springs from the eucharistic language of the church (which Jesus is anticipating), and now it becomes a metaphor for the interior life one should have with Christ. This is truly mystical spirituality, which echoes what we heard in chapter 4 concerning worship: Neither Jerusalem nor Samaria can provide the appropriate form of worship. This worship is to be done in Spirit and truth. Again, John is challenging religious forms and replacing them with an immediacy of spiritual experience mediated through the Holy Spirit. For John, the spiritual life is not simply a life of confession and obedience, but a life of *encounter.*

Does this mean that religious forms should be discarded? Some interpreters have seen John as strictly antisacramental, going so far as even to exclude any account of the Lord's Supper in the Upper Room. Some pastors want to promote this sort of spirituality, creating worship and experience untethered to religious forms and rituals. One major church in California even removed the Lord's Supper from worship altogether so that people would not become confused or dependent on it.[33] But this sort of response finds no sympathy from John. The apostle provides a critique of sacramental worship that has lost any connection with the life-giving Lord present in

---

32. J. Bernardin, *The Gift of Peace* (New York: Doubleday, 1998); cf. E. Kennedy, *My Brother Joseph: The Spirit of a Cardinal and the Story of a Friendship* (New York: St. Martin's Press, 1997).

33. At this church in Riverside, California, the Lord's Supper could be had in a private room following the worship service but was an entirely optional experience for the regular attender. Within months the congregation objected so strenuously that the pastor was compelled to return the sacrament to the regular worship service.

the church through the Spirit. I believe he would have us use the sacraments correctly so that they become true vehicles of encounter and not fossilized instruments of religiosity.

Rebellion. I am naive if I think that the confusion, anger, and outrage of the disciples at the end of the chapter is something unique to them, as if they have some deficit, some blindness, or some spiritual malady that makes them incapable of embracing the profundity of Jesus' revelation. Hearts that are religiously inclined can become angry when the formulas change, when things don't show up as predicted, when conventions become upset. It is a religious rebellion that in some fashion disguises itself as piety, as light—but in the end is darkness nonetheless. I assume that as a follower of Christ I bear pure light into a world of darkness. But the truth is that Christ's brilliance makes every light (even my own) appear as darkness.

Christ may have things to say that we cannot accept. We may hear ourselves saying, "This is a hard teaching. Who can accept it?" (6:60). We have built our religious structures and justified them with verses from the Bible. We have forged coalitions of people like us who are sensible, biblical, and theologically orthodox. We have a history to protect, an agenda to promote, a vision to foster, and any who impede our progress—no, God's progress—deserve our militancy.[34]

I must forever keep in mind that Judas Iscariot's traitorous act is born when Jesus reveals the deeper things about himself. Was this man not a coworker with Jesus for three years? Did Jesus not choose each of the Twelve, including Judas (6:70)? Judas worked miracles in Galilee and preached for Jesus. He evangelized villages and brought converts into the fold. Even his fellow apostles did not detect anything unusual in him (13:29). He was *not* chosen by Jesus simply so that he would play the role of betrayer. Something happened, some overwhelming despair engulfed him, some virus-strength cynicism settled in his heart—and he decided to stand against the man in whom he believed. In the end, it was a decision he regretted profoundly (Matt. 27:5). Perhaps he liked the way things were in Galilee, and when they arrived in Jerusalem and Jesus disclosed his identity as the Messiah and Son with abandon, he simply couldn't bear it. The Jesus Movement, he concluded, might do better without Jesus.

Do the grumbling disciples and the fiercely rebellious Judases live today in the ranks of the church? Arming ourselves against God, we may not want to hear any new thing Jesus may have for us.

I realize that for some readers, my story of a young evangelical woman spiritually rescued in a Catholic monastery will offend. Does God *really* work

---

34. For an interesting defense of evangelical militancy, see M. Olasky, "21st-century Amish: Shall We Go Gently into the Cultural Night?" *World* (Nov. 22, 1997), 30.

through the Catholic Church?[35] When Christian leadership worked to support the civil rights of blacks in America in the 1960s, some of us grumbled. Does God speak for political activism? When the charismatic renewal was born in the 1970s, many of us were angry. Can this be God's inspiration? When Christians spoke up for justice in South Africa and Palestine in the 1980s, many of us complained. It can be as small as introducing a contemporary worship service at church and as large as promoting women in ministry. But when God tries to lead us into things outside our zone of comfort, we bathe our objections in religious language and rebel.[36]

Even the line of thought in these paragraphs will inspire frustration. When *evangelicals* rebel, they are defending what is true, aren't they? But this is just the point. Each of us—evangelicals included—produce our own set of religious assumptions and defend them in the name of God. We become inquisitors and crusaders, pursuing what we think is a divine work. But Jesus and his mission are more complex and profound than any Christian tradition. With Peter we must always be willing to relinquish our position, to hold our assumptions loosely, and to say in faith, "Lord, to whom shall we go? You have the words of eternal life" (6:68).

---

35. A recent coalition called "Evangelicals and Catholics Together" receives regular criticism from evangelical ranks. See the remarks of Timothy George (dean, Beeson Divinity School), "Evangelicals and Catholics Together: A New Initiative," *Christianity Today* (Dec. 8, 1997).

36. In 1997 I wrote an article for *Christianity Today*, appealing to the evangelical church that we reclaim the noncognitive simplicity and awe of worship ("Are Evangelicals Missing God at Church?" *Christianity Today* [Oct. 6, 1997], 20–27). Letters to the editor ran for two subsequent issues; letters to my office seemed to go on forever. To challenge the traditional evangelical structures of worship for some seemed outrageous.

John 7:1–52

‌❧

A FTER THIS, JESUS went around in Galilee, purposely staying away from Judea because the Jews there were waiting
to take his life. ²But when the Jewish Feast of Tabernacles was near, ³Jesus' brothers said to him, "You ought to leave
here and go to Judea, so that your disciples may see the miracles
you do. ⁴No one who wants to become a public figure acts in
secret. Since you are doing these things, show yourself to the
world." ⁵For even his own brothers did not believe in him.

⁶Therefore Jesus told them, "The right time for me has not
yet come; for you any time is right. ⁷The world cannot hate
you, but it hates me because I testify that what it does is evil.
⁸You go to the Feast. I am not yet going up to this Feast,
because for me the right time has not yet come." ⁹Having said
this, he stayed in Galilee.

¹⁰However, after his brothers had left for the Feast, he
went also, not publicly, but in secret. ¹¹Now at the Feast the
Jews were watching for him and asking, "Where is that man?"

¹²Among the crowds there was widespread whispering
about him. Some said, "He is a good man."

Others replied, "No, he deceives the people." ¹³But no one
would say anything publicly about him for fear of the Jews.

¹⁴Not until halfway through the Feast did Jesus go up to
the temple courts and begin to teach. ¹⁵The Jews were
amazed and asked, "How did this man get such learning
without having studied?"

¹⁶Jesus answered, "My teaching is not my own. It comes
from him who sent me. ¹⁷If anyone chooses to do God's will,
he will find out whether my teaching comes from God or
whether I speak on my own. ¹⁸He who speaks on his own does
so to gain honor for himself, but he who works for the honor
of the one who sent him is a man of truth; there is nothing
false about him. ¹⁹Has not Moses given you the law? Yet not
one of you keeps the law. Why are you trying to kill me?"

²⁰"You are demon-possessed," the crowd answered. "Who is
trying to kill you?"

²¹Jesus said to them, "I did one miracle, and you are all
astonished. ²²Yet, because Moses gave you circumcision

(though actually it did not come from Moses, but from the patriarchs), you circumcise a child on the Sabbath. ²³Now if a child can be circumcised on the Sabbath so that the law of Moses may not be broken, why are you angry with me for healing the whole man on the Sabbath? ²⁴Stop judging by mere appearances, and make a right judgment."

²⁵At that point some of the people of Jerusalem began to ask, "Isn't this the man they are trying to kill? ²⁶Here he is, speaking publicly, and they are not saying a word to him. Have the authorities really concluded that he is the Christ? ²⁷But we know where this man is from; when the Christ comes, no one will know where he is from."

²⁸Then Jesus, still teaching in the temple courts, cried out, "Yes, you know me, and you know where I am from. I am not here on my own, but he who sent me is true. You do not know him, ²⁹but I know him because I am from him and he sent me."

³⁰At this they tried to seize him, but no one laid a hand on him, because his time had not yet come. ³¹Still, many in the crowd put their faith in him. They said, "When the Christ comes, will he do more miraculous signs than this man?"

³²The Pharisees heard the crowd whispering such things about him. Then the chief priests and the Pharisees sent temple guards to arrest him.

³³Jesus said, "I am with you for only a short time, and then I go to the one who sent me. ³⁴You will look for me, but you will not find me; and where I am, you cannot come."

³⁵The Jews said to one another, "Where does this man intend to go that we cannot find him? Will he go where our people live scattered among the Greeks, and teach the Greeks? ³⁶What did he mean when he said, 'You will look for me, but you will not find me,' and 'Where I am, you cannot come'?"

³⁷On the last and greatest day of the Feast, Jesus stood and said in a loud voice, "If anyone is thirsty, let him come to me and drink. ³⁸Whoever believes in me, as the Scripture has said, streams of living water will flow from within him." ³⁹By this he meant the Spirit, whom those who believed in him were later to receive. Up to that time the Spirit had not been given, since Jesus had not yet been glorified.

⁴⁰On hearing his words, some of the people said, "Surely this man is the Prophet."

⁴¹Others said, "He is the Christ."

Still others asked, "How can the Christ come from Galilee? ⁴²Does not the Scripture say that the Christ will come from David's family and from Bethlehem, the town where David lived?" ⁴³Thus the people were divided because of Jesus. ⁴⁴Some wanted to seize him, but no one laid a hand on him.

⁴⁵Finally the temple guards went back to the chief priests and Pharisees, who asked them, "Why didn't you bring him in?"

⁴⁶"No one ever spoke the way this man does," the guards declared.

⁴⁷"You mean he has deceived you also?" the Pharisees retorted. ⁴⁸"Has any of the rulers or of the Pharisees believed in him? ⁴⁹No! But this mob that knows nothing of the law—there is a curse on them."

⁵⁰Nicodemus, who had gone to Jesus earlier and who was one of their own number, asked, ⁵¹"Does our law condemn anyone without first hearing him to find out what he is doing?"

⁵²They replied, "Are you from Galilee, too? Look into it, and you will find that a prophet does not come out of Galilee."

JESUS' RELUCTANCE TO RETURN to Judea is understandable when we recall the events of his last visit (see ch. 5).[1] The subject of his death arose then (5:16), and it rises again (7:1, 7, 19). In fact, this is Jesus' last visit to Jerusalem (in September/October); in the coming spring he will be crucified. Jesus never returns to Galilee following chapter 7. Much like the Synoptic story line (see Mark 9:30–33), Jesus moves from Galilee to enter Judea, only to face the threat of death. John 7 sets the same stage. Arrest (7:30, 44) and death (7:1, 7, 19, 20, 25) are constant themes as he approaches and enters Jerusalem. Nevertheless his brothers (cf. 2:12) urge him to go and to make his identity plain (7:3–4), but their intentions are not in Jesus' interest since, as John states clearly, "they did not believe in him" (7:5). But Jesus knows what will really happen in this city. There is even a subtle Johannine play on words in 7:8. Jesus will "go up" (Gk. *anabaino*) to

---

1. The close link between chs. 5 and 7 has been used frequently to argue for a rearrangement of these chapters of John (see comments on ch. 5). Brown (*John*, 1:308) even compares the three requests made of Jesus in John 5 and 7 with the temptation stories in the Synoptics (king/kingdoms, 6:15; bread, 6:31; show power in Jerusalem, 7:3).

Jerusalem; in 20:17 *anabaino* is used again to describe the ascension. In the autumn of his final year Jesus heads south in order to "go up"—both to the city and to heaven.

I have suggested that the literary outline followed by John in chapters 5–10 is organized around the festivals of Judaism (see comments on ch. 5). Chapter 5 centers on the weekly feast of Sabbath, while chapter 6 is organized around Passover. Jesus appears at these festivals, exploits some feature of their imagery, and launches major discourses in which he identifies himself and his mission through their historic themes.

Jesus' visit to Jerusalem now at the Feast of Tabernacles (John 7–9) follows this same pattern. Tabernacles was the third of three pilgrimage feasts anchored in the agricultural cycle of Judaism. The first was Passover, which recognized the beginning of the grain harvest in spring. Then came Pentecost, seven weeks later, celebrating the end of the grain harvest. The last one was Tabernacles (also called Booths or Ingathering), which celebrated the autumn harvest of tree and vine. Since the crop in autumn had to be protected, Israelite farmers built temporary shelters in the fields (Heb. *sukkoth*, hut, booth). Theologically this reminded them of the temporary shelters of the desert wandering; thus the feast was set not simply to praise God for the harvest, but to study the desert period and its meaning (Lev. 23; Deut. 16).

For each of these festivals, Jewish men were required to come to Jerusalem and worship at the temple (cf. Ex. 23:14–17; 34:23; Deut. 16:16), although it is uncertain how rigorously this was observed. The Festival of Tabernacles was observed for seven days and celebrated with numerous sacrifices of bulls, rams, and lambs, building to a climax on Day Seven, when special ceremonies were conducted (which John 7 interprets). No doubt since Jesus' family was faithful to Jewish law and worship, Jesus likely came to Jerusalem at least three times per year for these celebrations. His instinct to "go up" to the city now fits that pattern.

Since the Festival of Tabernacles takes place in September or October (on the fifteenth day of the Jewish month Tishri), it coincided with other interesting phenomena. People in the ancient world observed the length of days carefully, charting the solstices as well as the fall and spring equinox. Tabernacles coincided with the autumn equinox, when day and night are equal length and from which point on the calendar the nights lengthen and the days become shorter. Jewish ritual practice recognized this "dying of the sun" and incorporated into the festival ceremonies of light to hallmark the passing of the season. Jesus knows this and in the discourse of this feast will exploit images of light to make his point (John 8:12).

In addition, the late autumn was a period of drought in Israel. Strong, drenching rains had not been seen since spring. Cisterns were low. Springs were becoming weak. The hills were barren and parched. The ground could not be renewed without water. Therefore Tabernacles incorporated another set of symbols, depicting a prayer for water to replenish the country agriculturally as well as refresh the land spiritually. In fact, rainfall during Tabernacles was a sign of strong blessing from God in the coming season.[2] Jesus likewise knows these images and in the present chapter exploits their themes as well (7:37–39).

To sum up, it is almost impossible to interpret John 7 without some detailed acquaintance with the Jewish Feast of Tabernacles and how it was celebrated in Jerusalem in the first century.[3] It was an old festival of agriculture from the ancient Near East that adopted the Israelite story of redemption. To this were added Jewish intertestamental motifs of water and light, and even these the rabbis interpreted spiritually. Tabernacles then blended a variety of images from agriculture (harvest), climate (sun and rain), and theological history (desert wandering). Jesus makes these motifs serve his purposes as he stands in the feast and makes his identity known. John 7 even uses the sequence of the feast as its literary structure:

- The beginning of the Feast (7:1–13)
- The middle of the Feast (7:14–24)
- The last, great day of the Feast (7:37–52)

Threaded through these days are *questions* posed to Jesus (7:15, 20, 25–26, 35) by leaders and the crowd, who are trying to interpret what Jesus is saying. The chapter also describes a series of *reactions* to Jesus as people must decide if indeed he is a man to be followed (7:3–5, 12, 30–31, 40–44, 45–59). But there is no doubt that in Jerusalem a storm is brewing, and words of condemnation recur with surprising frequency: Some want to arrest him (7:30, 44) while others want him killed (7:19, 20, 25).

The Beginning of the Festival (7:1–13)

IT HAS BEEN six months since the Passover Festival (John 6), and Jesus has been avoiding Judea because he knows the depth of hostility waiting for him there (7:7). It is not inappropriate to hear cynicism in the encouragement of Jesus' brothers for him to attend the autumn festival (7:3). They may be reminding him of his religious obligation (despite the danger) or even pushing him

---

2 Even today Arabs in countries surrounding Israel see rainfall during the Jewish Tabernacles Feast as a hopeful sign of a good agricultural season.

3. The background of the festival can be gained from most thorough Bible dictionaries. In addition, see G. W. MacRae, "Meaning and Evolution of the Feast of Tabernacles," *CBQ* 22 (1960): 251–76.

to place his messianic identity into full public view. Either way, they do not believe in him (7:5) and do not see in the Jerusalem visit a fruitful disclosure of the truth about him. In another sense they portray precisely the view found in chapter 6. The brothers acknowledge that Jesus can do miracles, but miracles do not necessarily lead to faith (6:25–34). Only God can provide the divine insight needed for a person to comprehend fully the identity of his Son (6:44–46).

This failure to comprehend is represented in yet another way. Throughout this Gospel we have seen how misunderstanding becomes a typical Johannine theme to explain how Jesus' self-disclosure is beyond the human imagination. When Jesus says that he will not "go up" at the festival, he explains that he cannot because it is not yet his time (7:8). "Going up" in Greek can mean both pilgrimage to Jerusalem (Mark 10:33; John 12:20) or ascension (John 20:17). For him, "going up" is symbolic of his "hour" of betrayal, death, resurrection, and ascension. Thus in 7:30 when they do try to arrest him at the festival, they fail because "his time had not yet come." Jesus knows that his departure from this world must await the coming Passover in the spring.

Jesus' brothers, however, take his words at face value. They see things from an earthly perspective and assume that Jesus is simply going to avoid the feast. Jesus intends no deception and attends the feast on his own, keeping his identity as quiet as possible in order to avoid those who would like to harm him. Jesus' arrival in secrecy is paralleled in the Synoptic Gospels in Mark 9:30, where Jesus moves from Galilee to Judea with limited fanfare. Since the Synoptic picture is severely condensed, John's story describes more fully how Jesus came to Judea and worked in secret for many months prior to his dramatic Passover entry into the city.

John's description of the anticipation of the crowd (7:11–13) sets the stage for what is to come. Jesus' arrival brings controversy and division. The crowd is "whispering" (7:12)—*gongysmos*, a word that reminds us of 6:41 and the desert grumbling (Ex. 17:3; Num. 11:1).[4] In their search for Jesus some from the crowd describe him as "good" while others describe him as a deceiver, a fraud. But overshadowing all is the fear of the common person for the Jewish leaders (not "the Jews" in general), who have decided to kill him. The behavior of the crowd parallels that of Jesus: They will not speak "publicly," just as Jesus cannot come to Jerusalem publicly. Both Jesus' appearance and the crowd's questionings must be done privately.

---

4. This motif of "grumbling" fits the desert wandering theme embedded in Tabernacles. For an opposite view, see Barrett, *John*, 314.

The Middle of the Festival (7:14–36)

AT THE MIDPOINT of the feast, Jesus enters the temple courts for the first time and teaches publicly. The discourse represented in 7:14–36 follows the pattern already well-established in this Gospel. Questions are launched by Jesus' listeners that permit him to describe his identity and mission more completely. But the questions do more. They disclose how little his audience really understands (similar to Nicodemus's questions about rebirth). Buried in each of Jesus' answers are ironic messages fully beyond the grasp of his listeners. Three scenes are anchored to three questions with three ironic answers:

Scene	Question	Jesus' response
One	Where did Jesus go to school? (7:15)	heaven
Two	Where is this man from? (7:25–27)	heaven
Three	Where is this man going? (7:35)	heaven

Scene One (7:14–24). Educational standards for rabbis were well established in the first century. Advanced study under a rabbinic scholar in a school was common (cf. Paul and Gamaliel).[5] Jesus possessed no such credentials. The Jewish leaders, in effect, wish to see these (7:15), and Jesus complies by saying that his diplomas are divine (7:16–18). God has taught and commissioned him; God has given him the things he teaches. Moreover, Jesus explains that if their lives are in harmony with God, they will recognize the character and source of his teaching (cf. 5:42ff., where Jesus said that if they had the love of God in their hearts, they would recognize God's teaching at once). Jesus' mission is to honor God, to deflect glory from himself, which is also a sign of his authority and veracity (7:18).

Jesus is actually explaining the nature of his religious authority. The Jewish notion of authority (Heb. *reshuth*) was specialized. No one possessed *inherent* authority; it was secondary and indirect. Authority was passed down and conferred from rabbi to rabbi through ordination. It was as if the *reshuth* of Moses was preserved through the generations this way through each successive ordination. If the chain was broken, *reshuth* might be lost.

Jesus' problem is that he is not ordained. On whose shoulders, then, is he standing? What traditions are his? Which rabbi has authorized his teaching office? What is the source of his *reshuth*? Jesus' answer is clear: His authority stems directly from God (7:14–18; cf. 17:1–2). That is, Jesus answers the rabbis in their own categories, namely, that his authority has been properly conferred to him, but his source of authority is unconventional, to say the least. Therefore Jesus is working and speaking in order to honor this One who

---

5 A. Culpepper, *The Johannine School* (SBLDS 26; Missoula: Scholars, 1975).

sent him, the One who commissioned and equipped him. Unlike a rabbi, Jesus is authorized to speak much like a prophet because he bears the words of God, not religious tradition.

It is clear from 7:19 that the Sabbath debate of chapter 5 still dominates Jesus' relation with these authorities. In that chapter Jesus healed a crippled man in Jerusalem and instructed him to carry his bed on the Sabbath. Rather than praise him for this miracle, the authorities criticized Jesus for violating religious law. Jesus here returns to his line of argument expressed then (5:39–47): Those who do not keep the law of Moses in its entirety should be reluctant about judging others. It is a variation of the later theme in the story of the adulteress woman: Those who are without sin may cast the first stone (8:7). Moreover, the leaders' plan to kill Jesus (5:18; 7:19) is a specific violation of the law. On more than one occasion the New Testament reports that some people were so intent on their hostility toward Jesus that they either made plans to kill him (Mark 3:6) or they tried to carry it out (Luke 4:29). The threat here in 7:19 is real: In these months before Passover, Jesus has to be cautious, protecting himself from those who want to assassinate him.

The crowd in 7:20 must be distinguished from the authorities arguing with Jesus in 7:15. Perhaps they have come from Galilee for the feast, but at least we can say that they are astonished by Jesus' claim and know nothing of an attempt to kill him. "You are demon-possessed" (7:20) likely carries no theological weight[6] and can simply be translated, "You're crazy!"

Jesus now expands his line of reasoning more fully (7:22–24).[7] The Sabbath law permitted a ceremony of circumcision if a male child became eight days old on the Sabbath. If a boy can be *partially* healed on the Sabbath in this context, why should not a man be *completely* healed on the Sabbath? Jesus argues from the lesser to the greater, using circumcision as a precedent. Jesus sees himself not simply liberalizing the law but fulfilling what the law was meant to do: to bring renewal and redemption to God's people.[8]

Seeing that Jesus makes a claim to not only interpret the Sabbath but also to work on the Sabbath (as God does, see ch. 5), the audience opens a new line of questioning that queries the origin of Jesus.

Scene Two (7:25–31). The force of Jesus' argument with the authorities seems to impress many in the audience who are either residents of the city or pilgrims in Jerusalem for the Feast of Tabernacles. A shift in subject springs from

---

6. Elsewhere in the Gospel there are no exorcisms and limited interest in demon-possession beyond Judas Iscariot's role (see 13:27; so Brown, *John*, 1:316; Barrett, *John*, 319).

7. Rabbi Jose said, "Great is circumcision since it overrides the stringent Sabbath" (*m Ned.* 3:11).

8. Note the parallel once again between Jesus and Moses (cf. 1:17; 9:28–29; etc.). Jesus has come to replace and fulfill all that had been partially offered in Moses.

Jesus' answer in Scene One: If Jesus' authority to work on the Sabbath indeed comes from God, then Jesus is making a spiritual claim (a messianic claim, 7:26b). And if he can make a spiritual claim, this opens the way to new questions about his origins—his divine origins. Even the failure of the authorities to stop Jesus (7:26a) lends intrigue to the crowd's observation: Perhaps some of them are reluctant to interfere. Are some of them secretly believing in him?

Once again the ironic misunderstanding of the crowd is displayed by their question in 7:27: "We know where this man is from; when the Christ comes, no one will know where he is from." In a culture without surnames, the place of origin was a means of personal identification. Jesus son of Joseph "of Nazareth" (1:45) or Joseph "of Arimathea" (19:38) are typical identifiers. The crowd is examining Jesus on an earthly level and think that since they can trace Jesus' human origins, he is disqualified from messianic status. We possess evidence that many Jews expected the Messiah to appear suddenly, mysteriously, since he would be commissioned supernaturally by God.[9] For these Jews, Jesus' commonplace appearance at the feast disqualifies him completely.

Jesus leaves the confusion unchallenged (7:28–29). If his origin is at issue, he does not deny that he has an identifiable human history ("the Word became flesh," 1:14) or that he is from a place like Nazareth. He may well think that this speculation about the "hidden Messiah" is unfounded. But Jesus goes on to make his claim more astounding. He has come from God, whom he knows with unparalleled intimacy (cf. Matt. 11:27; Luke 10:22). This is paramount to a divine claim that breaks with all of the canons of Judaism. A Messiah might be powerfully sent by God, but Jesus is claiming to know God and be something of a personal liaison or confidant—a Son!— who now has authority in Jerusalem not by virtue of his education alone (Scene One) but also by virtue of his origins (Scene Two). It is Jesus' ontological status with the Father that empowers not simply what he does but who he is. As in chapter 5, Jesus says again that the Jews' inability to comprehend this reality is evidence of their ignorance about God himself (7:28; cf. 5:42).

The episode with the crowd comes to a dramatic climax with a division within their ranks (7:30–31). It is a division we see throughout the Gospel, where some express openness to Jesus (7:31) while others either deny him or attempt to inflict harm (7:12, 32, 44). Some in the crowd try to arrest him for making divine claims, but their efforts are frustrated. Jesus is sovereign over his life and will choose when his time has come (10:17–18; 18:6–8). Luke records a similar attempt at the start of Jesus' ministry in Nazareth,

---

9. See *4 Ezra* 7:28; 13:32; *2 Bar.* 29:3. *4 Ezra* 13:1ff. describes the Messiah as arising out of the sea. Morris, *John*, 365n.54, cites Rabbi Zera in the *Babylonian Talmud (Sanhedrin* 97a), "Three come unawares: Messiah, a found article, and a scorpion." Most major commentaries give ample evidence of this Jewish mystical tradition.

and once more Jesus could not be apprehended (Luke 4:29–30). Jesus is now waiting for the coming of Passover in the spring, when his arrest and death will have a rich and important theological meaning.

Scene Three (7:32–36). The first two scenes raised ironic earthly questions about Jesus' schooling and Jesus' background, both of which found an unexpected answer: heaven. In Scene Three the audience shifts to the chief priests and Pharisees, who show their alignment with half the crowd at once. They enlist police from the temple to arrest Jesus.[10] This is a more serious matter than an impulsive attempt by the crowd to do the same (7:30), and no doubt it leads Jesus to think about his death at their hands.

It will only be a "short time" till this occurs (7:33); when it does, Jesus will view his death not as a tragedy but as a departure, a "going away," in which he returns to the Father (13:3). This departure will put him beyond the world's reach (7:34) since he will have returned to his glory in heaven (17:5). As in the previous scenes, this statement inspires earthly misunderstanding. The Jewish leadership cynically wonders where Jesus could be going (7:35–36). The only place they *will never* go is among the Gentiles (the Greeks), so they speculate that Jesus is simply leaving Israel. But Jesus is talking about where they *cannot* go: heaven. His departure will be a return to God. When this happens, there will be a divine reversal. Up to this point, Jesus has been at work in the world, searching for those who believe. Once he departs, once God's revelation is withdrawn, they will do the searching (7:36), trying to find what they have tragically missed.[11]

The Last Day of the Festival (7:37–52)

EACH DAY OF the feast witnessed a water ceremony in which a procession of priests descended to the south border of the city to the Gihon Spring (which flowed into the Pool of Siloam).[12] There a priest filled a golden pitcher as a choir chanted Isaiah 12:3: "With joy you will draw water from the wells of sal-

---

10. As we will see in John's Passion narrative (18:3, 12), the temple police serve with limited jurisdiction to enforce religious law at the whim of the Sanhedrin and priests.

11. Many scholars point out that the description of Jesus in this section owes a great deal to Old Testament and Jewish notions of divine Wisdom. Divine Wisdom had mysterious origins and could be found only by diligent searching (Prov. 1–8; Bar 3:14–15). God's people pray that Wisdom will descend from heaven so that pious, diligent searches for it will be satisfied (Wisd. Sol. 6·12; 9·10; Sir. 24:8). See Witherington, *John*, 164–78; Brown, *John*, 1.318.

12. The Gihon Spring originally flowed into the Kidron Valley on Jerusalem's east side, but was rerouted by King Hezekiah in order to fill a pool on the southwest side of the lower city. By Jesus' day, the original spring had been closed over and forgotten, and the Pool of Siloam (filled by the running Gihon Spring) was erroneously viewed as the Gihon.

vation." The water was then carried back up the hill to the "Water Gate," followed by crowds carrying a *lulab* in the right hand (tree branches reminiscent of the desert booths) and an *ethrog* in the left hand (citrus branches reminiscent of the harvest).[13] The crowd would shake these and sing Psalms 113–118. When the procession arrived at the temple, the priest would climb the altar steps and pour the water onto the altar while the crowd circled him and continued singing. On the seventh day of the festival, this procession took place seven times.

Judaism saw this water ceremony on multiple levels. On the one hand, it was a plea to God for rain since the autumn is a time of threatened drought in Israel. On the other hand, it was a source of rich symbolism. In the desert, God brought water from a rock (Num. 20:8, 10), and here water was flowing from the sacrificial rock altar of the temple. Zechariah and Ezekiel had visions of rivers flowing from the temple in a miraculous display of God's blessing (Ezek. 47:1; Zech. 14:8). In a drought-stricken land, it was a spectacular vision of water, life-giving water flowing from God's life-giving temple.[14]

On this final day of celebration, Jesus steps into public view and makes his most stunning pronouncement of the feast. As seven water processions are climbing the steep hill of south Jerusalem, he proclaims, "If anyone is thirsty, let him come to me and drink." This announcement parallels symbolically what Jesus did in John 6 at Passover. Just as earthly bread led to memories of heavenly bread (manna), which concluded with Jesus offering himself as the bread of life (6:35), so now Jesus is doing the same. Needed rainfall and water ceremonies lead to memories of miraculous desert water, water given from heaven, which concludes with Jesus' offering himself as the source of the water of life.

The punctuation of 7:37–38 has inspired numerous debates among scholars. The NIV follows the tradition of the Eastern Fathers (Origen, Athanasius) and numerous scholars[15] who punctuate the verses to make *the believer* the one in whom the living water is flowing: "If anyone is thirsty, let him come to me and drink. Whoever believes in me, as the Scripture has said, streams of living water will flow from within him."[16] This view puts a full period after "drink" and makes the participle ("whoever believes") the subject of the Scripture citation.

---

13. For details of the feast, see A. Edersheim, *The Temple* (New York: James Pott, 1881), 238; J. Jeremias, "λίθος," *TDNT* 4:277–78; Brown, *John*, 1:327; m *Sukkah*.

14. Judaism quickly united the themes of paradisal streams in Jerusalem and the rock of Meribah. Schnackenburg, *John*, 2.156 cites P. Grelot, "Jean VII,38: eau du rocher ou source du Temple," *RB* 70 (1963): 43–51, who identifies this union in the rabbinic Tosephta tradition, *Sukka* 3:3–18.

15. Lightfoot, Westcott, Zahn, Bernard, Barrett, Lindars, Morris, Carson. For a full defense, see J. B. Cortez, "Yet Another Look at John 7:37–38," *CBQ* 29 (1967): 75–86.

16. The NRSV makes a startling expansion of the Gk. text of 7:37–38: "Let anyone who is thirsty come to me, and let the one who believes in me drink. As the scripture has said, 'Out of *the believer's* [Gk. his] heart shall flow rivers of living water.'"

A second Western or Christological punctuation views Christ as the source of the living water and enjoys not only the support of antiquity (Justin, Hippolytus, Tertullian, Irenaeus) but contemporary scholars as well.[17] "If anyone is thirsty, let him come to me. And let him drink—who believes in me. As the scripture has said, 'Streams of living water will flow from within him.'" This view interprets the participle (the believer) as the one who drinks. The Scripture citation now stands on its own with Christ as the source of living water. A superior translation reflecting the nuances of the Greek might read: "If anyone thirsts, let him come to me—and if he believes, let him drink. As the Scripture has said, 'Streams of living water will flow from his belly.'"[18]

It is important not to gloss over the importance of this punctuation debate, for the theology of the entire chapter depends on it. The second Christological view is compelling for a number of reasons. Not only is it grammatically defensible, but theologically it fits the literary setting of both John 6 and 7, wherein Jesus supplies the spiritual gifts promised in the festival. We have already seen how Jesus is the new temple in John's theology (see 2:21), and just as Jewish eschatology predicted the temple to be the dramatic source of water (displayed in the water ritual), so now Jesus is announcing himself as a replacement for the temple once again. Those seeking eschatological water need to look no further. Jesus is the source of Zechariah's fountain. Jesus is the source for what Tabernacles seeks.

Another difficulty in this passage is the Scripture citation in 7:38, but here too the Christological interpretation assists us. This quote does not appear in the Old Testament (either the LXX or the Hebrew text), and most scholars believe we have a composite quotation describing visions of the coming blessings of the messianic age (Isa. 43:19; 44:3; Ezek. 47:1–11; Zech. 14:8). John also has in mind the desert water image of the rock struck by Moses at Meribah to feed the Israelites and their flocks (Num. 20:2–13).

This theme was popular in Judaism (Ps. 78:15–16; 105:40–41; Isa. 43:20; 48:21) and symbolized how God miraculously can reverse the threats of drought and disaster. It comes as no surprise that Paul identifies Jesus with this rock: "They ... drank the same spiritual drink; for they drank from the spiritual rock that accompanied them, *and that rock was Christ*" (1 Cor. 10:4, italics added).[19] At the Feast of Tabernacles, then, Jesus is saying he is not only

---

17. Abbott, Brown, Bultmann, Dodd, Dunn, Hoskyns, Jeremias, Painter. For a full defense of this view, see G. M. Burge, *The Anointed Community The Holy Spirit in the Johannine Tradition* (Grand Rapids: Eerdmans, 1987), 88–93.

18. This emphasis is reflected in the NLT, the NEB, and the RSV margin.

19. In early Christian catacomb art, the rock in the desert is the most frequently painted Old Testament scene (Brown, *John*, 1:322)

the new temple and source of living water, but also the eschatological rock that, when struck, will yield life-giving water. Is it any surprise that when Jesus is struck on the cross with a spear (as Moses struck the rock with his staff), his "belly" (lit. trans. of *koilia* in 7:37b) yields blood *and water* (19:34)?

John's theological comment in 7:39 is likewise critically important. (1) He explains that Jesus was referring to the Holy Spirit in this pronouncement. This links with a standard Jewish interpretation of the Feast of Tabernacles, well-attested in our sources. The rabbis did not merely see the ceremonies as a literal plea for rain, but as a plea for eschatological blessing as well. The water of Zechariah 14 was viewed as a promise of the Holy Spirit.[20]

(2) This gift of the Spirit is not available during Jesus' earthly ministry. It must await his "glorification" in order to be distributed. By this John is referring to Jesus' death and resurrection, subjects that will be closely linked in Jesus' Farewell Discourse (John 13–16). The Spirit, then, is closely tied to Jesus' life (and death), and as we watch the Passion story unfold, we will do well to observe how the Spirit becomes a signal feature of Jesus' departure from the world and return to the Father.

The ample allusions to Moses' activity in the desert both here and at Passover lead the crowd to the same result: This Jesus may be the prophet-like-Moses anticipated from Deuteronomy 18:15. Others simply refer to him as the Messiah ("Christ" in 7:40–41), but this at once stumbles on the same line of questions in 7:41–42. At the middle of the feast, Jews who viewed the Messiah as "hidden" spoke their objections to Jesus (7:27). Now we meet Jews who hold that the Messiah will fulfill prophecy, descend from David, and be born in Bethlehem. The crowd only knows that Jesus is from Galilee, and if the prophetic fulfillment is important, Jesus is disqualified (7:41–42).

But this is misunderstanding at work once again. John knows (and assumes his audience knows) that Jesus was born in Bethlehem. Thus, once more knowledge about Jesus is just out of reach of those tying to grasp it. The result parallels the previous Tabernacles section: The crowd divides into those who are potential believers and those who wish to harm Jesus. But they cannot determine the hour of Jesus' arrest (only Jesus can), and so they do not lay a hand on him.

The complete frustration of the Sanhedrin and the erosion of opposition to Jesus becomes clear in 7:45–52. Even the temple police are impressed with Jesus (7:46)—to such a degree that they fail in their assignment to

---

20. Evidence is given in Strack-Billerbeck 2:434. The *Jerusalem Talmud* (*Sukka*, 55a) says, "Why was the place called the place of drawing? Because there the Holy Spirit was drawn in virtue of the saying [Isa. 12:3]: with joy you shall draw water out of the wells of salvation."

arrest him. Nicodemus, a member of their body, speaks up in Jesus' defense, urging caution and fair play (7:51; cf. Gamaliel a few years later, Acts 5:34–39). But Jesus' primary opponents are those in political and religious leadership in Jerusalem's high council. Their contempt for the masses is well-established in Jewish sources where the peasantry, uneducated in the law, were not considered truly pious since through their ignorance, they could not possibly keep the law (*m. P. Aboth* 2:6; 1QS 10:19–21). The irony, of course, is that these are the very people who seem to have the only hunch about Jesus' true identity.

The Sanhedrin's objection that Jesus cannot be a prophet since he has come from Galilee is outlandish and unfounded. Their call to investigate the matter (7:52) is a challenge to search the Scriptures, but remarkably, two prophets, Jonah and Nahum, came from this very place. These words mirror the parallel discussion in 5:39–47, where Jesus describes their "search" for the Scriptures and how these Scriptures will judge their readers. According to Rabbi Eliezer (about A.D. 90), no tribe of Israel failed to produce a prophet at some time (*b. Sukkah* 27b)!

Two important Greek manuscripts (p^{66} and p^{75}), however, provide an alternative reading. These texts read, "*The* prophet does not come out of Galilee." The addition of this definite article suggests that it is not any prophet that the Sanhedrin meant, but "the prophet-like-Moses" described earlier in 7:40. Later Christian scribes could have easily misread an ancient original and omitted the article (a mere 'o').[21] If the article is retained, the sharp irony of 7:42 is sustained even to Jerusalem's leaders.[22]

THE TRIAL CONTINUES. The theological substance of chapter 7 must be read together with chapter 5 since one simply carries on the debate of the other. Jesus healed a crippled man in Jerusalem; now on his subsequent visit to the city, further rumors and accusations are being attached to Jesus' name.[23] As I mentioned in my discussion of chapter 5, these narratives in John are conscious of the "trial" of Jesus that will come up later in the story. Indeed a "trial motif" seems to shape how these stories

---

21. The weight of textual evidence does, however, supports the shorter reading ("a prophet .. ").

22. Most ancient manuscripts do not include the story of the woman caught in adultery (7:53–8:11). In order to retain the coherence of Jesus' Tabernacles discourse, 8:12 should follow 7:52.

23. We should keep in mind the suggestion of many scholars that the order of chs 5 and 6 should be reversed (see comments on ch 5). This would link chs. 5 and 7 directly.

are told: Jesus' crime is described (healing on the Sabbath), his accusers speak up (generally the religious leadership), evidence for and against Jesus is provided (his authority, his origins, witnesses for his case), and a decision must be made.

John 7 concentrates on the final aspect of this "trial" scenario. The three major sections of the chapter (7:1–13, 14–36, 37–52) each conclude with a divided audience: At the beginning of the feast, some say that Jesus is a good man while others call him deceptive; at the middle of the feast, some put their faith in him while others try to seize him; and at the end of the feast, the crowds split into those who are receptive ("He is the Christ," 7:41a) and those who are not ("How can the Christ come from Galilee?" 7:41b), in the same way that the religious leaders experience a parallel division—the guards and Nicodemus express interest and respect for Jesus while the Pharisees utter curses (7:49). No doubt it is this latter group (the Pharisees and their colleagues) whose shadow looms large over the chapter. Verse 13 says clearly that everyone is afraid of them, a fear that limits the public freedom to speak openly about Jesus.

As I suggested in chapter 5, these chapters are not only portraits of Jesus' trial in history, but a window into the struggles and experiences of John's church. John's understanding of what he experienced in his world was shaped by his understanding of what had happened to Jesus. Jesus himself had promised, "If the world hates you, keep in mind that it hated me first" (15:18). At the end of his life Jesus prayed to God, "I have given them your word and the world has hated them, for they are not of the world any more than I am of the world" (17:14). Jesus' life was a model of Christian proclamation and rejection.[24] The truth of Jesus split any audience (Jesus' or John's) into those who believed and those who refused to believe. As John penned these chapters, he stylized them in a manner that created literary (and theological) characters that played the same role on the Johannine church stage.

As I try to look at this narrative and cull from its words a message for my context, I see something similar: *Jesus is on trial in my world as well.* As it was in Jerusalem, so today audiences will be divided. Some appear open and receptive, others appear cynical and hostile. Moreover, there is also the specter of fear: Just as the earliest crowds around Jesus were alert to the judgments of those in power, so too audiences today assess the risks of publicly identifying with Jesus. The tone of these early Gospel debates is severe, and this too

---

24. It is important to affirm that by viewing John as offering a "window" into the Johannine church, this is not to deny the historical character of the Gospel. Scholars in recent years have frequently viewed the Gospels as mere foils for later church history. This view is incorrect. However, it is also true that story-telling also tells us something about the speaker and his/her world

should enter into the equation that will surround our understanding of Jesus' trial. John did not expect, nor should we, that the debate about Jesus will always be civil. John 7 portrays a struggle for ultimate religious commitments; in this debate passions can run furiously high. In particular we gain in this chapter a profile of religious leadership in Jerusalem that is vehemently opposed to Jesus and willing to employ any resources at its disposal to dispense with him.

Individuals in the crowd. Not only does John introduce the notion of division into the story, but the literary drama of John 7 also analyzes the role of individuals in the crowd. No doubt as John looked at his world (just as we look at our own), there were discernible players who always stepped to center stage. As he forges his narrative, he understands too that the same "types" played on the stage of Jesus during his earthly ministry. Among the crowds, there are those who are simply curious (7:14, 25–26, 41–42) while others are open and receptive, willing to exhibit faith (7:12, 26–27, 31, 40–41, 46). Still others in the crowd are openly antagonistic (7:3, 13, 20, 30, 44). The Jewish leadership becomes a cast of its own: Some express anger (7:15, 47–48, 52) and want to arrest him (7:32); others are simply ignorant (7:35). One man, Nicodemus, stands out as genuinely open (7:51).

All of this invites interesting questions about the actors in our world, indeed the actors in our own churches. In John 6 we saw that it was not simply the crowds who stumbled over Jesus' deeper teachings, but his followers too. How are these roles being played today?

The Spirit. Finally, Jesus has made a profound theological statement in this festival. In my comments I explained how at the Feast of Tabernacles Jewish symbols of water were spiritualized to include expectations of the Holy Spirit. John 7:39 makes the symbolism of Jesus' language plain: He was speaking about the Spirit, but the Spirit had not yet been given because Jesus had not yet been glorified. In the theology of this Gospel it is important to understand *when* Jesus is glorified and from this moment interpret the coming of the Spirit. John is intentionally linking Jesus and the Spirit in order to give us a precise understanding of the origin of the Spirit and his relation to Christ.

It is also significant that in the midst of Jesus' most severe debate thus far, he offers the very thing his antagonists expect least. His religious opponents express themselves in all their shrill excitement at the end of the chapter. *What do they want?* At the very least they want Jesus to conform to their understanding of religious observance. But in doing so he must relinquish his claims to privileged status with God. He must deny that he is the Christ and make himself less offensive. He must shape himself to fit under their leadership. Instead Jesus increases the offense. He offers himself as the eschatological temple of the end of time and aggravates them further. Rather than promote a religious experience with God that catalogues obedience to law, he offers the Spirit—a gift of sheer unexpected immediacy with God. Jesus offers the tools of mysticism among those who cannot see beyond their own strident legalism.

QUESTIONS CHRISTIANS SHOULD ASK. A teacher or preacher working with John 7 has to make a fundamental decision. Once I understand the nature of the conflict Jesus has with the Jerusalem authorities and the theological nuances of the Tabernacles symbolism, I have to decide *where I stand* on this Johannine stage. Do I see myself standing with Jesus (and those who are persecuted), or is it truer to admit that I stand with Jesus' opponents? John penned this story not simply to record one of Jesus' visits. He is conveying meaning to readers in the Christian church, many of whom were his own followers.

Virtually every commentator assumes that this passage recounts the conflicts of Jesus in order to encourage those who likewise experience trial and persecution. We thus become bearers of the Light, allies of Jesus, and spokespersons for God. In some cases this is a true reading of the story. There are many times when I suffer as Jesus suffered, and Jesus promises that we will have such experiences ("If they persecuted me, they will persecute you also," 15:20).

But there may be another message, a more difficult message, that we are reluctant to see. Just as Jesus' followers argued with him concerning his words and mission in John 6, so too John 7 provides another scenario about religious debate. Can Christians become religious debaters? Can they ever oppose a new thing God may be doing? Are they genuinely affected by the sinful impulses that permeate the audiences in John 7? John understands that even those who claim to believe in Jesus sometimes choose to reject his word and deny him his way (6:66). As an interpreter bringing this passage to my generation, I have to wrestle with the sobering truth of this possibility and its implications.

Standing with Jesus. The most obvious application of John 7 has to do with the reactions of the world to the revelation of Jesus Christ. Again and again throughout this Gospel John has emphasized the difficulty and unwillingness of the public to accept what God is doing in Christ. In the prologue to this Gospel we learned about the rejection of the Word in the world ("The light shines in the darkness, but the darkness has not understood it," 1:5) and his rejection among his own people ("He came to that which was his own, but his own did not receive him," 1:11). Now for seven chapters we have witnessed how Jesus enters as "light in darkness," revealing the condition of the human heart.

John 3:19 describes this invasion of light as a type of judgment: Light penetrates darkness and unveils what is hidden there. But those who love darkness will hate the light and struggle against it. Similarly here in John 7 we read about Jesus in Jerusalem among his own people, struggling for recognition, being battered by questions, and in the end, being condemned by those who are experts in theology.

In this respect it is naive for Christians to think that the "good news" of the Gospel is going to enjoy a warm reception when it is given in the world. It is naive to think that if people simply understand the truth correctly, if they have the message of Christ fully explained, or if they meet a "true" Christian, they will be converted. It is presumptuous to think that the world is an eager, receptive vessel waiting to be filled by the presence of God. *The world is in rebellion.* It is skilled at asking religious questions and feigning spiritual interest, but such inquiries are nothing more than disguised, sophisticated rebellion. *Is this man from Galilee? Where did this man get all this learning? Isn't the Messiah supposed to arrive mysteriously? Why doesn't he show himself to the world?*

Jesus fields such questions in this chapter just as he has been interrogated throughout the centuries by men and women eager to engage in religious dialogue but reluctant to meet God. John's cosmology is strictly dualistic: There is darkness and there is light, the above and the below, truth and falsehood, God and Satan. As Jesus moves through the world, he unmasks the opposition wherever it is hiding.

There are, however, men and women in whom God is moving, who have had the courage to step near the light, to probe its truth, and to question the reality of the darkness—men and women who confess their ignorance, sin, and willfulness, with God's help (6:65). They are potential saboteurs on the world's stage, willing to pry open uncomfortable questions. *But isn't he a good man? Have the authorities concluded that he is the Christ? Should we put our faith in him? Have you ever heard a man speak like this? Doesn't our law expect us to provide every man with a just hearing?* Jesus surely hears their voices and knows that they are allies, witnesses to his cause, fledgling believers (no matter how feeble, 8:31).

When the gospel is preached in the world, Jesus goes on trial. Every hearer must choose which voice he or she will embrace, which "side" he or she will choose, for there is no middle place. Will our voice be filled with anger? cynicism? fear of the authorities? shame? courage? I am convinced that we really do not know what voice is ours until there is risk involved in speaking up. As soon as the opponents of Jesus express their will—and John 7 is filled with hints of conflict and violence—the crowd must decide if their faith is stronger than their fear.

Standing against Jesus. But there is a deeper motif here that haunts this chapter. It is not simply the world in all of its pagan self-indulgence that settles in as Jesus' great opponent. It is religious authority, spiritual experts hailing from the most religious city in the Bible, who stand militantly before him. We see this in chapter 1 when a delegation from Jerusalem arrives to question John the Baptist. We also see it in chapter 3 when Nicodemus talks to him at night. We observe this in chapter 5 when religious leadership try to disqualify Jesus on the grounds that he does not understand or respect God's will (concerning the Sabbath). Here at Tabernacles (which continues through ch. 8) the leadership's unrestrained contempt for Jesus shows itself in all its fury.

Just as there is a worldly opposition to Jesus, there is likewise a "religious" opposition to Jesus. What does this opposition mean? As a Christian interpreter do I simply leave this conflict on the first-century horizon and record for posterity the opposition of the temple to Jesus? Or is the malady deeper? Does the religious reflex that came alive in the temple—a reflex that builds and preserves religion, that weighs obedience to its statutes, that finds quibbling ways to dissect fidelity to its mission—does this reflex ever come alive in the church? Does Jesus ever go on trial *in the church?* Are we exempt from *dark religious reflexes?*

If the synagogues and the temple were eager to interrogate him, would we do the same if he came and challenged our dearly held assumptions about religious commitments and ceremonies and faith? We assume that since we are Christians, since we possess the "light," since we confess our creeds and trumpet our testimonies, there is no possibility of religious antagonism against any who would speak a prophetic word. But we are naive as well if we think we cannot be counted among the temple authorities.

The first time I reflected on this reading of the New Testament came when I read Karl Barth's famous commentary on Romans.[25] His comments on Romans 1–3 bore a power that completely amazed a generation of theologians following World War I. Today I assign this volume to undergraduate students, and they stand amazed again. Barth describes with sweeping authority the nature of sinful rebellion that permeates pagans and Christians alike (many of whom participated in the horrors of World War I).

But the most interesting exegetical decision Barth makes is his refusal to leave the historic religious position of Judaism something unique to the synagogue. The religious person who boasts (Rom. 2:17) is both a Jew and a Christian, each of whom have the capacity to build religious systems—houses of worship, colleges, seminaries, mission agencies—that promote a fallen human agenda rather than an agenda of God. *These are people who can argue with God about theology!* So I ask, should I be reading John 7 as Barth read Romans 2?

---

25. K. Barth, *The Epistle to the Romans* (Eng. trans.: Oxford. Oxford Univ. Press, 1918, 1933).

Standing in contrast to the arguments about law and religion is Jesus' promise of the Holy Spirit (7:37–39).[26] While religious officials are debating Jesus' alleged disrespect for the Sabbath, the proper meaning of messianic fulfillment, the preservation of tradition, and the correct venue for judgment, Jesus is talking about the Spirit. Ironically, this Spirit will not be released until Jesus is glorified (7:39), until the authorities have their way with him and he is killed.

Jesus is offering a spiritual mysticism and encounter with God that *always* makes the custodians of traditional religion nervous. This can be especially true in those tightly drawn circles of conservative theology that seem impenetrable. To propose new freedom, new spontaneity, new thought—that is, to step outside the canons of orthodox behavior or thinking—is to experience what Jesus experienced at the Feast of Tabernacles.

---

26. If one follows Barth's reading of human sin in Romans, the only possibility for humanity is God's divine intervention from outside, not only to save, but also to renew through the Holy Spirit (Rom. 8).

John 7:53–8:11

THEN EACH WENT to his own home.
8 ¹But Jesus went to the Mount of Olives. ²At dawn he appeared again in the temple courts, where all the people gathered around him, and he sat down to teach them. ³The teachers of the law and the Pharisees brought in a woman caught in adultery. They made her stand before the group ⁴and said to Jesus, "Teacher, this woman was caught in the act of adultery. ⁵In the Law Moses commanded us to stone such women. Now what do you say?" ⁶They were using this question as a trap, in order to have a basis for accusing him.

But Jesus bent down and started to write on the ground with his finger. ⁷When they kept on questioning him, he straightened up and said to them, "If any one of you is without sin, let him be the first to throw a stone at her." ⁸Again he stooped down and wrote on the ground.

⁹At this, those who heard began to go away one at a time, the older ones first, until only Jesus was left, with the woman still standing there. ¹⁰Jesus straightened up and asked her, "Woman, where are they? Has no one condemned you?"

¹¹ "No one, sir," she said.

"Then neither do I condemn you," Jesus declared. "Go now and leave your life of sin."

FEW PASSAGES IN the New Testament bring to the interpreter the bewildering variety of problems found in the story of the woman caught in adultery. Most translations either footnote the textual questions or render the passage in a smaller typeface in order to indicate some irregularity. Commentaries either ignore the passage completely by assuming its inauthenticity[1] or discuss it in an appendix.[2] Still others will try to integrate it into the text of the Gospel.[3] There is considerable

---

1. See the commentaries of Bultmann and Dodd.

2. See the commentaries of Witherington, Barrett, Bernard, Hoskyns, Morris, Marsh, and Hunter.

3. See the commentaries of Carson, Brown, Schnackenburg, MacGregor, Lindars, and Westcott.

237

scholarly literature that has weighed the merits of the text and its textual tradition.[4]

The dilemma we face has two dimensions. On the one hand it seems clear that the weight of evidence mitigates against the originality of the story. That is, this brief account is probably not original to the Fourth Gospel. On the other hand, the story has every suggestion of historical veracity, suggesting that it was indeed an event that occurred in the life of Jesus and was a story worthy of collection and recitation. These two factors give the interpreter an interesting problem of canon: Should a beloved story with weak manuscript attestation and a doubtful setting in John's Gospel be the subject of sermons today?

Authenticity of This Passage

THE MANUSCRIPT EVIDENCE. This story is absent from all of major Greek manuscripts that bear the strongest, earliest witness to John's original form. In these texts, John 7:52 is followed by 8:12. Even the early versions (Syriac and the Coptic dialects Sahidic and Bahairic) fail to record it. Byzantine manuscripts begin showing the text in the ninth century but even there, scribes expressed reservations about it by making editorial marks in the margin of the text.

The early patristic writers are the same. With one exception, in the East no Greek Father mentions the passage for one thousand years.[5] Lectionaries and commentaries alike fail to mention it. Origen's commentary on John moves from 7:52 to 8:12. Even where Tertullian gives judicial directions for cases of adultery, he makes no reference to this most obvious passage from John.

However, the story was alive and well in the West. It appears in the writings of Ambrose (d. 397), Ambrosiaster (d. 350), and Augustine (d. 430). When Jerome began working on the Latin Vulgate in the fourth century, he says he found the story in many Greek and Latin codices (*Against Pelagius*, 2:17). He included it in the Vulgate and so it entered into the mainstream Latin text tradition and the Western church canon.

But hints of the story's existence abound in early years. Eusebius (the church's first historian) says he learned a story coming from Papias (c. A.D. 60–130) about a woman who was maliciously accused before Jesus con-

---

4. G. M. Burge, "A Specific Problem in New Testament Text and Canon: The Woman Caught in Adultery," *JETS* 27 (1984): 141–48 (see bibliography).

5. B Ehrman, "Jesus and the Adultress" *NTS* 34 (1988): 24–44, shows from a recently discovered manuscript that it was likely known to Didymus the Blind, a fourth-century monk in Alexandria, Egypt. The only major Gk. manuscript antedating the eighth century with the story is Codex Bezae

cerning her sins, and he recorded it in the *Gospel of the Hebrews*. In the Syriac *Didascalia Apostolorum* (2:24)[6] bishops are exhorted to receive mercifully those who repent, whereupon an illustrative story is mentioned about a woman deposited before Jesus by her accusers and his refusal to condemn her.

To sum up, despite these hints of the story in Eusebius and *The Didascalia*, the absence of the account from the earliest Greek manuscript tradition is important. The whole range of Greek patristic literature virtually ignores it while it seems to have a strong currency only in the West.

Internal evidence. The story also seems artificial to the narrative of John 7 and 8. This account appears in some manuscripts in different places: Some place it after John 7:36, after 7:44, or at the end of the Gospel. One group of manuscripts places it after Luke 21:38, another after Luke 24:53. Some scholars think it may have originated from the pen of Luke.

A simple glance at its literary setting in the Fourth Gospel makes its awkwardness more clear. Jesus is speaking to a crowd in 7:37–39, and when 8:12 resumes, a crowd is still before him. But in 7:53–8:11 Jesus is left alone (8:9). Without the story, the Tabernacles narrative flows smoothly from 7:1 to 8:59. This must explain the numerous textual variants in the story as scribes tried to smooth over this awkwardness.

Scholars also point to numerous words and grammatical forms that are not Johannine. Sentences, for instance, are connected with the Greek word *de* ("and, but," which John uses less than half the number of times as, say, Matthew). Moreover, the vocabulary of 8:2 contains several expressions that appear elsewhere only in Luke–Acts or in Matthew.

In other words, this story was likely an independent account that circulated freely for some time and was only later attached to John. But why was it placed here? The answer is that the theme of 8:14ff. turns on judgment: Jesus judges no one (8:15). The story illustrates this well. Not only have the woman's judges disappeared, but Jesus himself will not join their ranks. Derrett, by contrast, thinks that the story turns on the idea of evidence. At Tabernacles the authorities are trying to weigh the admissibility of Jesus' claims about himself. This leads to a rabbinic debate about the character of evidence, which our story illustrates.[7] Scholarly opinions are almost unified that the passage is foreign to the Gospel of John, interrupts the flow of thought in chapters 7–8, and is likely not from the pen of the fourth evangelist.[8]

---

6. This is a third-century church order written originally in Gk. but now surviving only in Syriac.

7. J. D. M. Derrett, "The Story of the Woman Caught in Adultery," *NTS* 10 (1963–64): 1–26; also in his *Law in the New Testament* (London: Darton, 1970), 156–88.

8. Z. Hodges has recently argued for the authenticity of the story in "The Woman Taken in Adultery," *BSac* 136 (1979): 318–72; 137 (1980): 41–53.

Historical authenticity. While scholars are reasonably convinced that this story does not belong to the Fourth Gospel, many are confident that it is an ancient narrative that stems from the same pool of stories that contributed to the Synoptic Gospels. This is a typical Synoptic "conflict" story in which Jesus is placed on the horns of a dilemma. He chooses to stand against the representatives of the law in favor of the needs of the woman. We also have evidence that in the first century there was an ongoing debate about the death penalty (stoning or strangling) and here, typically, Jesus refuses to get embroiled in the legalism of sinners who want to judge sin.[9]

However, there is good reason why the text was either ignored or suppressed in the early church for a long time, only to be discovered in the West in the fourth century and in the East centuries later. Ethical perfection and penance were hallmarks of teaching in the patristic period (*Didache* 15:3; *1 Clem.* 48:1). But certain sins demanded more severe warnings. In Paul's lists of sins, adultery and immorality appear repeatedly (1 Cor 6:9ff.; Gal. 5:19ff.; Eph. 5:3ff.; Col. 3:5), and these warnings are no doubt tied to the frightful immorality that pervaded the Roman empire. For Paul, this moral chaos pointed to the godlessness of the pagan world (Rom. 1:26), and so he calls for immorality not to be even named among Christians (Eph. 5:3) and in one case calls for a man's removal from a church because of it (1 Cor. 5:5).

The postapostolic writers emphasize this concern about sexual sin. In the *Acts of Paul and Thecla*, we have a story of a woman who converts to Christianity and becomes a model of chastity and holiness. When it comes to sexual sins, writers such as the person who wrote *The Shepherd of Hermas*, Clement of Alexandria, and Cyprian indicate lengthy, severe penance for readmission to the church. Adultery is listed along with homicide and apostasy, and at least for Tertullian, Origen, and Cyprian, sexual sins were especially heinous and *without* forgiveness.

It is against this background in the second, third, and fourth centuries that the story of the woman caught in adultery is struggling for recognition. Jesus' refusal to condemn her was at odds with the outlook of the day. How could a lengthy penance be reconciled with such immediate forgiveness? How could a sexual sin be excused so readily? The story was not removed from the New Testament, but rather it never gained access to the manuscript tradition once the story competed for credibility.[10]

It was not until the fourth century that the church was firmly established

---

9. See Schnackenburg, *John*, 2:170–71. Derrett ("The Story of the Woman") shows how some Jews felt that stoning would violate the doctrine of the resurrection and so stood against it.

10. Luke has another story about an adulteress in the house of Simon the Pharisee (Luke 7:36–50). But this story was preserved because it had elements that could be readily adapted to teaching on penance (the flask, tears, kneeling). John's story makes no such allowances.

in society through the efforts of Constantine. Its care of souls and disciplines had stabilized and bishops were admonished to demonstrate mercy. Thus Basil of Caesarea could set the penance for an adulteress at fifteen years. John Chrysostom tells of the conversion of a notoriously sinful actress in Antioch who turned from her adulterous ways to holiness through penance. She traveled to Jerusalem in men's clothes and lived as a recluse in a grotto on the Mount of Olives for the rest of her life. In this era our text emerges as a model for the penitent adulteress and is embraced by the leading theologians. On St. Pelagia's Day (October 8) our story became the Gospel text in most fifth-century Western lectionaries, honoring a seeming variety of women martyrs who either preserved their virginity through martyrdom or repented and led a life of chastity.

The Woman Caught in Adultery (7:53–8:11)

THIS STORY HAS numerous arresting details that richly repay careful study and provide excellent insight into the thought and ministry of Jesus. The setting of the story must have been typical of Jesus' ministry in Jerusalem, particularly during his final visits there (from Tabernacles to Passover in his final year). He taught regularly in the temple courts in the early mornings (8:2), and many people crowded around to hear him. In the evenings he retired east of the city to the Mount of Olives (8:1).[11] Luke presents this picture in Luke 21:37: "Each day Jesus was teaching at the temple, and each evening he went out to spend the night on the hill called the Mount of Olives." Mark says that Jesus stayed in Bethany (Mark 11:12), where we know that Jesus had three good friends, Mary, Martha, and Lazarus (John 11). Since Bethany is simply on the east slope of the Mount of Olives, this is likely his destination every night.

On this particular day, the group with Jesus is joined by Pharisees and teachers of the law (Gk. *grammateus*, sometimes trans. scribes).[12] These two groups had many mutual interests. Scribes were a valued profession in a world with limited literacy, and since biblical law was one of the chief subjects of theological discussion, the Pharisees (who were completely committed to the law) made good use of scribal skills.

The most important cultural element within the story is the nature of the accusation against the woman.[13] The religious leaders make their charge

---

11. This is typical of the non-Johannine character of the story. John does not refer to the Mount of Olives elsewhere in his Gospel. But it is a commonplace reference in the Synoptics. Luke refers to it four times, Matthew and Mark three times each.

12. Again, this is a non-Johannine phrase. *Grammateus* occurs frequently in the Synoptics (Matt. 22 times, Mark 21 times, Luke 14 times) but nowhere else in John.

13. Derrett's article on the legal background of the story is essential reading for exegesis (see "The Story of the Woman").

explicit, "Teacher, this woman was *caught in the act* of adultery" (italics added). The Greek construction of the sentence makes it clear that these men are making a legal claim: They possess the evidence the law requires to convict the woman.

What evidence do they need? So that suspicious husbands could not accuse their wives unnecessarily, the law required strong testimony from two witnesses who saw the couple in a sexual context: lying in the same bed, unmistakable body movements, and positive identities. The two witnesses had to see these things at the same time and place so that their testimonies would be identical. Such evidence virtually required the witnesses to set a trap.

Numerous problems, however, accompany their charge this day in the temple. (1) The law also expected that if a person witnessed another about to commit a sin, compassion required them to speak up. These witnesses stand silently, neglecting their moral obligation to give guidance to the woman. They want to catch her and use her.

(2) We must ask if the woman is married or betrothed to another man. A woman who is sexually unfaithful to her fiancé was to be stoned to death along with her lover (John 8:5; cf. Deut. 22:23–24). Unfaithful wives were likewise killed (Lev. 20:10; Deut. 22:22), but the law did not indicate the method of death. The *Mishnah* (which was oral law in Jesus' day) specified that unfaithful fiancés should be stoned, but wives strangled (*Sanhedrin* 7:2). In the present passage, the woman therefore must be engaged.[14] But if so, where is her lover? If they were caught in the act, he was caught too. The accusers have permitted him to get away clean.

(3) These witnesses bring the woman to Jesus before a crowd and heap public shame on her. They could have kept her to one side and brought her case to Jesus privately. But their approach to the problem indicates that they wish to trap Jesus, and her personal life is incidental (8:6). They have no interest in a trial. They are thinking about a public lynching, and they want Jesus to make a judgment.

It is impossible to know what Jesus wrote in the dust (8:6). For some interpreters, Jesus was simply drawing to give himself added time. More likely, however, a detail like this had some importance. Most believe that he began to write in Hebrew some verse from the law that would shape his response to the dilemma. The traditional view is that Jesus wrote Jeremiah 17:13: "Those who turn away from you will be written in the dust because they have forsaken the LORD, the spring of living water." Derrett thinks Jesus began to

---

14. In this culture it would be highly unlikely for her to simply be a "single" woman as we think of it today. A culture of arranged marriages seals a woman's marital plans long before adolescence.

write Exodus 23:1, "Do not help a wicked man by being a malicious witness."[15] This is a test of law, and certainly whatever Jesus wrote alluded to the law and demonstrated his displeasure with how these men were applying it.

If his writing seemed to stall things, 8:7 indicates that these men persist to force the question of judgment on him before the crowd. Jesus responds with his often-quoted statement, "If any one of you is without sin, let him be the first to throw a stone at her." This does not mean that this woman's accusers must be sinless or morally perfect in order to bring charges against the woman. In such a case, accusations would be impossible at any time. This is simply a direct reference to Deuteronomy 13:9 or 17:7, which says that those who witness a crime and bring home a successful accusation must be the first to stone the victim.

But then the accusers must engage in self-examination. The world of antiquity was little different from our own when it came to sexual sins. Women who transgressed social mores could find themselves in legal jeopardy much more quickly than their partners. Jesus may thus be cutting through the double standard in order to force the men to reflect on their own hypocrisy.

Jesus resumes his writing (8:8), and the religious leaders begin departing one by one (8:9). John uses an imperfect verb here (conveying continuous action) to build a picture of one teacher departing, who is then followed by a succession of people eventually walking away, so that the accusers arrayed against the woman crumble bit by bit. No doubt they are stunned, and perhaps the audience is embarrassed. But in the end, Jesus and the woman are left alone.

Because Jesus must have been sitting and the woman standing, he now straightens up (8:10) and speaks to her for the first time. His use of the title "woman" is not harsh, but a typical sign of respect that Jesus uses even with his mother (cf. 2:4; 4:21; 19:26; 20:13, 15; also Matt. 15:28; Luke 13:12; 22:57). His questions do not imply that the woman is innocent since in 8:11 he warns her to cease a sinful life that has been her habit.[16] He simply points to the absence of accusers. They have disappeared. Her response shows considerable respect for Jesus.

Jesus' final words ("Then neither do I condemn you") again do not imply innocence, but reflect his sovereignty to forgive sin (Mark 2:5ff.). Borchert writes, "Sin was not treated lightly by Jesus, but sinners were offered the opportunity to start life anew."[17] The story's crisp ending captures the

---

15. Derrett, "The Story of the Woman," 20. He also points to Ex. 23:7, "Have nothing to do with a false charge and do not put an innocent or honest person to death, for I will not acquit the guilty."

16. The Gk. form used in 8:11 (*hamartane*) is a present imperative.

17. Borchert, *John*, 1:376.

seriousness with which Jesus views sin and judgment—even the sin of those who accuse the woman—and his gracious, forgiving outlook on those who are caught in its grip.

THE FIRST QUESTION any interpreter must answer is whether to teach and preach from this passage at all. Should I even carry this text into my church context today? When Erasmus developed his famous Greek text in 1516, he doubted the origin of the story, but because of its popularity included it anyway, leading to its incorporation into the *Textus Receptus* (and the King James tradition). Augustine felt the same dilemma in 397. He knew the story but suspected that anxious husbands had removed it from the Bible so that it could not be abused by their wives! We share a similar dilemma. The popularity of the story is beyond question, and to announce from the pulpit that this story ought to be excised from the Bible would bring strong reactions. I imagine that early Christians teachers felt the same. This was a free-floating story that everyone loved, but it had no home. That home was eventually found in John (and Luke).

For Roman Catholics, the issue is quickly decided. Once the story was admitted into the Vulgate by Jerome in 382, it received universal recognition. When the Council of Trent pronounced the Vulgate to be the authoritative Scripture of the church in 1546, the matter was settled. But for Protestants, it is less easy. While we respect (and defend) the earlier councils of the church (such as Nicea), we are less sure about the later decisions of medieval Catholicism. Protestants are fond of pointing to the earliest canonical list penned by Athanasius in 367 in his Easter Letter. However, we have no idea what text of John Athanasius was promoting or whether that text carried this story.

If our notion of canonical authority rests in the books of the Bible themselves—that is, those literary units called Gospels and letters penned by inspired authors—then our passage cannot be a part of the canon. Textual evidence confirms what a literary study only suggests: The story is a later insertion. Nevertheless, scholarly research points to its antiquity and authenticity, and a cursory study of patristic history provides a good explanation for our story's disappearance.

Furthermore, the story edifies the church and has been a vehicle through which the Spirit has worked. Are these the grounds of the Protestant canon? If so, the passage should remain firmly anchored in the New Testament. The evangelical Gerald Borchert thus writes: "This little story captures magnificently both the gracious, forgiving spirit of Jesus and his firm call to the transformation of life. I consider this text to be divinely inspired and fully authoritative for life."[18] But if the criterion of text criticism is upheld, the story should slip into the margin as an edifying extrabiblical story about Jesus.

Thus Christians must make a theological (canonical) decision whether or not to use this story. If I choose to preach on it, no doubt the themes of unyielding judgment (which lacks compassion) and unmerited mercy (which is overwhelmed by God's love) should be placed center stage. This is a powerful story because it paints a strong picture of harsh judges who have neglected their responsibility to care for the soul of the woman. She is disposable. Their aim is to corner Jesus, and her life is a tool in their theological gambit to make him either condemn her (thus sacrificing his commitment to grace) or forgive her (thus sacrificing his commitment to God's law).

The portrait of the woman is equally powerful. As a woman *caught in the act* of adultery, she is completely vulnerable, completely at risk. She is encircled by hostile men willing to sacrifice her through their unyielding commitment to the law. Certainly, she must have thought, this man named Jesus, this man known as a rabbi, would know the law and uphold it. *That is what it means to be a rabbi.* His implied judgment on her accusers and his mercy mixed with exhortation sets her free in a manner she never expected.

THIS IS A POWERFUL drama of sin and forgiveness and has always been one of the favorite stories of the church (which makes the question of canon and authority much more complicated). As I speak to an audience from this story, however, it is too easy to set my focus entirely on the woman, the depth of her sin, and the power of Jesus' forgiveness. That theme is important. But there are other subsidiary themes that also require reflection, and these can have an equally powerful message today. Here I am thinking about the position of the woman's accusers, their attitude, and their aims in making these charges. Thanks to research into the law in rabbinic Judaism, we can have a far more sophisticated look at what was occurring in these men's minds.

Moreover, it is interesting that the charges brought against the woman had to do with sex, not with theft or blasphemy or any other of the countless crimes listed in the Jewish law. Religious communities are often swift in their judgment on those whose unrighteousness includes problems with sexual rules (premarital sex, abortion, adultery, divorce, etc.).

---

18. Borchert, *John*, 1·376

There is a final level at which the story comes to life: It is terribly important that the "accused" in the story is a woman. In the first century, Judaism had stereotyped women as instigators whenever sexual sins were committed and labeled them as lacking the spiritual and moral fiber needed to uphold the law. The sexual passions of adolescence, for instance, were viewed as coming from the seductive attractions of females. The absence of the woman's lover in the story is crucial. Allowances may be made for men who experiment with sexual adventures, but this was forbidden to women. A woman who committed the sexual sin was "marked," but the man was not. This has been a continuous theme of women who interpret John, but it rarely shows up in contemporary commentaries.

The woman. In order to reset the stage of this drama, I must begin with potent images of men and women who have sinned and who have been forgiven. The tension in the drama centers on the gravity of the woman's sin and the shocking forgiveness she experiences in the words of Jesus. She does not have a minor problem. Her life is in jeopardy. She has broken the law. According to that law, it is fully appropriate for her to die. There is no quibbling about the evidence; the witnesses "have her." Through the story she moves with shocking speed from death to life.

The sort of profile I have in mind is like that of Karla Faye Tucker. Karla Faye was twenty-three years old in June, 1983, when she and her boyfriend (Daniel Garrett) broke into a Houston home in order to "case" the house for a robbery. High on drugs for days, Tucker and Garrett ran into a couple in the home and murdered them with a hammer and a pickax. Both bodies had more than twenty stab wounds. Following their trial and conviction (which was widely reported around the United States), each received the death sentence. Garrett died in prison in 1993, but Tucker remained on death row for many more years.

Karla Faye Tucker's story is more than one more senseless homicide because three months after her imprisonment, she became a Christian. A puppet ministry team came to her cell block, and since everyone else was going, she joined the crowd out of boredom. She stole a Bible at the meeting (not knowing they were free) and secreted it away that night in her cell. Later that night, she accepted Jesus into her heart. "When I did this," Karla wrote later, "the full and overwhelming weight and reality of what I had done hit me. I realized for the first time that night what I had done. I began crying that night for the first time in many years, and to this day, tears are a part of my life."[19]

19. From Karla's letter to Governor George W. Bush and the Texas Board of Pardons and Paroles, 1998. The texts of Karla's letters and the full story can be found in the archives of Cable News Network, CNN (www.cnn.com).

The transformation of Karla's life was tangible. Christ was alive in her. For over fourteen years she was a powerful Christian presence in the prison, in 1995 marrying the prison chaplain who worked with her (Dana Brown). Her life was gripped by the horror of what she had done. "I feel the pain of that night and I feel the pain that goes on every day with others because of what I did that night. I know the evil that was in me then, and I know that what took place that night was so horrible that only a monster could do it."[20] Her life was hallmarked by the radiant joy of experiencing Jesus' forgiveness.

In 1997 a date was set for Karla Faye's execution: February 3, 1998. At once she was a media sensation. Was this conversion real? Would Texas execute its first woman since the Civil War? On January 14, 1998, Karla Faye was interviewed by Larry King on CNN. King tried to exploit the gruesome details of the 1983 murder (which Tucker resisted) and could not believe this was anything more than a "jailhouse conversion." Perplexed by her positive attitude weeks before her death, King asked, "Are you still up? You have to explain that to me a little more. It can't just be God." Karla Faye responded simply, "Yes, it can. It's called the joy of the Lord." Tough questions pressed Karla Faye to explain her feeling about the impending execution. She said she was calm and peaceful, and she hoped that the families of her victims would see her love and forgive her. Her only regret was that she could not continue a life of ministry within America's prison systems.

On February 3, 1998, in Gatesville, Texas, Karla Faye Tucker was executed by lethal injection. Her final words spoke of love and forgiveness. Final appeals to the governor of Texas, George W. Bush, were fruitless. Appeals from Christians around the world fell on deaf ears.

Karla Faye's conversion is poignant and helpful because the power of her Christian life was so directly tied to the power of her sin. She did not live a day without reflecting on her sin and on God's forgiveness. She did not deny the crime any more than the woman caught in adultery denied her wrongdoing. In each case the possibilities for freedom from sin were the result, not of threat and law, but of forgiveness and love. Karla Faye was a changed person, and she demonstrated that change for fourteen years. The woman caught in adultery would be changed too because Christ set her free. Sadly, the parallel stops there. Jesus understood the power of grace and released the woman; the state of Texas did not, and Karla Faye was killed.

Christ's forgiveness in each of our lives diminishes as we lose touch with the depth of our own sinfulness. When we no longer see ourselves in the drama of the woman, when we feel we are free from accusation and judgment, we lose sight of God's grace. Jesus is not simply committed to the requirements of the

---

20. Ibid.

law, but to the care and transformation of the woman before him—and every person who likewise brings a debt of sin into the circle where he sits. This drama of Jesus and the woman gains power when I become that woman and reflect on the seriousness of my own jeopardy. Through this new vision, I gain a new glimpse of Jesus' love and mercy.

The judgment. There are other subsidiary issues that the drama raises, and we would do well to think about them today. Despite the woman's sin and the requirements of the law, Jesus does not permit the accusers to carry out the punishment. *The woman does not die.* The story forces us to ask troubling questions about what to do with convicted sinners in our own society. Evangelicals are comfortable finding in this story a spiritual message about the state of my sinful life and God's forgiveness (all in the abstract). But we rarely venture into the complex problem of what to do with people who have grievously sinned in society (thieves, murderers, etc.), who repent, and who discover a new life. The fact remains, Jesus did not punish the woman. As I argued above, this fact is precisely why the story was not appreciated in the church for three hundred years. There is no punishment, no penance, no restitution. Should not the woman do public service at an orphanage for a couple of years in Jerusalem?

Karla Faye's story similarly raises enormous questions about capital punishment and the purpose of the penal system in the United States. On the night of February 3, a phalanx of international reporters crowded the prison gate at Gatesville with opposing groups of Texans. Some held a silent prayer vigil for Karla Faye, while others yelled for her "to pay." The scene was surreal. The alignment of sides reminds me again of this story of Jesus and the woman.

I am not suggesting that our story teaches us to free all convicted criminals. But it does raise questions about the purpose of capital punishment. What is being satisfied when an inmate is executed? Is this revenge? Is it preventive? Is this about justice? Despite what we think about the function of the punishment itself, what happens when a person is truly transformed by the Spirit of God in the prison system? Through Chuck Colson's ministry, Prison Fellowship, I have had the opportunity to meet a number of former convicts who are now growing Christians. One meeting with them and suddenly we will carry the burden of new questions that did not trouble us before. If Jesus can forgive, transform, and set free in the temple, what happens if he does it in our prisons? Will we join him or those religious leaders who prefer to see one woman dead?

The accusers. Perhaps one of the most troubling aspects of the drama is the approach these men have toward this woman. These are religious men, leaders in their community, men known for upholding the law. If asked, they would say that they bring glory to God because they uphold his expectations for righteousness. Their attitudes remind us of the Pharisees and teachers of the law, with whom Jesus often debated. In Matthew 23:23, Jesus tells them how they pursue the fine details of religious obedience and miss important things: "But you have neglected the more important matters of the law—justice, mercy and faithfulness. You should have practiced the latter, without neglecting the former."

Of course the deeper motive among these men is to trap Jesus. Their strategy includes trapping the woman. Perhaps entrapment characterizes a good portion of their religious effort. They are religious police, and here in Jesus they seem to have found a man who bends the rules. Thus they find a woman who has broken a rule and demand to see if Jesus will bend one more. These teachers no doubt think that both the woman and Jesus are guilty and deserve discipline.

The Pharisees understood the mercy and grace of God, though they struggled with its application. They were not the religious henchmen we sometimes make them out to be. However, they expected that men and women once redeemed would obey God's law with passion. Religious obedience, they could argue, ought to be visible in external forms of righteousness. This was a "responsive legalism" that did not see righteous living as a prerequisite to grace, but as a necessary and enforceable feature of the godly person's life. These rules for living (illustrated amply in the *Mishnah*) could become a central concern—a preoccupation even—among the leadership.

People with religious obsessions like this rarely see themselves this way. Evangelicals who take godly righteousness seriously rarely see themselves this way either. The story of the woman probes our reflexes toward people who do not fit our religious expectations. Are we religious police? Does our healthy commitment to righteousness ever lapse into an obsessive preoccupation with the details of people's personal lives? Any newcomer to the evangelical world will at once tell us that the answer is "yes," but that we barely see it in ourselves.

Sex and sin. I am intrigued that the sin brought before Jesus has to do with a sexual crime. If the strategy of the Pharisees is to provoke a public response against Jesus, if they want to ignite an issue that will make the evening news, if they want to draw a crowd and arouse interest, sex works like magic. They assume no doubt that even though Jesus has a reputation for breaking a law or two on the Sabbath, he will not fail to enforce a law that has to do with sexual taboos. These leaders are guaranteed popular support. Folks who may be fatigued to hear about one more sinner will find energy to invest in a story of sex and scandal![21]

---

21. As I write, the sex scandals of President Bill Clinton are everywhere in the media. Lurid details now fill the national news. And the ratings of the talk show hosts (e.g., Jay Leno and David Letterman), for whom this has provided an endless supply of humor, have increased measurably.

Jesus is not moved by any of it. Sin is sin, and sexual sin does not evoke a different response. Yet as I look at the contemporary church, I am fascinated to observe how we do not share the same impassive reaction of Jesus. There are certain sins for which we extend forgiveness. Then there are other sins (often sexual sins) for which the grace of Christ is not (apparently) sufficient. If a pastor is once divorced, what does that mean for his or her job prospects for ministry? There is an unwritten rule in many evangelical institutions that divorce is the unforgivable sin. In colleges and churches that have nothing about divorce in their statements of faith, candidates for the faculty or staff can be bypassed intentionally because of this personal disgrace. In some cases, people are victims of divorce. A friend of mine is a brilliant New Testament scholar whose wife left him and his two children. After she divorced him, he found employment impossible as a result of this history.

The church has a special category for sins linked to sexuality, and we have strong reactions for them: abortion, adultery, and premarital sex can easily be included. Imagine for a moment the status of a man who desires to join the church but admits he is gay, celibate, and desiring God's healing. Will he be treated the same as a man who claims he is prone to gossip, repentant, and likewise desiring God's healing? If an elder has an extramarital sexual affair, is our reflex to judge and expel or to forgive and heal?

I am not compromising the seriousness of sexual sin. Neither was Jesus. But Jesus had different reflexes. He could say to the sexual sinner: "Then neither do I condemn you. . . . Go now and leave your life of sin." The story before us forces me to check my reflexes because there are many, like the woman, who believe that because their sin is sexual, there is no room for them among God's people.

Women, sex, and sin. We should be deeply troubled that the Pharisees have decided not to drag a woman *and a man* before Jesus. If it is true that sexual sins evoke a strong public reaction (as I argued above), it is all the more true when the culprit is female. In this case, the man was as guilty as the woman, yet it did not seem necessary (or advisable?) to bring him into judgment. This is an important detail that we generally overlook. What does this mean?

Societies have a higher tolerance for male misconduct than female misconduct. "He's all boy" is a convenient label for a child who challenges the rules and tears his jeans. "He's out sowing his wild oats" is another convenient label for boys when they are much older. Throughout the centuries societies have indulged men as they experimented in the boundary waters of acceptable behavior. Sexual activity is no exception. The irony for women historically is that men have sinned *with them*—and then later accused them of sexual misconduct. It is like the picture of Jimmy Swaggert, the southern evangelist who ranted and raved against sexual promiscuity during the 1980s while all the while visiting prostitutes in cheap, local motels.

If it is true that gender plays a role in our perception of wrongdoing, what does it mean for women when they are unmasked in their sin? When men accuse them? Is there a different level of severity? Different levels of tolerance? Are the social ramifications different? Are signals sent and labels made that mark the woman permanently? These are troubling questions that require soul-searching honesty if we are to get to the heart of them. No doubt the place to begin is to ask *a woman* what it means when she *alone* is dragged before the religious authorities. Many of us men might hear some surprising answers.

John 8:12–59

WHEN JESUS SPOKE again to the people, he said, "I am the light of the world. Whoever follows me will never walk in darkness, but will have the light of life." ¹³The Pharisees challenged him, "Here you are, appearing as your own witness; your testimony is not valid."

¹⁴Jesus answered, "Even if I testify on my own behalf, my testimony is valid, for I know where I came from and where I am going. But you have no idea where I come from or where I am going. ¹⁵You judge by human standards; I pass judgment on no one. ¹⁶But if I do judge, my decisions are right, because I am not alone. I stand with the Father, who sent me. ¹⁷In your own Law it is written that the testimony of two men is valid. ¹⁸I am one who testifies for myself; my other witness is the Father, who sent me."

¹⁹Then they asked him, "Where is your father?"

"You do not know me or my Father," Jesus replied. "If you knew me, you would know my Father also." ²⁰He spoke these words while teaching in the temple area near the place where the offerings were put. Yet no one seized him, because his time had not yet come.

²¹Once more Jesus said to them, "I am going away, and you will look for me, and you will die in your sin. Where I go, you cannot come."

²²This made the Jews ask, "Will he kill himself? Is that why he says, 'Where I go, you cannot come'?"

²³But he continued, "You are from below; I am from above. You are of this world; I am not of this world. ²⁴I told you that you would die in your sins; if you do not believe that I am the one I claim to be, you will indeed die in your sins."

²⁵"Who are you?" they asked.

"Just what I have been claiming all along," Jesus replied. ²⁶"I have much to say in judgment of you. But he who sent me is reliable, and what I have heard from him I tell the world."

²⁷They did not understand that he was telling them about his Father. ²⁸So Jesus said, "When you have lifted up the Son of Man, then you will know that I am the one I claim to be and that I do nothing on my own but speak just what the

Father has taught me. ²⁹The one who sent me is with me; he has not left me alone, for I always do what pleases him." ³⁰Even as he spoke, many put their faith in him.

³¹To the Jews who had believed him, Jesus said, "If you hold to my teaching, you are really my disciples. ³²Then you will know the truth, and the truth will set you free."

³³They answered him, "We are Abraham's descendants and have never been slaves of anyone. How can you say that we shall be set free?"

³⁴Jesus replied, "I tell you the truth, everyone who sins is a slave to sin. ³⁵Now a slave has no permanent place in the family, but a son belongs to it forever. ³⁶So if the Son sets you free, you will be free indeed. ³⁷I know you are Abraham's descendants. Yet you are ready to kill me, because you have no room for my word. ³⁸I am telling you what I have seen in the Father's presence, and you do what you have heard from your father."

³⁹"Abraham is our father," they answered.

"If you were Abraham's children," said Jesus, "then you would do the things Abraham did. ⁴⁰As it is, you are determined to kill me, a man who has told you the truth that I heard from God. Abraham did not do such things. ⁴¹You are doing the things your own father does."

"We are not illegitimate children," they protested. "The only Father we have is God himself."

⁴²Jesus said to them, "If God were your Father, you would love me, for I came from God and now am here. I have not come on my own; but he sent me. ⁴³Why is my language not clear to you? Because you are unable to hear what I say. ⁴⁴You belong to your father, the devil, and you want to carry out your father's desire. He was a murderer from the beginning, not holding to the truth, for there is no truth in him. When he lies, he speaks his native language, for he is a liar and the father of lies. ⁴⁵Yet because I tell the truth, you do not believe me! ⁴⁶Can any of you prove me guilty of sin? If I am telling the truth, why don't you believe me? ⁴⁷He who belongs to God hears what God says. The reason you do not hear is that you do not belong to God."

⁴⁸The Jews answered him, "Aren't we right in saying that you are a Samaritan and demon-possessed?"

⁴⁹"I am not possessed by a demon," said Jesus, "but I honor my Father and you dishonor me. ⁵⁰I am not seeking glory for

myself; but there is one who seeks it, and he is the judge. ⁵¹I tell you the truth, if anyone keeps my word, he will never see death."

⁵²At this the Jews exclaimed, "Now we know that you are demon-possessed! Abraham died and so did the prophets, yet you say that if anyone keeps your word, he will never taste death. ⁵³Are you greater than our father Abraham? He died, and so did the prophets. Who do you think you are?"

⁵⁴Jesus replied, "If I glorify myself, my glory means nothing. My Father, whom you claim as your God, is the one who glorifies me. ⁵⁵Though you do not know him, I know him. If I said I did not, I would be a liar like you, but I do know him and keep his word. ⁵⁶Your father Abraham rejoiced at the thought of seeing my day; he saw it and was glad."

⁵⁷"You are not yet fifty years old," the Jews said to him, "and you have seen Abraham!"

⁵⁸"I tell you the truth," Jesus answered, "before Abraham was born, I am!" ⁵⁹At this, they picked up stones to stone him, but Jesus hid himself, slipping away from the temple grounds.

ANY ANALYSIS OF John 8:12—59 must begin with a reminder of its setting. The story of the woman caught in adultery is an interruption to Jesus' Tabernacles discourse (see comments on 7:53—8:11). Thus, we must link 7:52 with 8:12 in order to continue the themes of this festival. Earlier we observed how the discourse is advanced through a series of questions and reactions that follow the progress of the festival from its beginning (7:1—13), to its middle (7:14—36), and to its final, great day of celebration (7:37—52). On this final day Jesus has just made a tremendously important announcement about himself (7:37—39): He is the source of the living water that Tabernacles promises through its symbolic rituals. Just as Jesus had done on Sabbath (ch. 5) and Passover (ch. 6), so here he takes up images from the Jewish celebration and uses them in order to make clearer his identity as the Messiah and God's Son.

Thus, when we turn to 8:12, Jesus is still at the Festival of Tabernacles and is likely still standing in the temple on the final day.¹ Religious motifs from that final day of the feast will continue informing what we find in 8:12—59. Just as water is an important image at Tabernacles, light likewise plays an important role, which is precisely Jesus' theme in 8:12.

---

1. The first Greek word of 8:12 is "again," implying a continuation from a previous section.

Moreover, 8:12–59 forms an important unity with chapter 9. The setting of the Feast of Tabernacles is also presupposed in that chapter. In 8:12 Jesus announces that he is the light of the world; then in the very next chapter he prophetically *plays out that message* by giving light to a blind man. A man who once lived in darkness experiences divine light, and (ironically) those who claim to possess the light (the Pharisees) are told that they live in darkness.

"I Am the Light of the World!" (8:12–20)

THIS IS JESUS' second "I am" saying that is followed by a predicate: "I am the light of the world."[2] Tabernacles occurred in the late autumn and celebrated the harvest of tree and vine (see comments on ch. 7). In addition to the water ceremonies (which recalled the need for water in the dry autumn), the calendar also marked the passing of the long summer days. The autumn equinox (where night and day are of equal length) provided the context for a light ceremony that was popular in Jerusalem and orchestrated during Tabernacles.

Zechariah 14 sets the theological context for both ceremonies: In the Day of the Lord not only will there be abundant water flowing from Jerusalem, but that day "will be a unique day, without daytime or nighttime—a day known to the LORD. When evening comes, there will be light" (Zech. 14:7). The imagery also pulls from the desert stories of water flowing from the rock and the pillar of fire and light that guided Israel for so many years (Ex. 13:21–22; Num. 14:14). Thus, Tabernacles witnesses the converging of multiple motifs; harvest, drought, the coming winter darkness, desert wandering, and eschatological vision all merge in the temple ceremonies.

The *Mishnah* chapter on Tabernacles (*Sukkah*) provides lavish descriptions of both the water and light ceremonies and explains that whoever has not seen these things has never seen a wonder in his or her life! Four large stands each held four golden bowls; these were placed in the heavily-used Court of the Women.[3] These sixteen golden bowls (reached by ladders) were filled with oil and used the worn undergarments of the priests for wicks (*m. Sukkah* 5). When they were lit at night (so the rabbis said), all Jerusalem was illumined.[4] In a world that did not have public lighting after dusk, this light

---

2. Cf. 6:35 and comments, where Jesus says, "I am the bread of life."

3. To recreate this setting, readers would do well to review the layout of Herod's temple. The Court of the Women was the first elevated court restricted to Jews only and was east of the Court of Israel (or Men).

4. There is some debate if the lamps were lit only at the beginning of the festival or every night This will impact the significance of Jesus' words in 8:12. If the lamps were dark (so Morris), then Jesus' announcement would contrast with the darkness of the final evening.

shining from Jerusalem's yellow limestone walls must have been spectacular. Choirs of Levites would sing during the lighting while "men of piety and good works" danced in the streets, carrying torches and singing hymns.

On this final day of Tabernacles, Jesus is teaching in the treasury (8:20) located within the Court of the Women (so that men *and women* could give offerings, cf. Mark 12:41). Imagine the scene! In the very court where the lighting ceremony takes place, Jesus stands beneath sixteen lit bowls of oil and says that he is not only the true light of Jerusalem, but of the whole world!

The spiritual use of "light" was common throughout the ancient world. Parallels are available from Judaism, the Old Testament, Qumran, Hellenistic religions, and later gnostic writings. However, Jesus' use here—and the entire scene we have just built—is thoroughly Jewish. Jesus is referring to the countless times that God's saving work in the world is described as "light."[5] John 1:5 reflects this tradition, "The light shines in the darkness, but the darkness has not overcome it" (cf. NIV note). God's first creation was light (Gen. 1:3). God even led the Israelites in the desert with light (Ex. 13:21–22; Ps. 78:14), and they were taught to sing, "The LORD is my light and my salvation—whom shall I fear?" (Ps. 27:1). God's wisdom given to the world is thus a light that illumines his people (Prov. 8:22). Hence, Psalm 119:105: "Your word is a lamp to my feet and a light for my path." In rabbinic Judaism, this light was defined further as God's Word (Torah), which guides and provides wisdom through study.

Since in John's Gospel Jesus is the realization or incarnation of God's own presence in the world, it is not surprising that "light" is used to describe the work of Christ sixteen times. Even the Johannine letters use it. "God is light; in him there is no darkness at all" (1 John 1:5). If Jesus is the light, walking "in the light" is a description of discipleship (1:7).

Jesus' self-reference as light guiding people through darkness (as the pillar of light guided the Israelites in the desert) is quickly challenged (8:13–19). The Pharisees' argument in 8:13 echoes what occurred during Jesus' last visit to Jerusalem in chapter 5, when he referred to the legal qualifications of judicial witnesses, "If I testify about myself, my testimony is not valid" (5:31). The Jewish law required more than one witness to validate any testimony (Deut. 17:6; 19:15; Matt. 18:16; 2 Cor. 13:1; *m. Ketuboth* 2:9). Jesus knows this law (John 8:17). Unfortunately his opponents have forgotten that in the earlier Jerusalem debate, Jesus showed that there were ample witnesses verifying his claim: John the Baptist (5:33), his miraculous works (5:36), the Father (5:37), and even the Scriptures (5:39). Now Jesus must repeat again that his Father is a second witness (8:18).

---

5. In the NIV English text of the Old Testament, "light" is mentioned over 130 times.

But something important has now been added. Jesus would hardly say that whenever he speaks alone his words are invalid, as if they must be weighed by the double-witness judicial rule. This is what it means to judge "by human standards" (Gk. *kata sarka*, lit., "according to the flesh," 8:15a). Jesus does not judge in this manner (8:15b),[6] and he encourages others likewise: "Stop judging by mere appearances, and make a right judgment" (7:24). Jesus' judgment is true, and his words are true, not because of their inherent persuasiveness, but because of their *origins* (8:16b). This is the new unexpected authority behind Jesus' testimony.

Those who judge by worldly standards cannot understand this (see 2 Cor. 5:16).[7] Jesus comes from the Father. He does not speak on his own authority but is echoing what the Father has told him to say (John 3:34; 14:10, 24; 17:8, 14). The root problem with Jesus' opponents, then, is that they do not know the Father (8:19). They are incapable of having true spiritual discernment because they do not know the source of all spirituality, God himself. This criticism is the same one we heard in 5:42 during Jesus' last visit to the temple. Without a deep knowledge of God and his love, it is impossible to recognize his Son.

This interchange takes place in the "temple area near the place where the offerings were put" (8:20a), that is, in the Court of the Women. There were thirteen money chests built in the shape of a *shofar* (a ram's horn, 1 Chron. 25:5) in this court, each indicating how the money was going to be spent (*m. Shekalim* 2:1; 6:1, 5). In Mark 12:41–44 these are the receptacles that the widow uses to deposit two small copper coins. John goes on to remark that Jesus is not seized by the Pharisees at this time (John 8:20b), not because they are suddenly content with his answers, but because his "time had not yet come." The hour of Jesus' departure will include his capture and arrest, but only he himself determines when it will occur (2:4; 7:30; 8:20; 12:23).

"I Am Going Away!" (8:21–30)

THERE ARE NUMEROUS parallels between this section of the discourse and 7:25–36. The question of Jesus' origins remains at the center of the discussion. Jesus will depart eventually to return where he came from (cf. 7:33b and

---

6. There is an important exegetical debate in these verses. Some scholars argue that Jesus is changing the meaning of Gk. word *krino* (to judge) in 8:15–16. Jesus does not condemn (8:15b) but he nevertheless provokes judgment (8:16). This wordplay is found in the Gospel: Jesus does not *condemn* (3:17; 12:47; using *krino*), but he does come to judge (9:39; 5:22; using *krino* and *krima*). Other scholars (myself included) believe that Jesus' judgment in ch. 8 is being contrasted here with *worldly* judgment (cf. 7:24).

7. "So from now on we regard no one from a worldly point of view [*kata sarka*]. Though we once regarded Christ in this way [*kata sarka*], we do so no longer."

8:21a), and even though many will look for him (7:34a; 8:21a), they will not be able to come (7:34b; 8:21c). This leads to remarkable misunderstandings. In chapter 7 the Jewish leadership concluded that Jesus must be going to the Gentiles since such a journey would be prohibited to orthodox Jews. There is an ironic truth here because this is precisely where Jesus' ministry eventually leads (through the work of evangelists like John and his church). Here in chapter 8, the crowd concludes that Jesus must be going to his death—a departure they would prefer to avoid for themselves. Here is another ironic truth: Jesus will indeed die, and this departure will be a return to his Father in heaven.

Jesus' answer in 8:23–29 provides a critical insight into his identity and his incomprehensibility before his listeners. It also explains the urgency of humanity's condition: Once Jesus departs, once the opportunity to hear him and believe in him is gone, the world is lost. "You will die in your sins— unless you believe that I am" (8:24, pers. trans.). The crowd naturally asks, as it were, "You are—what?" (8:25).

But the crowd misses the point altogether. It is God's divine name ("I am") that they cannot understand since they are "from below," since they judge "according to the flesh." Jesus is not simply a prophet with divine things to communicate, but he bears divinity in himself. He is not a man with religious insight (from below, from the world), but God's Son (from above, from heaven). This prompts his audience to ask its most important question. Not: "What do you mean?" But: "Who are you?" (8:25). It is Jesus' divine identity, his mysterious divine incarnation that makes everything about him important. But, John indicates, this sort of insight is beyond their grasp (8:27).

The supreme moment of revelation is when Jesus is "lifted up" (8:28), which is not merely the cross, but the series of events that lead to his glorification: betrayal, trial, crucifixion, resurrection, and ascension. Through these events, the world will see *not* that Jesus is simply telling the truth (NIV), but that he is the bearer of God's divine name ("I am"). "When you have lifted up the Son of Man, then you will know that I am." Again, 8:28 leaves off the predicate, making Jesus' audience wonder and marvel at the amazing claims he is making.

In the Synoptic Gospels there are three instances when Jesus specifically predicts his coming death in Jerusalem (Mark 8:31; 9:31; 10:33–34). In Mark's arrangement, Jesus is moving closer and closer to Jerusalem as he describes the doom that awaits him. His disciples, on the other hand, express increasing incomprehension, denial, and fear that Jesus will actually die and that they too may suffer. The Fourth Gospel parallels this with three statements about the "lifting up of the Son of Man" (3:14; 8:28; 12:33–34); in each we see John emphasize how it is God's sovereign will that determines his Son's fate ("so the Son of Man must be lifted up," 3:14 and 12:34; "I do nothing on my own," 8:28b; "the one who sent me is with me," 8:29). Jesus' remarkable sense of the Father's presence, even as he describes the cross that awaits him, is linked to his perfect obedience to God's will: "I always do what pleases him."

The faith of some of the Jews in his audience (8:30) provides an interesting counterpoint to what we learned in 8:20. In the first section (8:12–20) the discussion concludes with speculation about Jesus' capture. Now we have a description of some who believe. These two reactions parallel what we observed elsewhere in the Gospel where Jesus' audience divides: Some completely oppose him while others are receptive and welcoming. Nevertheless (as the next section shows) those who believe may find difficulty once Jesus' full identity is disclosed.

Spiritual Ancestry (8:31–59)

THE DISCUSSION NOW moves on to address those "who had believed" (8:31). Yet as the story unfolds, it is evident that despite their interest in Jesus, they are unwilling to accept the deeper truths about him. In fact, this audience becomes the very audience that launches the most severe criticisms of Jesus in the entire Gospel. In the end they argue that Jesus is demon-possessed. And Jesus even says that rather than acting like children of Abraham, they are behaving like children of the devil.

This recalls the close of chapter 6 when the believing disciples of Jesus, confronted with the truth of his personhood, stumble, yet declare that they must remain with him: "To whom shall we go? You have the words of eternal life." Now Jewish "believers" who are not his disciples stumble as well; but in the end, they repudiate Jesus and even try to kill him (8:59). This is a deep irony, and we can see here the division sharpening as Jesus and his opponents stand against each other. The section opens with a surprising declaration of belief, but it ends with an attempt on Jesus' life. True discipleship is tested with "if you hold to my teaching" (8:31b). It may be one thing to follow a Jesus whom we have engineered in our religious consciousness; it is quite another to stay with Jesus when he discloses who he really is.

This section of the discourse carries features that we have seen in the other discourses most clearly: The failure of Jesus' audience to perceive his true identity leads to acute misunderstandings; however, these misunderstandings become opportunities for Jesus to clarify his position and press his hearers to deeper levels of discussion. The common thread that holds everything together is the subject of Abraham (8:37, 39, 40, 53, 56, 57, 58), who his true children are, and how they should behave.

In the first round of debate (8:31–41) Jesus challenges a widely held assumption in Judaism. From the earliest chapters of the Old Testament

(Gen. 22:17–18; Ps. 105:6) the people of Israel understood the importance of their election. They would be a blessing not only to God but to other nations. However, the sense of obligation and responsibility that this inspired was eventually replaced with feelings of privilege and protection. In the Lazarus parable (Luke 16:24) the Jews expressed shock that a "son of Abraham" could go after death to the place of suffering. John the Baptist announced that God could make "sons of Abraham" out of Judean stones (Matt. 3:7–10). Jesus said that strangers would be seated with Jews in the heavenly banquet (8:11–12). When Jesus said in 23:9, "And do not call anyone on earth 'father,' for you have one Father, and he is in heaven," he was likely referring to the Jewish reflex to find in the Abraham lineage security that simply was not there.[8]

With its history of slavery and bondage, freedom was a precious treasure among the Jews. Yet, Jesus claims, it is not religious heritage that brings true freedom, but truth (John 8:32). "The truth will set you free." But to be set free means that there is a bondage from which you need to be freed. This inspires a major objection at once. Jews, of course, had been subject to countless nations' sovereignty: Egypt, Assyria, Babylon, Persia, Greece, and Rome. But Jesus' audience is likely referring to spiritual or inward freedom. *One can be a slave and nevertheless still be free.* At the siege of Masada in A.D. 73, Eleazer the priest boasted to his fellow beleaguered Jews, "Long ago we determined to be slaves to neither the Romans nor anyone else."[9] This was idealism at its best. Similarly, Rabbi Akiba commented that the Jews saw themselves as "sons of the kingdom despite their conquests" (cf. Matt. 8:12).[10] Just as in Mark 2:17 those who claimed they were whole did not need a physician, so here those who are free feel they need no deliverance. But they are wrong on both counts.

The captivity, of course, to which Jesus points is a bondage to sin. This is a theme we meet frequently in Paul (Rom. 6:17; 8:2) and in John's letters (1 John 3:4, 8, 9). Jesus is urging that the more devastating bondage is not to any political power, but to spiritual and moral depravity. He then moves to a parabolic saying about the *status* of slaves (John 8:35). The Jews consider themselves to be free (sons of Abraham), but in actuality, Jesus insists, they are slaves (of sin). Slaves can be sold and traded. Slaves have no security.

---

8. Paul makes these same challenges when he spiritualizes the true nature of circumcision in Rom. 2 and when he claims in Gal. 3:16, 29 that the *true* descendents of Abraham have little to do with blood line, but it is a matter of faith. Similarly, Rom. 9:7, "Nor because they are his descendants are they all Abraham's children."

9. Josephus, *Wars*, 7.8.6, cited in Brown, *John*, 1:363.

10. *b. Shabbath*, 128a.

Thus, because they are slaves, their residence in God's family can be in jeopardy. Hence, sinners who claim to be sons of Abraham may discover that they have lost that which they prize. Lineage from Abraham is a matter of faith, and claims to blood heritage that brings spiritual privilege always stand in question (Gal. 3:6ff.; cf. again Rom. 9:7). Sin ruptures a relationship with God. The "son" who is secure and permanent is likely Jesus himself.[11] If the son in such a large household sets a slave free, he will be free indeed (8:36). Imagine, then, if the Son of God sets a slave free. The freedom enjoyed will be indescribable.

Jesus acknowledges that his audience bears the bloodline of Abraham but because of their desire to kill him and their refusal to accept his word, they betray that their lives are not guided by the Father, whose voice Jesus obeys (8:37–38). Blood lineage does not guarantee spiritual lineage. In the Old Testament Abraham had descendants who did not receive his blessing (e.g., Ishmael, Gen. 21). Paul does not miss this parallel to make the same point (Gal. 4:21–31). True Jewishness is inward, not physical and outward (Rom. 2:28–29). Judaism likewise taught that there were features of conduct that gave away "sons of Abraham" (*m. Pirke Aboth* 5.22, "a good eye, a lowly spirit, a humble mind are the makers of the disciples of Abraham our father"). So here, the unrighteousness of Jesus' opponents places in question their claim to possess any link with Abraham. Jesus implies that their activity points to another spiritual father (John 8:38b).

"Abraham is our father" (8:39) now sounds hollow, given Jesus' suggestion that their behavior (8:40) can undermine their claim to heritage. For a second time Jesus' refers to "your own father," as if to suggest he knows the lineage that controls them (8:41). But as the argument unfolds Jesus' opponents see clearly where he is leading. Without Abraham, they cannot belong to God's people. "We are not illegitimate children" is now a defense and an attack. "We" is emphatic and implies comparison: *We* are not illegitimate (but you certainly are), and some scholars argue for a hint here of speculation about Jesus' extraordinary origins and its irony. By claiming to have God as Father, Jesus cannot have a human father, which is precisely the argument from the Synoptic nativity stories. Yet illegitimacy was a slur used by Jews against the Samaritans (and visa versa), and this will come up in 8:48 for Jesus.

If Jesus will not permit them Abraham, certainly (they think) he cannot forbid them an appeal to God (8:41b). But even this is rejected. Since Jesus himself has come from God the Father, then if their parentage stemmed from God the Father, they would love the things of Jesus (1 John 5:1). But in fact

---

11. Gk. reads *"the* son," not as in NIV, "a son." Throughout this Gospel "the son" refers to Jesus. In the Johannine literature, Christians are described as "children" of God.

they do not. The problem is not with the clarity of Jesus, as if he was failing to communicate effectively; the fault rather lies with their role as obedient listeners (John 8:43). They do not "belong to God" (8:47) and are therefore working against his purposes. It is not as if Jesus' opponents disagree with him; the problem is more essential. Given who they are, they cannot recognize the truth, the Father, or anyone sent from the Father speaking the truth. The problem is not necessarily intellectual, but spiritual.

The climax of these implications is finally given in 8:44. His opponents' desire to kill Jesus unmasks the true nature of their spiritual ancestry: Satan. The murder the devil promoted "from the beginning" refers either to Cain and Abel or to the fact that it was through Satan's work that death came into the world, making him the architect of death (Rom. 5:12–14). This is contrasted with Jesus, the architect of truth (John 1:17; 14:6).

The opponents of Jesus now turn back accusations on him (8:48). If it is true that his opponents are children of the devil, then he must be a Samaritan and demon-possessed. This is a radical dishonoring. (1) "Samaritan" (see comments on John 4) refers to those people living north of Jerusalem near Shechem, who had compromised the purity of their faith. By Jesus' day, the enmity between Jews and Samaritans was intense (Luke 10:29–37). This slur likely had become a curse, much like "heretic" or "unbeliever," so Jesus does not even take the time to refute it. (2) The charge of demon-possession is far more serious (cf. also John 7:20; 8:52; 10:20). Rather than seeing God's work in Jesus, his opponents now point to Satan. Note that this charge appears in the Synoptic Gospels as well, where Jesus considers the glib confusing of God and Satan to be serious and unforgivable (Mark 3:22–27).

Jesus has made numerous absolute claims. He comes from the Father and bears the truth; their inability to see this truth betrays their separation from the Father and his purposes. Is this self-promotion? Is Jesus consumed with his own place? Is this a feature of Satan's handiwork? Jesus denies this (8:50), but he cannot deny the essential relationship he has with the Father. The Son glorifies the Father and likewise the Father glorifies the Son (cf. 16:14; 17:5). If his opponents cannot understand the truth about Jesus, they cannot understand this either.

Jesus' original claim centered on freedom and slavery, and objections were voiced vigorously. Now Jesus makes a claim about life and death (8:51–58), and the same reaction results. That Jesus can promise life eternal to those who obey him sets him apart from every spiritual luminary in Judaism, Abraham included. But rather than seeing that Jesus may be pointing to eternal life, the crowd misunderstands him through a material rendering of his meaning. Abraham and the prophets have died and were buried. Is Jesus promising that mortality will be reversed? That he and his followers will not see death?

The force of 8:53 is literally, "What are you making of yourself here?" It is antagonistic and aggressive. But Jesus' defense is that he is *not* glorifying himself again; instead, he is faithfully witnessing to his relationship with the Father. Jesus is simply living in fidelity to his word (8:55), and because God is the author and sustainer of life, all who know him will share in that life.

If Judaism could make an appeal to their ancestry in Abraham, Jesus now makes a parallel appeal (8:56). Many rabbis in this period taught that Abraham possessed tremendous gifts of prophetic insight. God had given to him the secrets of the coming ages, which included an awareness of the coming Messiah. Even his "rejoicing" at the birth of his son Isaac (Gen. 17:17; 21:6) was a foreshadowing of the blessing that would come to the world through his lineage. No rabbi would object to Jesus' claim that Abraham would see the messianic era. But Jesus does not say this. Instead, he says: "Your father Abraham rejoiced at the thought of seeing *my day*; he saw it and was glad" (italics added). The messianic era is now fulfilled in Christ.

But how can Jesus and Abraham know each other since Jesus is not even fifty years old?[12] An important variant in 8:57 reverses the subject of the sentence and is likely the original. Rather than Jesus' seeing Abraham (NIV), some variants read: "and Abraham has seen you?" This accords with the rabbinic understanding of Abraham and his dramatic prescience.[13]

The climax of the entire chapter arrives at 8:58: "'I tell you the truth,' Jesus answered, 'before Abraham was born, I am!'" The seriousness of this statement is confirmed by Jesus' preface (lit.): "Truly, truly [Gk. *amen, amen*] I say to you," a phrase Jesus uses some twenty times in the Gospel (see comment on 1:51). This is an absolute claim to preexistence anchored in the absolute "I am" (Gk. *ego eimi*) language we have already seen in this Gospel (cf. 4:26). "I am" possesses no predicate (as in "I am the bread of life," 6:35) and so stands alone, no doubt echoing the Greek translation of God's divine name given in Exodus 3:14.[14] To exist before the birth of Abraham—and yet to stand here today—is the boldest claim Jesus has yet made. It recalls the affirmation of the prologue that the Word existed even at the beginning of time. His existence has been continuous since his life is completely drawn from God's eternal life.

---

12 This verse suggests that perhaps Jesus was in his 40s since otherwise his opponents would have objected, "You are not yet forty years old!" Luke says that Jesus began his ministry when he was "about thirty years old" (Luke 3:23). The notion that Jesus enjoyed a three-year ministry is merely conjecture taken from the three annual Passover festivals recorded in John. It is plausible that his ministry lasted much longer. See M. J Edwards, "Not Yet 50 Years Old: Jn 8:57," *NTS* 40 (1994): 449—54.

13. T. Baarda., "Jn 8:57b: The Contribution of the Diatessaron of Tatian," *NovT* 38 (1996): 336—43.

14. The LXX translates Ex 3:14 as *ego eimi ho on.*

That Jesus' audience interpreted his words as a divine claim is seen in their reaction (8:59). They are furious because they believe they have heard blasphemy, for which stoning is the legal response (Lev. 24:16; *m. Sanhedrin* 7:4; Josephus, *Ant.* 17.9.3). Jesus slips away not as a result of his own ingenuity, but because God has appointed an hour when his death will be necessary (John 7:30, 44; 8:20; 18:6; cf. Luke 4:29). There is a divine plan, and no action of a mob will interrupt it. In John 10:18 Jesus explains, "No one takes it [my life] from me, but I lay it down of my own accord. I have authority to lay it down and authority to take it up again."

THIS LONG CHAPTER sustains numerous arguments between Jesus and his opponents in the city of Jerusalem. Charges and counter-charges tumble over one another until the tension between Jesus and the "theologians" of Jerusalem reaches a crescendo at the end of the chapter. His opponents hurl a devastating criticism at him, "You are a Samaritan and demon-possessed" (8:48), while Jesus offers the most elevated Christological self-description yet in the Gospel, "Before Abraham was born, I am." The battleground is truth and identity with God: Is Jesus fraudulent or are his accusers? One bit of artillery in the fight is the rhetoric that surrounded the famous image of Abraham in Jewish history and lore.

Hostility from "the Jews." Certainly any interpreter of this chapter must address the breathtaking hostility that Jesus experienced in Jerusalem. But as we do so, we must affirm again (and yet again) that Jesus' opponents are not "the Jews," as some translations (such as the NIV) have it. Jesus himself is Jewish, as are the apostles. The church we know today has been grafted into a Jewish olive tree rooted in the traditions of Abraham, Isaac, Jacob, Moses, and David.

The rhetoric of the debate between Jesus and Jerusalem here is described through the lens of a later era, when the church was locked in struggle with synagogues that denied Jesus' messiahship and sonship. It was later, when the church distinguished itself from Judaism, that the nomenclature "Jesus versus the Jews" took shape, for in the second half of the first century messianic Jews and Gentile Christians struggled with just these opponents.[15] I say this because chapters such as John 8 and 10 have often inspired anti-Semitism.

15. However, such critical language of "the Jews" was not unknown in the earliest period Note how the Jewish rabbi Paul describes the bitter struggles in Judea in 1 Thess. 2:14–15, "For you, brothers, became imitators of God's churches in Judea, which are in Christ Jesus. You suffered from your own countrymen the same things those churches suffered from the Jews, who killed the Lord Jesus and the prophets and also drove us out."

Jews as well as Jewish-Christians would have us be careful and discriminating in how we use this material.

Nevertheless, religious leadership and institutions of Jerusalem, which have been the custodian of divine things for centuries and have enjoyed the temple and the revelation of priest and prophet, cannot accept what God is doing in Christ. Their cynicism evolves from disbelief to antagonism, and then leads to full-scale hostility to Jesus. Given the tone of the debate in John 8 it is no surprise that Jesus is finally crucified in the city less than a year later. In fact, we should read these verses with a sense of awe: Anyone who would teach and argue like this will ultimately get himself killed.

Is there a message in this hostility for us? My instinct is to align myself with Jesus and portray his opponents as those who do not accept the gospel. Jesus' opponents become my opponents. The theologians of Jerusalem who fight with Jesus correspond to the irreligious and cynical of my day. But this hermeneutical decision is a tremendous presupposition. It is like watching a film and identifying with the hero, the winner, the righteous. Such a decision frees me from the vulnerability of rebuke, setting me on God's side and against all comers.

Such a reading of this Gospel might be legitimate, for at times we may find ourselves standing with Christ, defending his claims to divinity, and experiencing the hostility of the world. Jesus tells us, "If the world hates you, keep in mind that it hated me first" (15:18). But there also may be times when we are the residents of Jerusalem, when we are the defenders of orthodoxy, and when we cannot tolerate a new word from God. I am naive to think that if I had lived in the days of Jesus, I would have stood with him at all times. Many of us would have been arguing against him in the courts of the temple.

Ancestry and traditions. Another motif that stands out sharply is the defense used by Jesus' opponents. They make the claim that their ancestry (historical and spiritual) bears definitively on their standing before God. They possess the traditions, the heritage, the temple, the Scriptures, and the institutions. They live in the "city of God" and so should not have to listen to voices challenging their religious instincts. This reflex is a timeless problem that bears on us as well. To what extent do our traditions become impediments to hearing God's voice? To what extent do we rely on our religious heritage too ("I am a son of Luther!" "I come from a long line of Presbyterians!") and use it to insulate ourselves from a prophetic word from God?

In the end it is not the teaching of Jesus that scandalizes his audience. Nor is it his provocative activity. What finally divides Jesus and his followers from the religiously inclined in Jerusalem is his ultimate claim about himself. Jesus is not simply one more prophet gracing the streets of Jerusalem. He is not one more upstart rabbi from Galilee, now in town to challenge the theological giants at the temple. Jerusalem has seen these types of men before. What sets Jesus apart—and in the minds of his enemies, what qualifies him for death—is his outrageous and unacceptable claim to unity with the Father. Whenever the church is locked in dispute for the truth of the gospel, Jesus' absolute authority, his unity with God, and his divine mission will always be the crux of the debate.

There is something ultimate and final about Jesus' call in this discourse. "I am the light of the world." "I am going away, and you will look for me, and you will die in your sin." "If the Son sets you free, you will be free indeed." "If anyone keeps my word, he will never see death." In this Gospel, Jesus brokers all personal access to God and life. "Jesus" thus cannot be an optional experience, an addendum to some religious system. He is the light, the life, and the freedom everyone seeks. In other words, he is not merely the bearer of these things, he possesses these things in himself, and to embrace him, to believe in him, and to follow him mean that we acquire these things by being "in him."

To bring this passage into my own generation means that I must deal with some of the text's more troubling and difficult aspects. I have to talk about hostility and the gospel. I have to talk about religious tradition and spiritual impediments. And I have to talk about the ultimate truth claims in this Gospel that cannot be compromised lest the heart of Jesus' gift to us (light, life, and freedom) be lost. But in each case I have to be sober about where I plant my feet.

THE CUSTODIANS OF TRADITION. Christianity will always experience hostility in the world. We expect that unbelievers will reject our message, persecute the church, and bring untold suffering. The stories of Christian displacement and martyrdom throughout the centuries of the church, including the stories of Christian suffering today in places like Sudan and Egypt, all speak of the same truth. Those who choose to live a godly life in this world, who follow Jesus Christ, and who possess a public witness will be persecuted (2 Tim. 3:12). But this is not the main theme of John 8.

The deepest paradox of John 8 is that Jesus suffers *religious* persecution. These are not godless masses whose pursuit of paganism has deemed Jesus inconvenient. Jesus is confronting the "world," to be sure, but it is a religious world—a world of unbelief, yes, but a religious world with spiritual appetites. The Judaism embraced by Jesus' opponents was a deeply spiritual religion that earnestly sought its Messiah, prayed fervently to God, followed the Scriptures, and worshiped regularly. Those whose hearts were inclined to hear

God's new voice in the world quickly recognized this voice in Jesus and followed him. Yet those who were entrenched in the traditions of their religious world, whose spiritual passions betrayed them and closed their eyes and ears, were singularly unable to find anything redeeming in Jesus' life work.

The paradigm of the passage is then set: Jesus steps into a religiously devout environment and immediately splits his audience. Those who follow him become passionate believers. Those who stand opposed, who defend their traditions with zeal, suddenly become zealous opponents, enemies of God's work in the world. This passage warns the custodians of tradition that their defense of these spiritual habits and rituals may well be their undoing.

Paul expresses a similar prophetic critique in Romans 2:17–29. In his argument with his Jewish opponents, he urges that the tradition of circumcision in itself has minimal effect: "A man is not a Jew if he is only one outwardly, nor is circumcision merely outward and physical" (2:28). The preservation of the tradition is not in itself a spiritual asset. Instead, circumcision is something inward, spiritual. "Circumcision is circumcision of the heart, by the Spirit, not by the written code" (2:29).

In our passage Jesus' audience argues in the same manner regarding their natural ancestry: "Abraham is our father," they insist (John 8:39a). But Jesus argues that lineage from Abraham is evidenced not through bloodline but through spiritual disposition (8:39b–40). This too is the same line that Paul picks up in Romans 4. Abraham is the father of *those who have faith*, not simply those who keep the Jewish traditions and possess his bloodline. Ancestry and tradition offer false promises to those who think that God is found in them alone.

When Karl Barth wrote his remarkable commentary on Romans in 1919, he looked at these passages on circumcision (Rom. 2) and Abraham (Rom. 4) and made a critical decision. The religious complacency that Paul confronts points not simply to ancient Judaism, but to today's church. Even Paul understands that the story of Abraham told in Romans 4 was written not only for the sake of the ancients, but *for us* (4:23–35). Those who point to religious ancestry and tradition as their badges of religious security will actually find themselves in serious jeopardy.

Barth describes their life. It is the life of people who are headed on a long journey and along the way find a sign pointing them westward. The signpost is there to convey them to their destination, but instead they stop and create a life for themselves under its painted words. They build a civilization there, celebrating the signpost and telling stories of how they arrived at the marker. Rituals evolve and songs are written. Books are published and liturgies follow. A few travel on and return, confirming that the sign does indeed lead to the place promised. But the second and third generations have built a life around the signpost and have forgotten the meaning of the journey. Their lore is built on stories of past travel, not on stories of arriving or on the prophetic call to get on with the journey themselves.

Jesus in our century. It is a troubling question, but we must face it. If Jesus stepped into our century, if he walked into our evangelical churches, if he picked up a religious symbol (as he did at the Jewish Feast of Tabernacles) and challenged the symbol's original meaning, would we cheer or would we fight? Suddenly we might find ourselves defending *Christendom* instead of the Christian faith. We might explain that the old meaning, the old songs, the old forms had worked just fine for generations. We might challenge this newcomer and demand that he verify that he was indeed a messenger from God. And when he pressed his claims powerfully, suddenly we would be forced either to let go of our former position and become a believer or argue and rebel.

This reflex that cannot see God in the prophetic voice of Jesus, that rebels and fights and attacks, is the work of Satan (8:45). It is Satan's work among *religious* people. It is a work that appeared within Judaism and that appears just as often within the Christian church. It is the work of darkness that is commonplace to the human heart. It is work that denies the true authority of the Son and robs him of his credentials to speak (8:13). It is work that puts Jesus before the bar of secular examination, when the examiners are discovered to be philosophers or theologians or historians (8:15). It is work that refuses to admit that his voice is not merely another human voice, but a divine voice sent by God (8:26–27, 40). It is work that distorts the truth, that lies about what it knows to be real, and that defends instead its own religious prerogatives (8:44). Above all, it is a voice that makes a human voice preeminent to the voice of God.

When Jesus arrived at Tabernacles, he found strict opposition among the religious leadership of Judaism. I fear to think how I would have responded were I living in the city at that time. Here I am, a religious professional, a devout believer, one who serves and defends the institutions built in the name of God. I have religious investments and religious commitments. Perhaps I would see it as an act of devotion and piety to stop anyone who would upset what *we had built* in God's name.

Are evangelicals any different today? Can our piety become life under the "signpost"? Can it be simply a recitation of ancestry and tradition, a defense of all that is holy and good and spiritual but that knows little of God? In 8:47 Jesus says that the problem is that his audience "does not hear" any longer. This, he suggests, is evidence that they do not belong to God.

John 8:12–59 is a severe call to Judaism that it must repent. But it is a call for us too, who have taken up the mantle worn by the temple leadership of Jerusalem.

John 9:1–41

A S HE WENT along, he saw a man blind from birth. ²His
disciples asked him, "Rabbi, who sinned, this man or
his parents, that he was born blind?"

³"Neither this man nor his parents sinned," said Jesus, "but
this happened so that the work of God might be displayed in
his life. ⁴As long as it is day, we must do the work of him who
sent me. Night is coming, when no one can work. ⁵While I am
in the world, I am the light of the world."

⁶Having said this, he spit on the ground, made some mud
with the saliva, and put it on the man's eyes. ⁷"Go," he told
him, "wash in the Pool of Siloam" (this word means Sent). So
the man went and washed, and came home seeing.

⁸His neighbors and those who had formerly seen him begging asked, "Isn't this the same man who used to sit and beg?"
⁹Some claimed that he was.

Others said, "No, he only looks like him."

But he himself insisted, "I am the man."

¹⁰"How then were your eyes opened?" they demanded.

¹¹He replied, "The man they call Jesus made some mud and
put it on my eyes. He told me to go to Siloam and wash. So I
went and washed, and then I could see."

¹²"Where is this man?" they asked him.

"I don't know," he said.

¹³They brought to the Pharisees the man who had been
blind. ¹⁴Now the day on which Jesus had made the mud and
opened the man's eyes was a Sabbath. ¹⁵Therefore the Pharisees
also asked him how he had received his sight. "He put mud on
my eyes," the man replied, "and I washed, and now I see."

¹⁶Some of the Pharisees said, "This man is not from God,
for he does not keep the Sabbath."

But others asked, "How can a sinner do such miraculous
signs?" So they were divided.

¹⁷Finally they turned again to the blind man, "What have
you to say about him? It was your eyes he opened."

The man replied, "He is a prophet."

¹⁸The Jews still did not believe that he had been blind and
had received his sight until they sent for the man's parents.

¹⁹"Is this your son?" they asked. "Is this the one you say was born blind? How is it that now he can see?"

²⁰"We know he is our son," the parents answered, "and we know he was born blind. ²¹But how he can see now, or who opened his eyes, we don't know. Ask him. He is of age; he will speak for himself." ²²His parents said this because they were afraid of the Jews, for already the Jews had decided that anyone who acknowledged that Jesus was the Christ would be put out of the synagogue. ²³That was why his parents said, "He is of age; ask him."

²⁴A second time they summoned the man who had been blind. "Give glory to God," they said. "We know this man is a sinner."

²⁵He replied, "Whether he is a sinner or not, I don't know. One thing I do know. I was blind but now I see!"

²⁶Then they asked him, "What did he do to you? How did he open your eyes?"

²⁷He answered, "I have told you already and you did not listen. Why do you want to hear it again? Do you want to become his disciples, too?"

²⁸Then they hurled insults at him and said, "You are this fellow's disciple! We are disciples of Moses! ²⁹We know that God spoke to Moses, but as for this fellow, we don't even know where he comes from."

³⁰The man answered, "Now that is remarkable! You don't know where he comes from, yet he opened my eyes. ³¹We know that God does not listen to sinners. He listens to the godly man who does his will. ³²Nobody has ever heard of opening the eyes of a man born blind. ³³If this man were not from God, he could do nothing."

³⁴To this they replied, "You were steeped in sin at birth; how dare you lecture us!" And they threw him out.

³⁵Jesus heard that they had thrown him out, and when he found him, he said, "Do you believe in the Son of Man?"

³⁶"Who is he, sir?" the man asked. "Tell me so that I may believe in him."

³⁷Jesus said, "You have now seen him; in fact, he is the one speaking with you."

³⁸Then the man said, "Lord, I believe," and he worshiped him.

³⁹Jesus said, "For judgment I have come into this world, so that the blind will see and those who see will become blind."

⁴⁰Some Pharisees who were with him heard him say this and asked, "What? Are we blind too?"

⁴¹Jesus said, "If you were blind, you would not be guilty of sin; but now that you claim you can see, your guilt remains.

THE STORY OF the Feast of Tabernacles now goes to a type of narrative we frequently encounter in the Synoptic Gospels, namely, a healing followed by controversy. It is also a story that has numerous parallels with the healing account given in John 5. A man is healed on the Sabbath, the temple leadership (and in John 9 the neighbors) raise questions, Jesus later finds the man and encourages him, and finally Jesus enters into an extended debate with Jerusalem's theologians about the meaning of his authority.

The healing of the blind man is also closely linked with the preceding narrative in 8:12–59. Jesus is still at the Feast of Tabernacles, and the reader should review the temple light ceremonies alluded to in 8:12 (see comments). Chapter 9 can almost be described as a "case study" of Jesus' message in the second half of chapter 8. It is a magnificent summary of what Jesus has been saying about himself throughout the festival. He is the true light that surpasses anything available in the temple; he is a messenger from God, bearing God's word for the world and giving life to all who believe.

In the present chapter, a man who lives in "darkness" is miraculously given "light." Through the story of this man's healing we see another parable beginning to unfold. Physical healing becomes a symbol of spiritual healing while physical blindness is replaced with spiritual blindness. At the end of the story a splendid reversal appears: The man who once lived in darkness now has light (in both eye and heart), while those arrayed against him have sound eyes but nevertheless live in spiritual darkness. Tabernacles light has truly come to Jerusalem and everyone needs it. Yet only those who believe in Jesus will have the opportunity to enjoy it.

The chapter can be conveniently organized in three units. First is the account of the healing itself (9:1–7). This is followed by the interrogation of the blind man by his neighbors and the Pharisees (9:8–34)—a section that ends with the man being expelled from his synagogue (9:30–34). Finally Jesus reenters the story to provide a parabolic teaching that sums up the lessons of the story: how one sightless man gained vision while others are told they are blind (9:35–41). John delights in double meanings, which we must watch for as the story unfolds. John 9 provides a refreshing interlude from the dense argumentation of chapters 6–8. It is, as Raymond Brown has remarked, Johannine "dramatic skill at its best."[1]

The Healing of the Blind Man (9:1–7)

THE SYNOPTICS PROVIDE numerous examples of Jesus healing blind people. In some respects this sort of miracle was a hallmark of his ministry (Matt. 11:5; Luke 4:17; 7:22). Jesus healed the blind man Bartimaeus in Jericho (Mark 10:46–52; Luke 18:35–43), two blind men in Galilee (Matt. 9:27–31), a blind man without speech elsewhere (possibly in Capernaum; Matt. 12:22–23), a blind man in Bethsaida (Mark 8:22–26), and one more in Jerusalem following his cleansing of the temple (Matt. 21:14). Jesus was a healer especially of the blind. They came to him in order to see if he would deliver them from their suffering (Matt. 21:14).

Blindness was a problem in antiquity, far more common than we would think. Eye disease had few cures, and unsanitary conditions (especially in water) increased risks considerably. In Jesus' day blindness was so well known that he includes the blind in his parables about whom to invite to parties (Luke 14:13). He even uses it metaphorically to represent spiritual darkness, precisely as he does in John 9 (Matt. 15:14; 23:16, 17, 19, 24, 26; Luke 6:39).

The man whom Jesus meets at the Feast of Tabernacles has been blind from birth (9:1). This leads his disciples to ask about the origin of his suffering (9:2). They assume there must be a connection between sin and suffering, so they probe who is responsible, the man or his parents. Jesus rejects this entire line of questioning (9:3). However, the NIV and most English translations invite gross confusion with Jesus' answer. The NIV reads: "Neither this man nor his parents sinned," said Jesus, "but this happened so that the work of God might be displayed in his life."[2] It hardly takes a careful reader to see the theological implications following this line of thought: God brought suffering to this man so that he might glorify himself in his healing. While a sound theology cannot doubt God's sovereignty to do as he pleases, thoughtful Christians may see this as a cruel fate in which God inflicts pain on people simply to glorify himself.

However, the "purpose clause" of 9:3b ("so that the work of God . . . ") can just as well be applied to 9:4, and no doubt it should. Such clauses (introduced by Gk. *hina*) may begin the main sentence rather than follow it. Of eleven uses of the Gk. *all' hina* ("but so that," 9:3b) in John, four of them precede their main sentence (1:31; 13:18; 14:31; 15:25). If 9:2–4 follows this pattern, we may translate it as follows: "'Neither this man nor his parents sinned,' said

---

1. Brown, *John*, 1:376.
2. The words "this happened" do not appear in the Greek text and are an interpretation added in the NIV.

Jesus. 'But so that the work of God might be displayed in his life, we must do the work of him who sent me while it is still day.'"

The purpose clause now explains that Jesus must work *so that* God's work may be displayed in this man's life. God had not made the man blind in order to show his glory; rather, God has sent Jesus to do works of healing in order to show his glory. The theological nuance of the two translations cannot be more different. Jesus' work must not be interrupted because he is the light that illumines the day, and night is coming (9:4b–5) when he will be absent and such miracles at his hand will cease.

Jesus then makes a mud plaster of saliva and soil and applies it to the man's eyes (9:6). In antiquity spittle was thought to have medicinal power. Thus, Jesus' action is not unusual.[3] Mark records two other instances where Jesus does the same thing (Mark 7:32–35; 8:22–25). Jesus then tells the man to go and wash in the Pool of Siloam (9:7). John indicates in a parenthesis that "Siloam" means "sent" (which it does in Hebrew).[4]

This pool was at the south end of the city of Jerusalem and is an important detail for two reasons. (1) It was the source of water in the Tabernacles ceremony (see comments on 7:37–52). This is the pool built after Hezekiah redirected the Gihon Spring by tunneling west under the city of David. It was the only source of spring water in the city and thus had religious, ceremonial value.[5] If Jesus is the source of the Feast of Tabernacles water (7:37–39), this man has now experienced such water in a profound way.

(2) The name of the pool bears symbolic importance for Jesus. More than twenty times in this Gospel, Jesus is described as the one who has been "sent" by God (e.g., 4:34; 5:23, 37; 7:28; 8:26; 12:44; 14:24). In other words, the blind man is being told to go wash in the place called "sent," by the One who was "sent" by God. Jesus, then, is the source of his healing, not the pool.[6] The man is obedient (9:7) and is healed.[7] John reports no fanfare or disturbance.

---

3. In antiquity there was enormous superstition surrounding the "spittle" of a renowned person. Both the Greek healing cult of Asclepius and Jewish popular belief gave spittle magical power. The rabbis were generally critical of such superstition (K. Rengstorf, "πηλός," *TDNT* 6:118–19).

4. In Hebrew the word was *shiloah*, which the LXX usually translates *siloam*. Josephus calls it "Siloa."

5. Today the pool can be seen south of "David's City," below the Arab village of Silwan. One can walk through Hezekiah's Tunnel (where the spring begins) and exit at the Pool of Siloam.

6. Some scholars point out that in Judaism during this period, *shiloah* had messianic overtones. Isa. 8:6 says, "Because this people has rejected the gently flowing waters of Shiloah," which the LXX translates as "Siloam." A similar name appears in Gen. 49:10 (Shiloh). Both of these were interpreted by Jews and Christians as messianic. In our present passage Judaism is rejecting Jesus, just as in Isa. 8 they rejected "Shiloah."

7. Compare the similar healing/washing story of Naaman and Elisha in 2 Kings 5:10–14. Naaman's trip to the Jordan River is an act of obedience to show his respect for the prophet.

Interrogation (9:8–34)

THE DRAMATIC HEALING of this man must have made a significant stir among his immediate friends and family. While in antiquity numerous people might claim to possess healing powers, miracles such as this *that could be verified* caught everyone's attention. The ancient world had few answers for severe illnesses and disabilities, which led many to look to magic and superstition. But here was a healer who did what he promised. A man well known as a beggar blind from birth now could see; this was unparalleled (9:32).

The community's investigation of this man's experience is given to us in abbreviated form in the following verses. We can imagine hours of debating and discussing as the community tries to verify not only the identity of the man *as blind* but the identity of the healer, Jesus. How did he do this? Can it be repeated? Can he do this to still more people? And where does his authority come from? Is this power something unique, something that unveils God's working in him? Is this divine power?

(1) **The neighbors (9:8–13).** John provides a cycle of four scenes where questions are launched concerning the man and his healing. It is instructive to make a careful comparison of these four to see what implied messages they bear. In the first scene (9:8–13), the neighbors interrogate the man and in disbelief work to verify that he is indeed the man they knew as blind. They do not reject the miracle, but they look to the Pharisees, the established theological leaders in the synagogue, for counsel. These leaders sat on the high court of Israel, the Sanhedrin, but for minor, community matters, they were accessible for the average person.

(2) **The Pharisees (9:14–17).** The Pharisees question the man about the healing, but their chief worry is about a violation of the Sabbath. Because Jesus has done this on the Sabbath, they conclude that he must be a sinner and consequently, he cannot be acting in the power of God.

(3) **The man's parents (9:18–23).** The Pharisees turn next to the man's parents in order to confirm that indeed a miracle has occurred. The leaders are incredulous, but the parents fear them because they know of a conspiracy that will expel anyone from the synagogue who stands with Jesus. They deflect the Pharisees' questions and direct them back to their son.

(4) **The formerly blind man (again) (9:24–29).** The leaders turn to the man for a second time. While he can hardly make a comment about Jesus' sinfulness, he cannot deny the miracle. In exasperation, he presses the Pharisees boldly and the tension of the story mounts. The miracle demands an explanation, and its sheer magnitude points to only one source: God. But if this is the case, since God does not listen to sinners—and God has listened to Jesus—Jesus cannot be a sinner. Here we have the sharpest division between the man (who supports Jesus) and the leaders (who do not). "We are

disciples of Moses," they claim. These words point not merely to the division within Jesus' audience, but to the later harsh division that will erupt between synagogue and church in coming decades.

Each of these scenes probes the identity of Jesus, and each betrays a deeper literary function. As the story progresses, Jesus is more closely revealed by name: He is "Jesus" (9:10), then he is called a "prophet" (9:17), then "the Christ" (9:22), and finally, he is declared to be "from God" (9:33). It is easy to see the Christological progression of each name as the story develops. While the Pharisees repudiate Jesus and his role, the discussion drives home his true identity.

Ironically, the entire episode of interrogation ends with an accusation hurled at the man from the leaders: "You were steeped in sin at birth; how dare you lecture us!" (9:34). This is telling since it echoes the verses that began the chapter. Recall the question raised in 9:1–2 about the man's birth and sin. Jesus' rejected this question (9:3) as a cause of his infirmity, just as he rejected the Pharisees' attempt to dismiss this man again as a sinner (9:34). In the former instance, sin supposedly brought physical blindness; in the latter, his sin supposedly brought spiritual blindness (or religious ignorance). They are wrong on both counts. Nevertheless the interrogation ends with the healed man experiencing the very thing his parents feared: He is expelled from the synagogue. We are not told if the discipline extends over a few days, a month, or permanently. Each may have been possible (though the latter seems unlikely).

Some scholars have viewed the expulsion of 9:34 as evidence that the story comes from a later period (generally the late 80s or 90s), when synagogue/church tensions were acute and the formal language of expulsion was imbedded into Jewish liturgy and law. Some point to the Jewish Council of Jamnia and expulsion decrees established in the late 80s. But others today are doubtful if Jamnia is determinative and think that it should be "relegated to the limbo of unestablished hypotheses."[8] It is thus not necessary to see the discipline for the present story as a formal excommunication from the synagogue, but a quick rejection of the man from their presence.

Spiritual Blindness (9:35–41)

THE STORY CLOSES with Jesus' return visit to the now-healed blind man. He has heard that as a result of the healing this man was expelled from the synagogue community. Jesus similarly "found" the paralytic in chapter 5 following his healing on the Sabbath (5:14). But while the paralytic's disobedience to

---

8. J. Lewis, *ABD*, 3:634–37, cited in D. Wenham, "A Historical View of John's Gospel," *Themelios* 23:2 (1998). 5. Lewis continues, "It should not be allowed to be considered a consensus established by mere repetition of assertion."

Jesus in refusing to remain silent led to Jesus' increased persecution, the blind man becomes a model of faith and goodness.

Jesus meets with the blind man privately to unveil the true depth of what he experienced. His confession of faith ("Lord, I believe" 9:38) and his worship indicate that he no longer lives in "darkness" in any sense. This does not imply that the man simply believes in the reality of the miracle or the ability of Jesus. He has been arguing for this all along. The fact of his regained eyesight is beyond dispute. This rather is an open embrace of Jesus—a commitment to him as the Messiah of Israel. Jesus' use of the title "Son of Man" does not evoke images of the coming conquering hero that we see so often in the Synoptics. In John's story it is a commonplace title for Jesus as the divine messenger from heaven (3:13–14; 5:53; 6:27; 12:23).

The blind man thus becomes a model of every believer who embraces Jesus' lordship and suffers persecution as a result (15:18–16:4). This is evident particularly in the double use of the Greek word *kyrios* in 9:36 and 38. In the first instance, *kyrios* simply means "sir" (NIV), to reflect the respect the man has for Jesus (cf. 4:11; 5:7; 12:21). But once Jesus unveils the true meaning of his personhood, the man's attitude is transformed. Thus in 9:38 *kyrios* ("Lord") parallels Thomas's attitude of worship in 20:28; both men recognize that they are standing before a revelation of God.

The Pharisees, by contrast, have come forward to judge both the man and Jesus. But in the end, Jesus judges them. Once again we can find a parallel in the narrative of John 5. Following the accusations of that Sabbath controversy, Jesus' discourse unveils the spiritual sickness of his accusers. Judgment is thus reversed as Jesus' accusers suddenly stand accused. The same is at work in John 9. The light/darkness motif that surrounds the Feast of Tabernacles creates a delightful double meaning. Jesus' opponents are physically sighted, but in reality they are spiritually blind. The blind man has had both conditions reversed (he can see perfectly clearly in both respects now).

But the most serious condition these opponents possess (9:41) is their insistence that they are innocent, that they understand fully the theological point Jesus is making, and that they reject it. Because they *claim* that they can see, their guilt is underscored since they are self-affirming in their religious position against Jesus.

The drama of chapter 9 has played out in full the meaning of Jesus' announcement at the Feast of Tabernacles that he is "the light of the world" (8:12). Light has triumphed over darkness both in the blind man's eyes and in his heart. But the light has also come as a symbol of judgment. This motif of light and judgment came out clearly earlier in 3:19–21. The Pharisees and the blind man have each stood in the light, and it has unmasked their spiritual dispositions:

Light has come into the world, but men loved darkness instead of light because their deeds were evil. Everyone who does evil hates the light, and will not come into the light for fear that his deeds will be exposed. But whoever lives by the truth comes into the light, so that it may be seen plainly that what he has done has been done through God.

TWO HORIZONS. This dramatic story is as much about my life as a reader as it is about the first-century experiences of one blind man. But I cannot neglect the historical importance of Jesus' Tabernacles revelation (about which this story is the climactic episode), for it sets the tone of Jesus' visit to Jerusalem. Since chapter 7 we have witnessed how the authorities have firmly stood against Jesus, making condemning accusations. In this chapter the ultimate gulf seems firm. To the blind man they say, "You are this fellow's disciple! We are disciples of Moses!" (9:28). In other words, the man must make a choice concerning whom he will follow.

The implication is that once a person becomes Jesus' disciple, no longer can he or she be considered Moses' disciple. This is a truly unfortunate decision since all of the earliest Jewish-Christians saw themselves as fulfilling what Moses and the patriarchs would have desired. As in 8:57, Abraham has seen Jesus' day—indeed, Jesus himself—and rejoiced. But here we see that a decision to follow Jesus and proclaim him to be Messiah had severe religious consequences in the synagogue.

But the story goes further. The man and his opponents play out their story on a stylized literary stage, speaking not simply of history but of the present. The man is the protagonist in whose life we can easily see ourselves. The opponents are the literary antagonists, whose position is predictable and repeatable. For some scholars, this literary form is proof that the story is not historical, but stems from the Johannine church decades later.

But such a conclusion is unnecessary. John is rather writing on two horizons, recording a tragic, revealing episode in Jesus' life and letting that story speak powerfully to any who would listen in their own context. The man thus becomes a model of the ideal convert (and no doubt should be contrasted with the healed man in chapter 5): He is healed by Jesus, he is persecuted, he chooses to believe in Jesus, he becomes a disciple. Jesus' opponents likewise are stylized characters, who stand in their religious convictions (much like the opponents of ch. 8) and instead of seeing the miracle, point to Jesus' violation of the Sabbath. In the end, they are found to be blind in their religious "wisdom."

Occasionally John lets us watch "double meanings" at work among the characters of his story, such as when Nicodemus wrestles with the notion of rebirth in chapter 3. But in chapter 9, Jesus lets these double meanings work between the text and the reader. We are observers who see things not even the actors see. And the meaning (missed on them) can be ours if we have the sight, the spiritual insight, that Jesus is offering in chapter 9. Spiritual insight and physical sight move back and forth as we watch the actors play their roles.

For instance, the blind man confesses twice that he does not "know," that he is ignorant (9:12, 25). Even when he meets Jesus in the end, he betrays how little he understands (9:36). Even his parents confess their ignorance (9:21). Yet at the end of the story, this man gains not only physical sight but spiritual insight (9:34–38). The religious leaders, by contrast, possess physical sight, but in the end are told that they are blind (lacking spiritual wisdom) even though two times they proclaim to "know" (9:24, 29). They even make pronouncements betraying their confidence in their knowing (9:16). The message here is fascinating: What one claims about spiritual insight cannot always be trusted. Sometimes those with numerous academic degrees and positions of religious power know less truth than the simple religious inquirer.

The antagonists, therefore, enjoy boasting in their confidence; the hero of the story comes to Jesus in complete emptiness. The empty man is filled; the men who claim they "need [no] doctor" (Matt. 9:12) are left in their darkness. The story is thus about open hearts and closed hearts. But here an element is added that we did not see in the controversies of chapter 8. These opponents boast in their knowledge, they are confident in their knowing, and yet they do not realize that they are actually unwise, ignorant, and misdirected. Guilt is attached to this boasting ("But now that you claim you can see, your guilt remains," 9:41). In chapter 8 we simply met opponents who expressed religious antagonism. In chapter 9 we meet religious antagonism that springs from religious hybris.

As a reader I watch this drama unfold. However, the drama is working its magic on me as well. I too must choose. Will I believe the evidence of the miracle? *Was this man blind from birth? Were these his parents?* Will I decide that whoever can do such a miracle may come from God? *Was Jesus a sinner? Does his Sabbath violation invalidate his claims?* And will I choose to believe? *What about the consequences? What about threats of persecution?*

I am invited to believe. Just as we witnessed in chapter 4, the narrative of John 9 supplies me with what I need to properly identify Jesus. Titles for Jesus spill over each other, creating a catalogue for my study: Rabbi (9:2), Jesus (9:3), the light of the world (9:5), Sent (9:7), from God (9:16), prophet (9:17), Christ (9:22), Son of Man (9:35), Lord (9:38). Everything is here except the title Son of God (cf. 3:18; 5:25; also 10:36), and one can argue that this theme is presupposed in 9:16 and 33 (to be "from God" is to be God's authoritative emissary or Son).

Hence, there are two principle "loci" in the story that I can interpret and bring into my generation. (1) There is the experience of the blind man, and here I can draw a dramatic picture of his infirmity, his begging, his healing (physical and spiritual), and his expulsion from his synagogue. (2) I can explore the experience of Jesus' opponents—filled with questions aimed to hobble Jesus' good work, puffed up in their theological knowledge, and in the end are judged by the Lord. Each locus is placed before me and I am invited to participate in the story. John has crafted the story so that I am forced as the reader to make the same judgment as Jesus' audience. All the evidence of the miracle and Jesus' identity are here. Now will I believe—with the blind man—or will I ask antagonistic questions—with the leaders?

THE HEALING OF the blind man in John 9 has always played an important role in the instructional work of the church. Along with the stories in John 4 (the Samaritan woman) and 5 (the paralytic), the blind man appears in early catacomb art as an example of conversion/baptism. In all three stories water is the agent of regeneration, and the patristic and early medieval church quickly applied them to its baptismal rites. New converts were generally taught through the season of Lent, and these three stories were central to its liturgies.[9] In eleventh-century Milan, for instance, the third Sunday in Lent was "the Sunday of the Blind Man." Baptism was then celebrated during Easter week. John 9 served this too since it showed the healing power of water when it is employed for a spiritual work of God.

As early as the third century, we have evidence that examinations were also given to baptismal candidates during Lent. Three tests were given, and before the third, "the great test," John 9 was read aloud.[10] Since questions were asked of this man in chapter 9, it was a fitting model of what it meant to be a Christian who was ready to answer for his or her faith. If the candidate passed these tests, passages about cleansing water were read before baptism. Then the confession of the blind man was read aloud, "I do believe, Lord" (9:38).[11]

The blind man: a model of belief and conversion. This man's life should be depicted as a hopeless tragedy. While he later shows himself to be spiritually astute, his day-to-day life enjoyed none of the protection or charitable assistance often given to the blind today. We have to forget images of

---

9. See Hoskyns, "The Use of the Fourth, Fifth, and Ninth Chapters of St. John's Gospel in the Early Lectionaries," *John*, 363–65.

10. Brown, *John*, 1:380, citing Braun, *Jean*, 158–59.

11. In Catholic liturgies many of these traditions remain (see Mass liturgies for the Fourth Sunday in Lent).

seeing-eye dogs and Braille books. He sat at the roadside and begged. No employment, no prospects for marriage, no social honor. He was at the bottom of the social ladder. His future was bleak and he knew it. He was like the paralytic of chapter 5, only worse. This man's world had foreclosed on him. There was no social net to catch people like this.

This hopelessness and darkness provide us with a potent image because John describes men and women without Christ to be in a crisis no less desperate. In 8:12 and 12:35 Jesus refers to those who "walk in darkness," and this is precisely the condition of the blind. They stumble and get lost. Jesus lifts this image above the commonplace in order to make it a spiritual metaphor for the condition of the world that he has come to remedy.

The glory of this man's healing stands in stark contrast with the desperation of his condition. Jesus did not simply give him sight; he gave him life. Some features of the story bear reflection. (1) Healing was important to Jesus' work, and likewise it should be important in the church's work today. I do not want to spiritualize this story utterly, making the spiritual renewal of the blind man the only important thing. Jesus also recognized that making the blind man whole was a gesture of his love for the man. Unfortunately many of us are predisposed not to believe in healing such as this.

There is an entire literature on this subject, and I imagine that anyone aiming to duplicate Jesus' ministry (as found in John 9) needs to grapple with it. Some approaches wrestle with intellectual questions (such as C. S. Lewis's *Miracles*). But others (Kathryn Kuhlman, Benny Hinn) seem to discredit a healing ministry for the thinking pastor. For many (myself included), the writings of Francis MacNutt have been compelling. As a Catholic priest, MacNutt entered into this ministry during the height of the Catholic charismatic renewal thirty years ago. His experiences there, along with his Ph.D. in theology from Harvard, give him maximum credibility to address the issue.[12]

(2) God is glorified when ministry happens in this manner. This is ministry that invites God to act in a powerful, dramatic manner to utterly transform. I fear sometimes that evangelicals are prone to view ministry through the lens of a twenty-first-century scholasticism. The work of God (which Jesus was eager to do) was simple: He brought the power of God to bear on one man's life. The man was healed and transformed, and this led to an accurate, articulate confession of Jesus' personhood. We often look for such testimonies without supplying the power of healing Jesus offered.

---

12. See his many books: *The Power to Heal* (1977); *Healing* (1974, 1984, 1988); *Prayer That Heals* (1984); *Overcome by the Spirit* (1990); and *Deliverance from Evil Spirits* (1995). Another helpful writer is Agnes Sanford.

The model of this man's conversion, however, is not simply about desperation and healing. He is courageous. He valiantly holds fast to what he cannot deny. His thinking runs as follows: Jesus had healed him; only God can do such things; therefore, Jesus must be from God. But his intellectual courage is matched by his personal fearlessness as he suffers persecution for his courage. The intellectual and religious leaders despise his testimony and want him to pay a price for holding to it. This drama is also a part of John's conversion model. To embrace faith in Jesus Christ will come with consequences: social isolation, punishment, perhaps martyrdom.

It is significant that John's story moves quickly away from the sheer fact of Jesus' miracle-working capacity to the identity of the One who heals. The man's faith is not in the miracle-working ability of Jesus. This is only the springboard. His faith quickly connects with the true identity of who Jesus is. He is "the Lord," and he rightly ought to be worshiped. To my mind, this is the ultimate test of any healing ministry, and this is what makes me suspicious of some healing ministries today that enjoy a national profile. To what extent is Jesus glorified and worshiped? Are the miracles themselves center stage or is Jesus Christ, whose power and work is displayed through them?

There is one final note that most American evangelicals probably miss in this story. As far as the Jewish leaders are concerned, in order to follow Jesus the blind man can no longer be considered a follower of Moses. The sharp line they draw in 9:29 between being *Jewish* and *Christian* (to use modern terms) seems clear to them, though it is unresolved yet today. This is problematic for two reasons. (1) Jewish-Christians today insist that they have not given up their Judaism, but they are severely criticized by the Jewish community. In modern-day Israel, a Jew can give up everything about his or her faith, even becoming an atheist, and still be considered a Jew in order to take up Israeli citizenship. The one thing that invalidates "Jewishness" is belief in Jesus. The deep irony is that an atheist is still Jewish, but a "messianic Jew" is not.[13]

(2) Theologically as a Christian, I need to say that I am still a follower of Moses when I believe in Jesus. By believing in Jesus I am doing what Moses would have done. Jesus does not break with Moses; rather, he fulfills what Moses began. In this sense, Christians are being faithful to the Jewish tradition inasmuch as they are embracing a Jewish Messiah. The rabbi Paul would have considered himself no less a Jew even though he believed in Jesus.

The temple leadership: a model of spiritual intransigence. Perhaps the most troubling questions to surface in this passage have to do with the profile

13. This dilemma presents grave problems for messianic Jews who want to move to Israel. Many keep their faith secret until they are granted citizenship.

of Jesus' opponents. The image of them in chapter 9 is different from that given of Jesus' opponents in chapters 5 and 8. These are theologians, religious leaders, whose rejection of Jesus is based not simply on his refusal to conform to their religious system, but on their knowledge of who he is. They stand against Jesus from an informed theological standpoint. They are aggressive, and according to the end of the chapter, because they are self-affirming, claiming that "they know," their sin cannot disappear. If they rejected Jesus out of ignorance, it would be a different matter. But they reject Jesus out of knowledge, and so their "guilt remains" (9:41).

(1) John opens a question that he does not answer. Is it possible to "be blind" and yet not guilty of sin (9:41a) because of genuine spiritual ignorance (9:41b)? I imagine that this would be a person who is in the darkness, who cannot recognize God's work in Christ, and who thus rejects Jesus—but the rejection is based ignorance. Certainly John would affirm that anyone who is in the darkness is in spiritual jeopardy regardless of his or her intellectual, religious position. But he has here framed the question in a provocative, unexpected way. I think, for instance, of a Jewish neighbor I had in Chicago, for whom the Holocaust had forever made Christianity a horror. He entered a Catholic church one weekend for the first time in twenty-five years in order to attend a wedding, and the crucifix above the altar paralyzed him. There on the wall was one more dying Jew. He could not hear the name of Jesus without hearing the voice of Nazis.

(2) John's real interest is to examine the position of a person who has a knowing, willful religious rejection of Jesus. Of course, we could point to the old debate between synagogue and church and project that into our current generation. But in the church there has always been (and continues to be today) those from within our own ranks who reject Jesus knowingly. They know the rudiments of the orthodox faith, they know our theological traditions, they may have experienced the life of a Christian, but they say "No." This is called heresy or apostasy, and we need to be able to name it when it appears.

I am always reluctant to provide an example since it is impossible to know what private spiritual work God may be doing in someone's life. But an example does come to mind. John Shelby Spong is an Episcopal bishop in Newark, New Jersey. He is a prolific writer, whose work chiefly dismantles most of the sacred beliefs of the church. In *Living in Sin: A Bishop Rethinks Human Sexuality* (1990) he called for the church to recognize same-sex marriages and homosexual ordination. In *Rescuing the Bible from Fundamentalism: A Bishop Rethinks the Meaning of Scripture* (1992) he argued that Paul was gay. In *Born of a Woman: A Bishop Rethinks the Birth of Jesus* (1994) he argued that the virgin birth was a tactic to cover up Jesus' illegitimacy and that Jesus himself may have married

Mary Magdalene. His most current work is *Why Christianity Must Change or Die* (1998), where he argues that the worldview of Christianity is outdated and that all theism and supernatural assumptions must go if the church is going to speak to a modern world. Other religious systems have died, he says, and Christianity is simply the next system on the chopping block. He likes shock value. Typically he writes, "I would choose to loathe rather than to worship a deity who required the sacrifice of his son."

Here is an educated, ordained theologian who knows his Bible well and understands the basic tenets of orthodox Christology. He plainly admits that from the view of traditional Christianity, what he writes is "heresy." This is precisely what we need to be willing to say to those who (like Spong) make a major departure from belief in Jesus.

Of course, the challenge for us is to determine who fits this profile and what beliefs qualify as heresy. But our fear of launching attitudes last seen in the Inquisition have made us unable to judge religious error for what it is. In C. S. Lewis's wonderful book *The Great Divorce*, Lewis describes a busload of folks who travel from hell to heaven. The roster of tourists has as many intellectuals as it does base heathen. As I often tell my students, hell will have more than its share of thoughtful theologians.

John 10:1–42

I TELL YOU the truth, the man who does not enter the sheep pen by the gate, but climbs in by some other way, is a thief and a robber. ²The man who enters by the gate is the shepherd of his sheep. ³The watchman opens the gate for him, and the sheep listen to his voice. He calls his own sheep by name and leads them out. ⁴When he has brought out all his own, he goes on ahead of them, and his sheep follow him because they know his voice. ⁵But they will never follow a stranger; in fact, they will run away from him because they do not recognize a stranger's voice." ⁶Jesus used this figure of speech, but they did not understand what he was telling them.

⁷Therefore Jesus said again, "I tell you the truth, I am the gate for the sheep. ⁸All who ever came before me were thieves and robbers, but the sheep did not listen to them. ⁹I am the gate; whoever enters through me will be saved. He will come in and go out, and find pasture. ¹⁰The thief comes only to steal and kill and destroy; I have come that they may have life, and have it to the full.

¹¹"I am the good shepherd. The good shepherd lays down his life for the sheep. ¹²The hired hand is not the shepherd who owns the sheep. So when he sees the wolf coming, he abandons the sheep and runs away. Then the wolf attacks the flock and scatters it. ¹³The man runs away because he is a hired hand and cares nothing for the sheep.

¹⁴"I am the good shepherd; I know my sheep and my sheep know me—¹⁵just as the Father knows me and I know the Father—and I lay down my life for the sheep. ¹⁶I have other sheep that are not of this sheep pen. I must bring them also. They too will listen to my voice, and there shall be one flock and one shepherd. ¹⁷The reason my Father loves me is that I lay down my life—only to take it up again. ¹⁸No one takes it from me, but I lay it down of my own accord. I have authority to lay it down and authority to take it up again. This command I received from my Father."

¹⁹At these words the Jews were again divided. ²⁰Many of them said, "He is demon-possessed and raving mad. Why listen to him?"

²¹But others said, "These are not the sayings of a man possessed by a demon. Can a demon open the eyes of the blind?"

²²Then came the Feast of Dedication at Jerusalem. It was winter, ²³and Jesus was in the temple area walking in Solomon's Colonnade. ²⁴The Jews gathered around him, saying, "How long will you keep us in suspense? If you are the Christ, tell us plainly."

²⁵Jesus answered, "I did tell you, but you do not believe. The miracles I do in my Father's name speak for me, ²⁶but you do not believe because you are not my sheep. ²⁷My sheep listen to my voice; I know them, and they follow me. ²⁸I give them eternal life, and they shall never perish; no one can snatch them out of my hand. ²⁹My Father, who has given them to me, is greater than all; no one can snatch them out of my Father's hand. ³⁰I and the Father are one."

³¹Again the Jews picked up stones to stone him, ³²but Jesus said to them, "I have shown you many great miracles from the Father. For which of these do you stone me?"

³³"We are not stoning you for any of these," replied the Jews, "but for blasphemy, because you, a mere man, claim to be God."

³⁴Jesus answered them, "Is it not written in your Law, 'I have said you are gods'? ³⁵If he called them 'gods,' to whom the word of God came—and the Scripture cannot be broken—³⁶what about the one whom the Father set apart as his very own and sent into the world? Why then do you accuse me of blasphemy because I said, 'I am God's Son'? ³⁷Do not believe me unless I do what my Father does. ³⁸But if I do it, even though you do not believe me, believe the miracles, that you may know and understand that the Father is in me, and I in the Father." ³⁹Again they tried to seize him, but he escaped their grasp.

⁴⁰Then Jesus went back across the Jordan to the place where John had been baptizing in the early days. Here he stayed ⁴¹and many people came to him. They said, "Though John never performed a miraculous sign, all that John said about this man was true." ⁴²And in that place many believed in Jesus.

JOHN 10 CONTINUES the series of festival sermons and controversies that we have been following since chapter 5. Jesus has appeared at Sabbath, Passover, and Tabernacles, revealing his identity and work through the festival imagery; now he appears at Hanukkah. Symbols employed in story or ritual (e.g., bread, water, light) have become avenues of revelation by which Jesus unveils his heavenly mission.

The first problem we encounter in John 10, however, is deciding if we must divide the chapter.[1] The festival itself is not mentioned until 10:22; in most cases, John refers to the festival at the head of the relevant section (5:1; 6:4; 7:2). Therefore 10:1-21 could almost be seen as a continuation of the debate that concluded chapter 9. No new audience is assumed, and 10:21 refers again to the healing of the blind man. In fact, the blind man who refuses to follow the Pharisees is like the sheep of 10:5, who will not follow "because they do not recognize a stranger's voice." Thus, the failed leadership of the Pharisees described in chapter 9 is given a severe critique. They are "false shepherds" compared with Jesus, the true shepherd.

There are a few difficulties, however, when we link 10:1-21 with the end of chapter 9 exclusively. (1) There is an abrupt change of subject in chapter 10. From discussing "light" Jesus suddenly moves to the motif of shepherds. Thus, it seems plausible that we are now in a different setting. (2) In 10:26-27 (during Hanukkah) Jesus continues to refer to sheep and assumes the same audience he had in 10:1-21. The Feast of Tabernacles (ch. 9) and Hanukkah (ch. 10) are almost three months apart, and certainly John wants us to assume that the audience for all chapter 10 is the same. (3) John 10:1-21 is also an excellent preface to a theme that was central to the Hanukkah Festival. During this season Israel recalled the failed leadership of the temple during the Maccabean era; during its ceremonies Ezekiel 34, the powerful criticism of Israel's "false shepherds," served in the Hanukkah liturgy.[2]

Yet even though the events of chapters 9 and 10 are months apart, John no doubt wants us to see a *literary* unity between them. John 10:1-21 points both backward and forward. It is Jesus' final public discourse and concludes his severe criticism of Jerusalem's leadership (dramatically played out for us in the blind man story). But it also launches the principal theme of Hanukkah: identifying the true shepherd of God's people.

---

1. Scholars have often believed they could "improve" the Fourth Gospel by rearranging its chapters. Reuniting the related themes of chapters 9 and 10 is common.

2. A Guilding, *The Fourth Gospel and Jewish Worship: A Study of the Relation of St. John's Gospel to the Ancient Jewish Lectionary System* (Oxford. Clarendon, 1960), 129-32.

The chapter divides into three main units. In 10:1–5 Jesus supplies his parable, which concludes with the failure of his audience to understand (10:6). Jesus then interprets and expands the parable (10:7–18), which is followed by a division in the audience: Some wonder if Jesus is demon-possessed while others are impressed by the compelling power of his words (10:19–21). Jesus closes the discourse by arguing for his messiahship from Psalm 82 (John 10:22–38). This forces his audience into a crisis: Some try to seize him while others choose to believe (10:39–42). The entire chapter, then, carefully follows the reactions of the audience, indicating how the coming of Christ divides the world (cf. 3:19–21; 9:5).

The Good Shepherd (10:1–18)

JESUS IS STEPPING into a venerable Old Testament tradition when he describes himself as the good shepherd of Israel. The culture of Jesus' day understood shepherds and their sheep well. In the Synoptics Jesus commonly uses shepherding as a metaphor in his speech (Matt. 9:6; 10:6, 16) and a subject in his parables (Matt. 25:32; Luke 15:4). This becomes the principal image for describing leadership and is easily expanded into a metaphor for everyday life.

In the Old Testament, God is the shepherd of Israel (Gen. 49:24; Ps. 23; 78:52–53; 80:1). Note especially Isaiah 40:10–11:

> See, the Sovereign LORD comes with power....
> He tends his flock like a shepherd:
>> He gathers the lambs in his arms
> and carries them close to his heart;
>> he gently leads those that have young.

Moreover, shepherding became a helpful image explaining the spiritual and practical leadership among God's people (see Isa. 56:9–12; Jer. 23:1–4; 25:32–38; Ezek. 34; Zech. 11). Moses and David, for example, were shepherds. Impious kings in Israel were commonly called "false shepherds" (1 Kings 22:17; Jer. 10:21; 23:1–2).

The occasion for this discourse, John reminds us, is the Festival of Hanukkah (10:21). This is the only reference to this minor, intertestamental festival in the Bible. Since the conquest of Alexander the Great in 332 B.C., Greek influence in the Middle East not only controlled the political aspirations of people like the Jews, but gradually assimilated them into the Greek way of life. Within 150 years, Israel had adopted numerous Greek cultural and religious habits. Even the Bible was translated into Greek (the Septuagint, abbreviated LXX) for Jews who could no longer read Hebrew.

Jewish resistance to this Hellenization (in the party called the Hasidim) met opposition not only from Greeks but also from Jews who had compromised their commitment to Jewish culture and their faith. Priests such as Jason and Menelaus (2 Macc. 4—5) were corrupt and contributed to the demise of Jewish temple worship, while Greek soldiers desecrated the temple with pig's blood, outlawed Jewish ritual (e.g., circumcision), burned Scripture scrolls, and erected a pagan idol in the temple.

In the 160s B.C. the Maccabean War erupted, pitting conservative Jewish fighters against Greeks and Hellenized Jews. Its first leader, Judas Maccabeus, captured Jerusalem's temple and in 165 B.C. rededicated it. Hanukkah is a Hebrew word meaning "dedication," and it became the name of the winter festival in Jerusalem that remembered these events. Sometimes (as in the NIV) it is called "The Feast of Dedication" (10:22).[3] In the first century, it was celebrated for eight days in Jerusalem (recalling eight miraculous days when Judas's supply of oil burned in the temple).[4]

Hanukkah thus became a season that asked hard questions about failed leadership and false shepherds. How did the temple leadership lose its way during this Greek period? Where were the shepherds? What must shepherds do today? During the week when Jesus gave his good shepherd sermon, synagogues were reading prophetic critiques of leadership.

> "This is what the Sovereign LORD says: Woe to the shepherds of Israel who only take care of themselves! Should not shepherds take care of the flock? You eat the curds, clothe yourselves with the wool and slaughter the choice animals, but you do not take care of the flock. You have not strengthened the weak or healed the sick or bound up the injured. You have not brought back the strays or searched for the lost. You have ruled them harshly and brutally. So they were scattered....
>
> "Therefore, you shepherds, hear the word of the LORD: As surely as I live, declares the Sovereign LORD, because my flock lacks a shepherd and so has been plundered and has become food for all the wild animals, and because my shepherds did not search for my flock but cared for themselves rather than for my flock, therefore, O shepherds, hear the word of the LORD: This is what the Sovereign LORD says: I am against the shepherds and will hold them accountable for my flock...." (Ezek. 34:2—10)

Jesus builds on this motif in his figurative saying in John 10:1—3. Sheep must discern the shepherds who enter by the gate (with the endorsement of

---

3. Josephus (*Ant.* 12:316—25) tells us that the feast was also called "the Festival of Lights." According to 2 Macc. 1:9, because of its parallel use of light, the feast was also called "the Feast of Tabernacles in the month of Chislev" (approx. December).

4. Judas Maccabeus had only one day's supply of oil, which God made burn for eight. The Hanukkah menorah has eight candles (while the temple candelabra had seven).

the gatekeeper) and those who climb over the wall (whose intentions are destructive). God's people have had excellent shepherds in the past as well as shepherds who have harmed the sheep.

Jesus assumes his audience understands the scene he is constructing. In the desert at night sheep were often herded into walled enclosures that either backed up against a cliff face or were at the end of a canyon. Such enclosures (still used today by Palestinian shepherds in the Judean desert) had waist-high stone walls topped with thorny branches. Such a pen was entirely for safety so that the sheep would not become prey to wild animals. One small doorway (or opening) in the wall served as the only entrance and exit. The shepherd would either close this area with dry thornbushes or would himself serve as sentry in the opening.

Not only can sheep identify rightful shepherds by their access through the main gate, but they also recognize the voice of their shepherd (10:3-5). The Middle Eastern shepherd is well known for having a personal devotion to his sheep. He talks to them and sings to them. Often shepherds will carry a short flute and use a repeated tune so that the flock has a consistent auditory cue to follow. Jesus notes that this shepherd does not simply lead any sheep but rather leads "his own" (10:3b). That is, just as Arab shepherds today can separate personal sheep from larger flocks by using peculiar calls, so Jesus knows his own sheep, they can recognize his voice, and he leads them (10:4). Note that this shepherd does not *drive* the sheep; rather, he is out in front, leading the way.

The reverse is also true. Just as false shepherds might climb over the wall to get access to the sheep (10:1), now we learn that their voice is unrecognizable to the sheep (10:5), and the sheep flee from them.

It is not surprising that Jesus' audience does not understand the figurative saying. They understand the nature of shepherding, but they fail to grasp the spiritual point he is making. The word for "figure of speech" used in 10:6 is unusual in the New Testament (Gk. *paroimia*) and occurs only two other times in John (16:25, 29) and once in 2 Peter 2:22. In the Synoptics the word generally used for such sayings is "parable" (Gk. *parabole*), but there is likely little difference between the two words.[5]

The Middle East delights in the "dark saying" that must be unpacked, and every good teacher must know how to use the proverb and the symbolic story. In the Synoptics the parables generally explain the "kingdom of God." Frequently the audience does not understand (Mark 4:13). In John the theme

---

5. There is one Hebrew word that likely stands behind both words: *mashal*. A *mashal* is a figure of speech, a proverb, or a cryptic saying that requires further explanation. It can either be a lengthy story or a one-sentence statement (Luke 4:23).

is consistently Jesus' identity; stories unveil who he is. But in each case, the problem is not necessarily intellectual. The problem is often an unwillingness to respond to the challenge of the saying.[6]

Jesus' explanation (10:7–18) turns the story creatively. The setting of the sheep pen in the parable invites reflection particularly at three points: the gate, the shepherd, and the sheep. (1) The first image of the parable that Jesus does not interpret concerns his entry into the sheepfold. The watchman permits him entry, making him God's shepherd. He is the rightful leader who goes through the gate. He has authority to lead the sheep (while others do not).

(2) In his interpretation Jesus shifts some of the images. He now is *the gate*. He alone is the sentry, the one through whom access to the sheep can be found (10:7–8). He stands in the gate, and any who enter without his permission (who sneak into the flock) are not to be trusted. This implies some endorsement of those who enter into leadership in Christ's name, leaders who come after him whom he knows. But it also implies a warning, for there are illegitimate shepherds whose entry he prohibits. Who are these "thieves and robbers" who have come before Jesus (10:8)? Some have argued that they are false messiahs in the first century, and we know that there were many. But the most likely target of Jesus' criticism is the Pharisees, who have been the subject of Jesus' teaching since chapter 9. Since the Maccabean era Jerusalem had witnessed many leaders who qualified as "false shepherds."

But there is another nuance. Since Jesus is the gate for the sheep too (10:9a), only those sheep who find him will enter the sheepfold and find safety. They alone will know his leadership and exit to find safe, lush pasture (10:9b). This thought parallels 14:6, "I am the way and the truth and the life. No one comes to the Father except through me." The image here is a flock of sheep in a threatening desert. Food and water are scarce. Predators are everywhere, and they know the sheep are vulnerable. Jesus' image is that of well-fed sheep whose shepherd knows how to lead them to pasture and water daily, and who at night gives them safe rest in the sturdy walls of the sheepfold. These are sheep that flourish and are content, thanks to the skill of the shepherd. Psalm 23 describes this sheep's life in full ("The LORD is my shepherd, I shall not be in want" 23:1). Similarly Psalm 118:20 describes this gate and our entry: "This is the gate of the LORD through which the righteous may enter."

(3) At the final level of his interpretation, Jesus claims that he is the "good shepherd" (10:11–18). It is important not to overly sentimentalize the image given here.[7] This is not a portrait of a kindly man holding cuddly lambs.

---

6. Brown, *John*, 1:392.
7 Carson, *John*, 386

"Good" (Gk. *kalos*) can just as well be translated "noble." The shepherd's job was severe, tiring, and hazardous. The point of contrast here is the "bad shepherd" or the hired hand (10:12), who is distinguished by his lack of commitment to the sheep. When danger comes, he flees (10:13) and the flock is attacked. His own self-preservation, his own self-interest (he "cares nothing for the sheep," 10:13b), characterizes his career and no doubt refers directly to the leaders of Israel graphically chastised during the Hanukkah Festival. The good shepherd, by contrast, "owns the sheep" (10:12a), which speaks to his unique, passionate commitment to them.

The most important feature of Jesus' role as shepherd is that he lays down his life for the sheep (10:11b, 15, 17–18). Of course, his intention is to live and protect them. But the point here is that he cares for them so much that he is willing to come between his flock and danger. He is *willing to die* for them. Jesus has in mind a flock under siege—perhaps a flock in its sheepfold, shuddering under the terror of an attack by wild animals—and the shepherd standing firm at the gate using stones and staff, unwilling to sacrifice even one of his animals to satisfy the enemy. To die "for" (Gk. *hyper*) the sheep is significant. Throughout the Fourth Gospel *hyper* is used almost exclusively in a sacrificial context, generally describing Jesus' sacrificial death on behalf of others (e.g., 6:51; 10:11).[8] Therefore Jesus is pointing to the depth of his love for the flock of God and his commitment to die for them in obedience to God's will (10:18).

Perhaps the most startling feature of Jesus' interpretation is his description of the intimacy of the sheep and their shepherd. We have already learned that the sheep "know" the shepherd's voice (10:4), but now we learn that this knowledge is mutual and exhaustive (10:14). Moreover, the model for this intimacy is the mutual knowledge shared between the Son and the Father—and here Jesus slips out of the parable and speaks directly of himself and God (cf. Matt. 11:27). His profound relationship with God characterizes the intimacy he seeks with his followers (17:21); as he and the Father share profound love, so too Jesus and his flock share this quality of love (15:9–10).

This explains the willingness of Jesus to die for his sheep. This is not merely about obedience to God nor is it his personal honor. Rather, Jesus is willing to die because of his profound commitment to the ones he loves.[9] As

8. The Gk. word *hyper* is used thirteen times in John, of which eleven imply or refer to sacrificial death (6:51; 10:11, 15; 11:50, 51, 52; 13:37, 38; 15:13; 17:19; 18:14; the other two occurrences are 1:30, 11:4).

9. Interpreters must be warned that this passage is not describing a divine unity that results in a deification of the believer (such as might be found in ancient Hellenistic systems or modern New Age religions). C. K. Barrett, *John*, 376, comments that here in John's thought, "This makes any kind of identification between God and the worshipper unthinkable; man is not deified but delivered."

Paul writes, "Christ loved the church and gave himself up for her ... to present her to himself as a radiant church, without stain or wrinkle or any other blemish, but holy and blameless" (Eph. 5:25, 27).

An interesting digression appears in John 10:16. The picture we have thus far consists of a sheepfold filled with animals and Jesus, the good shepherd, calling his own sheep from this fold with his voice. This flock constitutes his sheep, his followers, and those who do not know his voice presumably refers to unbelieving Jews from which Jesus' followers come. However, Jesus says, there are "other sheep" that do not come from this sheepfold. If they come from a different fold, they come from outside of Judaism, which no doubt refers to Gentiles.[10] They too will recognize Jesus' voice and follow him, so that there will be one flock and one shepherd. This is Jesus' vision for the unity of the church: Jewish believers and Gentile believers living together under Christ's leadership. For the first time, Jesus is anticipating in detail the wider scope of his ministry to reach the world. We will learn of it in full in John 17.[11]

The unique love and intimacy between the Father and the Son is the model that determines the relationship of Jesus to his flock. Jesus now probes the deeper meaning of the Father's love for him (10:17–19).[12] The fundamental element in this relationship is Jesus' dependence on and obedience to God's will. This is expressed utterly in his willingness to die on the cross. We must avoid the idea that in giving his life, the Son wins the Father's love. The Father gives everything into the Son's hands (3:35), shows him everything (5:20), gives him life (5:26), and gives his own glory (17:24) and name (17:26). Indeed, the Father has loved the Son from the "creation of the world" (17:24). Jesus' voluntary death therefore is a hallmark of his union with the Father's will and an expression of the love they share together.

This is underscored at the beginning of 10:18. "No one takes it [my life] from me." Jesus is not a victim of human conspiracies. He was not a martyr whose life was ended as a tragedy. He obediently participates in the plan of God. The early Christians who interpreted Jesus' death reinforced this view. It meant that the sacrificial act of Jesus pointed to the saving work of God,

---

10. Morris, *John*, 455, reminds us of Acts 18:9–10, where the Lord speaks to Paul in a vision at Corinth, "Do not be afraid . because I have many people in this city."

11. For many scholars, this description of the "flock of Jesus" speaks to the composition of John's church and its struggle for unity (cf. 1 John). See further R. J Karris, *Jesus and the Marginalized in John's Gospel* (Zacchaeus Studies, New Testament; Collegeville, Minn.: Liturgical, 1990).

12. Ridderbos, *John*, 365, suggests that "love" in 10 17 is synonymous with "know" elsewhere in the chapter: "It is not to be understood so much in the sense of an affective relationship between the Father and the Son as of the effective 'being' of the Father 'with' the Son."

not the attempt of Caiaphas and Pilate to end his life. Peter remarked to the Jerusalem crowd on Pentecost (Acts 2:23–24; cf. 4:27–28):

> This man was handed over to you *by God's set purpose and foreknowledge;* and you, with the help of wicked men, put him to death by nailing him to the cross. But God raised him from the dead, freeing him from the agony of death, because it was impossible for death to keep its hold on him. (italics added)

The final aspect of Jesus' uniqueness as the good shepherd—and one more feature of his union with the Father—is the authority he bears not only to die but to retake his life in resurrection (10:17b–18). The resurrection, therefore, is not an afterthought wherein God rescues his Son from an unexpected tragedy. The empty tomb was encompassed in the plan of Golgotha, and Jesus predicted this clearly (Mark 9:31). Here we see that the power that opened the tomb was a power that could not be held back. As the tomb could not contain God, so too Jesus, in his union with the Father, possessed the authority and power to vanquish the death he had embraced on Good Friday. He takes his life up again.[13]

But even in this act he is not working independently, as if he submits to God's plan of sacrifice, but recovers through his own power of resurrection. "This command I received from my Father" (10:18b) means that all of Jesus' authoritative, powerful activity, from Good Friday to Easter Sunday, operates in harmony with God, who has authorized and directed it.

The Reaction of the Crowd (10:19–21)

JOHN REPORTS THAT the crowd is once again "divided." This happened before, and this is now the third time that Jesus has divided his audience (7:43; 9:16; 10:19). The NIV accurately translates that "the Jews" were the audience, but this refers to his general audience in Jerusalem during the feast, both priests and bystanders.[14]

John's chief interest here is in the opposite reactions now forming. Some believe that Jesus is "demon-possessed and raving mad." This is the fourth time such a charge is made (7:20; 8:48–49, 52), and it is curious that unlike the Synoptics, each time "demon" is mentioned it is applied to Jesus (never other

---

13. Elsewhere in the New Testament the resurrection of Jesus is described as an act of God (see Acts 2:24). John views the union of the Son and the Father as so comprehensive that the resurrection is an act of God (carried out by the Son). Elsewhere the New Testament describes the resurrection as Jesus' work (Acts 17:3; 1 Thess. 4:14).

14. This is a good example of why some scholars prefer translating *Ioudaios* as "Judeans," to reflect the geographical identity of the audience.

people). These two terms may well say the same thing. Given the impious and presumptuous claims of Jesus (they argue), he must be out of his mind and thus not worth listening to. But this may be a genuine charge of demon-possession, and because he is thus possessed, he is insane. Either way, the reaction is antagonistic.

Still others in the audience are impressed with Jesus (10:20). They point to his miracle of opening the eyes of the blind man and make a claim not unlike that of the audience and the blind man of chapter 9: A miraculous sign points to God's hand in this man's life. Here in chapter 10, this part of the crowd fails to identify Jesus accurately or exhibit belief. Nevertheless, they are open to new possibilities and unwilling to judge Jesus outright.

The Controversy Intensifies (10:22–42)

JOHN INDICATES THAT the Feast of Dedication (or Hanukkah) was then tak-ing place (10:22).[15] This reference to the feast alerts us at once to the sym-bolic power of all Jesus' words thus far. The shepherd imagery (as outlined above) spoke directly to the festival's recital of the corruption of the temple priesthood, the desecration of the temple by the Greeks, and its rededica-tion under Judas Maccabeus (see comment on 10:1). That Jesus is continu-ing his shepherd sermon is indicated by 10:26–27. But as his audience presses him concerning his claims to messiahship, Jesus will further exploit the imagery of the festival, quoting Psalm 82 in defense of his claims.

This final section is a critical revelation for the Fourth Gospel. This is Jesus' final public disclosure of himself to his people. It will be an ultimate disclo-sure of his complete identity. The account ends with his returning to where it all began—the Jordan River, where John had baptized him (10:40).

Hanukkah is celebrated in winter during the Jewish month of Chislev (November to December). The main courtyard of the temple was surrounded by massive covered colonnades on all four sides, which were open to the court itself, but walled facing the outside. Solomon's Colonnade (10:23) was on the east and though built by Herod I, took its name from the temple's first builder, King Solomon.[16] In winter, teachers used these porches as a shelter

---

15. The English "then" (Gk. *tote*) is replaced by "and" (Gk. *de*) in numerous early manu-scripts and signals the calendar problem of 10:1–21 I mentioned earlier, *"Then* came the feast. . ."* Scribes were likely trying to link the two halves of the chapter together with the reference to Hanukkah.

16 The dramatic size of these porches has been discovered in the excavations at the southwest corner of the temple. In A D 70, when the temple was destroyed by the Romans, the porches were thrown from the temple and evidence of their destruction is now in the ruins at the temple platform base

from the cold weather. Jesus is walking here, and suddenly people who have heard him before "gather [*kykloo*] around him" (10:24; lit., "circle in on him"). The note here is ominous; this Greek word is used elsewhere in the Gospels only at Luke 21:20 to describe how Rome would "surround" Jerusalem before its destruction.[17]

The crowd is looking for an unambiguous statement about Jesus' identity. "How long will you keep us in suspense?" (10:24) can also be translated, "How long will you annoy us?" Are these people seeking clarity or are they antagonistic? What they want is an open, clear statement from Jesus about his messiahship, and no doubt they are poised to judge him if his answer is not to their liking. Thus far Jesus has not made an explicit, public claim to be the Christ. He did this privately to the Samaritan woman (4:26) and the blind man (9:35–36), and many have already offered this statement of faith.

But given the explosive, highly politicized views of the Messiah in this period, it is not surprising that Jesus has used restraint so far. He has used images in the festivals and allusions from the Old Testament. Now his audience wants a "plain" statement (cf. 7:4, 13). But we have already learned that even if Jesus were to speak plainly, only his "sheep" would recognize his voice (10:26). Ironically, his shepherd sermon was just such a disclosure, but they have not "heard" it.

The root problem is unbelief (10:25b). The character of Jesus' life and his works or miracles wrought by God's power (or "name") indicate his true identity. As we learned in chapter 5, these works should be seen as evidence pointing to Jesus' authority as God's messenger and Son. But the true problem, which is a deep theological issue, is that only those who are Jesus' sheep can understand these things (10:26–27). The "other sheep" cannot understand his voice, he does not know them, and they do not follow (10:1–18). This does not excuse them; it simply says that nothing in Jesus' life is happening outside of the sovereign plan of God.

Not only is this faith a gift, but so are eternal life and security (10:28–30). This shepherd will die for his sheep, but those outside the fold will remain in jeopardy. Jesus' assignment has been to gather up "all that the Father gives" him (6:37–40; 10:29). Therefore his skill as the good shepherd secures them from all predators (10:12) and thieves (10:1, 8). The word "snatch" (Gk. *harpazo*) denotes violence and is used in 6:15 for the crowds who wish to kidnap Jesus. In 10:12 it describes the attack of the wolf. But the true power

---

17. In Acts 14:20 *kykloo* describes how the disciples surround Paul after he is stoned at Lystra. In Heb. 11:30 it describes how Jericho was surrounded by the Israelite army. These are its only uses in the New Testament.

behind Jesus is the Father (10:29). Thus it is the Father who is the true pre-
server of the sheep because no one is greater than he.[18]

The astounding affirmation given in 10:30 serves as a high point in the
chapter. Jesus' unity with the Father is the basis of the Father's participation
in the preservation of the sheep. But we must be clear about what Jesus is saying. Earlier he spoke about his working in cooperation with the Father (5:17,
19) and in accordance with the Father's will (6:38; 8:26, 28; 10:18). The
sheep here belong both to the Father and the Son (17:10) and enjoy fellowship with both simultaneously (14:23; 17:21–23, 26). "One" in Greek is
neuter and does not refer to "one person." Therefore, Jesus is affirming a
unity of purpose and will. The protection of the sheep results from the joint
work of Father and Son.

However, we must quickly say that this is not a denial of the ontological
unity of the Father and the Son, which is at the heart of John's Christology.
From beginning (John 1:1) to end (when Thomas exclaims to Jesus, "My
Lord and my God!" 20:28), this Gospel affirms more. A suggestion of this may
lie in the present passage. This formulation of oneness is stronger than what
we see elsewhere, and the response of the crowd in 10:31, 33 suggests that
they hear something different too. This is not a man who is saying he has
joined his efforts with God; this is a man who is saying something dangerous, something more, something blasphemous.

Hoskyns comments here: "The unity is neither merely a moral unity or
agreement of character, since the Jews would not presumably have treated
as blasphemy, the idea that a man could regulate his words and actions
according to the will of God."[19] Later Jesus will say, "Anyone who has seen
me has seen the Father" (14:9). Jesus is the vehicle of divine revelation and
salvation. He is God's agent in the world, not merely a righteous man or
divine spokesman.[20]

Such statements by Jesus demand a response. In chapter 8 Jesus' summary disclosure of his relationship to Abraham ended in an attempt to stone
him. The same thing happens here. The perceived problem is not Jesus' miracles (10:32) but his words (cf. 6:42, 60; 7:29–30). Stoning in the first cen-

---

18. John 10.29 contains a well-known set of variants. The chief problem is locating the
subject of the sentence. The NIV follows the popular reading: "My Father, who (Gk *hos*) has
given them to me, is greater than all." The NRSV, NIVmg, and others read. "What (Gk. *ho*)
my Father has given me is greater than all else." An excellent summary of variants can be
found in Schnackenburg, *John*, 2.307–8.

19. Hoskyns, *John*, 389.

20. In the early theological debates of the church, this passage was deemed of utmost
value in refuting those who undermined the authority of Jesus. See T Pollard, "The Exegesis of John 10:30 in the Early Trinitarian Controversies," *NTS* 3 (1957): 334–49.

tury tended to be a mob action. Roman justice systems supervised civic punishments, which tended generally to be crucifixion or beheading (for Roman citizens). The Jewish law stipulated stoning for a variety of crimes: witchcraft (Lev. 20:27), worshiping other gods (Deut. 13:10), immoral conduct (22:24), violating the Sabbath (Num. 15:35–36), and blasphemy (Lev. 24:23). While charges have been given against Jesus' illegal work on the Sabbath, here the problem is blasphemy. His opponents believe he is claiming to be God (John 10:33). This statement is likely John's typical use of irony, where the antagonist affirms the very truth about Jesus. As later Caiaphas will say that Jesus must die for the nation (11:50), indeed here we learn that Jesus is truly a man who is to be compared with God.

Jesus' defense in 10:34–39 is carefully nuanced and takes advantage of the symbolic motifs present at the Hanukkah Festival. He defends himself by citing Psalm 82:6. This psalm was well known and provided a critique of Israel's failure to respond to God (82:5–7):

"They know nothing, they understand nothing.
They walk about in darkness;
all the foundations of the earth are shaken.
"I said, 'You are "gods";
you are all sons (Heb. *beni*) of the Most High.'
But you will die like mere men;
you will fall like every other ruler."

The relevance of the passage is striking. The absence of knowledge and understanding is a fitting description of Jesus' audience. *They do not know the shepherd's voice.* But the single point Jesus is making centers on Psalm 82:6. Rabbinic interpretation argued that this psalm was addressed to Israel's tribes as they received the law at Mount Sinai.[21] It recalled Exodus 4:22–23, "Israel is my firstborn son, and I told you, 'Let my son go, so he may worship me.'" If the word "god" can be applied to those other than God himself in the Scriptures—if someone can be called a "son of God" here in God's unbreakable word—why are Jesus' words blasphemy? In John 10:36 Jesus calls himself "God's Son," and this is surely an echo of this historic context.

Moreover, Jesus is the one whom God "sanctified" (Gk. *hagiazo*; NIV "set apart") and sent into the world. The NIV obscures 10:36a with a paraphrase. The Greek verb *hagiazo* means to consecrate or make something holy. This points to the meaning of Hanukkah itself. Recall that Judas Maccabeus had reclaimed the temple after he conquered his Greek oppressors. In 1 Maccabees 4:48 we read, "They also rebuilt the sanctuary and the interior of the

21. For opinions on this verse in early Judasim, see Beasley-Murray, *John*, 175–77.

temple, and consecrated [*hagiazo*] the courts." Jesus, then, is the object of Hanukkah's interest. He is the "sanctified place," the "holy place," the "temple" of God celebrated in this season. Not only is his title "Son of God" justified by Psalm 82, but his identity as the locus of God's presence, as the divine courier from heaven, gives him an incomparable status.[22]

In 10:38 Jesus goes on to put his affirmation in strong language again. "The Father is in me, and I in the Father." But this becomes too much, so that (10:39) the crowd again tries to arrest him. But they are not the ones who will control his fate. He escapes, yet as we learned in 7:30 and 8:20, we may interpret here: Jesus' hour had not yet come.

Jesus' departure from Judea (10:40–42) is as much a theological statement as it is geographical. He is moving away from the area of conflict in Jerusalem and returning across the eastern deserts near the Jordan River, where John the Baptist had worked. As such it forms a "literary bookend" that matches the John the Baptist stories at the start of the gospel (1:19–51; 3:22–36; 4:1–6). Jesus has come full circle. He has concluded his public ministry among his people, and now it is time for him to "stay" (10:40b) there until his hour does come. It is winter, and in a few months he will appear in Jerusalem at Passover to be glorified as God has planned.

For the last time, John the Baptist's role is affirmed. Echoing the words of 3:22ff., his ministry is placed in perspective. He was a trustworthy and reliable witness to the truth about Jesus. Jesus alone has provided divine signs that point to the hand of the Father in his life (10:38), but John provided a voice, a voice in the desert calling men and women to faith.

Ironically, the evangelist adds, "And in that place many believed in Jesus." Jesus finds faith not among the ranks of the "religious" in the holy city of Jerusalem. Rather, he finds it when he moves to the desert and works among those who must travel at some hardship to find him. "Many people came to him" in the desert by the Jordan and believed in him, recognizing that this was God's hand behind Jesus' works and God's voice within his words. But the leaders of Jerusalem will not see him again until they are given an opportunity to crucify him.

CHRISTIANS AND THEIR LEADERS. The important universal theme behind this chapter centers on the relationship of people to their leaders. The historical crisis of the Maccabean period is an essential background. Israel's leaders failed them, having guided them into

---

22. G. Yee, *Jewish Feasts and the Gospel of John* (Wilmington, Del.. M. Glazier, 1989), 83–92.

spiritual bondage and almost destroyed their country by assimilating it into the world of Hellenism. This reminds me that in my generation the possibility always exists that the leaders whom I follow may not be worthy of my devotion and loyalty. This, of course, is true of all leaders, but in particular John 10 underscores the role of spiritual leaders. While called to represent the truth about God before their people, they sometimes fail and bring harm.

Jesus has been at work since his baptism presenting the evidence of his messiahship. He has stepped into numerous Jewish settings—from weddings to festivals—attempting to persuade his audience of his relationship with the Father. He has demonstrated this relationship through the wisdom of his words as well as through his works (or signs). While some have come to faith, the leadership of Jerusalem has failed to accept him. They have not embraced him as Messiah.

This means two things. (1) The failure of these spiritual leaders to acknowledge the work of God in Christ puts in question the legitimacy of their leadership. As an interpreter I must probe who such people might be in my own generation. It may well be church leaders, but the subject is wider than this. It is any voice that draws people away from God, any voice that inflicts harm particularly on God's people. Jesus is remarkably bold with these people. They are "robbers" and "thieves" about whom we must be warned. And the litmus test for us is whether what they say and do coheres with the work and witness of Jesus Christ. Using Jesus' sheepfold image, he alone is the gate that gives access to the sheep. Those who enter "over the wall," whose voice is foreign to the voice of Jesus, who bring no safety and protection, are to be rejected.

(2) This story provides an exhortation to the sheep as well. Sheep must recognize the voice of the one who can lead and feed them. They must know how to find the sheepfold and safety. As an interpreter, such an exhortation means that I must speak honestly (though compassionately) to the people of God about their lives: Whom do they follow? What voices do they recognize? Where do they go for shelter? What are the characteristics of shepherds that can be followed and shepherds that must be avoided? This is a teaching about discernment since individuals constantly must assess those authoritative voices demanding obedience in their lives.

The importance of this theme was borne out inside the history of John's own church. It is impossible to read 1 John without reflecting on the crisis that swamped John's community. False "shepherds" had infiltrated the ranks of the community, teaching that Jesus is not the Christ (1 John 2:22), deceiving believers (2:26), and leading a "flock" of people out of the church. They employed charismatic authority, buttressing their teaching with claims of the Holy Spirit (4:1–3); in the end, however, they brought destruction.[23] These were shepherds who sabotaged the flock, broke over the sheepfold wall, and destroyed the safety of the sheep. Therefore John must teach his followers how to recognize true shepherds and to recognize when they truly belong to the flock of God. As I think about applying the lessons of John 10 today, I would do well to consider the lessons gleaned from the Letters of John as he addressed the problem of false shepherds.

This story is virtually an allegory. The flock of Christ (the church) is led by the good shepherd (Jesus himself). Yet many interpreters are wary of taking the symbolism further. In fact some deny that John has any interest in the allegory beyond making a Christological affirmation about Jesus Christ.[24] But this is surely wrong. The story is a warning as well as an affirmation. Jesus is telling us about himself to be sure, but he has done this all along in the Gospel. Now he is warning us about those detractors who damage the flock of God. In fact, the merits of all other leaders must now be tested against his leadership.

Are there risks in this teaching today? Absolutely. Perhaps this is what concerns some interpreters. Should the sheep now begin to examine every shepherd in their midst? Pastors? Teachers? Should the sheep be the new arbiters of who is qualified to lead them? To encourage discernment is to invite judgment. And legitimate leaders may find themselves to be the unfair object of scrutiny. But this is not Jesus' intent. He rather desires to help sheep become discerning of those who bring genuine harm, leaders who come to hurt and destroy.

Ancillary issues. Several ancillary issues fan out from the primary image of shepherds and sheep. (1) The suggestion in 10:16 that there are "other sheep" invites us to reflect on the exclusivity of the flock of Christ today. They are members, but they are outside the fold. Yet when Jesus says that he desires to see "one flock and one shepherd," we must probe the implications for today. Is this a comment about the unity of the church? Does this challenge or affirm those with a "one true church" theology? At the very least, it suggests that there are *unexpected sheep* that must be considered a part of the fold— sheep that the present fold does not know and might not recognize. This too invites some reflection as I bring John 10 into my own setting and world.

(2) This chapter sounds a strong note in favor of the overwhelming sovereignty of God. Jesus' opponents are not a part of his flock (10:26) because the Father has not given them to him (10:29). This theme seems clear, but

---

23. I have explained this struggle in the Johannine church fully in my commentary *Letters of John* (NIVAC; Grand Rapids: Zondervan, 1996), 27–33.

24. G. Sloan, *John. A Bible Commentary for Teaching and Preaching* (Atlanta: John Knox, 1988).

it must be balanced against Jesus parallel call for these people to believe (10:38). There is thus both human responsibility and divine participation in the building up of the flock of Christ. But how does this tension impact our view of the nature of the church today and evangelism? John would hardly accept a view that makes men and women "elect" purely by God's choice, leaving no room for human responsibility. Yet the theme of sovereignty sounds so strongly here that any presentation of the text must address the problem.

(3) Finally, it is clear that the separation of Jesus from Jerusalem in 10:40 sounds an ominous note. He has finished his revelation, and he has spoken God's word and completed God's works (with the exception of his Passion). Now he separates himself. The same theme will appear at the close of chapters 11 and 12. Here too we find a provocative theme. Does this mean that once God has revealed himself to a people, he too withdraws? Is there an act of judgment on the unresponsive heart in which God declines to pursue the faithless? How could such a motif be formed in a contemporary setting?

WHEN I EXPLAIN this chapter to the modern audience, I find that they need to have some sense of the dangers of the desert and the skills of a shepherd if they are to understand the themes that are instinctive to Jesus and his audience.

The desert. Let me begin with the desert. The desert in Israel is tremendously important in order to understand the Bible. It can be found along the eastern fringe of every major city in the central mountains of Israel, from Hebron to Shechem. From Jerusalem one simply has to climb over the Mount of Olives (a mere forty-five minute walk) to be hiking in the beginning of the desert near where Jesus was tested following his baptism. It stretches for thousands of miles across the Jordan River, into the eastern plateaus, and on through Saudi Arabia and Iraq. Today Middle Eastern children (both Arab and Jew) tell adventure stories of the desert, much like Canadian or European children might tell stories of deep, dark forests. In fact, the biblical stories about Abraham, Moses, Jacob, David, Elijah, and even John the Baptist and Jesus all contain "desert motifs" well known to this part of the world.

Villagers living along the fringe of this desolate region use it for their sheep. From October to March a good rain will suddenly make the desert bloom with a surprising number of plants, and all of these make excellent pasture for the sheep. But during the bulk of the year, the desert is inhospitable to life. Water is scarce, food is rare, and dangers are everywhere. In fact, the eastern deserts of Judea have steep, eroded cliffs that present a drop of a thousand feet in many places. Psalm 23 is an excellent source of what it means to be a competent shepherd in this environment. Such a leader can find food ("green pastures," 23:2a), water ("quiet water," 23:2b[25]), safe paths ("paths of righteousness," 23:3), and places of safety from danger ("in the presence of my enemies," 23:5). Competent shepherds must have skills and tools or else their sheep will become prey either to the elements or to wild animals in this region.

We cannot downplay the life-threatening danger of this environment. The parable of the lost sheep in Luke 15 gives a glimpse of how serious the life of the flock is weighed. To lead a flock through a desolate region with bandits and hungry animals is still serious business. Shepherds commonly carry a four- or five-foot wooden staff that serves chiefly as a defense weapon. They are also skilled with a sling and stones (much like the biblical shepherd David).[26] When the flock is attacked, a "good" shepherd will never throw a lamb to the attacking animals in order to save the flock. He tries to find a sheep pen (described above on 10:1—18) and then stands between the flock and danger.

As already mentioned, Arab shepherds are well known for knowing their sheep personally. During the Palestinian uprising in the late 1980s the Israeli army decided to punish a village near Bethlehem for not paying its taxes (which, the village claimed, simply financed their occupation). The officer in command rounded up all of the village animals and placed them in a large barbed-wire pen. Later in the week he was approached by a woman who begged him to release her flock, arguing that since her husband was dead, the animals were her only source of livelihood. He pointed to the pen containing hundreds of animals and humorously quipped that it was impossible because he could not find her animals. She asked that if she could in fact separate them herself, would he be willing to let her take them? He agreed. A soldier opened the gate and the woman's son produced a small reed flute. He played a simple tune again and again—and soon sheep heads began popping up across the pen. The young boy continued his music and walked home, followed by his flock of twenty-five sheep.

This is precisely the image that I need to construct for my audience. The desert is a desperate place. Our shepherd is skilled and courageous. If we remain under his leadership, if we recognize his voice, we will find safety and flourish. To make this come alive, I need to recognize the perilous environment of my life, my need of guidance, and the requisite skill that can tell the right voices from the wrong voices.

---

25. Sheep need standing (not running water) for drinking. Shepherds will dam small brooks near springs in the desert in order to make watering pools.

26. I have seen Palestinian boys watching their sheep in the desert of Judea and demonstrating incredible, lethal skill with sling and stone.

It takes little convincing to show that the environment of the world is as treacherous as a Judean desert. I was speaking at a conference recently in the mountains above Santa Cruz, California, and listened to the pastor of a large Santa Cruz church describe the dangers of secular life in his city for his children. It was not simply the illicit sexuality and overwhelming pressure to "do drugs" that bothered him. It was the persuasive moral atmosphere that said, "God is irrelevant and there are no rules."

It is not simply the stereotypical immorality of California's beach cities that is threatening our lives today. The environment of the world is hostile at every turn. A friend of mine is a rock musician from a rural Illinois town. Recently we were exploring together the violence, aggression, and amoral worldview served up in modern rock music. As an adult convert with a history in this industry, he argued that the threats were severe.

We do live in a modern desert. But John 10 demands that we ask a different sort of question. In the midst of this moral chaos, in this threatening desert, whose voice, which shepherd, do we follow? A youth leader of a large high school ministry summarized for me a study conducted recently by George Barna. The study asked high school students where they would turn first in times of tension, confusion, or crisis. Their fathers were ranked about No. 25 on the list. Mothers came in about No. 11. Music and personal friends scored at the top. In time of tragedy, young people may well look to the wrong leaders when coming out of the desert. To illustrate, many sitcoms today oriented to young adults (such as *Seinfeld* and *Friends*) display this tendency generously. In times of crisis, where do these apartment-dwelling singles go for their answers?

But adults respond to false voices as well. The *Chicago Tribune Magazine* recently reported on a woman in the city who called herself an "intuitive healer." She claimed to have supernatural power to diagnose people's diseases. She could even do it over the phone. While most of us would find such an article little more than entertaining, what disturbed me most was the number of people, patients as well as physicians, who relied on her powers. When people are in crisis, when they are surrounded by the dangers of the desert, they will turn to any shepherd offering a way out. Friends of mine who are missionaries in France have told me the breathtaking number of New Age healers that work in the country. Recently the cost of using these healers is covered under France's health coverage.

Not long ago I read in a British newspaper how married couples have sought to address the problem of infertility through the council of witches.[27] As hard as it is to believe, "pagan pastors" make claims to curing infertility in

27. *The Observer* (Aug. 23, 1998).

thirty minutes through the use of secret potions and ceremonies—and assigning the couples to make love on ancient, ceremonial stones located around the country. The mind boggles. The point here is that British society finds an interest in this and is willing to put it on some of the leading pages of one of its most respected newspapers.

Testing. These are just a handful of examples, but every communicator of biblical truth needs to sound the alarm and point his or her audience to their need of a true shepherd who can genuinely lead them from the desert. When Eastern Europe and Russia became open to Western missionaries (following the close of the Cold War), the Russian government was in a dilemma. They wanted the good things that "religion" could bring to healing their land. The Russian military even contacted the United States Navy, asking for chaplain consultants so that they could bring chaplains into their armed forces. But how could they tell what groups were trustworthy and what ones were dangerous? In the Russian desert, which of the religious voices could be trusted? In a curious behind-the-scenes assignment, leaders from a number of evangelical organizations and colleges helped interpret the mass of religion pouring over Russia's borders.

John has given us a direct and simple solution. Jesus is the true shepherd, and he is the only one who can endorse others who will lead the sheep. The final test of a shepherd's credentials is his or her fidelity to the leadership of Jesus. When someone makes a claim on the sheep, when a new voice emerges over the horizon, the first question we should ask is whether this voice echoes the voice of Jesus we know in the Scriptures. When John was trying to teach his congregation—and us—how to discern the false voices calling for attention, he wrote again and again that they had to recall what had been given to them "from the beginning" (1 John 1:1; 2:7, 13, 14, 24; 3:8, 11; 2 John 1:5). That is, John underscored the value of testing would-be prophets and leaders against the historic revelation we have of Jesus Christ, which springs from Jesus' earthly ministry.[28]

Ancillary issues. I mentioned above that there are three provocative ancillary questions that this chapter raises but does not resolve. Nevertheless each of them invites a contemporary expression that might bear a powerful meaning today.

(1) That Jesus has "other sheep" not of "this fold" means in its historic setting that Jesus has sheep among those on the margins of Jewish society (most likely, the Gentiles) that must be included in his flock. Hints of Jesus' inter-

---

28. To interpret John's pastoral setting directly, he is in effect saying in his letters, "If you want to discern the validity of a new would-be shepherd, test his profile against the profile of Jesus you have read in my Gospel."

est in those outside the traditional "flock of Judaism" increases as we near the end of the Gospel. But this means that for his immediate followers, they dare not express arrogance over their control of the flock. These sheep are "outside," they are different, but they are nevertheless equally loved and valued. Jesus' desire is to see one body, one genuine unity, in which all of his sheep move as one flock.

When the body of Christ—or the flock of Jesus—embraces these "other sheep," remarkable things happen. As a modern interpreter, I need to wrestle with the identity of these sheep for the church in which I live. Who lives on the margin of my world? Recently I had the privilege of speaking at a week-long family camp for a large urban Presbyterian church in Illinois. There I witnessed sights of diversity and wonder as the "other sheep" of Christ were invited into full participation: the elderly, the socially awkward, young children, blue collar, and white collar—each had a place at the table. Imagine observing the camp's talent show filled with music and song, including a mentally impaired man's performance of "Jesus Loves Me." Then imagine as the congregation, whose love for this man is tangible, begins to sing with him as he forgets the words. He may be one of the "other sheep."

Or imagine a sock-hop one evening where on the dance floor I watch little children, seniors, and regular middle-aged couples dancing to Patsy Cline. Then I observe one more miracle of the flock. A dancer sweeps over and takes the wheelchair of a young woman who last year lost both legs in a car wreck, and she dances with her hands and her wheels. She too is one of the "other sheep." Another young woman takes the hand of a mentally impaired gentleman and draws him in, and he dances and laughs with glee. He too is a part of this flock. One more of Jesus' "other sheep." I lean over to the pastor of the church and comment, "You know, you don't see a sight like this in the world. This is the kingdom of God." "Yes," he remarks, "it is amazing. This is the peaceable kingdom."

Of course no church is perfect, and this one in Illinois has challenges on its horizon. As an old inner-city church with chiefly a white population, it is thinking hard about the fact that the demographics of its city have changed. The church is surrounded by a growing Hispanic community. Jesus has "other sheep" here too, and these Christians are wrestling with how to open their flock to them.

This is a comforting word for sheep who have been marginalized. But it is also a warning to those sheep whose control of the fold has made it homogenous and exclusive. These other sheep are "Jesus' sheep," not random sheep aspiring to gain a better identity, a better fold. The vision here is for a unity that breaks the bonds of racial, economic, and cultural divisions, that sees a person's identity in Christ first, while all other markers fall away. In the mid 1990s I had the privilege of leading a short retreat for pastors in Bethlehem in Palestine (Israel). There I watched while courageous Palestinian pastors and messianic Jewish pastors discovered the beginnings of reconciliation that went beyond the historic, violent divisions imposed by their societies. I vowed that if Arab and Jew can overcome differences in Palestine/Israel through their identity in Christ, there is no excuse for me to fail at any reconciliation and work for the unity of the church.[29]

(2) The second ancillary question concerns the divine sovereignty alluded to throughout the chapter. Every theologian recognizes the problem of understanding the sovereignty of God and the responsibility of his people. Thinking Christians will pick up on this immediately. "If God's will is sovereign, then there are no autonomous human decisions." Every theologian likewise knows that in some fashion we have to strike a balance that pays appropriate respect to both of these themes. This is particularly true for the theology of the Gospel of John.[30]C. S. Lewis was not a professional theologian, but he had a gift for providing excellent illustrations of complex themes. In an important chapter in his famous book *Mere Christianity*, Lewis denies the validity of a view which would make humans responsible in a world where they possess no freedom. Nevertheless, Lewis recognizes that any theology that does not embrace God's power is truly inadequate. His picture is that of a child playing a piano, whose hands are guided note-by-note by the experienced fingers of an artist. At first the expert may play the melody and the child is invited to rest his or her fingers on the skilled fingers. Then perhaps they change places, the child's fingers working under the guidance of the skilled hands. The point here is that God continues to work in powerful ways, but his work always invites our participation, or even demands our participation. In John 10 Jesus' sheep are those whom God has given into his hand, and they are also sheep who have decided to believe.

This synthesis of divine aid and human effort should give us confidence when we present the truth claims of the gospel to an unreached listener. But it should also help us to understand that indeed humans have the capacity to disbelieve, to resist God's efforts on their behalf. As Lewis once said, there are only two sorts of people in the world: those who say to God, "Thy will be done," and those to whom God says, *"Thy* will be done."

(3) Finally, I am troubled by the nuanced ending of the chapter. While we hold firmly that God's love will not be withdrawn from any person, still, the suggestion here is that once Jesus has completed his direct revelation within

29. On the remarkable globalization of the church and its growth outside the West, see M. Hutchinson, "It's a Small Church After All· Globalization Is Changing How Christians Do Ministry," *Christianity Today* 42 (Nov. 16, 1998): 46–55.
30. See D. Carson, *Divine Sovereignty and Human Responsibility* (Atlanta: John Knox, 1981)

Judaism, he is ready to remove himself and remain outside Judea until the coming festival of Passover, when he is killed. The same motif also concludes both chapters 11 and 12. Following the raising of Lazarus Jesus "withdraws" to the desert (11:54), and in the midst of his final Jerusalem plea he "leaves and hides" (12:36).

Perhaps the application of this theme points to the limited opportunities we possess to hear the gospel. Practically, the messenger from God who speaks to me the gospel may not be there tomorrow. Consequently, "today" must be the "day of salvation" (2 Cor. 6:2). But this motif is not simply about a lost opportunity. It is a word of judgment. In the letters to the seven churches, the Ephesian church is told that unless it repents, its "lampstand" may be removed (Rev. 2:5). This is a similar act of judgment in which God removes the privilege of a church to exist as *his church* in a given locale. Could the same happen in other contexts? Can a nation or a city become so utterly godless, so utterly pagan and thoroughgoing in its repudiation of the gospel, that it experiences a diminution of God's activity?

John 11:1–57

NOW A MAN named Lazarus was sick. He was from Bethany, the village of Mary and her sister Martha. [2]This Mary, whose brother Lazarus now lay sick, was the same one who poured perfume on the Lord and wiped his feet with her hair. [3]So the sisters sent word to Jesus, "Lord, the one you love is sick."

[4]When he heard this, Jesus said, "This sickness will not end in death. No, it is for God's glory so that God's Son may be glorified through it." [5]Jesus loved Martha and her sister and Lazarus. [6]Yet when he heard that Lazarus was sick, he stayed where he was two more days.

[7]Then he said to his disciples, "Let us go back to Judea."

[8] "But Rabbi," they said, "a short while ago the Jews tried to stone you, and yet you are going back there?"

[9]Jesus answered, "Are there not twelve hours of daylight? A man who walks by day will not stumble, for he sees by this world's light. [10]It is when he walks by night that he stumbles, for he has no light."

[11]After he had said this, he went on to tell them, "Our friend Lazarus has fallen asleep; but I am going there to wake him up."

[12]His disciples replied, "Lord, if he sleeps, he will get better." [13]Jesus had been speaking of his death, but his disciples thought he meant natural sleep.

[14]So then he told them plainly, "Lazarus is dead, [15]and for your sake I am glad I was not there, so that you may believe. But let us go to him."

[16]Then Thomas (called Didymus) said to the rest of the disciples, "Let us also go, that we may die with him."

[17]On his arrival, Jesus found that Lazarus had already been in the tomb for four days. [18]Bethany was less than two miles from Jerusalem, [19]and many Jews had come to Martha and Mary to comfort them in the loss of their brother. [20]When Martha heard that Jesus was coming, she went out to meet him, but Mary stayed at home.

[21]"Lord," Martha said to Jesus, "if you had been here, my brother would not have died. [22] But I know that even now God will give you whatever you ask."

²³Jesus said to her, "Your brother will rise again."

²⁴Martha answered, "I know he will rise again in the resurrection at the last day."

²⁵Jesus said to her, "I am the resurrection and the life. He who believes in me will live, even though he dies; ²⁶and whoever lives and believes in me will never die. Do you believe this?"

²⁷"Yes, Lord," she told him, "I believe that you are the Christ, the Son of God, who was to come into the world."

²⁸And after she had said this, she went back and called her sister Mary aside. "The Teacher is here," she said, "and is asking for you." ²⁹When Mary heard this, she got up quickly and went to him. ³⁰Now Jesus had not yet entered the village, but was still at the place where Martha had met him. ³¹When the Jews who had been with Mary in the house, comforting her, noticed how quickly she got up and went out, they followed her, supposing she was going to the tomb to mourn there.

³²When Mary reached the place where Jesus was and saw him, she fell at his feet and said, "Lord, if you had been here, my brother would not have died."

³³When Jesus saw her weeping, and the Jews who had come along with her also weeping, he was deeply moved in spirit and troubled. ³⁴"Where have you laid him?" he asked.

"Come and see, Lord," they replied.

³⁵Jesus wept.

³⁶Then the Jews said, "See how he loved him!"

³⁷But some of them said, "Could not he who opened the eyes of the blind man have kept this man from dying?"

³⁸Jesus, once more deeply moved, came to the tomb. It was a cave with a stone laid across the entrance. ³⁹"Take away the stone," he said.

"But, Lord," said Martha, the sister of the dead man, "by this time there is a bad odor, for he has been there four days."

⁴⁰Then Jesus said, "Did I not tell you that if you believed, you would see the glory of God?"

⁴¹So they took away the stone. Then Jesus looked up and said, "Father, I thank you that you have heard me. ⁴²I knew that you always hear me, but I said this for the benefit of the people standing here, that they may believe that you sent me."

⁴³When he had said this, Jesus called in a loud voice, "Lazarus, come out!" ⁴⁴The dead man came out, his hands and feet wrapped with strips of linen, and a cloth around his face.

Jesus said to them, "Take off the grave clothes and let him go."

⁴⁵Therefore many of the Jews who had come to visit Mary, and had seen what Jesus did, put their faith in him. ⁴⁶But some of them went to the Pharisees and told them what Jesus had done. ⁴⁷Then the chief priests and the Pharisees called a meeting of the Sanhedrin.

"What are we accomplishing?" they asked. "Here is this man performing many miraculous signs. ⁴⁸If we let him go on like this, everyone will believe in him, and then the Romans will come and take away both our place and our nation."

⁴⁹Then one of them, named Caiaphas, who was high priest that year, spoke up, "You know nothing at all! ⁵⁰You do not realize that it is better for you that one man die for the people than that the whole nation perish."

⁵¹He did not say this on his own, but as high priest that year he prophesied that Jesus would die for the Jewish nation, ⁵²and not only for that nation but also for the scattered children of God, to bring them together and make them one. ⁵³So from that day on they plotted to take his life.

⁵⁴Therefore Jesus no longer moved about publicly among the Jews. Instead he withdrew to a region near the desert, to a village called Ephraim, where he stayed with his disciples.

⁵⁵When it was almost time for the Jewish Passover, many went up from the country to Jerusalem for their ceremonial cleansing before the Passover. ⁵⁶They kept looking for Jesus, and as they stood in the temple area they asked one another, "What do you think? Isn't he coming to the Feast at all?" ⁵⁷But the chief priests and Pharisees had given orders that if anyone found out where Jesus was, he should report it so that they might arrest him.

AS WE MOVE to chapter 11, we cross an important literary divide in this Gospel. Thus far we have examined the way Jesus' ministry takes advantage of the various institutions and festivals of Judaism, making them interpretive vehicles for his self-revelation. In fact, chapter 10 concludes this section with a "closing frame": Just as the narrative began with the story of John the Baptist (1:19ff.), so it ends on the same note (10:42). John the Baptist's work frames the entire revelation of Jesus.

However, John 11 and 12 stand together as marking a new and significant step in the life and work of Jesus. Jesus now makes his final move to the region of Jerusalem by coming to the village of Bethany (a short walk from Jerusalem) to attend to his friend Lazarus. Here we read the story of the most dramatic, provocative miracle in this Gospel. Jesus is master of life and death and proves it by bringing Lazarus back from the grave. But he is also prepared for his own death. Mary anoints him for burial (12:3), and at last we learn that the hour of Jesus' glorification, the hour we have anticipated since chapter 1, has arrived (12:23). Jesus describes himself as a grain of wheat that must fall into the earth and die (12:24).

Therefore these two chapters are about both death and life. The Lazarus story is a story about one man whom Jesus rescues from the grave; but it is also a parabolic story, telling us far more about Jesus, his power, and his upcoming experience in the grave. In order to help us understand this deeper message, the story employs double meanings in the same manner we have observed in previous chapters. For instance, in 11:12 Jesus comments that Lazarus is asleep, but his followers take this literally: "Lord, if he sleeps, he will get better." But Jesus means death in its fullest sense. Ironically death for Jesus is much like sleep because Lazarus must be awakened. Death does not bear the same finality for Jesus as it does for every other person.

Chapter 11 has invited numerous scholarly criticisms over the years, but it is not within the scope of this book to address them all. Objections have been raised, for instance, against the sheer enormity of the miracle itself. This is certainly Jesus' most dramatic sign. Those who have difficulty with the miraculous will find themselves stumbling here. However, John's entire theology aims to affirm that God has indeed intervened in the history of the world. An incarnational theology at once makes room for a story like this, in which this God who comes into history has power over the natural human processes over which he is master.

Other scholars have posited that this story is simply a reworking of the Lazarus parable of Luke 16:19–31. True, both stories use the same name and center on a resurrection motif. But actors in Jesus' Synoptic parables generally remain anonymous, and in this case the parallels between the two accounts are limited.[1] The name of Lazarus was popular in the first century (as can be attested from both literary and archaeological remains). Moreover, the two stories serve different purposes. The Lazarus parable is an exhortation to obey the words of the prophets; the Lazarus miracle points to Jesus' lordship over the grave. It may be that the parable took the name of its central actor from the miracle, whose resurrection was well known.[2]

---

1. Lazarus "from Bethany" named here is as specific as "Philip from Bethsaida," whom we met in 1:44, or "Judas Iscariot" (meaning "Judas, man from Kerioth," 6:71).

2. See Beasley-Murray, *John*, 200.

The Death of Lazarus (11:1–16)

BETHANY WAS A village just east of Jerusalem over the Mount of Olives, about one and a half miles away (11:18). In the fourth century Eusebius located it at the second Roman milestone from Jerusalem to Jericho, and today the Palestinian town of El-Aziriyeh (taken from the name of Lazarus) is located here.[3] Jews traveling from Jerusalem to Galilee commonly took the route east to Jericho and then north to Galilee in order to avoid Samaria. This explains Jesus' frequent movement through Jericho (hence the stories of Bartimaeus, Mark 10:46; Zacchaeus, Luke 19:2; the good Samaritan, which takes its setting from this road, Luke 10:30–37) as well as his familiarity with Bethany, which was along this road. When he was in Jerusalem, Jesus used Bethany as his base (as he used Capernaum in Galilee). This is why the Gospels contain multiple stories related to the village (Matt. 21:17; 26:6) and why Jesus likely lived here during the final week of his life.

Here in this small Judean community live a family extremely dear to Jesus. Two sisters, Martha and Mary, are the centerpiece of a story in Luke 10:38–42. Martha is likely the oldest since in Luke's story she is the host, and even here in John 11 she is named as the representative of the family (11:5). Their brother, Lazarus,[4] lives in the village as well; the three of them may have become something like an extended family for Jesus. No indication is given that they live together and we should not assume it. It would be most natural for them all to be married. That Jesus loves this family is affirmed again and again (John 11:3, 5, 36)—in this Gospel only the Beloved Disciple is described like this (13:23). John assumes that Mary (11:2) is so well known to his readers that he can refer to her as the one who anointed Jesus with oil even before he describes the scene (12:1–8).[5]

The women send a report to Jesus, not mentioning Lazarus by name but referring to him as "the one you love" (11:3). Jesus would know immediately whom they mean. It is interesting that the women know how to find Jesus. Does this suggest that they have been keeping up with his movements? Or is there a network of supporters the sisters tap? Although they do not request Jesus to come, it is implied since he is well known as a healer and later both

---

3. The Bordeaux Pilgrim in A.D. 333 located it 1500 steps east of the Mount of Olives. Today a number of fourth-century Byzantine churches have been uncovered. Pilgrims today are often shown "the tomb of Lazarus," but it has a doubtful claim to authenticity. Nevertheless walking from Bethany to Jerusalem (through Bethphage) over the Mount of Olives accurately retraces Jesus' daily steps in this last season of his life.

4. Lazarus is an abbreviated Hebrew name taken from Eleazar, which means "God has helped." It is a fitting description of those events about to occur in the story.

5. This may be a signal to us that John assumes we have read the Synoptic story. The anointing of Jesus by Mary is recorded in Mark 14:3–9 (though her name is not given there).

women express regret that if Jesus had only come on time, Lazarus would not have died (11:21, 32). No doubt they are in a dilemma. They know about the hostility of the Jerusalem's leadership toward Jesus (11:8) and conclude that for Jesus to visit would mean considerable risk.

When Jesus hears the report about Lazarus's illness, his response (11:4) parallels his comments about the man born blind (9:1–5). The final result of this tragedy is that God will be glorified, not that death will win the victory. It is not a denial of Lazarus's death since this is the thrust of the whole story, but that death will not gain the final word in this man's life. The tragedy is not by God's design, but God will use it for an opportunity to glorify his Son.

After affirming Jesus' love for these three followers once more (11:5), John reports that Jesus does not respond immediately and come to Bethany (11:6). Paradoxically, he waits two days. Note that Jesus' delay is not the cause of Lazarus's death (as if a prompt response would have avoided it). According to John 11:17, when Jesus arrives in Bethany Lazarus has been dead for four days. We know from 10:40 that Jesus is now in "Bethany across the Jordan" (i.e., in Perea), and surely it does not take four days to travel to Bethany near Jerusalem.[6] It likely took the messengers one day to find Jesus, Jesus continues to work where he is two days, and then he takes one more day to travel to Bethany. This means that Lazarus likely died right after the departure of the messengers. When they meet Jesus, Lazarus is already buried.[7]

Nevertheless, we should assume that in the narrative Jesus has divine knowledge of what is happening in Bethany (just as he could see Nathanael in 1:48 and the Samaritan woman in 4:18). He tells his followers before they arrive that Lazarus is asleep (11:11), which invites the usual Johannine irony of misunderstanding: "Lord, if he sleeps, he will get better." But Jesus must say clearly that Lazarus is dead (11:14). If Jesus has this knowledge and if he knows the moment of Lazarus's death, his delay serves not to promote the death, but to heighten the significance of his own miraculous work. Jesus is proceeding with his own sense of timing, in which he can say again and again that the urgency felt by others is not necessarily the same as the divine timing within which he works (2:4; 7:5–9). His aim is to reveal the glory of God's work in him and thereby to promote the faith of his followers (11:15).

---

6 Some scholars suggest that Jesus was in Batanea in the far northeast (modern Golan Heights), which was eighty-five miles away. This explains why it took four days for Jesus to reach Bethany. But this suggestion seems to strain the evidence of 10:40–42 and 1:28 (see comments). John the Baptist's death in the Synoptics occurs because he was working in a region controlled by Antipas (Perea) on the border of Nabatea. Residents of Jerusalem would likely not come to visit John (1:19) in Batanea. On the contrary, John's ministry was centered on the Jordan River south of Galilee

7. In this culture, deceased persons were generally buried immediately Cf. Acts 5:1–10.

The decision finally to go up to Judea must have been frightening to Jesus' disciples (11:8). Throughout the story we have learned of the growing tensions surrounding Jesus' contact with the religious leadership. During the previous autumn celebration at the Feast of Tabernacles the authorities tried to arrest him (8:44), and rumor was out that they wanted to kill him (7:25). At one point a crowd tried to stone Jesus (8:59). A few months later at Hanukkah they tried to arrest him (10:39), and again there was the threat of stoning (10:31). The events of John 11 are set sometime between the winter Hanukkah Feast and the upcoming spring when Jesus is crucified—and the tension must have been palpable. The threat is not simply to Jesus but to his disciples as well, so that Thomas speaks up, "Let us also go, that we may die with him" (11:16).[8]

While in the Synoptics Thomas only appears in the lists of Jesus' disciples, in John he appears here and in three other places. He offers a question in the Upper Room (14:5), he appears a week after Easter in the famous "doubting" narrative (20:24), and he is fishing with Peter in the final resurrection miracle (21:2). But here he shows himself with courage and faithfulness (even though Thomas is certainly filled with misunderstandings about Jesus).[9]

Some interpreters suggest that if we take into account the profile of Thomas elsewhere in the Gospel, we should see in these words a cynicism characteristic of the man who refused to believe in the resurrected Jesus until he gained his own personal audience with him. I prefer to see these words as another case of Johannine irony. Even if Thomas is less than sincere, he likely does not understand the profound truth he utters. This parallels the role of Caiaphas later in the chapter (11:49–50), when the high priest says that Jesus' death will be expedient for the nation. Indeed it will be—but not as Caiaphas imagines it. So too being a disciple will pose dangers, even martyrdom, for anyone who follows Jesus (as Peter learns in 21:18-19).

Jesus' reassurance to Thomas and his followers appears in 11:9–10. We should remember that Jesus has described himself as "the light" (8:12; 9:5). Thus, to walk in the light of day is in some manner to walk in concert with the work of Jesus. So long as they are with him—and since he understands the "hours" of his life and work—they can be confident that he will guide

---

8. "Thomas" is a Hebrew name; its Greek equivalant is *Didymos* (which means the same thing, "twin"). We have no suggestion, however, who his twin might be. The apocryphal literature that venerated the image of Thomas calls him the twin of Jesus—or simply that he looked like Jesus (*Acts of Thomas*, 11, 31). But this is unlikely.

9. In a lengthy monograph, J. H Charlesworth argues that the Beloved Disciple of the Fourth Gospel is actually Thomas, who later inspired a "school" and an entire body of apocryphal literature. See *The Beloved Disciple Whose Witness Validates the Gospel of John?* (Vally Forge, Pa.: Trinity, 1995).

them through this treacherous trip to Judea. But the reference to "twelve hours" means more than this. It means that there is work to be done and that the day cannot be extended. Jesus must move to Bethany because *night is coming.* There is a crisis awaiting on the horizon (a tragedy that will be turned to glory nonetheless), but it is a crisis that is within the control of Jesus' will (10:17–18).

Jesus Comes to Bethany (11:17–37)

WHEN JESUS FINALLY arrives in Bethany Lazarus has been dead for four days. This note is significant. There was a well-known Jewish belief (attested from about A.D. 200) that the soul of a dead person remained in the vicinity of the body "hoping to reenter it" for three days, but once decomposition set in, the soul departed.[10] John wants us to know clearly that Lazarus is truly dead and that the miracle of Jesus cannot be construed as a resuscitation.

Lazarus's death was not a private period of mourning for his family. Life in New Testament Palestine was lived publicly and community ties were strong. As in today's Middle East, relatives whom Westerners would consider distant cousins still had intimate contact with each other. Thus, many Jews (friends and relatives) have come to Bethany even from nearby Jerusalem to comfort Martha and Mary (11:19). There would be great wailing and crying (cf. Mark 5:38; Acts 8:2), some beating their chests in grief (Luke 18:13; 23:48). Hiring flute players was also common (Matt. 9:23; *m. Ketuboth* 4:4); even the Jewish oral law encouraged it.

Formal mourning lasted for seven days, called in Hebrew the *shibah* (cf. Sir. 22:12), and it commenced immediately on the day of burial, which took place on the same day as death.[11] We can assume that Lazarus was buried in a rock-cut tomb of the type that have been discovered throughout the hills of Judea.[12] Inside a cave room (perhaps ten to fifteen feet square) burial benches were carved in stone along the inner wall. The body was prepared here and then laid in horizontally cut burial tunnels (Heb. *kochim*) about six feet deep and there left to decompose. After a year or so, the body was removed from the *koch* and the bones placed in a limestone "burial box" (an ossuary). The tomb was closed (and reopened for further burials) with a wheel-shaped "rolling stone" fitted to cover the entrance in a stone channel.

---

10. Similarly, the *Mishnah* says that in judicial cases deceased persons can only be identified up to three days (*Yebamot* 16:3).

11. The Jewish tractate *Semahot* (Heb. 'joys'), appended to the Talmud, outlines the legal rules for burial and mourning.

12. Perhaps the best example of a first-century tomb complex to illustrate Lazarus's burial (and Jesus' too) is that of Queen Helena of Adiabene in northeast Jerusalem. It is called the Tomb of the Kings in guidebooks.

Therefore when Jesus arrives on the outskirts of Bethany, Lazarus is buried in a *koch*, the tomb is "closed," and there is tremendous commotion surrounding Martha and Mary. The extent and passion of mourning reflect the honor and esteem of Lazarus in the village. Friends and family from far off came to join the scene. By referring to Jerusalem (11:18) the text increases our sense of Jesus' jeopardy when he arrives. His presence in Bethany just over the Mount of Olives would certainly become known to his enemies in Jerusalem. He could not slip into Bethany incognito and comfort the sisters.

The story follows the two sisters as each makes contact with Jesus. First Martha (11:20–27), then Mary (11:28–37), talk with Jesus; this is followed by the miracle itself (11:38–44). Commentators are quick to make comparisons between the two women and contrast their activity here with that given in Luke 10. In both narratives the key is that Martha is the oldest and so has the responsibility of hospitality and food preparation (cf. Luke 10) as well as overseeing the activities of this day and greeting Jesus (John 11). It is wrong, therefore, to look for nuances in the story (Doesn't Mary fall at his feet in devotion?) and make key points from them. The sorrowful complaints of both women (11:21, 32) are virtually the same.

Martha meets Jesus before he enters the village (11:30), and her words in 11:21 are an affirmation of faith in Jesus' healing ability. "Lord" here is a polite form of address (much like "sir"). Despite what she says in 11:22, she likely does not expect Jesus to raise Lazarus from death since in 11:39 she objects when Jesus wants to roll open the tomb. Instead, she is expressing faith, not wanting to imply any criticism of Jesus since he was not in Bethany to rescue her brother. Martha's words can be paraphrased: "If you had been here, you could have healed Lazarus. Nevertheless, I still believe in you, that God works through you mightily." Martha continues to be confident in Jesus.

But Jesus pushes Martha to a second, deeper level of discussion (11:23–27). "Your brother will rise again" can be seen on one level as words of comfort, appealing to the common Jewish belief in the end-time resurrection.[13] Lazarus would enjoy eternal life. Martha misses entirely the more immediate application Jesus has in mind. His correction leads to one of the most famous and significant "I am" sayings in John's Gospel. Jesus does not say that he can provide resurrection and life (though this is implicit). That in itself would be astounding. In fact, the Synoptics recount stories of Jesus' authority over death and his ability to call someone back to life (e.g., the widow's son in Nain in Luke 7:11–17; Jairus's daughter in Mark 5:21–43). But Jesus says that *he is* resurrection and life.

---

13. This was a view popularly defended by the Pharisees but denied by the Sadducees (cf. Mark 12:18–27; Acts 23:8, *m Sanhedrin* 10:1).

In other words, eternal life and rescue from the finality of death are not merely gifts obtained by appeal to God; they are aspects of what it means to live a life in association with Jesus. If Jesus is life, then those who believe in him will enjoy the confidence and power over death known by him. This does not mean that Jesus' followers will not die a physical death (11:25b), but that life will be theirs beyond the grave; they will not suffer death in eternity.[14] Moreover, they will have a life now and do not have to await the end of human time and history in order to enjoy the benefits of Jesus' power.

Jesus' question to Martha, "Do you believe this?" has little to do with her faith in Jesus' ability to bring her brother from the grave. Nor is Jesus pointing to her commitment to the end-time resurrection. Jesus is asking if her faith can embrace a belief in Jesus' lordship over death itself. If it is true that in Jesus the power of resurrection life is present in Bethany, the logical implication is that this may lead to something for Lazarus. Lazarus's resurrection becomes a proof of Jesus' statement.

At this point, however, Martha cannot draw this conclusion directly. Her affirmation (11:27) shows that she is following Jesus' thinking. She says "yes" when undoubtedly the implications of this "yes" are beyond her comprehension. She is trusting in Jesus' power as a personal commitment, but she is also ready to make a cognitive commitment to who Jesus must be. If he has this sort of authority, by extension he must also be the "Christ [the Messiah], the Son of God," whom Judaism sought on its future horizon.

Mary then enters the scene (11:28) while Jesus is still outside the village and inaccessible to the crowd. It is a deeply touching scene since Jesus knows that his ministry here is not simply to Lazarus, but to both of these women whom he has known. When Mary runs from the house, she is followed by other mourners (11:31), which once again reinforces the public context of this scene. Mary (like her sister) explains in dismay their sorrow over Jesus' absence while Lazarus was alive and then is overcome with grief (11:33). The NIV's "weeping" leaves the impression of quiet tears of sadness, but the Greek tells a different story. The verb *klaio* describes loud wailing and crying, which is echoed by the people standing around Mary. Such loud public displays of grief (relatively foreign to us in the West) were common in this culture.

When Jesus sees and hears their wailing, he is moved powerfully. But there is confusion in how to translate an important phrase in 11:33. The meaning of "in spirit" is clear enough; these words refer to Jesus' deepest self

---

14. The affirmation in 11:26, "whoever lives and believes in me will *never* die," employs an emphatic negative in Gk. (*ou me*), reinforcing the notion: "Whoever lives and believes in me will *absolutely never* die."

(not to the Holy Spirit). But the NIV's "deeply moved" may not be the best reading of the Greek verb *embrimaomai*.[15] In classical Greek this word describes the snort of a horse (in war or in a race). For humans it describes outrage, fury, or anger. This nuance appears in its Synoptic uses (Matt. 9:30; Mark 1:43; 14:5) and undoubtedly must be applied here.[16] Beasley-Murray cites Schnackenburg: The word "indicates an outburst of anger, and any attempt to reinterpret it in terms of an internal emotional upset caused by grief, pain, or sympathy is illegitimate."[17] This is further seen in the explanation John attaches: Jesus was not only outraged but "troubled."[18]

But what arouses Jesus' anger? Why is he outraged in the deepest level of his being? He is certainly not angry at Martha, Mary, or their mourners. Rather, he is overcome by the futility of this sorrowful scene in light of the reality of the resurrection. God's people possess knowledge of life; they *should* possess a faith that claims victory at the grave. But here they stand, overcome in seeming defeat. And here stands the One in whom victory, life, and resurrection are powerful realities. Jesus is angry at death itself and the devastation it brings. His only interest now is to locate the tomb (11:34) and begin to demonstrate divine power over humanity's foe.

Jesus' tears (11:35) are not for Lazarus, whose removal from the grave is imminent and whose life is going to show God's glory.[19] He knows what good surprises are in store for his good friend! Jesus' tears should be connected to the anger he is feeling so deeply. The public chaos surrounding him, the loud wailing and crying, and the scene of a cemetery and its reminders of death—all the result of sin and death—together produce outrage in the Son of God as he works to reverse such damage.

As happens so often in John's stories, the audience provides different responses (11:36—37). The same will happen later in the chapter when the

---

15. The entire English Bible translation tradition beginning with the KJV finds in the word some emotional distress for Jesus. Hence, the Good News Bible, "his heart was touched"; the Jerusalem Bible, "in great distress."

16. So the commentators Westcott, Hoskyns, Barrett, Brown, Carson, Beasley-Murray. The NLT rightly uses, "Jesus was moved with indignation."

17. Beasley-Murray, *John*, 193.

18. Jesus is "stirred" (*tarasso*), which most versions translate "troubled." But this is a metaphorical use of the word. Its literal meaning occurs in 5:4, 7 when water is stirred. Throughout John 1–11 water is a theological symbol for the Spirit, and in chapter 11 we find one of the few chapters that fails to mention it. Its active use here may refer to the Spirit (as living water) within him (7:37–39; 19:34). See C. Story, "The Mental Attitude of Jesus at Bethany, John 11:33, 38," *NTS* 37 (1991): 51–66; E. K. Lee, "The Raising of Lazarus," *ExpTim* 61 (1950): 145–47. This idea was originally presented to me in a research paper of Deborah Leighton, "John's Seventh Sign" (Wheaton College, Dec. 6, 1999).

19. This is now a different Gk. verb (*dakruo*) than that used to describe Mary's wail in v 33. It is not a funeral cry.

Sanhedrin makes its judgments. Here before the tomb, some witness the depth of Jesus' love for Lazarus and are duly impressed; others recall the stories of Jesus' works of healing (such as the blind man, ch. 9) and marvel that of all the people Jesus might heal, certainly Lazarus should have been one of them. Are they merely confused? Is this sincere questioning? Or is this cynicism and disbelief?

Lazarus is Raised to Life (11:38–44)

AS JESUS STEPS to the tomb itself (11:38), he is "once more deeply moved." The verb used here is the same one as in 11:33 (*embrimaomai*), which suggests he is outraged at what he sees. The Lord of life is now directly confronting his opponent, death, symbolized in the cave-tomb before him. The description of the tomb indicates that it is a "rolling stone" tomb (see notes above), which was designed to be opened. The vertical "wheel" could be rolled back, permitting access to the main receiving room of the burial cave.

Martha's response in 11:39 is critical for John's report of the scene. Note how Martha is described as "the sister of the dead man." She further warns that since Lazarus has been dead four days, decomposition has set in and there will be an odor. In an early medieval Jewish tradition (which may well go back to the first century) Jews would return to the cemetery after three days to check to see if the person was living (*b. Semahot* 8:1). All of this serves to remind us that Lazarus is truly dead and that the miracle of Jesus is not simply one of resuscitating his friend. He must be "awakened" (11:11) *from death.* In 11:4 Jesus had explained to his followers that Lazarus's illness would result in the glory of God. Although he has not said this directly to Martha, his exhortation to her in 11:40 serves as a summary of what he meant in 11:21–27. God's glory will lead to the glorifying of his Son (11:4).

When the stone is rolled back, Jesus prays (11:41–42). This prayer is interesting on several counts. (1) It implies that Jesus had prayed *already* for Lazarus and that he is now coming to this great miracle fully prepared for what will take place. This is not a "last minute" request.

(2) Jesus prays publicly, and he does so "looking up" (no doubt with hands upraised). This was a common posture for Jewish prayer. Audible prayers were more common in Jesus' world than private prayers. Jesus is certainly not praying to impress the audience of mourners. But his followers could use prayers to learn things about the life and thought of their Master (cf. the Old Testament prayers of Moses). Thus Jesus is aware that his prayer is also for the benefit of these bystanders (11:42).

(3) Jesus addresses God as "Father" (not "our" father) and shows his personal intimacy with him (12:27–28; 17:1). He also demonstrates that his work is done in concert with God's will, for he never acts autonomously. In

5:19, Jesus remarked, "I tell you the truth, the Son can do nothing by himself; he can do only what he sees his Father doing, because whatever the Father does the Son also does."

The dramatic high point of the story is reached in 11:43 when Jesus calls to Lazarus "in a loud voice" to come out. This is not a whisper or a firm request. It is a shout of raw authority. The Greek *kraugazo* is used six times in John—in addition to here, once for the crowds on Palm Sunday (12:13) and four times for the cries of the crowds calling for Jesus' crucifixion (18:40; 19:6, 12, 15). When Lazarus emerges from the tomb, he is bound in grave wrappings, which were strips of fabric wound around his limbs and filled with burial spices. Jewish burials likewise tied the jaw closed and covered the face with a linen cloth.[20]

Lazarus's coming from the grave must have been an amazing spectacle witnessed by a growing crowd of people, many of whom carry news of this miracle back to Jerusalem (12:9, 17). Lazarus stands before Jesus wrapped tightly. Jesus is no doubt talking to him (what does he say?), and the crowd undoubtedly shrinks back in awe. Jewish superstitions took great interest in cemeteries (as do most cultures), and strict ritual laws of purification (clean/unclean) were attached to dead bodies. Should anyone come near the man? Martha? Mary? Jesus loved Lazarus, and it is not hard to imagine him being the first to embrace his friend. Jesus had a reputation for touching those deemed "untouchable" (Matt. 8:3; 9:20), and while the text is silent, such an embrace here would have left the crowd stunned. Jesus remains in command and orders that someone unbind him (John 11:44).

The Sanhedrin Plots to Kill Jesus (11:45–57)

MOST OF THE miracles and discourses in the Book of Signs (John 1–12) led to a sharp division in the audience. The same occurs here. Many of the Jews in Bethany who witnessed the events of that day "put their faith in him" (11:45)—one of John's favorite phrases to express true belief in Jesus.[21] They have seen the glory of God at work (as promised) and rightly link it to the person of Jesus. John's sharp contrast with the "others" (11:46), who go directly to the Pharisees, suggests they do not believe.

The popularity of Jesus and the sheer power of this breakthrough sign on the outskirts of Jerusalem bring a crisis to the ruling council of Jerusalem (the Sanhedrin). Even if the story of Lazarus were untrue (as some of the leaders no doubt contend), still the rumor of it will spread in the city like wildfire.

---

20. Often we discover that coins had been placed on the eyes of buried first-century Jews.

21. The precise Gk. phrase used here (*episteusan eis auton*) occurs seven times in this Gospel.

The Sanhedrin deliberations (11:47–50) are noteworthy. (1) There is genuine fear that the populace will accept Jesus as the Messiah. This is not simply religious rivalry, but a paralyzing concern that if a messianic claimant is embraced by the city, the Roman armies will suppress it. "Our place" (11:48) refers to the Jerusalem temple (NRSV, "our holy place"; cf. Acts 6:13–14; 7:7; 21:28). The Romans had shown their intolerance to this sort of messianism in the past (viewing it as a political challenge), and Jerusalem's leadership know the seriousness of the threat now.

(2) John summarizes the view of the reigning high priest, Caiaphas (11:49–50). This man ruled the Sanhedrin from A.D. 18 to A.D. 36 and took personal responsibility for the political stability of the country.[22] He worked for ten years alongside the Roman governor Pilate, and together the two men forged an uneasy peace in the country.[23] For Caiaphas, then, political expediency is the key: If there must be a sacrifice, better to lose one man than the entire nation. Therefore the high council begins planning how they can kill Jesus (11:53).

Just as Jesus' discourses have double levels of meaning, so too these voices say more than even they expected. John knows this (11:51–52) and tips us off to look beneath the surface. Indeed, both of the comments from the Sanhedrin bear some truth. (1) The Romans will eventually come and bring their judgment on the city and its temple. From A.D. 66–70 Jerusalem was under siege, which concluded with the burning of the temple. (2) But also Caiaphas is right in a way he cannot perceive. Jesus will die for the salvation of the nation. An unwitting prophecy here points to the cross since the salvation Judaism needs has less to do with Rome than it does with Jerusalem's spiritual jeopardy.

John knows that the death of Christ will perform a work that is far more profound than anyone imagines. It is not simply the city of Jerusalem or the people of Judaism that will be saved, but the "scattered children of God" (11:52). To a Jew, such a phrase would describe Jews living in the "Diaspora" (or the dispersion) of Gentile countries around the Mediterranean. But here John is no doubt referring to Gentiles, who likewise need to come into the family of God. This thought parallels what we read in 10:16, that Jesus is a good shepherd whose flock includes many unexpected sheep. His work is to bring together into unity the diversity of God's people.

The formalized threat to Jesus leads him to make a judicious political move (11:54). Today we would say that he goes "underground"—Jesus cannot

---

22. Recent archaeological work has uncovered the burial box (ossuary) of Caiaphas. It is on display in the Israel Museum located in West Jerusalem.

23. Pilate ruled from A.D. 26–36, overlapping Caiaphas for ten years. In A.D. 36, when Pilate was removed forcibly from office, Caiaphas immediately lost his hold on the high priesthood.

risk being a public figure in the same manner any longer. He knows the hour of his glorification and will not permit anyone or anything to interrupt his mission. With characteristic geographical precision, John says that Jesus moves to Ephraim, a small town likely near Bethel, about a dozen miles north of Jerusalem (cf. Old Testament Ephron, 2 Chron. 13:19).[24] Here Jesus is safe from the Sanhedrin, but he is also close enough to attend the upcoming Passover in Jerusalem.

As an orthodox Jew, Jesus would have faithfully obeyed the requirement of attending the annual pilgrimage festivals such as Passover. As men and women begin moving toward the city from throughout the country (11:55), they look for Jesus. Residents of Jerusalem no doubt spread the story of Lazarus (12:9), and the city is buzzing with talk about the intentions of the religious authorities (11:57). An open announcement of arrest is circulating for Jesus. If he is seen, he will be captured. With the crowds filling the city, "Jesus stories" added to the excitement. There will be a showdown. What about his supporters from Galilee? Will his twelve followers try to defend him? What will this do to the upcoming Passover celebrations?

But from Jesus' point of view, his public ministry among his people is completed. No longer will he provide any miraculous signs for them. No longer will we hear of new audiences of Jews "believing in him." Jesus is finished. He now will spend concentrated private time with those families (e.g., Martha, Mary, Lazarus), friends, and followers who know him, trust him, and believe in him. Jesus will indeed return to the public square once more during the Passover Feast following his triumphal entry, but only to give an impassioned plea for belief (12:44). No longer will he provide public signs that evoke belief. The next time after this he appears in public, he will be a prisoner.

Bridging Contexts

THIS IS A profoundly ironic chapter in the Gospel of John. As one of its longest narratives, it draws us into the story with excellent dramatic development. It records the most remarkable miracle in Jesus' ministry. Its climax is Jesus' gift of life to his dead friend Lazarus—and here is the irony—its conclusion finds his enemies (represented by Caiaphas) plotting Jesus' death. The Lord of Life demonstrates that he is victor over death and in the end, he has death pronounced on himself. He dispenses life while his enemies try to take it away.[25] We are even given

---

24 Today this is likely the modern Palestinian village of El-Tayibeh.

25. A similar irony occurs in Mark 3:1–6. After Jesus gives a man life (forgiving his sins and then healing him), his enemies plot how to destroy Jesus

signals in 11:55–57 pointing us to the festival (Passover), which is going to be the final feast of Jesus' life. Life and hope as well as dread and doom hang over the chapter ominously.

The nature of Jesus' work. We should see this chapter as an important statement about the character of Jesus' work. John includes this story so that Jesus' message does not "sink into a general symbolic mysticism."[26] His works are concrete. He is not just the light; he gives sight to a blind man. Jesus is not just the resurrection and the life; he brings a man from the tomb. The revelation of Jesus does not take place apart from concrete acts in history. Therefore the historicity of this passage (so often assailed in modern criticism), the truth about this story, is not to be found in the inspiring narrative it builds but in the deed it records. Something happened in Bethany that was unparalleled. God (who alone is sovereign over life) has acted decisively in Jesus Christ.

This follows the general pattern of John's message in his Gospel. Jesus has entered into human history and brought a number of "signs" that point us to his true identity. As such the raising of Lazarus is the seventh and final sign of Jesus.[27] It is interesting to compare the first and seventh signs of Jesus— Cana and Bethany—for in each Jesus unveils his glory in the company of personal friends (2:11; 11:4, 40).

It is no accident that the final number (seven) is a symbolic biblical number of completion, since it is the most important sign of all. It not only unveils the ultimate power of Jesus, but it points to what may be the ultimate and all-encompassing sign of all, the death and resurrection of Jesus. As we will note later (see comments on chapters 19–20), the story of Lazarus's empty tomb anticipates the story of Jesus' empty tomb. The Lord who has power over life has power over his own life as well. "The reason my Father loves me is that I lay down my life—only to take it up again" (10:17). If resurrection is the final, climactic sign, how much more will Jesus' glorification be the ultimate sign of the Gospel!

There are four principal themes (and a number of secondary ideas) that step from this chapter and deserve our closest attention as we try to communicate this text in a modern setting. The story is telling us a great deal

---

26. Hoskyns, *John*, 460.
27. Altogether John records seven signs of Jesus:
    1. Wine at Cana.
    2. Healing the nobleman's son.
    3. Healing the lame man.
    4. Feeding the five thousand.
    5. Walking on water.
    6. Healing the blind man.
    7. Raising Lazarus.

about Jesus in history and this cannot be neglected. It will not do simply to say that the Lazarus story is about men and women coming from death to life metaphorically, having their grave clothes removed as they are converted to Christ.[28] This is an important theme, but is better suited to John 3 or 4, where people move toward faith out of their religious (and irreligious) contexts. John 11 is about real life and real death. It is about Jesus' death (and life) as well as our own.

A reverse pattern. This is the first Johannine narrative that reverses the pattern of sign and discourse. In all of the chapters we have seen thus far, Jesus works a miracle (a sign), which is then followed by a thoroughgoing explanation. In John 9, for example, Jesus heals the blind man; this event is followed by clarifications (buried in the drama) that unfold for us the deeper meaning of the sign.[29] In John 11 the explanation comes in the dialogues with Martha and Mary, particularly 11:25–26, which tell us explicitly that the coming miracle is an opportunity to glimpse the glory of Christ. This coaches us so that we will not miss the importance of the sign. John wants his readers to comprehend and believe.

Once again John tells us that there are many who will witness the sign and fail to believe. Of course, people such as Martha and Mary (who share the revelation we enjoy as readers) will believe since they have been told what this sign means. But others (11:46) resist belief and instead go to the authorities. What does this mean in the revelation of Christ? Must explanation accompany sign? How should this be integrated into the ministries of the church?

The lordship of Jesus. The narrative is built to tell us about Jesus, not Lazarus. This may seem obvious to some, but many miss this basic point when explaining the chapter. The Lazarus story is a vehicle to take elsewhere, to help us reflect on the confidence and power of the person of Christ, and to wonder at the truth and glory of his presence on the earth. As we have seen in other chapters (e.g., chs. 1, 4, 9), John 11 provides another catalogue of names for Jesus so that we as readers will not miss who this central character is (Jesus, rabbi, Lord, Christ, Son of God, he who is coming into the world, the resurrection and the life). Therefore John 11 teaches us not

---

28. As R. Fredrikson, *John* (The Communicator's Commentary, Waco: Word, 1985), 200, contends.

29. Beasley-Murray, *John*, 200-201, points out that while six of the signs employ the literary pattern of sign-revelation, this seventh sign reverses it (revelation-sign). This reversal is also the pattern of the Gospel generally. The prologue gives us an explanation of what will happen, followed by a narrative describing the "Word become flesh." Similarly, the Farewell Discourse "interprets" Jesus' departure, which is then followed by his glorification on the cross.

simply about an idea, but about a person. And knowing *right things* about this person, such as his identity and his relation to his Father, are important to getting the story right.

We have seen John's Christological interests throughout the Gospel. The new vision we have of Jesus here is his lordship over death. Jesus is confident when he faces the grave of his friend Lazarus. He has prayed that God will work in and through him. If anything, the chief emotions we see are anger and grief. Lazarus has become a victim of something Jesus yearns to defeat. What does it mean to face a grave in the company of Jesus? How do we take seriously the genuine suffering of women like Martha and Mary—and our own anguish at the threat of death—and still maintain faith in the power of Christ?

The looming crucifixion. If the lordship of Jesus over death is the chief motif in this chapter, the prospect of Jesus' own crucifixion is a theme that comes close behind. The drama of Jesus' trial began at the very start of this Gospel, and I suggested that John may have even designed it with a "courtroom drama" in mind (see the discussion of the trial motif in the comments on John 5). Here too we have hints (ironic hints) that if indeed Jesus is master over the grave, he will have an opportunity to demonstrate this mastery by dying himself. At the beginning of the chapter Jesus is warned that people in Judea wish to stone him (11:8); as it closes, we listen to the Passover crowds in Jerusalem speculating whether Jesus will appear and meet his accusers face-to-face (11:55–57). The disciples understand soberly what it means to approach Jerusalem. Even they may die (11:16). The shadow of death stalks the entire chapter.

But we are given advance notice that this death is not going to be a tragedy. What Jesus can do for Lazarus by opening the Bethany tomb is now foreshadowing what he can do for himself. The tomb that cannot contain Lazarus cannot hold him either. Moreover, we are told that the death of Jesus is not simply an obstacle to be overcome by resurrection. Caiaphas tells us that Jesus' death will be purposeful. Jesus will die for the people and the nation (11:50). Jesus will give life only by giving his own life. Central to any explanation of this chapter, therefore, must be a confident and compelling explanation of Jesus' saving death and his personal victory over his own grave.

Tension between life and death. We would be remiss if we did not explore the implications of this tension between life and death within the experiences of the characters in the narrative. All the themes of grief and dismay and loss are appropriate subjects for careful exploration. When we do so, we should place ourselves in the narrative and identify what it means to lose someone to death who is as close to us as Lazarus was to his sisters. We dare not trivialize death. We dare not say that Martha was wrong to grieve because Jesus was present. Even Jesus himself wept. But it is clear from his conversation with Martha that Jesus expects God's people to have an understanding of death and possess confidence in God's power.

However, there is an unexpected turn in the story. Martha is gently corrected (11:24) so that she will see that her hope is anchored not merely to the far future resurrection of the last day, but to a present experience with Jesus Christ. There is something in Christ that exceeds the hope we have on the Day of Judgment. Jesus brings a present reality to our victory over death. But how is that realized for us today? It is one thing to say we are "saved," but quite another to understand what it means to possess "life" now in the present. How do I proclaim this? How do I possess this without denying the reality of death?

JOHN 11 TOUCHES on themes that are immediately relevant to the modern heart. Every age struggles with the finality of the grave and the incomprehensibility of death. Throughout history societies have surrounded death and burial sites with mystery and superstition, and this is no less true of modern, Western society.

In some respects, we also live in an age that does its best to deny death. People rarely die at home surrounded by their loved ones. Their bodies are no longer "dressed" and prepared for burial by the family (as they were not too many decades ago). Today this process has been sanitized, taken over by professional hospitals, hospices, and morticians. As a result, few of us have seen someone die, and I dare say that before the twentieth century there were few who had *not* seen someone die. We build coffins that look like plush, oversized jewelry boxes and cemeteries that evoke the peace and serenity of a botanical garden. We use euphemisms ("Mrs. Taylor *passed away* on Tuesday") to gloss over what we dare not say. All of this is cultural, springing from the heartfelt wish to make death pleasant. But it masks a profound anxiety that even the prettiest funeral service cannot disguise.

Perhaps this is why in the work of the church, funeral services become such potent opportunities for ministry. Here the raw vulnerability of our lives stands naked and we are confronted by a personal fate we would rather not look at directly. The story of Lazarus draws us directly into the pathos so deeply rooted in our hearts. Lazarus is a friend who has died. He is a brother whose illness should never have been terminal. His grave is a reminder of every grave we have visited and a parable of the grave we must all visit—our own. Numerous themes come from the story that make for fruitful reflection today.

Sign and explanation. In Luke 16 Jesus tells the parable of the rich man and Lazarus (Luke 16:19–31). While there are limited links with John 11 (see comments above), the conclusion of the parable says something provocative. While the poor man Lazarus is being comforted in Abraham's bosom, the rich man calls out for help. When none is forthcoming, he pleads with Abraham to send a messenger to his home to warn his five brothers what the afterlife may hold for them. Then Abraham gives a stunning answer:

> "Abraham replied, 'They have Moses and the Prophets; let them listen to them.'
>
> "'No, father Abraham,' he said, 'but if someone from the dead goes to them, they will repent.'
>
> "He said to him, 'If they do not listen to Moses and the Prophets, they will not be convinced even if someone rises from the dead.'"

According to Jesus, even a resurrection miracle will not be sufficient to persuade some people of the power and the reality of God. This is apparent in John 11. There were many standing among the mourners of Bethany that day who were friends with Lazarus, who knew he was dead, and who participated in his burial. But when he stepped from the grave, they refused to believe in Jesus. This is amazing. Signs alone cannot provoke faith. Miracles do not of themselves transform lives. "They will not be convinced even if someone rises from the dead." Since Luke is writing from a vantage that already knows about Jesus' resurrection, he no doubt is thinking about Jesus' resurrection too. People living in Jerusalem refused to believe despite Jesus' return from death. As John writes this chapter for us, he knows the Christian story too. Even when Jesus came from the grave, some refused to believe.

This understanding of the limited success of the miracle is at the root of John's link between "sign and explanation" (or miracle and discourse). A sheer experience of the power of God is insufficient to persuade the human heart. It is incomprehensible, easily misunderstood, fleeting. And if it does become the basis of faith, the event itself becomes the object of faith rather than the One who has worked such a mighty deed.

Therefore, in the activity of the church, words must accompany deeds. It is foolhardy to think that if God supplies us with a compelling miracle, our spiritual communities will be energized. Signs from God must have a spiritually true context to be understood correctly, to be grounded as they should. This explains, for instance, Luther's argument that whenever the sacraments of the church are presented in worship, *the gospel must be preached.* Word must accompany deed. It also provides a worrisome critique of churches whose worship pursues spiritual encounters as ends in themselves. When spiritual activity—from acts of healing to eucharistic worship to praise choruses—is engaged without a richly rooted theological context, we are vulnerable.

I recall talking recently with a friend from Central America. There in his homeland, the traditional Catholic churches did not have a tradition of practical instruction and teaching. He explained how a great deal of pagan superstition (from native religions) had joined with Christian practice to give "deeper meaning" to ceremony and worship. People sought mystical, power experiences with God; because of a lack of theological guidance, this had taken thousands of Christians far from their traditional faith.

Not long ago I attended a worship service that had almost an hour of praise singing that left little time for the sermon. "Never mind," someone said to me afterwards, "the worship was wonderful and that's what matters." This is the pursuit of power and experience—of signs—without explanation or context. John insists that these two dimensions be wed or else misunderstanding of God's interests will result. Sign must be linked to explanation; spiritual experience must be united with spiritual teaching or preaching.

The power and confidence of Jesus. When Paul prays for the Ephesians at the beginning of his letter, he asks God to confirm in their hearts the features that come with having an identity completely wed to the person of Jesus Christ. Listen to his words:

> I pray also that the eyes of your heart may be enlightened in order that you may know the hope to which he has called you, the riches of his glorious inheritance in the saints, and his incomparably great power for us who believe. That power is like the working of his mighty strength, which he exerted in Christ when he raised him from the dead and seated him at his right hand in the heavenly realms.... (Eph. 1:18–20)

Paul prays that Christians will know the hope and the power available to them in Christ. He prays that the reality of their rich inheritance will transform them and that they will have a glimpse of the power of God at work when Jesus came from the grave. This is an apt description of the sort of confidence he carried as he stepped into Bethany that afternoon: God is victor over death. Jesus, as his Son, likewise understood God's "incomparably great power" to call a man like Lazarus out of the tomb.

As I stand at a graveside today, I need to ask: What difference does it make that my Lord is this Jesus who possesses power over the tomb? One remarkable feature of leading a funeral service is the array of reactions visible in the audience. Grief and anxiety affect Christians who know the hope they possess, but who are overwhelmed with the sorrow of the moment.

When I was in seminary, I had my first internship at a Lutheran church where I was asked to lead a group of high school students. It was a wonderful experience, in which I was mentored for the first time by a pastor and experienced lay leaders. The layperson working closest to me was a woman named Barbara. She was a model of conviction and hope, whose heart was devoted to the church and its ministries. For six months I valued every moment in which she provided advice and inspiration to continue in the ministry. And then one day Barbara gave me a phone call I will never forget. She said she had a brain tumor, which explained the gradual deterioration of her otherwise athletic physique. Most remarkable of all, the tumor was inoperable. I watched as Barbara wasted away. Two months later, just before she died, I remember Barbara taking my hand and talking with confidence about her faith. She knew this was hard for me. And her last words to me were these: "Don't worry about me. I'm about to go on the greatest adventure of my life." Soon after, she died.

This story is important because it says that Barbara's confidence in death was not a shallow optimism that denied the anguish of her experience. She looked it straight in the eye. Nor was she persuaded concerning the doctrine of the resurrection, as if that alone would hold some importance to her. Her confidence was grounded in the strength of her knowledge of Jesus Christ. She knew him. She knew who he was. She knew his power and his ability. And she knew that he was waiting for her the moment she died. Therefore the Christian's confidence at the grave has little to do with our intrinsic potential to survive death. It has everything to do with our understanding and confidence in the power of Jesus. Jesus overpowered death at the tomb of Lazarus. Jesus likewise overpowered the dread of death for Barbara.

The raising of Lazarus does not mean that now this man and believers like him are no longer subject to mortality and death. Lazarus eventually died (again!). Barbara died. But imagine for a moment Lazarus's thoughts as he laid on his "second" deathbed some years after the death and resurrection of Jesus. Normal feelings of worry and fear were there in the corners of his soul, no doubt. But he had confidence. He knew that Jesus had a relationship with death like no other. Jesus was "resurrection and life," and so he was not going to the grave alone.

Jesus' death and resurrection. When tourists come to Jerusalem, one of the most important places for them to visit is the church commemorating Jesus' burial and resurrection.[30] Guidebooks written in English refer to it as "The Church of the Holy Sepulchre." Arabs and Jews are used to this, so

---

30 There is some debate as to the location of this church (as with virtually every holy site in Israel). The present Church of the Holy Sepulchre is likely the right location. Archaeological research has demonstrated beyond doubt that the "Garden Tomb" is not from the first-century era of Jesus, although it serves a vital ministry in the city.

when they find pilgrims wandering around Jerusalem's "Christian Quarter," they send them in the right direction. But the ancient churches of Jerusalem have a different name for this church. For countless centuries, Arab Christians have known it as "the Church of the Resurrection," recalling the truly important events that happened here. If you ask an Arab Christian for the "church of Jesus' tomb" *in Arabic,* he likely will not know what you mean. The church recalls not the tomb, but the resurrection life that came from this place. It is a place of victory and life, not sorrow and defeat.[31]

John is taking the long view of Jesus' work when he describes the events that surround Lazarus's new life. Jesus proves he has power over death; but more, we also learn that Jesus' death will play a role in the work that he still has to do. That Jesus must die is said explicitly in the chambers of the Sanhedrin (11:51). Moreover we learn that Jesus is the one man who must die *for the people* (11:50). We also know that Jesus is "the resurrection and the life" (11:24). Therefore in order to vanquish death for himself and in order to bring the benefits of his work to the world, he too will demonstrate his power by his own resurrection from the tomb. This is why the Jerusalem Christians are right in refusing to let their central church become a memorial to Jesus' death. It is not. This is a monument to Jesus' completed work, by which he embraces death fully and defeats it, standing triumphant before his own grave.

The raising of Lazarus thus provides us with theological foreshadowing. It points us elsewhere, reminding us that Jesus' work is greater even than this. Jesus is not demonstrating that death has a limited grip over humanity. It does not. But *his own death and resurrection* affect the reality of death permanently for those who believe in him.

Paul reminds us of this same idea. Reconciliation and salvation are achieved by both the death of Christ and his resurrection (Rom. 4:25; 5:10). Baptism connects us to Christ's death (6:3), but it also connects us with his resurrection (6:4). Paul summarizes, "If we have been united with him like this in his death, we will certainly also be united with him in his resurrection" (6:5). The point here is that the work of Christ is not simply a matter of reliance on the work of the cross. The work of Christ is his *comprehensive* effort by which he enters the world as a human, embracing the totality of our humanity. He dies on the cross, becoming a sacrifice for our sins, and he is raised to new life, bearing with this life the very humanity he has embraced. To use Paul's words, death no longer has dominion over Christ (Rom. 6:9;

---

31. The chief ceremony at the church is the Easter festival of Holy Fire that commemorates Jesus' resurrection. See T. A. Idinopulos, "Holy Fire in Jerusalem," *Christian Century* 99 (1982): 407–9.

1 Cor. 15:21ff.). Therefore in Christ humanity has found a way to defeat death, and we are joined to the benefits of Christ's work through faith.

Our graveside experience. We have seen that Christ understood the power of God just as he understood the nature of his own mission. Christ overwhelmed the grim scene of Lazarus's grave with his own power, and he faced the specter of his own death with the confidence that the same power of God would rescue him from the grave. John 11 is thus a story designed to encourage us, to give us strength to face our own mortality (or the death of someone near to us) by virtue of the Lord whom we worship. Resurrection is not now a new principle imposed on human life; the Lord *who is resurrection* has now imposed life where there was only the prospect of death.

While the chief thrust of chapter 11 is theological, the dramatic setting of the story also invites reflection. (1) In some Christian circles Jesus' power over the grave is embraced with such conviction that there is no permission to mourn the tragedy of death. To grieve is to show a lack of faith; funerals are to be celebrations of eternal life and victory. To a degree this is true, but it denies a basic human need to express the sorrow and dismay that comes with loss. One obvious thing about John's story is a thing we may pass over quickly: Martha and Mary were crying. Jesus did not say to Martha, "If you believe in the resurrection, why are you wasting your time and your tears?" He did not say to Mary, "If you have victorious faith, you should stand clear-eyed and confident because I am here." No. Jesus did not impede this family's grieving; instead by joining with them, he gives generous permission. It is right to describe death as terrible and painful and horrible without compromising the quality of our faith. Jesus himself cried in anger at the wreckage death brought to one family. Death is a foe that in Christ is being defeated.

(2) Jesus is telling us that the reality of the resurrection is not something that simply awaits us in the end of time. As we saw, Judaism held this belief popularly. But Jesus is expressing a truth that is sometimes missed. Resurrection describes an aspect of life that we can experience *now*. Martha says that Lazarus will be raised in the future. But Jesus says that Lazarus is going to be raised *now*. This means that there is a real power available in the present experience of Christ that is unknown to the Jewish framework of Martha and Mary. The power of God resident in our lives today is the same power that will enable us to live for eternity. John no doubt hopes that this will be no small comfort for us. As L. Morris puts it, "Death is but a gateway to further life and fellowship with God."[32] As we think about death, it should be a passageway, not a terminus. Jesus' power is in us and it will continue to

---

32. Morris, *John*, 488.

carry us through that darkest hour, for nothing can ever separate us from God's mighty love (Rom. 8:35–39).

Two minor notes. John 11 has two minor notes with some genuine practical importance. (1) We saw in 10:16 that Jesus is conscious that there are other sheep "not of this fold," who likewise must be included in his flock. In 11:52 this idea is reinforced. Jesus must die not only for the nation (of Israel) but "to bring [the scattered children of God] together and make them one." As Jesus leaves the mainstream of Judaism (where his self-revelation is complete), he shows how his kingdom extends beyond the usual national, racial, and cultural boundaries of Judaism. The same theme will appear in John 12, when some Greeks come to see Jesus at the temple (12:20). In other words, we may not limit the work of Christ to a particular people, excluding some as Judaism excluded the Gentiles. As modern Christians we need to wrestle with our worldviews, inquiring who are those "scattered people" for whom Christ died.

(2) I find it interesting that Jesus treats Martha and Mary with such respect. In 11:28 Martha calls Jesus "teacher." This reminds us of Jesus' appearance in Martha's home in Luke 10, where Jesus is teaching these women. Even in John 11 we have a description of Jesus teaching Martha (11:21–27). This is important because women were not taught by the rabbis in the first century. Jesus dignifies these women as full participants among his followers. If he is their rabbi, they are his disciples (not unlike the other men who followed him). When Lazarus becomes fatally ill, his sisters know immediately how to locate Jesus despite the fact he is far away. Were they well-connected among the Jesus' followers in Judea? Were they "women of prominence," not unlike Prisca, Junia, Phoebe, and Mary, whom Paul greets in Romans 16?

John 12:1–50

SIX DAYS BEFORE the Passover, Jesus arrived at Bethany, where Lazarus lived, whom Jesus had raised from the dead. ²Here a dinner was given in Jesus' honor. Martha served, while Lazarus was among those reclining at the table with him. ³Then Mary took about a pint of pure nard, an expensive perfume; she poured it on Jesus' feet and wiped his feet with her hair. And the house was filled with the fragrance of the perfume.

⁴But one of his disciples, Judas Iscariot, who was later to betray him, objected, ⁵"Why wasn't this perfume sold and the money given to the poor? It was worth a year's wages." ⁶He did not say this because he cared about the poor but because he was a thief; as keeper of the money bag, he used to help himself to what was put into it.

⁷"Leave her alone," Jesus replied. "It was intended that she should save this perfume for the day of my burial. ⁸You will always have the poor among you, but you will not always have me."

⁹Meanwhile a large crowd of Jews found out that Jesus was there and came, not only because of him but also to see Lazarus, whom he had raised from the dead. ¹⁰So the chief priests made plans to kill Lazarus as well, ¹¹for on account of him many of the Jews were going over to Jesus and putting their faith in him.

¹²The next day the great crowd that had come for the Feast heard that Jesus was on his way to Jerusalem. ¹³They took palm branches and went out to meet him, shouting,

"Hosanna!"

"Blessed is he who comes in the name of the Lord!"

"Blessed is the King of Israel!"

¹⁴Jesus found a young donkey and sat upon it, as it is written,

¹⁵"Do not be afraid, O Daughter of Zion;
    see, your king is coming,
    seated on a donkey's colt."

¹⁶At first his disciples did not understand all this. Only after Jesus was glorified did they realize that these things had

been written about him and that they had done these things to him.

[17]Now the crowd that was with him when he called Lazarus from the tomb and raised him from the dead continued to spread the word. [18]Many people, because they had heard that he had given this miraculous sign, went out to meet him. [19]So the Pharisees said to one another, "See, this is getting us nowhere. Look how the whole world has gone after him!"

[20]Now there were some Greeks among those who went up to worship at the Feast. [21]They came to Philip, who was from Bethsaida in Galilee, with a request. "Sir," they said, "we would like to see Jesus." [22]Philip went to tell Andrew; Andrew and Philip in turn told Jesus.

[23]Jesus replied, "The hour has come for the Son of Man to be glorified. [24]I tell you the truth, unless a kernel of wheat falls to the ground and dies, it remains only a single seed. But if it dies, it produces many seeds. [25]The man who loves his life will lose it, while the man who hates his life in this world will keep it for eternal life. [26]Whoever serves me must follow me; and where I am, my servant also will be. My Father will honor the one who serves me.

[27]"Now my heart is troubled, and what shall I say? 'Father, save me from this hour'? No, it was for this very reason I came to this hour. [28]Father, glorify your name!"

Then a voice came from heaven, "I have glorified it, and will glorify it again." [29]The crowd that was there and heard it said it had thundered; others said an angel had spoken to him.

[30]Jesus said, "This voice was for your benefit, not mine. [31]Now is the time for judgment on this world; now the prince of this world will be driven out. [32]But I, when I am lifted up from the earth, will draw all men to myself." [33]He said this to show the kind of death he was going to die.

[34]The crowd spoke up, "We have heard from the Law that the Christ will remain forever, so how can you say, 'The Son of Man must be lifted up'? Who is this 'Son of Man'?"

[35]Then Jesus told them, "You are going to have the light just a little while longer. Walk while you have the light, before darkness overtakes you. The man who walks in the dark does not know where he is going. [36]Put your trust in the light while you have it, so that you may become sons of light." When he had finished speaking, Jesus left and hid himself from them.

³⁷Even after Jesus had done all these miraculous signs in their presence, they still would not believe in him. ³⁸ This was to fulfill the word of Isaiah the prophet:

"Lord, who has believed our message
and to whom has the arm of the Lord been revealed?"

³⁹For this reason they could not believe, because, as Isaiah says elsewhere:

⁴⁰"He has blinded their eyes
and deadened their hearts,
so they can neither see with their eyes,
nor understand with their hearts,
nor turn—and I would heal them."

⁴¹Isaiah said this because he saw Jesus' glory and spoke about him.

⁴²Yet at the same time many even among the leaders believed in him. But because of the Pharisees they would not confess their faith for fear they would be put out of the synagogue; ⁴³for they loved praise from men more than praise from God.

⁴⁴Then Jesus cried out, "When a man believes in me, he does not believe in me only, but in the one who sent me. ⁴⁵When he looks at me, he sees the one who sent me. ⁴⁶I have come into the world as a light, so that no one who believes in me should stay in darkness.

⁴⁷"As for the person who hears my words but does not keep them, I do not judge him. For I did not come to judge the world, but to save it. ⁴⁸There is a judge for the one who rejects me and does not accept my words; that very word which I spoke will condemn him at the last day. ⁴⁹For I did not speak of my own accord, but the Father who sent me commanded me what to say and how to say it. ⁵⁰I know that his command leads to eternal life. So whatever I say is just what the Father has told me to say."

Original Meaning

JOHN HAS NOW finished recording the events of Jesus' public ministry. John 12 is the final chapter of the "Book of Signs," in which the evangelist records three events in the days just prior to Passover: Mary anoints Jesus in Bethany (12:1–11), Jesus enters Jerusalem in his triumphal entry (12:12–19), and Greeks who are attending Passover visit

Jesus (12:20–36). These are followed by John's theological explanation of the unbelief of Judaism (12:37–43) and Jesus' final plea for faith (12:44–50).

The drama of John's account of Jesus' life has now taken a critical turn. Two stories are building as we come to this juncture. On the one hand, Jesus is being praised by growing numbers of people. At Bethany, the Lazarus miracle led many to faith (11:45; 12:17), so that enthusiasm for Jesus is growing. When Jesus crosses the Mount of Olives from Bethany to enter Jerusalem, crowds gather to cheer him on (12:12). Even non-Jews are intrigued and show interest in him. On the other hand, the authorities are increasingly determined to stop him. From their point of view, Jesus' popularity has become a problem (11:48; 12:19), and he must be arrested. No compromise seems possible. Jesus must be eliminated or the stability of Jerusalem will be at risk (11:45–53).

These two dramatic threads in this Gospel will climax at one place: the cross. Ironically, it is not as if these two interests collide, destroying each other's momentum. That would be a surface reading of the story. The *deeper story* is that the work of the Sanhedrin will propel Jesus toward further glory. "But I, when I am lifted up from the earth, will draw all men to myself" (12:32). The cross will not be a place of humiliation, but of glory. Therefore we have in this final page of the Book of Signs a variety of themes rolling over one another: excited popularity, imminent death, promised glorification, rejection, and unbelief.

Mary Anoints Jesus in Bethany (12:1–11)

AFTER THE RAISING of Lazarus, Jesus knew that the threat to his own life was serious. He therefore departed and remained in the region north of Jerusalem, near Bethel (see comment on 11:54). However, as the Passover approaches, he returns to Bethany and remains with the family of Lazarus, Martha, and Mary.[1] The family is no doubt living with a keen sense of fear and are dreading the tragedy of Jesus' arrest that seems to lie on the near horizon. Mary feels the weight of these momentous days. During a meal hosted by Martha (in Martha's home?) she anoints Jesus with costly ointment.

The account of Jesus' anointing in Bethany is recorded in Matthew and Mark (Matt. 26:6–16; Mark 14:3–9) as well as here in John.[2] Matthew and Mark offer a similar version and, on one view of the Synoptic problem, Matthew may be dependent on Mark's account. Most likely Mark and John are recording the same story. Note this comparison of their details:[3]

---

1. Bethany, a village on the fringe of Jerusalem's life, was located just east over the Mount of Olives (see comment on 11:1).

2. There is another anointing story in Luke 7:36–38; while there are few parallels, it has a completely different setting.

3. See Brown, *John*, 2:450.

Mark 14:3-9	John 12:1-11
Bethany	Bethany
two days before Passover	six days before Passover
house of Simon the leper	[house of Martha]
a woman	Mary
[x]	a pound
alabaster jar	[x]
breaks jar	[x]
"expensive [*polytelos*] perfume"	"expensive [*politimos*] perfume"
genuine nard	genuine nard
anoints Jesus' head	anoints Jesus' feet
[x]	wipes Jesus' feet with her hair
disciples angry	Judas angry
value: more than 300 denarii	value: 300 denarii
Jesus defends the woman	Jesus defends Mary
"Leave her alone"	"Leave her alone"
"Poor always with you"	"Poor always with you"
Jesus anointed for burial	[x]
reported to the whole world	[x]

These parallels are extensive and the major differences really only work to supplement one another. The chief contextual difference is that Mark and Matthew record the anointing following the triumphal entry, whereas John records it before. However, Synoptic chronologies are often fluid. Mark also says that Jesus' head was anointed (John refers to feet). Most of the other details can be easily integrated to create a consistent picture. For instance, the "pound" of ointment mentioned by John would be too much for Jesus' feet. Even though Mark explains that Jesus' head was anointed, Jesus later says that his body was anointed (Mark 14:8). Therefore Mary likely took this large amount of perfume and liberally placed it on Jesus, only drying his feet with her hair. We will look at the details more closely below.

Jesus' arrival six days before Passover (12:1) immediately opens a complex subject concerning how John dates the Passover and Jesus' crucifixion. I will look at this in some detail on 13:1 (and 19:14, 31), but for now can anticipate those conclusions. John can be harmonized with the Synoptic chronology, making the onset of Passover Thursday night (hence the meal recorded in chapter 13 is indeed a Passover meal). This means that Jesus arrives in Bethany six days before the next Thursday evening (remembering that Jewish days start just after dusk), which is to say that he arrives late on Friday just as Sabbath begins. The meal described in 12:2 may refer to a meal on Saturday evening (following the close of Sabbath), since by then word of Jesus' arrival would have spread through the village and people would be free to travel. On the following day (12:12) Jesus enters Jerusalem in triumph.

It is difficult to be precise concerning the location of the meal. Is it Martha's home? Mary's? Do they live together? No evidence is available. Some have tried to harmonize Mark's account and suggested that Simon the Leper (Mark 14:3) is the father of Lazarus (and the women), but this is speculative. It may also be that since lepers could not live in Israelite villages, this is traditionally "Simon's" house and the family of Lazarus now lives there.[4] Mark only tells us that it was Simon's home, not that he is at the meal. At any rate, it is an important meal attended by many who want to honor Jesus publicly and remember the great event of Lazarus's life (John 12:9). Jews reclined at formal meals in the first century (12:2); this will become an interesting aspect of Jesus' Passover meal in chapter 13 (see comment on 13:25).

It goes without saying that Mary's dramatic gesture (which fits her portrait in Luke 10:38–42) is astonishing. While Judas objects (12:4), Jesus finds in it a pleasing expression of devotion. Nard was a rare and precious spice imported from northern India. The Latin writer Pliny gives us a full description of it in his *Natural History*.[5] Nard is a shrub whose leaves and "shoots" were harvested and taken by caravan to the west. Sometimes it was mixed with its own root to increase its weight. Note that Mary's gift is called "pure" nard, meaning it had no additives. Nard smelled like gladiolus (gladiola) perfume (Pliny: "a sweet scent") and had a red color. It could be used in a variety of ways: in medicinal recipes, as an aromatic wine, as a breath scent, and as a perfume (for clothes and body).

A pound of the spice would have been huge and lavish. Its value of three hundred denarii represents one year's wage for a day-laborer (Matt. 20:1–16). Some cheaper nard cost one hundred denarii per pound (depending on its origin: Gaul, Crete, or Syria), but our story shows that Mary has purchased the very best.[6] Such a gift invites us to speculate how Mary can acquire this perfume. Are they a wealthy family? Is this from some family heirloom? At least we know that the average Jewish family would not be able to do such a thing.

Mary anoints Jesus generously, not simply on his feet (12:3) but also his head (Mark 14:3), which no doubt runs down and perfumes his garments (cf. Mark 14:8). Mark says that Mary "breaks the bottle" when she pours it. This refers to her breaking the stopper-seal at the top of the alabaster vase.[7] The

---

4. Haenchen, *John*, 2:86.

5. Pliny, *Natural History* 12.24–26.

6. R. K. Harrison, "Nard," *ISBE* 3:490–91; G. H. R. Horsley, *New Documents Illustrating Early Christianity* (North Ryde, Australia: Macquarie Univ., 1981), 1:85 [Entry 41].

7. Such vases (broken and unbroken) have been found in Hellenistic-era Egyptian tombs, confirming the method of opening and pouring.

quantity is so great that the entire house is filled with its fragrance (John 12:3), which underscores the extravagance of the gift. John emphasizes Jesus' feet to show the sheer act of humble devotion on Mary's part and to provide a contrast with the foot-washing of the next chapter. That she uses her hair to dry his feet is peculiar; in a similar story in Luke 7:38, such behavior inspires sharp criticism from the dinner host. Women did not let down their hair in public, and the only one who saw a woman's hair was her husband. Mary is acting with abandon, extravagant abandon, hoping that the close circle of friends will understand.

That Judas objects (12:4) comes as no surprise. This gift is astounding. Although John does not say it, some of the other disciples probably feel similar things. The legitimacy of Judas's complaint is tarnished, however, by his own reputation. As treasurer of the group he would steal money from their holdings (12:6). But John reminds us that Judas is also the one who will betray Jesus (12:4). This is not a prophesy, but derives "from the shocking force of hindsight."[8] John cannot tell any story about Judas without his treacherous deed overshadowing his image.

Jesus' defense of Mary (12:7–8) is difficult to translate. What is Mary "to save"? The perfume is all gone (cf. Mark 14) and it cannot be kept till later. Some believe that the memory of this deed will be kept. Ancient scribes often edited the text at this point to clear up the point. The NIV gives a paraphrase that extends the Greek but likely gives the best interpretation ("It was intended that she should save this perfume for the day of my burial"). The idea is no doubt that she had kept this perfume for some later use, but now (unknowingly) has kept it for Jesus' embalming.[9] Like Caiaphas in 11:50–51, her deed (like his words) bears a meaning far beyond what is intended. Jesus has now been prepared for burial (figuratively) as he heads toward the day of his death and glorification.

Jesus' final words in 12:8 place in tension pure personal adoration and social responsibility (also in Matt. 26:11; Mark 14:7). To acknowledge the endless needs of the poor was not unusual (Deut. 15:11). Jesus' presence among them, however, is unique.[10] This is not to deny our responsibility to the poor, but it alerts us to the wonder of who Mary and Martha are hosting that day.

Following the story of Mary in Bethany, John provides a narrative link to the next episode (12:9–11). Many people begin to arrive in Bethany. Jesus' reputation has spread through Jerusalem and its surrounding villages. Now

---

8. Carson, *John*, 428–29.

9. But Mary's nard will not be used later. Nicodemus embalms Jesus with 100 pounds of spices (19:38–42) and Mary's perfume does not appear again.

10. The Gk. construction places sharp emphasis on Jesus.

there is a double reason to see him: Not only is Jesus in Judea, but they can see Lazarus too. Lazarus has become a source of new faith in Jesus. Is he talking about this miracle? How can he not? Therefore the Sanhedrin determines that Lazarus must likewise die (12:11). And this supplies some not-so-subtle humor. They wish to return Lazarus to the place he belongs (the grave), and no doubt from Lazarus' perspective, it is a plot that has been emptied of its threat. Lazarus now knows the power of Jesus over the grave.

Jesus' Triumphal Entry into Jerusalem (12:12–19)

IF WE ARE right that Jesus meets with crowds on Saturday and that rumor of his presence in Judea is alive in Jerusalem (12:12), his grand entrance into the holy city the next day ("Palm Sunday") stirs the populace even more. This account is recorded in all four Gospels (cf. Matt. 21:1–11; Mark 11:1–11; Luke 19:29–38), which shows the importance of this event. On the Sunday of Jesus' final week, he climbs the back (or east) side of the Mount of Olives (departing Bethany) and comes to the next village of Bethphage (Mark 11:1), where, according to the Synoptics, he borrows a young donkey to ride into the city (John 12:14).

John's abbreviated account omits some of the Synoptic details and focuses on the crowds, who likewise have come to Jerusalem to celebrate the feast of Passover. Such festival participation is a religious obligation,[11] and we can expect that crowds of pilgrims, including many from Galilee, have arrived and are living on the outskirts of the city. Many are in the Kidron Valley (which separates Jerusalem and the Mount of Olives), and as Jesus crosses the crest of the mountain, they join the crowd already accompanying him.

It is important to keep in mind the significance of these crowds. Many scholars believe that the regular population of Jerusalem in this period was about 50,000 and that during Passover it grew to perhaps 100,000 to 120,000.[12] The social dynamic of this change was immense. The city could not contain the population and as a result, thousands of people lived on the hillsides surrounding the city. The crowds brought tension to the leadership of the city (12:19), who knew that any social disruption that began at a festival could explode violently.

---

11. Old Testament law required Jews to come to Jerusalem for three pilgrimage festivals: Passover (the start of the barley harvest), Pentecost (the end of the wheat harvest), and Tabernacles (the harvest of tree and vine). Each celebrated religious events in Israel's history (the Exodus, the giving of the law, and the desert wanderings).

12. Josephus records one Passover hosting over 2.5 million, but this is surely an exaggeration. In 1961 the entire population of Galilee was only 190,000 and in antiquity it was likely less. For a full catalogue of evidence, see J. Jeremias, "Excursus: The Number of Pilgrims at the Passover," *Jerusalem in the Time of Jesus* (London. SCM, 1969), 77–84

The branches from date palms (12:13) were abundant in Israel, and their use here is important for symbolic reasons. Palms had become a symbol of Jewish nationalism. When the temple was rededicated during the Maccabean era, palms were used in the celebration (1 Macc. 13:51; 2 Macc. 10:7). In the extrabiblical tradition, palms were used by Levi as a symbol of ruling power (*T. Naph.* 5:4). During both major wars with Rome, reliefs of palms were stamped on the coins minted by the rebels. Thus this act of celebration is by no means neutral. It symbolizes Israel's national hopes, now focused on Jesus, being hailed as he enters the city.

The cry of "Hosanna!" is an Aramaic phrase meaning "Save us now!" and it occurs in a number of the psalms (esp. Ps. 118:25). The following words ("Blessed is he who comes in the name of the Lord") likewise continue to quote from Psalm 118:26 and announce a blessing on the pilgrim arriving in Jerusalem. But what comes next ("Blessed is the king of Israel!") is not in the psalm and departs considerably from its intent. Suddenly we gain the impression that the crowds are greeting a national liberator.

"Triumphal entries" were common in the ancient world. A conquering hero or king would return to his city, bringing the spoils of his battles and stories of conquest.[13] This imagery would not be missed on any Greek-speaking audience on the eastern edge of the Roman empire. When John says that the crowd "went out to meet him," this is a common expression used for cities meeting their triumphant, returning king.[14] In a Jewish context, "Hosanna" was used to greet such incoming kings (2 Sam. 14:4; 2 Kings 6:26). In fact, Jewish culture understood these "royal welcomes" so well that it adopted such forms commonly.[15]

Therefore this scene is awash in Jewish political fervor. The palms, the entry, and the cries all remind us of what happened in John 6:14–15. After Jesus fed the five thousand, the crowd announced that Jesus is "the Prophet who is to come into the world" and promptly attempted to take him "by force" and "make him king." Jesus was misunderstood then; now he is misunderstood again. The Lazarus miracle that fuels the crowd's enthusiasm is now twisted into something linked to Jerusalem's political aspirations.

Jesus' use of a young donkey (12:14) is an attempt to calm the zeal of the crowd, which John interprets for us with a quote from the Old Testament. "Do

---

13. Following Titus's conquest of Jerusalem in A.D. 70, his triumphal entry in Rome was celebrated by a "triumphal arch," which can still be seen in Rome. On the arch are carved reliefs depicting the destruction of Jerusalem and the captivity of its citizens. For a complete study, see B. Kinman, *Jesus' Entry into Jerusalem* (Leiden: Brill, 1995); idem, "Jesus 'Triumphal Entry' in the Light of Pilate's," *NTS* 40 (1994): 442–48.

14. See Brown, *John*, 1·462, for Hellenistic and Jewish parallels.

15. For Jewish evidence, see Kinman, *Jesus' Entry*, 48–65.

not be afraid" may either come from Zephaniah 3:16 or Isaiah 40:9, while the balance of the quote is cited from Zechariah 9:9. These are reassurances of God's presence in Jerusalem to work on behalf of the people. However the larger context of Zechariah 9—surely assumed by the crowd—is helpful. Matthew knows this and cites the passage more widely (Matt. 21:5). The triumphant king is "gentle and riding on a donkey." This "gentle [humble] king" is not a man of chariots and war horses, swords and bows (Zech. 9:10), but one who will bring peace to all nations. His gift is a gift of life, not conquest. Hence, Jesus is forcing a messianic reinterpretation of his purposes for the crowd, which is caught up in a frenzied passion for Jesus' kingship.

John concludes this part of his story with a "transitional" section (12:16–19) that sums up what has transpired thus far as this "Jerusalem drama" reaches its crescendo. Not only do the crowds fail to understand the true nature of Jesus' "kingship," but the disciples likewise misunderstand "all this." (They understand the messianic nature of Jesus' acts, but they cannot see beneath the surface to the true meaning of Jesus' mission.) John's editorial comment about their misunderstanding recalls 2:22, following Jesus' cleansing of the temple. It was not until Jesus was glorified—when they saw the nature of Jesus' person and work and were filled with God's Spirit—that they understood the true picture of what was happening.

John reminds us that the catalyst for the crowd's excitement was the raising of Lazarus (12:17–18). At this point we are also reminded that the Pharisees have begun to despair at Jesus' popularity (12:19). This parallels similar concerns voiced by Luke. When Jesus reaches the city, his popularity swells and some of the Pharisees tell him to silence the crowd (Luke 19:39). When Jesus teaches in the temple, the Pharisees despair, recognizing that so many people "hang on his words" (Luke 19:47–48).

But double meaning is still at work in John. When the Pharisees say "the world" has gone after him, the deeper irony is that these words point to the fulfillment of Jesus' primary mission. "For God did not send his Son into the world to condemn the world, but to save the world through him" (3:17). The "world" in Johannine thought generally refers to those men and women who stand in disbelief, refusing to acknowledge God or his Son. Now we learn that the "world" is running to Jesus. It is no accident that the next episode records characters from that larger Mediterranean world, namely, some Greeks who are eager to see Jesus.

The Hour Has Come (12:20–36)

THE WORD "GREEKS" (Gk. *Hellenes*, 12:20) does not necessarily describe someone from Greece, but was a label for anyone not Jewish—that is, from a Jewish perspective, "Gentiles." They are also likely not converts (proselytes) to Judaism or else something more descriptive would be given (cf. Acts 6:1). These Greeks who come up to the feast are likely "God-fearers," Gentiles who admire the Jewish faith and respect its traditions. An example of such a person might be the centurion of Capernaum, who respected Judaism so much he built a synagogue (Luke 7:5). Cornelius is likewise described as a God-fearer in the book of Acts: "He and all his family were devout and God-fearing; he gave generously to those in need and prayed to God regularly" (Acts 10:2, 22). Even Paul distinguishes them in his public addresses: "Men of Israel and you Gentiles who fear God, listen to me" (Acts 13:16, 26).

The lands surrounding Israel (e.g., the Decapolis) were filled with Greek-speaking peoples. Sepphoris, the capital of Galilee, for instance, had a population of about twenty thousand, who knew and admired these grand festivals. Such Gentiles were invited to the feasts but were permitted to go no further than the Court of the Gentiles, the largest forecourt surrounding the temple sanctuary. A short wall stood between them and the inner courts, warning that for a Gentile to pass beyond was viewed as a capital offense (cf. Eph. 2:14).

The interest of these Greeks in Jesus may have come from the gossip spreading through the city or from his cleansing of the temple, recorded here by the Synoptic Gospels.[16] Either way, they approach Philip from Bethsaida (1:44–46; 6:5–7), probably because he has a Hellenistic name and comes from a Greek region (Bethsaida, 1:44). But for John it is their theological symbolism that is important. These God-fearers represent the "scattered children of God" of 11:52. They are the "other sheep" of 10:16. The question they ask in 12:21 is reminiscent of the language of discipleship we have seen earlier in the gospel. They want to "see" Jesus. On one level it refers to an opportunity to talk with Jesus and ask questions (cf. "see" in Luke 8:20; 9:9). However, the verbs of seeing often mean far more.[17] They are invitations to belief; these are foreigners who now stand ready to join the flock of Christ.

Curiously, the arrival of these God-fearers triggers "the hour" we have been hearing about throughout the gospel (12:23). Many times we have listened to Jesus say that the hour has not yet arrived (2:4; 7:30; 8:20). The "hour of glorification" points to his return to the Father through his death on the cross, his resurrection, and his exaltation. Therefore something has changed; the Greeks signal the closing of a chapter for Jesus. His ministry in Judaism is finished and he now belongs to the wider world.

---

16. John records the cleansing of the temple in 2:13–22. On the relation between John's placement and the Synoptics', see comments on John 2.

17. The verbs *horao* and *blepo* occur eighty-four times in the Gospel of John. To "come and see" is almost a formula for discipleship.

Rather than engage these God-fearers (who now disappear from the story), Jesus offers an extended discourse (12:24–36) that gives insight into the meaning of this hour. What are the chief elements here? Jesus begins by offering a parable that explains the "law of the kingdom of God."[18] Just as a seed must "die" in order to give life, likewise Jesus must die in order to give life to the world. This same law applies to disciples (12:25). To relinquish one's hold on life—to give it up—is the key to participation in the kingdom.[19] This thought appears in the Synoptic tradition as well (Matt. 10:39; 16:25; Mark 8:35; Luke 9:24; 17:33), which shows its importance in the minds of all the evangelists.

But we should note that the results of this sacrifice are different for Jesus and for the disciples. Jesus' sacrifice brings about life for others, but his disciples must practice this discipline so that they can procure life for themselves. Jesus' fidelity to this law is one reason the Father loves him (John 10:17); likewise, Jesus says, such service will be the basis of God's honoring his people (12:26b). Following Jesus therefore involves self-sacrifice (12:26a)—an echo of similar Synoptic sayings about bearing one's cross (Matt. 16:24; Mark 8:34; Luke 9:23). The chief difference in the Johannine version, however, is a promise: " . . . and where I am, my servant also will be." While most commentators believe this promise points to a unity of purpose between Jesus and his servants, it also points to a guarantee that such servants will be with Jesus in heaven (14:3; 17:24).

One of the hallmarks of John's Gospel is Jesus' confidence as he moves toward the hour of glorification, now imminent as the days of Passover unfold. The Synoptic Gospels describe this period as a time when Jesus both affirms his complete commitment to do God's will and struggles with the horror of what it means to die in crucifixion. While John records no scene that parallels Jesus' Gethsemane agony (e.g., Mark 14:32–42), John 12:27–33 gives us a glimpse into Jesus' struggle and perseverance.

Jesus' turmoil (Gk. *tarasso*, 12:27) recalls his agitation and anger when he stood before Lazarus's tomb (11:33) and will come up again when Judas betrays him (13:21). This turmoil should not be minimized. Thus, he wonders what he should say (12:27a). The words in 12:27b can be read either as a question (so NIV, RSV, NRSV, NLT, etc.) or as a statement. If a question, it implies that this is something Jesus does not really pray ("What shall I say? 'Father, save me from this hour'? No!"). But if it is a genuine prayer (which is

---

18. Beasley-Murray, *John*, 211.

19. The language of Jesus here ("the man who *hates* his life . . . ") reflects the Semitic taste for vivid contrasts (see Deut. 21:15; Matt 5:30; 6:22–24; Mark 10:25; Luke 14:26). The dynamic meaning of this phrase in English might be "those who deny their life" or "those who despise their life in this world" (NLT).

likely), it can be read as a statement in the following manner: "What should I say? [pause] Father, save me from this hour—but no! It was for this very reason that I came to this hour."

Here we are listening to Jesus' genuine anguish and the strength of his obedience as he conforms his life to his Father's will (5:19–23; 6:37; 8:29; 38; 14:31; cf. Heb 5:7–10). In this sense, the prayer is similar to Jesus' words in Gethsemane, "Take this cup from me," which are followed with a word of obedience, "Yet not what I will, but what you will" (Mark 14:36). The prayer that concludes Jesus' spiritual wrestling (John 12:28) unveils his final commitment: "Father, glorify your name!" This is a request that has controlled his entire life (8:29, 50).

Jesus' prayer is a conversation with God, who now responds audibly (12:28b). Such words from heaven were not viewed as uncommon in Judaism, and while the rabbis thought they were inferior to prophesy, such words were seen as legitimately from heaven.[20] God affirms that he has *already* glorified himself in his Son; here we no doubt should think of the Incarnation (by which God has entered the world) and the work of Jesus (by which God has shown his power in the world). But he says he will glorify it again; this will be the final act of glory, the cross.

As with the other signs of Jesus, so now, the crowd struggles to understand what has happened (12:29–30). Some think the voice is only thunder. Others assign it to an angel. But typically, the world can barely comprehend the magnitude of what is transpiring in Jesus Christ. Thus, naturally, there is misunderstanding. This voice, Jesus says, is for those listening, not for him. God is continuing to supply the world with evidence of himself.[21]

If the long-anticipated hour is breaking forth, the "lifting up" (or crucifixion, 12:33) of the Son of Man (12:31) will be *the* climactic event for the world.[22] The judgment inaugurated by the cross is not about some future day when believers and unbelievers are separated. The glorification of Christ brings catastrophic change to everything right now. The "now" of 12:31 must be underscored and taken seriously. The cross of Christ inaugurates judgment. It unmasks those aligned with Satan and opposed to God, who will crucify the Son. The cross also identifies those who are children of the light, who believe and are saved. Thus Jesus' ironic phrase, "lifting up," is an apt

---

20 Such heavenly words (Heb., *bath qol*, or "the daughter/echo of a voice") appear both at Jesus' baptism and at the Transfiguration.

21. Note how the voice from heaven is directed to the disciples rather than to Jesus in the Transfiguration (Mark 9:7); cf. Beasley-Murray, *John*, 213.

22. This is now the third reference to the "lifting up" of the Son of Man (see 3:14; 8:28; 12:32–34). These three passages may parallel the three predictions of the cross found in the Synoptic Gospels (Mark 8:31; 9:9; 10:33).

euphemism for crucifixion (cf. 3:14–15). As he is lifted up from the earth in crucifixion (en route back to heaven), he is visible to all. Like light shining in darkness with all of its radiance, so now every hidden darkness will be exposed.

The crowds who have just celebrated Jesus' kingship (12:13–15) now hear clearly what Jesus is intending (12:34):[23] A grain of wheat must die; Jesus must lose his life; Jesus will be lifted up; all of this will bring about his glorification. This is perplexing because according to popular belief in Judaism, the Messiah (or the Christ) would not be a victim; rather, he would triumph over his foes and establish Israel as his permanent kingdom (*Ps. Sol.* 17:4).[24] Jesus' view seems incomprehensible. The same response of incomprehensibility appears in the Synoptic Gospels when Jesus specifically says he is going to die (Mark 8:32). "Who is this 'Son of Man'?" is not a request for Jesus to identify himself (e.g., "Are you the Son of Man?"), but a question that asks: What sort of Son of Man or Messiah is this who finds glory in death?

Jesus denies them an answer (12:35–36a), refusing to enter into speculation about the theological role of the Messiah in popular thought. Instead he appeals to them to believe. Now the urgent tone of his appeal is based on the limited opportunity of the crowd. Jesus is the light (1:4, 7–9; 3:19–21; 8:12, etc.), but it will not shine in the world forever (except through the later ministry of the Spirit). Therefore the crowd must make a choice and *make it quickly* before the light disappears. To become a "son of light"[25] (12:36) means to become a disciple, one who reflects the life of the master (cf. 1:12). But to fail to embrace the light, to refuse to believe, means that one will become a victim of the darkness (12:35).

To reinforce this urgency and to model what he means Jesus disappears (12:36b; cf. 11:54), intentionally hiding himself from them. The public revelation of Jesus is now complete. His signs have been displayed in full. Men and women must come to terms with the revelation that has been placed in the world. Yet this is the mystery of Jesus' life: Even though "light has come into the world . . . men loved darkness instead of light" (3:19).

John 12:37 recalls Moses' words in Deuteronomy 29:2–4, where that great leader reminds Israel of all God has done for them: "With your own eyes

---

23. The crowd may have had in mind Ps 61.6–7. See G Bampfylde, "More Light on Jn 12:34," *JSNT* 17 (1983)· 87–89 Or this may be a reference to Isa. 52:13, "See, my servant will act wisely; he will be raised and lifted up and highly exalted." See B Chilton, "John 12:34 and Targum Isa 52:13," *NovT* 22 (1980): 176–78.

24. The crowd refers to "the law" (meaning the entire Old Testament). But it is difficult to know what verses they have in mind Some have pointed to Ps. 72:17; 89:35–37; Isa. 9:7; or Ezek. 37:25.

25. This is a Jewish phrase now attested in the Dead Sea Scrolls (cf. Eph. 5:8, 1 Thess. 5:5).

you saw those great trials, those miraculous signs and great wonders." Nevertheless, Moses says, "the LORD has not given you a mind that understands or eyes that see or ears that hear." It only remains for John to supply an "addendum" (12:38–43) that will help us understand this mystery.

The Dilemma of Unbelief (12:38–43)

JOHN 12:37–38 IS a watershed in the theology of the Gospel of John. Jesus' public work is completed; his signs have been displayed in the world; his discourses have been delivered. *And yet, the signs have been rejected.* His own people have failed to believe the messenger sent by God. We were warned that this would happen in John's opening prologue, "He came to that which was his own, but his own did not receive him" (1:11). How does John explain this? How can the Christians in John's church (many years later) interpret the story of Jesus' life that leads to rejection? Has God failed? Has unbelief triumphed? Is John 1:5 wrong; that is, has the darkness won the victory over the light?

John echoes the thinking of other New Testament writers when he leads us first to Isaiah 53:1. Isaiah 53 provided the earliest Christians with a poignant description of the Suffering Servant, whose image helped interpret the anguish and suffering of Jesus.[26] And Isaiah 53:1 sums up the Servant's rejection: Neither his words ("our message") nor his deeds ("the arm of the Lord") has found any reception in Israel. John then takes us to Isaiah 6:10, which became the classic New Testament explanation for Israel's rejection of Jesus. Paul cites it in his final speech in Acts (Acts 28:26–27), and the Synoptic Gospels use it to explain why the people cannot comprehend the parables of Jesus (Matt. 13:13–15; Mark 4:12; Luke 8:10).

The theological message of John 12:38–40 is thus anchored to Isaiah's experience. God called Isaiah to speak to Israel but forewarned him that his words would find no acceptance. People would hear, but fail to understand; they would see, but fail to comprehend. Therefore Isaiah did not fail; rather, he fulfilled God's purposes. Likewise, Jesus did not fail in his ministry, but he was continuing the prophetic experience of Isaiah; he was simply filling up or completing what Isaiah described in his own time.[27] The Jews should

---

26. John's theological vocabulary for "lifting up" and "glorify" both appear in the LXX of Isa. 52:13, "See, my servant will act wisely; he will be raised (*doxazo*) and lifted up (*hypsoo*), and highly exalted." The citation in John 12:38 is taken directly from the LXX of Isa. 53:1.

27. The Gospels commonly cite quotation formulas (e.g., "it is written" or "this happened that Scripture might be fulfilled") to show how Jesus fulfilled the Old Testament. John only points to fulfillment (Gk. *pleroo*) beginning at 12:38–39 (see also 13:18; 15:25; 17:12; 18:9; 18:32; 19:24, 19:28; 19:36–37). For John, the hour of glorification (and the failure of Judaism) is the premier moment of Scripture fulfillment.

therefore hear John's words and see them as an exhortation to repent of their disbelief and turn to the messenger who can save them.

The intention of John (and indeed Isaiah) is not to provide a rigid predestinarian explanation for unbelief. In fact, it is doubtful if biblical writers like Isaiah or John were thinking about a philosophical causality as some would argue for it today. In John's Gospel, God's sovereignty and human responsibility are held together consistently. Jesus calls for people to believe (12:36), and we learn that many do indeed make this choice (12:42). Throughout the Gospel John never compromises the demand Jesus makes for decision and faith.

However, John is describing what we might call a "judicial" hardening that settles on a people who are already guilty. When revelation comes, we must believe. But if we refuse to believe, the light disappears (12:35–36); and when God's light departs from the world, the darkness (which is the default state of the world) closes over unbelieving hearts.[28] (In John's literary schema, this is why Jesus disappears in 12:36b.) Paul makes a similar argument in Romans 1. The consequence of the world's sin and unbelief is God's judgment, in which he "gives them over" to their sinful instincts (Rom. 1:24, 26, 28).[29] Note that John changes the order of Isaiah 6:10. While Isaiah refers to "heart, ears, eyes," John begins with "eyes." This fits the literary motif he has developed since chapter 9. Will blind eyes see? It also underscores the importance of Jesus' signs, which must be seen and believed.

It is also important to see that rejection is hopeful in the plan of God. God's sovereignty looks to accomplish wider purposes: In Isaiah 6:11–13 blindness must remain until the thoroughgoing judgment of God on Israel is complete ("until the cities lie in waste"). In John's understanding, the hardness of Israel is likewise purposeful: Through Christ's rejection, salvation will be won for Israel at the cross and the glory of God revealed.[30] Unbelieving Jews will crucify him. Moreover, through their refusal the gospel now comes to the rest of the world. Paul makes the same claim in Romans 9:22–33: God is at work sealing judgment in the present in order to achieve a long-term purpose.

---

28. Some interpreters have tried to soften the causality of 12:40 by saying that it is not God ("he") who blinds and hardens, but Satan Most scholars reject this view vigorously.

29. St. Augustine wrote, "God thus blinds and hardens, simply by letting alone and withdrawing his aid: and God can do this by a judgment that is hidden, although not by one that is unrighteous" (Confessions 63 6; cited in Morris, *John*, 537n.115). See further D. A. Carson, *Divine Sovereignty and Human Responsibility Biblical Perspectives in Tension* (London: Marshall, Morgan, Scott, 1981), 195–97

30. C. Evans, "The Function of Isa 6.9–10 in Mk 4.10–12 and Jn 12:39–40," *NovT* 24 (1982)· 124–38.

The link with Isaiah is further reinforced in John 12:41, "Isaiah said this because he saw Jesus' glory and spoke about him." This brings us back to Isaiah's vision in Isaiah 6:1–4, where the prophet saw the Lord "high and exalted" and surrounded by "his glory." Isaiah had seen the Messiah (cf. John 8:56 and Abraham), and the glory witnessed there glimpsed something of the glory Jesus will presently reveal in his "hour."

Jesus' Final Plea for Belief (12:42–50)

THE STRUGGLE FOR belief in the world has now entered its final stage. Some believe and are eager to become "children of God" (1:12). Others are willing to betray Jesus (such as Judas Iscariot, 12:4), and still others are plotting his demise (11:53). Others are asking questions but remain in the darkness (12:34). Now John introduces us to yet another group (12:42–43): leaders in Judaism, such as Nicodemus (3:1; 7:50), who are keenly interested in Jesus and some of whom have decided to believe in him.[31] But they refuse to make this faith public, so that many of their colleagues do not even know about them (7:48). John is harshly critical of them, and the stinging rebuke given in 12:43 reminds us of Jesus' judgment on his accusers in 5:43–44. John provides models of excellent discipleship in 1:35–51; 4:1–42. To follow Jesus is to go and tell your friends despite the social consequences. Nicodemus's story (recorded near these chapters) fails to show the basic elements of belief and testimony.

The Book of Signs closes with Jesus' making a final plea for belief, probably in the precincts of the temple. For John this is no doubt a final theological summary, comprising the main motifs that have been publicly revealed in the ministry of Jesus. Many of its themes are now familiar: Jesus has been sent by the Father (12:44, 49); the Father is the sole authority in his ministry (12:45, 49); and he is light shining in darkness (12:46), trying to bring salvation (12:47) and eternal life (12:50) to those who will show faith (12:44, 46).

But we also have a warning. Just as Moses' word will judge Israel (5:45), so now Jesus' word will remain as a deposit of revelation by which human lives may be judged (12:48). Moreover, discipleship is not just a matter of knowing Jesus' word; it is also a matter of "keeping" and "doing" what Jesus has said (12:47; cf. 8:31; Matt. 7:24–27; James 2:14–26).

The seriousness of Jesus' revelation is reinforced in the end when he returns to his first subject: the Father (John 12:50). Without doubt, the presence of the Father in the life and work of Jesus is the theme John does not want us to miss. The Book of Signs began with a lofty description of Jesus' origins with

---

31. Acts 6:7 describes "a large number of priests [who] became obedient to the faith." See R. Brown, *The Community of the Beloved Disciple* (New York: Paulist, 1979), 71–81.

God himself (1:1–5). Throughout the course of the book we have read about how this light has been shining in the darkness (1:5). The greatest error of all is for a man or woman to see this light and reject it, thinking it has no connection with God. As Jesus will make clear in his private teachings among his disciples (14:10), when the world sees Jesus, when the world makes a decision about Jesus, it is really making a decision about God.

IT IS IMPOSSIBLE to understand the dramatic forces at work in John 12 if someone has not watched the story of Jesus' life unfold for the past eleven chapters. John 12 is a turning point, a critical juncture in the story—the close of the Book of Signs. It cannot be studied in isolation as if these episodes somehow stand independently of John's longer story. The struggle between light and darkness, described in the prologue (1:1–18), now reaches a fever pitch. The light is shining with brilliance in the world, calling people to join its ranks. At the same time, the forces of darkness are working to extinguish it. Men and women are being forced to choose which side is theirs, and Jesus is passionately urging them to join with God. "Put your trust in the light while you have it, so that you may become sons of light" (12:36).

The chapter provides four scenes, each one weaving its stories into the larger tapestry of the Gospel's drama. Some point back to earlier chapters, picking up motifs we have already studied (such as the misunderstood popularity of Jesus or the "other" sheep of Jesus). Other scenes point us forward to those things still to come (such as Mary's devotion to Jesus in Bethany). These scenes provide intriguing possibilities for reflection in the church today.

Mary's anointing of Jesus. The scene of Mary's anointing of Jesus with costly perfume presents as many interpretative problems as it invites inspiring reflections.[32] The story barely addresses Judas's complaint. Was this money being wasted? Can the needs of the poor be set aside? Instead, Judas's charge is dismissed quickly because of his reputation and because of what will happen later when he betrays Jesus.

This story is all about devotion, and Mary is the perfect character to model this. Wherever she appears both in this Gospel and in Luke, she appears at Jesus' feet. This is a symbol of her interest as a devoted disciple of Jesus, and it is significant that Jesus defends her, giving her a respected place as one who knows better even than Jesus' apostles. I have often thought

---

32. J. R. Michaels, "John 12:1–11," *Int* 43 (1989): 287–91.

about the importance of this gift to Jesus. If we integrate Mark's version of the story, then we understand that Jesus was anointed all over. Even his garments were covered with the strong, sweet scent of nard. It is likely that Jesus kept this scent on his body through the following week. When he was suffering the anguish of crucifixion, Mary's gift remained. It was the last truly beautiful fragrance he smelled as he went to the cross.

The scene of Mary's anointing thus points us forward. Embalming spices were commonplace in the first century (12:7; 19:39), and the quantity of Mary's perfume evokes images of an embalmed body. While the men surrounding Jesus will ask questions in the Upper Room and will find Jesus' decision to die incomprehensible (13:36ff.), here is the image of Mary who asks no questions but gently begins to prepare her Lord for the grave. She has accepted Jesus' humble mission long before Jesus' leading disciples have understood it.

The comparison with the disciples of Jesus is apt from another angle. Inasmuch as Mary bathes Jesus' feet in perfume, she has anticipated the footwashing scene in chapter 13. In fact, Mary is the only one who does precisely what Jesus will ask in 13:14 before he asks it.

Thus this story is really about the cross, about Mary's courageous understanding and acceptance of Jesus' death. It is a profound signal to us (as readers) that Jesus is really going to die. It is also a statement that no gift can be too precious that shows gratitude for what Jesus is about to do.

How can I show Mary's devotion today? If she is a model disciple here— and we have every suggestion that she is just that—how can I emulate her deed? Does one pound of nard simply become a metaphor for personal piety and devotion?

The triumphal entry. The second scene provides a stark counterpoint to Mary's pure and extravagant devotion. On the surface, we could say that the celebration of Jesus' arrival in Jerusalem shows the crowd's enthusiasm for Jesus, and certainly John wants us to see it that way. But as I have sought to demonstrate, there is a darker motif in the story. The crowd is cheering a fantasy: *Their* messianic hero is a victor bringing a triumphant messianism to Jerusalem. But Jesus is a humble servant, and I imagine he wondered a great deal about the source of these people's zeal. Nevertheless, here we have celebration. For John, even if players in his story do not know the deeper meaning of their actions (e.g., Caiaphas in 11:51), John is willing to identify the error and permit us to see the double meaning. Jerusalem is celebrating the arrival of its king despite the erroneous motivations of Jewish nationalists on that day.

But as we bring this text into the modern setting, we have to ask the same questions we asked when we probed the meaning of John 6. Does our zealous celebration of Jesus sometimes contain mixed motives? Does God accept the praise of his people even when it is faulty, incomplete, and broken?

Philip and the Greeks. We dare not miss John's story about Philip's meeting with the God-fearers in Jerusalem (the "Greeks"). Resting as it does at the dramatic turning point in the story, this episode is saying something important about Jesus' mission. It parallels what we hear in the Synoptics about Jesus' primary commitment to Israel, his own people: He was called to come exclusively to Israel and to reveal his messiahship. Jesus once even remarked, "I was sent only to the lost sheep of Israel" (Matt. 15:24; cf. 10:6; Rom. 1:14–15). Ministry among those on Israel's periphery (the Decapolis, Samaria) was secondary. But now his ministry in Israel is complete. Suddenly people not within the traditional "sheepfold" of Israel are coming to him.

This widening of the circle of "Jesus' flock" was a hurdle for the earliest Christians, and a passage such as this would have been important if preached in John's church. Consider, for instance, the tension described in Acts 6, when Greek-speaking believers in Christ (who were also Jews) expected equal participation in the church. There was discrimination. Imagine what might happen if Greek-speaking God-fearers were converted to Christ! Would their entry pose problems for culturally conservative believers such as James and Peter? Would this cultural and racial diversity be acceptable?

This is precisely the story found in Acts 10–11, where Peter receives a vision and converts the Roman Cornelius in Caesarea. When Peter submits his report to the leadership in Jerusalem (11:11–18), his most telling words address the cultural problem directly, "So if God gave them the same gift as he gave us, who believed in the Lord Jesus Christ, who was I to think that I could oppose God?" (11:17). The conclusion meant that God was also at work among the Gentiles (11:18).

Therefore this episode in the Jerusalem temple bears tremendous significance. Without rejecting Israel, this story affirms a new direction in the ministry of Jesus. Jesus is committed to men and women who live outside the cultural norms of Jewish society. And John suggests that this commitment, this widening of ministry, signals the start of "the hour" (12:23). To embrace "the Greeks" means that Jesus is now headed on the path that will lead to death for the world.

I am forced, then, to ask what it would look like for us to embrace this same "widening ministry" of Jesus. As we asked in chapter 10, who are the "other sheep" who are not yet in Jesus' fold (10:16)? Is there a signal for us too, that to embrace that wider mission is to incur risk (a "cross"?) and to walk down the same path of Jesus? Is this what Jesus has in mind when he follows the story of the Greeks with an exhortation about discipleship leading to self-sacrifice?

The unbelief of the world. We need to struggle with the unbelief of the world that is described in 12:37–50. We cannot miss the importance of the dilemma that faced John and the early Christians. Certainly the problem of unbelief was as problematic during Jesus' ministry as it was following the resurrection. Jews no doubt later argued that they could hardly be expected to believe in Jesus as the Messiah when, during his lifetime, many Jews rejected him. This problem was current among many leading New Testament writers. Paul anticipates this same criticism in Romans 9–11, when he must explain the consistent failure of Judaism to completely embrace Jesus. Just listening to Paul in Romans 9:1–5 gives us a glimpse into the apostle's anguish:

> I speak the truth in Christ—I am not lying, my conscience confirms it in the Holy Spirit—I have great sorrow and unceasing anguish in my heart. For I could wish that I myself were cursed and cut off from Christ for the sake of my brothers, those of my own race, the people of Israel. Theirs is the adoption as sons; theirs the divine glory, the covenants, the receiving of the law, the temple worship and the promises. Theirs are the patriarchs, and from them is traced the human ancestry of Christ, who is God over all, forever praised! Amen.

What was the explanation? Had God's efforts in the world failed? Was God still in control even though his people lived in rebellion? Were there precedents from sacred history that perhaps could resolve the problem? As I pointed out above, John's answer is in the experience of Isaiah. While some may point to a rigid Johannine determinism that claims God sovereignly elects all whom he desires and leaves in darkness those whom he rejects, there may be more satisfying interpretative alternatives. The fact is, Jesus clearly calls *all persons* to faith, and this is anchored to God's love for the entire world (3:16). The hardening described by Isaiah may be a "judicial hardening," namely, a decision by God to leave unbelievers in their unbelief, to leave them with the consequences of their refusal to embrace God.

But then we are again on the horns of a dilemma: How does anyone come to faith? How is the believing remnant any different? Has God's sovereignty not successfully called them to life and faith? We must come to grips with the responsibility of human response.[33]

No subject could be more timely for today. Unbelief is rampant in the modern world. Today men and women love darkness just as they did in the first century. Are we safe to draw conclusions about God's "judicial activity" even today? If God hardened the hearts of Isaiah's audience and if God hardened the hearts of Jesus' audience, does he still harden hearts today?

---

33. For an examination of this theme, see I. H. Marshall, *Kept by the Power of God* (London: Epworth, 1969), 176.

Secondary themes. Finally, I think the chapter invites us to reflect briefly on a few secondary themes. They are not central to the thrust of the entire chapter, but they are by no means minor. (1) John gives us a candid, personal glimpse into the heart of Jesus when he prays to his Father. The cross was a terrible fate, and Jesus knows the profundity of his sacrifice. We need to see in 12:27 that Jesus genuinely struggles, yet his obedience to his Father's will is greater than his anxiety.

(2) John 12:35–36a could not provide a clearer evangelistic charge. We too must make a decision. The Greek tense of 12:36a underscores the force of Jesus' words carefully, "that you may become sons of light." This is an event, a threshold crossed, a line drawn. People do not inherit status as children of the light. *They must choose.*

(3) I am intrigued with John's description of the "fearful believers" in 12:41–43. Were they truly followers of Jesus? Did their unwillingness to stand with Jesus publicly invalidate their faith? What does this say to men and women in the modern context who have privatized their faith and are unwilling to "go public" among those who have prestige and power?

FEW CHAPTERS IN the Gospel of John are as potentially controversial as chapter 12. Here we have the stuff that has kept Christians debating for centuries: social responsibility, politics, pluralism, and divine sovereignty. If that were not enough, the chapter ends describing a circle of believers who decide that the social risks to being a public follower of Jesus are just too much. They fear people in established, prestigious authority. John implies (with little subtlety) that their faith is inadequate. It is not that these ideas are unclear; it is that their modern application is difficult, even controversial. I am confident that every reader will find something disagreeable in at least half my suggestions!

Mary's extravagant gift of nard. It is easy to say that the expensive gift of Mary to Jesus simply has a temporal application. Jesus is on his way to the cross, and this is a gift that will prepare him. It is a luxurious perfumed reminder of her devotion that he can possess even as he is being tormented and tortured by the Roman garrison in Jerusalem. Since Mary's gift is serving this once-for-all event, it may be impossible for us to do anything with it. There is no suggestion in Scripture that we are to imitate such a deed since Jesus is not in our presence in the same manner as he was in Bethany.

Of course, the extravagance of the gift is a problem. Since the average day worker in Israel at this time received about one denarius per day, Mary's gift is the equivalent of almost one year's salary. Let's translate that into modern terms. Assuming a minimum wage of $5 per hour, one denarius would equal $40. Three hundred denarii would then be equivalent to $12,000. Imagine! Mary pours $12,000 out of an alabaster bottle in a couple of minutes, simply in an effort to cherish and honor Jesus. It is breathtaking. Surely she could have poured half the bottle and sold the rest. Maybe she could have instead sold the entire bottle and used the money to honor the work of Jesus in some way (an endowed scholarship or trust somewhere?).

Judas's complaint would likely be echoed by virtually every church elder today. If we have that many disposable assets, perhaps we should do the godly thing and strategize how that money might advance the work of the gospel in the world. We could feed the hungry or house the homeless. Perhaps we could use the money to advance ministry or support missionaries. Other (more thoughtful) elders may argue: "Of course, if Jesus were here today as he was in Bethany, no cost would be too much. But he isn't. And that's the problem. Therefore we cannot duplicate the gift of Mary." Jesus' difficult words in 12:8 ("You will always have the poor among you, but you will not always have me") now cannot apply. Jesus is not here, but the poor are.

For some Christians this has resulted in a spirituality that has promoted personal austerity and commitment to the poor as the highest virtues. Personal piety must be translated into personal compassion for it to have value. It may be that Jesus was trying to launch this sort of complex discussion when he told the parable of the good Samaritan. While we are quick to chastise the priest and Levite who bypass the suffering stranger, it may be that these two men were genuinely trying to do the right thing *so that they might serve God*.[34] Jesus is not attacking the Jewish establishment in this parable, nor is he opposing priests and Levites. Neither is this a parable about failed legalism. But it asks: How do I weigh my religious priorities when it comes to serious matters of spiritual discipline (the law) and practical need (the poor)?

Evangelicals are comfortable with this discussion. We quickly point to how we sell our "nard" in order to build ministries and institutions for the kingdom. But we are less comfortable looking at this problem from another angle. In its boldest terms: Is it possible to cherish and honor Jesus today in the world in ways that seem extravagant? When an impoverished African community pools its resources in order to build a church on a scale that is "extravagant" by local standards, is this "nard" that has been wasted? In both Rumania and Palestine orthodox priests have shown me their church sanctuaries and said that this "glorious extravagance" is here to honor Jesus. Western visitors

---

34. See the recent important article by R. Bauckham, "The Scrupulous Priest and the Good Samaritan: Jesus' Parabolic Interpretation of the Law of Moses," *NTS* 44 (1998): 475–89.

will look at the poverty surrounding the church and see such expense as misdirected. But the poor may see it otherwise.

In the West, is it possible to build a beautiful church, or simply invest in an aesthetically pleasing sanctuary, as a gesture of praise to Jesus? When I enter a European cathedral (despite the political history of the cathedrals), can I appreciate legitimately pure motives—a desire to glorify God? When a cathedral builder wants to radiate the glory of Christ behind the altar with pure gold, is there not something right about this decision? When a senior citizen in my church wants to take some of his lifelong savings and purchase an extravagant and glorious communion set for worship, is this not "nard" put to good use?

Of course there can be abuses, and that is where the debate begins. When extravagance is pursued at the expense of the ministry to the poor, there is a problem. And there may be an extravagance that discerning Christians may consider completely out of bounds. Nevertheless, I would like to argue that Mary's gift may be something we may worthily imitate today—with caution and with discernment, of course, but nevertheless it is there. At the simplest level this tension surfaces when a church board debates refurbishing a tattered, dark sanctuary and one person piously remarks, "Jesus would have us feed the poor, not install new carpet and lights." There it is. Mary's nard has been sold, and another congregation has been forbidden to honor Jesus in a way that may be fitting.

Celebrating Jesus in Jerusalem. The familiar Palm Sunday story is often seen today as a pure, unblemished celebration of Jesus as he comes into Jerusalem one week before his crucifixion. There were, of course, Galilean pilgrims camped on the west side of the Mount of Olives who believed in Jesus and celebrated his arrival in the city. Today when we have our children wave palms in the pews of our churches, we are joining those pilgrims who saw Jesus and remembered the wonderful things he had done. If we had been there on that day before Passover (we say), we would have joined these voices of praise. Such praise for Jesus is appropriate. Celebrating the re-creation of this great day in Jesus' life is something we ought to do. Luke 19:40 reminds us that if Jesus' followers do not do this, nature itself will cry out.

But the story has another side—a side that most of us each spring do not pause to hear. Palm Sunday is a happy day, a day of flowers and dresses and new shoes. But another message carries a warning about our vision of Jesus as we celebrate. The crowd in Jerusalem had many who understood both the needs of the day and the charismatic power of Jesus. In some fashion (which perhaps they did not entirely understand) they assumed that Jesus and his movement would serve their cause. Their vision for society and Jesus' presence could together make changes they dearly desired. As the gospel story unfolds further, Jesus' failure to satisfy those visions (religious, political, and social) leads to a cry for crucifixion one week later.

In what manner do we likewise use Jesus to fuel our own visions for social and political change? Do we ever take up the name of Jesus and attach it to our own agendas? I recall, for instance, a gay lobbyist in the Presbyterian Church (USA) making a claim for gay ordination: "Jesus loved everyone, and today he would stand with the gay community affirming its rights in society and the church. Anyone who does not stand with us stands against Jesus."

For conservatives it is easy to produce such an illustration and condemn it as a political misuse of the name of Christ. But things feel considerably more painful when we ask the same question about ourselves. Evangelicals likewise have agendas for social change, which they wed to their religious convictions. To be "biblical" is to affirm a platform of political commitments, and to question them is to place in jeopardy one's theological orthodoxy. Of all the evangelical writers who have pointed this out with power and courage, Tony Campolo has done a great deal to stir the conscience of American evangelicals.[35]

It is tempting at this point to provide examples of evangelical misuses of Jesus' name and illustrate the times when we have wrongly hailed Jesus as our hero.[36] But to do so would simply invite a debate about the merits of the particular agenda promoted instead of leading to reflection about a phenomenon every generation must face squarely. Jesus wants our praise and celebration. But too often we only see him through the issues of the day, issues about which we are confident he stands with us.

The arrival of the Greeks. If the early Christians in Jerusalem struggled with the arrival of Gentiles after Peter's dramatic vision in Joppa (Acts 10), imagine the stir that must have followed when suddenly in Jerusalem, non-Jews ("God-fearers") began coming to see Jesus. If Stephen was criticized by the temple authorities because as a Hellenistic Jew he expressed openness to the wider Mediterranean world (Acts 7), imagine how Jesus' meeting with these Greeks might jeopardize his standing with the theologians of Jerusalem. Peter or James may well have urged Jesus, "Look, if a leading Jerusalem Pharisee challenges your orthodoxy, you will lose your hard-won popularity." For Jesus to be seen with a Greek would bring that sort of risk.

In order to understand what is at stake here, we must have some comprehension of Israel's passionate commitment to racial purity. Beginning with

---

35. See two of his recent books, *20 Hot Potatoes Christians Are Afraid to Touch* (Dallas: Word, 1993) and *Following Jesus Without Embarrassing God* (Dallas: Word, 1997).

36. To simply browse the "social issues" section of a large, conservative bookstore would in itself uncover a fascinating list of these.

Moses' call for the Israelites to remain separate from the Canaanites, Israel remained suspicious of those who diluted Judaism's racial identity through marriage to Philistines, Phoenicians, Persians, Greeks, or Romans. The world was divided into harsh categories: clean and unclean. And keeping oneself "clean" was a religious pursuit of the highest order.

The entry of Samaritans, God-fearers, or Gentiles, therefore, into the early church was not just a matter of racial diversity and tolerance. It was a profound theological statement that cut across the heart of one of Judaism's primary commitments. To argue that Cornelius is indeed a child of God was one of Peter's most dramatic moments. For the rabbi Paul to announce that he was an "apostle to the Gentiles" must have shocked his former professional peers in Jerusalem.

This is the wider context of John 12:20–26. There is tremendous risk for Jesus to meet with these Greeks who want to see him. But for John's own church (which was likely in Ephesus), a passage like this would have been extremely useful. If John's Ephesian church had a number of Gentiles, this story would have served as a strong reassurance. If the church had struggled with the issue of racial diversity, this passage would have been a sobering exhortation.

John 3:16 is the radical charter of Jesus' mission. "God so loved the world . . ." means that God loves the *entire* world, that Christ died for the entire world (1:12, 29; 1 John 2:2). He does not reserve his affections and commitments for special races or nations. Today we may live in an era that talks openly about racial diversity, but not far beneath the surface racial divisions flourish. I have heard Edinburgh shopkeepers speak severely about "Italian tourists" (as if it were a blight to be avoided), and Greek Christians barely able to acknowledge their Turkish neighbors. Ireland, Lebanon, Israel, America, Rwanda—it is all the same. The name "Kosovo" should forever be burned into our hearts, speaking to us about what happens when ethnocentrism (and sometimes racism) is unleashed with a fury. These divisions are central to the human experience.

I have a wonderful memory of singing the very same praise songs in evangelical churches in Cairo, Egypt, Aberdeen, Scotland, Jerusalem, Israel, and Chicago. When the overhead switched on in Cairo and Arab voices (accompanied by a worship band) began singing a familiar tune in their native Arabic, one of my daughters whispered to me, "Hey! That's our song from home." When I heard the same song in a city on Scotland's North Sea coast, I could not help but marvel at how the worship of Jesus has the ability to transcend culture. Jesus loves the "Greeks"—which means that he loves the "Gentile" or any person I may classify as racially different. Andrew and Philip do not object and say to these people, "I'm sorry, but our teacher does not talk to

Gentiles." Any Christian who fails to welcome a "Greek" does not understand the radical nature of Jesus' community.

It has become commonplace to say that in America, 11:00 A.M. on Sunday is the most segregated hour of the week. If we do not understand the radical mandate of Jesus or his willingness to take the social risk of being with Greeks *in the Jerusalem temple*, we do not comprehend Jesus' extreme love for the world. At the same time, we have to understand the risk. After hearing about the Greeks, Jesus immediately speaks of sacrifice and the cross. The same risks pertain to us who likewise see Jesus' vision and take a parallel social risk of being with "Greeks" *in the local evangelical church*.

Belief and unbelief. When John describes the hardening of Jesus' audiences in 12:37–41, he is not saying that God has forced into unbelief men and women who otherwise would have believed. It is wrong to conclude from 12:37–41 that John supports an extreme determinism in which God assigns otherwise neutral people to faith and others to unbelief. John's comment here is that people who refuse to believe will experience judgment. For these men and women "the eschatological verdict has already come. For this reason they cannot believe. For them it is too late."[37] Paul has this same view in 2 Thessalonians 2:10–12 when he describes those who have aligned themselves with Satan and have refused to love the truth and be saved. "For this reason God sends them a powerful delusion so that they will believe the lie and so that all will be condemned who have not believed the truth but have delighted in wickedness."

The significance of this is twofold. (1) It underscores the urgency of coming to faith. The natural state of the world we inhabit is darkness, which God's light has penetrated in Christ. Those who refuse the light will find it extinguished and the darkness closing over them. (2) It assures us that when we are confronted with hardened unbelief, it does not mean that God has lost control, but that God is "active in judgment as well as in salvation."[38]

These are potent words for the mission of the church. To use theological jargon, it means that the realized eschatology of John now is genuinely at work in the experience of faith. The decision to which we call people is an ultimate decision with eternal consequences. It is not an invitation to "believe" so that in the distant future we will be saved from judgment. *Judgment begins now. Salvation begins now.* The consequences of our decision begin to work themselves upon our lives in the present. It is like a person with a curable disease. The antibiotic begins to reverse the effects of the disease at once; without it, the doom of the infection grows daily. Jesus' urgent words

---

37. Carson, *Divine Sovereignty and Human Responsibility*, 196.
38. Ibid.

are therefore grounded in this sort of drastic framework. To refuse the medicine is to succumb to the disease. To refuse to have faith is to be swallowed by the darkness.

The implication of this section is sobering. As Jesus hid from his audiences in Jerusalem (12:36)—as God blinded those who refused the sight offered by him (12:40)—likewise, God's judgment can fall in the present on an era and a people who have utterly rejected him.

John 13:1-38

❧

IT WAS JUST before the Passover Feast. Jesus knew that the time had come for him to leave this world and go to the Father. Having loved his own who were in the world, he now showed them the full extent of his love.

²The evening meal was being served, and the devil had already prompted Judas Iscariot, son of Simon, to betray Jesus. ³Jesus knew that the Father had put all things under his power, and that he had come from God and was returning to God; ⁴so he got up from the meal, took off his outer clothing, and wrapped a towel around his waist. ⁵After that, he poured water into a basin and began to wash his disciples' feet, drying them with the towel that was wrapped around him.

⁶He came to Simon Peter, who said to him, "Lord, are you going to wash my feet?"

⁷Jesus replied, "You do not realize now what I am doing, but later you will understand."

⁸"No," said Peter, "you shall never wash my feet."

Jesus answered, "Unless I wash you, you have no part with me."

⁹"Then, Lord," Simon Peter replied, "not just my feet but my hands and my head as well!"

¹⁰Jesus answered, "A person who has had a bath needs only to wash his feet; his whole body is clean. And you are clean, though not every one of you." ¹¹For he knew who was going to betray him, and that was why he said not every one was clean.

¹²When he had finished washing their feet, he put on his clothes and returned to his place. "Do you understand what I have done for you?" he asked them. ¹³"You call me 'Teacher' and 'Lord,' and rightly so, for that is what I am. ¹⁴Now that I, your Lord and Teacher, have washed your feet, you also should wash one another's feet. ¹⁵I have set you an example that you should do as I have done for you. ¹⁶I tell you the truth, no servant is greater than his master, nor is a messenger greater than the one who sent him. ¹⁷Now that you know these things, you will be blessed if you do them.

¹⁸ "I am not referring to all of you; I know those I have chosen. But this is to fulfill the scripture: 'He who shares my bread has lifted up his heel against me.'

¹⁹"I am telling you now before it happens, so that when it does happen you will believe that I am He. ²⁰I tell you the truth, whoever accepts anyone I send accepts me; and whoever accepts me accepts the one who sent me."

²¹After he had said this, Jesus was troubled in spirit and testified, "I tell you the truth, one of you is going to betray me."

²²His disciples stared at one another, at a loss to know which of them he meant. ²³One of them, the disciple whom Jesus loved, was reclining next to him. ²⁴Simon Peter motioned to this disciple and said, "Ask him which one he means."

²⁵Leaning back against Jesus, he asked him, "Lord, who is it?" ²⁶Jesus answered, "It is the one to whom I will give this piece of bread when I have dipped it in the dish." Then, dipping the piece of bread, he gave it to Judas Iscariot, son of Simon. ²⁷As soon as Judas took the bread, Satan entered into him.

"What you are about to do, do quickly," Jesus told him, ²⁸but no one at the meal understood why Jesus said this to him. ²⁹Since Judas had charge of the money, some thought Jesus was telling him to buy what was needed for the Feast, or to give something to the poor. ³⁰As soon as Judas had taken the bread, he went out. And it was night.

³¹When he was gone, Jesus said, "Now is the Son of Man glorified and God is glorified in him. ³²If God is glorified in him, God will glorify the Son in himself, and will glorify him at once.

³³"My children, I will be with you only a little longer. You will look for me, and just as I told the Jews, so I tell you now: Where I am going, you cannot come.

³⁴"A new command I give you: Love one another. As I have loved you, so you must love one another. ³⁵By this all men will know that you are my disciples, if you love one another."

³⁶Simon Peter asked him, "Lord, where are you going?"

Jesus replied, "Where I am going, you cannot follow now, but you will follow later."

³⁷Peter asked, "Lord, why can't I follow you now? I will lay down my life for you."

³⁸Then Jesus answered, "Will you really lay down your life for me? I tell you the truth, before the rooster crows, you will disown me three times!"

Original
Meaning

JOHN 13:1 OPENS the second half of this Gospel. For some scholars, it serves as an introductory heading to the entire Book of Glory.[1] The "Book of Signs" (John 1–12) centers on Jesus' *public* ministry within Judaism. Jesus provides a series of signs and discourses that rely heavily on the Jewish institutions and festivals of his day. His audience is wide-ranging as he seeks men and women who will believe. He provokes crises of faith, and in many of the chapters there is a division within his audience: Some choose to believe while others remain in unbelief.

The "Book of Glory" (John 13–21), however, shifts our attention to Jesus' *private* ministry, to the hour of his glorification (the cross) that has been promised throughout chapters 1–12. His audience has narrowed to the circle of those who truly believe. From chapters 13–17 Jesus is alone with his disciples; chapters 18–21 record Jesus' final glorification.

The focus of the first half of John is on *the signs* of Jesus, evidences of his identity borne by miraculous works. The focus of the second half of John is on *the hour*. Jesus now must say farewell to his followers and begin his return to the Father through his arrest, crucifixion, resurrection, and ascension. In 13:1 Jesus recognizes that "his hour" has come to depart out of the world, and he focuses his attention on "his own," whom he has loved.

Throughout the Book of Signs we observe a link between sign and discourse. That is, when Jesus offers a sign (such as the feeding of the five thousand), he generally provides an explanation (a discourse) that unveils its deeper meaning. He explains that he is the light of the world and then heals the blind man (chs. 8–9). In the Book of Glory there is one sign, one event of momentous importance: Jesus' death on the cross. In a similar fashion, the lengthy teaching of chapters 13–17 is Jesus' "final discourse" that explains this "final sign."

Raymond Brown likes to compare the literary form of the Gospel of John with the arc of a pendulum.[2] Its swing begins up high, reaches a low point, and then returns to its original elevation. Even the prologue of John reflects this structure: In 1:1 the Word exists in the realm of God; in 1:10 there is the crisis of rejection; in 1:18 Jesus is once again identified with God. Likewise, John's Gospel introduces Jesus as the Word that enters the world in his incarnation. He gloriously reveals his identity to Judaism through miraculous signs. But as the story unfolds, hostility increases. Although Jesus is divine light shining in the world, the darkness is coming, threatening to extinguish him. At its lowest ebb, Judas departs to betray him, at "night" (13:30). The

---

1. For a complete examination of the structure of John, see the Introduction.
2. R. Brown, *John*, 2:541.

Book of Glory is now the upswing of the pendulum as the Book of Signs is the downswing.

Why is this an important observation? I stress it because in the theology of John's Gospel, the death of Jesus is not a tragedy. The cross is not a low point (as perhaps in Mark's story). It is the highest moment of Jesus' glory. John thus uses language that reinterprets Jesus' crucifixion glory: The Son of Man will be "lifted up" (12:32), and when he does he will draw everyone to himself (cf. 3:13—14; 8:28). In 19:19—20, when Jesus is on the cross, he is proclaimed "king" in all the chief languages of the world. The cross is thus where Jesus is "elevated" above all, hailed as glorious ruler; through his resurrection, he is empowered to return to his place in heaven.[3] As the prologue points to the gift of eternal life for those who believe and become children of God (1:12), so the Book of Glory ends with Jesus' giving his Spirit to his disciples (20:22), truly making them his own.

The problem of the meal in John 13. John 13 tells us that Jesus is eating a supper with his disciples during his final discourse (13:2). Many readers readily assume that this is Jesus' Passover meal described in the Synoptic Gospels (Matt. 26:17—19). However, there is a puzzle here that every interpreter must study. Many commentators believe that John is at odds with the Synoptic chronology. But as I hope to suggest, this is not an impossible problem.[4]

In first-century Jewish culture, days began following sunset.[5] Therefore a day beginning after dusk on, say, Thursday, was the same "day" as the following Friday morning and afternoon. Such days had months and dates based on a lunar calendar (e.g., Nisan or Tishri, 5 or 6). Passover occurred in the springtime month of Nisan. Nisan 14 was the "day of Preparation," when the Passover lambs were killed; the immediately following evening (a new day) began Nisan 15, when Jews ate their Passover meal. Thus a Jewish family might slaughter their lamb on one afternoon at 3:00 P.M. (Nisan 14) and be eating it four hours later on Nisan 15 (both events happening on different "days").

According to the Synoptics, Nisan 14 began on Wednesday evening and continued through Thursday. On Thursday morning Jesus told Peter and John to go ahead of him and prepare his Passover (Luke 22:7—13). Thus Nisan 15 (Passover) began Thursday evening with its Passover meal (Mark 14:16) and continued through Friday. Jesus was arrested late Thursday night and

---

3. Ibid., 2:541—42.

4. For a comprehensive and understandable presentation of the complex issues, see I. H. Marshall, *Last Supper and Lord's Supper* (Exeter: Paternoster, 1980). See also J. Jeremias, *The Eucharistic Words of Jesus* (London: SCM, 1966), 15—84.

5. This was the Jewish pattern. In the Roman world, days began following midnight, exactly as we count them today.

crucified the next day (both events occurring on Nisan 15). However, this was an unusual Passover since it came close to Sabbath. Jesus was removed from the cross because Sabbath would begin Friday after sundown (Mark 15:42). Hence on this week, Thursday night/Friday was viewed as a "day of Sabbath Preparation" as well as the Passover. To sum up, the meal of Jesus on Thursday evening was indeed a Passover meal according to the Synoptics.

The main problem in John's Gospel is that the author says Jesus was crucified on the "day of Preparation"—presumably when the Passover lambs were being killed (John 19:14, 31). Therefore if Friday was Nisan 14 (the day of Preparation), then the meal of Jesus Thursday evening was also Nisan 14 and could *not* have been his Passover meal. John (by this reading) holds that in this week, Passover came one day later than the Synoptics report.

Solutions to this problem have come in four forms. (1) Some have argued that the Synoptic Gospels have it right and that John has a theological motive for placing Jesus on the cross on Nisan 14 (thereby making him a Passover lamb).

(2) Others argue that John is correct. Jesus was hosting a formal guest meal that night, and the Synoptics have a theological motive for making Jesus' final meal a Passover meal.[6]

(3) Still others argue that *both* accounts (though different) are correct. F. F. Bruce, for example, thought that Jesus was hosting an "irregular" Passover meal one day early.[7] But in order to take this view, scholars have suggested that the Passover was eaten *both* on Nisan 14 and 15 for a variety of reasons—either because of the congestion in the temple and the number of lambs slain, the proximity of Passover to Sabbath, rival calendars (one lunar, one solar), regional differences (Galilee, Judea), or rival ways to mark days (sunset/sunset or sunrise/sunrise). I. H. Marshall offers his solution succinctly: "Our conclusion is that Jesus held a Passover meal earlier than the official Jewish date, and that he was able to do so as a result of calendar differences among the Jews.[8] Each of these are plausible suggestions.

(4) There is also a fourth view that many find intriguing and attractive. It is clear that John understands this meal to be the same meal as the Synoptic meal. The reference to Judas Iscariot (13:21–30; cf. Matt. 26:20–25) solidly links the two. John also implies that this was indeed a Passover meal: Pilgrims must eat it in Jerusalem, as the law required (John 11:55; 12:12, 18, 20); it was a ceremonial meal with formal "reclining" (required at Passover); Jesus did not leave the precincts of Jerusalem after the meal (as the law

---

6. R. T. France, "Chronological Aspects of Gospel Harmony," *VE* 16 (1986): 50–54; Brown, *John*, 2:555–57.

7. F. F. Bruce, *New Testament History* (1969), 191ff.

8. Marshall, *Last Supper and Lord's Supper*, 74.

forbade) but went to Gethsemane;[9] Passover alms were distributed (13:29); and the disciples were in a state of "levitical purity" (13:10) required at Passover.[10] Therefore the Johannine meal clearly suggests a Passover meal.

But what do we do with the passages that imply Jesus was crucified on the "day of Preparation?" The argument that according to John Jesus was crucified on Nisan 14 (the day of Preparation) is anchored to five texts that imply that the Passover had not yet happened when Jesus is crucified.

- 13:1–2: "It was just before the Passover Feast. Jesus knew that the time had come for him to leave this world and go to the Father.... The evening meal was being served...."
- 13:29: "Since Judas had charge of the money, some thought Jesus was telling him to buy what was needed for the Feast, or to give something to the poor."
- 18:28: "To avoid ceremonial uncleanness the Jews did not enter the palace; they wanted to be able to eat the Passover."
- 19:14: "It was the day of Preparation of Passover Week, about the sixth hour."
- 19:31: "Now it was the day of Preparation, and the next day was to be a special Sabbath. Because the Jews did not want the bodies left on the crosses during the Sabbath, they asked Pilate to have the legs broken and the bodies taken down."

We will look at these verses later in the commentary, but for now we note that they do not necessarily imply that the meal in John 13 was before Passover.[11] In 13:1 "before the Passover Feast" probably describes when Jesus knew his hour had come, and the meal mentioned in 13:2 refers to the Passover itself described in 13:1. John 13:29 records that Judas must make a purchase for the feast, but this may well be something they need at the moment or something needed for the next day. In 18:28 the authorities fear defilement from Gentile contact, but such ritual uncleanness would expire at sundown (if it were Nisan 14). These men likely refer to eating an afternoon meal (the *chagiga*) on the day following the night of Passover (Nisan 15).[12]

---

9. Jesus could not return to Bethany since the village was outside the formal boundary of Jerusalem. Bethphage was the village furthest east that remained in Jerusalem's precincts. This rule was based on a rabbinic interpretation of Deut. 16:7.

10. See C. C. Torrey, "In the Fourth Gospel the Last Supper Was a Passover Meal," *JQR* 42 (1952): 237–50.

11. For discussion, see C. Blomberg, *The Historical Reliability of the Gospels* (Downers Grove, Ill.: InterVarsity, 1987), 175–80; I. H. Marshall, *Last Supper and Lord's Supper*, 69–71; D. A. Carson, *John*, 455–58; C. C. Torrey, "The Date of the Crucifixion According to the Fourth Gospel," *JBL* 50 (1931): 227–41.

12. See C. C. Torrey, "The Date of the Crucifixion, " 240–41.

Finally, the "day of Preparation" referred to in 19:14 and 19:31 does not necessarily refer to preparation for the Passover. It may refer to preparation for the Sabbath. In fact, 19:31 makes the connection with Sabbath explicit. Mark 15:42 refers to Jesus' day of crucifixion (Friday) in this manner as well ("It was Preparation Day [that is, the day before the Sabbath]"). Moreover, we have no extrabiblical evidence describing Nisan 14 as "the day of Preparation for the Passover."[13] Many scholars think the phrase may simply be an idiom meaning "Friday of Passover week" (or, "the day of Sabbath preparation within the week of Passover").

If this fourth line of reasoning is correct (and I am now compelled to think it may be), John's chronology fits the Synoptic outline perfectly. Thursday evening began Nisan 15, when Jesus hosted a Passover meal; on Friday afternoon Jesus was crucified "on the day of [Sabbath] Preparation of Passover Week." I recognize that this explanation has been long and perhaps complex. But it is important. In critical discussions of the historical reliability of John's Gospel, the problem of chronology and the Johannine Passion narrative always come up for examination.

Jesus Washes His Disciples' Feet (13:1–17)

IT MAY SEEM odd that although John records Jesus' final meal (13:2) before his arrest (18:12), he does not record the well-known details of the Lord's Supper as we have them in the Synoptic Gospels (Matt. 26:17–19; Mark 14:12–16; Luke 22:7–13) and Paul (1 Cor. 11:23–26). This is certainly not because John felt the meal was irrelevant (as Bultmann once argued). John 6:52–58 shows his genuine interest in the meal. As we will see, allusions to the meaning of the meal appear in chapters 13–16. Others have argued convincingly that John realizes he is writing for Christians who know the meal well. Perhaps he is consciously writing for Christians who have already read Mark.[14] He may be conscious of a "Eucharist narrative" that contributed to the creation of Mark. If so, John wants to supplement (or interpret) the well-known tradition with new things that will give a more complete theology of the sacrament not seen elsewhere.[15]

In the Synoptic setting, two important motifs appear. (1) Jesus uses the imagery of Passover bread and wine to point to his death (body broken, blood poured out). Joined to this is the account of Judas's betrayal (whose

---

13. Jeremias, *Eucharistic Words*, 80.

14. R. Bauckham, "John for Readers of Mark," in R. Bauckham, ed., *The Gospel for All Christians Rethinking the Gospel Audiences* (Grand Rapids/Edinburgh: Eerdmans/T. & T Clark, 1998), 147–71; this is the general outlook of Barrett's commentary.

15. Beasley-Murray, *John*, 226; Schnackenburg, *John*, 3:46.

deed triggers Jesus' arrest) and Peter's denial. (2) Luke tells us that there was a dispute about greatness that night, and Jesus responds by telling the disciples about true servanthood (Luke 22:24–27). John weaves these themes together in the Upper Room as he shows Jesus speaking about and modeling true servanthood as well as declaring in clear terms his death and departure. In John 13, these two themes appear in sequence: the spiritual cleansing work of Jesus (13:2–11) and the moral mandate for humble service (13:12–20). In fact, later Jesus will even supply a homily on the vine (cf. Mark 14:25, "fruit of the vine") to illustrate his intimate connection with his followers (John 15:1–11).

If I am correct that John views the meal as a Passover meal (see above), 13:1 likely hints that the footwashing was an event that took place just prior to the celebration of the dinner. As the meal is being served (13:2)[16] Jesus interrupts the ceremonies in order to demonstrate the depth of his love for his followers (13:1b).

The footnote about Judas Iscariot in 13:2 reminds us that Jesus is completely aware of the cost of this love, for already the darkness, driven by the devil, is working its plans through Judas. The Greek at this point is uncertain: "The devil had already put in *his* heart that Judas should betray him [Jesus]" (lit. trans.). But whose heart is this? Our assumption that it belongs to Judas (NIV) is not altogether clear. The phrase "put in his heart" also means "made up his mind," and according to some Greek manuscripts, Judas is not yet the object of the devil's work. The sense is most likely: "When the devil had decided that Judas should betray Jesus...."[17] It is not till 13:27 that Satan enters Judas. Either way, Judas becomes one who has refused to believe (12:46); since he is surrounded by the darkness, he is ready to become a pawn of Jesus' adversary, Satan.

Jesus' decision to wash his disciples' feet is anchored in his assurance of his relationship with God (13:3). He knows both his origins and his destiny and as such understands the authority he has been given. This gives him the courage to do something his followers never expected. Footwashing was commonplace in Greco-Roman and first-century Jewish culture and appears as a ritual of daily cleansing, as a religious act (such as washing the hands and feet in hot water before Sabbath), or as a token of hospitality when some-

---

16. There are important variants in the Gk. text specifying the timing of the meal. An aorist tense ("after the meal ..." KJV) or a present tense ("during supper ..." RSV, NRSV; "the evening meal was being served ..." NIV) controls its meaning. Since the meal is still being served in 13:26, the sense of the verse cannot be that the meal is completed when Jesus washes the disciples' feet.

17. So Barrett, *John*, 439; the alternate translation: "when the devil prompted Judas to betray Jesus...."

one first entered a home.[18] This was a world where roads were dusty and sandals were worn daily. In Luke 7:36–50 Simon the Pharisee's failure to wash Jesus' feet was correctly interpreted as a gesture of hostility. In 1 Timothy 5:10 washing the feet of the saints may be a metaphor for humble service.

The task of footwashing was so menial that according to some Jewish sources, Jewish slaves were exempt and the job kept for Gentiles. One story reports how Rabbi Ishmael returned home and his wife tried to wash his feet. He refused, claiming it was too demeaning. She took the question to a rabbinic court, arguing that it was in fact an honor.[19] In the splendid romantic Jewish book of *Joseph and Asenath*, Joseph's bride, Asenath, is so overcome with love for Joseph that she offers to wash his feet. When Joseph protests and sends for a servant girl, Asenath interrupts him. "No, my Lord, because you are my lord from now on and I (am) your maidservant. For your feet are my feet and your hands are my hands ... another woman will never wash your feet" (20:4).[20]

At the very least, all our ancient sources show that footwashing was a degrading and lowly task. When done by a wife (for her husband), a child (for his/her parents), or a pupil (for his teacher), it was always an act of extreme devotion. But since it was an act with social implications, in no way do we find those with a "higher" status washing the feet of those beneath them. When Jesus "takes off his outer clothing" and wraps a towel around himself (13:4), he is adopting the posture of a slave.

While the circle of disciples seems to accept Jesus' gesture (13:5), Peter reflects how shocking the deed must have seemed (13:6). The depth of his devotion to Jesus defines the strength of his objection. But Jesus is not simply giving them a lesson in humble service (this will come in 13:14); he is doing something that symbolizes his greater act of sacrifice on the cross (13:7). Only after "the hour" when Jesus is resurrected will any of this make sense (cf. 2:22; 12:16). But Peter continues to object in the most strenuous way, and Jesus' rebuke is carefully worded. "If *I* do not wash you ..." means that the question is not simply one of washing, but a question of *who* does the washing. Peter must participate in the work of Jesus (13:8–9). He lacks a cleansing that only Jesus can supply.

The language of 13:8 is peculiar. If Peter is not washed, he cannot have any "part" (Gk. *meros*) in Jesus. Throughout the LXX, the *meros/meris* word group

---

18. Gen 18:4; 19:2; 24:32; 43:24; Judg. 19:21; 1 Sam. 25:41. For first-century Judaism, see the pseudepigraphal *Testament of Abraham* (ch. 3), where Abraham washes his guests feet. Also see Homer's *Odyssey*, 19.343.

19. Carson, *John*, 462; Barrett, *John*, 440.

20. See J. Charlesworth, ed., *The Old Testament Pseudepigrapha* (London: Darton, Longman, Todd, 1985), 2:234. Joseph and Asenath was written between 100 B.C. and A.D. 100.

refers to tribal land promised in Canaan that Israel was to inherit (Num. 18:20; Deut. 12:12; 14:27). It was one of the principal gifts of the covenant. But this gift of God is no longer "land," but life with Jesus (cf. also ch. 15). Jesus is talking about eternal life and union with him (cf. 14:3; 17:24). If so, then the footwashing is symbolic of something more than a gesture of fellowship. It is only the death of Jesus (and its acceptance by the believer) that brings eternal life.

Peter's zeal to gain this inheritance (13:9) is one more example of Johannine misunderstanding. Peter concludes that if footwashing gains an inheritance with Jesus, what would a thoroughgoing "washing" gain? Jesus' correction in 13:10 brings us to perhaps one of the more controversial verses in the Gospel. "He who has bathed does not need to *wash, except for his feet*, but he is clean all over" (RSV, italics added).[21] The italicized phrase is included in a wide range of Greek manuscripts and so is found in most translations, such as the NIV. But it is missing in a number of others. Most modern commentators reject it as an artificial scribal insertion.[22] A later scribe may have thought that the bath initially referred to by Jesus was a previous cleansing. When Jesus says that he does not need to wash, this would not make sense since Jesus is about to wash their feet. The phrase clarifies: If one has bathed, one need not wash except his feet (which Jesus is doing).

But Jesus' initial reference to bathing points to his own work.[23] This is the bathing that makes one "clean all over." The plain sense of Jesus' words seems clear and almost proverbial: If you have been cleansed already, you don't need to wash further. The cleansing work of Jesus—footwashing, symbolizing spiritual cleansing on the cross—is complete in itself and therefore Peter does not need to pursue more. Ongoing footwashing will remain Jesus' mandate (13:14), but it does not need to be anchored in 13:10.

The curious return to the subject of Judas in 13:10b–11 (cf. 13:2) indicates that Jesus' work of footwashing has not changed Judas's heart. The fact alone that Jesus washed Judas's feet is stunning and is a testimony to Jesus'

---

21. The NIV obscures the Gk. grammar with a paraphrase, "A person who has had a bath needs only to wash his feet, his whole body is clean."

22. Barrett, Brown, Bultmann, Carson, Dunn, Hoskyns and Davey, Lindars, Marsh, Tasker. For a full survey, see J. D. G. Dunn, "The Washing of the Disciples' Feet in John 13:1–20," *ZNW* 61.3 (1970)· 247–52; A. Hultgren, "The Johannine Footwashing," *NTS* 28 (1982): 539–46; J. C. Thomas, " Note on the Text of John 13:10," *NovT* 29.1 (1987): 46–52. The phrase is omitted by Codex Sinaiticus, ancient Latin manuscripts, and Origen.

23 John uses two verbs in 13:10. "A person who has had a bath [*louo*] needs only to wash [*nipto*] his feet." The first generally refers to complete bathing, the second to partial washing (9:7). But John often uses pairs of verbs as if they were synonyms (to know, to send, to love, etc.); the same is likely here.

patience and love for his followers (even the man who betrays him). Judas is now a man in the grip of the darkness.

As with so many of Jesus' powerful acts, here too he provides a discourse explaining what he has just done (13:12–17). But while the subject of the footwashing in 13:2–11 pertained to Jesus' salvific work on their behalf, his teaching now points to how they might imitate his deeds.[24] These themes are different, though related. Jesus' sacrifice will be the supreme token of his overwhelming love for the world. In his Farewell Discourse, Jesus now wants his followers to exemplify that same love to one another. His act of sacrifice cannot be repeated, but his model of self-giving love can become a natural feature of the community that follows him and imitates him (13:14–15). Later Jesus will say that our love for one another should be like his in yet another way: We may be called to lay down our lives for our friends (15:12–13).

Jesus' proverb in 13:16 echoes well-known words from the Synoptics: "A student is not above his teacher, nor a servant above his master" (Matt. 10:24; cf. Luke 6:40; John 15:20). His prefacing words, "I tell you the truth" conceal the phrase "truly, truly" (Gk. *amen, amen,* see comments on John 1:51). Jesus is reinforcing the importance of this often-repeated truth. Servants should not consider themselves to be greater than their masters; if this is so, what is applicable to the master (sacrifice) is likewise applicable to the servant.

Jesus Predicts His Betrayal (13:18–30)

FOR THE THIRD time, the subject of Judas's betrayal enters the story (13:2, 11, 18–19). The first footwashing section ended with a reference to Judas (13:11), and now Jesus' interpretation returns again to thoughts of him (13:18–19). This builds the impression that Jesus is troubled about this matter (13:21) and that the betrayal of this man weighs heavily on him. Jesus makes clear that his choice of Judas was no mistake. The blessing pronounced in 13:17 is not directed to Judas, whose intentions Jesus knows perfectly. "I know those I have chosen" should not be read to say that Jesus chose the eleven and Judas has been rejected from the beginning. Brown's translation serves the passage well: "What I say does not refer to all of you: I know the kind of men I chose. But the purpose is to have the scripture fulfilled. . . ."[25]

Jesus knows each of these men now with him in the room. There have been no surprises after so many years together in ministry. Jesus wants *each*

---

24. This difference between 13:2–11 and 13:12–20 has led some to think that this is a "second" interpretation of Jesus' footwashing. For scholars who look for editorial additions to John, 13:12–20 (they argue) was added at a later date. As I will argue, such a view is unnecessary.

25. Brown, *John,* 2:549.

of them. In 6:70 we have the same idea: "Have I not chosen you, the Twelve? Yet one of you is a devil!" Therefore this betrayal has not taken Jesus unawares nor should it shock his disciples (13:19; cf. 14:29; 16:4; Matt. 24:25). But the realization of the betrayal now fits the pattern of Scripture (13:18b), where earlier in Israel's history David (prefiguring the Messiah) was likewise betrayed. Jesus' citation of Psalm 41:9 (LXX 40:10) underscores the personal affront that this betrayal meant. To "eat bread" is a cultural symbol that refers to personal intimacy, and to expose the bottom of the foot is another symbol of personal contempt.[26] Jesus possesses divine wisdom into these events and yet experiences bewildering dismay as they unfold.

John 13:18–19 is really a digression. Jesus returns to his subject of the servant and the master in 13:20. As servants are obligated to reflect the work of their masters in every respect, so too such servants enjoy the respect and the authority that comes from working in their master's name. Both 13:16 and 13:20 are proverbs (preceded by "truly, truly"), and both echo well-known sayings in the Synoptics (Matt. 10:40).

This is the third and final time we read that Jesus is "deeply troubled" (12:21, Gk. *tarasso*; cf. its use at Lazarus's tomb, 11:33, and at the prospect of the cross, 12:27). His words predicting his betrayal in 13:21 were firmly fixed in the Gospel tradition and appear almost identically in Matthew 26:21 and Mark 14:8 (cf. Luke 22:22). In all four Gospels the Twelve immediately begin questioning the identity of the betrayer. But since the Fourth Gospel is preserving the eyewitness testimony of the Beloved Disciple (19:35; 21:24), it is not surprising that John records a story unlike any other.

Since the disciples are eating a Passover meal (see above), it is necessary for them to recline (13:23).[27] Jews in this period adopted the Roman *triclinium* table, a low three-sided table shaped like a "U." Guests reclined on cushions around the perimeter (hence on three sides) while the interior of the table setting provided access for servers. The body was supported with the left arm (or elbow), the right hand was used for eating, and the feet were extended away from the table (cf. Luke 7:38).

The Beloved Disciple enjoys a place of honor, seated on Jesus' right (cf. Mark 10:37, where James and John want to sit on Jesus' left and right in glory). This explains why he can easily lean back and place his head near Jesus' chest and speak to him privately, asking Jesus to divulge the name of the betrayer (13:24). Peter is not as near and so must call to the Beloved Disciple (13:23). Judas likewise has a place of honor near Jesus (on his left?) because Jesus is able to dip some bread into a common dish and serve the morsel to him (13:26).

---

26. These symbols are true even today in the Middle East.
27. This is according to Jewish tradition; see Jeremias, *Eucharistic Words*, 22–26.

This is the first time we have encountered the phrase "the disciple whom Jesus loved." He will make an appearance at the cross (19:26–27), at the tomb (20:2–9), and at the resurrection in Galilee (21:1, 20–23), and his authority will be "stamped" onto this Gospel at its very end (21:24–25). There are no references to him in the Book of Signs (cf. 1:35). In the Introduction, I surveyed the possible options given for this figure and concluded that the traditional solution that this is John son of Zebedee is not unreasonable. Even though Lazarus is the only disciple specifically named as being "loved" by Jesus (11:2, 5, 36), here we learn that the Beloved Disciple was one of the Twelve and present in the Upper Room (this was not true of Lazarus). The Beloved Disciple also appears together with Peter in the Fourth Gospel both at the tomb (ch. 20) and on the sea (ch. 21). A similar link between John and Peter is also a Synoptic motif.

But if this is John himself, is it not curious that he would describe himself with a title like this? Some desire to see this as a self-designation in which John is pointing to "his sense of indebtedness to grace" and his desire to give himself a lower profile next to Jesus.[28] In the Introduction, I suggested instead that this is rather the name given to John by his followers. John 21:20–21 seems to indicate that John has died and 21:24 suggests that his own disciples ("*we* know that his testimony is true") have placed the finishing touches on his Gospel. This title is their tribute to their beloved teacher and pastor.

Meals were eaten with flat baked bread, and a broken portion of this bread was then dipped into common bowls on the table. Jesus says that the betrayer is the one to whom he provides some dipped bread (13:26), and then he promptly serves Judas (13:27). To serve someone a morsel from the table like this was not unusual (see Ruth 2:14), and the disciples could have taken it as a simple honoring gesture for Judas. If so, it is particularly ironic since this gesture of respect is the last thing Jesus can do for Judas, and it compares with Judas's last gesture of betrayal in the garden (18:3–11).

At this point, Satan controls Judas's fate (he "entered into him"; cf. Luke 22:3), and Jesus dispatches him to pursue the course he has set for himself. Even though the disciples seem unaware of what is happening (13:28) and speculate that Judas is leaving to purchase things for the feast, the story implies that John understood everything. He had been given the key to the morsel, and he sees the consequences of the gift.

The departure of Judas is "at night" (13:30). No doubt we should see this as both literal and symbolic. Night represents the antithesis of Jesus, who is the light. It is the darkness of unbelief and opposition (9:4), where people stumble (11:9) and find themselves in a fruitless search for life (21:3). It is the

---

28. Carson, *John*, 473.

setting of Nicodemus, a man who must choose to leave the darkness and be reborn to join Jesus (3:2; 19:39). Therefore Judas represents a person described in 3:19: "Light has come into the world, but men loved darkness instead of light because their deeds were evil" (cf. also Luke 22:53, where Jesus describes the moment in the Garden of Gethsemane as the time "when darkness reigns").

Some scholars have urged that 13:29 ("some thought Jesus was telling him to buy what was needed for the Feast") proves that this could not be Jesus' Passover meal. But this argument fails for three reasons. (1) The Passover continued throughout the next day and provisions would still be needed. Shops were likely open Thursday night during Passover to supply the many needs of the meal that night. (2) If Passover was the following night (Friday), Judas would have the entire next day to collect the needed items. (3) The disciples also wonder whether Judas is giving alms to the poor (13:29b). Such nighttime almsgiving was a Passover tradition. This was the only night of the year when the temple gates were left open (Josephus, *Ant.* 18:29–30). The *Mishnah* even suggests that worshiping Jews invite a poor person from the street to eat the Passover with them.[29]

Jesus Begins His "Farewell" (13:31–38)

THE DEPARTURE OF Judas into the night (13:30) marks a solemn divide in the plot of this Gospel. Jesus is now left with "his own" (10:27), those who are his intimate followers, to give them his final instructions. The arrival of the Greeks in 12:20 signaled that the "hour" was near at hand. Now in 13:31 it has arrived: "Now is the Son of Man glorified and God is glorified in him." Except for Jesus' personal exchange with Peter in 13:36–38, he addresses the entire group of Eleven even when he is interrupted by Thomas (14:5), Phillip (14:8), and Judas (not Iscariot, 14:22). In fact, 13:31 to 17:26 comprises Jesus' lengthy "Farewell Discourse," in which he not only talks specifically about his departure, but prays a "departure prayer" in a tradition with deep roots in the Old Testament.

Numerous academic studies have compared Jesus' Farewell Discourse with those of dying teachers and leaders in antiquity. Jacob's last words in Genesis 49 are typical of this form, as is Moses' farewell in Deuteronomy 31–34. Not only does Moses identify his successor, but he gives teachings that must be recorded and a final blessing. Apocryphal Jewish literature from Jesus' day offers more tantalizing parallels. In the *Testaments of the Twelve Patriarchs* each of the twelve sons of Jacob give farewell instructions, blessings, and prayers. In the *Testament of Moses*, we overhear Moses' final words to Israel and Joshua. We

---

29. *m. Pesach* 9:11; see Jeremias, *Eucharist Words*, 54.

even possess "testaments" of Solomon, Job, Isaac, and Adam[30]—fictionalized farewells imagined by Jewish authors between 100 B.C. and A.D. 200.

Jewish testaments imagine the dying (or departing) person surrounded by his most intimate friends and family. Standard literary elements generally appear. For instance, they always show a concern for the comfort and encouragement of those left behind. Often there is an exhortation to obey the law, and a deposit of writings is left behind.[31] In some cases, the departing person passes his "spirit" to his followers or successor. Moses and Elijah do this respectively for Joshua and Elisha (Num. 27:18; Deut. 34:9; 2 Kings 2:9–14).

In the farewell of Jesus many of these elements appear. He encourages his disciples and comforts them (John 14:1). He also urges them to be obedient (13:34; 15:12), and from John's perspective the "literary deposit" Jesus leaves behind is the Fourth Gospel itself. Moreover, Jesus promises that his Spirit will indwell and empower his followers following his death (14:17, 26; 15:26; 16:3, 13). In other words, we have in John 13–17 all of the elements of a Jewish farewell.

With the departure of Judas Iscariot, Jesus speaks directly of his glorification. Note that Jesus uses the past tense (Gk. aorist tense, 13:31), saying that *already* the glory of God has been revealed in his life (leading to reciprocal glorification).[32] Throughout Jesus' life of perfect obedience, God has been honored. God's power has also been made visible through the many signs of Jesus' ministry. Now the hour of glorification has dawned; even in washing his disciples' feet, Jesus has revealed something more of God's glory. Jesus' glory thus occurs when God's glory radiates through him.

The supreme place where this divine radiance will be visible will be on the cross ("God *will glorify* him at once," 13:32, italics added).[33] This future glorification, then, is not some distant event at the end of time or in heaven. It is the series of events that will unfold at the end of this momentous week: Jesus' death, resurrection, and ascension.

If Jesus' glorification is tied to his imminent death, he then must speak directly to one of the chief themes of a farewell discourse: his departure

---

30. These and many other "testaments" can be found in J. Charlesworth, *The Old Testament Apocrypha*, 2 vols. (London: Darton, Longman, Todd, 1983).

31. In 4 Ezra we are told that Ezra dictated ninety-four books of wisdom in forty days before his death (4 Ezra 14:44)! Moses instructs Joshua to keep his "book" of promises for perpetuity (*T. Moses* 10:11).

32. Jesus uses the title "Son of Man" to refer to himself (see comments on 1:51; 3:13; 5:27; 6:27, 53, 62, 8:28, 9:35; 12:23, 34). This is the final reference to the Son of Man in the Gospel.

33. The phrase "if God is glorified in him" in 13:32a is missing from a number of important manuscripts. But this has likely happened by scribal error. It is easier to explain how the phrase was lost than why a scribe might have added it.

(13:33). "Little children" is an affectionate expression occurring only here in John (but seven times in 1 John); it was a title of address used by Jewish rabbis for their students. In 7:33–34 and in 8:21 Jesus had told his public audiences that he was departing, and in each case there was profound misunderstanding. His theme to these previous Jewish leaders was that in his departure they would no longer be able to find him, that his revelation would be closed, that he would be inaccessible.

John 13:33 is thus a crucial thought for the Farewell Discourse. It is balanced by the words of assurance that are threaded through the balance of the discourse for his intimate friends. He is departing so that he can prepare for their arrival (14:1–7). His desire is not to abandon them or to orphan them (14:18), but to enjoy their fellowship in perpetuity. Jesus possesses life that goes beyond the grave, and those who believe in him will possess the same life with him (14:19). Therefore Peter will shortly be assured that soon after Jesus' departure he "will follow" his master to where he is (13:36).

The "new commandment" mentioned in 13:34–35 is also explained in 15:12–17.[34] That the disciples are to love one another is nothing new (Lev. 19:18). That they are to love each other with the sort of love modeled by Jesus is something dramatic. Love characterizes Jesus' relationship with God (14:31), and love characterizes God's relationship with Jesus (3:35; 15:9–10). Jesus' love is manifested in his obedience to the Father's will ("the world must learn that I love the Father and that I do exactly what my Father has commanded me," 14:31). Therefore disciples are to reflect the sort of love known to Jesus—a love expressed through committed obedience. "As I have loved you" points to Jesus' most immediate act of love (the footwashing) and means that to truly love another, we must pursue a life of servanthood and sacrifice.

But the word "new" (Gk. *kainos*) may mean something more. We can recall that in this Synoptic supper setting Jesus also talked about "newness" in another respect. He referred to the "new" covenant established in his sacrifice, and he also said he would not again drink wine until he did it "new" in the kingdom of heaven. This "new command" may be a signal that Jesus is talking about life in a new era, a messianic era. In that era love must characterize his followers—a love patterned on the generous, loving act of God that saves his people.

Peter's immediate response to Jesus' announcement (13:36–38) includes two traditions about the apostle: Peter is to follow Jesus in death, and Peter is to deny Jesus shortly. Peter's bravado and Jesus' prediction of his denial are well known to the Synoptics (Matt. 26:32–34; Mark 14:27–30; Luke 22:31–

---

34. The phrase "new commandment" is characteristic of John. It occurs in 1 John fourteen times and in 2 John four times.

34). Peter is eager to be with Jesus even if it costs him his life, and his words echo the language of the good shepherd (10:11, 15). Whereas Jesus will depart in "a little [while],"[35] Peter must wait till "later." Jesus must first do his work on the cross that makes possible Peter's eternal life.

Jesus goes on to prophesy that Peter's nerve will fail at the last moment. His good intentions to lay down his life, uttered so bravely, will not hold when confronted with genuine danger. Peter's eventual death ("but you will follow later") is not mentioned in the Synoptics but will come up again in John 21:18–19. Peter will have an opportunity to show his faithfulness in death and so "glorify God" (21:19); this is reinforced when Jesus returns from the grave.

AS ONE OF the most popular chapters in the Gospel of John, chapter 13 presents unique challenges to us in the contemporary setting. The literary picture of the chapter—that is, the inner world of its drama—is potent. If we simply repeat the cultural forces at work in this first-century Passover setting (the drama of Jesus' shocking the disciples, Peter's refusal, Judas's preoccupation with betrayal, Jesus' announcement of death and departure), we should be able to recreate the gripping story that was so well known to John. *This is a good story.* But unfortunately those of us who know it too well, who know the outcome already, forget its power.

A growing list of scholars is convinced that the Gospels were written for illiterate audiences. Some estimate that only 10 to 15 percent of the Roman world was literate (and the average among Christians was lower still).[36] This means that primarily the Gospels were *heard* by the ancient audience. It is hard for us to imagine a world in which we cannot read or write, but in antiquity it was common. Thus, anyone who wrote a gospel had to take its presentation into account. Churches acquired the skill of excellent reading and rhetoric. That the Gospels lend themselves to such a presentation can be seen in the recent oral production of Mark's Gospel in the King James Version by Alec McCowen. Matthew's Gospel has even been dramatized in film (with only the words of Matthew used). The Gospels make for good storytelling. In our presentation of this chapter, we must keep the story itself alive. If we miss its drama, we have failed to recreate John's literary skill.

---

35. The Greek *mikros* occurs eleven times in John, nine of which are in the farewell discourse. This is Jesus' clarification of his imminent death.

36. R. Burridge, "About People, by People, for People: Gospel Genre and Audiences," R. Bauckham, ed., *The Gospels for All Christians* (Edinburgh/Grand Rapids: T. & T. Clark/Eerdmans, 1998), 113–45; also W. V. Harris, *Ancient Literacy* (Cambridge, Mass.: Harvard Univ. Press, 1989).

The footwashing. Three themes stand out in the chapter as offering strong potential for bridging to the modern context. We begin with the amazing picture of Jesus' washing the disciples' feet. As I argued above, the setting of this scene is the Lord's Supper of the Synoptic Gospels. If indeed John assumes his readers know the details of a Gospel like Mark (see comment on 13:1), then we must make the hermeneutical decision whether to integrate John 13 into the themes of the Lord's Supper. I believe such a decision is legitimate. The wider context of Jesus' gesture of washing his disciples' feet finds its significance in his death. This is why Peter's washing is a prerequisite to his inheritance with Jesus (13:8); it will provide eternal life.

The washing parallels the picture we have in Mark when Jesus breaks bread and pours out wine. It is his life poured out—his work as a servant—that brings everlasting life. Therefore a practical application of John 13:1–11 can be found at a Eucharist service. Jesus is a servant who bears lowly tasks; his ultimate service is on the cross. Our union with this divine work brings about our salvation (cf. John 6:53, "I tell you the truth, unless you eat the flesh of the Son of Man and drink his blood, you have no life in you").

Jesus' gesture is also linked with his repeated teaching that he is a servant who embraces the unacceptable role. In Mark, for instance, Jesus predicts three times that he will die (8:31; 9:31; 10:33). Following his third prediction he remarks, "For even the Son of Man did not come to be served, but to serve, and to give his life as a ransom for many" (10:45). This describes a service that leads to a purposeful death, a servant's death. When a dispute breaks out in the Upper Room this night among the disciples and they debate who is the greatest, Luke records Jesus' answer: "But you are not to be like that. Instead, the greatest among you should be like the youngest, and the one who rules like the one who serves. For who is greater, the one who is at the table or the one who serves? Is it not the one who is at the table? But I am among you as one who serves" (Luke 22:26–27).

Paul likewise describes to the Philippians that the work of Jesus was in emptying himself in service: "But [he] made himself nothing, taking the very nature of a servant . . . he humbled himself and became obedient to death—even death on a cross" (Phil. 2:7–8). The humility we see, therefore, in the footwashing of John 13 must be seen through the lens of Jesus' ultimate "washing," namely, his sacrificial death, which cleanses us of our sins (Acts 22:16; 1 Cor. 6:11; Eph. 5:26; Titus 3:5; Rev. 7:14).

If the footwashing points to Jesus' death and if disciples need to be "washed" in order to be a part of Jesus' following, is this washing also a symbol for baptism? This is a shorter step than we might expect. The Greek verb "to bathe" (*louo*, 13:10a) also appears in the New Testament for baptism. In Acts 22:16, for example, Ananias says to the converted Paul, "Get up, be baptized and wash [*apolouo*[37]] your sins away" (see also 1 Cor. 6:11; Eph. 5:26; Titus 3:5; Heb. 10:22). Added to this is a strong patristic tradition that interpreted John 13:10 as a reference to baptism (e.g., Tertullian, Cyprian). "A person who has a bath needs only to wash feet; his whole body is clean" then may become a secondary exhortation underscoring the importance of baptismal washing for the believer.

The surprising extension of this footwashing is that Jesus not only says that we must be washed, but that we must "wash one another's feet" (13:14b). How do we do this? There is a long tradition in the church that has taken this literally.[38] In some ancient liturgical traditions, footwashing became a part of Maundy Thursday rituals. Benedictine monastaries practiced footwashing as a part of their hospitality to guests. In early England, Catholic monarchs used to wash the feet of twelve poor men each Maundy Thursday. In the Greek Orthodox tradition in Jerusalem, the archbishop re-creates the footwashing scene with twelve priests, washing and kissing each of their feet.[39] Other ancient interpreters, however, saw the command as a symbol of lowly service and nothing more (e.g., Augustine).

Today modern interpreters are similarly divided. For some, it is a general command to humility and service, while others believe that John's church in the first century and their churches today should make footwashing a standard feature of the Christian life. At the very least the command of Jesus is that we take on a role that is similar to his: If he has washed our feet (bearing all of the symbolism appropriate in the first century), we ought to do something similar.

The betrayal of Judas. Another theme that stands apart in this chapter is the betrayal of Judas Iscariot. This is not a minor motif in John, for Jesus returns to it again and again (13:2, 11, 18, 21, 26–30). Jesus had chosen this man as one of his disciples. They had spent at least three years working together. The fact that he was the group's treasurer (13:29) no doubt tells us that he held a place of trust and esteem. In the Upper Room Jesus even washes his feet. When did it dawn on Jesus that Judas would be his betrayer? (The first hint follows the miraculous feeding, 6:71.) What was it like for Jesus to wash this man's feet? What was it like for Judas? Even Jesus' gesture of giving Judas a morsel of food (13:26) reminds some interpreters of the Lord's Supper served to them in this room.[40] Judas participated in this supper (Luke

---

37. The verb *apolouo* is a combination of *louo* plus the preposition *apo*.

38. For a thorough survey of the history of the interpretation of footwashing in the church, see C. Thomas, *Footwashing in John 13 and the Johannine Community* (JSNTSup 61; Sheffield: JSOT Press, 1991), 11–19.

39. See Hoskyns and Davey, "The Liturgical Use of the Pedivalium or the Washing of the Feet," *John*, 520–24.

40. F. Maloney, "A Sacramental Reading of Jn 13:1–38," *CBQ* 53 (1991): 237–56.

22:21; but see Mark 14:17–25), and if this morsel represents the sacred elements of the meal, it is striking that immediately after taking it, Judas falls to Satan's control.

This story is more than a description of one man's demise. Throughout the Gospel we have been warned about the struggle between light and darkness. In 1:5 we noted the absolute hostility between the two. As the Gospel unfolds, we hear again and again about those who choose the darkness despite their exposure to the light. Audiences divide following Jesus' revelation of himself—some believe and some refuse. But in Judas we have a man who could be no closer to the revelation. In spite his proximity to the light, he chooses the darkness. John invites us to reflect on the horror of this. Does the same thing happen in the church today?

The command to love. The final theme deserving our attention is Jesus' command to love. Note how this command follows immediately after the footwashing. Thus it is not a sentimental attachment Jesus expects among his followers. Rather, this is love that translates into a decision to act in profound ways. The closest Synoptic parallel to the command comes in Jesus' Sermon on the Mount, where he teaches, "You have heard that it was said, 'Love your neighbor and hate your enemy.' But I tell you: Love your enemies and pray for those who persecute you" (Matt. 5:43–44). For some scholars, the "new commandment" in 13:34 is a lesser command since it does not include our enemies. But this is a misdirected criticism. John's Gospel speaks generously of God's love for the world (John 3:16). Jesus' mission is to save the world (4:42), to give it life (6:33) and light (12:46). The disciples are commanded to go into this world to continue Jesus' work (17:18; 20:21).

But Jesus has specialized interests in the present setting. He wants his followers to show a quality of love unparalleled in the world. Carson puts it well: "At the risk of confounding logic, it is not so much that Christians are to love the world less, as that they are to love one another more. Better put, their love for each other ought to be a reflection of their new status and experience as the children of God."[41] The theme of community love, while not compromising our commitments to the world, matches another perspective in John concerning the world.

A mere perusal of John's use of the term *world* uncovers a reality about our environment that may be sobering.[42] A commitment to the world must take into account the reality of the world's hostile attitude toward the light. There-

---

41. Carson, *John*, 485

42. "World" (Gk. *kosmos*) occurs seventy-eight times in this Gospel (1:9, 10, 29; 3:16, 17, 19; 4:42, 6:14, 33, 51, 7:4, 7; 8.12, 23, 26, 9.5, 32, 39; 10:36; 11 9, 27; 12:19, 25, 31, 46, 47; 13·1; 14:17, 19, 22, 27, 30, 31; 15:18, 19; 16.8, 11, 20, 21, 28, 33; 17:5, 6, 9, 11, 13, 14, 15, 16, 18, 21, 23, 24, 25; 18:20, 36, 37, 21:25)

fore the community of believers must be a refuge, a place of unparalleled affections and service that will at once set it apart from its environment.

Such a theme is relevant today. We live increasingly in a world that is experiencing fractured communities. As a result, Jesus' new commandment is a challenge to us to examine how we live as Christ's followers and how we demonstrate the quality of love he extended.

 TO APPLY THESE three themes in our present generation will take some skill. We will have to leave many questions unanswered and speculate broadly on others. Did Jesus expect his followers to literally wash his disciples' feet? Or is this a symbol of humility? Is Judas merely an actor in history or a literary model set before us as a warning?

Jesus and footwashing. In order to bring the power of Jesus' actions into my generation, I have to reconceptualize the significance of what he did. We could, of course, reintroduce footwashing into the church, and some churches (especially in the Pentecostal tradition) have done this.[43] But footwashing is foreign to us and may evoke responses today never intended in the original biblical setting. But it was not foreign to Jesus and his followers. Jesus' act was powerful not because of the footwashing itself, but because of the role he was assuming by doing it. To sweep a floor is commonplace, but for Queen Elizabeth of England to come and sweep my kitchen would be upsetting, not because sweeping is significant but because the Queen is doing it. It is the person of Jesus tied to this lowly role that brings power to this image.

It is impossible for us to imitate this lowly role of Jesus (13:14) unless we have a clear understanding of what he has done for us. Jesus only expects his disciples to wash someone else's feet *after* they have been washed themselves. Similarly, Jesus does not expect us to work on behalf of another until we see the depth of that person's work on our behalf.

John understands the logic of this precedence. In his first letter, he wrote, "This is love: not that we loved God, but that he loved us and sent his Son as an atoning sacrifice for our sins. Dear friends, *since God so loved us,* we also ought to love one another" (1 John 4:10–11, italics added). Without a prior, life-consuming experience of God's love for us, we will be singularly ill-equipped to love anyone else.

This is what often characterizes the lives of people who have given themselves to profound acts of Christian service around the world. The story of

---

43. Can such footwashing, when it becomes a feature of regular church life, become routine? That is, is it possible to wash someone's feet and then forget what it is meant to convey concerning lowly service?

their pilgrimage begins with an overwhelming encounter with God's goodness, which never fades for them. This is precisely what Jesus has done. He has given his disciples a concrete image—a concrete experience, no less—of what it means to be loved. I am sure that this experience of *being washed* led to remarkable later reflections on what it meant to *be saved* after Jesus had died on Calvary.

This transforming experience of God's grace is precisely what fueled the missionary work of the apostle Paul. He served because he had been served. Paul writes, "I have been crucified with Christ; it is no longer I who live, but Christ who lives in me; and the life I now live in the flesh I live by faith in the Son of God, who loved me and gave himself for me" (Gal. 2:20 RSV). The motivating force behind Paul's life was not the law or a desire to promote his Jewish religiosity. The apostle realized that he had been washed, that God had given himself to him; therefore he can now freely and joyfully give himself to others.

To serve *as Jesus served* requires humility. It requires sacrifice. It means taking up the "lesser role" for the benefit of someone else. Many stories illustrate this point, but one always comes to my mind. Dr. Robertson McQuilkin was for many years the president of Columbia Bible College and Seminary in Columbia, South Carolina. In about 1980 Dr. McQuilkin began to see signs of memory loss in his wife, Muriel. For the next decade he watched as his wife's career of conference speaking, radio shows, and television began to erode and disappear. In the mid–1980s she was diagnosed with Alzheimer's, and her deterioration continued to advance rapidly.

This situation naturally posed a crisis for Dr. McQuilkin. As president of a thriving college and graduate school, how could he meet the needs of both his wife and his job? Many Christian friends encouraged him to give Muriel over to professional care (i.e., a nursing home), but he could not bear the thought. As her condition worsened, he made a decision that was "a matter of integrity" (his words). He resigned from Columbia to care for his wife full time. "It was a choice between two loves," he writes. Columbia wisely and compassionately supported his decision and began seeking his replacement.

The striking thing about McQuilkin's personal story is its theological underpinnings. For some, he was choosing a task at remarkable social and professional cost. He was throwing away his career. Not so. His decision was grounded in God's love for him, experienced also through Muriel's unselfish forty-two-year love for him. This made his service a joy.

It is more than keeping promises and being fair. As I watch her brave descent into oblivion, Muriel is the joy of my life. Daily I discern new manifestations of the kind of person she is, the wife I always loved. I also see fresh manifestations of God's love—the God I long to love more fully.[44]

Another tremendous story is that of Henri Nouwen, the popular author and Catholic priest whose books *The Wounded Healer* and *Creative Ministry* are on virtually every seminarian's bookshelf. This theologian, who has taught at Notre Dame, Yale, and Harvard, moved in 1986 to a community called Daybreak, a residental communty serving a hundred mentally impaired people. He writes:

> L'Arche [the ark] exists not to help the mentally handicapped get "normal," but to help them share their spiritual gifts with the world. The poor of spirit are given to us for our conversion. In their poverty, the mentally handicapped reveal God to us and hold us close to the gospel.[45]

Here again we have a man whose life has been so deeply touched by the gospel that it transformed him and gave him the joy of service. He had been washed by Jesus, and so he was washing others' feet.[46]

These are two illustrations of what it means to take the teaching of John 13 to heart. Such service may not come in the dramatic forms described by McQuilkin or Nouwen, but the service we may enjoy will certainly be motivated by the same power that touched the lives of Jesus' disciples. Jesus' love and service for us transform us and empower us. Without such knowledge we *cannot* wash another person's feet as Jesus would have us.

Judas Iscariot's betrayal. Theologians have speculated endlessly about the person of Judas and what made him betray Jesus. Some have appealed to his disillusionment with the course of events in Jesus' life. Others have suggested that Judas was actually trying to intervene and save Jesus from a messiahship gone wrong. One recent writer has used every effort to cleanse Judas's reputation and show him to be Jesus' foremost servant, handing him over to the Sanhedrin as Jesus wanted.[47]

The truth is that our evidence into the inner workings of Judas is extremely limited. But one feature does stand out. In the great struggle between light

---

44. R. McQuilkin, "Living by Vows," *Christianity Today* 35 (Oct. 8, 1990): 38—40; the full story is now in a book, *A Promise Kept* (Carol Stream, Ill.: Tyndale, 1998).

45. A. Boers, "What Henri Nouwen Found at Daybreak," *Christianity Today* 38 (Oct 3, 1994): 28—31.

46. H Nouwen's care of one mentally impaired man can be found in *Adam· God's Beloved* (New York: Orbis, 1997).

47. W. Klassen, *Judas: Betrayer or Friend of Jesus?* (Minneapolis: Augsburg, 1996). In order to accomplish this rewriting of Judas's image, Klassen must critically dismantle much of the Gospels.

and darkness, between truth and falsehood, between God and Satan, Judas became a vessel of God's opponents. While the actual "handing over" of Jesus occurs in chapter 18, the critical moment in Judas's life takes place in 13:27: "As soon as Judas took the bread, Satan entered into him." From this juncture, Judas is barely his own person. He has been absorbed by darkness. The last image we have is a man filled with regret, who tries to return his payment for the betrayal. But it is refused, and Judas commits suicide (Matt. 27:1–10; Acts 1:16–20).

Here we have a man who stood closer to the revelation of God than many. Judas heard Jesus teach and witnessed his miracles. While Peter expresses doubts about Jesus' announced crucifixion and Thomas later doubts the resurrection, we have no description of Judas that shows him as anything but faithful. In the Upper Room, Peter refuses to have his feet washed. But Judas (apparently) complies, accepting the humble role of Jesus. Something happens to intervene in this man's pilgrimage. He changes sides. To use John's language, he flirts with the darkness to such a degree that he becomes one of its own.

C. S. Lewis is well known for his children's books (*The Narnia Chronicles*) and his Christian apologetics (*Mere Christianity, Miracles*). But perhaps one of his best efforts appears in his Space Trilogy (*Out of the Silent Planet, Perelandra, That Hideous Strength*). Here Lewis tells the story of a man named Ransom, who travels first to Mars and then to Venus, only to discover that his own Earth is viewed by the universe as the Silent Planet, the planet of disarray and corruption. Creatures elsewhere have not "fallen," and they live in blissful harmony with the spiritual forces of the universe.

Lewis's interest in the trilogy is his study of the nature of corruption. Two men, Weston and Divine (symbolic names for the 'divine' Western world), introduce corruption where it has never been seen before. The first bullet flies on Mars, killing an innocent creature called a Hross—much to everyone's shock. And on Venus, Ransom watches a new world born, and he meets Eve as she rules her kingdom and is sickened as Weston tries to tempt her to sin. It is the garden of Eden revisited.

What is most telling in these books is the progressive corruption of Weston and Divine. They are academics who have had access to the greatest wisdom the world has known. In their arrogance, they jettison their humility and flirt with ideas that make God obsolete and manipulate the course of history. In the course of their work—this is the important point—they become the unwitting pawns of Satan. On Venus Ransom finally confronts Weston in a life-and-death struggle as he fights to rescue Eve. But, Ransom observes, Weston has changed. Satan has become his co-conspirator; Satan has not so much possessed the man as absorbed him.

This is the picture of Judas. He made a wrong turn somewhere and courageously pressed ahead instead of admitting his mistake, going back, and retracing his steps. Before long he is in the realm of the darkness. In 13:11 Jesus knows this and can call him "unclean." Then, ever so gradually, Judas becomes a pawn of the evil one. It is frightening to watch Judas run out into the "night," where people stumble (11:9; 13:30). This is where the light is despised.

Is this betrayal a possibility that pertains not simply to the circle of Jesus' immediate followers, but to his followers today as well? The setting of the Upper Room was a spiritual turning point in which Jesus was doing profound spiritual work. But at the same time, where God is most deeply at work, Satan's attack is that much more acute. It is significant that in Luke's version of the Lord's Supper, at this point Jesus tells Simon Peter that Satan wanted him as well (Luke 22:31–32). This is stunning. Satan's desire to sabotage the followers of Jesus reached more levels than we realize. Are those most intimately connected with Christ's life and work today similarly vulnerable?

Judas is a parable and a warning. We read his story as "insiders," thinking it depicts someone else. But Judas is a more disturbing figure than Pilate or Caiaphas or any of the Jewish leaders. He saw the light and understood it, but chose the darkness anyway. "Judas is the reminder that every day is judgment day and that on any day some faithful follower, like Judas—or like you and me—might turn tail on the light and stumble out into the darkness, caught up in evil or caught up by evil's prince."[48]

We too, then, are in danger—in danger of misunderstanding Jesus and of being seduced by our own dreams and visions for life. In doing this work, we betray Jesus. Paul is brutally honest with the threat of this possibility. He warns about those who may "follow Satan" (1 Tim. 5:15) and who may be snared by the devil "to do his will" (2 Tim. 2:26). John's own pastoral experience made him face Christians who knew the faith well but corrupted it and stood against Christ. He named such people "antichrists" (1 John 2:18, 22; 4:3; 2 John 1:7).

Is this a description of famous theological heretics? Is it a profile of people like John G. Bennett, who stole over eighty million dollars from evangelical organizations in a fraudulent investment scheme?[49] Is it believers who leave the community of Christ and then do irreparable harm to the church? In different degrees, it is all of these things. The "betrayer" is someone who "hands over" Christ to his enemies and who (unwittingly or not) serves the forces of darkness rather than the light.

---

48. D. L. Bartlett, "John 13:21–30," *Int* 43 (1989): 393–97 (citation on p. 394).

49. T. Giles, "Double-Your-Money Scam Burns Christian Groups," *Christianity Today* 39 (June 19, 1995): 40–42; "New Era's Bennet Pleads 'No Contest' to Fraud," *Christianity Today* 41 (May 19, 1997): 62.

The love command. Jesus uses the strongest possible language in 13:34. In the Gospel of John the Sanhedrin gives commands (11:57), the Father gives commands to the Son (10:18; 12:49, 50; 14:31), and Jesus gives commands to his followers (13:34; 14:15, 21; 15:10, 12). For Jesus, this is not a "suggestion" any more than the Father's words to him were suggestions. This command to love bears all the weight of the person who uttered it.

The command to love was one of John's foremost concerns. Throughout his letters he refers to it again and again as the hallmark of those in whose lives the presence of God is being reflected (1 John 3:11, 23; 4:7, 11; 2 John 1:5). No doubt as a pastor he has seen a church torn viciously by strife (1 John 2:11), so that showing Christ's love ranks in importance to having faith in Christ (1 John 3:23).

The problem with this verse is that it may be impossible to order someone to love. The psychologist John Sanford writes in his meditations on John:

> The difficulty from a psychological point of view with this command is that love cannot be willed. The person who tries to love by an act of will is likely to wind up with a persona that looks like he or she is loving, but with a shadow side hidden in the unconscious that negates it. Love must come from the heart if it is to be genuine; it cannot be feigned, not even with the best of intentions.[50]

Sanford goes on to describe the many complex ways that "love" can become an artificial manipulative response that disguises deeper levels of rivalry, brokenness, and anger. One key to Jesus' ability to love is provided in 13:3. Jesus knew himself well; he knew his origins and his future and through this self-knowledge found the ability to love his disciples in the remarkable scene of the footwashing. Sanford would urge us to do the same.

The love command puts in abstract words what Jesus meant in 13:14 when he told his disciples to wash one another's feet. As we discovered above, the same rule applies here: Unless one has a profound experience of being loved, it is virtually impossible to express profound love for another. I recall talking about this theme one day in a class when a student came forward to confide that she had no memory of ever being told "I love you" by her parents. Hers was a sterile family of no spoken emotion and rare gestures of physical affection. I could not help but wonder what this meant for her at twenty years old. Was her ability to love handicapped?

For evangelicals, the command to love has often been translated into a command to "love the world." This fully appropriate attitude is then tied to

---

50. J. Sanford, *Mystical Christianity A Psychological Commentary on the Gospel of John* (New York: Crossroad, 1995), 259.

evangelism and used to increase the work of the church in the world. But Jesus is talking specifically about how we love one another within his church. For instance, John Ortberg has pointed out that among evangelicals who are fighting for "the truth," our opponents do not often qualify for love. "An old saying suggests that the first casualty of war is truth," Ortberg writes. "This is not quite true. The first casualty of war is love."[51] He goes on to describe the Pharisees as representing rigorously orthodox thinkers of his day who stood on the right side of all the tough issues, yet they had the most difficult time loving those whom Jesus loved, people whom Jesus was willing to make a part of his community. Imagine how shocked they were when Jesus claimed confidently that the entire law was summed up in this command to love (Mark 12:28–34)!

When Christians disagree—in national debates on major cultural issues or in local congregations—there is an unresolved tension between the degree of our passion for truth and the command Jesus has given us to love. I have former students serving now in conservative churches who write to me with pain about how former friends have declared doctrinal war on them. I have had evangelical friends describe how they have discovered a new commitment to some social cause (the poor, the AIDS community, Palestinian rights), only to be ostracized and hurt by their churches. Zeal for truth and the command to love have sometimes been at odds in our evangelical world.

The same can be true in the local church. The command to love has its first application within the body of Christ. When a non-Christian steps foot inside a church, this should be his or her first observation: "By this all men will know that you are my disciples, if you love one another" (13:35). In the early third century, Tertullian wrote, "It is mainly the deeds of a love so noble that lead many to put a brand upon us! 'See,' they say, 'how they love one another . . . see how they are ready even to die for one another.'"[52] In the earliest church the social caring and commitment of Christians to one another was a profound testimony in a Roman world with its sharp social divisions.

Nothing so astonishes a fractured world as a community in which radical, faithful, genuine love is shared among its members. There are many places you can go to find communities of shared interest. There are many places you can go to find people just like yourself, who live for sports or music or gardening or politics. But it is the mandate of the church to become a community of love, a circle of Christ's followers who invest in one another because Christ has invested in them, who exhibit love not based on the mutuality and attractiveness of its members, but on the model of Christ, who washed the feet of everyone (including Judas).

---

51. J. Ortberg, "Do They Know Us By Our Love?" *Christianity Today* 41 (May 19, 1997): 25.
52. Tertullian, *Apology*, 39, cited in Hendricksen, *John*, 254.

John 14:1–31

D O NOT LET your hearts be troubled. Trust in God; trust also in me. [2]In my Father's house are many rooms; if it were not so, I would have told you. I am going there to prepare a place for you. [3]And if I go and prepare a place for you, I will come back and take you to be with me that you also may be where I am. [4]You know the way to the place where I am going."

[5]Thomas said to him, "Lord, we don't know where you are going, so how can we know the way?"

[6]Jesus answered, "I am the way and the truth and the life. No one comes to the Father except through me. [7]If you really knew me, you would know my Father as well. From now on, you do know him and have seen him."

[8]Philip said, "Lord, show us the Father and that will be enough for us."

[9]Jesus answered: "Don't you know me, Philip, even after I have been among you such a long time? Anyone who has seen me has seen the Father. How can you say, 'Show us the Father'? [10]Don't you believe that I am in the Father, and that the Father is in me? The words I say to you are not just my own. Rather, it is the Father, living in me, who is doing his work. [11]Believe me when I say that I am in the Father and the Father is in me; or at least believe on the evidence of the miracles themselves. [12]I tell you the truth, anyone who has faith in me will do what I have been doing. He will do even greater things than these, because I am going to the Father. [13]And I will do whatever you ask in my name, so that the Son may bring glory to the Father. [14]You may ask me for anything in my name, and I will do it.

[15]"If you love me, you will obey what I command. [16]And I will ask the Father, and he will give you another Counselor to be with you forever—[17]the Spirit of truth. The world cannot accept him, because it neither sees him nor knows him. But you know him, for he lives with you and will be in you. [18]I will not leave you as orphans; I will come to you. [19]Before long, the world will not see me anymore, but you will see me. Because I live, you also will live. [20]On that day you will realize

that I am in my Father, and you are in me, and I am in you.
²¹Whoever has my commands and obeys them, he is the one
who loves me. He who loves me will be loved by my Father,
and I too will love him and show myself to him."

²²Then Judas (not Judas Iscariot) said, "But, Lord, why do
you intend to show yourself to us and not to the world?"

²³Jesus replied, "If anyone loves me, he will obey my teaching. My Father will love him, and we will come to him and
make our home with him. ²⁴ He who does not love me will not
obey my teaching. These words you hear are not my own;
they belong to the Father who sent me.

²⁵"All this I have spoken while still with you. ²⁶But the
Counselor, the Holy Spirit, whom the Father will send in my
name, will teach you all things and will remind you of everything I have said to you. ²⁷Peace I leave with you; my peace I
give you. I do not give to you as the world gives. Do not let
your hearts be troubled and do not be afraid.

²⁸ "You heard me say, 'I am going away and I am
coming back to you.' If you loved me, you would be glad
that I am going to the Father, for the Father is greater than I.
²⁹I have told you now before it happens, so that when
it does happen you will believe. ³⁰I will not speak with
you much longer, for the prince of this world is coming.
He has no hold on me, ³¹but the world must learn that I
love the Father and that I do exactly what my Father has
commanded me.

"Come now; let us leave."

Original
Meaning

JOHN 14 IS a continuation of the Farewell Discourse that began in 13:31 after Judas's departure
from the Upper Room. In the previous chapter
we saw how Jesus is adapting a "farewell formula"
well known in Judaism. He comforts his disciples in light of his impending
departure by explaining what will come, how the Spirit will arrive, and how
they will flourish as his followers. Throughout these verses (beginning in
ch. 13) we can feel how distraught the disciples must have been. They have
entered Jerusalem for the last time and Jesus is speaking clearly about his
death. They are facing profound shame, disillusionment, and fear. Peter was
the first to express their worry (13:36). Jesus now begins to provide answers
to their many spoken (and unspoken) questions.

A great deal of scholarly energy has been spent on deciphering the literary structure and theological purposes of John 14. Scholars prone to locate sources behind this Gospel and to reconstruct the compositional history of the chapter claim to find complex cycles of thought here that really tell us more about John's thinking than about Jesus. But much of this work seems dubious at best.[1] The primary theme of the chapter is the departure and return of Jesus. This discussion is advanced through the questions of various disciples: Peter (13:36), Thomas (14:5), Philip (14:8), and Judas (14:22). Jesus likely taught for a long time during this supper and what we have here are summaries of his words. These disciples' questions are thus literary devices that push the subject along, raising important themes and advancing the chapter to its climax.

We can discern a shift in subject at 14:18. From 14:1–14 Jesus is addressing the disciples' despair over his leaving. This is followed by his first promise of the Spirit (14:15–18). Jesus then turns to the subject of his return in 14:18, which is followed by yet another promise of the Spirit (14:25–31).

But the themes of "departure and return" are more complex than we might imagine. Jesus' departure refers to his glorification (that mix of subjects that begins with the arrest and concludes with his ascension). His return is likewise complex: In 14:18–19 Jesus' return seems to describe his "Easter return," when his disciples will see him. But in 14:21 we learn that another "coming" of Jesus to his disciples will result in his indwelling them spiritually (14:23). In each case—Jesus leaving, Jesus returning—the Holy Spirit plays a vital role in comforting, empowering, and reassuring the followers of Christ. The entire chapter ends in a blessing of "peace" (14:27–31) that Jesus bestows on his followers.

Jesus' Departure from this World (14:1–14)

ON THREE PREVIOUS occasions we learned of Jesus' deeply troubled feelings (Gk. *tarasso*): when he faced Lazarus' tomb (11:33), when he contemplated the cross (12:27), and when he reflected on the betrayal of Judas (13:21). Jesus' confidence in the greater power and purposes of God made it possible for him to confront each of these crises. Now the disciples must face the same feelings (14:1). Jesus' answer can be read either as an indicative ("You [already] believe in God and you believe in me") or as

---

1. F. F. Segovia, "The Structure, *Tendenz* and *Sitz-im-Leben* of John 13:31–14:31," *JBL* 104 (1985): 471–93. For Segovia the chapter is shaped by John's need to explain the failure of Jesus to return in his second coming. John's solution, according to him, is that the coming of the Spirit replaces the coming of Jesus.

an imperative ("Believe in God! Believe also in me!"), since the Greek forms for the indicative and imperative are identical in this case.[2] The imperative for both verbs seems preferable (as it is in 12:36; 14:11) since Jesus is charging his disciples to hold fast in light of the upcoming crisis. This follows the majority readings of current translations, such as the NIV: "Trust in God; trust also in me."

One of the reasons to trust is that Jesus' departure will be purposeful. In his departure he will be working on their behalf, preparing a place for them (14:2). The KJV "mansions" (for Gk. *monai*, "rooms") was a seventeenth-century expression for modest dwellings; thus, 14:2 should not build a picture for us of heavenly palatial residences. This is not Jesus' point. God's "house" refers not to the church but to the heavenly dwelling where he lives (cf. Heb. 12:22; Rev. 21:9–22:5), and a *mone* is a place of residence there with him. This word is related to the common Johannine verb *meno*, to remain or abide. To "remain" with Jesus is the highest virtue in John's Gospel (15:4–10), and he is promising that death will not interrupt intimacy enjoyed with him.

To have a place in heaven reserved for us is one thing; confidence in getting there is quite another (13:36–37). But Jesus promises that he "will come back."[3] The image is straightforward: Jesus is leaving for heaven and there will prepare a place for his followers; then he will return to take them there. But when will this "coming" occur? At Easter? At the coming of the Spirit? At our death? At his second coming? Scholars have pointed to each of these. For some, it is each one together, so that the verses represent a sweeping all-inclusive promise of encouragement.

Even though it is Christ who comes in each event, the best view takes 14:2–3 as a plain promise of the Second Coming.[4] As the chapter develops, Jesus points to other returns he will make (14:18, 23), but these are separate from what he affirms here. John has a genuine future eschatology that expects a dramatic climax to history (5:25ff.; 1 John 2:28). But here his interest is not like that found in the apocalyptic drama of Mark 13:24–26; rather, it is in comforting and reassuring his disciples that they have not been forgotten.

---

2. It is also possible that the translation could be indicative/imperative: "You believe in God; now also believe in me!" Compare Mark 11:22–24, where Jesus exhorts his followers to believe in God during the last critical days in Jerusalem.

3. Even though the tense of the verb here is present (Gk. *palin erchomai*), John often uses *erchomai* with a future force (see 1:15, 30; 4:21, 23; 14:18, 28; 16:2). The following verb, "will ... take" (*paralempsomai*), is future.

4. A popular view argues that John begins the chapter with the promise of the Second Coming and then works to correct it, reinterpreting this "coming" with the coming of the Holy Spirit (14:23). See R. Gundry, "In My Father's House Are Many *Monai*," *ZNW* 58 (1967): 68–72.

While Jesus affirms (14:4) that they know where he is going,[5] Thomas speaks up and presses for more clarification. He claims that they know neither the *destination* of Jesus nor the *way* he will take to get there. This reflects the disciples' inability to comprehend that the cross will be the way Jesus will return to the Father—a way, if they understood, they would have trouble accepting.[6] Peter had already asked about Jesus' destination (13:36) but this had been left unanswered. Thomas now picks it up again and adds another element.

Jesus' answer in 14:6 is the premier expression of the theology of this entire Gospel: "Jesus answered, 'I am the way and the truth and the life. No one comes to the Father except through me.'" Of the three terms, emphasis surely falls on the first, "the way." Access to the Father's presence in heaven will only be through Jesus and no other. He is the only one who can lead his followers back to the places he will prepare.

This is the case because Jesus is *the truth*, the authoritative representative and revealer of God. He hears what God says and obeys what God tells him to do (5:19; 8:29). He discloses God exhaustively unlike anyone else can because he has seen God (1:18). Those who follow Jesus, who come to the Father through his "way," will be the ones who gain eternal "life" (cf. 11:25, "I am the resurrection and the life"). Thus, this verse places Jesus in the role of mediator, creating the only avenue to God. Bruce has written, "All truth is God's truth, as all life is God's life; but God's truth and God's life are incarnate in Jesus."[7]

Such an absolute statement leads, of course, to a different series of questions. Jesus has disclosed more than anyone expected. Instead of simply defining his destination (the Father, heaven), he says that he alone is the way to get there. *But only God can lead us to himself.* Jesus takes the next inevitable step, therefore, a step no doubt that the disciples can barely comprehend: Only the Father can lead us to himself—*and the Father is genuinely present in Jesus.*

This is an echo of the prologue (1:1–2), which explained the ultimate union (and differentiation) of the Son and the Father. Jesus Christ is God in complete human form (1:14) and so has the capacity to accomplish divine tasks. Hence if his followers know Jesus, they will know the Father as well

---

5. Because of the difficult Greek construction, a variant adds a longer reading: "You know where I am going *and you know* the way." This may come from the influence of 14:5, where Thomas asks a question about the "way." The shorter reading (NIV) is best· "You know the way where I'm going." The disciples should know where Jesus is going (heaven) but the way (Jesus is "the way," 14:6) will still be shown.

6. Compare the multiple accounts of the disciples' struggle with Jesus' decision to go to the cross (Mark 8:31; 9:31; 10:33).

7. Bruce, *John*, 298–99; cited in Smalley, *John*, 253.

(14:7). This is not a rebuke,[8] but a promise pointing to a deeper revelation that will come if they continue with Jesus (14:23). Since they have known him, there is more to come, and they will discover the Father who is present in him. Moreover, they have seen the Father *already* (14:7b).

Philip's question (14:8) now concentrates on Jesus' last phrase. "Lord, show us the Father and that will be enough for us." This is perhaps a typical "misunderstanding" that we have seen in numerous Johannine discourses. Philip does not understand that *no one* has seen God (1:18a). It is beyond the human capacity. Even Moses' request on Mount Sinai was refused (Ex. 33:18–23). But in Christ Philip has before him the full embodiment of God as it *can* be seen by humanity. Nevertheless, Jesus now says with utter clarity what Philip could not comprehend before (14:9). In seeing Jesus Philip is seeing God. This is one of the high points of John's Christology. Jesus is not simply a religious teacher or guide, nor is he simply the means to some other destination. He is also the end, the goal. He is the One in whom God can be found. The exhaustive and exclusive nature of this astonishing claim cannot be missed (cf. 10:30, 37–38).

Such a claim requires justification, and Jesus supplies it (14:10–11). At its most basic level, Jesus is God's envoy. In the ancient world, a duly authorized representative (an agent) had the power to speak and act in the name of his sender. Thus the rabbinic saying "A man's agent is like himself" (*m. Berakoth* 5:5) means that Jesus (as God's agent) is authorized both to work for and to speak for his Sender.

But "agency" barely touches the surface of Jesus' thought. Jesus and the Father enjoy a reciprocity of life: The Father is in him and he is in the Father. This is not merely a functional unity, as if Jesus' life could be summed up by his obedience. This is an exhaustive, substantial unity—an ontological unity—that at last explains statements hinted in the public ministry: "I and the Father are one" (10:30; cf. 10:38).

The First Promise of the Spirit (14:12–17)

THE GOAL OF Jesus' words from the beginning of this discourse has been to encourage and comfort his followers. John 14:12–14 begins a change of subject. If it is true that the power of God is resident in Jesus and that the disciple is invited to know Jesus and gain life from him, then in some manner the disciple will share in God's power. (1) It is of utmost importance to

---

8. The NIV follows a variant reading that makes the verse punitive. In 14:7 the first verb is perfect ("If you have come to know me . . . ") and the second may be perfect (" . . . you *would know* my Father also") or future (NIV note: " . . . you *will know* my Father also"). Strong manuscript evidence supports the future tense of verse 7

note that the astonishing promise of 14:12 points to the future. Jesus must first go to the Father before the promise of remarkable works and realized prayer can come.

(2) In addition, there can be no diminishing of what these verses say: The works of Jesus refer to his miraculous signs, and in some respect every believer (14:12a, "anyone who has faith") will be able to participate in such work.

(3) Whatever believers do must be done in the name of Jesus so that as God is glorified in Jesus' work, they will do mighty works in Jesus' name. Jesus' works glorify the Father, and disciples (whose lives continue the work of Jesus) continue to glorify the Father.

Once Jesus departs, two promises will be realized in the community of faith: Great works will accompany those who believe (14:12) and prayer will be answered (14:13). Note that the promise of 14:12 does not simply point to miracles. What Jesus has been doing includes deeds of humility, service, and love as well as miraculous signs. Jesus' followers will do works that are "greater" even than these.

This promise can hardly mean that the efforts of disciples will exceed those of Jesus, who, for instance, provided the stupendous miracle of raising Lazarus from the dead. What is "greater" is that these works will be done by regular people in whom the power of Christ has taken up residence following his glorification. This is why the departure of Jesus is crucial, for only through that can the Holy Spirit become a reality to all who follow him (7:37–39). Recall 10:41, where we learned that John the Baptist (surely one of the greatest men in the era before Jesus' glorification) could do no signs. He (and the present disciples) lived in an era completely different from what is to follow. The coming of the Spirit after Christ's glorification will inaugurate an eschatological reality not known in the world.

One hallmark of the intimacy shared between Jesus and his disciples will be their ability to hear one another's voice. In 10:3 a mark of the good shepherd is that his sheep can hear his voice. Now we learn that the shepherd can hear their voices in the same manner (14:13–14; cf. 1 John 5:14–15). This theme that Jesus will do what his disciples ask (in prayer) is frequent both in the Farewell Discourse (John 14:13, 14; 15:7, 16; 16:23, 24, 26) and in the Johannine letters (1 John 3:21–22; 5:14–15).[9] Such prayer is given in "Jesus' name" and directed to Jesus.

However, John can just as easily refer to this prayer as directed to the Father (15:16; 16:23); no doubt we should not make too much of this difference since every prayer must come in "Jesus' name." This promise of answered prayer is really a continuation of what is given in 14:13. Such

---

9. See also the similar Synoptic sayings: Matt. 7:7–8 (Luke 11:9–10); Matt. 18:19; 21:22.

answered prayer is another "great work" that Jesus will accomplish among them. The disciples' lives will be continuation of Jesus' life in the world. Both great deeds and answered prayer glorify the Father because it is Jesus who is at work still accomplishing them. But because this is so, such prayer is predicated on the assumption that it fits with the will and purposes of Christ in the world (14:15). Later John will write essentially the same thing in his first letter: "This is the confidence we have in approaching God: that if we ask anything according to his will, he hears us" (1 John 5:14).

Thus far we have learned nothing about the coming of the Spirit following Jesus' glorification. At the Feast of Tabernacles John noted explicitly that the Spirit had not yet been given because Jesus had not yet been glorified (7:37–39). Now as Jesus anticipates his departure, he describes the Spirit that is coming (14:15–17). The Spirit's gift in these verses is controlled by verse 15a, "if you love me."[10] The gift, then, is an outgrowth of the loving relationship between Jesus and his disciples, not an entitlement earned by the disciple.

Jesus uses an unusual term in 14:16 for the Spirit. The NIV "Counselor" translates the Greek *parakletos*, often transliterated "Paraclete." This word is unique to John in the New Testament. Of the five Spirit promises in this discourse (14:16, 26; 15:26; 16:7; 16:12–14), four of them include this title (14:16, 26; 15:26; 16:7). A fifth (and final) use occurs in 1 John 2:1, where Jesus is called a *parakletos*.

Extensive scholarly debate as well as every commentary on John tries to probe the meaning of this word.[11] It comes from a verbal root that describes someone "called alongside"[12] and occurs in secular Greek literature for an advocate in a court of law, who comes "alongside" a person to speak in his or her defense and provide counsel. The Greek term became popular in the first century and was even a loan word in Hebrew and Aramaic for a similar judicial setting (*P. Aboth*, 4:11).[13] The word does not mean "comfort" (as in the KJV "Comforter") except in the old English understanding of someone who strengthens (from Latin, *confortare*, to strengthen; *fortis*, strong). "Counselor" (RSV, NIV) is a popular translation, but today its therapeutic connotations can be misleading. Rather, one must think of a "legal counselor." Thus the best translation is "Advocate" (NRSV), so that

10. Barrett, *John*, 451.

11. For summaries, see R. Brown, "The Paraclete in the Fourth Gospel," *NTS* 12 (1966–67): 113–32; G. Burge, *The Anointed Community*, 3–31, Morris, "Additional Note F: The Paraclete," *John*, 587–91.

12. The Gk. *parakletos* is related to the verb *parakaleo* and is similar in force to the participle, *ho parakeklemenos*.

13. Burge, *Anointed Community*, 14–15.

Jesus is pointing to the Spirit's judicial or legal service (see comments on 15:18–27; 16:7–11). Many scholars prefer to leave the word untranslated (though no modern translation has done so).

It is interesting that Jesus calls the Spirit *another* Paraclete. This should not be taken to mean that the Father will send "another person, namely, a Paraclete." First John 2:1 makes clear that John views Jesus also as a Paraclete ("But if anyone does sin, we have an *advocate* with the Father, Jesus Christ the righteous," NRSV, italics added)[14] Jesus is thus a Paraclete, who is now sending a second Paraclete. This means that the ongoing work of the Spirit will be a continuation of the work of Jesus during the disciples' lifetime.

In John's mind, this serves his "judicial" framework for the Gospel (see comments on John 5): Jesus has been on trial and like an advocate he has produced evidence and witnesses for the truth about God. The Paraclete, then, will pick up where Jesus leaves off. It is no surprise that he is also called "the Spirit of truth" (14:17; also 15:26; 16:13). He communicates the truth about God, which is the essence of God's work in Christ (1:17; 4:24; 5:33; 8:32, 40). Moreover, we know that Jesus is "the truth" (14:6), and inasmuch as the Spirit duplicates and sustains Jesus' work, he will continue to defend the truth of Jesus.

In John's Gospel, the world (14:17b, Gk. *kosmos*) refers to the human environment that is in rebellion against God (1:10; 3:16, 19; 7:7; 8:23; 12:31; 14:30) and in need of salvation (4:42; 6:14, 33, 51; 8:12). Like the Pharisees in chapter 9 who belong to this world, Jesus recognizes that such people cannot perceive or penetrate the deeper things of God, such as the mystery of the Holy Spirit (9:39). The disciples, however, can know the Spirit of truth because he (i.e., Jesus) has been with them all along—and will be in them in the future (i.e., in the Spirit).[15]

Jesus' Return to His Disciples (14:18–24)

JESUS HAS ALREADY reassured his followers that he will return in the drama of the Second Coming to rescue his disciples from this world (14:1–4). In the

---

14. Unfortunately the NIV disguises the use of *parakletos* in 1 John 2:1 with a dynamic paraphrase, "But if anybody does sin, we have *one who speaks* to the Father *in our defense*—Jesus Christ, the Righteous One." The italicized words represent the single Greek word *parakletos*.

15. John 14:17c, "for he *lives* with you and *will be* in you," hides a number of variants related to the tense of the two verbs, coming from the fact that *menei* (to dwell, abide) can either be future or present (when printed without accent marks, as in ancient manuscripts). Variants show: μένει (present)/ἔσται (future); μενεῖ (future)/ἔσται (future); μένει (present)/ἐστιν (present). The third option denies the later role of the Spirit. The second option denies Jesus is a Paraclete. The first draws a theological line between the functions of Jesus and that of the Spirit.

meantime (following his glorification), they will be empowered by the Spirit to sustain his mighty work in the world (14:12–17). Moreover, the Spirit will not be merely an ambiguous force coming upon them, but in a genuine way will sustain what they have loved about Jesus thus far. The Spirit-Paraclete will be "another" Paraclete, another presence who will recreate the person of Jesus within them.

But the crisis of the present moment still hangs heavy in the disciples' hearts. In the near term, what comfort will Jesus give in light of his imminent death? It is fine for Jesus to promise the Spirit, but it is Jesus whom they will miss. "I will come to you" (14:18b) means that Jesus will not leave them desolate (NIV "orphans").[16]

But does this refer to the coming of the Spirit (14:16–17)? The Second Coming (14:3)? Easter? Scholars have defended all three as possible answers.[17] Subtle clues, however, suggest that this is Jesus' coming after his resurrection on Easter. The time frame is specific ("before long"), and the disciples are to look for "that day" (14:20). Now it is not just a matter of the world failing to see him, but of the disciples having a private visual experience (14:19). Moreover this promise needs to be compared with 16:16–24, which uses similar language and makes the Easter promise specific. In other words, while from the world's perspective Jesus will disappear from view (in his death), in his resurrection he will return to them alone and validate that the power of the Father has been with him all along (14:20).

But the coming of Jesus on Easter will mean more than a mere return of Jesus to life. His aim is to establish the sort of intimacy and unity he has promised throughout the discourse. The oneness he enjoys with the Father (14:20a) parallels the oneness the disciples will enjoy with him (14:20b). *Thus the Easter return will be the bridge that will inaugurate the spiritual union Jesus wants with them.* The call to obedience (14:21) is similar to that given in 14:15 and is a clue that Jesus is speaking of a union that will include the coming of the Spirit. This is precisely what happens when on Easter Jesus appears to them and in that setting they receive his Spirit (20:22).

If the question of Jesus' return (after death) has now been clarified, Jesus has just connected another thought to it. Out of love for his disciples Jesus will "reveal" (14:21; NIV, show) himself to them, which will result in a profound spiritual union beyond the world's comprehension. The question of

---

16. In rabbinic Judaism, disciples who had lost their teacher were considered "orphans" (Brown, *John*, 2:640). The same was said for disciples of Greek teachers (e.g., Socrates).

17. Many critical scholars have argued that John has demythologized in 14:18 an original expectation of the Second Coming and converted it into an expectation for the Spirit. Thus (so it is argued) the verses are surrounded by two "Spirit sayings" (14:16, 26).

Judas (who is not Judas Iscariot)[18] presses Jesus on the nature of his appearance to the disciples (14:22), which will exclude the world. Surely, the disciples are thinking, the revelation of Jesus must happen *before the world* so that Jesus' testimony and indeed, their testimonies, will be validated publicly.

Again (for the third time) Jesus talks about obedience as a key to what is planned (14:23): Those who love Jesus show it by their fidelity to his word. Out of love, the Father and Jesus will come to them and make their home with them (14:23). But the reverse is also the case (14:24). Those who fail to invest faith in Jesus—who do not love him and refuse to obey him—are not connected either to Jesus or the Father (who is behind and within Jesus' words and mission) and so cannot share in this divine union.

The delicate play on words in chapter 14 should not be missed. Jesus "will come" to the disciples. This reality must be seen at three distinct points: Jesus' climactic second coming, his Easter return, and now his "coming" to them in the interior experience of the Holy Spirit. Moreover, in 14:2 we learned that Jesus will depart in order to make heavenly "rooms" (*monai*) for his followers. Later he will come and take them there (14:3). But when he returns at Easter ("before long," 14:19), he and the Father will reside within them, making a "home" (Gk. *mone*) within them (14:23). That is, the places of dwelling promised in 14:2 will be realized as places of "indwelling" in 14:23.

The Second Promise of the Spirit (14:25–31)

THE SECOND PROMISE of the Paraclete (14:25–26) brings further clarity to the role of the Spirit, since now he[19] is described specifically as the "Holy Spirit."[20] The Paraclete is without doubt the Spirit of God experienced in the lives of disciples. The rudimentary Trinitarian implications of 14:25–26 are

---

18. Besides Judas Iscariot, there were several other men named Judas in the New Testament. The two most important are: (1) Jude (the same name as Judas in Gk.), who was a brother of Jesus (Mark 6:3) and so was the brother of James. He likely penned the letter of Jude (see Jude 1). (2) Jude "of [son of?] James" mentioned in Luke's list of apostles (6:16). Since Matthew and Mark do not list this name among the Twelve, he is traditionally identified with Thaddaeus. Most view John's Judas in 14:22 as the apostle listed by Luke.

19. It is helpful to describe the work of the Spirit as "he." While "Spirit" is a neuter noun in Gk., Paraclete is masculine, and in 14:26 (also 15:26; 16:8, 14) John uses a masculine pronoun (*ekeinos*) with a neuter antecedent (*to pneuma to hagion*) to underscore the personal character of the Spirit. Most telling, in 16:13 *ekeinos* is used again without the noun *ho parakletos*. English provides no inclusive singular pronoun that bears this personal nuance intended by John. "It" cannot bring out this meaning.

20. A few manuscript variants omit "holy," while others read "Spirit of truth" (harmonizing the verse with 14:17). The present reading (NIV) is important since some scholars have refused to identify the Paraclete as the Holy Spirit (e.g., G. Johnston, *The Spirit-Paraclete in the Gospel of John* [Cambridge: Cambridge Univ. Press, 1970]).

---

inescapable: The Father will send the Spirit in the name of Jesus. Therefore this spiritual revelation promised by Jesus is in fact the effort of God himself (in every dimension) working for our benefit.

Jesus now emphasizes the conserving and teaching roles of the Spirit. The concept of "remembering" occurs multiple times in this Gospel (2:17, 22; 12:16; 14:26; 15:20; 16:4, 21) and is linked to the "misunderstanding" of the disciples. During the earthly ministry of Jesus, understanding was difficult. But now, Jesus promises, the Spirit-Paraclete will recall the things he has done and said and fix them in the minds of his followers.

We can see this at work in John's own Gospel. After Jesus cleansed the temple (2:13–23) John adds the editorial comment, "After he was raised from the dead, his disciples recalled what he had said. Then they believed the Scripture and the words that Jesus had spoken" (2:22). It was the resurrection—and its gift of the Spirit—that provided the meaning of Jesus' works. The inspiration of the Spirit, therefore, does not bring forward new revelations about Jesus, but simply gives correct applications and meanings for what he did in history.[21] Just as Jesus' primary work was revealing the Father (1:18), so now the work of the Spirit-Paraclete is revealing the "Jesus of history" to his followers.

The discourse of chapter 14 closes with words of reassurance similar to those offered at the beginning. "Peace" refers to the Hebrew greeting *shalom* and for Jesus refers to the aim of his work on earth: to restore the equilibrium and richness of humanity's relationship with God (Rom. 5:1).[22] Nothing in the world can offer such a gift. Jesus' *shalom* not only brings an end to the brokenness caused by sin, but it will be the fruit of the Spirit given when he departs. Thus when Jesus meets the disciples following his resurrection and gives them the Spirit, *shalom* is what he brings (20:19, 21, 26).

As in 14:1, Jesus mentions again that his disciples are troubled (14:27). Thus far his encouragement has described the benefits that his departure will bring: a new intimacy with God (and himself) wrought through the eschatological gift of the Spirit. Within the promise "I am going away and I am coming back to you" (14:28), the latter phrase is all that concerned the disciples. Now Jesus points to himself. Their love for him should lead to celebration because he is returning to where he began, to the Father. It is the Father who sent him, who gave him his words, and whose love for the world initiated Jesus' mission and the planned indwelling of the Spirit.

---

21. Barrett, *John*, 467. No doubt this "remembering" role of the Spirit was important for John in his production of the Gospel itself.

22. This *shalom* was prophesied as the achievement of the Messiah (see Isa. 9:6–7; 52:7; 57:19; Ezek. 37:26; Hag. 2:9; cf. Acts 10:36; Rom. 5:1; 14:7). As a result, it became a standard greeting among Christians (e.g., Rom. 1:7; 1 Cor. 1:3; 2 Cor. 1:2; Gal. 1:3).

To receive the Father's gifts is blessed; to return to live with the Giver is beyond comprehension.

Few verses have caused more controversy than 14:28b, "I am going to the Father, for the Father is greater than I." Controversy centers on the many places in this Gospel where the equality and oneness of Jesus and the Father (e.g., 1:1–18; 5:16–18; 10:30; 20:28) are juxtaposed to affirmations describing the dependence of the Son on the Father (4:34; 5:19–30; 8:29; 12:48–49). Theologians have often pointed to one set of verses at the expense of the other.[23] The phrase "is greater than" suggests (in some views) that Jesus simply cannot be God in the fullest sense, so that this verse has been used to deny the divinity of Christ.

Taken in isolation, this may appear to be the meaning of 14:28b; but if so, this verse jars the overwhelmingly divine portrait we have of Jesus in this Gospel. Making Jesus a lesser divinity or a lesser God would offend the solid Jewish monotheism of the Gospel. Making Jesus merely a human being loses the plain sense of his origin and unity with the Father in places such as the prologue, where incarnational Christology seems clear.

Classic exegesis has taken one of two paths out of this interpretative forest. Some interpreters have sought to make this "lesser" status refer to Jesus' humanity limited in the Incarnation (Augustine, Ambrose). Others have pointed to eternal distinctions between the Father and Son that do not compromise the Son's divinity. To use the language of another century, the Son is subordinate in person but not in essence (Tertullian, Athanasius). But these views owe more to later theological Trinitarian debates than the Gospel itself. Arguments about ontology are likely far from John's mind. There is no thought of the creation or subordination of the Son (despite Arian uses of the verse). The Father's greatness springs from his role as the origin and sender of Jesus, just as a ray of light might refer to the sun from which it came.

The word picture Jesus often uses to describe his life is the agent sent on a mission (17:4–5) and completing the assignments of his Sender (4:34; 5:30; 6:38–39; 9:4; 10:32, 37; 17:4). Within this agent/sender relationship, the originator of the mission has greater authority. In 13:16, Jesus cites the proverbial saying: "I tell you the truth, no servant is greater than his master, nor is a messenger greater than the one who sent him." Later he repeats it for his disciples, who will be *his* agents in the world (15:20).[24] As courier of God's message, as the agent devoted to divine service, Jesus is acknowl-

---

23. See T. E. Pollard, *Johannine Christology and the Early Church* (Cambridge: Cambridge Univ. Press, 1970); C. K. Barrett, "The Father Is Greater than I' (John 14:28): Subordinationist Christology in the New Testament," *Essays on John* (London: SPCK, 1982), 19–36.

24. Brown cites the Jewish *Midrash Rabbah* 78:1 on Gen. 32:27, "The sender is greater than the one sent" (*John*, 2:655).

edging the relationship, the source, of what has brought that message to life (14:24b, 31a).

Not only should the disciples take comfort and rejoice because Jesus is returning to his origin (and then sending gifts), but they should realize that the events unfolding in Jerusalem for him are not controlled by Satan (14:30). In fact, his specific description of these matters (14:29) should prove to encourage their faith because when they occur, the disciples will recall his words and see his predictions fulfilled (cf. Mark 14:41–42). Moreover, Jesus' obedience to God's plan (14:31a) within these events should be seen as an example of his love for the Father (a love, hopefully, every disciple will imitate, 14:21).

Following the discourse Jesus says, "Rise; let us leave" (14:31b). This verse presents a notorious problem since Jesus and his disciples do not leave. Jesus teaches for three more chapters. In fact, one can easily read 18:1 directly after 14:31 and build a coherent picture, "When he had finished praying, Jesus left with his disciples and crossed the Kidron Valley." Without the intervening chapters (chs. 15–17) the scene makes perfect sense: The discourse is found in chapter 14 and the group leaves for the Kidron Valley.

Scholars have offered various attempts to make sense of the literary problem, and few will satisfy every reader.[25] (1) Many critical scholars argue that at some point, chapters 13–17 were edited (by John? by his followers?); these scholars then rearrange John 13–17 so that 14:31 is followed by 18:1. Bultmann, for instance, rearranged the discourse thus: 13:1–30; 17; 13:31–35; 15; 16; 13:36–14:31. He noted that other literary "seams" were evident in the chapters (e.g., 16:5, where Jesus says that no one has asked him where he is going, but in 13:36 this was Peter's very question). Bultmann's rearrangement solves this problem too.

(2) Other scholars suggest that 14:1–31 was the original discourse and that John has expanded it with his own theological insights in chapters 15–16. This may explain why, perhaps, there is so much duplicate material in chapters 14 and 16. If John did this, it is apparent that he was not a skilled storyteller or else he would have removed the problem in 14:31. Haenchen likes the idea that 14:31 came to John from Mark 14:42 (a verse John wanted to use) but found that 18:1 blocked its way. Its placement at 14:31 was an "emergency" insertion.[26]

(3) The oldest solution is to take the text at face value. Even if editorial theories are correct, *someone* thought that the text in its present form made sense, and interpreting it in its present context is the exegetical task. (a) One

---

25. For an excellent summary of the options, see Carson, *John*, 477–79.
26. Haenchen, *John*, 2:164. The phrase is identical in both Mark and John.

view suggests that while Jesus tells his disciples to get up and go, they linger longer in the room. Therefore despite 14:31, chapters 15–17 take place in the Upper Room. But if this is so, why does John include 14:31 at all?

(b) Morris (following Lightfoot and Dodd) argues that the words "let us go" do not refer to a change of setting, but to a change of topic (e.g., "let's go on . . . "), a signal that Jesus is switching themes.[27] But this seems implausible.

(c) Others suggest that we should take the text as it is: Jesus does leave the room at 14:31, so that the words spoken in chapters 15–17 take place en route to the Kidron Valley. Perhaps Jesus even enters the temple and sees the golden vines on the temple gates, which then inspire his discourse in chapter 15 ("I am the vine . . . "). Westcott once made an eloquent case that the words of chapters 15–17 find their best setting in the temple (where in chapter 17 Jesus gives a priestly prayer).[28] If Jesus is in the temple following 14:31, the departure of 18:1 refers to his departing the temple as he climbs east into the Kidron Valley.

THE APPLICATION OF chapter 14 is significant since for the first time in this Gospel, Jesus speaks in detail to his followers concerning their experience in the church following his departure. Of course throughout the Gospel we have been able to bridge themes that arose during Jesus' ministry and apply them to the current setting. But here we have something different. This chapter is filled with promises addressed directly to the community of faith, not to the leadership of Jerusalem or to audiences in Galilee. Jesus is now anticipating that the community he has built, a community centered on his twelve apostles, will continue his work when he is gone.

A number of theological themes spring from this chapter, each of which could become a starting point for long excurses on numerous subjects (such as Jesus, the Spirit, eschatological hope, and salvation).[29] Our first challenge is to distill them into units that will make sense for a clear presentation of their key themes. Three general areas of inquiry seem evident:

The departure of Jesus. Jesus speaks openly and honestly about his departure. Throughout the Synoptic Gospels and indeed here in John, Jesus has continued to say that he will die on the cross; this event will be a dramatic return to the Father. Jesus affirms what he has said throughout this Gospel:

---

27. Morris, *John,* 587.

28. Westcott, *John,* 2:238.

29. See the lengthy exposition by D. A. Carson, *The Farewell Discourse and the Final Prayer of Jesus An Exposition of John 14–17* (Grand Rapids: Baker, 1970).

His death will not be a tragedy orchestrated either by men who desire to stop him or by Satan, who thinks that by using Judas like a pawn he has foiled God's plan; but it will be a glorious return to God the Father. As we have heard elsewhere in John, this death should be described as Jesus' "glorification."

But here in chapter 14 Jesus tells us something about his aims: He is going to prepare a place (a "room") for us. Immediately this means that we need to have a different perspective on the "dwellings" we possess in this world. Jesus has gone ahead of us, and there is now something ready for us. The implications of such a teaching are profound and timely. Our perspective on this world as well as on the eternal life God has prepared for us both come into view.

But if Jesus is indeed someone who can return to the Father and make a place for us, then this leads naturally to reflections about his identity and the access he can provide to these heavenly dwelling places. The flow of the discourse, including the successive questions of Peter, Thomas, Philip, and Judas, all point in this same direction. If heaven is Jesus' destination and if this heavenly work is Jesus' mandate, then who is Jesus? What is the nature of his divine power and influence? To what degree is God himself present in him? Such questions lead immediately to the next field in reflection.

The identity of Jesus. This chapter invites us to think deeply about the identity of Jesus and his relation to the Father. This is the direction of Philip's thinking in 14:8. Discerning that Jesus is offering more than simply knowledge about God and the way to heaven, Philip pursues the subsequent reflection. Is Jesus substantially different than the rest of us? Or is he simply a wise leader who can show the way to heaven? We discover (and it came no doubt as some surprise to Philip and his fellow disciples) that fellowship with Jesus was a prerequisite for fellowship with the Father. To see Jesus is to see the Father.

Jesus is therefore not making a claim simply to possess some functional equivalence with the Father, saying in effect that he is doing what the Father does, so that to participate with him is to participate in the Father's work. No, Jesus is saying more. Resident within his person is some aspect of the Father's life, some feature of divine reality that sets him apart. *It is not simply that Jesus is sent on a divine mission on behalf of the Father, but that the Father himself is on a divine mission in the life of his Son.* In 14:10 Jesus explicitly says that the Father is *living in* him. This exploration of the Father and Jesus is a direct working out of the implications of the prologue of the gospel.

> In the beginning was the Word, and the Word was with God, and the Word was God.... The Word became flesh and made his dwelling among us. We have seen his glory, the glory of the One and Only, who came from the Father, full of grace and truth. (1:1, 14)

Later in the chapter a final step is taken. Jesus tells us about his obedience to God's will, his fidelity to God's word, and a union of profound intimacy between them. But then another feature is included. The Spirit is likewise a part of this union, and the Spirit's indwelling in the believer will create a unity between God and the Christian that reflects the intimacy between Father and Son. While many of us in the church find discussions of the Trinity opaque and confusing, here in John 14 we cannot miss the basic elements of Trinitarian thought implicit in this description of God. Jesus is promising not simply to fill his disciples with the Spirit, but to come to the disciples himself and there take residence.

To sum up, the Father is resident in the life of the Son, and the Son will return to his disciples in the form of the Spirit. Jesus can say in 14:23 that both Father and Son together will indwell the disciple. These are profound contributions to our understanding of God.

Jesus' return. The third area of thought concerns Jesus' return to his followers. Throughout John 14 Jesus brings comfort to his disciples by reassuring them of his imminent return. But in our exegesis we had to wrestle with the timing of this return (vv. 1–3, 18, and 23). When Jesus says, "I will come again," is he referring to his Second Coming? To Easter? Or to his coming in the Holy Spirit? We noted that Jesus makes all three affirmations. Thus any application of this subject of "Jesus' coming" must explore each of these themes carefully.

(1) *The promise of the Second Coming.* The promise of the Second Coming appears throughout the Johannine literature both explicitly (21:22; 1 John 4:17) and implicitly (when Jesus refers to the resurrection on the last day, John 6:54; 11:24–27). We can also find this theme in the Synoptic Gospels, which describe Jesus' "appearing" (Gk. *parousia*) to his followers at the end of time (Matt. 24:3, 27, 37–44; Luke 17:26–35). Any treatment of John 14 must embrace some sense of Jesus' eschatological vision for his disciples. Their comfort will not simply be found in a newfound strength to endure the things of the world (a strength found in the Spirit). Jesus also says that some day he will "come again" and take us to himself (14:3).

(2) *Jesus' death.* The most pressing immediate concern for the disciples is the threat of death that Jesus describes so clearly. Here he says confidently that he will return "before long" so that they can see him. The appearance of Jesus in the Upper Room following the cross is one of the most important events in Christian history. Jesus' return from an empty grave is the bedrock of early Christian testimony. It is found not only in the Synoptic Gospels (Matt. 28:1–10; Mark 16:1–8; Luke 24:1–9; cf. John 20:1–18) but also in Paul in virtually a creedal form (1 Cor. 15:1–6). The promise of Jesus' coming at the end of time took faith. The promise of Jesus' coming in the Spirit may

have seemed ambiguous and open to interpretation. But here in this promise, Jesus provides objective, concrete proof that validates his identity and power. Any attempt to defend the divine power of Jesus Christ today does well if it begins here.

(3) *The Holy Spirit.* The climax of the chapter describes the "coming" of Jesus in the Holy Spirit. As we saw in the Original Meaning section, the "rooms" of heaven in 14:2 parallel the "home" built by the Son and Father in the disciple's life (14:23). In other words, the Christian experience of the Holy Spirit cannot be viewed apart from an experience of Jesus. In theological jargon, our pneumatology (doctrine of the Spirit) must have a Christological basis. To experience the Spirit is to experience Jesus. While this may seem to be of peripheral value, its theological ramifications are profound, and they are in desperate need of clarity in the church today.

This experience of the Spirit promised by Jesus also points to benefits that are truly astounding. Believers will sustain the miraculous works of Jesus (14:12), they will have intimacy with God in prayer (14:13–14), and they will recall God's word with conviction (14:25; 1 John 2:22–27)—all with the aid of the Spirit. A brief perusal of the book of Acts shows that this is exactly the profile of the earliest Christians, and it is safe to assume that this must have been the experience of the believers in John's church. Christians were reproducing not merely the work of Jesus; they were continuing the *presence of Jesus* in the world. Perhaps we could put it this way: As the Son incarnated the Father's presence in the world, so now the Spirit brings the Son's presence into the world through the life of the believer.

These three themes have sweeping importance for the church today. We live in an age that is eager for spiritual experiences. John 14 provides us with guidance on how to interpret and understand them.

IN THE CONTEMPORARY Significance section of John 1:18–51, I referred to the testing of biblical and theological literacy we at Wheaton College have done on the incoming freshmen. We as professors were delighted by our incoming students' zeal for the Lord but were surprised at their illiteracy about the stories of the Bible and the classic doctrines of the Christian faith. I mention this here again because as I think about the contemporary significance of John 14, I sense the temptation to pursue the promises of this chapter without examining the theological structures that undergird them.

We live in an age that is eager for experience. Sermons are often measured by the "emotional work" that can be done in twenty minutes. The comment "that was a great service" can easily refer to the worship band. Preaching themes are often filtered through therapeutic categories, and for many Christians, the final validity of the Christian walk is not what I believe (a cognitive category) or how I live (a moral imperative) but what I have experienced. All three are an essential part of the Christian life. John 14 invites us to have profound experiences with Christ-in-Spirit, but it also instructs us in how to think rightly about Jesus and the Spirit.

The departure of Jesus. John 14:1 is often used at a funeral. "Do not let your hearts be troubled. Trust in God; trust also in me." In one respect this is not a precise use of 14:1–2 since Jesus is actually saying that the solution to the disciples' despair will be found in his dramatic second coming.[30] But there is another sense in which it is appropriate. Jesus expects his followers to have a confidence in his power that is equal to their confidence in God. His departure is not simply an exodus from humanity, it is a continuation of his work on behalf of humanity. *Jesus then has a postresurrection ministry and authority.* He will be glorified above all creation and seated on God's right hand (Rom. 8:34; Heb. 1:3; 10:12). From this position he serves on our behalf. "I am going there to prepare a place for you" is a promise that his work will continue until we are united with him for eternity in heaven.

It is valuable to look carefully at the words of 14:2. The passage does not mean that these rooms need to be built, for the Father's house has these rooms already (14:2a). Rather, it is *in Jesus' returning* to the Father (a departure through the cross) that *the way* to these rooms will be constructed. And it is *in his arrival* there that the place will be prepared completely for us. Our experience of coming to this place will be one of overwhelming gratefulness to God's grace for bringing us there. We will not take pride in any private residence, but will discover that this residing is a life that is invited into the residence, the presence, the "rooms" of Jesus *himself*. Prepared rooms are rooms where Jesus lives, which are the places he desires us to enter.

As noted above, the word translated "rooms" does not refer to the quality of the place Jesus is preparing (as in the KJV, "mansions"). The concern on the hearts of the disciples is their loss of Jesus' fellowship. The "room" in Greek refers to an abode, a place of residence, a place "with your name on it." Jesus is saying to them (and to us) that heaven is awaiting our arrival. The experience of heaven will not be merely one of bliss, but it will be one of fellowship when Jesus renews his presence with us.

Possessing such an anticipation for heaven builds in us what I call an eternal vantage point. I live in a world that continually offers me temporal securities and comforts, a world that keeps my eye on the near horizon of the

---

30. Carson, *John*, 487.

present, that denies the limitations of my own mortality. My "life of work" aims not simply to make a contribution to my career, but to provide a means of security in the world: a home, a stable income, an investment scheme, a retirement program. While Jesus is clear that these securities are foolish and unreliable (Matt. 6:19–20; Luke 12:31–21), here he offers a positive incentive. Our true home, our complete security has already been built for us by him in heaven. Once we embrace the significance of this notion, our attitudes toward this world completely change.

Perhaps this is why some of the most creative and thoughtful conversations I have ever had have been with the senior members of my church. These are men and women in their late seventies and eighties who are firm in their faith and aware—very aware—that their hope rests in the Lord and nowhere else. John 14:1–3 are key verses for them. They possess this "eternal vantage," and when I ask them to think about the many years of their life, they always say that they wish they had this eternal perspective when they were younger. "I would have spent more time giving and less time acquiring," one friend told me. This is an eternal perspective that has put a check on our investment in earthly rooms.

Jesus and the Father. I believe that John's deepest desire is for us to see that Jesus is the revealer of God and in this revelation, to find life. This is not the same as saying that Jesus had wisdom that unveiled the inner workings of God (although this is true). Nor is it the same as saying that Jesus lived a life so attuned to God that simply by imitating him, we might know God (although this is true too). *Jesus does not show us the way to the Father; rather, Jesus is the way to the Father.* We have to pause to let the nuance of this idea settle in.

In a world of religious pluralism, anyone making an exclusive truth claim will find opponents who will object not necessarily to the religious system offered, but to the *exclusivity* of any such claim. In general our age views all religious systems as offering variations on the same theme. Judaism, Islam, Hinduism, Christianity, Taoism—all religious systems possess historical, cultural accretions that must be removed as dispensable byproducts, but essentially they point the way to God through principles of belief (the oneness and goodness of God) and life (charity and love). But to stand in one of these traditions and affirm that there is something ultimate, something unrepeatable, something unparalleled is offensive to the reasoning of our day.

But this is precisely the truth claim we have in Christianity. Jesus does not merely point the way, he is the Way. Jesus does not just teach us truth, he is the Truth. He does not represent one avenue to life, he is the Life. This is an exclusive claim that cannot be compromised. In a word, the human quest for God ends in Jesus Christ. There are those who with Philip might say, "I wish

God would just show himself! This would end the spiritually debilitating ambiguity of life." To such people the answer is: God *has* shown himself; God *has* spoken—in Jesus.[31] Even Bultmann in his critical study of John's Gospel saw this same absolute claim in John 14:

> The implication behind the reproachful question [of Philip] is that all fellowship with Jesus loses its significance unless he is recognized as the one whose sole intention is to reveal God, and not to be anything for himself; but it also implies that the possibility of seeing God is inherent in the fellowship with Jesus. What need is there for anything further?[32]

The theological idea that anchors this belief—and this is the important point—is that God *himself* was in Christ. The Word was not a creature (as we are). There was not a time "when he did not exist," and so he shares in the same substance (or essence or being) as God himself. Of course, I am using the language of the first council of the church (Nicea, A.D. 325), but I argue that it is not an anachronism to press this language back into John. It was the image of Jesus given in John (and elsewhere in the New Testament) that presented the Christological dilemma that Nicea tried to articulate.[33] "He who has seen me has seen the Father." Throughout the chapter Jesus is pictured as enjoying an intimate unity with the Father (14:10, 20, 21, 23)—a unity not just of purpose, but of "essence."

Therefore the exclusive claim of Christianity about Christ is *not* centered on our belief that Jesus was right about God. It is centered on our claim that God was fully present in Christ to reconcile the world to himself (2 Cor. 5:18). It is the theological claim *about* Jesus that makes the spiritual claims of Jesus potent. Jesus' words are right because those words are God's words (14:10b). Jesus "way" is not superior because it promotes a higher ethic or because it champions values that resonate with our spiritual sensitivities. Jesus' way is true because *in him* we find God drawing us to himself.

A young woman told me recently that for her Christianity was true— Jesus was true—because she had experienced him as true in her heart. I asked what would happen if these feelings of certainty went away. She

---

31. G. Fee, "Expository Article. John 14:18–17," *Int* 43 (1989): 170–74.

32. Bultmann, *John*, 608–9; also cited in Smalley, *John*, 253.

33. At the Council of Nicea, Arians, fearing the compromise of monotheism, argued that Christ was one of God's creatures ("There was a time when he was not"). Athanasius and the majority of the church rejected this, arguing that Christ shared the same eternal "essence" (*homoousios*) as the Father. Today these same Arian claims are made by Jehovah's Witnesses. See W. Harding, "An Examination of Passages Cited by the Jehovah's Witnesses to Deny Jesus Is God," in R. L. Harris, ed., *Interpretation and History* (Singapore: Christian Life, 1986), 273–80.

admitted quietly, "I guess I would not be very sure about God if that happened." The validity of spiritual truth cannot be found entirely in spiritual experience. There is an objective reality here ("You have seen the Father!"). John knows this well, and as he writes his first letter, he affirms again and again that the basis of our faith is "that which was from the beginning," "that which we have heard . . . seen . . . looked at . . . touched" (1 John 1:1; 2:7, 13, 14, 24; 3:8, 11; 2 John 1:5, 6). The objective historical reality of Christ supplies our confidence in our knowledge of the truth and the certainty of our spiritual pursuits.

Our survey of evangelical college students has a parallel in the similar surveys of David Wells at Gordon-Conwell Theological Seminary.[34] Young seminarians reflect the same reluctance to embrace absolute theological truth claims. Many of us in the church need to pause and take notice of the results. The exclusive and absolute claim of Christ anchored in an incarnational theology may be slipping from evangelical thinking. Nothing could be further from the truth in John's mind in John 14.

Jesus is coming. If John 14 has an organizing idea, it may be found in 14:18: "I will not leave you orphans; I will come to you." Throughout the chapter Jesus is assuring his followers that whatever may occur in their experience in the world, they will never be on their own. They will not be left desolate. He will continue to shepherd them and protect them. Of course, the immediate occasion for their worry is the threat of Jesus' arrest and death, which he is willing to accept as God's will. But threaded throughout the discourse, Jesus says, in effect, "I will come again," in three different contexts (14:1–3, 14:18, and 14:23).

(1) The Second Coming. Many interpreters agree that when Jesus refers to his return in 14:1–3, he is referring to the Second Coming.[35] That is, these verses fit with the descriptions in the Synoptic Gospels describing the triumphant return of Jesus at the end of time. It is significant that in 14:3 Jesus does not simply promise his return, but adds, "I will come back *and take you to be with me* that you also may be where I am" (italics added). Jesus' return will encompass a reunion with his disciples and a departure that escorts them to another place, where Jesus is.

Older conservative writers with an interest in dispensational eschatology have suggested that 14:1–3 may refer to the Rapture, the dramatic end-time removal of the church described by Paul (1 Thess. 4:12–18; 2 Thess. 2:1;

---

34. D. Wells, *No Place for Truth or Whatever Happened to Evangelical Theology* (Grand Rapids: Eerdmans, 1993).

35 Some have suggested that it may refer to Jesus' coming to the believer at his death (Lightfoot, *John*, 275–76; Bultmann, *John*, 602) or that it is simply an ambiguous "coming" at any time (Barrett, *John*, 157).

cf. 1 Cor. 15:23).[36] Curiously, few (if any) evangelical commentators note this.[37] While 14:3 does not provide any detail, it does dovetail with Paul in one respect: When Jesus returns, the rescue of his followers will be one of his first aims. The description of eschatological "removal" in Luke 17:34–35 even uses the same verb (and tense) as in John 14:3 ("[I will] take you").[38]

For many of us, the notion of the Second Coming has evolved from being a longed-for experience and has instead become a doctrine we defend and teach.[39] In the 1960s and 1970s this hope flamed brightly. In 1978 American newspaper editors were asked by *The People's Almanac* to consider what would be the most sensational headline they could write. "Jesus Returns to Earth" was their answer.[40] One wonders if this answer would be the same today.

My experience among young people in their twenties is that they hold a sense of historical despair equal to any in the 1960s: War, population, environmental crises, infectious disease, and moral decline are some of the items they will check off quickly. Oddly, when asked to describe their hope in this apparent "mess," the "blessed hope" of the Second Coming rarely comes to view. Jesus' promise is that he will come, that he will return to save his church and rescue his followers. This teaching needs to be revitalized in the church today.

(2) *The empty tomb.* Jesus' promise to return from the grave is another central belief for the church. Paul could not be more firm when he writes, "If there is no resurrection of the dead, then not even Christ has been raised. And if Christ has not been raised, our preaching is useless and so is your faith" (1 Cor. 15:13–14). In John 14:18ff. Jesus' resurrection is not merely a display of his divine power over death, but it is motivated by his interest in coming to his followers and aiding them. While the resurrection is a step in Jesus' glorification and return to the Father, it also provides an opportunity for him to meet with his disciples, encourage them, and equip them. Disciples today need to have a confident grasp of the meaning of this return. In virtually every sermon in the book of Acts, Jesus' return from the grave lies at the center (e.g., Acts 2:24, 32; 3:7, 15; 4:10; 5:30; 7:37; 10:40; 13:22, 30, 33–34, 37; 17:31; 26:8).

(3) *The Holy Spirit.* The chief thrust of Jesus' teaching lies here. The "coming of Jesus" will also be experienced in the "coming" of the Spirit (14:23).

---

36. J. N. Darby, *Lectures on the Second Coming* (London: Broom, 1869), 10; L. S. Chafer, *The Kingdom in History and Prophecy* (Chicago: Moody, 1915, 1944), 87; J. W. Hodges, *Christ's Kingdom and Coming* (Grand Rapids: Eerdmans, 1957), 195–96.

37. In addition to the major commentaries, note its absence in S Travis, *I Believe in the Second Coming of Jesus* (London: Hodder, 1982), 99–100.

38. G. Beasley-Murray, *Jesus and the Future* (London: Macmillan, 1954), 237.

39. See recently, C. Blomberg, "Eschatology and the Church: Some New Testament Perspectives," *Themelios* 23.3 (1998): 3–26

40. Travis, *I Believe in the Second Coming,* 100.

Yet in a manner similar to the other themes we have explored, there are crucial theological issues that affect our experience. Jesus promises that we will receive the Holy Spirit (14:16) and then goes on to promise that he and the Father will indwell his followers (14:23). What are the implications of these thoughts?

(a) We have seen that God *himself* was in Christ restoring and loving the world. Christ was not a courier sent on a mission to change God's mind; Christ came from the Father to express God's mind. Therefore the divinity of Jesus (the ontological unity of Christ and the Father) cannot be compromised. Now in a parallel manner, we see that the Spirit is not an independent agent sent on a mission to equip and inspire us. The Holy Spirit is God's Spirit; the Holy Spirit ushers to us the presence of Father and Son to indwell us and to share fellowship with us. Hence, as God was at work on the cross in Christ to save us, so now God is at work in the Spirit to transform us. I cannot underscore sufficiently how important this is. God is on our side. He is at work renewing us and loving us. This is the gospel.

(b) John 14 has been in one of the most difficult controversies in church history, one that in 1054 split the Eastern Orthodox Church from the Western Roman Church. Here we can only skim its surface. In a word, does the Spirit come from the Father, or does it come from the Father and the Son together? In John 14:16, 26 Jesus says that the Father will send the Spirit. In 15:26; 16:7–8 Jesus says that he will send the Spirit. Which is it? The East argued it was the Father alone; the West argued that it must be the Father *and the Son* (and so a pope in Rome changed the Nicene Creed and was promptly denounced by Orthodox bishops).[41]

Rather than an arcane theological squabble, much was (and is) at stake. The East preferred to see the Spirit as an independent person, coming directly from the Father. As Irenaeus put it, the Son and the Spirit are the two separate hands of God at work.[42] But this distinction came at the expense of showing how the Father, Son, and Spirit were unified and how the Son plays an indispensable role in the Spirit's work. Where has this led? According to some, it can inspire a "Christless mysticism," in which the Spirit is an inspiration apart from Jesus.[43] It can also lead to more radical theologies that seek

---

41. This change in the West resulted in the changing of the Nicene Creed so that in Catholic and Protestant churches it reads, " . . . and we believe in the Holy Spirit, who proceedeth from the Father *and the Son*." The phrase "and the Son" (in Latin, *filioque*) was the medieval addition.

42. *Against Heresies*, 2.1.1.

43. K. Barth, referring to Russian Orthodoxy, *Church Dogmatics* I:1 (Edinburgh: T. & T. Clark, 1975), 481; cited by T. Smail, *The Giving Gift: The Holy Spirit in Person* (London: Hodder, 1988), 125.

a spirituality apart from Jesus, a spirituality that seeks to unite with other world religions. It is also evident today in some charismatic/Pentecostal theologies, in which the Spirit is distinguished from Jesus as a subsequent experience—theologies that promote inspiration and illumination quite apart from the Jesus of history.[44]

The West (going back to Augustine) objected to this view. The Father begets the Son and together the Son and the Father breathe out the Holy Spirit. In this, the Father wins the priority, but still, the Son cannot be separated from the Spirit. The Father and the Son are *one*—and so the Spirit cannot glorify the one without the other. This means that one cannot claim to have the Spirit without having the Son. One does not have a complete Christian experience if he or she embraces the Son and has not had a life-transforming experience in the Spirit. This theological squabble means everything for how we understand, experience, and interpret the Spirit. How deeply is the Spirit connected to the person of Jesus?

But there is perhaps an easy way to reconcile this tension on the origins of the Spirit. In Great Britain, there is a train called the Flying Scotsman, which runs between Edinburgh, Scotland, and King's Cross Station, London. It also passes through a number of other English cities. In watching this famous train arrive at King's Cross, you could say "The Flying Scotsman has just come from Edinburgh," or you could say "This train has come from Edinburgh and York," or "This train has come from Edinburgh through York." All three statements are true.[45]

John 14 urges us to see the Spirit as intimately tied to Jesus. The Spirit is *another* Paraclete, continuing the work of Jesus (14:16). The Spirit is dependent completely on Jesus' glorification before he can come (7:37–39; 16:7). Even each of the numerous tasks of the Spirit as outlined in John 14–16 have direct parallels in the life of Jesus in the Gospel.[46] As the disciples come to the Upper Room on Easter day, it is the breath of Jesus that conveys to them the Holy Spirit (20:22), indicating that this Spirit is his Spirit indwelling them.

The unity of Jesus and the Spirit means that we should not talk about receiving Jesus without incorporating some notion of receiving the Spirit. To receive Jesus, to "have Jesus in your heart," is to experience the Spirit dwelling within. And charismatics likewise should not promote a "two-stage" doctrine that in some manner offers the Spirit as something subsequent to Jesus.

---

44. Of course, Orthodox theologians are sensitive to these criticisms and argue that their view of the Trinity does not demand this result. Moreover, the excesses that thrive in the West are the result of Protestant thought that has united Jesus and the Spirit!

45. This explanation was given first by Michael Ramsay, former Archbishop of Canterbury. See T. Smail, *The Giving Gift*, 138

46. For a list see Burge, *The Anointed Community*, 140–42.

The work of the Spirit-Paraclete is to usher to our hearts the ongoing life and presence of Jesus-in-Spirit.

To have this Spirit is to have the catalogue of gifts listed in this chapter. Powerful works (14:12), effective prayer (14:13), and the peace of God (14:27) all deserve careful application today. But this does not mean that the work of the modern minister will exceed the work of Jesus. As remarkable as this thought sounds, such a view is often heard among certain African Pentecostal leaders, who claim supernatural power superior to Christ. This is not Jesus' point. It is the distribution of his powers to the wider world that facilitates a remarkable outpouring of mighty works (promised in 14:12).

A quick glance at the church in Acts shows that the earliest Christians took these promises to heart and experienced these gifts as they lived in the power of the Spirit. But among these John directly connects the coming of the Spirit with the preservation of Jesus' word (14:25–26). Jesus says that the Spirit "will teach you all things and will remind you of everything I have said to you." Does this refer to the historical reminiscences of the apostles as they protected and recorded the words of Jesus? Did John experience this as he wrote his Gospel? Does this refer to the Spirit's work in providing us with the inspired Scriptures we treasure today? Or does this refer to the inner illumination of the Spirit as we work within God's Word, delving deeply into its meaning?

No doubt John would say "yes" to each of these. The Spirit in 14:25–26 is a conserving, recalling power in the church. As Jesus faithfully spoke the words given to him by the Father, the Spirit faithfully recalls Jesus' words, never deviating from the things he taught. New ideas, therefore, new spiritual "insights" must always be tested against the historic revelation we have in the Gospels (cf. 1 John 2:22–27).

John 15:1–16:4a

I AM THE TRUE vine, and my Father is the gardener. [2]He cuts off every branch in me that bears no fruit, while every branch that does bear fruit he prunes so that it will be even more fruitful. [3]You are already clean because of the word I have spoken to you. [4]Remain in me, and I will remain in you. No branch can bear fruit by itself; it must remain in the vine. Neither can you bear fruit unless you remain in me.

[5]"I am the vine; you are the branches. If a man remains in me and I in him, he will bear much fruit; apart from me you can do nothing. [6]If anyone does not remain in me, he is like a branch that is thrown away and withers; such branches are picked up, thrown into the fire and burned. [7]If you remain in me and my words remain in you, ask whatever you wish, and it will be given you. [8]This is to my Father's glory, that you bear much fruit, showing yourselves to be my disciples.

[9]"As the Father has loved me, so have I loved you. Now remain in my love. [10]If you obey my commands, you will remain in my love, just as I have obeyed my Father's commands and remain in his love. [11]I have told you this so that my joy may be in you and that your joy may be complete. [12]My command is this: Love each other as I have loved you. [13]Greater love has no one than this, that he lay down his life for his friends. [14]You are my friends if you do what I command. [15]I no longer call you servants, because a servant does not know his master's business. Instead, I have called you friends, for everything that I learned from my Father I have made known to you. [16]You did not choose me, but I chose you and appointed you to go and bear fruit—fruit that will last. Then the Father will give you whatever you ask in my name. [17]This is my command: Love each other.

[18]"If the world hates you, keep in mind that it hated me first. [19]If you belonged to the world, it would love you as its own. As it is, you do not belong to the world, but I have chosen you out of the world. That is why the world hates you. [20]Remember the words I spoke to you: 'No servant is greater than his master.' If they persecuted me, they will persecute you also. If they obeyed my teaching, they will obey yours

also. [21]They will treat you this way because of my name, for they do not know the One who sent me. [22]If I had not come and spoken to them, they would not be guilty of sin. Now, however, they have no excuse for their sin. [23]He who hates me hates my Father as well. [24]If I had not done among them what no one else did, they would not be guilty of sin. But now they have seen these miracles, and yet they have hated both me and my Father. [25]But this is to fulfill what is written in their Law: 'They hated me without reason.'

[26]"When the Counselor comes, whom I will send to you from the Father, the Spirit of truth who goes out from the Father, he will testify about me. [27]And you also must testify, for you have been with me from the beginning.

[16] [1]"All this I have told you so that you will not go astray. [2]They will put you out of the synagogue; in fact, a time is coming when anyone who kills you will think he is offering a service to God. [3]They will do such things because they have not known the Father or me. [4]I have told you this, so that when the time comes you will remember that I warned you.

IN CHAPTER 14 the answer to Jesus' departure was resolved in the assurance of his coming, that he would not leave his disciples desolate (14:18). In chapter 15 Jesus' theme is no longer "coming" but "remaining." He paints an intricate picture of a vine trimmed by its gardener that produces generous fruit. He applies this image to his disciples, charging them to remain vitally attached to him so that they may produce the fruit borne of love and obedience. The twin themes of this image are mysticism and fruit-bearing.

Jesus is looking at the lives of the believers who will live in the world following his departure (the church). His interest here is not dissimilar to that in John 14. The interior life of intimacy with God described in 14:23 is now posed in a new form: "Remain in me, and I will remain in you" (15:4a). In order to sustain a genuine spiritual life in the world, believers must remain intimately attached to Christ.

If it is true that the disciples will be in the world personally connected to God in the Spirit, Jesus also warns them about the conflicts they will have with the world. Chapter 15 shifts abruptly to a second subject in verse 18, a theme that continues to 16:4. Here the controlling motif is in 15:20: "No servant is greater than his master." If Jesus experienced hostility and trial in the world, the same will be true of his followers. Nevertheless, in this trial Jesus has given them an Advocate—the Spirit-Paraclete (15:26)—who will strengthen their witness and keep them from falling away. This is Jesus' third promise of the Spirit (14:16, 26; 15:26).

Another way to organize the chapter is to see it as outlining the relationships of the believer: With Christ there is a relationship of *remaining* (15:1–11); with fellow believers there is a relationship of *love* (15:12–17); with the world there is a relationship of *hostility* (15:18–25, 16:1–4a); and with the Spirit there is a relationship of *cowitness* (15:26–27).[1] This has a slightly different topical arrangement but follows the main outline given below.

The Vine and the Branches (15:1–17)

THE FORM OF the vineyard metaphor is comparable to the story Jesus tells in chapter 10. There Jesus took the image of a shepherd and transformed it into a parabolic saying to describe his own life and work. Here Jesus takes the image of a vineyard and transforms it into an extended metaphor (15:1–8), followed by an interpretation and application (15:9–11).[2]

What prompts Jesus to use this image? His figures (shepherd, bread, water, light) all came from ancient Jewish traditions. If Jesus left the Upper Room in 14:30, he may have stopped at the temple to teach and to pray (not entering the Kidron Valley until 18:1).[3] At the entrance of the Holy Place (west of the altar), steps led to a linen curtain covered with purple, scarlet, and blue flowers (Josephus, *Ant.* 15.394; *Wars* 5:207–14). Solid gold chains hung alongside the curtain from the door beam. Above the curtain (beneath the roof line) grew a gigantic grapevine of pure gold, representing Israel (*Ant.* 15.395). Wealthy citizens could bring gifts to add to the vine (gold tendrils, grapes, or leaves), and these would be added by metal workers to the ever-growing vine (*m. Middoth* 3:8). Josephus claims that some of the grape clusters were the "height of a man."[4]

---

1. C. J. Laney, "Abiding Is Believing: The Analogy of the Vine in John 15:1–6," *BSac* 146 (1989): 55–66

2. Scholars are divided on how to divide the parable and its interpretation (vv. 7, 8, and 9 are all suggested). R. Bauckham believes that unlike the shepherd story in John 10, chapter 15 does not contain the parable at all, but only its interpretation. He thinks a fragment of the original parable may be found in the *Acts of Thomas* 146. "The Parable of the Vine: Rediscovering a Lost Parable of Jesus," *NTS* 33.1 (1987): 84–101.

3. This would be possible since Passover was the only night when the gates of Jerusalem and the temple were kept open all night to serve the many pilgrims.

4. Josephus says that when the Romans sacked the temple in A.D. 70, the amount of gold taken from its precincts was so great that it depressed the value of gold in Syria by half (*Wars*, 6.316–18). See C. T. R. Hayward, *The Jewish Temple: A Non-Biblical Sourcebook* (New York: Routledge, 1996).

The vine and the vineyard were old and sacred images in Judaism (as in most Mediterranean societies). The vine represented the covenant people of God, planted and tended by him so that Israel would produce fruit (Ps. 80:8–18; Isa. 5:1–7; Jer. 2:21; 12:10–11; Ezek. 15:1–5; 17:1–6; 19:10–15; Hos. 10:1–2). Generally in the Old Testament when Israel is depicted as a vine or vineyard, the nation is being chastised for not bearing fruit as God expects. The following two passages are representative:

Restore us, O God Almighty;
>make your face shine upon us,
>that we may be saved.
You brought a vine out of Egypt;
>you drove out the nations and planted it.
You cleared the ground for it,
>and it took root and filled the land. (Ps. 80:7–9)

Now you dwellers of Jerusalem and men of Judah,
>judge between me and my vineyard.
What more could I have done for my vineyard
>than I have done for it?
When I looked for good grapes,
>why did it yield only bad?
Now I will tell you
>what I am going to do to my vineyard.
I will take away its hedge,
>and it will be destroyed;
I will break down its wall,
>and it will be trampled. (Isa. 5:3–5)

The vineyard image continued to be a favorite in Judaism and appears in much of its literature (and even on its coins) in the New Testament period (Sir. 24:17–21). Jesus likewise used it regularly as a teaching device (Matt. 20:1–7; 21:28; Mark 12:1–11; Luke 13:6–7). But here in John 15 he makes a departure. In his final "I am" saying in this Gospel, Jesus declares that *he* is the true vine (15:1). That is, in this ancient imagery he has taken the place of Israel as God's true planting.[5] The new concept is that God's vineyard holds *one vine* and Israel must inquire if it is attached to him. No longer is Israel automatically seen as vines growing in God's vineyard. Men and women are now branches growing from one stock.

As in the Old Testament picture, God is eager to see fruit coming from his work tending the vines (15:2). Jesus presses the idea, using the time-honored

---

5. In most of the Johannine discourses, Jesus takes up a role reminiscent of God (e.g., the good shepherd).

skills of viticulture. Vine dressers both trim branches so that they will produce more fruit and cut away dead branches that have no life in them. In each case the assumption is that fruit-bearing is the test of life-giving attachment to the vine.

The picture of attachment to Jesus as a branch is attached to a vine is an apt description of the interior spiritual life Jesus has described since chapter 14. Here, however, the key word is "remaining" or "abiding" (Gk. *meno*), which is used throughout the discourse (15:4, 5, 6, 7, 9, 10). The growing disciple in whom the Father and Son live (14:20, 23) through the Spirit (14:16, 25; 15:26) is one whose life is utterly dependent on Christ. Discipleship is not just a matter of acknowledging who Jesus is; it is having Jesus spiritually connected to our inner lives.

That connection also means being "pruned" (15:2b). The Greek word for trimming (*kathairo*) is closely related to the adjective in 15:3, "You are already clean [Gk. *katharos*] because of the word I have spoken to you." Those who remain in the vine (such as Jesus' disciples) are being readied for more fruit-bearing by the word Jesus is giving them.

But with this comes a warning (15:6). To fail to "remain" in Christ, to fail to find life in the vine (i.e., Jesus), risks separation from the vineyard and consequent destruction. There is only one evidence if a branch is truly alive: Does it produce clusters of grapes (15:5)? Note carefully, however, what the metaphor is not saying. Fruit-bearing is not a test; that is, a branch does not have to demonstrate a level of productivity to be safe from destruction. Rather, fruit-bearing is a byproduct. "Apart from me you can do nothing" (15:5b). To be connected to the vine means that the life of Jesus is flowing through us, and this leads to fruitfulness. Fruitfulness will be the inevitable outcome of an interior spiritual life with Jesus (cf. Gal. 5:22—23).

Jesus concludes the metaphor in 15:7—11 by drawing out some of the implications that come from "remaining" in him, many of which repeat what we already have learned in chapter 14. Verse 7 compares remaining in Jesus and remaining in his word. No doubt this recalls the commands to obedience (14:15; 15:10), in which keeping Jesus' word is how we demonstrate love for him. Those whose lives are so in harmony with Jesus will find their prayers controlled by his word, and such prayers will be answered and bring added glory to God (15:7b; cf. 14:10—12). The branch produces what the life coursing through its limbs desires, that is, the "fruit of the vine." But the outcome is not a mechanical productivity of fruit. The disciple steps into a relationship of love with both Jesus (15:9) and the Father (15:10), out of which a transformed life, a fruit-bearing life, will flow.

The "peace" promised in 14:27 is now matched to "joy" in 15:11. Note that this joy is not merely a human happiness. Jesus desires "that *my joy* may be in you" (italics added). It is likewise a gift of the Spirit, a gift of Jesus dwelling within, that makes this joy supernatural and substantial. Jesus' joy has come through his reliance on God and his obedience to his Father's will. We inherit not only his joy but the capacity given through the Spirit to enjoy God in the same manner. The theme of joy will return in the discourse (16:20–24; 17:3) and will remain a personal emphasis for John (1 John 1:4; 2 John 12; 3 John 4).

In 15:12 the subject shifts to the character of life among Jesus' followers. In chapter 13 we viewed the same shift: Jesus models and describes his work on their behalf (13:1–11) and then charges them to imitate what he has done (13:12–20). Having described the life-giving vine and our need to share in his life and love in order to live, Jesus moves on to describe life among the branches. For some scholars, these six verses are the center of Jesus' Farewell Discourse.[6] Note that the unit is framed by two statements of the love command (15:12, 17).

This is the second time that Jesus has commanded his followers to love one another (cf. 13:34). This is the true test that will always put his followers in high relief (13:35). The same theme is sounded throughout the letters of John. "Dear friends, since God so loved us, we also ought to love one another. No one has ever seen God; but if we love one another, God lives in us and his love is made complete in us" (1 John 4:11–12). Such love for one another is a fulfillment of God's love for us and in us (4:17), and to refuse to love leads John to describe such people as "liars"—people who show that they have neither seen or experienced God's love (4:20).

This human love cannot be viewed in isolation, as if simply exhibiting such love satisfies the call to discipleship. Such love is an outgrowth of a life that has witnessed the dramatic quality of God's love (15:13) when his Son died on behalf of those he loves. Such love requires that we also love God with our entire heart, soul, and, strength (Deut. 6:5).

Jesus now calls his disciples "friends" (15:14–15) to distinguish them from servants, who do not know the deeper thoughts of their masters. What characterizes such friends is that they obey him.[7] In the Old Testament both Abraham (2 Chron. 20:7; Isa. 41:8; cf. Jas. 2:23) and Moses (Ex. 33:11) are called friends of God.[8] This title is unusual and speaks of the highest relationship possible between God and a human being. This friendship is not our doing; rather, Jesus chooses us as friends (15:16a), which gives us tremendous security that his affection for us will not disappear.

---

6. F. J. Moloney, "The Structure and Message of John 15:1–16:3," *ABR* 35 (1987): 35–49.

7. Carson, *John*, 522.

8. Today Arabs call the city of Hebron *el-Khalil* (Arabic, friend). Hebron is where Abraham, "the friend of God," is buried.

Where true friendship exists, true disclosure (or revelation) accompanies it (15:15b). Disciples possess the word of Jesus (thanks to the Spirit, 14:25–26), and they will receive ongoing revelations of Jesus (also brought by the Spirit, 16:12–13). Disciples thus know "God's heart." When they therefore pray, their desires and God's will harmonize, making them participants in God's efforts in the world (15:16; cf. 15:7).

Conflict with the World (15:18–25)

JOHN 15:18–16:4a FORMS a unified section that centers on the topic of persecution and hostility in the world. It is preceded by the charge to love (15:12–17) and followed by the detailed work of the Spirit (16:4b–15). Of all the sayings in the Farewell Discourse, it enjoys numerous parallels to teachings given by Jesus in the Synoptic Gospels (Matt. 10:17–25; 24:9–10; Mark 13:9–13; Luke 6:40; 21:12–17).[9] Essentially Jesus says that discipleship will be a costly endeavor and whoever chooses to follow Jesus must be ready to experience the sort of conflict he has seen and will soon endure. But Jesus will send the Spirit, who will provide a vital function in these conflicts.

Jesus explains the hatred of the world (15:18–21) as a continuation of the hatred he personally witnessed throughout his public ministry. Jesus has been hated because as the light, he exposes the world's deeds (3:20) and unmasks them as evil (7:7). Because the disciples are now separated from the world by virtue of their faith in Jesus, they qualify for similar treatment. No doubt the story of the man born blind in chapter 9 speaks on two levels in this regard: It tells one man's story *and* warns future disciples reading the Gospel what may come. In his prayer recorded in John 17, Jesus says, " . . . and the world has hated them, for they are not of the world any more than I am of the world" (17:14). Christians have passed from "death to life" (1 John 3:13–14), they are not "of the world" (3:19) and so should not expect the world's affections.

Jesus repeats the proverb about servants and masters (John 15:20; cf. 13:16)—not to compromise his disciples' status as friends ("No longer do I call you servants," 15:15), but to teach that they now share his status as *persona non grata*. This anticipation of conflict recalls the role of the prophets in the Old Testament. As bearers of God's word, they expected harsh treatment when their announcements were unpopular (Ezek. 3:7). For example, when Micaiah spoke the truth to Ahab and Jehoshaphat concerning their siege on Ramoth-Gilead and the Syrians, he was struck, imprisoned, and starved (1 Kings 22:24–27). In this sense, Jesus bears God's word and expe-

---

9. For an analysis of the detailed parallels, see Brown, *John*, 2:692–95.

riences hostility; now his disciples bear his word. In Matthew 10:40 he said, "He who receives you receives me, and he who receives me receives the one who sent me."

Jesus discusses the guilt of the world in 15:22–25 by explaining that it is accountable before the revelation of God. Jesus' ministry provided both words (15:22) and works (15:24) that pointed to God. Now that they have seen and heard him, their guilt is immovable (15:24). For instance, in the story of the healed blind man (ch. 9), the Jewish leadership refused to accept the miracle as a sign from God. Yet because they claimed to see, Jesus pronounced their guilt (9:41).

This same statement of accountability closed the Book of Signs. "Even after Jesus had done all these miraculous signs in their presence, they still would not believe in him" (12:37). Similarly, following Jesus' debate with the leaders on Sabbath, he claims that the historic revelation given by Moses will be their judge (5:45–47). The cumulative effect of this is to undermine the justification of the world's hostility against Jesus. When Jesus cites the Old Testament ("They hated me without a cause," 15:25; cf. Ps. 35:19; 69:4), he ironically points to even more revelation that judges their unwarranted anger.

The Third Promise of the Spirit (5:26–16:4a)

THE THIRD PROMISE of the Spirit-Paraclete (see 14:16, 26) fits this judicial, conflictual setting well. As we learned earlier (see comments on 14:16), *parkletos* (generally translated "Counselor" or "Comforter") should be taken as "Advocate," since it is a judicial title describing someone aiding a legal argument. The Spirit-Paraclete will not only live in the disciples, enabling them to recall the words of Jesus (14:26); now he will become a witness, supporting their trial (either literally or figuratively).

The promises of the Spirit in the Synoptic Gospels fit this setting precisely. Jesus says that in the midst of persecution (Matt. 10:16–18) his followers should not worry about what to say since the Spirit will speak through them (Matt. 10:19–20; Mark 13:11). The Spirit will also instruct, "for the Holy Spirit will teach you at that time what you should say" (Luke 12:12). But there is a partnership, for *"you also* must testify" (John 15:27a, italics added). "You" is emphatic in Greek here, underscoring that we are not permitted a passive role. The disciples are witnesses and the Spirit will bear witness; the disciples possess the historical record of Jesus' words and work ("you have been with me from the beginning," 15:27b), and they now will be empowered as they deliver that message to the world.

No doubt this also helps explain the title "Spirit of truth" (15:26b; cf. 14:17; 16:13). The disciples will be forced to witness about Jesus as they are confronted. But the words they utter will be "the truth" because they are speaking about the work of God in Christ through the power of the Holy Spirit. Other utterances given in the world, in the darkness, are simply falsehoods.

But this truth is also a faithful rendering of what they know about Jesus' ministry. "From the beginning" (15:27b) recurs with great frequency in John's letters as does the word "truth." The truth (this Spirit of truth) is not a compelling spiritual experience in the first instance; it is the capacity to point faithfully to what is known about Jesus' historic ministry from its onset.

The final paragraph of the section (16:1–4a) summarizes why Jesus has taught them "all this" (16:1, referring to 15:18–27). He has warned them so that they will not "go astray" (Gk. *skandalizo*). This word refers to someone who stumbles, such as when a person trips because of darkness (12:35). When Jesus spoke of eating and drinking the Son of Man's flesh and blood in chapter 6, those who failed to see beneath the metaphor were "scandalized" (6:61), and many fell away. The greatest thing, therefore, that the disciples have to fear is that they will renounce their faith or commit apostasy. Here Jesus refers to expulsion from the synagogue.

Throughout his ministry Jesus was candid about the social consequences that came with discipleship. Suffering and even martyrdom may be theirs. In Luke's version of the Sermon on the Mount Jesus says, "Blessed are you when men hate you, when they exclude you and insult you and reject your name as evil, because of the Son of Man" (Luke 6:22). Matthew records Jesus' harsh prophetic words to the Pharisees about God's messengers: "Some of them you will kill and crucify; others you will flog in your synagogues and pursue from town to town" (Matt. 23:34). In John's own Gospel the story of the blind man (John 9) serves as a paradigm of what is to come: For refusing to deny Jesus this man was "put out of the synagogue" (9:22; cf. 12:42). To embrace Jesus as Messiah early on became a matter of synagogue discipline, and none other than Saul of Tarsus served in this capacity (Acts 9:1–2).

But Jesus' point is that to know in advance is to be equipped (16:4a). To step into suffering and recognize that it follows the pattern of Jesus' life and fulfills his word may strengthen men and women for whom faith comes at a severe cost. John 16:4a does not refer to "when the time comes" (NIV) but "when *their hour* comes." Throughout John "the hour" refers to Jesus' death and glorification, but now it is the "disciples' hour" that will test their devotion to their faith.[10]

---

10. The possessive pronoun "their" is omitted in a number of significant manuscripts, but it is likely original. Scribes may have omitted it to make it conform to the Johannine form "the hour," which generally occurs with only the definite article.

IN THIS CHAPTER (as in John 14) Jesus is speaking directly to the needs and experiences of disciples who will believe in him following his departure. It is important to recall his audience: He is surrounded by his closest followers. This provides the chapter with an immediacy and applicability for the church today. These words are guidelines for discipleship, instructions for how the disciple (and the church) ought to live out life in a world that is at odds with God's Word but nevertheless in need of it.

Two major themes stand out, each of which carries additional secondary lines of thought that at first glance may go unnoticed. But there is also a third theme in the passage that is less central to the thrust of the text, but no less significant for the evangelical church today.

Christian experience. This chapter places in sharp relief our definition of the Christian experience. Is discipleship a commitment to doctrinal beliefs concerning God and Jesus? Is it a way of life, a way of "love" perhaps, that sets disciples apart from the world? Or is it an experience, a mystical spiritual encounter that transforms? I believe it is all three: Discipleship is a way of thinking (doctrine), a way of living (ethics), and a supernatural experience that cannot be compared with anything in the world.

John 15 emphasizes that neither doctrine nor ethics can alone define Christian discipleship. It reminds us that remaining in Christ, having an interior experience of Jesus (as a branch is nourished and strengthened by a vine), is a nonnegotiable feature of following Jesus. Many words could be used to describe this: mysticism, interiority, spiritual encounter. But without some dimension of an interior experience of the reality of Jesus, without a transforming spirituality that creates a supernatural life, doctrine and ethics lose their value.

This theme of spiritual experience will be at home to some but foreign and threatening to others. What will this experience look like? How is it measured or quantified? Is this just another way to talk about the charismatic renewal or Pentecostalism? What are the dangers inherent in a discipleship that talks about "remaining in" Jesus?

Flowing from this motif are three secondary issues that the passage touches on but does not explore. (1) Many commentators see here a secondary (or even primary) reference to the Lord's Supper. This evening Jesus initiated a sacred meal that used the "fruit of the vine." Does John understand that eucharistic participation[11] is an avenue to this interior life? (2) One

---

11. The "Eucharist" is an ancient and noble word for the Lord's Supper, coming from the Greek word *eucharisteo* (to give thanks, cf. its use in Mark 8:6; Luke 22.19).

outcome of this life is prayer that brims with confidence (15:16). But how do we understand this as we pray today? (3) What do we make of the branches that are "broken off"? If a branch (i.e., a disciple) bears no fruit, what is its fate? Can dormant branches be removed and burned? John 15:6 has inspired considerable debate on the subject of eternal security and assurance.

Conflict and the world. The second major theme of this section focuses on conflict and the world. Throughout the Gospel we have seen how in John's thought the "world" consists of that place—those hearts—where faith is refused and God is opposed. In the first century, tensions often flared up between the early Christians and the local synagogues from which they came. The stories of Stephen (Acts 7:58–60) and James (12:2–3) illustrate well the hostilities. Even Paul refers to the number of times he was persecuted, often by his own people, as he preached the gospel (2 Cor. 11:24; 1 Thess. 2:14). Tensions continued until the church finally won the empire in the fourth century and returned the favor, setting a pattern of shameful anti-Jewish persecution that has remained even to the twentieth century. Nevertheless, John no doubt knew these struggles well and includes for us and his disciples warnings about conflict and persecution.

This theme, then, centers on the nature of the world and its hatred of those who follow and love God. But this leads to a number of questions: Does this develop an unhealthy worldview of suspicion and foster a sectarian view of the church? How can evangelism go forward if a disciple harbors feelings of fear and suspicion of the world? What does Jesus mean when he says that his followers (while in the world) are nevertheless not "of" the world? Does this mean that life among non-Christians is a necessary evil and we should carefully limit the penetration of its values whenever and wherever possible? This, of course, raises the old tension between "Christ and culture."

Once we establish an understanding of the nature of the world, two secondary themes follow. (1) If I am being persecuted, what does this tell me about the nature of my own faith? Is this a true sign of my fidelity to Christ? Is persecution something to be sought, almost as a badge proving that I have been on the "front lines" with the world? (2) What are the resources of the Holy Spirit in the midst of this persecution? What can we expect? Is the Spirit-Paraclete simply a source of encouragement, or is this genuine assistance? In a word, how will the Spirit "bear witness" within my witness as I speak courageously before the world?

The vineyard metaphor. The third theme in this chapter, often left unnoticed, would have been explosive in Jesus' day. When Jesus employs the vineyard metaphor, he is touching one of the most-used images in Judaism to express God's relationship with his people. We saw that instead of describing God's people as planted vines rooted in the soil of Israel, Jesus describes them as branches attached to himself, the one true vine. Something important has happened here. God's people are defined not as people now planted in the vineyard of Israel, but as people attached to Jesus.

What does this mean for Israel's historic attachment to the land, the geography of the Middle East between Be'er Sheva and Dan? In his major speech in Acts 7, Stephen similarly challenges Israel's self-definition anchored to a national political identity. He not only challenges the sanctity of the land (as the goal of religious life) but the temple (as the sole place of access to God). This costs him his life. Is Jesus making the same prophetic challenge in John 15? Now the vineyard consists of *one vine*, and the question for God's people is no longer, "Do I live in the vineyard?" but instead, "Am I attached to Jesus, the vine?"

 THE TWO PRIMARY themes of spiritual attachment and persecution as well as this third theme of the vineyard provide a number of opportunities for explanation and application today. Sadly these have also been topics that have inspired misunderstanding, division, and abuse. Therefore, anyone wishing to bring John 15 to a modern audience must think carefully about what the text of the chapter is saying and what it is not saying about our identity as Christians.

Spiritual attachment. In my first seminary internship, I had the privilege of working in a traditional Lutheran church under the guidance of a wise, experienced pastor. For the first time I found myself teaching both college students and adults. One adult class covered the basics of the Christian life, and one Sunday morning an older, longtime member asked a very basic question: How does somebody become a Christian anyway? It is interesting to pause for a moment and answer this question thoughtfully.

Of course, our traditions provide us with a theological starting point, be they Arminian or Calvinist in orientation. For many of us our answers are a quick part of our repertoire, an answer we have used so many times we barely think about the theological assumptions it contains. But at this particular moment in the 1970s, in my first term of seminary, I could think of nothing other than Campus Crusade's Four Spiritual Laws, which I dutifully outlined on a blackboard. My only excuse could have been that I had not taken systematic theology yet. "Accept Jesus Christ?" the man asked. "I was baptized when I was a baby and I was confirmed at twelve. Is that enough?" I'll never forget the look on the associate pastor's face as he watched me field the question before thirty-five of his most valued members.

What struck me about this moment was how few in that circle had contemplated the notion that there is an *experiential* dimension to Christianity. Assurance came from sacramental participation, just as evangelical assurance often comes through intellectual assent (belief) or a personal, public decision. John 15 does not necessarily address either of these belief systems, but it does invite a host of fundamental questions. Discipleship here is viewed in terms of attachment and fruit-bearing. The believer is like a living branch attached to a living vine. It is the vine that gives life to the branch. Nourishment from the vine enables the branch to bear good fruit. *How one becomes attached is not the issue.* But that one must be attached, that one will bear fruit as a result of this attachment, means everything. One should be able to look at a branch, see its fruit, and say, "This branch is living, it is attached, it is vital and growing from the vine."

This means that Christianity is not simply about believing the right things (though this is important). Nor is it simply a matter of living a Christ-like life (though this is important too). Christian experience must necessarily have a mystical, spiritual, non-quantifiable dimension. To be a disciple means having the Father, Son, and Holy Spirit living in us (14:23–26). It means having a supernatural, interior experience that is completely unlike anything available in the world. It is a way of believing (doctrine) and a way of living (ethics), but these are nurtured by the life-giving connection with Jesus Christ. Today's world is not hardened in a rigid demand for rationalistic religious proof as it was in another generation. It is bona fide spiritual experience that authenticates religious truth in our world, and this is precisely what Jesus is describing.[12]

What are the outcomes of this sort of life? The fruit Jesus expects from the branches is first and foremost love. The love command has been repeated throughout this Upper Room discourse, and Jesus repeats it here (15:12).[13] This spiritual awakening, this transforming encounter does not always lead to fantastic signs and powers (though these may come, cf. 14:12). It leads principally to a life that has features of Jesus' life running through its veins. As Jesus enjoyed the Father's love and reflected it to his followers, so now his

12. I recently had a conversation with a young Christian Science scholar doing theological research at Cambridge University (where I am presently writing). She commented that evangelical arguments for truth don't really matter. She predicted a resurgence of Christian Science since it blends so well with postmodern religious instincts about experience. "Once you've been healed by divine principles, Christian doctrine doesn't matter as much anymore."

13 It is interesting that when the apostle Paul critiques the spirituality of the Corinthians (1 Cor. 12–14), he places a premium on love as the central outcome of the Spirit's presence (1 Cor. 13).

love should fill their lives. Fruit then becomes a sign of spiritual life and vitality; fruit is not an evidence by which we demonstrate that we belong in the vineyard.

The confident prayer described in 15:17 is a byproduct of the intimacy with Jesus offered in 15:15–16. To be a branch, to be a disciple, does not mean that we can make some claim on the vine and demand it to produce what we wish. Prayer "in my name" is not a formula that guarantees we will get what we want. Centuries of Christian experience bear this out. But prayer that is *itself* inspired by the spiritual presence of Jesus, that is in harmony with his will, that is in accord with what he is doing in nurturing the vineyard—this prayer will succeed.

Can branches be broken off? This is the clear teaching of 15:2, 6. But does this mean that branches once nourished by the vine (i.e., disciples once saved) can then lose their salvation and be removed from Christ? Jesus' analogy here has not been missed in recent theological debates about assurance and faith. Zane Hodges of Dallas Seminary, for instance, attempts to shore up eternal security by arguing that it is possible to be genuinely saved but bear no fruit.[14] Others have disputed this view strongly.[15]

What are our options on this issue? (1) Arminians have often argued that the removed branches are Christians who have lost faith and hence lost salvation. But this seems hard to square with passages like John 10:28: "I give them eternal life, and they shall never perish; no one can snatch them out of my hand." (2) Some have suggested that breaking off branches depicts Christian discipline (death perhaps?), aimed at bringing restoration in the end. But the description in 15:6 seems to evoke images of eternal judgment ("such branches are picked up, thrown into the fire and burned"). (3) A third view argues that these branches are people who have some superficial external identity with Jesus but no internal, spiritual unity with him. Throughout John's Gospel we have met people who are interested in Jesus but show inadequate belief (12:41–43). They live on the margin of the community of faith and enjoy its activities, but they have not embraced its truth for themselves.

The chief problem here is that Jesus' vine image is being pressed to answer questions it was not intended to answer. The viticulture of the Middle East teaches us that every good farmer knows how to read the health of his vines. Living branches are trimmed; dead branches are removed insofar as they do not have the life of the vine coursing through them. The principle is simple:

---

14. Z. Hodges, *The Gospel Under Siege* (Dallas: Redencion Viva, 1981); see also C. R. Smith, "The Unfruitful Branches of John 15," *Grace Journal* 9 (1968): 10.

15. J. MacArthur, *The Gospel According to Jesus* (Grand Rapids: Zondervan, 1988); cf. Laney, "Abiding Is Believing"; J.C. Dillow, "Abiding Is Remaining in Fellowship: Another Look at John 15:1–6," *BSac* 147 (1990): 44–53.

Jesus (and the vine) are the source of life; to fail to have him is to fail to have life. To refuse to "remain in Jesus" (15:6a) is to refuse the gift of life he offers. Elsewhere Jesus refers to his gift as living water or the bread of life. The image is the same. He provides this analogy to talk about his essential, life-giving work, not to discuss the history of individual branches.

Spiritual attachment and the Eucharist. While the metaphor of the vine finds its first meaning in the symbolism of attachment to Jesus, many writers (Catholics, Orthodox, and Protestants) wonder if John's audience would not have found another meaning in the story. Early Christian readers who knew the institution of the Lord's Supper (see 1 Cor. 11:23–26) would recall how the contents of the cup are described as "the fruit of the vine" in Mark 14:25 and Matthew 26:29.[16] Further, the saying of the vine is given on the very night in which Jesus provides the Lord's Supper. In this paragraph he even refers to his sacrificial death (John 15:13). Surely (many suggest) there must be eucharistic overtones here.

We must also compare to this the most explicit eucharistic language found in John (6:51–58). Here, eating and drinking Jesus parallels remaining in him as outlined in chapter 15. But the climax of John 6—and this is the important part—is that its graphic imagery is symbolic of the Spirit (6:63). As the flesh and blood of the Son of Man give life (6:53), so the Spirit alone gives life (6:63). The consumption of Jesus represents the acquisition of Jesus-in-Spirit, the very theme of the Farewell Discourse. Eucharistic participation, then, is not mere ritual, but is intended to reinforce and genuinely provide a life-giving attachment to Jesus.

Christians who do not come from a liturgical background will at once object to this reading of John 15. Many of us are eager to see spiritual realities in the chapter but less so to see them as linked to ritual observances or sacraments. I would urge that learning to see spiritual reality within liturgical ritual is a gift. Those who possess it hold something precious.[17]

One story will suffice. I remember talking with a young woman in her late twenties who had been a Christian for perhaps five years. Her ongoing sin troubled her, and she wanted to experience the reality of Jesus' forgiveness and attachment to him. Evangelical sermons about forgiveness and eloquent words about assurance felt like disembodied truths, ideas without substance—gnostic perhaps. Her church had spiritualized or abstracted the reality of

---

16. The earliest Christian Eucharist liturgy we possess (in *Did.* 9) has this blessing, "We thank you, our Father, for the holy vine of David your servant, which you revealed to us through Jesus your servant" (9:2).

17. I have explored the problem of evangelicalism and its loss of the numinous in "Missing God at Church? Why So Many Are Rediscovering Worship in Other Traditions," *Christianity Today* 41 (Oct. 6, 1997): 19–27.

Jesus so that her attachment to him could only be seen in her imagination (a world cluttered with as much darkness as light).

Then by accident she attended an Anglican eucharistic service. As she knelt before the apse of a stone church, a priest in flowing robes (divinely attired, she thought) prohibited her from touching the Eucharist with her hand ("I was too unclean," she said), and a chalice was brought to her lips. She was fed, she was nurtured, she was forgiven. The priest laid his hand on her head, saying words of forgiveness and assurance.

The physical, incarnational reality of the Lord's Supper is now one avenue through which this woman experiences attachment to Jesus. Our incarnational Christology insists that God's work in Christ took seriously the natural, material world in which we live. God used the form of this world, the full humanity of our lives, in order to accomplish his work. To this woman God is still using "the things we need," the concrete things of this world, to attach himself to us.

Conflict with the world. A religious community generates a worldview that in some fashion defines it over against its surrounding environment. In most cases these views are unconscious as believers either separate themselves from the world or integrate fully with its environment. (1) Some communities are "world-embracing." Such churches view the world as more or less benign and believers feel free to join its life. Many mainline denominations fit here.

(2) Other communities are "world-suspecting." These churches are cautious about the world, believe firmly in its fallenness, and see the church as a refuge. Many evangelical and fundamentalist groups identify themselves here. They may continue to participate in secular politics and social life (such as public education) but do so with care lest they are forced to compromise the essentials of faith.

(3) Finally, some churches are "world-rejecting." These communities have experienced such hostility and rejection in the world that they see nothing to be gained in it. They may be sectarian and disengage entirely from public life. In our century some fundamentalist and Pentecostal groups fit this category, as do Jehovah's Witnesses. Such groups have formed a worldview based on experiences of conflict. Feeling marginalized and powerless, they separate themselves for the sake of self-preservation.

John's Gospel has preserved some of Jesus' most stringent teachings about the world and its ill will. It is uncertain whether this is to be explained by the context of John's own church or his perspective of the wider church in the first century. The first century was a difficult time for believers. The church struggled for survival among antagonistic synagogues and suspicious Roman authorities. Christian martyrdom became commonplace before the century was finished.

Here in 15:18—16:4a we have dramatic words outlining the "hatred of the world." It would not be far wrong to see that the worldview John offers is "world-rejecting." Such teaching needs to be balanced against other teachings in the New Testament that express God's love for the world and the readiness of the world to be evangelized. "The harvest is plentiful but the workers are few" (Matt. 9:37). But this teaching also needs to be placed in reserve for times when the world's hostility is acute and when suffering, including martyrdom, may come to us.

Today such threats are rarely ours in the West. But it is still the experience of many Christians around the world. I think, for example, of the church in China (over one hundred million strong), whose pastors are arrested and imprisoned as leaders of a fanatical cult simply because they lead unregistered house churches.[18] One pastor, Peter Xu Yongze, was last year sentenced to serve three years in hard labor ("re-education through labor") for leading a banned religious cult, comparable, argued the government, with the American David Koresh.[19] Some estimate that thousands of Christian leaders have been arrested and jailed in China in the 1990s. If this is not our experience at present in the West, we need to support those who suffer and ready ourselves for a day when we may. When this happens, 15:18—16:4 will be vital to us.

Those who do suffer offer eloquent testimony to what Jesus teaches in these verses. The Spirit promises to join with our testimony and to provide the courage and strength to sustain our witness before increasingly hostile audiences. Remarkably, despite persecution, unflinching courage and spiritual revival are hallmarks of Christian life in China. In order to survive, the church must wrestle with temptations to cooperate with the Communist government in order to have a reprieve from persecution. Those in "registered churches" (ten to fifteen million believers) must ask when their participation in this "world," this sinful godless system of life, has compromised their spirituality altogether. A "world-rejecting" worldview may be an appropriate strategy after all.

The world always has the potential to "turn" on the church and see it as an impediment to some social, political, or ideological program—just as Jerusalem "turned" on Jesus and found in him a dangerous inconvenience. "If they persecuted me, they will persecute you also" (15:20).

The vineyard and the land. Jesus' use of the vineyard analogy contains theological implications that would not be missed by any thoughtful Jewish

---

18. See "A Tale of China's Two Churches: Eyewitness Reports of Repression and Revival," *Christianity Today* 42 (July 13, 1998): 30—39; P. Marshall, *Their Blood Cries Out* (Waco, Tex.: Word, 1997).

19. Koresh led the Branch Davidian cult in Waco, Texas, and died in 1994 when the FBI laid siege to his compound.

theologian in the first century. The subject of "the Land" (i.e., the territory of Israel) was prominent in Jewish thought. Israel was considered the center of the world, Jerusalem was the center point of the Land, and the temple was the center of Jerusalem. According to the book of *Jubilees*, Mount Zion is the "center of the earth's navel" (*Jub.* 18:19)! Jews living outside of Israel (called the Diaspora) desired to be buried in Israel; it was like being buried on an altar of atonement.[20] Thus to neglect Judaism's "land consciousness" is to neglect a significant theme presupposed in the first century.

Why is this significant? We have already seen that the vineyard was one of Israel's most prized historic symbols of its nationhood and inheritance. In the Synoptic Gospels, for example, Jesus uses this symbol to express judgment in the parable of the vineyard and the tenants (Matt. 21:33–44; Mark 12:1–11): "'Therefore, when the owner of the vineyard comes, what will he do to those tenants?' 'He will bring those wretches to a wretched end,' they replied, 'and he will rent the vineyard to other tenants, who will give him his share of the crop at harvest time'" (Matt. 21:40–41). Imagine the explosive implications of this answer! The vineyard will be given to new people, who will be faithful tenants!

John 15 is the Fourth Gospel's most profound theological relocation of Israel's "holy space."[21] Jesus is here revising Israel's theological assumption about territory and religion. He is changing the place of rootedness for the people of God. Unlike the Synoptic parable that employs the traditional Old Testament categories of vineyard and vine, Jesus here says God's vineyard has one vine, he is that vine, and attachment to God comes through attachment to him. It is no longer a matter of possessing the vineyard; it is now a matter of knowing the one true vine. Branches found in the vineyard that are not connected to him are gathered and burned. "The only means of attachment to The Land is through this one vine, Jesus Christ."[22] Jesus is thus pointing away from the vineyard as place, as territory of hills and valleys, cisterns and streams. *In a word, Jesus spiritualizes the Land.* He replaces the image of the vine and the promise of the Land held so sacred in Judaism.[23]

---

20. M. Wilson, *Our Father Abraham· Jewish Roots of the Christian Faith* (Grand Rapids. Eerdmans, 1989), 260; the seminal study on "the Land" is W. D. Davies, *The Gospel and the Land. Early Jewish Territorial Doctrine* (Berkeley: Univ. of California Press, 1974); idem, *The Territorial Dimension of Judaism* (Minneapolis: Fortress, 1992).

21. See G. M. Burge, "Territorial Religion and the Vineyard of John 15," in J.Green and M. Turner, eds., *Jesus of Nazareth: Lord and Christ Essays on the Historical Jesus and New Testament Christology* (Grand Rapids: Eerdmans, 1994), 384–96. See also P. Walker, *Jesus and the Holy City· New Testament Perspectives on Jerusalem* (Grand Rapids: Eerdmans, 1996).

22. Burge, "Territorial Religion," 393.

23. This vine metaphor is one more example of the "replacement motif" we have observed throughout the Gospel of John.

The practical implications of this are profound. Christians, particularly Western evangelicals, have been quick today to endorse the territorial agenda of modern Israel *for theological reasons.* Often it is a zeal for eschatological fulfillment that has prompted some evangelicals to make commitments to Israeli nationalism. However, deep within the New Testament is an announcement of a reversal, a radical reversal. The Christology of the New Testament makes obsolete those avenues of religious pursuit today pulled from the Old Testament. Just as Jesus is a replacement for the religious functions of the temple, so too Jesus replaces the religious inheritance of the Land. Jesus is the locus of God's habitation. He is the sole link to the vineyard, and to promote a vineyard without him, to promote a territorial salvation, is to miss entirely the thrust of his message about the Land.

Today Palestinian pastors plead with Western evangelicals to recognize them as brothers and sisters and to see that because of Israel's territorial religion, their people are suffering by losing land, becoming refugees, and being imprisoned. Pastors like Naim Ateek of Jerusalem,[24] Mitri Raheeb of Bethlehem,[25] Elias Chacour of Galilee,[26] and Audi Rantisi of Ramallah[27] have powerful stories to tell about what happens when misplaced religious commitments are unleashed in modern Israel.[28]

---

24. N. Ateek, *Justice and Only Justice* (Maryknoll, N.Y.: Orbis, 1989); idem. with M. Ellis and R. Ruether, *Faith and the Intifadah: Palestinian Christian Voices* (Maryknoll, N.Y.: Orbis, 1992).

25. M. Raheeb, *I Am a Palestinian Christian* (Minneapolis: Fortress, 1995).

26. E. Chacour, *We Belong to the Land: The Story of a Palestinian Israeli Who Lives for Peace and Reconciliation* (San Francisco. Harper & Row, 1990).

27. A. Rantisi, *Blessed Are the Peacemakers: A Palestinian Christian in the Occupied West Bank* (Grand Rapids: Zondervan, 1990).

28. I have surveyed this topic on a popular level in *Who Are God's People in the Middle East? What Christians Are Not Being Told About Israel and the Palestinians* (Grand Rapids: Zondervan, 1993); see also W. Pippert, *Land of Promise, Land of Strife. Israel at 40* (Waco, Tex.: Word, 1988). From a nonevangelical view see R. Reuther, *The Wrath of Jonah· The Crisis of Religious Nationalism in the Israeli-Palestinian Conflict* (San Francisco: Harper and Row, 1989).

John 16:4b–33

IDID NOT tell you this at first because I was with you. ⁵"Now I am going to him who sent me, yet none of you asks me, 'Where are you going?' ⁶Because I have said these things, you are filled with grief. ⁷But I tell you the truth: It is for your good that I am going away. Unless I go away, the Counselor will not come to you; but if I go, I will send him to you. ⁸When he comes, he will convict the world of guilt in regard to sin and righteousness and judgment: ⁹in regard to sin, because men do not believe in me; ¹⁰in regard to righteousness, because I am going to the Father, where you can see me no longer; ¹¹and in regard to judgment, because the prince of this world now stands condemned.

¹²"I have much more to say to you, more than you can now bear. ¹³But when he, the Spirit of truth, comes, he will guide you into all truth. He will not speak on his own; he will speak only what he hears, and he will tell you what is yet to come. ¹⁴He will bring glory to me by taking from what is mine and making it known to you. ¹⁵All that belongs to the Father is mine. That is why I said the Spirit will take from what is mine and make it known to you.

¹⁶"In a little while you will see me no more, and then after a little while you will see me."

¹⁷Some of his disciples said to one another, "What does he mean by saying, 'In a little while you will see me no more, and then after a little while you will see me,' and 'Because I am going to the Father'?" ¹⁸They kept asking, "What does he mean by 'a little while'? We don't understand what he is saying."

¹⁹Jesus saw that they wanted to ask him about this, so he said to them, "Are you asking one another what I meant when I said, 'In a little while you will see me no more, and then after a little while you will see me'? ²⁰I tell you the truth, you will weep and mourn while the world rejoices. You will grieve, but your grief will turn to joy. ²¹A woman giving birth to a child has pain because her time has come; but when her baby is born she forgets the anguish because of her joy that a child is born into the world. ²²So with you: Now is your time of grief, but I will see you again and you will rejoice, and no one will

take away your joy. ²³In that day you will no longer ask me anything. I tell you the truth, my Father will give you whatever you ask in my name. ²⁴Until now you have not asked for anything in my name. Ask and you will receive, and your joy will be complete.

²⁵"Though I have been speaking figuratively, a time is coming when I will no longer use this kind of language but will tell you plainly about my Father. ²⁶In that day you will ask in my name. I am not saying that I will ask the Father on your behalf. ²⁷No, the Father himself loves you because you have loved me and have believed that I came from God. ²⁸I came from the Father and entered the world; now I am leaving the world and going back to the Father."

²⁹Then Jesus' disciples said, "Now you are speaking clearly and without figures of speech. ³⁰Now we can see that you know all things and that you do not even need to have anyone ask you questions. This makes us believe that you came from God."

³¹"You believe at last!" Jesus answered. ³²"But a time is coming, and has come, when you will be scattered, each to his own home. You will leave me all alone. Yet I am not alone, for my Father is with me.

³³"I have told you these things, so that in me you may have peace. In this world you will have trouble. But take heart! I have overcome the world."

THE BALANCE OF the Farewell Discourse (before Jesus' final prayer in ch. 17) continues many of the themes already introduced in the Upper Room. Struggles with the world, the need for the Spirit's assistance, the trauma of Jesus' death and departure, and the reassurance of his imminent return all find attention here. In fact, there are so many parallels between chapter 16 and chapter 14 that some scholars have wondered if perhaps this is a duplicate version of the earlier chapter, or perhaps Jesus is replowing ground already covered.

Other scholars point to the seemingly final remark in 14:31c ("Come now; let us leave") and the question in 16:5, "Now I am going to him who sent me, yet none of you asks me, 'Where are you going?'" Note that this is precisely the question Peter asked in 13:36 and Thomas in 14:5. This has inspired numerous rearrangement theories for the Farewell Discourse (see comments on ch. 14). For some, Jesus' words in chapter 16 were some of the *first* words he taught that evening. But as I have made clear in my comments on chapter 14, this does not have to be our only understanding of these chapters (see further below).

The two chief themes Jesus concentrates on in this chapter concern the work of the Spirit-Paraclete (16:5–15) and Jesus' anticipated return (16:16–33). This divides the chapter into two neat divisions. (1) Jesus continues the subject of the hostility of the world (begun at 15:18) and explains the function of the Spirit to convict the world as a prosecutor might make a persuasive argument in court. He also explains that the Spirit has a revelatory role quite different from the one we studied in 14:26, for he will unveil things not yet revealed to the disciples. John 16:12 offers a genuine prophetic role for the Spirit in the followers of Jesus.

(2) Beginning at 16:16, the Greek word *mikron* ("a little while") is repeated again and again to reassure the disciples that their separation from Jesus will be short-lived. The emphasis here is on the cross and the resurrection (as John 14 emphasized the Second Coming), saying in effect that Jesus' "return" from the grave will be a spectacular source of joy. From this point on, the intimacy they share with Jesus, the knowledge they have of his will, will be unsurpassed.

The Fourth Promise of the Spirit (16:4b–11)

JESUS' CANDOR ABOUT the coming sufferings stems from his awareness that he will not be with them to absorb the hostility of the religious authorities. In past times he has been with them (16:4b); but in the future, while he will be within them in the Spirit, they will have to bear the brunt of persecution. As in the earlier chapters Jesus' departure brought dismay (13:31ff.), so now Jesus returns to the subject of his going away.

Jesus' statement in 16:5 (" . . . yet none of you asks me, 'Where are you going?'") has perplexed many since in 13:36 and 14:5 this is precisely what Peter and Thomas ask. Numerous solutions have been proposed: Bultmann and Bernard, for instance, rearranged the Farewell Discourse, placing chapter 16 earlier than 14 (solving the problem of 16:5) and linking 14:31 with 18:1. But these schemes often generate even more complications and today are unpopular.

Others (such as Brown and Schnackenburg) point to an editor (even John himself) who perhaps assembled these chapters from sources and out of respect for the tradition, did not correct the problem. But would John (or a disciple) have left such a wrinkle in his text and not taken the time to iron it out?

Still others (Carson, Beasley-Murray) argue that the details of the text provide insights that reconcile these verses. Hoskyns reasonably argues that in fact the disciples have not grasped the reality of Jesus' departure and so the question must be asked again. Carson thinks that the first questions were rhetorical, focusing on their dismay and not really on Jesus' destination.

Note that in 16:5 Jesus speaks in the present tense: "No one *is* asking...." His interest here is that in light of his disclosures about persecution, no one is pressing him about his departure. This question thus must be linked to 16:6. Sorrow has so swamped the disciples' lives that they have forgotten that Jesus' death is not the end of everything, it is the beginning. They are concentrating on the wrong subject. "No one is asking me, '*Where* are you going?'" Peter's earlier question was about the reasonableness of the cross. Thomas was asking about the way of Jesus' departure. But now, Jesus says, these are secondary. The point is the goal of his glorification, namely, the Father's presence.

Moreover, from their perspective Jesus' departure will bring a direct benefit. John 7:37–39 taught that the Spirit could not be given until Jesus was glorified. John 16:7 says the same thing. The Spirit-Paraclete[1] can only be sent to the disciples after Jesus' departure. If he does not go away, if he is not glorified, then the Spirit cannot come. In some fashion, then, it is mutually exclusive to have both this Spirit and Jesus on earth. The Spirit is a gift that must await the trigger of Jesus' going.

In 16:8–11 Jesus gives another description of what the Spirit will do in this difficult relationship with the world. Let's summarize what we have seen so far. The world cannot know the Spirit-Paraclete because it does not know or love God (14:15–17). Amidst the hostilities of the world, the Spirit-Paraclete will defend believers, strengthening their witness (15:26–27) and their recollection of the things Jesus has taught (14:26). All of this is defensive. Now in 16:8–11 the Spirit-Paraclete "passes to the attack."[2] As if in a court of law, the defender now becomes prosecutor and judge. Note carefully that this is precisely the role of Jesus in the Gospel of John. He who is on trial, who must defend his signs and words, will finally judge his accusers. This happened in chapter 9 when in 9:35–41 Jesus personally came to the aid of the blind man. The Spirit (who theologically becomes Jesus' *alter ego*) plays the same role.[3]

Precisely how we are to understand the work of the Spirit in these verses has been difficult. While we cannot survey all of the issues here,[4] we can

---

1. On the word *parakletos* (Paraclete; NIV "Counselor") see comments on 14:16.
2. A. E. Harvey, *Jesus on Trial: A Study of the Fourth Gospel* (London. SPCK, 1976), 118; similarly, Barrett, *John*, 487.
3. Older commentators once thought that we needed to search for angelic models to explain the personal features of the Paraclete's work. Today such efforts are passé. The personal features of the Paraclete come from the personality of Jesus himself.
4. See D. A. Carson, "The Function of the Paraclete in John 16:7–11," *JBL* 98 (1979): 547–66, who surveys the problems. Also see G. M. Burge, *The Anointed Community*, 208–10.

nevertheless give the general contours of the problem. One important issue involves the Greek verb *elencho*, translated "prove wrong about" in the first edition of the NIV: "[The Spirit] will prove the world wrong about sin...." Here the idea is that of *convincing* the world about the truth of its wrongdoing. Brown thinks this contradicts 14:17, since there the world cannot accept the Spirit-Paraclete.[5] But this is a different matter: In 14:17 Jesus is talking about receiving the Spirit, not hearing its message.

If this issue is not about convincing the world, perhaps *elencho* means to *convict* the world, exposing its sin and judging it. If so, then the problem is that we must explain the three clauses from 16:9–11. Does the Spirit convict the world concerning *its* sin, *its* righteousness, and *its* judgment? If so, how is the world "righteous"? Perhaps the Spirit convicts the world of *its wrong ideas* concerning sin, righteousness, and judgment. Or note the 1978 revision to the NIV: "When he comes, he will convict the world of *guilt in regard to* sin and righteousness and judgment" (italics added). Even though the italicized phrase is absent in the Greek, the sense here is that the Spirit is a prosecuting counsel, now exposing the world of its sinfulness.

In the New Testament, *elencho* occurs seventeen times and in most cases describes an instance where someone's sin is exposed (leading to the related idea "to convict"). Thus John the Baptist exposes and convicts Herod of sin (Luke 3:9). Similarly, prophecy has the power to convict (1 Cor. 14:24), and we are charged to convict or rebuke sinners (1 Tim. 5:20; James 2:9; Jude 1:5) and antagonists to the faith (Titus 1:9). Therefore the meaning of the verb has to do with exposing sin and its guilt.

In John the judicial context sharpens it further: This is exposure leading to conviction and judgment. The fundamental idea is that the world has already conducted its "trial" of Jesus and found him guilty and deserving of death. But in fact, Jesus is innocent and the world stands accused of error and sin. The Spirit-Paraclete "unveils to the world the real nature of sin and righteousness and judgment in light of what God was doing in Jesus."[6] The clauses that follow 16:8 may therefore indicate cause ("... about sin, because it ..."; so Carson, Barrett) or further explain the substance of the accusation ("... about sin, inasmuch as ..."; so Smalley, Brown, Morris).[7] In 16:6–11 the words "sin and righteousness and judgment" possess no article; thus, the

---

5. Brown, *John*, 2:711.

6. Beasley-Murray, *John*, 281.

7. Carson argues both in "The Function of the Paraclete" and in *John*, 535–38, that the clauses must be causal and that each must possess the same symmetrical reference to the world ("its sin, its righteousness, its judgment"). But such symmetry is unnecessary. Morris, *John*, 619, suggests that John's meaning may include various nuances and no idea should be excluded.

Spirit unveils the truth about these ideas, not specific instances of the world's sin, and so on.

To sum, the world is now put on notice: Its guilt will be exposed. The Spirit will bring to light the true meaning of sin and righteousness and judgment and expose the world's fatal errors. As in a grave and major trial, the verdict will be announced with absolute clarity: The world is guilty. The world *may* be persuaded to accept it, but it cannot deny that the verdict has been given any more than a criminal can miss the judgment passed on the final day of his or her trial.

The work of the Spirit here is an operation on the "conscience of the world."[8] But since the world cannot receive the Spirit, this operation will be effected through the work of the church, which has the Spirit and which provides a bold testimony to the truth. The disciples who have been wrongly accused are affected too. This word from the Spirit confirms their confidence in the truth, assuring them that the accusations against them are false and that a divine prosecution of the world has already begun because the world has rejected Jesus.

The three clauses given in 16:9–11 each offer important descriptions of the errors of the world and the bases of its conviction. (1) The first error (16:9) is the refusal to believe. That this is a primary sin is clear (1:11; 3:19; 15:22). It does not refer to ignorance, as if at issue is a problem of intellect; it is a problem of will and so implies rejection (cf. 5:43–47; 9:39–41).

(2) The second error (16:10) thinks that through Jesus' death his *unrighteousness* will be demonstrated for all to see. But God plans to reverse this and make the cross a place of glorification in which Jesus' innocence and righteousness are proclaimed. The surprising reversal is that it is the world that lacks true righteousness (see 3:19–21; 7:7; 15:22, 24). So when the world celebrates "the end of Jesus" at the tomb because he cannot be seen any longer (16:10b), the disciples can celebrate the true circumstances of his absence: He has been enthroned with the Father. This is the essence of the church's Easter proclamation.

(3) The third error concerns judgment (16:12). Jesus has not been judged by his trial; rather, the world has been judged. Jesus has described the world's ability to judge as perverse and darkened (7:24; 8:16), and therefore it is incapable of making correct decisions about God. In 12:31 and 14:30 Jesus identifies the source of this error to be the "prince of this world" (no doubt Satan). While the absolute hold of Satan has been broken and he has been judged through the cross, he still has power over the present world (1 John 5:19; cf. Eph. 2:2; 6:12). Thus as the hour of glorification approaches, Jesus

8. Barrett, *John*, 487.

realizes that it is the world's "hour" as well: "Now is the time for judgment on this world; now the prince of this world will be driven out" (12:31). This Jesus who has been rejected and who now sits enthroned has become the world's chief judge.

The Fifth Promise of the Spirit (16:12–15)

THIS FINAL PROMISE of the Spirit (again called "the Spirit of truth," see comments on 14:26) brings to a climax the range of the Spirit's work among the followers of Jesus. But something new and important here is added. While the work of the Spirit in 14:26 stressed "remembering" the historic words of Jesus uttered in his ministry, 16:12–15 suggests that the Spirit will provide supplementary revelations that the disciples have not yet heard.[9]

Some commentators have genuine difficulty with these verses. But on closer inspection, such apparent problems dissipate. For instance, in 15:15 Jesus said that he has told his disciples everything he has heard from the Father. But 16:12 describes the work of the Spirit who will have new things to say, things the disciples have not yet heard. This is now a different time, a different experience. Nor does this verse stand in contradiction with 14:26, where Jesus describes a different function of the Paraclete, namely, recalling and preserving the historic words of Jesus. Here in 16:12–13 Jesus speaks of a future time when new things will be disclosed. Both of these passages work together. The historical Jesus and his ministry stand alongside the ongoing living Jesus-in-Spirit, who is continuously experienced in the church.

But this new revelatory work, this ongoing divine voice of the Spirit, has its limitations. The Spirit is dependent on Jesus for everything he says (16:13). Note the tense of these verbs: The Spirit is not only going to reiterate the things Jesus has said (remembering, 14:26), but he will convey the things that Jesus will say (revelation). The revelation of Jesus will continue in the community and the Spirit-Paraclete will be the authoritative channel through which he is heard. Yet these revelations may not depart from what Jesus uttered in his historic ministry. Historic revelation must always be the measure by which new revelations are tested. Revelations that fail to glorify Jesus (16:14), that fail to recognize Jesus' preeminence and glory, dishonor the Father since it is he who is the source of everything Jesus has (16:15). The Father is at work in the Son, the Son is at work in the Spirit; any revelation that disrupts the glory of these is not from God.

"What is yet to come" in 16:13b may refer to the events of the trial and crucifixion that are coming, but this would be odd since the Spirit will not be received until after these events. Thus, this phrase more likely refers to a

---

9. See Burge, *The Anointed Community*, 214–16.

genuine prophetic gift that will disclose the future—a gift like that exercised in the book of Revelation and described in 1 Corinthians 12:29–30. The Spirit's "making known" is not of Jesus' previous historic teachings[10] nor is it confined to the eyewitnesses of the apostolic era, whose prophetic work will close with the canon.[11] As Bernard wrote, "this is the only place in John where any of the Pauline *charismata* of the Spirit are mentioned."[12]

Jesus' Return, the Disciples' Joy (16:16–22)

ONE PROMINENT FEATURE of the promises of the Spirit in chapter 14 had to do with the second coming of Christ. That is, Jesus was indeed "coming back" (14:3) but in some fashion the realization of the Spirit at Pentecost would satisfy many of these desires of reunion with the Lord. We might say that the Parousia (or return) of Jesus is being interpreted in light of the Spirit. Now in 16:16–24 something similar is afoot. While the question in chapter 14 may have turned on *how* Jesus would return, the question in 16 is *when*. Here the focus is on the events of Easter.

The departure of Jesus and its distress for the disciples has been a constant theme in the Upper Room. Jesus does not let them ignore the reality of his going, and in 16:16 he brings it up again: "In a little while you will see me no more, and then after a little while you will see me." Jesus had said almost the same thing in 14:19. Now seven times in this chapter (16:16–19) Jesus refers to "a little while" (Gk. *mikron*), which prompts the central question of the section: "What does he mean by saying, 'In a little while. . . '?" (16:17a). The confusion of the disciples is understandable. In 16:10 Jesus has said that he is going to the Father and they will not see him any longer. Now he says that they will see him, and it won't be long. What can he mean? The confusion swirls through the circle of disciples from verses 17–19.

This is not intentional ambiguity on Jesus' part, nor is this an attempt to provide a double meaning (Barrett). Jesus is not talking about his second coming either (Brown). Rather, he is simply referring to his return in resurrection. He is departing from the world in his glorification and the world will no longer have access to him. When he returns in resurrection, it will be his followers' final opportunity to see him as he has always been.

---

10. So Brown, *John*, 2:708.

11. So Carson, *Farewell Discourse*, 149–50; *John*, 540–42. Carson skews the interpretation of these verses by arguing that even 16:12 refers to the Spirit's work within the apostolic eyewitness testimony. But 16.12 does not show this. If anything, the evidence of 1 John suggests that a prophetic gift like that described here was active in John's church and in fact was causing problems.

12. Bernard, *John*, 2:511.

What clues point to the resurrection? (1) The opening words of 16:20 underscore the seriousness of Jesus' answer. The NIV's "I tell you the truth" disguises the Greek "truly, truly."[13] The celebration of the world (16:20b) can only point to Jesus' crucifixion, which is contrasted with a time of sorrow for the disciples (16:20a), triggered by their shock at Jesus' death. Weeping and mourning were common descriptions of sorrow at death (Jer. 22:10 LXX; Luke 7:32; cf. John 11:31, 33; 20:11, 13, 15). But this sorrow will be transformed into "joy" because Jesus will *not* be defeated by the grave.[14] Note that when the disciples do in fact see Jesus again on Easter, they are filled with "joy" (20:20).

(2) Jesus twice says "you will see me" (16:17, 19). This is the one-line identification employed on Easter by Mary (20:18), the disciples (20:20, 25a), and Thomas (20:25b). Seven days after Easter Jesus invites Thomas to "see" him (20:27, 29). John himself knows that this promise of "seeing" was at the heart of his confidence about Jesus (1 John 1:1, "That ... which we have seen with our eyes ... this we proclaim concerning the Word of life"). There is no doubt that it is the resurrection of Jesus when the joy promised in 16:20 will be fulfilled.

(3) The analogy Jesus uses in 16:21–22 of a woman in labor and childbirth was frequently used in the Old Testament to illustrate the anguish Israel (or a person) might have to endure before God's wonder and blessing were finally experienced (Isa. 21:2–3; 26:16–21; 66:7–10; Jer. 13:21; Hos. 12:13; Mic. 4:9–10; cf. Rev. 12:2–5; 1QH 3:18). The woman's suffering (Gk. *thlipsis*) also recalls the suffering of God's people before the Lord brings final deliverance (Zeph. 1:14–15; Hab. 3:16; Mark 13:19, 24).

Isaiah 26:16–31 is particularly important since it combines the ideas of "a little while" and the picture of a woman in labor. "As a woman with child and about to give birth writhes and cries out in her pain, so were we in your presence, O LORD." Then God answers through the prophet: "Go, my people, enter your rooms and shut the doors behind you; hide yourselves *for a little while* until his wrath has passed by" (Isa. 26:17, 20, italics added).

Since these ideas—suffering and dramatic deliverance—are properly eschatological, this has led some commentators to say that Jesus is actually referring to the Second Coming in 16:16 (or at least that John is confusing the Second Coming with Easter, or reinterpreting it). But such a view is unnecessary. The cross and resurrection represent a dramatic deliverance; but more, they truly inaugurate an era in which eschatological gifts such as the Spirit are given.

---

13. Gk. *amen, amen* (see comments on 1:51).

14. This transformation cannot refer to the Parousia since the era in which Christians await the Second Coming should be described as joyous. "I have told you this so that my joy may be in you and that your joy may be complete" (John 15:11).

Prayer and Understanding (16:23–33)

THIS JOY AT seeing Jesus will not only result in a renewed relationship with him, but it will have two notable effects: the joy of understanding (16:23a) and the joy of efficacious prayer (16:23b–24).[15] The confusion described in 16:16–18 will no longer be theirs. At last they will understand (see 16:25–30). The momentous event of the resurrection will at once dispel their apprehensions.

Of course, these faithful men had on many occasions asked God for things in prayer. But the new theological order stipulates that they ask *in Jesus' name*, which is something new, something that belongs to the new spiritual era inaugurated by Jesus' work (see comments on 14:13–14; 15:7, 16). Hoskyns quotes Swete: "The name of Christ is both the passport by which the disciples may claim access into the audience chamber of God and the medium through which the Divine answer comes."[16] Jesus is their shepherd, their patron who will take care of their needs. The intimacy that will result from his indwelling them and their obedience to his word assures their success.

Jesus recognizes that his ministry had used parables and sayings that were difficult to understand. The misunderstanding of the people is a characteristic of the Synoptic portrait of his ministry. Both the crowds and the apostles could not understand many things he did and said (Mark 9:32). In John we have seen in the Book of Signs how often misunderstanding became a literary motif, showing us as readers the world's inability to comprehend the complete significance of Jesus.

Jesus had taught "figuratively" (16:25), but the Greek word used here (*paroimia*) does not simply mean illustrative speech or the use of metaphor and parable; rather, it is speech that is obscure and enigmatic. It occurs in the good shepherd sermon, "Jesus used this figure of speech [Gk. *paroimia*], but they did not understand what he was telling them" (10:6). For the Middle Easterner, this is the "dark saying," which typically possesses prophecy or wisdom.

The "hour" (16:25; NIV, "time") that is coming, however, is not the time immediately following, but the "hour of glorification," that passage of Jesus out of this world when he returns to the Father and sends to them the Holy Spirit (2:4; 7:39). As we have seen many times, *hora* ("hour") is a theological term for John. This will be a new era, when revelation of Jesus will be spoken "plainly" (Gk. *parresia*). No doubt we should again look to the work of the Spirit, through whose efforts the Father's words given through the Son are brought to the disciples (14:10; 15:15), and through whose presence the Father and the Son indwell the disciples (14:23).

---

15. Beasley-Murray, *John*, 285.

16. H. B. Swete, *The Last Discourse and Prayer of Our Lord: A Study in John 14–17* (London: Macmillan, 1914), 141, cited in Hoskyns, *John*, 579.

This "hour" is about access. Jesus himself has mediated the Father's presence to the world (16:27b; cf. 14:9), and now the Father himself is accessible (16:26–27). There is a new circle of fellowship possible, which now includes not simply Jesus and the disciple, but Jesus, the disciple, *and the Father.*[17] As Augustine commented, "The Son does not ask the Father," but the Father and the Son alike listen to those who ask."[18]

One might call 16:28 a terse, or "plain" (cf. 16:25b), summary of John's doctrine of Christ. His origins are divine and he comes from God; he was sent on a mission to the world; he will return to the Father after completing his work. This is the essence of the Christian faith, distilled to its most essential form. It shows the paradox of the incarnational service of the Son.

The disciples immediately celebrate this "plain speech" (16:29–30) and feel confident that in Jesus they have gained access to unsurpassed wisdom. But this is one more example of tragic misunderstanding, such as we have seen in every other discourse. This final discourse too must end on the same note. The time of complete understanding is coming with the hour of glorification, when the Spirit is given to them as a powerful and unique endowment. It is the Spirit who will give this insight and wisdom from Jesus, and this gift must await "the hour." It cannot happen now. So Jesus must abruptly censure their exuberance (16:31–32).

The language of 16:31 does not make a declaration (as in NIV: "You believe at last!"), as if Jesus now finally can rejoice in their brilliant insights about him. The disciples have not at last discovered faith. This misses the point. Instead, Jesus is asking a question (RSV/NRSV: "Do you now believe?"), placing some doubt on their achievement.[19] They do not believe with the rigor or insight that they think. *Now* they think they've got it? At the "hour," in fact, they will be scattered in their fear (16:32; cf. Matt. 26:56). If they had understood, if they had believed fully, they would have the strength to cross this obstacle, but they do not.

While his disciples will desert him, Jesus says that nevertheless he will not be alone because the Father will never leave him (John 16:32b). This verse does not contradict Jesus' cry of desolation on the cross (Mark 15:34, "My God, my God, why have you forsaken me?"). In John, Jesus is comparing the faithfulness of God through the hour of glorification and contrasting it with the faithlessness of his disciples. Mark records Jesus' moment of agony when he cites Psalm 22:1, which reflects something of the mystery

---

17. Barrett, *John,* 496.

18. Cited in Hoskyns, *John,* 581.

19. The Greek text has two words, *arti pisteuete* ("now you-believe"). In phrases like this only inflection of voice will indicate if it is a question; sometimes the context will give clues (BDF sec. 440). In this case, the criticism of 16:32 is our best clue.

of his complete humanity, a humanity that could experience desolation even at this depth.[20]

John 16:33 records Jesus' final words to his disciples before his arrest. Last words are always precious. These words given by Jesus are doubly so. Luther wrote of them in a letter to Melanchthon, "Such a saying as this is worthy to be carried from Rome to Jerusalem upon one's knees."[21]

Jesus does not continue his chastising words of 16:31–32 but instead supplies comfort and reassurance. His exhortation was for their benefit since the days to come will be difficult for each of them. He has already referred to peace (14:27) and joy (16:20, 22) as two gifts belonging to his followers, but these must be seen together with the struggle (NIV "trouble") and conflict they have in the world. Discipleship is about learning how to discover peace when surrounded by threat, how to possess tranquillity despite those hostile to your faith. The solution is "courage" (Gk. *tharseo*, 16:33b; NIV "take heart!"). This word occurs only here in John but is used in the Synoptics to describe the attitude Jesus sought in the disciples during the Galilee storm (Matt. 14:27; Mark 6:50). It was also the word given by the Lord to Paul in Jerusalem when he was surrounded by enemies (Acts 23:11). Despite the circumstances, the victory of Jesus ("I have overcome the world") outweighs the jeopardy of the present crisis.

Bridging Contexts

CHAPTER 16 PROVIDES an array of practical possibilities. While there are numerous relevant themes that can be brought into our generation, interpreters have not always agreed on how some of them ought to be applied. This is particularly true of the work of the Spirit in 16:8–11 and 16:12–14. Among those interpreters who stress the ongoing work of the Holy Spirit in the church today, these verses have a great deal to say. But among those who confine the Spirit's revelatory work to the apostolic age and see the development of the canon of Scripture as the chief effort of the Spirit, these verses have a restricted applicability.

In John 16 Jesus continues to talk about the equipment of the church as he anticipates his departure. He began this lengthy sermon in 13:31; therefore, students of chapter 16 should begin their study there in order to see how themes woven throughout the discourse are presupposed in the present verses. Foremost on Jesus' mind is the gift of the Holy Spirit, which he

---

20 According to many scholars today, Jesus probably did not simply cite Ps. 22:1. He likely recited the entire psalm, which ends on a note of faith and confidence.

21. D. G. Miller, "Tribulation, but   " *Int* 18 (1964): 165

promises five times in chapters 14–16. He even supplies a unique name for the Spirit, the "Paraclete" (see comment on 14:16).

This Spirit will not only bring gifts to the church, but will supply the ongoing presence of Jesus in the church. In this sense, throughout the discourse Jesus and the Spirit are closely aligned. The Spirit virtually becomes the *alter ego* of Jesus (as I termed it above), continuing Jesus' work and reiterating his words. In chapter 14 Jesus makes a subtle play on the language regularly used for his second coming. "I will come back" (14:3) evolves to "I will come to you" (14:18) so that by the end of the chapter, we find ourselves learning that Jesus' "coming" might well be an apt description of the indwelling of the Spirit-Paraclete.

Now in chapter 16 a different theological question comes into view. If it is true that the "coming" of Jesus can also be found in the coming of the Spirit, the disciples now inquire *when* this will happen. Chapter 16 thus gives us numerous clues that point to the day of resurrection, Easter, as the great day when all questions will be dispelled and when Jesus' relationship with his followers will be perfected in the Spirit.

Keeping this wider theological framework in mind, there are at least four themes that come to the fore in any application of the chapter. John provides our two final descriptions of the work of the Spirit; to these should be added the theological meaning of the resurrection not only as a validation of Jesus' divine sonship, but as an experience for disciples solidifying their understanding of Jesus. Finally, the chapter ends with a candid description of the tensions inherent in the Christian life, a life of empowerment and victory that simultaneously experiences difficulties in the world.

The duties of the Spirit. In 16:4b–11 (the fourth promise of the Spirit) Jesus outlines some of the remarkable duties of the Spirit. An interpreter must first decide the meaning of the Greek verb *elencho* (see above, 16:8). Does this describe convincing or convicting? If the Spirit *convinces*, who is his audience: disciples in their witness before the world or the world itself? The latter option is difficult to defend since the world is rarely convinced of its error as it stands in stark opposition to Christ. Despite its value as an apologetic tool, this view of the Spirit in 16:8–11 will have to go.

But if the Spirit *convicts* (as I have argued), then the audience is most naturally the world, which (ironically) is really on trial here before God. The courtroom scenario of the Fourth Gospel (or the "trial motif") we have seen since chapter 5 now undergoes a dramatic reversal: The Spirit will empower the testimony of the church, making its word incisive and its indictment of the world clear. The message of the church is not only about a "better product" or a better life that might entice the unbeliever. The message of the church is also prophetic: It incriminates the moral and spiritual bankruptcy of the world around us. The world lives under the judgment of God; its institutions are infirm and impotent. When the church announces its indictment in the power of the Spirit, there will be trouble.

The revelatory role of the Spirit. In John's fifth promise of the Spirit (16:12–15), Jesus discloses that the Spirit will have a revelatory role, unveiling things that the disciples have not yet heard. These verses complement what we read in 14:26, and the two sections must be read closely together. John's understanding of revelation has two foci: (1) There is historical remembering, in which the words from Jesus' earthly ministry are recalled accurately by the Spirit. (2) There is ongoing illumination, which either (a) *applies* these historic words to new contexts or (b) *opens up new vistas,* new ideas, that the church has not known before.

Evangelicals have traditionally preferred to see this work of the Spirit as closely tied to the development of Scripture and its use. This is in part an exegetical decision that believes that the promises of this section belong not to the church universal but to the apostles only. "I have much more to say *to you*" (16:12, italics added) points to Jesus' immediate audience. Hendriksen's well-known commentary on John thus sees this ongoing revelation in 16:12 as fulfilled in the writing of the book of Acts and Paul's letters.[22]

But if the Spirit's work goes beyond the production of the Scriptures—that is, if we have here a genuine prophetic gift that provides ongoing revelation—we then have to discern the guidelines and limitations for such revelation. Is this promise (like so many biblical promises) extended to every Christian? I would argue that it is.[23] If so, what are the limits of its use? Calvin, for instance, writing in 1553 on these verses, lapses into nothing short of a tirade here as he outlines the "wicked abuses" of medieval Catholics, who (in his mind) use the verse to justify the "most stupid and absurd things imaginable."[24] Some would argue that the Protestant church in the modern era has been subject to similar abuses.

---

22. Hendriksen, *John,* 328.

23. Interpreters who refuse to apply this promise of the Spirit to the postapostolic church must then justify how they can apply other spiritual promises to the church. Who owns the promise, "I will come again and take you to myself" (14:3) when it was addressed to the Twelve? These promises, just like the command to "love one another," belong both to the circle of apostles *and* to the later church.

24. Calvin, *John,* 375–76. What sounds amusing today was no doubt deadly serious in Calvin's day as the Reformers debated the institutions and the power of the dominant Catholic church in Europe. "Did the Spirit have to come down from heaven for the apostles to learn by what ceremony to consecrate cups and altars, baptize church bells, bless holy water, and celebrate Mass? . . . It is perfectly clear that the Roman Catholics are mocking God when they claim that those things came from heaven." Happily this sort of rhetoric has no place in the church today.

Jesus and his disciples. The incomprehensibility of Jesus' words and deeds not only frustrated the disciples (note 16:29, "Now you are speaking clearly") but must have frustrated him as well. He is their friend (15:15), and friends share a mutual understanding that is impossible with strangers. Yet Jesus knows that it is impossible for them to comprehend the totality of who he is and of what God is doing in the world before the time of his glorification. In particular, his resurrection will change everything when they will no longer need to ask him questions (16:23). "Seeing Jesus" is the solution, and this "seeing" will take place on Easter when the tomb is opened (16:16) and all questions disappear.

This means a couple of things for us. (1) The resurrection should be the center point of our proclamation about Jesus. It is not one more event in a series of events, it is *the event* that climaxes Jesus' self-revelation in the world. It is a historical confirmation that God has penetrated our world and begun to set things right.

(2) But this proves to be a dilemma for those of us who live on the other side of the resurrection. *We have questions.* We have not had the privilege of "seeing Jesus" as the early apostles had it. And while we might say that Jesus is with us in Spirit, this is not what Jesus is offering to his disciples. In addition to the Spirit, he says that the objective, historical event of the resurrection will resolve many of their doubts. Evangelicals might say that we possess the Scriptures (which were unavailable to the apostles) and that these should supply renewed confidence. But would Jesus expect the generations that follow the apostles to be satisfied *without* seeing him? It is interesting that in 20:29 Jesus offers a special blessing on us in this circumstance when he speaks to Thomas, "Blessed are those who have *not* seen and yet have believed." What then is the basis of *our* confidence?

Life in the world. All along we have listened to Jesus talk about the reality of life in the world. He has not been subtle. "If the world hates you, keep in mind that it hated me first" (15:18). John uses the term *world* eighty times, and fully one-third of these describe the world as a place of unbelief and conflict. Yet Jesus also says that he has overcome the world (16:33) and that Christians who live in the world should have peace and joy (16:20, 33).

This produces a theological tension that has led to numerous mistaken spiritualities. In a word, how do I combine the victory of Jesus and the trouble of the world? Is it a sin or a failure of faith to admit to suffering and despair in the world? To admit to illness? Does this deny the victory of Jesus? For others is the acceptance of struggle and spiritual battle—to acknowledge the world in all its power—a concession that has no place for Christ as victor? Where is the power of God when the power of the world sometimes seems so overwhelming and we feel defeated?

AT LEAST FOUR areas of current application are possible in this chapter. True, there are other themes embedded here, such as the promise of efficacious prayer in 16:23 or the implied Trinitarian relationships, but most of these have been discussed in earlier sections (since 13:31).

The conviction of the world. The presupposition of the convicting work of the Holy Spirit is a courageous belief in the spiritual, moral, and intellectual bankruptcy of the world. The problem with most of us is that we have adapted to the world so successfully that we no longer *truly* believe that its systems of belief, life, and thought are wrong. Like the proverbial frog slowly cooked in a warming pot of water, we don't realize our jeopardy till it is too late.

In his Farewell Discourse, Jesus provides two promises regarding the Spirit and the world. In chapter 15, he describes the hostility of the world and promises that the Spirit will come as a ready aid to strengthen the witness of the church (15:26). However, in chapter 16, it is not the defensive posture of the church that is at issue but the *offensive efforts* of Christians. That is, in 16:8–11 the Spirit works to prosecute the moral and spiritual catastrophe of the world in which we live.[25]

There is a brilliant image that C. S. Lewis provides in his well-known space trilogy. The hero of the series is Ransom, a university philologist who accidentally finds himself on a spaceship headed to Mars. There he witnesses the attempted corruption of the planet by two diabolical humans (who are a "bent" species, the Martians say), and he also learns about the true nature of the universe. He meets Eldils, for instance, who are spirit-beings serving The Great Spirit who made the universe. Each planet has its own chief Eldil, and in due course he meets these "gods" of Mars and Venus, who have kept their planets (and their residents) from falling into sin. Earth, on the other hand, is "the Silent Planet," for in it darkness reigns. The point of the series is Lewis's exploration into the nature of human fallenness, and after Ransom explores Mars and Venus in the first two books, in the third volume he finds himself on Earth, confronting the darkness, the wretchedness of the "world." The divine forces of the universe have decided that the evil of Earth must be extinguished before its corruptions spill over into other spheres.

One evening for the first time Eldils from deep heaven begin their descent and siege of Earth. Suddenly they appear in dazzling brightness in Ransom's quarters. They are like shining pillars of light, powerful and dangerous, spinning at a speed he cannot fathom. But the important part lies

---

25. This general application of the Spirit's work is explored in the exposition of L. Newbigin, *The Light Has Come* (Grand Rapids: Eerdmans, 1982), 211–14.

here: They are not exactly vertical columns but seem to stand about ten degrees off. The impression Ransom has, however, is not that they are "off 10 degrees" but that they are in fact connected to "true vertical" and that the entire world is "off 10 degrees." For the first time Ransom sees "true vertical," and it makes the entire world seem irregular. Forever Ransom knows that the floor is not quite level.

In one of the most creative portrayals of human wretchedness and fallenness I have read, Lewis builds a portrait of human depravity that is stunning. The books are a rebuke: We need to be reminded that the sin of the world should stun us, but it does not.

One mission of the church, therefore, is to be the *one voice* that holds an honest assessment of the world, that speaks of the way it twists the meaning of sin, righteousness, and judgment, and that describes boldly its absence of justice and compassion and its failure to promote true virtue in the fear of God. The church's testimony should uncover "true vertical" so that the world can see how it has skewed our reality. This is the courageous testimony that the Spirit seeks to engage and empower.

"In the name of God! We know not what we should say to this.... Against the ungodliness and unrighteousness of men there is revealed the wrath of God."[26] These are some of the opening words furiously penned by Karl Barth in his Romans commentary on Romans 1:18–21, Paul's indictment of the world that Jesus describes in John 16. As Lewis wrote following the horror of World War II, Barth wrote at the close of World War I—and both men loathed what they saw when they looked into the heart of humanity. It is not just that individuals have a propensity to sin, but that corruption is universal and unavoidable and that whole systems of life have been built to sustain a darkness the world calls light, to keep in place injustices that only the world calls fair.

Therefore the mandate of John 16:8–11 is for us—in prayer, guided by the Holy Spirit, listening for the voice of Christ—to identify and diagnose the true nerve-system of this world in our own generation. "The prince of this world now stands condemned" (16:11b)—which means that the moral and spiritual struggle is not only about sinful humans, but about humans whose communities and organizations, governments and politics have been manipulated by Satan. To diagnose the injustice, say, of racially discriminatory programs becomes spiritual warfare. To unmask the dishonesty or deviousness of political systems that sustain suffering and anguish around the globe or around the corner is spiritual warfare too.

---

26. K. Barth, *The Epistle to the Romans*, 6th ed. (1918, 1928[6]; ET: Oxford: Oxford Univ. Press, 1932), 42.

Sometimes such activity will be labeled as unpatriotic (when we name political or military evil) or antisocial (when we identify the key players in evil deeds). But true vertical, once seen, demands that all floors be straightened and leveled. All floors! Every floor in this world, because each one has been bent by the world on which it rests.

If the church talks about the Holy Spirit only in terms of the emotional healing it may bring or the praise and worship it may generate, the church has missed part of the Spirit's work. Charismatic gifts, healings, and signs and wonders are only part of the Spirit's mission. The Spirit is also engaged in the prosecution of the world. The Spirit is likewise about battle and struggle and winning so that the kingdom of God described by Jesus will begin to emerge like a mustard seed, whose shrub stands visibly on the landscape (Matt. 13:31–32).

The Spirit and revelation. The book of Acts records a remarkable story in chapters 10–11, which we often refer to as the conversion of Cornelius, but I think of it as the conversion of Peter. It was not missionary passion or liberal theological views that led Peter to travel from Jewish Joppa to Gentile Caesarea in order to convert the Roman military centurion. Lesslie Newbigin writes:

> It was the Spirit that put him there, and it was the Spirit that shattered all of Peter's strongest religious certainties by giving to Cornelius and his household exactly the same experience of deliverance and joy as the apostles themselves had received. In the presence of that *fait accompli* Peter, and—later—the whole church, had simply to follow where they were led.[27]

Peter was forcefully directed by the Spirit to move into new theological territory that must have seemed completely uncertain. This is what Jesus describes in John 16:12–14. The Spirit will be "the Spirit of truth," guiding his followers into all truth, which they could not then bear to hear but which Jesus no doubt wanted to tell them later.

Here is the heart of the question: Does the Spirit simply lead each generation to apply the truths of Jesus in new ways? Certainly this is true. But does the Spirit also lead into new territory, new doctrines, and new activities unknown in Jesus' historical ministry? In the present example, one could argue that Peter's mention of clean and unclean in Acts 10:14 may echo Matthew 15:11 (Mark 7:19; cf. Rom. 14:14), where Jesus redefines "unclean" with new parameters. The Spirit has simply pressed the apostles to apply this truth in an unexpected way. But others have argued that the conversion of a

---

27. L. Newbigin, *The Light Has Come*, 216.

Gentile was something wholly unexpected. To cross a racial and cultural frontier is something Jesus did not predict and only now does the Spirit disclose it.[28]

John is the only Gospel that gives us some idea of the relationship between the Spirit and interpretation. John is fully aware that the deeper meaning of Jesus' words only came once he had been glorified and the apostles had experienced the Holy Spirit. In two places John specifically states that the plain meaning of Jesus' words remained veiled in their original setting and that it was only after Jesus' glorification (with its attendant gift of the Spirit) that true understanding came (2:22; 12:16). This is what Jesus means in 16:25 when he points to a time when plain speech will disclose the exact meaning of his words. Veiled revelation will be gone; clarity of spiritual insight will be an apostolic gift.

We can extend this perspective to John's overall effort to "write up" the story of Jesus' life in the Gospel itself. It was the Spirit that recalled to his mind the things Jesus had said and done (14:26), and it was the Spirit that led him into "all truth," probing beneath the surface of Jesus' mission. This also explains John's use of irony and "misunderstanding" as a motif in the Gospel: Jesus' audience misunderstood his purposes at many points, and it was only with the gift of the Spirit that his followers could really see his meaning.

Therefore in the first instance the work of the Spirit brings a Spirit-directed illumination as we interpret the Bible. This is God's Word, which now God's Spirit opens for us. With Calvin and a host of Protestant interpreters, the "all truth" of 16:13 refers to Scripture, opened and examined with divine guidance.[29]

But this explanation of 16:12–14 is inadequate if it is all we say about the Spirit and revelation. Jesus says that the Spirit will unveil things they have *not* heard. Such an understanding, of course, has led to countless abuses over the centuries as self-appointed teachers and new-age prophets have laid claim to the Spirit's authority as they unveiled new, unbiblical teachings. These abuses have made modern exegetes understandably cautious about such ongoing revelation, and some of them claim that we are doing nothing more than pressing modern issues of church life on John's ancient text.[30] But this is not the case.

---

28. See Matt. 10:5–6, "These twelve Jesus sent out with the following instructions: 'Do not go among the Gentiles or enter any town of the Samaritans. Go, rather, to the lost sheep of Israel.'"

29. J. Calvin, *John*, 375. Calvin points to 2 Tim. 3:17 and shows how the Spirit not only inspires the text of Scripture but equips us to use it. Also similarly see Carson, *The Farewell Discourse and Final Prayer of Jesus*, 150–51; Brown, *John*, 2:716.

30. So Carson, *John*, 542.

The best evidence for the view that John's followers understood the Spirit to have ongoing revelatory power can be seen in the abuses John had to combat in his first letter.[31] Since many false prophets have gone out into the world, John's followers need to start testing the spirits to see if they belong to God (1 John 4:1). John does not disqualify the spiritual endowment in his argument with these teachers; he calls for the testing of the gift. The problem arises from false teachers exploiting a prophetic understanding of the Spirit, who now are leading the church into false doctrines. Here John gives strict guidelines: "This is how you can recognize the Spirit of God: Every spirit that acknowledges that Jesus Christ has come in the flesh is from God, but every spirit that does not acknowledge Jesus is not from God" (1 John 4:2–3). This is the same test Jesus outlines in John 16:14–15. The Spirit will glorify Jesus and not depart from what he has revealed already. To refuse to glorify Jesus is to invalidate one's prophetic voice.

Therefore, as we look at the work of the Spirit today, we see that not only does the Spirit recall, authenticate, and enliven the teaching of Jesus for each generation, but *also* the Spirit works creatively in the church, bringing a new prophetic word.[32] This word never contradicts the historic word of Jesus and never deflects glory away from Jesus, but it may faithfully bring the church to see its message and mission in a new way. The "all truth" of 16:13 may be something unexpected, some new frontier (like a modern Gentile Caesarea), or some new work Jesus desires to do in the present time. The task of the church and its leadership is to discern with great care what that work might be.

To restrict the Spirit's voice to the work of historic recitation, that is, to the application of the biblical text, is to restrict the Spirit's effort to speak to contemporary issues. It is interesting that in Paul's writing, he lists prophets and teachers in the second and third places of authority after apostles (1 Cor. 13:28). In Acts 13:1 prophets and teachers led the church at Antioch where there were no apostles. The Spirit both equips those who guide the church into the deeper meaning of Scripture (teachers) and those who have a contemporary word, a dynamic word for the church in its world today (prophets).

Resurrection and resolution. Running through John 16 is Jesus' repeated assurance that "in a little while" his disciples will see him again. As I argued above, this "seeing" points to the resurrection, for "seeing the Lord" becomes a watchword on Easter for having encountered the resurrected, glorified Jesus. The importance of this is even underscored in 1 John 1:1–3:

---

31. See Brown, *The Community of the Beloved Disciple,* 138–44.
32. See T. Smail, *The Giving Gift· The Holy Spirit in Person,* 75; notice how in Rev. 1:10 John himself, who is "in the Spirit," experiences Jesus speaking following his ascension.

That which was from the beginning, which we have heard, which *we have seen* with our eyes, which *we have looked at* and our hands have touched—this we proclaim concerning the Word of life. The life appeared; *we have seen it* and testify to it, and we proclaim to you the eternal life, which was with the Father and *has appeared to us.* We proclaim to you what *we have seen* and heard, so that you also may have fellowship with us. And our fellowship is with the Father and with his Son, Jesus Christ. (italics added)

There is no doubt that for John the concrete visual encounter he had with the resurrected Jesus was foundational to his testimony. This "seeing" was not simply a metaphor, as if now in his faith, belief in resurrection "dawned" on him. This Jesus is someone seen and "touched"; this is an objective anchor that he refers to with great relish throughout his letter (1 John 1:1, 3; 3:2, 6; 4:1, 12, 14, 20; 5:16; 3 John 1:11). These verses in 1 John link up with John's repeated reference to "that which was from the beginning" (1:1; 2:7, 13–14, 24; 3:11; 2 John 1:5), which reminds his followers that the strongest argument for the truth of Jesus was found on Easter morning. The resurrection validated Jesus' truth claims about himself and forced the apostolic leaders to look back on his earthly life and reflect more deeply (with the aid of the Spirit) on the meaning of these events.

Paul follows this same tack in 1 Corinthians 15. The truth about his faith is not to be found merely in self-validating spiritual experiences, but also in the reality of resurrection from the dead. "If Christ has not been raised then our preaching is in vain and your faith is in vain" (15:14).

For the earliest Christians, Jesus' resurrection was the starting point for evangelism and proclamation. "This [Jesus] ... you ... put to death by nailing him to the cross. ... But God raised him from the dead" (Acts 2:23–24). These words of Peter on Pentecost become the turning point in sermon after sermon in Acts (see Acts 4:10; 5:30; 10:40; 13:30, 34, 37; 26:8). The same should be true of our proclamation. The resurrection of Christ should be the bold, unflinching word we possess for the world. Jesus knows what this moment will mean for his followers. "You will rejoice," he says (John 16:22). "Your grief will turn to joy" (16:20). No doubt, Easter was the catalyst for the apostolic faith, and it inspired much of the reflection we read in the New Testament today.

But what about us today? We do not live in an era that can await such a moment of resurrection. The "little while" of chapter 16 is now long past. The resurrection of Jesus in Jerusalem is not a personal experience to which we can point, but instead has become a solid doctrinal position that we hold with fervor. I envy the Easter experience of John, Peter, James, and the other disciples. And I would wish that the blessing pronounced by Jesus in 20:29,

"Blessed are those who have not seen and yet have believed," did not belong to me and my generation. We live with spiritual imperfection and incompleteness, not unlike the disciples as they awaited Easter. Paul's candid admission is that our vision is opaque, like looking through a dark glass or an ancient mirror (1 Cor. 13:12). We yearn for the day when we will see "face to face" (13:12b) and discover that all our questions have disappeared (John 16:23a).

This is perhaps where an application of John 16 requires that we understand clearly that Jesus participates in four episodes of self-revelation. (1) There was Jesus' earthly ministry, which was filled with ambiguity for his followers. (2) His resurrection provided the confirmation and clarity they yearned to experience. (3) Jesus promised the Spirit, who would serve as his personal, indwelling presence during his absence. (4) We await his glorious second coming, when we once more will *see* him again.

Our experience (episode 3) is similar to that of the disciples (episode 1) inasmuch as we struggle to understand and yearn for perfect clarity. But we have one sterling advantage: We possess the Spirit, who gives us insight and understanding inaccessible even to the apostles. Jesus' resurrection was the disciples' ultimate confirming experience, and while we can only point back to it (as a confirmation of their authority), we must point *forward* to Christ's return. *That is, the Second Coming serves the church much the same way that the resurrection served the apostles.*

In theological language, this is tension between the "already" and the "not yet" of the kingdom of God. We are interim citizens. We live in the kingdom that has been inaugurated by Christ, yet we yearn for that kingdom's final consummation at the end of time. The *history of Jesus* (his miracles, his parables, his empty tomb) must join with our *experience of Jesus* (his lordship, his indwelling Spirit) to form a confident discipleship that remains faithful as it awaits the fulfillment of his promise to return, when we will "see" him again (cf. 1 John 3:2).

"In the world you have trouble." There is a misunderstanding afoot that pertains to Jesus' final words in 16:33: "I have told you these things, so that in me you may have peace. In this world you will have trouble. But take heart! I have overcome the world."[33] Does this mean that the "peace" of Jesus enables us to escape the ills of life, as so many popular preachers today claim? Does faith in Jesus automatically solve all our problems?

I have just suggested that we are interim citizens of the kingdom, looking back to the resurrection and forward to the Second Coming—equipped by the Holy Spirit and eager to see Jesus as his apostles did. In this interim

---

33. In this section I am indebted to the outstanding sermon of Donald Miller, the former president of Pittsburgh Theological Seminary, entitled, "Tribulation; but ... " (165–70).

citizenship we need to understand fully what will be the character of our lives. For some interpreters, possessing the "victory of Jesus" means being exempt from tragedy, conflict, poverty, struggle, and disillusionment.

It is curious that Jesus here speaks of peace and trouble in the same breath. This forces us to carefully define what this peace really is. One sort of peace means the absence of all enemies; the other is freedom from anxiety while struggling with enemies. Who could not be at peace when there is no trouble? But it is the latter notion, peace within the storm, that Jesus has in mind. Donald Miller illustrates:

> It is not noteworthy, for example, for a housewife to be at peace about her housework if she happens to have no children, little company, every modern convenience, and servants to do her menial tasks. It is astonishing, however, when a mother of five children, many visiting relatives, few conveniences, and no servants can work without excitement, without fretting, without worry, moving majestically through the confusion of her overburdened days with poise and dignity.
>
> This type of peace—serenity in the midst of confusion—is superior to the "easier" peace because it abides while conquering obstacles rather than avoiding them.[34]

Therefore it is essential that we keep in mind that peace and trouble do not negate one another. The peace of Jesus is a condition that takes the uncertainties and struggles of this world seriously, but like a seagull riding the surface of a turbulent sea, is able to climb swells and drop into valleys without worry.

We have seen again and again in this Gospel that the world is a place of genuine hostility to the things of God. For a disciple to live in it is necessarily to experience struggle, conflict, even battle. Its values, its vision, its morals, its pagan religious instincts—these are all inimical to the God of the Bible. In this sense, Christian discipleship is nothing short of a call to warfare. Again, permit me to quote Miller:

> As long as a Christian is in the world he will be pressed as though by a great mob; he will be crushed in spirit as though great crushing weights were lying on his chest; he will know spiritual anguish like that of a mother in labor. This, Jesus has told us. When he speaks, therefore, of peace, it is not the peace of unruffled days but the inner confidence of the warrior who is weary, thirsty, outnumbered, and wounded, but who fights bravely on, confident of the outcome, assured of victory. We are saved not *from* trouble; we are saved *in* trouble.[35]

---

34. Ibid., 166.
35. Ibid., 168

In the reality of this sort of world, Jesus says "Take heart" (16:33b). The Greek verb used here is the same one Jesus used for his men in the boat during the Galilee storm (Mark 6:50). More accurately, it means to "have courage." It means taking stock of the circumstances and still prevailing. But the basis of this encouragement is important in the balance of the verse. Jesus does not say, "Have courage—you will overcome the world." The Greek sentence structure is emphatic: "Have courage—*I* have overcome the world."

If Jesus had said, "Have courage, I have overcome the world—and you can too," there would be little good news for us. If a golf master nearly drives on the green from every tee and says to you, "Have courage, I did it! You can do it too!" there is no encouragement here. If the superior student performs perfectly on an exam and says to a less-gifted friend, "Cheer up! I did well, so can you!" such counsel only brings a sharper sense of hopelessness.

If Jesus was simply one heroic man who achieved a superior life, if he was simply a stellar example of what we hoped to be, then he has little value for us. *We have tried to overcome the world, but we have failed.* Jesus' example of superior humanity simply makes my inferiority more unbearable.

But if Jesus is more than a human; if he is indeed the Son of God who overcame the world not simply for his own sake, but for our sake as well—for all of humanity; if his victory in his life can become a victory that we enjoy, a victory extended to us when we embrace him in faith, then his triumph can become our triumph. He thus offers us genuinely good news, "Have courage! I have faced your enemy and vanquished him. I have fought your battle on the battleground of human experience where you must fight. I have routed the foe. You can never do it; but I have done it and I can do it again in you. Abide in me and my victory is yours."[36]

This is the great departure of Christianity from every other religious faith. It does not simply set out an ideal or a moral code; it offers a means of achieving it. Christianity is the offer of God to live in his followers and achieve in them the victory demonstrated in his Son Jesus Christ. And in that indwelling, an indescribable peace will be ours despite the fury and foment of the world around us.

36. Ibid., 169

John 17:1–26

A
FTER JESUS SAID this, he looked toward heaven and
prayed:

"Father, the time has come. Glorify your Son, that
your Son may glorify you. ²For you granted him authority over all people that he might give eternal life to all
those you have given him. ³Now this is eternal life: that
they may know you, the only true God, and Jesus
Christ, whom you have sent. ⁴I have brought you glory
on earth by completing the work you gave me to do.
⁵And now, Father, glorify me in your presence with the
glory I had with you before the world began.

⁶"I have revealed you to those whom you gave me
out of the world. They were yours; you gave them to
me and they have obeyed your word. ⁷Now they know
that everything you have given me comes from you.
⁸For I gave them the words you gave me and they
accepted them. They knew with certainty that I came
from you, and they believed that you sent me. ⁹I pray
for them. I am not praying for the world, but for those
you have given me, for they are yours. ¹⁰All I have is
yours, and all you have is mine. And glory has come to
me through them. ¹¹I will remain in the world no longer,
but they are still in the world, and I am coming to you.
Holy Father, protect them by the power of your name—
the name you gave me—so that they may be one as we
are one. ¹²While I was with them, I protected them and
kept them safe by that name you gave me. None has
been lost except the one doomed to destruction so that
Scripture would be fulfilled.

¹³"I am coming to you now, but I say these things
while I am still in the world, so that they may have the
full measure of my joy within them. ¹⁴I have given them
your word and the world has hated them, for they are
not of the world any more than I am of the world. ¹⁵My
prayer is not that you take them out of the world but
that you protect them from the evil one. ¹⁶They are not

of the world, even as I am not of it. [17]Sanctify them by the truth; your word is truth. [18]As you sent me into the world, I have sent them into the world. [19]For them I sanctify myself, that they too may be truly sanctified.

[20]"My prayer is not for them alone. I pray also for those who will believe in me through their message, [21]that all of them may be one, Father, just as you are in me and I am in you. May they also be in us so that the world may believe that you have sent me. [22]I have given them the glory that you gave me, that they may be one as we are one: [23]I in them and you in me. May they be brought to complete unity to let the world know that you sent me and have loved them even as you have loved me.

[24]"Father, I want those you have given me to be with me where I am, and to see my glory, the glory you have given me because you loved me before the creation of the world.

[25]"Righteous Father, though the world does not know you, I know you, and they know that you have sent me. [26]I have made you known to them, and will continue to make you known in order that the love you have for me may be in them and that I myself may be in them."

JOHN 17 GIVES us a glimpse into the heart of Jesus unlike any other chapter in the four Gospels. For many readers of this "beloved Gospel" it is the "beloved chapter," expressing so much of what Jesus aimed to express in his life and work.[1] It is the longest prayer that we have from Jesus. Luke often mentions Jesus at prayer (Luke 3:21; 5:16; 6:12; 9:18, 28–29; 11:1; 22:41–45; 23:46); perhaps the Lord's Prayer is comparable, but not even it provides the depth and range of ideas offered here.[2] Listening to the prayer of someone often provides a glimpse into the deeper recesses of that person's consciousness of God. Such is certainly true in this prayer. Over a hundred years ago one commentator wrote: "No attempt to

---

1 One can find devotional literature focused exclusively on this prayer, particularly from earlier days, such as H C. G. Moule's *The High Priestly Prayer* (London: Religious Tract Society, 1908). Moule writes (9), "Let him who would presume to comment upon it [this prayer] prepare himself first, as it were, kneeling to worship at its threshold."

2. See M M. B. Turner, "Prayer in the Gospels and Acts," in D. A. Carson, ed., *Teach Us to Pray. Prayer in the Bible and the World* (Grand Rapids· Baker, 1990), 58–83.

describe the prayer can give a just idea of its sublimity, its pathos, its touching yet exalted character, its tone at once of tenderness and triumphant expectation."[3]

In our introduction to the Farewell Discourse (see comments on ch. 14) we concluded that these chapters in John fit a defined literary form in Judaism. Dying or departing leaders, prophets, and rabbis commonly provided "final words" of instruction for their disciples who remained behind. This tradition also made use of a "departing prayer," which closes the farewell speech. Earlier we compared the farewell of Moses in Deuteronomy, and now we can return to it. That farewell (Deut. 32–33) has a form of prayer similar to that found in John 17. As Israel listens, Moses begins by praising God: "I will proclaim the name of the LORD. Oh, praise the greatness of our God!" (32:3). Following this lengthy prayer, Moses then turns to the Israelites and prays a blessing on them for their future (ch. 33).

This is the pattern of John 17. Jesus turns from his own concerns with God (17:1–8) to those of the church and its future (17:9–26). The same pattern is displayed in Leviticus when Aaron the priest learns how to sacrifice and pray. First he prays and worships on his own behalf (Lev. 16:11–14), then he offers a sin offering and prayer for the people (16:15–19).

Technically, while Jesus' prayer presents us with these two divisions, the second division of the prayer should be divided into two parts. Following his personal prayer, Jesus prays for his personal disciples (17:9–19) and then prays for those who will be *their* disciples (17:20–26). This then organizes the prayer into three separate sections: Jesus prays for himself, for his followers, and for the later church. This organization is so finely built that Brown has shown how each of the three parts even displays parallel themes:[4]

- Each part begins with what Jesus is asking or praying for (vv. 1, 9, 20)
- Each has the theme of glory (vv. 1–5, 10, 22)
- Each has an address to the Father partway through (vv. 5, 11, 21)
- Each mentions the followers given to Jesus by the Father (vv. 2, 9, 24)
- Each has the theme of Jesus' revelation of the Father to his followers (v. 6, "your name"; v. 14, "your word"; v. 26, "your name")

Such symmetry has led to numerous theories about the history of the prayer.[5] Its natural use of "Father" in its petitions anchors it securely to the usual

---

3. W. Milligan and W. F. Moulton, *Commentary on St. John* (Edinburgh, 1898), cited in L. Morris, *John*, 634.

4. Brown, *John*, 2:750.

5. M. L. Appold, *The Oneness Motif in the Fourth Gospel* (Tübingen: Mohr, 1976), 194–211. For another analysis of the symmetry of the prayer, see E. Malatesta, "The Literary Structure of John 17," *Bib* 52.2 (1971): 190–214 (includes folding charts).

custom of Jesus' habit of speech.[6] Some compare the prayer with the finely worked prologue of John (1:1–18) and wonder if this prayer was ever used separately, even liturgically, in John's own church. Note that Mark 14:26 says that at the end of their evening in the Upper Room, the disciples sang a hymn before departing. This has led some to speculate whether this prayer could have also been used in eucharistic worship.[7] But these are all theories, and proof for them is impossible. We can be confident, however, that the prayer did not originate on its own separate from the Farewell Discourse, for the themes found in it build on ideas already covered in the preceding chapters.

We should also try to understand the theological role of the prayer in the portrait we have of Jesus in this Gospel. In the Synoptics we read about Jesus in prayer before his arrest, struggling with the true meaning of his sacrifice (Matt. 26:36–33; Mark 14:32–42; Luke 22:41–45). However, the agony of Gethsemane is never suggested in John, for whom Jesus is confident and hopeful. The prayer is uttered just prior to Jesus' arrest (18:3), which places it chronologically in the right place with Jesus' Gethsemane prayer, but the atmosphere of the prayer cannot be compared.

But this does not mean that the prayers are at odds with one another. The combined portrait we find of Jesus is convincing: He simultaneously experienced the anxiety of the cross and came to resolution through his confidence in and obedience to God. The Synoptics all record Jesus' firm obedience to God ("My Father, if it is possible, may this cup be taken from me. *Yet not as I will, but as you will*"; Matt. 26:39, italics added) and his confidence that whatever should come this night is firmly rooted in God's will.

Many have called this chapter Jesus' "high priestly prayer," in which he prays for himself and intercedes for his followers. Such a view fits the work of Christ described in Romans 8:34 and Hebrews 7:25 (though this work is reserved generally for his service following his ascension). John knows this theme and in 1 John 2:1–2 can describe Jesus in his intercessory work. For others, this is Jesus' "prayer of consecration," in which he prepares himself for his death and glorification, readying himself to be a sacrifice for his followers. In John 17:19, for instance, Jesus seems to be heading to the sacrificial altar ("For them I sanctify myself, that they too may be truly sanctified"). Westcott tied in this idea with Jesus' departure from the Upper Room in 14:31 and concluded that since Jesus has not yet left the Kidron Valley (18:1), he may be praying in the temple, the com-

---

6. S. Smalley surveys the problem of the historicity of the prayer in *John. Evangelist and Interpreter* (Exeter: Paternoster, 1978), 188–90.

7. In this case, comparisons are made between John 17 and the earliest complete Eucharist service we possess recorded in the *Didache*. See O. Cullmann, *Early Christian Worship* (Naperville: Allenson, 1953), 110.

mon place of sacrifice.[8] Other scholars object that the chapter contains no notion of sacrifice, that the prayer is not "priestly," and that Jesus aims to simply reveal his unity with the Father.[9]

No doubt prayers of personal consecration and priestly intercession are central to the meaning of Jesus' words in this chapter. All is being said in the shadow of the cross, and Jesus is not only preparing himself for this momentous event, but thinking about his followers. But we also have to see the prayer as an opportunity for further revelation. We should not assume that Jesus' prayer was something said privately; rather, in the Jewish tradition it was said aloud and so was available for his followers to hear (cf. 11:41–42; 12:27–30; also Matt. 11:25–30; Luke 10:21–22). The disciples are invited (as are readers) to catch a glimpse of Jesus' intimate relation between himself and his Father and to learn of his origins and his future, his mission and its successes, his concerns and his hopes. As the last chapter before Jesus' arrest, trial, and crucifixion, this is the Gospel's final opportunity to sweep up the many ideas about Jesus given in every other chapter. John 17 is in this sense a summary of Jesus' ministry. As the prologue anticipated the major ideas of the gospel (1:1–18), this prayer reviews and consolidates them.

Three themes thread their way through many of the prayer's paragraphs. (1) Jesus prays about glorification, that his obedience in this hour will truly bring glory to God. (2) He also prays for his followers' survival. Will they survive the enmity of the world? Will they remain united despite their differences? Do they truly possess the tools he has given them: knowing God's love as well as his Word, obeying his commands? (3) Finally, he prays about holiness. Will his followers emulate the holiness he has shown them? Will their lives so reflect the life of the Son living in them that they become living testimonies to the world?

Jesus Prays for Himself (17:1–8)

IT IS NOT entirely correct to view this opening to the prayer as Jesus' "praying for himself" (in contrast to him praying for others in later sections). It is not as if he has a list of petitions that he offers to God. There is no self-seeking here. We find but a single petition—"Glorify your Son, that your Son may glorify you"—repeated in these verses. This section of the prayer finds Jesus talking to his Father about his efforts on earth to glorify God and to be obedient to his will. In this sense, the section presupposes the incarnational Christology of the prologue. But now, with the work of the Incarnation complete (which assumes Jesus' descent from heavenly glory), Jesus anticipates his ascent, his resumption of the glory he had before creation.

---

8. On Passover the gates of the city were left open all night to accommodate the many pilgrims in Jerusalem (Josephus, *Ant* 18.2.2).

9. This debate will concern us in our interpretation of 17:17–19.

The opening phrase ("After Jesus said this," 17:1) links the prayer to the Farewell Discourse that Jesus has now completed.[10] He assumes a common Jewish posture for prayer by raising his eyes toward heaven (cf. 11:41, at Lazarus' tomb; also cf. Ps. 123:1). In the parable of the tax collector one sign of the man's humility is his refusal to lift his eyes to heaven (Luke 18:13). When Jesus prayed, he also probably raised his hands in the same direction (Ex. 9:33; 17:11; Ps. 28:2). Jesus' culture was accustomed to physical gestures (speech, movement, sound) accompanying religious activity.[11]

Addressing God as "Father" was Jesus' habit, and in this prayer it occurs six times (see also 11:41; 12:27). In 17:11 it becomes "holy Father" and in 17:25 "righteous Father." Such intimate language for God was a hallmark of Jesus' spirituality and led no doubt to the early Christian preference of imitating Jesus' Aramaic title for God, *Abba* (Father), even by those who spoke Greek (Mark 14:36; Rom. 8:15; Gal. 4:6). Jesus says that the "hour" (Gk. *hora*; NIV "time") has come, which points to "the hour of glorification" we have anticipated throughout the Gospel (see comment on 2:4). That Jesus mentioned the arrival of this *hora* in 12:23 and 13:1 (cf. 13:31) indicates that this "hour" is an elastic period of time that will incorporate the many events of Jesus' departure (from his final night with his followers through to the cross and resurrection). Now, however, the words gain an added poignancy. Shortly the hour will accelerate when during this night Jesus is suddenly arrested (18:1–14).

What does Jesus mean when he asks to be "glorified"? The Greek word used here (*doxazo*) means to venerate, bring homage or praise (see 1:14; 12:28). For Jesus the cross is not a place of shame, but a place of honor. His oneness with the Father means that as he is glorified, so too is the Father glorified. His impulse, then, is not for self-promotion but glorification, *so that* the Father can be honored through his obedience.

This unique connection with the Father finds further explanation (17:2) inasmuch as Jesus also possesses a divine authority over all humanity (5:27; cf. Matt. 11:27; 28:18) so that he may distribute to them eternal life (John 3:35–36; 10:28).[12] The tension between God's sovereignty and election in 17:2 and his universal love for the world is a subject that comes up regularly in this

---

10. This point is important because of critics who suggest that the prayer is foreign to the Farewell Discourse. Bultmann (*John*, 486–522), for instance, moves the prayer so that it follows chapter 13 and sees no historicity in its words or linkage with the discourse.

11. This might be contrasted with a common traditional posture of prayer in the West: hands folded, seated, eyes closed, head bowed, and silence. Jewish worship and prayer was audible and animated by comparison. Today in the West worship is increasingly expressive.

12. Note a grammatical symmetry here: Jesus is glorified *so that* the Father may be glorified; the Son has authority *so that* he may give eternal life. Both phrases indicate Gk. *hina* clauses linked by *kathos* ("just as").

Gospel (see comment on 17:9). But John sees no confusion in it and can tie human responsibility together with election (see 6:37–44; 10:29). The devastating and controlling darkness of the world requires that God participate in our decision to come to the light, or else no one would be saved. Yet those who remain in the darkness, who do not come to the light, stand under his judgment for not availing themselves of this merciful opportunity.

This eternal life offered by Jesus takes on definition in 17:3.[13] However its interpretation must be carefully weighed. Eternal life comes through "knowing God." This theme occurs not only in gnostic literature but in a variety of world religions today. Some interpreters of John have used such language to show that indeed John's Gospel provides such a gnostic salvation.[14] But there are stark differences: This "knowing" is not about intellectual assent at all. The Hebrew notion of knowing encompasses experience and intimacy and for Christians this means obedience to and love for God.

Moreover, such knowledge *must include* a commitment to Jesus Christ, God's Son. As we will see, such knowledge is realized through the work of Jesus on the cross (17:19). To deny the Son is to deny any true knowledge of the Father (1 John 2:22–23). This is because the only true knowledge of God has been delivered to humanity through the incarnation of his Son (1:18). Without Jesus Christ, access to God is impossible (14:6–7, 11; 20:31).

The first accomplishment of the Incarnation was Jesus' display of God's glory for the world. John 1:14 describes it: "We have seen his glory, the glory of the One and Only, who came from the Father, full of grace and truth." Now Jesus says that he has accomplished this task God has given him to do (17:4). His life has glorified God.

But does Jesus say that he is *finished* at this point in his life?[15] Surely he cannot be finished, for his work on the cross lies still ahead. On the contrary, it is best to see this finished work as including the hour of glorification in which Jesus is now engaged. This work includes his death, resurrection, and return to the Father, as much as it includes his revelation of the Father to the world. The contrast of 17:4 and 5 is not between Jesus' incarnational work and his sacrificial work, but between his life on earth (when God was

---

13. Many commentators have suggested that 17:3 is a parenthesis in the prayer, perhaps penned by John (much like a modern footnote today). But its formal links with the surrounding verses do not require us to set it apart.

14. E. Käsemann, *The Testament of Jesus According to John 17* (Philadelphia: Fortress, 1968). Exhaustive parallels from Hellenistic religious can be found in C. H. Dodd, *The Interpretation of the Fourth Gospel* (Cambridge: Cambridge Univ. Press, 1953), 151–69

15. This is another instance where interpreters who see a gnostic salvation in John conclude that Jesus' work is done since knowledge of God has been given; no sacrifice on the cross is needed. But this is to interpret the chapter outside of the larger conversations in the Gospel.

glorified) and his resumption of his place in heaven (when God will glorify him again). Jesus has glorified God in his life and will continue to do so in his death; thus, he prays that God will glorify him in his return to the Father.

Some interpreters divide the text at 17:6 and describe these verses as prayer in the interest of disciples. But a change does not occur until 17:9 (and 17:20), when Jesus marks the prayer, showing a change of topic (using the Gk. verb *erotao*, "I pray"). On the contrary, 17:6–8 are simply an expansion that describes the work Jesus has accomplished in 17:4.

What then is Jesus' summary of the work he finished in his ministry? Jesus has revealed "God's name" (17:6).[16] Not only does Jesus mention this here but he returns to affirm it again in 17:26. In 17:11–12 Jesus prays that his followers will be kept safe "by that name." The idea of name is not a minor idea to Jesus. The "name" of someone represents the totality, the inner character, of their entire person. Thus in Exodus 3:13 it is important to Moses that he know the *name* of God so that he can indicate to the Israelites who their Savior really is. It is no accident that throughout the Gospel Jesus not only refers to his work as empowered by God's name (John 10:25) but also that people should believe in "his name" (1:12; 2:23; 3:18). Jesus bears the name of God, which is unveiled in the Gospel in its many "I am" sayings.[17] Thus, in revealing himself, he has disclosed the personhood (the name) of God to the entire world.

But this revelation has not been distributed without purpose. While it has been offered to the entire world, only those who have faith (17:8), who have received (17:8) and kept (17:6) Jesus' word, have truly understood what was happening in this divine revelation. They know that Jesus has come from God and his words are divine.

But this description of these recipients is only what we might call the human perspective, recording the responses of men and women who have joined Jesus' flock. That only a portion of Israel embraced God's Son should come as no surprise. This had been the history of Israel and its prophets. Despite the apparent absence of faith, God is always aware of preserving a faithful remnant who belong to him, who, like sheep, know the voice of their shepherd (10:3). In Elijah's day, for example, the prophet thought that he alone was left who had not bowed to Baal (1 Kings 19:14). But God corrected him, "Yet I reserve seven thousand in Israel—all whose knees have not bowed down to Baal" (19:18). God is at work in places we least suspect.

A similar role for God is assumed in 17:2, 6, and 10, so that Jesus' disciples can be described as followers who belonged to God—a remnant, whom

---

16. The NIV paraphrases, "I have revealed you to those whom you gave me out of the world."

17. See 8:24, 58. As we outlined earlier, the "I am" sayings in John represent Jesus' unique use of God's divine name given in Ex. 3 and later translated into Greek in the LXX.

God delivered to Jesus. Of course this at once sets in place a theological tension that we must examine (see below). How are we to interpret this divine sovereignty and human response?

Jesus Prays for His Disciples (17:9–19)

THE THOUGHT OF this remnant, this flock, that has recognized Jesus' voice and believed leads Jesus to pray for them specifically (17:9). They are precious because they belong to the Father and are now Jesus' responsibility (17:10). Jesus is not praying for the world (the arena of unbelief), though this does not mean that the world is outside God's love or that Jesus neglects the world. Nothing could be further from the truth. The failure to read these verses in the wider context of John's theology has led many to misrepresent them. God loves the world (3:16) and entered humanity in his Son for the sake of the world, to save it (1:29; 3:17; 4:42), offer it life (6:33, 51; 12:35), and bring it light (8:12; 9:5; 11:9; 12:46). Now Jesus' work in the world is near completion, and he is praying exclusively for his immediate followers who will be left behind as he departs. Like a shepherd about to lay down his life for his sheep (10:17), he prays for his flock whom he has led and who now must persevere in the wilderness.

Note the similarity between Jesus' prayer in 17:10 and that in 17:1. The pattern of glorification is now complete: God is glorified through his Son (17:1, 4, 5) and the Son is glorified through his disciples (17:10, 22). Therefore those features of Jesus' life that brought glory to God may likewise be the characteristics of discipleship that bring glory to Jesus. But since Jesus and the Father share a perfect unity, when a disciple's life bears fruit, God himself is glorified directly (15:8). Jesus is describing a pattern of divine life, of indwelling and mysticism, in which God and Jesus share an interiority that leads to this sharing of glory; he also anticipates that disciples will enjoy a similar unity with God (17:24; cf. 14:23) and each other (17:11, 22).

(1) Jesus' first concern, his first petition for his followers, is that they remain united (17:11). Remarkably he desires that his disciples enjoy an intimacy and oneness that are analogous to the intimacy and oneness he shares with the Father. The reason for Jesus' concern is that his service, providing leadership and unity, will end with his departure. In fact, he is already departing. Jesus uses the present tense, "and now I am no more in the world," which lends the prayer a mystical sense that the hour of glorification is pulling Jesus forward, lifting him already to the Father.[18]

---

18. The NIV translates the Greek as future, "I will remain in the world no longer," perhaps to support the chronology of Jesus' departure. The NLT captures it nicely: "Now I am departing the world."

His disciples, however, do remain in the world. This is the environment not just of unbelief and cynicism, but of abject hostility (15:18–27). The mission of the church, the task of Jesus' followers, is to challenge this world (16:8–11), to draw out those who love the truth and bring them into the flock. It is not an invitation to defeat. With the aid of the Spirit there will be genuine victory. "For everyone born of God overcomes the world. This is the victory that has overcome the world, even our faith" (1 John 5:4). This empowering, this confidence, is the source of their joy (17:13b; cf. 16:22).

(2) Jesus' next worry concerns his disciples' sustenance and strength in the world. Their assignment is dangerous, and so he prays for their equipment and protection. Jesus has given them his word (17:14a), and the Spirit will recall it and keep it secure (14:26). This word, this divine revelation, will become essential equipment in their testimony and survival in the world.

Jesus also prays for their protection, particularly from Satan (17:15b). He recognizes the power of evil for he lost one of his disciples to Satan (13:27; cf. 12:31; 14:30; 16:11; 1 John 2:13–14; 3:12), and now he understands that representing God in this world is an invitation to genuine battle. Later John will write: "We know that we are children of God, and that the whole world is under the control of the evil one" (1 John 5:19). Inasmuch as Jesus has worked in the world, he has been assaulted by Satan but never overcome (John 14:30). But his disciples must contend with these powers since they remain in this world (17:15). God's "name" will be a refuge (17:11), as the wise man wrote in Proverbs: "The name of the LORD is a strong tower; the righteous run to it and are safe" (Prov. 18:10).

(3) Jesus' third concern has to do with holiness (17:17–19). There is a spiritual dilemma that pertains to all disciples: They live in the world, and yet Jesus can say that they are not "of the world" (17:14, 16). This points not to their location geographically, but to their position spiritually. As we have seen throughout this Gospel, the "world" is not a place on a map but a spiritual domain, an atmosphere of darkness and unbelief (3:19). It possesses values inimical to God.[19] It is not the domain of a disciple's spiritual identity any more than it was the domain of Jesus' identity (17:16). A better translation of 17:16 reads, "They do not *belong* to the world."

Jesus prays that his disciples might be "sanctified" (Gk. *hagiazo*) in the truth (17:17).[20] This Greek word refers to something made holy, but the

---

19. John lists a few of these in 2 John 2.16: "For everything in the world—the cravings of sinful man, the lust of his eyes and the boasting of what he has and does—comes not from the Father but from the world."

20. The Gk. verb *hagiazo* is rare in John (10:36; 17:17, 19) and its adjective refers to the Holy Spirit (1:33; 14:26; 20:22), the Father (17:11), or God (6:69).

means to achieving this holiness is through separation. God is God by virtue of his difference, his transcendence, his otherness with respect to all creation. Anything (a mountain, a temple shovel, a priestly garment, a people) that belongs to him or serves his purposes should consider itself "holy" and set apart from common use. To be holy, then, is not in the first instance a description of perfection (though this is included). It refers to a life that is so aligned with God that it reflects God's passions completely (for good, against evil). Such a person can be considered "sanctified," holy, attached to God's purposes and presence. In this case Jesus understands that a complete attachment to the truth discovered in God's Word will be the means of achieving this holiness (17:17b).

In the manner described here Jesus likewise was "set apart" (Gk. *hagiazo*) and sent into the world (10:36). He was separated, made holy, for a divine mission. Sanctification is always for mission since it is God's activity in the world, bringing it truth and light and salvation. Thus the disciples have a mission similar to that of Jesus (17:18). They too should see their purposes for living as not their own, but shaped by the mission God has for them.

Perhaps 17:19 is one of the key verses in the prayer. When Jesus says that he *sanctifies* himself (Gk. *hagiazo*), to what does this refer? He may have in mind his self-dedication to his greater mission. Prophets and priests dedicated themselves thus. The Lord says to Jeremiah, "Before I formed you in the womb I knew you, before you were born *I set you apart*" (Jer. 1:5, italics added). Priests likewise set themselves apart (Ex. 40:13; Lev. 8:30; 2 Chron. 5:11). But here in John 17:19 we learn that as a result of Jesus' consecration, his disciples will benefit. In the phrase "for them," "for" (Gk. *hyper*, meaning "for the sake of") implies sacrificial death throughout John (see 6:51; 10:11, 15; 11:50–52; 13:37; 15:13; 18:14).[21] "This bread is my flesh, which I will give *for* [*hyper*] the life of the world" (6:51). Note that Deuteronomy 15:19 even provides an example of *hagiazo* used in the context of blood sacrifice.

We should likely merge these views. Jesus is recommitting himself to the mission assigned by the Father. This priestly mission of service involves his sacrifice. Through his death on the cross, the disciples will experience something never known before. His death will enable them to experience a new holiness, an identification, a deep attachment with God. It is no surprise that following the cross and before Jesus departs to go to his Father, he prepares them with these things listed here: They will receive the *Holy* Spirit (the Spirit *of truth*) and the mission that this consecration demands (20:21–23). Each of these italicized words play a prominent role in the prayer of chapter 17.

---

21. Cf. atonement passages elsewhere in the New Testament: Mark 14:24; Luke 22:19; Rom. 8:32; 1 Cor. 11:24.

Jesus Prays for All Believers (17:20–26)

JESUS IS AWARE that not only will he depart from the world, but likewise those who stand with him—his immediate circle of followers—will also depart to be with him in his glory (17:24). This will leave those whom they disciple, the church, to represent the kingdom in the world. Therefore Jesus now turns to pray for these followers whom he has not yet met, men and women who will follow the apostles, indeed the church today, which carries the mission set down by Jesus during his final week.

He first prays that they will have a unity (17:21) like that of his first disciples (17:11). This unity must be visibly based on love so that when the world sees them, it will know immediately that they represent Jesus. "By this all men will know that you are my disciples, if you love one another" (13:35; cf. 1 John 3:11). But this love and unity is not a moral effort powered by human energy; it is an outgrowth of the union Christians will enjoy with Jesus himself (17:21b), a union modeled on the oneness of the Father and the Son, a union born when the Father and the Son indwell the believers when they are given new birth.

Jesus here envisages a profound spiritual intimacy that changes human life. It is a unity encompassing the Father with the Son, the disciples with them both, and the disciples in union with one another (14:10; 15:4). Interpreters often point out that Jesus fails to refer to the Spirit in his prayer. But it is the Spirit (mentioned from chapters 14–16) who facilitates this intimacy. Later John will write in his first letter, "We know that we live in him and he in us, because he has given us of his Spirit" (1 John 4:13).

Inasmuch as the church bears the Spirit, it also bears the "call of God to the world, because it is the manifestation of the love and glory of God in the world."[22] Jesus was the bearer of God's glory, and now the church bears that glory alone. "I have given them the glory that you gave me ... to let the world know that you sent me and have loved them even as you have loved me" (17:22–23). After the Sinai covenant was given, the glory of God left the mountain (Ex. 24:16) and descended on the tabernacle to live in Israel (Ex. 40:34). In the Gospel Jesus has been that place of glory (John 1:14), replacing, as it were, the temple. But now the thought is of the glory of God passing to Jesus' followers, indwelling them. The confidence of the church's mission rests here: If it lives in the Spirit (and thereby in the Father and Son), if it reflects God's glory and love, if it shows a unity in its ranks born by a shared knowledge of God, its testimony will astonish the world.

But the final chapter in the church's story lies ahead. The disciples had witnessed the glory of the incarnate Christ (1:14), and to a degree they had

---

22. Hoskyns, *John*, 599.

received something of that glory inasmuch as they were filled with the Spirit and experienced Christ in them (17:22). However, Jesus prays that some day his followers will see the true glory, the true love, that has existed in heaven since the beginning of time (17:5, 24). This is where Jesus is headed, where he is yearning to return to, and Christians possess an invitation to join him (cf. 14:3).

This anticipated glory, however, finds its counterpoint in the prayer's last sentences (17:25–26). Jesus addresses God as "righteous Father," reminding us that it is God's righteousness that has led to his upright judgment of the world. The problem is not the world's access to the knowledge of God—he came not to condemn the world but to save it (3:17)—but that the world refused to acknowledge that God had sent Jesus.

But all those who accept the Son, who embrace him and the Father, will experience the ineffable love known only between Father and Son. *We are loved by God with the love he holds for his Son!* And our lives are transformed by the life of Jesus, who now takes residence within our own. These are the last words Jesus prays before his arrest: "that I may be in them." His last desire is to love his followers and indwell them, to fill them with the glory and joy he has known, so that their knowledge of God will be unsurpassed and overwhelming.

WHILE JESUS' PRAYER is profoundly inspiring, it presents special challenges for any interpreter wishing to bring its themes to the modern period. Rather than recording scenes in which Jesus teaches great truths about eternal life in his kingdom and demonstrates its power with signs (the Book of Signs), and rather than providing us with the promises of discipleship like those found in the Farewell Discourse, John 17 invites us to listen in on a conversation. It is a divine conversation of the highest order, in which Jesus speaks of the completion of his tasks on earth and prays earnestly for his followers, both present and future. Therefore it offers a glimpse of who Jesus truly is in relation to the Father, and it gives us a portrait of those things that are close to Jesus' heart in these last days of his life among his disciples on earth.

Two guidelines. Keeping these limitations in mind, we may benefit if we remember two guidelines. (1) There are themes in the prayer that must necessarily be seen in the wider context of the Gospel's theology. John has built his Gospel assuming his readers will read it straight through, watching themes build on one another. Therefore interpreters who examine the prayer in isolation or lift individual verses or paragraphs out of the wider context of the gospel can end up misrepresenting their meaning.

Two examples may suffice. (a) Throughout the prayer Jesus uses the language of "knowledge" for salvation. "Now this is eternal life: *that they may know you*, the only true God, and Jesus Christ, whom you have sent" (17:3). Such language appears frequently (about ten times). Some scholars, both ancient and modern, have argued that John's soteriology is based on enlightenment, wisdom, or *gnosis* (knowledge, Gnosticism), so that the classic themes of repentance and faith or Christ's saving death on the cross are unnecessary. But such a view would have never entered John's mind. To "know" God encompasses a wide range of understanding that includes these other categories explained elsewhere in the Gospel. To neglect the larger theological framework of the Gospel is to misrepresent this chapter.

(b) A second example has to do with determinism. It is true that Jesus is *not* praying for the world; he is praying exclusively for his immediate followers. "I pray for them. I am not praying for the world, but for those you have given me, for they are yours" (17:9). In fact the "world" (Gk. *kosmos*) enjoys frequent mention in this chapter (eighteen times), but not once is the world the object of Jesus' affections. Yet it would be erroneous to say that Jesus' ecclesiology is utterly sectarian in John 17, that his mission is to locate his elect few and lift them from a despised world. Such an interpretation would be as wrong as lifting the sentence I have just written out of its paragraph and using it to represent my theological views. Again, the wider context of John's theology in the Gospel is crucial. Any study or sermon on "the world" that uses John 17 must necessarily employ the many references to "the world" in the balance of the Gospel, that the "world" is loved and valued by God.

(2) The second guideline has to do with the literary form and setting of the literature we are reading. In chapters 1–12 we examined stories of Jesus in public ministry, providing miracles and signs as well as extended teachings. There were even brutal conflicts in which we were forced to understand certain paragraphs in light of the struggles of John's own day (e.g., the references to "the Jews"). The form of the story changes in chapter 13, however, when Jesus provides his formal "farewell." His audience is now no longer the world, but the closed circle of his disciples in the Upper Room. As a Christian I must make the hermeneutical decision that, indeed, these promises Jesus offers to them apply to me as well: I am a disciple, I am a recipient of Jesus' care and concern. I may not possess those privileges that are bound by the historical specificity of the first century (such as the resurrection appearances), but I do enjoy the timeless gifts (such as the comfort and defense of the Holy Spirit).

Now in the Farewell Discourse we have another form and setting. Jesus is not talking to his disciples, he is talking to God. We are invited to listen in. But if this is *private* prayer, if this is Jesus' personal conversation with God, what use is it to me? (a) We need to see such prayers as teaching vehicles. They are meant to be overheard so that disciples can study them and learn. In Ezra 9:6–15, Ezra offers to God a moving prayer of sorrow and repentance, and upon hearing his words the people are filled with grief (10:1). Ezra knows that this prayer not only moved the Israelites, but will move any who might read his account. In other words, his prayer was recorded for us (readers) as well. A similar role for prayers appears in Acts, where Luke records a lengthy prayer uttered by the church (Acts 4:24–30). *But again, it is a prayer recorded for us, the reader.* Therefore what we can glean from Jesus' own spiritual perceptions and interests is appropriate.

(b) Nevertheless, it is a focused prayer limited by the concerns of the moment, not by universal issues of the church in the first century or today. My presupposition about the prayer is that it has its origins in what Jesus said (not in what John's theology dictated) and therefore it is unfair for me to bring too many modern issues to it, looking for confirmation or direction. Jesus' original agenda must win the day throughout. The prayer must speak to us from *its concerns,* and we should be cautious when we hear modern themes supposedly anchored to Jesus' words here.

Jesus at prayer. With these provisions in mind, what themes can I bring from the prayer for current study and reflection? The most obvious item is the one most overlooked. *Jesus prayed.* We have hints throughout the Synoptic Gospels that Jesus was a man of prayer, but here we have a premier example of him praying. On the one hand, the prayer becomes a model prayer for us, illustrating the sort of intimacy and confidence we can experience. On the other hand, the prayer gives us insight into the character of relationship within God's selfhood. This is the Father and the Son exhibiting the intimacy, the community, that is native to their life. Thus the prayer invites us into that quality of intimacy. The oneness Jesus enjoys with his Father is a oneness into which we are invited to participate. "My prayer is ... that all of them may be one, Father, just as you are in me and I am in you. *May they also be in us* so that the world may believe that you have sent me" (17:20–21, italics added). Christians are thus invited into this conversation.

The interests of Jesus. It is also appropriate for us to examine the interests of Jesus as he prays. What assumptions was he making about himself and God? How does he pray? I see two chief themes coming forward: Jesus explores his own relationship with God initially and then moves quickly to his concerns for his followers. What is Jesus telling God about his life, its aims, and its accomplishments? What can we glean from these to help us understand more fully Jesus' mission and identity? Then Jesus moves on to explore the relationship he has with his followers. What attitude does he exhibit? What issues stand out as critical in his mind?

The character of the church. The third area of reflection is generally the subject most expositors explore immediately. What is the character of the church as Jesus envisages it in this prayer? Certainly verses 9–26 *cannot* be viewed as Jesus' exhaustive definition of what it means to be the church. Interpreters who press these words to that end do so foolishly. These words supplement what we have learned elsewhere in the Farewell Discourse (and indeed throughout the Gospel).

Catalogues of ideas tumble over one another, each of which is worthy of reflection. The church should reflect God's glory and love for the world, and it should exhibit a confidence in its knowledge of God since it bears Jesus' word, a word that has come from God himself. The church has the truth, not a set of opinions, and the world should sense the strength of its conviction. But among these themes, two stand out: The church must be unified and the church must have a mission.

Jesus returns to the subject of unity two times (17:11, 21), encompassing both his immediate followers and the church to come. What is the nature of this unity? What contributes to unity? And what perils does the pursuit of unity present to the church today?

But the church not only has a relation with God, it also continues to be in the world, living amidst unbelief and darkness. Jesus uses the term *world* in two ways: as the common domain of human existence (17:13) and as a metaphor for everything that is opposed to God (17:14). Thus Christians are "in" the world while not being "of" the world. How do we delineate this? What guidelines do we make? How do we live as if we do not belong to the world yet avoid the problem of sectarianism, or a secluded, sheltered life that cannot reach the world any longer?

Contemporary Significance

IN HIS SPLENDID exposition on John 17, Lesslie Newbigin, the great Anglican leader and missionary to India, writes:

When a man is going on a long journey, he will find time on the eve of his departure for a quiet talk with his family, and—if he is a man of God—will end by commending to God not only himself and his journey, but also the family whom he leaves behind. Very surely will this be so if his journey is the last journey.[23]

We understand this impulse. It reveals a great deal about us—our affection for our family and our personal commitment to God. Therefore when

---

23. Newbigin, *The Light Has Come*, 223.

we open the words of Jesus in John 17, we should let them speak to us out of the setting of his life and world. For at least three years, these men have been his closest companions. They have lived and worked together through many trials and joys. But now they have come to "the hour" that has pounded like a drumbeat through the pages of the Gospel. Judas's departure signaled its arrival (13:31), and now Jesus knows that his own departure out of this world is at hand. He is leaving. Yet the prayer unveils his incredible love for his followers and his eagerness to return to his Father.

We should see ourselves too as the subjects of this prayer. Jesus is *our* Lord and shepherd as much as he was the shepherd of this small circle of men. Therefore when he prays, he invites us to listen, to hear the quality of the love and honor shared between himself and God. He invites us to listen too as he prays for believers, "so that they may have the full measure of my joy within them" (17:13). We are the church, the body of believers built on the apostles' word (17:20b).

A sensitive, spiritual reading of chapter 17 may even convert its many "third person" sentences into "second person" in order to get the full force of Jesus' passion for us. When we do this, suddenly the prayer takes on a remarkable force. For example:

> But I say these things while I am still in the world, so that you may have the full measure of my joy within you. I have given you my Father's word and the world has hated you, for you are not of the world any more than I am of the world. My prayer is not that God would take you out of the world but that he would protect you from the evil one. You are not of the world, even as I am not of it. But I want you to be made holy by the truth; God's word is truth. As my Father sent me into the world, I am sending you into the world. I am sanctifying myself for you, that you too may be truly holy. (17:13–19)

Jesus and spirituality. Jesus' spirituality was visible. He exhibited a spiritual life of worship, prayer, devotion, and love that left an indelible mark on all his followers. When men and women witnessed it, they were changed. Such visible spirituality can have strong effects. I recall some years back when my first grandparent died. It was the first funeral of our gathered family. Perhaps what was most striking were the expressions of the children, my nieces and nephews, who were then from three to twelve years old. For the first time, they saw the spiritual convictions of their parents and grandparents at work; tears and prayers and words of faith poured forth. I remember the face of one nine-year-old as she took it all in, wide-eyed. That morning brought what was private out into the open and left permanent marks on not a few children's hearts.

This is why the Gospels point not only to Jesus' mighty works and profound words, but also to his personal relationship with God. On some occasions he went alone into the hills to pray (Mark 1:35), and at other times he told his followers that they had to do the same (Mark 6:31). But more often than we realize, when Jesus was "alone" in prayer, his disciples were by his side: "Once when Jesus was praying in private and *his disciples were with him*" (Luke 9:18, italics added). Jesus made his spirituality visible. I am convinced that this explains the detailed Synoptic record of Jesus' prayer in Gethsemane (Matt. 26:36–46).

One of the chief things Jesus shows us in this prayer is God's desire for relationships. That is, at this point in the Gospel it is clear to us that Jesus is God's Son, but this means that he bears the presence of the Father in the world. He is not a courier sent from God, he is God-in-flesh. Yet within the personhood of God is a social dynamic, a desire for community, a yearning for conversation.[24] Jesus talks at length to his Father, and we sense from his words that this is a conversation that has been going on for some time. One could expect from this divine Son a serene and silent tranquillity, a composure formed from his intimacy with God, not needing any social intercourse or expression. But this is precisely what we do *not* find. Jesus lives in a conversation with the Father. "Words" are the medium of their shared life together (17:8).

This means that as we are invited into life with the Father, as the Father and the Son indwell us through Holy Spirit, spirituality is not a static experience. It is not a creedal position or a status any more than a marriage can be described as a "vocation" or a status. Marriage is not defined as sharing the same address. Marriage is about transparency and intimate union and life as one. Marriage is a conversation. It is the same here. The Christian life is a conversation, a dynamic relationship in which, as a result of our new birth, the talking begins. God's "word" now becomes the medium of our relationship too and with it, our talking develops an intimacy with profound social dimensions.

Jesus' interests. Once Jesus' prayer gets underway, we learn something about him and his interests. We gain insight into his attitudes toward God—attitudes worthy of emulation. For instance, it is clear (if it has not been manifestly clear since chapter 1) that Jesus is not simply a mortal messenger on earth. He is God's Son, but this now has a definition we have not truly seen since the prologue: Jesus Christ, as the Word, has had a preincarnational life, just as he will enjoy a postincarnational life. In 17:5 and 24 Jesus acknowledges that he lived in the presence of God, enjoying divine glory *before* the world was made. This ties the prayer directly to 1:1–3 and places on Jesus'

---

24 R. Gruenler, "John 17:20–26," *Int* 43 (1989): 178–83.

lips the affirmation John gave at the start of the Gospel. No clearer language of preexistence is possible. Even Isaiah witnessed this glory (12:41).

However, in his prayer Jesus anticipates that after completing his work, he will return to that same status of glory he enjoyed once before. In other words, Jesus is returning—returning to a glory he enjoyed previously but which he set aside temporarily in order to minister on earth. To use spatial language, Jesus has "descended" and now will "ascend"—and the Incarnation consisted of his work in the interim. This Christological thinking parallels what Paul describes in Philippians 2:5–11. Jesus Christ possessed the form of God, yet rather than hold on to his equality with God, he emptied himself, incarnating himself in humanity and dying on the cross. As a result God has highly exalted him, glorifying him in heaven and on earth. Preexistence, descent, incarnation, ascent, glorification—like the swing of a pendulum. The Word (incarnate in Christ) is now returning to the elevation where he began.

This spiritual anticipation of *return* to heaven is precisely the orientation Jesus desires for us. "Father, I want those you have given me to be with me where I am, and to see my glory, the glory you have given me because you loved me before the creation of the world" (17:24). Jesus not only is preparing a place for us (14:3) but is eager for us to join him there, to see his glory, to witness the tremendous love the Father has for him (and us).

We are invited, then, to reflect on what such a vision means in our own spiritual lives. How will it change our living and our praying if we fill our imaginations with such a vision? How will it change our investment in the world (while not denying our commitment to the world, 17:18) if we, like Jesus, are *genuinely en route* to the place of God's glory? Christians are people in transit by train, with passports in hand, speeding through the countryside, talking to bystanders at the village platforms why they need to get on board. How will such a vision change our view of suffering? Of mission? Of ethics and evangelism? Of worldliness?

This leads to a related thought. What was the work Jesus "completed" (17:4) through this incarnation? What warranted this descent from glory, what assignment did he bear? Did he come just to die? Was his work on the cross his only vocation? Jesus understands as he prays this prayer that he has *already* accomplished much of what God had called him to do. The key lies here: Jesus' saving work began in Bethlehem, not on Golgotha. The Incarnation, God's union with our humanity, in itself was a saving deed. That is, by uniting with our humanity God not only made known who he was (revealing his glory) but also brought about the conditions to make Christ's death efficacious and powerful for us all.

In Christ God has embraced us, expressing his genuine affection for us. He is *not* standing far off and announcing a way of salvation through a messenger.

Rather, "in Christ *God* was reconciling the world to himself" (2 Cor. 5:19, NRSV, italics added). Jesus was God's powerful agent of this union. Jesus prays, "I have done what you asked." He has become one of us (1:14), having shown God to the world (1:18). In doing so he has brought the glory of God into the human sphere (1:14; 2:11; 11:40). Now he has only to bear this humanity to the cross.

This means we need to explore a new appreciation for what God has done in and through the Incarnation. We need to see the salvific dimensions of God-in-Christ. God has shown his love for us not simply in sending his Son to the cross, but in coming *himself* to be with us. The death of Christ is not the precondition of God's love for us, as if we were despised by him, as if we had angered him, and only at the cross was his feeling toward us reversed. "*God* was in Christ reconciling the world" (ASV, italics added). Jesus did not come to change God's mind; instead, he came to express God's mind. If God so loved the world (3:16), he loved us too.

Among Jesus' interests that appear in the prayer, one more should join the list. We can say that Jesus' prayer really consists of only one prayer.[25] In the Synoptic record it is, "Your will be done." In John it is, "Father, the time has come. Glorify your Son, that your Son may glorify you" (17:1). Jesus' aim in life has been to glorify God, and this theme is repeated throughout. In 17:4 we see that this has been the goal of all his effort on earth: "I have brought you glory on earth by completing the work you gave me to do."

The essence of this sort of prayer is that Jesus is so utterly dependent on the Father, so oriented toward what the Father wills, so desiring that God be glorified through his living and working, that it has controlled every aspect of his life. To live in association with God is to be set apart and be sanctified (17:19), to be his alone, and by virtue of this life to live in and reflect God's glory. Living within this glory describes the life of Jesus in heaven (17:5, 24). Likewise, when Jesus enters humanity his ambition is to let the world see the glory of God still radiant within him. He wants to honor God's glory— to show it visibly in his signs, to speak of it in his discourses, to announce it from the cross. Jesus' life is a participation in the glory of God.

What is striking in the prayer is that Jesus draws us not only into a divine union of life and conversation, but he invites us into participation with the glory of God. "I have given them the glory that you gave me" (17:22). As Jesus turns in the prayer toward the life of his followers and the church that follows, his chief concern is that they too live a life that glorifies God, that they will exhibit in all of their worship, their words, and their work the same glory that Jesus exhibited on earth.

---

25. C. D. Morrison, "Mission and Ethic An Interpretation of John 17," *Int* 19 (1965): 259–73; J. E Staton, "A Vision of Unity—Christian Unity in the Fourth Gospel," *EvQ* 69 (1997): 291–305.

This is the *essence* of Jesus' vision for the church. It is not a community that heals people just so that they will be whole (though healing is important); it is not a community that teaches so that people will be gratified by knowledge (though wisdom is valuable); it is not a community that evangelizes so that it will grow its ranks (though its mission to the world is crucial). The church is a community that invites people to touch the glory of God, to be changed by it, and to bear it to the world. "This is to my Father's glory, that you bear much fruit, showing yourselves to be my disciples" (15:8). *Spiritual fruit is essentially that which glorifies God.*

Such a concept forces us to ask hard questions about every aspect of what we do. "Is God glorified here?" is the refrain that should accompany every decision. And the answer will not always be obvious or easy. But it must be asked because in Jesus' vision, this was the essential mission of his incarnate life and now is the essential mission of the church.

Jesus and the church. How does the church bear fruit that glorifies God? What things come to Jesus' mind as he now thinks about our participation in the glory of God? What results will follow from such a life? Of course the thoughts outlined in chapter 17 must be supplemented by additional ideas taken from the balance of this Gospel (especially the Farewell Discourse) as well as the rest of the New Testament. But here I suggest four foundational elements that cannot be ignored—four basic roles that the church serves: transcendence, fellowship, teaching, and mission. Each of these is anchored in John 17.

(1) *Transcendence.* People are often looking for the reality of God. While modernity suggested that rationalism might well do away with religion, the postmodern world has proved just the opposite. Spiritual interest is everywhere today, and people will exercise it whether it is in a church, a mosque, or a New Age temple. This does not mean that they are looking for rational, religious certainties or the recitation of creed, nor does it refer to "religion" popularly built by choirs and pews and pulpits or by denominational structures. People are not "coming home" to Lutheranism or Presbyterianism or Methodism. They are seeking places where God seems present, where he can be felt, where spiritual ecstasy and mystical realities are commonplace occurrences.

The quality of worship is today of paramount concern to many. Witness, for instance, the successes of the Toronto Blessing in Canada, the charismatic movements in the United States and Europe, or Pentecostalism globally. Of the world's 700 million evangelical Christians, fully 350 million are charismatic.[26] And two-thirds of all Pentecostal Christians are found in Africa, Asia, and Latin America, where Christianity is growing at a fantastic rate.

---

26. M. Hutchinson, "It's a Small Church After All: Globalization Is Changing How Christians Do Ministry," *Christianity Today* 31 (Nov. 16, 1987): 46–49. Figures originate from D. Barrett's *World Christian Encyclopedia.*

Jesus prays that his followers will know just this sort of reality. Jesus prays that they will *experience* the indwelling of God brought about through the work of the Holy Spirit. The authenticity of this spirituality is found in the first instance is an experience of "otherness," of a God who is not quantified in natural categories, whose presence is as real as his nature is foreign. This is what it means to possess the "name" of God (17:6, 26), to be indwelt by him (17:22), to experience his glory (17:22) and his holiness (17:16–17), and to be transformed by the truth (17:19). Those who know this experience are filled with joy (17:13) and enter into a life with God that they never knew before. This is what humanity is seeking today. The rationalists among us should not disparage this quest; it is a genuine gift that Jesus promises in his final discourse.

(2) *Teaching.* But religious quests must be anchored in the truth. Men and women intuit that there are as many false paths, many charlatans—from the dangerous Jim Jones cult (which in 1978 led to the mass suicide of 913 people in Guyana) to faith healers of every stripe to self-appointed prophets. Therefore the church must give guidance; it must anchor its experiences in the word of God given historically in the person of Jesus Christ (17:6, 14). Without the objective guidance of historic revelation, the church becomes a ship without a rudder.[27] Jesus prays, "Sanctify them by the truth; your word is truth" (17:17).

Such teaching means that seekers after God should grow in wisdom and knowledge as well as in experience. And the first thing such knowledge teaches is that any experience that departs from loyalty to Jesus Christ is mistaken. The Spirit of God never contradicts what has been given to us by Jesus Christ in history (16:13b). The church abides in the vine (15:1ff.); the church knows its shepherd's voice (10:1ff.). The church always returns to "what was from the beginning" as it sorts out the meaning of its experiences today (1 John 1:1; 2:7, 13–14, 24; 3:8, 11; 2 John 1:5).

(3) *Fellowship.* Not only are people looking for transcendent spiritual experience and sound instruction, they are also looking for community. This is one of the recurrent themes of the close of the twentieth century. People feel alienated, lonely, and disconnected from place and kinship. Jesus prays that the church will be a genuine community of strong unity. Tracing the theme of unity through the chapter shows how much this subject weighs on Jesus' mind (17:11, 21–23). If we continue to follow this theme in the letters of John, we see that the disunity of John's church was not unlike the disunity

---

27. Or as one critic put it, "Jesus loves me this I know, for my experience tells me so." Many observers comment that one of the remarkable features of worship in some corners of the charismatic/Pentecostal world is the lack of solid teaching. I have attended such services which have dispensed with the sermon altogether.

478

we experience today. People live together in the name of Christ and then in his name contend for every manner of special interest. This explains why Jesus keeps repeating his "new commandment" that his followers love one another (13:34; 15:12, 17). Without an heroic love similar to Jesus' love, unity is impossible.

Jesus' prayer, however, links the unity of believers to their interior spiritual life. In 17:20–22 Jesus says that the oneness we experience with him should lead to a oneness we experience with one another. He has given us God's glory so that we may be one (17:22). This is a remarkable thought. Does it imply that unity is not so much a byproduct of discussion and diplomacy as it is worship, repentance, and prayer? Does it mean that the degree to which we seek God together will assist us to find common ground in our lives together?

We understand unity. We at least know what we ought to do. The problem is that we also know that there are times when unity comes at a high cost. That is, when individuals have differences, unity can only be achieved when concessions are given and someone at last "gives way" so that the peace is restored. I remember being told by a leader in my own Presbyterian denomination that the unity of the church came before my heartfelt criticisms of same-sex marriage. "Would you split the church over this issue?" he asked. There it is: It may be that the pursuit of unity will lead to compromises we are unwilling to make.

(4) *Mission.* The church possesses a mission, a cause, just as Jesus had a mission in the world. The unity of the church and the quality of its life and experiences lead not only to the glory of God but to a powerful testimony to the world (17:22). Christians do the work of Christ in the world. They are his hands and feet, bringing the kingdom to reality wherever they go. This means that when the church experiences severe conflict from its adversaries (17:14), its unity with Christ and with its members will serve as a profound witness to its opponents. This has been the story of twentieth-century Christians from places such as Vietnam, India, Sri Lanka, Ethiopia, and Sudan. When confronted with severe persecution, the church's unity so impressed its oppressors that many converted and joined its ranks.[28]

But another tension arises from this theme. As the church separates itself from the world, it begins to lose its ability to connect with those who are unbelievers living in the world. In other words, the pursuit of godliness may compromise the ability of the church to reach the world. In the former Soviet Union, for instance, pastor Sergei Nikolaev writes about what happened

---

28. The November 16, 1998, issue of *Christianity Today* provides a global report of the state of the church penned by local church leaders from every continent.

when the church was isolated for seventy-five years. They had lost a common language with secular Russians, and unbelievers felt as uncomfortable with Christians as Christians felt about those newcomers walking through their doors.[29] The purity, holiness, and necessary separation of the church from the world is sometimes at odds with a church that has a mission of witness to the world. Christian leadership must discern with care where those boundaries are to be found.

These qualities of the church's life—transcendence, teaching, fellowship, and mission—outline the essential things we seek and the things Jesus desires to see within his church. These are pillars on which any healthy congregation must be built. A consortium of independent charismatic churches in Great Britain has four organizational goals for every meeting: worship, word, welcome, and witness. When I have asked pastors what these really mean, I have discovered that they are the same. The church is to be an other-worldly community that experiences the supernatural God in power, that grounds itself in the word of God, that generates a family that nurtures its members, and that understands what it is to do for Christ in the world. Who can argue with a mandate like this?

I have kept this four-point outline in mind as I have worshiped in a variety of contexts. I have been in conservative churches where there has been tremendous teaching and a strong sense of community, but no transcendence. I have also been in churches with remarkable worship and little or no teaching.[30] Still others are completely committed to praxis, to mission (either for social causes or evangelism), but there is little instruction in God's Word or transcendent worship experiences. Each of us needs to examine the character of the communities we serve and to build and test them against the vision for his church Jesus offers in his final prayer.

Above all, this means that the church will have a quality of life that so stands out from what is available in the world that the world takes notice. And the world yearns for it. The key is that the church is not a creation of God that offers frivolous or useless gifts to the world. This may be the case when the church has lost its identity and has become a byproduct of the culture in which it lives. But the true church of Christ offers the world a priceless gift, something it seeks desperately. When Christians are one with Christ and one with each other, the growth of the church is virtually inevitable.

---

29. Ibid., 54–55.

30. To cite one example: In one dynamic church where I worshiped for six months outside the United States, the Lord's Supper was offered in house groups, yet the pastoral leadership did not teach the leaders how to lead such a service nor explain its theological meaning. Nor was the question ever asked who should lead such a service.

John 18:1–19:16a

WHEN HE HAD finished praying, Jesus left with his disciples and crossed the Kidron Valley. On the other side there was an olive grove, and he and his disciples went into it.

²Now Judas, who betrayed him, knew the place, because Jesus had often met there with his disciples. ³So Judas came to the grove, guiding a detachment of soldiers and some officials from the chief priests and Pharisees. They were carrying torches, lanterns and weapons.

⁴Jesus, knowing all that was going to happen to him, went out and asked them, "Who is it you want?"

⁵"Jesus of Nazareth," they replied.

"I am he," Jesus said. (And Judas the traitor was standing there with them.) ⁶When Jesus said, "I am he," they drew back and fell to the ground.

⁷Again he asked them, "Who is it you want?"

And they said, "Jesus of Nazareth."

⁸"I told you that I am he," Jesus answered. "If you are looking for me, then let these men go." ⁹This happened so that the words he had spoken would be fulfilled: "I have not lost one of those you gave me."

¹⁰Then Simon Peter, who had a sword, drew it and struck the high priest's servant, cutting off his right ear. (The servant's name was Malchus.)

¹¹ Jesus commanded Peter, "Put your sword away! Shall I not drink the cup the Father has given me?"

¹²Then the detachment of soldiers with its commander and the Jewish officials arrested Jesus. They bound him ¹³and brought him first to Annas, who was the father-in-law of Caiaphas, the high priest that year. ¹⁴Caiaphas was the one who had advised the Jews that it would be good if one man died for the people.

¹⁵Simon Peter and another disciple were following Jesus. Because this disciple was known to the high priest, he went with Jesus into the high priest's courtyard, ¹⁶but Peter had to wait outside at the door. The other disciple, who was known to the high priest, came back, spoke to the girl on duty there and brought Peter in.

17"You are not one of his disciples, are you?" the girl at the door asked Peter.

He replied, "I am not."

18It was cold, and the servants and officials stood around a fire they had made to keep warm. Peter also was standing with them, warming himself.

19Meanwhile, the high priest questioned Jesus about his disciples and his teaching.

20 "I have spoken openly to the world," Jesus replied. "I always taught in synagogues or at the temple, where all the Jews come together. I said nothing in secret. 21Why question me? Ask those who heard me. Surely they know what I said."

22When Jesus said this, one of the officials nearby struck him in the face. "Is this the way you answer the high priest?" he demanded.

23"If I said something wrong," Jesus replied, "testify as to what is wrong. But if I spoke the truth, why did you strike me?" 24Then Annas sent him, still bound, to Caiaphas the high priest.

25As Simon Peter stood warming himself, he was asked, "You are not one of his disciples, are you?"

He denied it, saying, "I am not."

26One of the high priest's servants, a relative of the man whose ear Peter had cut off, challenged him, "Didn't I see you with him in the olive grove?" 27Again Peter denied it, and at that moment a rooster began to crow.

28Then the Jews led Jesus from Caiaphas to the palace of the Roman governor. By now it was early morning, and to avoid ceremonial uncleanness the Jews did not enter the palace; they wanted to be able to eat the Passover. 29So Pilate came out to them and asked, "What charges are you bringing against this man?"

30"If he were not a criminal," they replied, "we would not have handed him over to you."

31Pilate said, "Take him yourselves and judge him by your own law."

"But we have no right to execute anyone," the Jews objected. 32This happened so that the words Jesus had spoken indicating the kind of death he was going to die would be fulfilled.

33Pilate then went back inside the palace, summoned Jesus and asked him, "Are you the king of the Jews?"

³⁴"Is that your own idea," Jesus asked, "or did others talk to you about me?"

³⁵"Am I a Jew?" Pilate replied. "It was your people and your chief priests who handed you over to me. What is it you have done?"

³⁶Jesus said, "My kingdom is not of this world. If it were, my servants would fight to prevent my arrest by the Jews. But now my kingdom is from another place."

³⁷"You are a king, then!" said Pilate.

Jesus answered, "You are right in saying I am a king. In fact, for this reason I was born, and for this I came into the world, to testify to the truth. Everyone on the side of truth listens to me."

³⁸"What is truth?" Pilate asked. With this he went out again to the Jews and said, "I find no basis for a charge against him. ³⁹But it is your custom for me to release to you one prisoner at the time of the Passover. Do you want me to release 'the king of the Jews'?"

⁴⁰They shouted back, "No, not him! Give us Barabbas!" Now Barabbas had taken part in a rebellion.

¹⁹:¹Then Pilate took Jesus and had him flogged. ²The soldiers twisted together a crown of thorns and put it on his head. They clothed him in a purple robe ³and went up to him again and again, saying, "Hail, king of the Jews!" And they struck him in the face.

⁴Once more Pilate came out and said to the Jews, "Look, I am bringing him out to you to let you know that I find no basis for a charge against him." ⁵When Jesus came out wearing the crown of thorns and the purple robe, Pilate said to them, "Here is the man!"

⁶As soon as the chief priests and their officials saw him, they shouted, "Crucify! Crucify!"

But Pilate answered, "You take him and crucify him. As for me, I find no basis for a charge against him."

⁷The Jews insisted, "We have a law, and according to that law he must die, because he claimed to be the Son of God."

⁸When Pilate heard this, he was even more afraid, ⁹and he went back inside the palace. "Where do you come from?" he asked Jesus, but Jesus gave him no answer. ¹⁰"Do you refuse to speak to me?" Pilate said. "Don't you realize I have power either to free you or to crucify you?"

¹¹Jesus answered, "You would have no power over me if it were not given to you from above. Therefore the one who handed me over to you is guilty of a greater sin."

¹²From then on, Pilate tried to set Jesus free, but the Jews kept shouting, "If you let this man go, you are no friend of Caesar. Anyone who claims to be a king opposes Caesar."

¹³When Pilate heard this, he brought Jesus out and sat down on the judge's seat at a place known as the Stone Pavement (which in Aramaic is Gabbatha). ¹⁴It was the day of Preparation of Passover Week, about the sixth hour.

"Here is your king," Pilate said to the Jews. ¹⁵ But they shouted, "Take him away! Take him away! Crucify him!"

"Shall I crucify your king?" Pilate asked.

"We have no king but Caesar," the chief priests answered.

¹⁶Finally Pilate handed him over to them to be crucified.

Original Meaning

WE HAVE OBSERVED a number of major literary transitions in the Gospel of John. The Book of Signs (chs. 1–12) and the Book of Glory (chs. 13–21) neatly divide the public ministry of Jesus from the events of Jesus' life days before his arrest. The Book of Signs was filled with miracles (signs) and public discourses. The Book of Glory begins with Jesus' words in the Upper Room, particularly following the foot-washing and Judas's departure (ch. 13). Jesus speaks at length and follows his exhortations and promises with a lengthy prayer (chs. 14–17), thus closing his life and ministry with his disciples.

John 18:1 opens an entirely new section of the Book of Glory. Jesus now moves toward the climax of the "hour" we have anticipated throughout the Gospel. If the Farewell Discourse was a preparation for the coming of the darkness, in chapters 18–19 the darkness arrives. Jesus is arrested and taken into custody. He is interrogated both by Judaism's high priest and by Pilate. Then he is crucified. As we will see, however, John introduces important theological nuances to the story, aiding us as readers to anticipate the triumph of resurrection recorded in chapters 20–21. "The light shines in the darkness and the darkness has not overcome it" (1:5, NIV note). At the close of the Gospel the pendulum swings back to its lofty original height. The glory of Jesus, his light and truth, radiate through the final chapters, showing that he indeed has overcome the world and death (16:33).

The Passion[1] Story in John

I MENTIONED IN the Introduction how the historical trustworthiness of John has always been a matter of academic debate. When C. H. Dodd worked on the "historical traditions in the Fourth Gospel" in 1963, he began his study with the account of Jesus' arrest, trial, and death since there was so much material that overlapped the Synoptic Gospels.[2] Today that debate continues, particularly where it touches the Passion narratives. Some scholars, like Dodd, have a renewed confidence in the historical character of the Passion story.[3] But others are skeptical.[4] It is of course impossible as well as unnecessary for us to review the nature of this debate and list its primary contributors. I will simply outline the major issues.

When the earliest stories about Jesus were penned and recounted, no doubt the Passion story was of signal importance because it answered a fundamental question: Why was Jesus arrested and killed? If he was a man of truth, if his miracles were compelling, it made no sense that his own people would kill him. Confidence in Jesus ran aground at the Passion story. If he was the Messiah, what happened to him in Jerusalem during the last days of his life?

All four Gospels share the same basic outline: Jesus was arrested near Jerusalem, he was tried and convicted, and he was executed on a cross. Within this outline, the Gospels offer numerous consistent details: (1) Jesus and the disciples depart from the city for a location on the West side of the Mount of Olives; (2) Judas arrives with a crowd to take Jesus into custody; (3) Jesus is examined by the high priest; (4) Jesus is examined by the Roman Pontius Pilate; (5) Pilate infers Jesus' innocence and offers to release one of his prisoners; (6) the crowd calls for Barabbas's release; (7) Pilate gives the order of death for Jesus; (8) Jesus is crucified with two men; (9) the soldiers divide

---

1. "Passion" is the term generally used by scholars to describe the account of Jesus' arrest, trial, and death. Passion comes from the Latin verb *patior, pati, passum sum,* "to suffer." Passion thus refers to Jesus' suffering.

2. C. H. Dodd, *Historical Tradition in the Fourth Gospel* (Cambridge: Cambridge Univ. Press, 1963), 21–151; see the critical review by D. A. Carson "Historical Tradition in the Fourth Gospel: After Dodd, What?" in R. T. France and D. Wenham, eds., *Gospel Perspectives II* (Sheffield: JSOT Press, 1981), 83–146; about 95 percent of John's stories are unique to John. Of the material that parallels the Synoptics, the bulk is found in the temple cleansing (ch. 2), the feeding miracle (ch. 6), and the trial sequence (chs. 18–20).

3. F. F. Bruce, "The Trial of Jesus in the Fourth Gospel," R. T. France and D. Wenham, eds., *Gospel Perspectives I* (Sheffield: JSOT Press, 1980), 7–20; J. A. T. Robinson, *The Priority of John* (London: SCM, 1985), 212–95; the magisterial presentation of the Passion story is available in R. E. Brown, *The Death of the Messiah*, 2 vols. (New York: Doubleday, 1994).

4. Most recently see J. Ashton, *Understanding the Fourth Gospel* (Oxford: Clarendon, 1991), 485–514, and the literature cited there.

Jesus' clothes among themselves; (10) Jesus is offered wine; (11) Jesus dies; (12) Joseph of Arimathea requests Jesus' body for burial.

John's Gospel shares this outline and these details. Thus it is absurd for anyone to suggest that John is not linked to sound historical traditions in his Passion account. But John does add numerous independent details, and he omits a few things. Among those omissions are the following: (1) the betrayal with a kiss; (2) Jesus' prayer in the Garden of Gethsemane; (3) the sleepiness of the disciples; (4) the healing of the servant's ear; (5) Simon of Cyrene; (6) the mocking crowds; (7) Jesus' cry from the cross.

John also adds a number of details: (1) Roman soldiers falling to the ground in the arrest scene when Jesus identifies himself; (2) Jesus' conversation with Annas; (3) Jesus' conversation with Pilate; (4) John's emphasis on the inscription on the cross; (5) a full description of Jesus' garments; (6) Mary given to the Beloved Disciple at the cross; (7) Jesus' body threatened with the breaking of his legs; (8) Jesus pierced with a soldier's lance; (9) Nicodemus's joining Joseph at Jesus' burial.

While these omissions and additions may seem significant, it is not difficult to bring them together into one coherent narrative thread. Nevertheless, for scholars who believe that John is directly dependent on Mark for his story (Barrett, Haenchen), John wins low marks as a trustworthy narrative. For scholars who see John as considerably independent of the Synoptics (Dodd, Beasley-Murray), John's story gains increased credibility insofar as the added stories may stem from sources parallel to the Synoptics. In fact some scholars are even convinced that while John may not be copying from the Synoptic account, he nevertheless assumes that his Gospel will circulate among those who have perhaps read the Gospel of Mark.[5]

For instance, John 18:13–28 records the Jewish interrogation of Jesus and includes two high priests: Annas (the emeritus high priest who wielded considerable power) and Caiaphas (the reigning high priest). Mark does not name his high priest but nevertheless records Jesus' trial with him. John is making clear that Jesus' meeting with Annas (18:13) was not the official Sanhedrin trial. Caiaphas is mentioned in 18:14, and when Annas is finished with Jesus in 18:24, John records, "Then Annas sent him, still bound, to Caiaphas the high priest." Readers of Mark will at once realize that the critical trial and decision of the temple's high council ensues here and that by 18:28, Jesus has been sent on to Pilate. Details such as this are legion, and we will examine most of them closely in the commentary below. Above all, keep in mind that John has heightened the dramatic tone of the story, includ-

---

5. R. Bauckham, "John for Readers of Mark," *The Gospels for All Christians: Rethinking the Gospel Audiences* (Grand Rapids: Eerdmans, 1998), 157–58.

ing names here and there, and has provided conversations and events that give us a clearer insight into what is transpiring.

Despite the possibilities of harmonizing the Passion story, there are important theological emphases in John that must be understood for us to follow the course of his presentation. (1) Martin Kähler once made the famous (and scandalous) remark that the Synoptic Gospels might be called "passion narratives with extended introductions."[6] That is, the Gospels themselves are dominated by the events in the last week of Jesus' life (for Mark this is 40 percent of his Gospel!). But, Kähler suggested, this was hardly true of John. John's Gospel does not *need* Jesus' death on the cross.

Years later E. Käsemann championed this view and took it further. He believed that the Passion of Jesus was an addendum, an "embarrassment" to John.[7] If we read John without any recollection of Paul's idea of sacrifice and atonement, or if we try to forget the story in the Synoptics, we may see John's view of the cross emerging. Gone is the pathos of Gethsemane; gone is the trauma of Golgotha. For John the cross is an instrument of exaltation. Jesus is exhibiting his glory, not unlike he has throughout the Gospel.

But Käsemann is wrong to think of the cross as a postscript to this Gospel. From its beginning the "hour" is the moment toward which we are pushed (e.g., 2:4; 7:30; 8:20), and this theme continues straight through the Farewell Discourse. Jesus' death and its effects have been alluded to (6:51–58) and have been described even by the likes of Caiaphas (11:49–50). But what John has done is to reforge one theological dimension of Jesus on the cross. Throughout his Passion Jesus is sovereign; he is not a victim. The cross is a fate that he has chosen voluntarily and that he controls.

Thus, at his arrest, Judas does not hand Jesus over, but he steps forward (18:4). Jesus asks the question (lit.): "Whom do you seek?"—a question that parallels Jesus' first words in the gospel in 1:38 (lit.): "What do you seek?" Jesus protects his followers (18:8) so that none will be lost (17:12). Similarly in 19:11 Jesus checks Pilate's presumption of power. On the cross, Jesus cries, "It is finished" (19:30), announcing that the cross is a work, a goal achieved. Ashton (perhaps too glibly) puts it thus: "If God is the author of this passion play, Jesus is the protagonist—but also the producer and director!"[8]

This theological emphasis on glory, victory, and sovereignty likewise appears in the literary structure of 18:28–19:16. In Jesus' meetings with Pilate, we witness one of the Gospel's final great misunderstandings. While one level

---

6. M. Kähler, *The So-Called Historical Jesus and the Historic Biblical Christ* (Philadelphia: Fortress, 1892, 1964); cited in J. Ashton, *Understanding the Fourth Gospel*, 495.

7. E. Käsemann, *The Testament of Jesus· The Gospel of John in Light of Chapter 17* (London: SCM, 1968).

8. Ashton, *Understanding the Fourth Gospel*, 490.

of the story simply reports Jesus' interrogation and the harm done to him, another level permits us as readers to see a deeper truth at work. The structure of the story is inverted and so outside "stanzas" must be read in relation to each in order to see the symmetry or parallelism. Note the following:

Stanza A, 18:28–32 (outside Pilate's chamber)
It was early
Passover
Jewish leaders cannot put a man to death (lawfully)
The type of Jesus' death
A Jewish plea for Jesus' death
 Stanza B, 18:33–38a (inside)
 Pilate does not speak on his own accord
 Jesus' origins: not of this world
 Jesus is passive: he is not of this world
  Stanza C, 18:38b–40 (outside)
  Pilate finds no crime in him
  Pilate brings Jesus out: he *may* be set free
   Stanza D, 19:1–3 (inside)
   1 Jesus flogged
    2 Jesus crowned
     3 JESUS ARRAYED IN A ROYAL ROBE
    2' Jesus hailed as "king"
   1' Jesus struck
  Stanza C', 19:4–8 (outside)
  Pilate finds no crime in Jesus
  Pilate brings Jesus out: will he be set free?
 Stanza B', 19:9–11 (inside)
 Pilate's power is not his own
 "Where are you from"
 Jesus is passive: Pilate's authority is from above
Stanza A', 19:12–16 (outside)
It was late (the 6th hour)
Passover
The Jewish crowds call for death
Crucifixion
The Jewish leaders obtain Jesus' death

Parallelism (or chiasm) like this has been recognized for a long time in the biblical text. As a story-telling vehicle, it structures development and form into the drama and in this case offers the significant number seven. One can even tag each stanza following Pilate's movements in and out of the palace (praetorium). In Stanza A he steps out, in B he is in, C: out, etc. Here in this interrogation sequence, the stanzas can be aligned in an inversion, and at once it becomes evident that parallel themes are treated (A and A'; B and B'; C and C'; D). But the most significant feature, the "climax" or turning point of the structure, is Jesus' coronation (D). The center stanza is itself an inversion, telling us that, ironically, Jesus is crowned and arrayed in a purple robe, and while these men meant it as harm, on a deeper level Jesus is actually being acknowledged as king. The same motif appears on the cross. Pilate refuses to change the title of the cross, "JESUS OF NAZARETH, THE KING OF THE JEWS" (19:19). Why? Because these events are (truly) linked to Jesus' coronation.[9]

The second major theological motif at work in this Gospel concerns the place of "the Jews" in John's trial narrative. We need to examine the evolution of the role played by the Jewish authorities in the Gospels during the Passion. In Mark, following the condemnation of Jesus, Pilate is "amazed" about these events (Mark 15:5). In Matthew, Pilate has "great amazement" (Matt. 27:14), receives a warning message from his wife (27:19), and washes his hands of all responsibility (27:24–25). In Luke, Pilate states three times that Jesus is innocent (Luke 23:4, 14, 22). When we come to John, Pilate not only affirms Jesus' innocence, but he shows a determined effort to free Jesus (18:38–40; 19:12a) and only agrees to the crucifixion when his loyalty to Rome is questioned (19:12b). All of this seems to shift the blame to the Jewish leadership. Incredibly, John refers to "the Jews" twenty-two times in chapters 18–19. For the next few centuries, Christian literature continued to promote this shift.[10]

This is no delicate matter for Christians, and heated debate has followed these chapters in our Gospel particularly during the twentieth century. The sensitivity of Jews today is comprehensible inasmuch as this portrait of Judaism has fallen into the hands of countless unscrupulous Christians bent on a program of unconscionable anti-Judaism. The West's legacy of hating Jews runs from medieval charges of "God-killers" to Nazi death camps and Bible-toting

---

9. Most commentators recognize some literary structure in these verses. See Bultmann, *John*, 501, 648; Brown, *John*, 2:857–59; idem, "The Passion According to John: Chapters 18–19," *Worship* 49 (1975): 126–34; idem., *The Death of the Messiah*, 757–59; B. D. Ehrman, "Jesus' Trial Before Pilate: John 18:28–19:6," *BTB* 13 (1983): 124–31; G. H. Giblin, "John's Narration of the Hearing Before Pilate (John 18:28–19:16a)," *Bib* 67 (1986)· 221–39.

10. Within the next three hundred years the shift is complete In the Gospel of Peter, Herod (not Pilate) makes the pronouncement of death. In the Syriac manuscript of Matthew, the story is rewritten so that the Jews alone mistreat and crucify Jesus. Tertullian even considered Pilate a Christian at heart and legends told of his conversion. In the Ethiopian and Egyptian Coptic traditions, Pilate and his wife Procla become saints, whose feast is celebrated on June 25. See further, Brown, *John*, 2:794–95.

white supremacy groups. Whatever we do with John's Passion story, we cannot tolerate anyone who will use it to fire racial hatred of any sort.

One solution (so often championed by scholars wanting to appease Jewish fears and to facilitate Jewish-Christian dialogue) is to dehistoricize this Gospel, making all reference to Judaism here some sort of later Christian campaign to persecute the synagogue. But to say that Rome was the *only* player in the Passion story is not historically respectable. Nor is it correct to say that the Jewish leadership was solely responsible for Jesus' death. It is better to say that many people played a role in this conspiracy. As Carson notes, it is the people in power who can do the persecuting, and everyone must agree that in Jerusalem in the mid-first century, the Sanhedrin leadership held power.[11]

Brown reminds us that we should expect considerable collusion between Caiaphas and Pilate. Caiaphas held office for eighteen years, the longest time of rule for a high priest from the period of Herod the Great to the fall of Jerusalem. And ten of those years he shared with Pontius Pilate.[12] Curiously the same year that Pilate was removed from office, Caiaphas was deposed as reigning high priest.

But the shared responsibility of Jewish leaders here is no license for racism. The earliest Christians who wrote the Gospels were Jewish. Their debate with the temple or synagogue leadership was not along racial but theological lines. "Anti-Semitism" is a historically inappropriate label for their thinking. The tensions that run through the Gospel's Passion story is an *inner-Jewish tension*, springing from inner-Jewish debates about Jesus' messiahship.

As we will see, moreover, it is incorrect to argue that John simply blames "the Jews" for the death of Jesus. One of the most prominent themes in John's story is the high profile role of Pilate. His soldiers figure conspicuously in this story, and Pilate not only spurns the truth, but we see him as a pathetic, powerless figure whom Jesus must instruct and direct.[13]

Jesus' Arrest (18:1–11)

THE OPENING WORDS of chapter 18 link the Passion story with the Farewell Discourse. Once Jesus completes these teachings (his farewell and prayer), he leads his disciples out of the city to a garden that he frequented (18:2; cf. Luke 22:39). The Synoptics also refer to this departure (Matt. 26:30; Mark 14:26; Luke 22:39). Since it is Passover, they are required to remain in the

---

11. Carson, *John*, 575.

12. Brown, *John*, 2:798.

13. See D. Rensberger, "The Politics of John: The Trial of Jesus in the Fourth Gospel," *JBL* 103 (1984): 395–411

city precincts that night, and Bethany is beyond the permissible limit. East of Jerusalem's walled city is a steep valley called the Kidron.[14] This valley is a riverbed that remains dry most of the year but flows only following winter rains.[15]

Here they find a garden named by the Synoptics "Gethsemane." We should not think of a decorative garden like those built for pleasure in Europe or North America. This is an olive grove ("Gethsemane" means olive press, Matt. 26:36; Mark 14:32), which grew along the west shoulder of the Mount of Olives.[16] At this point, the Synoptic Gospels record Jesus' prayer in the olive grove (Mark 14:32–42). John does not refer to it.

John's account of the arresting party's arrival (18:3–9) has dramatic interests that differ from the Synoptics (Mark 14:43–50). Judas (who departed the story in 13:30) knows the location as well (18:2) and therefore can lead the party to this location.[17] While the Synoptics only mention a Jewish guard at the arrest, John refers to "a detachment of soldiers" (18:3) who appear alongside the Jewish police.[18]

The appearance of a Roman "detachment" (Gk. *speiras*) in this posse has posed historical problems for many. A cohort could consist of a thousand men (760 infantry, 240 cavalry) and be lead by a *chiliarch* (lit., *leader-of-one-thousand*, generally translated commander, captain, or tribune). These soldiers were based no doubt at Jerusalem's Antonia Fortress, but it is not necessary to think that all of them are present. This is likely a detachment large enough to warrant bringing along their commander (18:12) and equipped with weapons (18:3b).[19]

During festival seasons the Romans were aware of the explosive atmosphere in the city, and reinforcements routinely came to Jerusalem. At the beginning, then, we have a signal of Roman interest in Jesus and a hint that Pilate may already be participating. The presence of chief priests and Pharisees recalls their appearances elsewhere in the Gospel (7:32, 45; 11:47, 57)

---

14. The Greek spelling is *Kedron*, but this reflects the LXX spelling. Kidron comes from the Hebrew and is the traditional name.

15. In the LXX (Num. 34:5) it refers simply to a river. In LXX 4 Kings 3:16 it is a valley.

16. Today this garden is remembered at The Church of All Nations with its ancient olive grove. Nearby, ancient olive presses have been discovered just north of these trees. The classical lexicon of Liddel and Scott shows how the term is used for orchards and any cultivated land.

17. John does not suggest that Judas took command of this group (as some critics charge). He merely led them to the well-known garden, and then his services were dispensed.

18. Some have suggested that these are not Roman soldiers, but John is using a Roman title for Jewish troops. But this is unlikely. In 18:12 the two groups are carefully distinguished, and there the Roman troops are described with their "commander" or tribune.

19. F. F. Bruce, "The Trial of Jesus in the Fourth Gospel," 9.

and indicates that these leaders, priestly aristocrats and teachers of the law, who had plotted Jesus' death earlier under Caiaphas's direction (11:53), are now putting their plan into action. Therefore John's portrait is clear: The entire world—both Jew and Gentile—has come against Jesus. Responsibility for what happens next rests with all of them.

But Jesus is not taken by surprise (18:4). In Mark 14:42 Jesus knows that Judas is coming before he arrives. Likewise here, Jesus' foreknowledge (1:47–48; 6:6; 13:1) gives him the ability to see the arrest before it unfolds. He does not shrink from the moment but has already made the decision to lay down his life under his own volition (10:18). Therefore Jesus steps forward and asks the first question, "Who is it you want?" (which echoes Jesus' first words in the Gospel; 1:38). The answer is surprising (18:5): "Jesus of Nazareth." In John, reference to Jesus from Nazareth appears only here, in the title on the cross (19:19),[20] and at 1:45. Although John does not refer to Nazareth stories, he is acquainted with sources also known to the Synoptics. It is likely at this point that, according to the Synoptics, Judas marks Jesus with a kiss (Mark 14:44).

Jesus identifies himself plainly (18:5–7) but this certainly means a great deal more than a mere self-identification. Jesus uses the "I am" formula we have seen elsewhere in the Gospel (e.g., 4:26; 8:24, 58), which no doubt recalls God's divine name.[21] John underscores this in 18:6, "When Jesus said, 'I am ...,' they drew back and fell to the ground."

This verse does not describe unruly soldiers backing away and stumbling (Carson), nor is it about the psychological effect of Jesus' personality on the mob (Morris). Rather, John creates another of his many ironic scenes: Jesus' words provoke a response that even those who hear it likely do not understand. This is the biblical response of holy fear before the Lord (Ezek. 1:28; Dan. 10:9; Acts 9:4; 22:7; 26:14; Rev. 1:17). This is a theophany in which God has been revealed before mortals and the only response is to fall prostrate (Barrett, Brown, Beasley-Murray; see Ezek. 1:28; Isa. 6:5).

Jesus not only steps forward (thus taking charge of his own arrest), but he protects his followers from capture (18:8–9) and so fulfills what he said in 17:12 (cf. 6:39). Of those whom God has given to him, he has not lost one. Twice Jesus makes his captors say that he alone is the one they seek (18:5, 7). This recalls the image we have of Jesus the shepherd in chapter 10—not only laying down his life for his sheep (10:11, 17–18) but also preserving them and not letting them become victims left to the wolves (10:12).

John alone tells us that Peter is the one who draws out his sword and strikes the high priest's slave, whom John names as Malchus (18:10–11; cf.

---

20. The title is commonly used in the Synoptics, Matt. 2:23; 26:71; Luke 18:37; and six times in Acts.

21. The Gk. phrase is *ego eimi*, used in Ex. 3:14. See comments on 4:26; 8:58.

Matt. 26:51–53; Mark 14:46–47; Luke 22:49–51). The suggestion that we locate the origin of the name Malchus in Zechariah 11:6 (*malchus* means "my king") is farfetched. It is not impossible, however, that John sees some ironic double meaning, insofar as the kingship of Jesus is one of the chief themes that runs through chapters 18–19. Peter's sword is a *machaira*, a short sword or a long knife (probably worn with everyday garments), and Peter's clumsy use of it shows something of the chaos of the scene. We know nothing more of the priest's slave except that both John and Luke tell us that he loses his right ear. Luke closes the scene with Jesus' healing of the man's ear.[22]

Jesus then points to the "cup" the Father has given him to drink (John 18:11). This reference recalls the Synoptic Gethsemane prayer (Mark 14:36; but cf. John 12:27–28), but now the struggle with Jesus' fate belongs to Peter, who cannot face the "cup" that includes the cross. Jesus, by contrast, understands that this is God's will and so will not hesitate to embrace it.

Jesus, Peter, and Annas (18:12–27)

ACCORDING TO JOHN'S rendition, Jesus is then taken to Annas (18:12–14), where he is interrogated (18:19–24) and simultaneously Peter is questioned in the courtyard (18:15–18, 25–27). The literary interlocking of these parallel stories invites us to contrast them and reflect on their symbolic value.

Under full armed arrest (note that both Roman and Jewish troops continue working together, 18:12), Jesus is brought to meet Annas, Caiaphas's father-in-law. From the Kidron Valley they walk west across the city, climbing its western hill where archaeologists have recently discovered the wealthy "upper city" of Jerusalem, where Annas likely resided.[23]

Annas is well known even though he appears second to Caiaphas in the New Testament (Luke 3:2; John 18:13, 24; Acts 4:6). Josephus indicates that he was appointed in A.D. 6 but was removed from office in A.D. 15 by Valerius Gratus, Pilate's predecessor. He continued to enjoy enormous influence, however, and considerable popular support since Judaism resented how the Romans controlled the high priesthood (his festival vestments were kept, for instance, in the Antonia Fortress). Five of Annas's sons became high priests as well as his son-in-law Caiaphas. Thus Annas enjoyed great power and was the patriarch of an influential priestly family, well known for its wealth, power, and greed.

---

22. Matthew adds a warning—"for all who draw the sword will die by the sword"—and explains that if violence were an option, Jesus has massive heavenly resources at his disposal.

23. The company may have entered the temple courts and crossed a bridge on its western wall (which ran the risk of meeting crowds); more likely, they traveled south across or around the current "City of David," climbing west into the newer, "upper" sections of the western city

That John refers to Annas as "high priest" should not confuse since he clearly understands Caiaphas to be the ruling high priest and Jerusalem can only have *one* (18:24). Judaism understood that appointment to this position was permanent (Num. 35:25), so that when Rome removed such men, the continued use of this title became a courtesy. The *Mishnah* supports the ongoing holiness of such deposed high priests (*Horayoth* 3:1–2, 4), and Luke follows this practice when he mentions Annas in his Gospel (Luke 3:2).

That Jesus is sent first to Annas is plausible if he is the de facto power behind Caiaphas. This meeting may have been arranged in advance if Caiaphas (who originally determined that Jesus should die, 11:49–51) is seeking to broaden his base of support vis-à-vis Rome. Since Jesus remains with Annas until 18:24, we should assume that all generic references to the "high priest" until then refer to Annas (18:15, 16, 19, 22). Thus the interrogation in 18:19–24 represents the gist of Annas's questioning.[24] Some interpreters wonder if perhaps Caiaphas and Annas are together during this interrogation (thus making the references to "high priest" refer to Caiaphas), but this view struggles with what to do with 18:24.[25]

Each of the four Gospels record Peter's denials of Jesus during his interrogation by the Jewish authorities. On one level Jesus has predicted this (13:38) and so his foreknowledge includes not simply the events of the arrest, but the responses of his followers. Nevertheless it is a tragedy since throughout the story (both in John and the Synoptics) Peter figures prominently and the denials represent Jesus' apparent loss of a major follower.

Peter is accompanied, however, by "another disciple," who remains unnamed (18:15). This is curious since John has been careful to name people carefully (Annas, Caiaphas, Simon Peter, Malchus). Is this the Beloved Disciple, who figures elsewhere in the Gospel and is commonly identified with John son of Zebedee (a not unreasonable position)? Many scholars object, wondering how a Galilean fisherman could be "known to the high priest" (18:15b), enter his guarded courtyard, converse with the maid, and bring Peter in (18:16). Perhaps this is an anonymous Jerusalem disciple. Or, as one interpreter unconvincingly suggests, maybe this is Judas (who would be well known to the authorities by this time).

---

24. Some manuscripts attempt to harmonize John with the Synoptics by attributing verses 19–23 to Caiaphas. Some move 18:24 to an earlier position or eliminate the word "then" (Gk. *oun*) from 18:24. The KJV follows this latter solution at 18:24: "Now Annas had sent him bound unto Caiaphas the high priest." This makes the previous five verses belong to Caiaphas. But these corrections to John are unnecessary. F. J. Matera suggests that John has embedded the essence of the Synoptic Caiaphas trial in the body of the Gospel (see "Jesus Before Annas: John 18:13–14, 19–24," *ETL* 66.1 [1990]: 38–55).

25. A. Mahoney, "A New Look at an Old Problem (John 18:12–14; 19–24)," *CBQ* 27 (1965): 137–44.

Yet the view that this is the Beloved Disciple has a great deal to commend it. Throughout the gospel the Beloved Disciple frequently appears alongside Peter (13:23–26; 20:2–10; 21:7–8, 20–24), a portrait also common in the Synoptics (Mark 5:37; 9:2; 13:13; 14:33). The Beloved Disciple faithfully follows Jesus even to the site of the cross, where Jesus talks to him (John 19:25–27). His presence at the arrest shows his profound loyalty to Jesus so characteristic throughout the Gospel. We also must be careful not to stereotype fishermen and think of them as poor, uneducated, and socially marginalized—and thus unable to know Jerusalem's leaders. John's father, Zebedee, had hired servants (Mark 1:20). Brown makes the interesting (and compelling) argument that John (of Zebedee) may have been related to Jesus, which also explains the Beloved Disciple's responsibility in 19:26–27 to take care of Jesus' mother (we will look at this theory in ch. 19).[26] If Jesus and John are cousins, then Mary's priestly connections in Jerusalem (Luke 1:36–45) may well have connected John with Jerusalem too.

When Peter enters the courtyard, the young woman guarding the gate recognizes him and immediately inquires if he is one of Jesus' disciples (18:17–18). Each of the Gospels note that a young girl asks this question; the form of this question (beginning with the Gk. word *me*) implies a negative answer. She is cautious but curious, and she implies that she knows there are many others who follow Jesus. We might paraphrase: "What's this? Not another of this man's disciples, is it?" Or: "You couldn't be another one of this man's disciples, could you?"

Peter feels his vulnerability because the small courtyard also hosts officers and other servants (18:18a). Some of them may even remember that he attacked Malchus—another slave, whom this woman may know. So at the gate, to gain entry, Peter refuses to acknowledge his discipleship. The "other" disciple's silence does not point to the maid's failure to recognize him, but to his unbroken fidelity to Jesus. Since it was now night (note that lanterns were used at the arrest, 18:3) and springtime, the bystanders in Annas's courtyard, including Peter and the Beloved Disciple, stand around a charcoal fire,[27] warming themselves against the cold.

John now shifts the scene to what is transpiring inside (18:19–24). In a formal Jewish trial, the judge never asked direct questions of the accused but rather called forth witnesses whose words determined the outcome. If two or more agreed with the charges, the verdict was sealed. But Annas may not see himself engaged in such a trial. If it were a genuine trial, Caiaphas would

---

26. Brown, *John*, 1:xcvii; 2:905–6.

27. This attention to detail is one more example of John's commitment to historical specificity based no doubt on eyewitness memory (see 19.35). Peter stands not simply before a fire, but a charcoal fire (as the Gk. word here implies; cf. also John 21:9).

be presiding, but he is not present (18:24). This is like a "police interrogation" of someone recently arrested. Yet if Jesus does utter something incriminating, Annas himself will become a witness against him.

The words recorded here no doubt represent the barest summary of Jesus' meeting with Annas, who probes two things: Jesus' teachings and his disciples (18:19). To what extent is he a genuine threat? Does he have a strong following? Is he promoting some sort of conspiracy? A secret conspiracy? To what extent does he threaten their interests? Jesus' sharp answer—pointing out that Annas should be talking to witnesses—unmasks the priest's attempt to make Jesus' incriminate himself. Twice Jesus demands that Annas produce witnesses and evidence; in other words, Jesus is demanding a trial.

When Jesus affirms that he has taught openly (in the temple and in synagogues) and many can verify his work, he may sense that Annas is maneuvering to accuse him of being a false prophet.[28] "False prophesy" is the classic charge against Jesus reported in the Talmud (*b. Sanh.* 43a). To qualify as a false prophet one must "secretly entice" or "deceive" the people (Matt. 24:11, 24; Mark 13:5, 22; Luke 21:8). The punishment for this was death (Deut. 13:1–11). Twice before this was precisely the suggestion uttered by the crowds (7:12) and the Pharisees (7:47).

Jesus has thus reminded Annas of judicial procedure, which the guards interpret as insolence. Thus, one of them strikes him (18:22). But note that Jesus here (as later) simply points to the truth (18:23). He speaks directly to the soldier. There are no witnesses accusing him. He has not been subversive. No evidence says he has led people astray. Nothing he has said can be construed as incriminating. Annas is at an impasse. His probing has been unsuccessful. Therefore Jesus is sent on to the reigning high priest, Caiaphas. If Jesus is going to be prosecuted, if his case is carried successfully to Pilate, it will be necessary to have the explicit support of the Sanhedrin, Jerusalem's high judicial council.

John understands that a major meeting of the Sanhedrin takes place under the direction of Caiaphas that evening (see Mark 14:53), for in John 18:24 Jesus is moved to a new location.[29] This is not shameless harmonizing, particularly if we presuppose that John realizes his readership already is aware of the story (esp. Mark's story; see comments above). John continues with the denials

---

28. Beasley-Murray, *John*, 324–25.

29. The traditional site of Jesus' interrogation and Peter's denial is today at the church "St. Peter Gallicantu" (St. Peter of the Cock-Crow). While this site has long been venerated (there is evidence of a sixth-century monastic church and a seventh-century document identifying the site), it is likely that Caiaphas lived in the Upper City further north where aristocratic homes have been recently discovered. The Armenians exhibit another "house of Caiaphas," adjacent to the Dormition Abbey.

of Peter in 18:25 (which he left off at 18:18); he assumes that Peter is still in Annas's courtyard (they are still at the fire, 18:25). But according to the Synoptics, Peter's denials take place at the house of Caiaphas at the close of the Sanhedrin meeting (Mark 14:64, 66). John has split the denials so that the first one happens simultaneously with the meeting with Annas while the second and third happen as Jesus is before Caiaphas (which is the Synoptic setting).

But when John says that Jesus is sent to Caiaphas, it does not mean necessarily that he moves to the other side of the city. He is moved *to Caiaphas*, who may well be nearby (like moving from one courtroom to another).[30] We can imagine that Jesus' conversation with Annas takes place while Caiaphas is gathering the needed members of the Sanhedrin in the same locale. According to the Synoptic outline, Caiaphas meets with Jesus during the night with numerous Sanhedrin members (Mark 14:55). Early the next morning it reconvenes in order to consolidate the decision (15:1). John's account points to the late night meeting; then we should assume a lengthy pause before 18:28, when Jesus is taken early in the morning to Pilate.

While Jesus is with Caiaphas, John reports Peter's ongoing failings as a witness in the courtyard (18:25–27).[31] That he is still warming himself (presumably by the charcoal fire, 18:25a) links this scene with that in 18:15–18. But now the drama tightens: Around the fire stand soldiers and servants and *they* try to identify Peter. "You are not one of his disciples, are you?" (18:25b, cf. v. 17). Peter utters his denial a second time. Then Peter's worries are confirmed: A relative of Malchus, the man whom Peter attacked, speaks up. "Didn't I see you with him in the olive grove?" (18:26). When Peter denies Jesus the third time, a cock crows, recalling Jesus' prediction of Peter's great failure (13:38).[32] Such crowing can take place in spring between 3:00 A.M. and 5:00 A.M. and was a time signal for a trumpet blast at the temple (*m. Sukk.* 5.4).

By weaving Peter's denials among the various interrogations of Jesus, John makes a theological point. Brown aptly comments: "John has constructed a dramatic contrast wherein Jesus stands up to his questioners and denies nothing, while Peter cowers before his questioners and denies everything."[33] Of course, Peter's triple denial will return in John's story, for in 21:15–17 Peter meets with Jesus in Galilee and is invited three times to affirm his love for him.

---

30. Barrett, *John*, 529.

31. For an excellent defense of the historicity of Peter's denials, see Beasley-Murray, *John*, 325–26.

32. The synoptics include a number of additional details. Luke mentions that when the cock crowed Jesus was in the courtyard and he looked directly at Peter. Mark notes that this was the second time the cock crowed. There is some debate whether Jerusalem prohibited the raising of fowl. See Jeremias, *Jerusalem in the Time of Jesus*, 47–48.

33. Brown, *John*, 2:842.

Jesus Before Pilate (Episode 1) (18:28–40)

EVEN THOUGH THE Sanhedrin was Israel's highest judicial court, it did not have the power of capital punishment (18:31). Therefore, if it were to prosecute Jesus with a capital offense, it had to enlist the involvement of the Roman governor. The power to execute criminals was one of the most closely guarded functions of local Roman governors.[34] The Sanhedrin possessed only one ongoing exception in this regard: Any who violated the sanctity of the temple could be killed even if that person was a Roman citizen. When the Roman general Titus laid siege to the temple in A.D. 70, even he hesitated to enter and reminded the Jewish defenders of Rome's pledge.[35]

Pontius Pilate was the fifth Roman governor[36] of the province of Judea, ruling from A.D. 26 to 36. As governor he had numerous troops stationed at Caesarea (his chief maritime link with Rome), where he spent most of his time. Jerusalem was the Jewish heart of the country; when there he likely used the old palace of Herod the Great on the city's western hill. Pilate also kept troops in a refurbished Jewish fortress on the temple's northwest corner called the Antonia (named after Pilate's patron, Mark Antony). Jewish and Hellenistic sources tell us a great deal about Pilate, most of which is extremely critical. He was a brutal ruler whose atrocities against the Jews were legendary. As a member of Rome's lower nobility he was always aware of his vulnerabilities and so controlled Judea harshly, with an eye on the pleasure of his masters in Rome (see below, 19:12).

Early in the morning the Jewish leadership brought Jesus to the "Praetorium" (NIV "palace of the Roman governor"), which refers to his residence (18:28). This could have been in the barracks of the Antonia or at Herod's Palace (though pilgrim tradition generally points to the former). Two historical notes are important. (1) They do not enter Pilate's quarters because they did not want to become "ritually unclean" through contact with a Gentile.[37] Ceremonial defilement could have different degrees; in some cases it could be alleviated through evening bathing, in other cases,

---

34. A. N. Sherwin-White, *Roman Society and Law in the New Testament* (Oxford: Oxford Univ. Press, 1963), 36; F. F. Bruce, "The Trial of Jesus in the Fourth Gospel," 12.

35. Josephus, *Wars*, 6:124; note that the charge against Paul in Acts 24:6 says that he has tried to desecrate the temple, thus putting his life in jeopardy. By rescuing him, the Romans took him out of the temple's jurisdiction.

36. During this time, Pilate would have been termed a "prefect" (Lat *praefectus*). His title and full name were discovered at Caesarea in Israel on the Mediterranean coast in 1961.

37. There is good evidence that Jewish fear about Gentiles and impurity was based on the widespread rumor that abortions and premature babies were buried in Roman homes or flushed through their sewers. This would render Jews unclean by "corpse impurity" (cf *m. Oholoth* 18:7: "The dwelling places of Gentiles are unclean").

through temple sacrifice. David's prayer in Psalm 51 reflects this desire: "Cleanse me with hyssop, and I will be clean; wash me, and I will be whiter than snow" (Ps. 51:7). Contacting a dead body, for instance, required that the person postpone Passover celebrations for seven days (Num. 9:6–11). This Jewish concern makes Pilate move in and out of the building throughout the story. These conversations could take place among the colonnades of the Praetorium since ritual impurity could not be contracted there (*m. Oholoth* 18:9).

(2) What meal do they wish to eat in 18:28 and so remain clean? I argued earlier that Jesus' meal on Thursday night was the Passover meal (Nisan 15, keeping it in accord with the Synoptic story; see comments on 13:1). On the day following the evening Passover meal there was another ritual meal, the *chagiga*, the feast-offering of the first full morning of Passover day (Num. 28:16–25). This day (Nisan 15) also began the seven-day festival of Unleavened Bread—a feast immediately following Passover.[38] Therefore any ritual contamination would make the leaders apprehensive, given their role in all these festivities. They were concerned not with the Passover meal the night before, but with the many meals and celebrations that week in the Passover season, which continued till Nisan 21.

Since the Roman authorities have already been involved in Jesus' arrest, we can comfortably assume that Pilate has been briefed by his officers concerning the nature of the Sanhedrin's charges. Or, as I suggested earlier, Caiaphas possessed sufficient political savvy to brief the governor himself. The deeper irony of the scene is that here the leaders, concerned about their religious purity, now plot Jesus' death and claim that *he* is an evildoer (18:29). Such a charge would be meaningless to Pilate, who viewed this no doubt as an inner-Jewish squabble. Therefore he refuses to entertain the investigation and tells them that their own judicial powers should suffice (18:30). But they urge that this is a capital case and so *require* his involvement.

This appeal to the governor leads Pilate to return to the Praetorium and begin a formal inquiry (Lat., *cognitio*) in order to elicit the facts of this case. If it happened to be an ordinary minor crime, there were provincial court systems set up to manage it. But where the crime might threaten the interests of the empire or where the execution of the accused was involved, the governor was held personally responsible. Thus Pilate's first question to Jesus (18:33b), "Are you the king of the Jews?" is loaded with political meaning.

---

38. The Passover and the Feast of Unleavened Bread had merged chronologically in New Testament times. Nisan 15 (the evening of eating the Passover lamb) was also the first day of Unleavened Bread, which lasted from Nisan 15–21. Against this view, see Morris, *John*, 688–89.

"King" was a political title not held by a Jew in this land since Herod the Great (Matt. 2:1; Josephus, *Ant.* 14:385). Rome had authorized no king since the coming of the governors (like Pilate).

But where did Pilate get the notion to ask this question? Clearly the Sanhedrin has given him this privately (cf. 18:35), or it is a part of their original charge against Jesus (abbreviated in John). This is what Luke reports: "And they [the Sanhedrin leaders] began to accuse [Jesus], saying, 'We have found this man subverting our nation. He opposes payment of taxes to Caesar and claims to be Christ, a king'" (Luke 23:2). Such a charge would clearly get Pilate's attention. Is Jesus involved in political sedition? Is he one more Jewish terrorist-revolutionary with a head full of messianic notions and a band of well-armed followers?

Jesus does not answer directly but probes the source of Pilate's question (18:34). A Roman political query would be: "Are you a claimant-king challenging Rome?" Here the answer would be "No." But a Jewish question would be: "Are you the messianic king of Israel?" Here the answer would be "Yes."[39] So what sort of king does Pilate mean? Is this *his* question—and if so, what does he mean by it? Pilate is already being forced to make a judgment, to evaluate Jesus. But Pilate recoils (18:35a), asking incredulously if Jesus thinks he would have any interest in matters related to Jewish theological squabbles. Nevertheless, if kingship is at issue, Pilate must uncover what sort of kingship it is. In the Synoptics Jesus simply echoes, "You say [that I am]," conceding that this is the label applied to him but not wanting to affirm the political meaning attached to the term (see 18:37).

Unlike the Synoptics, however, Jesus provides a definition of his kingship (18:36). This is one of the few places in John where Jesus refers to his kingdom (Gk. *basileia*; see also 3:3, 5; Matthew uses *basileia* fifty-five times). He deflects all political implications by pointing to the other-worldly nature of his rulership. It has not originated with this world, and he is not a rival to Caesar. The true test of his kingdom can be seen in the behavior of his disciples. They will not engage in combat or struggle against Rome's rule. He is no threat to Rome. The one instance of violence when Peter struck Malchus was promptly rebuked by Jesus (18:11).

But Pilate presses further, looking for a confession. If "king" is the self-chosen label for Jesus, this could still be the grounds of an indictment. A good paraphrase of 18:37a might be: "So you're telling me that you are indeed some kind of king?" Jesus' response (18:37b) is nicely phrased by Dodd: "King is *your* word, not mine."[40] Having said what his kingdom is *not*, Jesus

---

39. See Morris, *John*, 680.
40. Dodd, *Historical Tradition in the Fourth Gospel*, 99 (cited by Beasley-Murray, *John*, 331).

can now say what it is—a kingdom of truth. His mission began in heaven and so he possesses a divine charge: He has come to unveil the truth to the world—not to point out true things as he finds them, but to unveil himself, his voice (which is God's voice), and his words (which are God's words). Therefore "truth" does not refer to a commitment to truthfulness (or honesty) in the first instance. Rather, truth is a *theological* term. "Truth" is what we see when we see God. Jesus is thus "the truth" (14:6; 1 John 2:20–23). It is reality lived out in divine light, which by virtue of its spiritual link with God is thereby *genuinely* truthful and honest.

Of course, "truth" is no foreign idea to Pilate. Everyone wants at least to claim that his or her efforts are true. Thus, Jesus' revelation that he is working for the truth serves as an invitation for Pilate to join him. For Pilate to condemn Jesus is for him to condemn the truth. Jesus has thus reversed positions with Pilate. In 9:29 Jesus said that he came into the world for judgment, unmasking the heartfelt dispositions of humanity. Ironically Jesus has been asking Pilate questions from the beginning. Now Pilate has been challenged (Will he side with truth or falsehood?) and now he carries the burden of response. But his cynical question, "What is truth?" reveals his true position, that he cannot recognize the things of God and will avoid the light (3:21). He is not among those given to Jesus by God (17:6). He waits for no answer to his question because he does not believe there is any. He then leaves the room.

When Pilate returns to the Sanhedrin emissaries, he announces Jesus' innocence, "I find no basis for a charge against him" (18:38). Having given this verdict (which is repeated two more times, 19:4, 6), the deeper question for Pilate is whether he will act on the truth he *has* seen. He does not see a man here who threatens Rome; Jesus does not qualify as a terrorist. Pilate therefore appeals to a tradition of Passover amnesty in which one prisoner was released during the festival. While we have no extrabiblical evidence for this,[41] the Synoptics describe it as a practice of Pilate (Mark 15:6) or of the governor generally (Matt. 27:15). John says that it was a valued Jewish custom, thus placing the outcome of the amnesty entirely in the Sanhedrin's hands.

The deepest irony of all comes in 18:39–40 when Pilate refers to Jesus as "the king of the Jews." It is difficult to interpret his motive. By bringing up the amnesty it is clear that he wants to have Jesus released. By using this title, he is endorsing it as something that is meaningless to Rome. But John and his readers can see it as a true identification of who Jesus is. This is one more example of Johannine dramas happening at multiple levels.

---

41. The *Mishnah* may refer to this tradition in *Pesachim* 8:6.

But irony often shocks and the scene closes with the crowd calling instead for the release of Barabbas (18:40).[42] While Jesus was no political threat to Rome, Barabbas was. Translations differ on how to interpret *lestes*, the Greek word used to describe Barabbas. The RSV and KJV "robber" is certainly wrong; the NIV paraphrase is a bit nearer the mark ("Now Barabbas had taken part in a rebellion"). A *lestes* was a violent man who could rob (e.g., in the Samaritan parable, Luke 10:30; cf. 2 Cor. 11:26) or fight in uprisings. Josephus uses the term for Zealot leaders. Such a person was a guerrilla fighter or, as the Romans would view him, a "terrorist."[43]

In other words, a man who *is* a genuine threat to Rome, a man with proven capability to challenge the military occupation of Israel, a man with demonstrated tendencies toward violence, is poised to go free. Jesus, by contrast, a man in whom there is no danger and whose followers will not fight, remains in custody.

Jesus Before Pilate (Episode 2) (19:1–16a)

JOHN REPORTS A slightly different version from the Synoptics of what happens next. While the latter say that Jesus was whipped after the trial following Pilate's verdict (and just prior to the crucifixion, Mark 15:15), John records that Jesus was flogged during the second interrogation with Pilate (John 19:1). Similarly the Synoptics place the crown of thorns and the mocking of the soldiers after the trial but John records it earlier (19:3). That such abuse happened more than once is not unimaginable (*pace* Brown). But John shows that Pilate has another motive: This preliminary flogging is his gambit to set Jesus free. Luke 23:16 also hints that when the crowd calls for Barabbas, Pilate suggests that Jesus be punished and set free.

Roman law recognized three types of flogging: *fustigatio*, *flagellatio*, and *verberatio*, each representing ascending levels of severity, although it is uncertain if the Gospel's original readers would have understood these differences. The lowest form (*fustigatio*) was reserved for troublemakers who simply needed to be punished and warned.[44] The third level (*verberatio*) was the most severe and served as a part of a capital sentence, generally as a preparation for

---

42. The name Barabbas is not a personal name, but a surname identifying his father, such as in Simon *Bar-jonah* (Simon, son of Jonah). Bar-Abbas means, son of Abba (father). In Matt. 27:17 variant readings give his full name: Jesus Barabbas. Many regard the name "Jesus" as original and think it was removed by copyists who wanted no confusion with Jesus Christ.

43. Mark adds that Barabbas had been caught killing someone "in the uprising" (Mark 15:7), and Luke that he had participated in an "insurrection in the city," presumably the city of Jerusalem (Luke 23:19).

44. A. N. Sherwin-White, *Roman Society and Roman Law in the New Testament* (Oxford: Oxford Univ. Press, 1963), 27; R. E. Brown, *The Death of the Messiah*, 1:851–53.

crucifixion. No doubt when Jesus is prepared for crucifixion in Mark 15:15, this severe beating is what Mark has in mind, and we should assume the same in John 19:16 (although it is not mentioned it would be a part of crucifixion itself). In the present scene Pilate chooses to employ *fustigatio*, a beating (19:1), not only to teach Jesus to be more prudent in the future, but to satisfy the crowds who are demanding his death.[45]

Since the task of flogging generally belonged to soldiers, the same soldiers also begin to mock Jesus and hurt him. The mock crown may have been a woven circular crown of twigs and thorns, pressed down to inflict pain. As a mockery of kingship, it imitated crowns worn by "divine" rulers (whose images appear on numerous coins).[46] It may have been made of the thorny date palm, whose thorns can exceed twelve inches. These are woven together with some of the thorns sticking straight up around the entire crown (like an Indian headdress). This made him look like a god-king with "radiating" beams coming from his head.

The robe is likely a soldier's robe thrown on him, completing the picture of mock royalty. Since purple was expensive (the dye came from shellfish) this robe is likely dark red, imitating the "royal purple" of kings (Rev. 17:4; 18:16). With this costume on Jesus they jeer, "Hail, king of the Jews!" imitating a greeting reserved for Caesar, and they strike him. Mark adds (Mark 15:19) that they also hit him with his reed scepter, spit on him, and bow down before him in mock worship.[47]

When Pilate escorts Jesus outside (19:4–5), his clear intention is to display Jesus in cruel submission, bearing the marks of his punishment, and thereby obtain his release. John's famous "Here is the man" (*Ecce homo!* [Lat.]) records Pilate's words as he tries to evoke sympathy for Jesus' pathetic state.[48] Jesus is in sore condition; he no doubt is bleeding profusely and terribly bruised. Pilate also announces for the second time that Jesus is innocent (19:4), but Pilate's overture fails when his audience calls for Jesus' death (19:6). We can almost sense Pilate's anger. Rather than pitying Jesus, the leaders are calling for his crucifixion and in disgust Pilate calls back to them, saying as it were, "If you want a crucifixion, do it yourself; I find nothing to warrant it." Pilate is trying to

---

45. F. F. Bruce, "The Trial of Jesus in the Fourth Gospel," 15.

46. See H. St. J. Hart, "The Crown of Thorns in John 19:2–5," *JTS* 3 (1953): 66–75. Hart includes photographs of palms and coins as well as examples of radiant crowns made of palm placed on a bust in the Museum of Classical Archaeology, Cambridge.

47. Interpreters must be clear, however, that the details of the mockery and abuse in the Synoptics stem from a scene not *during* the trial (as in John) but following the trial as a preparation for crucifixion

48. In Jerusalem the Ecce Homo Convent (the Convent of the Sisters of Zion) is located in the remains of the Antonia Fortress, the traditional location of these events. The Ecce Homo Arch attached to it (which crosses the Via Dolorosa) belongs to the later period of Hadrian.

avoid responsibility for the death of an innocent man (here Matthew adds that Pilate washes his hands, discharging any responsibility, Matt. 27:24).

Already the audience has reminded Pilate of their inability to carry out an execution (18:31). Thus, they now must show Pilate that *according to their laws*, Jesus deserves death (19:7). In the Synoptic trial before Caiaphas, the charge of blasphemy determines Jesus' true crime (Mark 14:61–64), and the language here in John 19:7 springs from that earlier setting. Both Matthew and Mark show the high priest asking Jesus if he is the Son of God (Matt. 26:63; Mark 14:61). Jesus' answer (describing himself as the Son of Man) brings the death sentence. John's account echoes this same background: "We have a law, and according to that law he must die, because he claimed to be the Son of God" (John 19:7).

The Jewish leaders had earlier played their "political card," telling Pilate that Jesus was a king. Now they have a religious accusation: If Pilate truly discharges his duties in the province he will uphold local law (when it is irrelevant to imperial interests) and thereby keep the peace. Jesus has broken *their law* and so must die. According to Leviticus 24:16, "Anyone who blasphemes the name of the LORD must be put to death."

Was it illegal to claim to be the Son of God? This is hardly the case. The king of Israel enjoyed this title (see Ps. 2, 45, 89, and 110), and it appears for the Messiah in various writings of intertestamental Jewish literature (such as Qumran).[49] But the language veils another worry: by "son" Jesus has said more, implying that he bears the authority of God himself. John 5:18 is explicit: "For this reason the Jews tried all the harder to kill him; not only was he breaking the Sabbath, but he was even calling God his own Father, making himself equal with God."

Pilate is unnerved (19:8). John says that he is more afraid *than before*, which gives us an insight into his previous state of mind during the morning. There is something about this inquiry he does not like. Why are they so insistent on killing this man? While Pilate may not possess spiritual insight, he undoubtedly is highly superstitious and the idea that in some fashion gods could appear in the world was not uncommon. In Acts 14:11 this is precisely the claim made by the citizens of Lystra for Paul and Barnabas.

When Pilate escorts Jesus back into his Praetorium (19:9), his first question is a terse, "Where do you come from?" (which matches his other two questions in 18:33, 38). The question follows naturally from his worries in 19:8. This is not a question about Jesus' birthplace; it lies deeper.[50] Is Jesus a

---

49. W. Horbury, *Jewish Messianism and the Cult of Christ* (London: SCM, 1998), 109–27, 145.

50. In Luke 23:6–7, Pilate does ask a question about Jesus' regional origin, and when he learns it is Galilee, he sends Jesus to Herod Antipas, who was in Jerusalem for the feast.

"divine man," who has descended from heaven?[51] Jesus has "appeared" on Pilate's religious map and it worries him. But Jesus supplies no answer, knowing that to fit himself into Pilate's religious schema would be useless (cf. Matt. 27:14; Mark 14:61; 15:5).

Pilate's conversation with Jesus about power (19:10—11) compares with the earlier conversation in 18:33—38. These are the only episodes where Jesus speaks; in each case Pilate begins with a question that only inspires his frustration and annoyance. Jesus and Pilate talk "past" each other, responding to ideas on utterly different planes. Such misunderstanding is characteristic of discourses and conversations throughout this Gospel. A mundane question discovers a spiritually profound answer but cannot comprehend it. Of course Pilate has the power to crucify Jesus (19:10), but (like truth) Jesus' retort explains the nature of *true* power: It is derived from heaven ("from above"), and that is the origin of Jesus. The implication is telling. Jesus, who comes "from above," bears greater power; what power Pilate does enjoy is simply a privilege given (on one level) by Caesar, who ranks above him.

But even here Pilate no doubt misses the *double entendre*: The real power above both Caesar and Pilate is God, and so Pilate has no grounds for boasting. No one can take the Son's life away from him (10:18). *No one!* God has permitted Pilate to have this power over Jesus because it is a necessary aspect of what will happen in "the hour." Jesus must die. In the story Pilate has tried to use what power he enjoys to free Jesus, but it doesn't work. Pilate is *powerless* before God's plan in this hour.

The "greater sin" of 19:11b is difficult. The most obvious candidate who "handed over" (Gk. *paradidomi*) Jesus to prosecution is Judas, the "betrayer" (which uses this same Gk. verb), but he has disappeared from the story since the arrest (18:5). In 18:30 the Jewish leadership corporately "hand over" Jesus and the responsibility may rest here. But Jesus seems to point to a person ("*the one* who handed me over to you," italics added), and the best solution is to see this in the high priest Caiaphas. He was the catalyst for Jesus' arrest and formulated a rationale for Jesus' death (11:49—53).

The first conversation ended with Pilate trying to release Jesus (18:38); now the same happens again. The nature of Jesus' answers increases Pilate's conviction that Jesus' innocence is compelling and he must be freed. The verb in 18:12 is imperfect, meaning ongoing action ("Pilate *kept trying* to free Jesus"), but it is fruitless. Suddenly something dramatic happens. The Jewish leaders know they have one more weapon, one more bit of leverage on

---

51. Barrett, *John*, 542, who cites Dodd, *Historical Tradition*, 114: "The whole episode therefore is entirely in character, and to all appearance, it owes nothing to theological motives.... This is surely a very remarkable feature in a work so dominated by theological interests."

this governor that will make him pliable, like putty in their hands. "If you let this man go, you are no friend of Caesar." The last time these leaders "shouted," they had called for Jesus' crucifixion (19:6); now they shout again, using the same tone with Pilate, suggesting that he likewise will suffer.

"Friend of Caesar" was an official title (Lat., *amicus Caesaris*) bestowed on select persons such as senators who showed marked loyalty and service to the emperor.[52] If Pilate is not a friend, he is an enemy of Caesar, and Emperor Tiberius had a firm reputation for eliminating his enemies swiftly. Suetonius tells of Roman leaders killed for simply removing statues of Augustus or for criticizing him (*Lives of the Caesars*, 3.58).[53]

The irony of this situation is that these Jewish leaders, who come from a province seething with hatred for Rome, are here chastising the governor for not being sufficiently loyal. But Pilate has reason for worry. Jewish delegations were known to travel to the Roman Senate to complain about the work of governors, putting careers in danger. Pilate has seen this with some of his own friends.[54] Therefore Pilate's powerlessness is all the more apparent (19:11) and at once his resolve is broken. The fate of Jesus has returned to politics. If Jesus claims to be a king, no matter the truth (18:38), political exigencies demand he be killed.

From this point, things proceed swiftly (19:13–16). Pilate returns to the porch outside with Jesus, where he occupies the governor's judgment seat (or tribune; Gk. *bema*; Acts 25:6, 17; cf. Rom. 14:10; 2 Cor. 5:10) and prepares to render a decision (John 19:16). In a footnote John tells us that this was known as "the stone pavement" (Gk. *lithostrothos*) and adds the Hebrew (i.e., Aramaic) note that it was called the "Gabbatha" (which likely means "platform" or "high place").[55] But the important feature of the note is that as governor, Pilate is now positioned to speak with the voice of his office.

---

52. The argument of Bammel has never been overturned. E. Bammel, "φίλος τοῦ Καίσαρι (John 19:12)," *TLZ* 77 (1952)· 205–20; Brown, *John*, 2:879, provides additional references.

53. A good example of what happens when one loses the title *Amicus* comes from the earlier governor of Egypt, C Cornelius Gallus. Augustus withdrew his friendship from him, accusing him of ingratitude and treason. He could no longer enter the imperial provinces and was showered with denunciations and legislative resolutions in the Roman Senate. In 26 B.C. he committed suicide (Suetonius, *Lives of the Caesars*, 2.66). See E. Stauffer, *Jesus and His Story* (London: SCM, 1960), 109.

54. There is an interesting tangent that may connect with 19:12. Pilate's patron was apparently a man named Aelius Sejanus, of whom Tacitus writes, 'The closer a man's intimacy with Sejanus, the stronger his claim to the emperor's friendship" (*Annals*, 6 8). When Sejanus was overthrown in A.D. 31, many of his friends were executed. If this is the same era (as it may be), Caiaphas knows the power of this threat to Pilate, who fears his own vulnerability.

55. This "stone pavement" is today claimed to be uncovered in the Convent of the Sisters of Zion on Jerusalem's Via Dolorosa and is a valued traditional site to pilgrims. This pavement at the convent is within the ruins of the Antonia Fortress Josephus describes an outdoor judgment seat for the governor Florus in *Wars* 2.301.

An odd exegetical dispute has followed 19:13 for some time. Most translations today say that Pilate "sat down," but the verb used here (*kathizo*) can just as well be transitive, requiring an object. Hence, perhaps "Pilate brought Jesus out and set [*him*] down on the judge's seat."[56] If this interpretation is correct, it would mean that Pilate continues to mock Jesus, sitting *him* on the *bema* and announcing his kingship (19:14). But there would also be a double meaning (something John enjoys), since throughout the Gospel Jesus is known as bringing judgment (3:18–21; 5:22–30; 8:26; 9:39; 12:48); indeed, now Jesus sits enthroned as his accusers' judge. Jesus, already made king (19:1–3), now becomes judge.

But as enticing as this interpretation is, modern scholars and translations are reluctant to follow this reading. Would Pilate, following the serious threats given in 19:12, do such a thing? Bruce remarks, "There are some things which [Pilate] would not do and to make the accused sit on the judge's seat is one [of these]."[57] Moreover *kathizo* is used elsewhere intransitively (e.g., Josephus, *Wars*, 2.172, uses the same syntax to describe Pilate sitting on his tribunal). Thus, the symbolic (and theological) reading of the verse must give way to a more straightforward historical rendering of events: Pilate sits and makes his judgment.

The closing scene is filled with Pilate's sarcasm. "Here is your king" (19:14b) echoes "Here is the man"(19:5), and Pilate now offers to crucify this royal Jewish monarch. The audience of chief priests (the great "shepherds" of Israel) supplies an acid tone to the conclusion and lays the groundwork for their own blasphemy. "We have no king but Caesar" is a direct contradiction of the injunction of the Bible that God alone is Israel's king (1 Sam. 8:7; 10:19) and the kings that did reign (e.g., David) did so by divine appointment. By rejecting Jesus they have rejected God himself, as Jesus predicted, "He who does not honor the Son does not honor the Father, who sent him" (John 5:23).

John states that these things take place "at the sixth hour on the day of Preparation for the Passover" (NIV "the day of Preparation of Passover Week, about the sixth hour"). Two problems surface here. (1) Mark 15:25 tells us that Jesus was crucified at the *third* hour. Both Mark and John are likely counting time in which the hours of the day began at sunrise (both Romans and Jews used this convention). Mark thus places the crucifixion at 9:00 A.M. and John puts it at 12:00 noon. Various attempts to harmonize this problem have been offered: transcriptional error, Roman time computation (from midnight), even John's desire to have Jesus crucified at the start of Passover. But perhaps

---

56. This reading is introduced in the much later Gospel of Peter.
57. "The Trial of Jesus in the Fourth Gospel," 17.

we should see both references as approximations since precision like this was somewhat uncommon. No one used timepieces as we use them today. In other words, Jesus is taken for crucifixion in the late morning.

(2) If we understand that this is the day *before* Judaism's Passover meal (Nisan 14), John is pointing to a time when all work would end (the sixth hour was noon), the leaven was gathered out of homes and burned, and countless lambs were slaughtered at the temple. But to hold this view means that Jesus' meal the night before, Thursday, was not the Passover, as the Synoptics contend. At 13:1 (cf.13:29; 18:28; and 19:31) I argued that John agrees with the Synoptics that Passover was Thursday night and that Friday morning/afternoon is Nisan 15. The best way to interpret "preparation" (*paraskeue*) in 19:14 is *preparation for the Sabbath*, or Friday, as 19:31 implies. Note that Mark 15:42 uses *paraskeue* in just this way as well: "It was Preparation Day (that is, the day before the Sabbath)." No evidence has shown the words "day of Preparation" as relating to any other day but a Sabbath. *Paraskeue* means "Friday" and John is telling us that this happened on Passover-Friday, that is, the Friday of Passover week.[58]

When Jesus is "handed over" for crucifixion (19:16a), he is placed in the custody of the Roman garrison that ordinarily handled such matters.[59] Here Mark 15:15b introduces Jesus' full preparation for crucifixion (although John's only record of flogging takes place earlier, John 19:1). While Jesus had been given a remedial flogging by Pilate's men, now the soldiers inflict the *verberatio* (see comment on 19:1). We can barely improve on the description of Blinzler:

> The delinquent was stripped, bound to a post or a pillar, or sometimes simply thrown on the ground, and beaten by a number of torturers until the latter grew tired and the flesh of the delinquent hung in bleeding shreds. In the provinces this was the task of the soldiers. Three kinds of implements were customary. Rods were used on freemen; military punishments were inflected with sticks, but for slaves scourges or whips were used, the leather thongs of these being often fitted with a spike or with several pieces of bone or lead joined to form a chain. The scourging of Jesus was carried out with these last-named instruments. It is not surprising to hear that delinquents frequently collapsed and died under this procedure which only in exceptional cases

---

58 For an excellent and persuasive defense of this view, see Carson, *John*, 603–4; Morris, *John*, 708, while not persuaded by Carson's view on the Passover, nevertheless sees 19:14 as referring to "Friday of Passover week."

59 John literally says that Pilate hands him over "to them." This cannot be the Jewish leaders since they did not have the power of capital punishment. Pilate is giving Jesus over to the fate his captors demanded.

was prescribed as a death sentence. Josephus records that he himself had some of his opponents in the Galilean Tarichae scourged until their entrails were visible. The case of Jesus bar Hanan, the prophet of woe, whom the procurator Albinus had scourged until his bones lay bare ... also makes one realize what the little word *phragellosas* [to scourge] in Mark 15:15 means.[60]

While this is a dreadful and chilling description, it correctly portrays the dire condition Jesus is in as he is prepared for his walk to Golgotha (19:17). He is bleeding profusely, his clothes are soaked in blood , his thorn-laced crown now digs deeply and painfully into his head, and he is nearly in shock. Jesus carries the cross himself for a good while (19:17a), but according to the Synoptics, his condition becomes so severe that he cannot carry it all the way to the site. A man named Simon, a visitor from North African Cyrene (in present-day Libya), must carry it for him. Visitors watching on the Via Dolorosa ("The Way of Suffering") would have seen a stunning spectacle and a roadway running with blood.

As I NOTED at the beginning of this chapter (see comments on 18:1), the story of Jesus' arrest and trial was essential for the earliest Christians and perhaps was one of the first explanations about Jesus' life that circulated. It answered fundamental questions: *How and why did the Messiah die?* Therefore the story contains a precision and density that is striking, and it is not unusual to find incidental details of history anchoring it to eyewitness testimony. John reminds us explicitly that his story is based on an eyewitness report (19:35), and he adds footnotes along the way confirming his knowledge of the details (e.g., 18:1, 3, 10, 13, 18, 28; 19:13, 17, 20).

But this is also woven into a larger theological tapestry in which each Gospel writer—and John in particular—is giving an interpretation, a perspective of the meaning of these things. Our task, therefore, is not simply to understand the historical details of the story, but to discern the theological presentation. For instance, it is a historical fact that Jesus is given the title "king" during the trial and that this is tossed back and forth between Pilate and the temple leaders in seven carefully constructed scenes. But John so builds the story to disclose a deep irony in it, that Jesus is indeed Israel's king and this is his coronation.

---

60. J. Blinzler, *Der Prozess Jesu* (Regensburg: Verlag Pustet, 1969[4]), 321–22, trans. and cited by Beasley-Murray, *John*, 335–36. For a complete study of crucifixion in antiquity, see M. Hengel, *Crucifixion* (Philadelphia: Fortress, 1977).

Hermeneutical decisions. The interpreter's first task is to make some organizational decisions that will put the section into manageable units. The chapter divide at 19:1 is entirely arbitrary and was introduced no doubt so as not to interrupt the important sequence of events with Pilate. As the literary structure of the Pilate sequence shows (see above), this is a unified narrative designed for us to see its ironic climax at 19:1–5. The crucifixion narrative begins at 19:16b when Jesus is led away to Golgotha.

Therefore, what organization pattern might work best? I suggest that readers are well-served if they use the following outline on the section: (1) Jesus' arrest (18:1–11); (2) Jesus' Jewish trial (18:12–14, 19–24); (3) Peter's denials (18:15–18, 25–27); (4) Jesus' Roman trial divided into two subunits: (4a) Episode 1, kingship and truth (18:28–40); and (4b) Episode 2, preparation for the cross (19:1–16a). The cross and burial stories can easily be added as fifth (19:16b–37) and sixth (19:38–42) sections.

Our second task concerns the hermeneutical perspective from which the Passion story is told. There is always a tension in Gospel study since as an interpreter I have to choose between integrating the Johannine account into the details of the Synoptic story or reading John's story alone from within his inner literary world. I do not believe we can avoid the first reading strategy, particularly when we have so much material in John that overlaps with the other three Gospels.

Nowhere is this more evident than in John 18–19. Our audiences (like John's audiences) may know the rough outline, say, of Mark's account. They may recall that it was Caiaphas who interrogated Jesus, but then are surprised to learn that in John, Annas speaks for the Jewish leaders. Inevitably, as an interpreter I must be in control of all the historical details that have shaped the story since my interest is not simply in John's literary world, but *the historical events* that occurred in Jerusalem that Passover.

To integrate John with the other Gospels is a controversial decision, which would undoubtedly meet strong disagreement among many New Testament scholars. But it is a decision I feel I must make. *It is Jesus' suffering and death that I pursue as a theologian, not simply John's understanding of his death.* This means that I have to grapple with Synoptic parallels, even when merging these with John may be difficult or perhaps impossible. It also means that I have to grapple with extrabiblical materials that may illumine the significance of aspects of the story (such as the role of the Sanhedrin, the history of the Roman occupation, the nature of crucifixion)—details that John assumes his audience knows.

Once I have said this, however, I also want to listen to the voice of John. His story invites me to look through the lens of his particular understanding of these events. I must set aside the Synoptic story for a moment and concentrate on the portrait that he has carefully crafted for us. This means I need to experience the inner world of the Johannine Passion play, to know its stage well, to understand its symbols, and to see its characters unfold within the script.

To use an analogy: It is one thing to know the full details of the French Revolution; it is quite another to see it through the eyes of Victor-Marie Hugo's *Les Miserables*. The play invites us to leave the revolution in the background momentarily (but without forgetting its details) so that we can trace the struggle of a few of its players from 1815 to 1832. Of course, Hugo fictionalizes his story (in order to explore personal themes) whereas John does not do this. Yet John is selectively reporting this story, which permits him to show us a view we may otherwise miss. John has a view of the arrest, the trial, and the cross that is uniquely his own. His views do not distort the reality of what happened in that fateful week, but rather they place elements of it in high relief, seeing it through the eyes of faith.

The responsibility for Jesus' death. What then are the primary Johannine perspectives on the Passion of Jesus? Two major themes stand out. For one thing, John is making a claim about the responsibility for Jesus' death. He has developed the Pilate story in such a manner as to underscore the role of the temple leadership in Jesus' conviction. Multiple times Pilate calls for Jesus' release, charging that he is innocent. In response, the leaders call for Jesus' death and the release of Barabbas. Pilate again and again labels Jesus as "king" and ironically permits his troops to crown him, while the Sanhedrin leadership points to Caesar as their true king.

As I noted at the beginning of chapter 18, it is vital to remember that John is *not* pointing to the ongoing responsibility of Judaism for Jesus' death. Centuries of Christian anti-Semitism are indefensible and may not be anchored here. But having said this, we must face squarely the fact that John does see the responsibility lying with their leadership. Judaism was *betrayed* by its leaders this Passover. Caiaphas and Annas represent men whose devotion to their religious careers and the political status quo exceeded their willingness to see God at work in Jesus. They have become the dangerous shepherds of chapter 10, whose interest in the welfare of the flock has been superseded by their own self-preservation. Now as an interpreter I have to ask a difficult question: In my presentation of this material, do I simply tell the historical story (Jesus died at the hands of Pilate through the manipulations of the Sanhedrin), or do I go beyond the story and see here a paradigm, a model of bad shepherds at work?

The kingship of Jesus. The other major theme that threads itself through chapters 18–19 has to do with the kingship of Jesus. From the wounded man in the garden (Malchus, meaning "my king") to Jesus' sustained discussion with Pilate, the word "king" occurs over a dozen times. Even on the cross, Pilate insists that Jesus be labeled "King of the Jews" instead of the compromising "This Man Said, I Am King of the Jews" (cf. 19:21). The remarkable thing from John's perspective is that all of this is going on while the characters on his stage do *not* know it is going on. In a manner similar to the misunderstandings accompanying the signs and discourses, the divine revelation at work in the world in Christ cannot be perceived by the natural eye.

John the writer, however, has a dilemma. If he wants us to see this process at work, he must give his readers an "eye" that can see beneath the surface; he must make his readers "insiders" to the true story so that we can see the clouded vision and the incorrigible attitudes of these players. If we gain this view—if we see these people stumbling in the darkness, unable to see the true king in their midst—he has then challenged *us* with their predicament. If the kingship of Jesus was being submerged in the politics of Jerusalem, can this happen today? If political operators and renowned theologians exploited God's Son then, how might it happen again? Of course, what we have just done is made a hermeneutical decision, casting John's story out of the sphere of the historical and into the present century by looking within it for a paradigm of meaning that places us on the same stage as some of John's players.

But despite the darkness of the story, John is quick to assure us that God's glory is nevertheless as work. *This is the King of glory,* now arrayed before Israel. God is at work within these events (this is "the hour" he planned from the beginning) and Jesus is still in control. He asks the questions and makes the judgments. He alone has power that comes from "above." Despite the difficulties of the world's treatment of God and his Son, God will prevail. God's glory and power cannot be suppressed or be contained by the plots of human antagonists.

Secondary issues. In addition to these two themes there are a few secondary issues that spring from this passage, and we would do well to explore their implications. (1) When Jesus refers to Pilate's power in 19:11, is he acknowledging the divine authority of the state? Interpreters have frequently made this suggestion and it has had lasting implications for how the church has viewed the power of government.

(2) When Jesus describes his kingdom as "not of this world," is he giving us guidelines for how God's people, the church, ought to consider life in the secular world? Does this imply that Jesus' followers should be apolitical, disengaged? As Peter should not fight in the garden, so too should we not fight in Congress or Parliament?

(3) The denials of Peter are secondary to the main thrust of the chapters (even though they are some of the most frequently used verses in sermons). They convey something important about the frailty of discipleship and the

sovereign knowledge and sustaining power of God. Peter's role in this Gospel is important and we will look at it in chapter 21 with some care. But here we see the beginnings of a portrait not unlike that found in Mark.

ANY REFLECTIVE READING of these chapters demonstrates at once that John has offered us a highly nuanced presentation of Jesus' Passion. John is writing a superb story with layers of meaning, layers that we must unpack.

The betrayal of leadership. This is a story about collusion, not cooperation. This is *not* a story about priests and governors working amiably together for the public good. Of course Caiaphas, one of its chief actors, would like to make that claim: "You do not realize that it is better for you that one man die for the people than that the whole nation perish" (11:50). But as readers of the story we know better—that the benefit this death brings is not what Caiaphas comprehends. Caiaphas was right—and terribly wrong; that is the essence of John's satire.

This is a story about collusion, about secret agreements with some fraudulent purpose, about conniving and conspiring. This is a story about the betrayal of leadership, how Judaism's high priests abandoned all pretense of devotion to God and decided instead to conspire with the military arm of Rome. Remarkably the leaders are willing to trade Barabbas for Jesus (18:40) and Caesar for God (19:16); their pursuit of pragmatic goals makes them unable to discern the difference between a terrorist and a good shepherd, a statue of Tiberius and the God of Abraham. All Judaism did not reject Jesus—the crowds cheering him on Palm Sunday bear testimony to his many followers—but Judaism's leadership did everything in its power to sabotage his successes.

While it would be easy enough to chastise the Sanhedrin's behavior, tell its incriminating story, and outline its failure to uphold the excellent judicial system known in Jerusalem, John may yet have more to say to us. As we have seen multiple levels of meaning throughout this Gospel (the woman at the well is not just about Jewish and Samaritan worship, but our worship too, 4:21–24), I am troubled to think that this story may have a similar *double entendre*.

The most obvious actor in this drama is Pilate. He wins the greatest number of lines and appears at almost every major scene that directly affects the outcome of Jesus' fate. Even though he was not at the arrest, he is in the background, represented by his troops. No governor at this season would send a detachment this size to arrest a man without studying the issues.

John 18:1—19:16a

When Jesus is finally handed to him after an entire night's interrogation, Pilate asks all the right questions, but for all the wrong reasons. When he hears the truth he disputes it; when he is challenged he makes a mockery even of the concept of truth. "What is truth?" (18:38a) has a sinister and contemporary ring to it, and this is how John intends for us to hear it.

With Pilate we unmask the secular betrayal of leadership that surrounds us at every turn. When asked to produce its moral compass, when examined on the basis of its virtues, we can hear the words of Pilate ringing again. "What is virtue?" "What is right?" "What is truth?" One of the most famous scenes of 1998 shows Bill Clinton asking, "What is sexual intercourse?" as his defense crumbles and he finally admits to having a lurid affair with Monica Lewinski. It is Pilate replayed for another century. Thirty years earlier we heard Lyndon Johnson talking publicly about a "just and lasting peace" as B52 bombers pounded Vietnam. "What is peace?" was the question no one would answer. I was a Reserve Navy chaplain during the Gulf War in the early 1990s and recall pressing the moral virtue of carpet-bombing hundreds of thousands of forced conscripts on the Iraqi front, or starving hundreds of thousands of Iraqi children for many years with an embargo. "What is justice?" a senior Naval officer with four gold stripes asked me. He wore Pilate's uniform.

How often do the Pilates of our world pursue a course of pragmatism and expediency, protecting their own self-interest, using the rhetoric of righteousness, feigning an interest in truth—but when backed into a corner, when pressed to make a decision with social consequences, they crumble? "What is truth?" is the question you ask when truth is the last thing you want to hear. In the end, Pilate is of the "world" and so represents a system that is filled with darkness. He may intuit the light, as Pilate senses that something is wrong with this verdict, and he may make gestures toward truth, as when Pilate tries to free Jesus. But when the deal-makers arrive, when the pollsters report what it is that will secure the future, all commitments are tossed out like yesterday's newspaper. *Pilate killed Jesus.* He did not have the resolve to act on what his instincts were telling him ("I find no basis for a charge against him," 18:38). *He is a failed leader.*

But the most disturbing profile in this climax to the Gospel belongs to Annas and Caiaphas, figures who almost merge in the narrative. Caiaphas is the catalyst, the mover, the inspired leader of the Sanhedrin, who is willing to tell them all they are ignorant ("You know nothing at all!" 11:49) while he alone knows the secret of how to deal with Jesus. When word is out in the streets of Jerusalem that the leaders are seeking to kill Jesus (7:19, 25), we can sense Caiaphas' shadow in the background. At Jesus' arrest his temple guard serves alongside Pilate's soldiers. He even puts his small company of men under the leadership of Judas (a remarkable scene!) in order to bring Jesus into custody. It is Caiaphas who delivers Jesus to Pilate and from Jesus' point of view, Caiaphas will be held accountable for this decision (19:11).

It is curious that nowhere is Judas incriminated for his deed during these chapters. He is a lackey, a pawn in a larger game, and no doubt in Gethsemane he is summarily pushed to one side. Later when Jesus squares off with the true power-brokers of the temple, he has arrived at the nodal point of darkness.

The essence of Jesus' only interview with the temple leaders is that Jesus requests a fair trial. There is no theological debate (as in the Synoptics). We do not even hear Annas's voice. Jesus simply wants an honest hearing wherein the evidence can be displayed and witnesses heard. He wants the public things he has done made known so that everyone can see them and make a judgment. But Jesus does not get what he wants; his request is answered with a slap (18:23).

This request is *precisely* what we possess in the course of the *entire* Gospel. Signs, witnesses, discourses—all have been paraded before us so that we may make our judgment on the truth of Jesus. John has thus taken the essence of Jesus' trial and organized it into the structures of his Gospel.[61] We now hold in eighteen chapters the material evidence against Jesus. Therefore *we know* the evidence accessible to these leaders; *we know* the basis of their judgment; as we read the Gospel, we stand with these leaders, weighing what Jesus has said and done. As we hear the tone of chapters 5, 8 and 10, we can hear echoes of the tone that flew at Jesus during his late-night interrogation.

With Caiaphas and Annas we unmask the religious betrayal of leadership. But when we read between the lines, we learn that in the end theology does *not* matter for these men. Caiaphas is concerned about the preservation of the state and the outcome of politics (11:50). His lieutenants are primed to call for Barabbas's freedom as quickly as they can call for Jesus' crucifixion. They have done their homework. When they see Pilate vacillating, they play political hardball (19:12), issuing a fatal threat to the man's career and labeling Jesus as a genuine enemy of the empire. Their final words on this stage appear at 19:15, where they hoist up their patriotic flag higher than the highest temple rampart, putting Caesar above God.

What can we make of these men? This is *more* than a story about the miscarriage of justice. It is more than a disturbing parable of an innocent man dying without justice. This is a story of religious corruption, of spiritual leaders who slaughter the sheep and ruin the flock (cf. Ezek. 34). This is the

---

61. I explained this literary technique in the introduction to John 5. This view is explored by F. J. Matera "Jesus Before Annas: John 18:13–14, 19–24," *ETL* 66.1 (1990): 38–55.

story of priests who have bent the knee before Rome, not the temple; who have viewed God's people as a power base, a social construct, a force among other political forces, an agent of change in the politics of change, and themselves as worthy brokers with the pagan power-broker from the Roman Senate. In their secret conspiracy to eliminate one man, a man who could upset their carefully-built equilibrium, they sacrifice their souls.

In the end, they are in the world as much as Pilate is; yet, disturbingly, they do not show any of Pilate's reserve or regret. Being trained experts at ethics they know how ethics can be bent; being theologians adept at religious language, they know how to manipulate it for public consumption. *Caiaphas is a parable as much as he is a man.* He is a Christian in Washington cutting deals with political action groups. He is a theologian at denominational headquarters winning respectability by cutting out ancient and cherished beliefs— no, revising them for the modern world in order to gain the respect of Caesar, in order to make the church palatable for the world. *Caiaphas kills Jesus.* In his theological wisdom and hard-earned ecclesiastical prestige, he has lost sight of God. *He is a failed leader.*[62]

Jesus the king. Earlier in this chapter I outlined the literary structure of Jesus' conversation with Pilate in order to show that John's construction of the story is designed to focus on a central turning point located at 19:1–3. While the word "king" appears throughout the seven inverted sections, this central section could be deemed the "coronation" of Jesus, as ironically, Jesus is now given his robe and crown. Note how the lines "mirror" one another.

1 Then Pilate took Jesus and **had him flogged.**
　2 The soldiers twisted together a **crown** of thorns and put it on his head,
　　3 They **clothed him in a purple robe**;
　2′ went up to him again and again, saying, "**Hail, king of the Jews!**"
1′ And they **struck him** in the face.

This structure is a clue to us to look deeply at what is really going on within the narrative. John's Passion story is like a symphony, which seems to pursue one theme: the sorrow of Jesus' departure, his rejection by many, the dismay of the disciples, the betrayal of Judas, the denials of Peter, Jesus' immanent death—each of these are a part of the "hour" that beats its way through virtually every chapter of the Gospel. Particularly for readers who know the Synoptic version, this theme has all the makings of a tragedy.

---

62. Today there is yet another parable. Jesus' tomb is the pilgrim site of millions of pilgrims worldwide. Caiaphas's tomb and "bone box" were uncovered by a bulldozer recently in Jerusalem, and his burial box (ossuary) can be found today in a corner of the Israel Museum in West Jerusalem.

But then there is a counterpoint, a secondary theme that works its way to the surface and makes itself known confidently but unobtrusively, a theme that could be missed if you were not watching for it. This is not the tragedy we think; this is not a moment for panic; there is something hopeful happening, something we didn't see at first glance: This scene, this hour does not belong to Pilate or Caiaphas, *it belongs to Jesus.* Jesus is in control of the situation. John 18:4 reminds us at the outset that nothing will take Jesus by surprise. He asks the questions, he takes the lead, he steps forward and presents his captors with queries that make them stumble. It isn't just the guards who fall to the ground in Gethsemane (18:6), but Annas and Pilate discover themselves plunging head-over-heel, made captive to questions they cannot answer.

John's story reads like a medieval drama, where the true king of a tortured land, whose rightful rule has been temporarily overthrown, moves among the masses and is known only to a select few. He wears no crown, but the leather and wool of the commoner. But we who watch the play know that the usurpers are doomed. Even if the true king is captured and threatened with destruction, there will be some intervention (Merlin?!) that will reverse these events and win the day. Jesus is the true king, the hidden king, whose victory is about to be cheered.

A simple exercise brings the counterpoint to light. Take a pencil and circle every reference to "king" (or kingdom, kingship) in the story and watch what happens. Jesus is Israel's king, despite what his enemies are doing to him; Jesus is the *true* king, despite their refusal to recognize him. Perhaps when we see this, we see the greatest "misunderstanding" of the gospel. The spiritual irony John enjoys most is when people only apprehend the surface of Jesus' identity or message. A woman at a well thinks he may show her a river; a rabbi on a Jerusalem night thinks he offers a return to the womb. But John delights in accounts of men and women betraying their ignorance, but also by their words disclosing the truths that even *they* do not see. Of course in 9:40 the Pharisees are not blind—but then again, yes, they are. Of course in 6:15 Jesus is not a king, hailed by an unruly mob—but then again, yes, he is. Of course Jesus must be crucified as a pretender to the throne—but then again, yes, the throne is his!

John's theological message is that despite the darkness of the hour, this is in fact *the hour of glory.* Jesus will not be crucified, he will be "lifted up" (3:14; 8:28; 12:32, 34). He is not a victim, but a king assuming his throne, transforming death into a passage, a return, a celebration of his resumption of heavenly position. *And no matter what the world may think about or do to this glory, this regal glory cannot be suppressed.* People who least recognize the work of God inevitably pay homage to his presence, acknowledging that he is there. They intuit truth they try to suppress, but inevitably, the truth about God becomes known. This means, with Paul, that "they are without excuse. For although they knew God, they neither glorified him as God nor gave thanks to him, but their thinking became futile and their foolish hearts were darkened" (Rom. 1:20–21).

The Passion story of John is indeed a story of tragedy, but it is not Jesus' tragedy; it is a human tragedy as we witness the futile and tragic efforts of people blinded by darkness, unable to see the true king in their midst. Nevertheless, their reflexes (unknown to them) and their instincts still work. They are religious. They have spiritual fears and questions. "Where *do you come from?*" Pilate asks (19:9). But their life in the darkness has made them only intuit the light, not see it, recognize it, or submit to it.

Therefore John's story says that God will accomplish his purposes, revealing his glory despite what is happening in the world. No human being can stop it. No person is capable of stifling the glory of God if God intends for that glory to be shown. God is in control of history, even this hostile, seemingly darkened chapter of history that offers little hope. If he is sovereign in places like *this* Passover during this particular year in Jerusalem, if he can manifest glory and accomplish his purposes when to the observer everything seems like defeat and disaster, our history can be no different. If God could transform this "hour" with glory, so too he can transform any hour.

Three secondary issues. (1) *Church and state in 19:11.* During Jesus' final conversation with Pilate (19:8–11) the governor postures himself as a man of power. Pilate asks him: "Don't you realize I have power either to free you or to crucify you?" Jesus then responds, "You would have no power over me if it were not given to you from above." Is Jesus saying that Pilate enjoys a divinely authorized power? If so, this makes the passage fit closely Paul's words in Romans 13:1, "Everyone must submit himself to the governing authorities, for there is no authority except that which God has established. The authorities that exist have been established by God."

Among German interpreters (such as Bultmann) who have had to wrestle with the specter of Nazism and the abuse of state power, this text has become the source of real theological agony.[63] Their solution, sometimes seen today as a "reading in" of issues from another era, nevertheless bears some truth. Pilate is being reminded that his ultimate power does not come from the empire at all, but from God. It is not as if the work of the state enjoys a divine approval, but that the representatives of the state are being put on notice. Pilate thus must choose to follow either the truth revealed

---

63. See the notes of Haenchen, *John*, 2:182–83. See also T. W. Gillespie, "The Trial of Politics and Religion: A Sermon on John 18:28–19:16," *Ex Auditu* 2 (1986): 69–73.

by Christ, a truth that finds its origin in God, or he must choose the world and its devices. When the state renounces its submission to God, it is immediately darkened and controlled by the world. As one writer puts it: "In place of the Roman governor offering the Jewish people the choice, 'Which will you have, Jesus or Barabbas?' the Jewish people offer the governor the choice, 'Which will you have, Christ or Caesar?'"[64] Pilate has little interest in the death of Jesus; but now at this moment he is confronted with a choice. Does his real power derive from Caesar or God? Pilate chooses the former.

In other words, 19:11 understands that God is indeed at work within the work of the state (Rom. 13:1), but this is not said in order to provide an endorsement of God-given rights for the governor; it is to check the governor, to make him alert to the limitations of the excessive power he thinks he already owns. He too is accountable to God and subject to God's work in the world. In fact, from John's point of view, the best example of God's power at work is found in the role he has given Pilate in "the hour." Pilate has been assigned a task in the redemptive plan of God, whether he knows it or not.

(2) *Politics and religion in 18:36.* In his first conversation with Pilate, the governor asks Jesus about his kingship. No doubt Pilate saw Jesus' answer as a harmless, sentimental response he could all but ignore: "My kingdom is not of this world. If it were, my servants would fight to prevent my arrest by the Jews. But now my kingdom is from another place." In context, of course, Jesus is eliminating any anxiety Pilate may have that he is indeed a political threat. Jesus does not deny he is a king, but he refuses to make his domain the same as that of the empire. *Jesus is not a king in Pilate's terms.* He will not assume a secular interpretation of power.

But what does this mean for Christians? If our allegiance is to Christ, whose kingdom is not of this world, who is making no claim on the civil order of secular society, does this mean that Christians should be disengaged and passive? Verses like 18:36 have led to remarkable examples of Christian neutrality (or apathy) in the world.

While it is beyond the scope of this discussion to explore the theological problem of the church and the state (or "Christ and culture"), at least we can place some parameters on how this verse should be used. (a) Its exegesis is utterly bound to its historical setting. Jesus is refusing to accept the label and crown in Pilate's question. Jesus is not a secular monarch, vying for rule; he is not building an army and palaces like so many other Caesars.

(b) Jesus refers to his heavenly kingship in order to explain its *origins* (18:37b) and its character, not its domain. He is a *different* king from a *different*

---

64. C. E. Evans, "The Passion of John," *Explorations in Theology* 2 (London: SCM, 1977): 61.

place. He is not competing with Pilate for dominion. Jesus is sent by God, not assigned by the *Imperium Romanum*.

(c) Therefore 18:36 leaves open the possibility that indeed Jesus (and his followers), whose origins are from above, may speak to the world and its systems of governance while not envying the positions of power held by men like Pilate. Jesus may well have something to say to Pilate about the truth and the right use of power as he uses them in his rule. In fact throughout the course of the Gospel Jesus has been challenging the systems of the (Jewish) world at every turn. Christians are commissioned to do likewise.

(3) *Peter's denials in 18:15—18, 25—27.* The account of Peter's denials is not a unique feature of the Johannine story but has parallels in the three Synoptic Gospels. It is profitable to follow the profile of Peter up to this point in John's Gospel. Unlike Mark's Gospel, which provides a consistently critical portrait of the apostle's heroics and shortcomings, John gives Peter a sterling role till now. He was a model disciple and among one of Jesus' first converts (1:42). When many are scandalized at Jesus' shocking words, he alone stands fast, urging that there is nowhere else to go to find eternal life (6:68). Because he respects Jesus deeply, he refuses to let him wash his feet (13:6); then, when he learns that this is a prerequisite for discipleship, he asks for a full bath (13:9). In the Upper Room when the disciples hear clearly Jesus' prediction of his coming death, Peter is heroic, refusing to believe he will ever renounce his Lord (13:37). In the garden he impulsively, albeit sincerely, tries to defend his master with a sword (18:10). When Jesus is led away as a prisoner, Peter follows, refusing to let Jesus undergo this abuse by himself (18:15a).

But this great profile is overshadowed by his great failing at the high priest's house. Numerous lessons spin out from this. Despite Peter's prominence, despite his role as custodian of the faith and leader among the disciples, he can still deny it. This is a warning. Denial and faithlessness are always within reach for even the strongest disciple. I can understand Peter's denials as he stands by the fire feeling threatened by Malchus's relative and a circle of soldiers. But does he have to dispatch his faith the moment a young woman at the gate catches his sleeve? We dare not miss the pitifulness of this scene.

But perhaps what stands out in the Johannine story is Jesus' continued interest in Peter. We will see this again in chapter 21, but can anticipate it here. John reports that Jesus renews his relationship with Peter later when he meets him in Galilee (21:1—17). He is still a man deeply loved and forgiven, a man with work to do for his master.

It was the real Peter who protested his loyalty in the upper room; it was the real Peter who drew his lonely sword in the moonlight of the garden; it was the real Peter who followed Jesus, because he could not leave his Lord alone; it was *not* the real Peter who cracked beneath the tension and who denied his Lord. *And that is just what Jesus could see.* ... The forgiving love of Jesus is so great that He sees our real personality, not in our faithlessness, but in our loyalty, not in our defeat by sin, but in our reaching after goodness, even when we are defeated.[65]

---

65 W. Barclay, cited by Morris, *John*, 672n.60.

John 19:16b–42

‎

SO THE SOLDIERS took charge of Jesus. [17]Carrying his own cross, he went out to the place of the Skull (which in Aramaic is called Golgotha). [18]Here they crucified him, and with him two others—one on each side and Jesus in the middle.

[19]Pilate had a notice prepared and fastened to the cross. It read: JESUS OF NAZARETH, THE KING OF THE JEWS. [20]Many of the Jews read this sign, for the place where Jesus was crucified was near the city, and the sign was written in Aramaic, Latin and Greek. [21]The chief priests of the Jews protested to Pilate, "Do not write 'The King of the Jews,' but that this man claimed to be king of the Jews."

[22]Pilate answered, "What I have written, I have written."

[23]When the soldiers crucified Jesus, they took his clothes, dividing them into four shares, one for each of them, with the undergarment remaining. This garment was seamless, woven in one piece from top to bottom.

[24]"Let's not tear it," they said to one another. "Let's decide by lot who will get it."

This happened that the scripture might be fulfilled which said,

> "They divided my garments among them
>   and cast lots for my clothing."

So this is what the soldiers did.

[25]Near the cross of Jesus stood his mother, his mother's sister, Mary the wife of Clopas, and Mary Magdalene. [26]When Jesus saw his mother there, and the disciple whom he loved standing nearby, he said to his mother, "Dear woman, here is your son," [27]and to the disciple, "Here is your mother." From that time on, this disciple took her into his home.

[28]Later, knowing that all was now completed, and so that the Scripture would be fulfilled, Jesus said, "I am thirsty." [29]A jar of wine vinegar was there, so they soaked a sponge in it, put the sponge on a stalk of the hyssop plant, and lifted it to Jesus' lips. [30]When he had received the drink, Jesus said, "It is finished." With that, he bowed his head and gave up his spirit.

³¹Now it was the day of Preparation, and the next day was to be a special Sabbath. Because the Jews did not want the bodies left on the crosses during the Sabbath, they asked Pilate to have the legs broken and the bodies taken down. ³²The soldiers therefore came and broke the legs of the first man who had been crucified with Jesus, and then those of the other. ³³But when they came to Jesus and found that he was already dead, they did not break his legs. ³⁴Instead, one of the soldiers pierced Jesus' side with a spear, bringing a sudden flow of blood and water. ³⁵The man who saw it has given testimony, and his testimony is true. He knows that he tells the truth, and he testifies so that you also may believe. ³⁶These things happened so that the scripture would be fulfilled: "Not one of his bones will be broken," ³⁷and, as another scripture says, "They will look on the one they have pierced."

³⁸Later, Joseph of Arimathea asked Pilate for the body of Jesus. Now Joseph was a disciple of Jesus, but secretly because he feared the Jews. With Pilate's permission, he came and took the body away. ³⁹He was accompanied by Nicodemus, the man who earlier had visited Jesus at night. Nicodemus brought a mixture of myrrh and aloes, about seventy-five pounds. ⁴⁰Taking Jesus' body, the two of them wrapped it, with the spices, in strips of linen. This was in accordance with Jewish burial customs. ⁴¹At the place where Jesus was crucified, there was a garden, and in the garden a new tomb, in which no one had ever been laid. ⁴²Because it was the Jewish day of Preparation and since the tomb was nearby, they laid Jesus there.

Original
Meaning

THIS SECTION OF the Passion story is intimately connected to what has just transpired. Thus our preliminary comments on the nature of John's treatment of Jesus' trial and death (see comments on 18:1) may be applied to these verses. Jesus has been arrested in an olive orchard (or garden) in a valley east of Jerusalem, interrogated by the leadership of the Jewish high council (the Sanhedrin), and handed over to the Roman governor (Pilate), and he now has been readied for crucifixion (19:16a). Pilate's presence will still be felt as the story continues (19:19, 38) and many of the themes we observed in 18:1–19:16a will continue in John's record. Despite the apparent tragedy of the scene, Jesus is Israel's king, and

Pilate will reinforce this in the strongest terms possible. Jesus' cross does not announce that he claimed to be king, but Pilate writes, "JESUS OF NAZARETH, THE KING OF THE JEWS." It is a statement, an announcement, a challenge to the Sanhedrin leaders who want him to change it.

But John sees in Jesus' death more than the ironic drama of Christ's glory and return. He develops the story aware that these events have a theological significance as well. Jesus' death on the cross is not only about the return of the king (to heaven), but also about Jesus' care for his flock, his sacrifice, and the Spirit—all motifs discussed in the Upper Room as Jesus prepared his followers for the crisis of that afternoon. Thus John delights in seeing the symbolic meaning hidden in commonplace events. This will be true for the crucifixion and its attendant details (the title above the cross, Jesus' garments, Jesus' last words) as well as for other related scenes such as Jesus' mother, the breaking of legs, and the spear thrust.

Jesus Is Led to Golgotha (19:16b–24)

WHEN JESUS IS led away from the Praetorium, he has been fully "prepared" for crucifixion (see comments on 19:16a). He is bleeding profusely and nearly in shock. Nevertheless it was the tradition that under Roman guard, the victim had to bear his own cross to the site of death, so this is what Jesus does (19:17). John says that "they" take Jesus out; despite the ambiguity, we can safely assume that these are Roman soldiers (cf. a similar phrase in 19:1).

The vertical beam of the cross (Lat. *staticulum*) was generally kept at the site and the victim was forced to carry the crossbeam (Lat. *patibulum*).[1] The beam was placed over the neck, like a yoke, while the person's arms were pulled back and hooked around it. Ancient writers knew this practice well, and we should assume that John's readers would understand as well. But even this is too heavy for Jesus, and the Synoptic Gospels tell us that the soldiers must remove the beam and give it to a bystander named Simon, from North African Cyrene (Mark 15:21; Luke 23:26).

According to a later tradition recorded in the Talmud, women of Jerusalem's nobility would offer the condemned a narcotic wine in order to numb the senses (*b. Sanh.* 43a). In Luke we read that Jesus turns and addresses them (Luke 23:28–31). John offers none of these details and keeps the story to a bare minimum. The route of Jesus' walk (traditionally Jerusalem's *Via Dolorosa*) would have taken him from the Praetorium of Pilate to a location

---

1. This same term, *patibulum*, is used in Latin for the bar that closes a door or a ship's yardarm. Plutarch writes, "Every criminal who goes to execution must carry his own cross on his back," *Divine Vengence*, 554 A & B (Loeb, Plutarch, *Moralia*, 7).

outside the city walls, where people passing by would see the spectacle and some would even speak to Jesus or jeer (Matt. 27:39; Mark 15:29).[2] John skips any notation of the route and simply notes that the place of crucifixion is called "the place of the Skull" or (in Aramaic) "Golgotha."[3] Public executions "outside the walls" were designed to shock and warn the populace, but no doubt John sees another meaning here: Jesus is being lifted up so that now, on the highways of Jerusalem, Israel can see its king.

The practice of crucifixion is somewhat debated. We know that thousands of slaves and criminals were crucified, but we have no complete description of the process, and only one crucified skeleton has been found, as recently as 1968 in a burial cave in Giv'at ha-Mivtar, Jerusalem.[4] But literary references make clear that this was a death reserved for lower classes, slaves, foreigners, and criminals. The victim was laid on the ground with his arms stretched across the beam. After he was either nailed or tied, he was hoisted up and mounted on the vertical post.

Various postures on the cross were possible but the least likely appears in Christian art (with the nails inserted on top of the foot).[5] Romans nailed the ankles together, forcing the feet to lay sideways on top of one another. They also kept a peg on the vertical post (the *sedile*) for the person to sit on and hence not tear away. The key is to remember that nailing was not the means of death on the cross. Many factors, such as hemorrhaging, asphyxia, and shock, played a role. It is easy to see why Josephus (who watched many crucifixions during Titus's conquest of Jerusalem) referred to this as "the most wretched of deaths" (*Wars*, 7.6.4).

Each of the Gospels say that Jesus was crucified with "two others," and both Mark and Matthew refer to these men on either side of Jesus as "bandits" (Gk. *lestes*)—the same word used for Barabbas in John (see comments on 18:40). This word is best translated "terrorist" and increases the irony of

---

2. Today the Via Dolorosa in Jerusalem is a route that begins at the remains of the Antonia Fortress (The Sisters of Zion Convent, The Monastery of Flagellation) in the Muslim Quarter west of St. Stephen's Gate and continues west to the Church of the Holy Sepulchre in the Christian Quarter. The route is approximate since Jerusalem was destroyed in A.D. 70 and subsequently rebuilt many times.

3. The Latin equivalent is *calvaria*, which explains the origin of the Christian name, Calvary (popularized by Wycliff's translation). Excellent archaeological and historical evidence suggest that today's Church of the Holy Sepulcher is the best location of Jesus crucifixion (see comments on 19:38–42).

4. For a current survey of crucifixion, see R. E. Brown, *The Death of the Messiah*, 2:945–52.

5. We have records of crucifixions in numerous postures: some upside down, others crucified on a single post with hands nailed above the head. Crosses could also be shaped like an "X" but since Jesus carried a crossbeam, this form (and the single post form) could not apply to him.

Jesus' wrongful execution. Jesus is being aligned with terrorists while another terrorist has gone free (19:18). Each of the Gospels also refer to Jesus' position between them. This may refer to a place of prominence or it may echo Psalm 22:16 ("Dogs have surrounded me; a band of evil men has encircled me, they have pierced my hands and my feet"). Isaiah's Suffering Servant is likewise described as dying among "the transgressors" (Isa. 53:12).

John's story concentrates on the important details given in 19:19–22. It was customary for the Romans to provide a public, written notice of the criminal's name and activity, and this was paraded before him (or hung around his neck) en route to his crucifixion. John alone employs the technically correct term for this "title" (Gk. *titlos*; Lat. *titulus*). He is also the only writer who notes that it came by Pilate's order, and it may equally be true that this is "Pilate's revenge" on the Jewish high council.[6] When they arrive at Golgotha, the sign is affixed to the cross "over Jesus" (so Matt 27:37; Luke 23:38): JESUS OF NAZARETH, KING OF THE JEWS.

It is the language of the *titulus* that is important. It is written in Aramaic, Latin, and Greek. Jewish tombs often had multiple languages, and the cemetery at Bet Shearim in Galilee shows numerous examples of the presence of Hellenistic culture into this world. Romans would understand the Latin; the Jewish population would read the Aramaic; and Greek was the universal language of the Mediterranean world. Pilate has, in effect, placed on public display an announcement for the world. Jesus' kingship is now available for the entire world to see.

It comes as no surprise that the chief priests are furious and insulted (19:20–21). They understand that the sign implies a kind of sarcastic endorsement by Rome of Jesus' royal identity, and they do not like it. "This man said, 'I am King of the Jews'" (NRSV) is their biting alternative, but Pilate for the first time in the story stands up to them. He refuses to publish a lie (even though he did not have the courage to act on the truth). Thus the scene ends and Jesus' kingship stands secure.

It was common for Roman guards during a crucifixion to demand the right to the prisoner's clothing.[7] While the Synoptics are brief, John provides more detail (19:23–24). They take Jesus' "clothes"[8] and divide it into

---

6. Beasley-Murray, *John*, 346.

7. This raises the question of whether Jesus was crucified naked. We cannot be certain. This was certainly the Roman habit, but there is also Jewish evidence that Rome made concessions to the Jewish disdain for nudity. Hence Jesus may have worn a loincloth. However, among the earliest church fathers and in early art, Jesus is sometimes depicted as unclothed.

8. The Gk. *himatia* (in the plural, as here) may refer to "clothes" generally (Barrett, *John*, 550).

four parts; this no doubt gives us a clue that there are four guards oversee-ing the crucifixion. These four "parts" have led to speculation as to what Jesus possessed. No doubt they include a head covering, a belt, possibly san-dals, an outer cloak (13:4), and an "undergarment" or tunic. This last item draws special attention because of its value and the soldiers' interest that it not be torn in parts because it is "seamless." Such a garment was not neces-sarily unusual or a luxury item, and many peasants could have them. It was worn as a long, thin gown lining the outer cloak.

The soldiers gamble for the undergarment, which John sees as a ful-fillment of Psalm 22:18 (cited in John 19:24). It is no accident that John tells us about Jesus' seamless tunic since it becomes the focus of the entire scene. But the interpreter must be cautious here. John's tendency to enjoy double meanings sometimes leads us to look for them in texts where none is intended, and the seamless tunic of Jesus is a case in point. Josephus describes the high priests' tunic as "seamless" in these words: "Now this gar-ment was not composed of two pieces, nor was it sewn together upon the shoulders and the sides, but it was one long vestment so woven as to have an opening for the neck" (*Ant.* 3.7.4 [159–61]). Josephus's description seems to refer to a long outer robe decorated with gold thread and fringes. It is difficult to know if this is what John has in mind; if so, this may be an allusion to Jesus' priestly work on the cross (a common New Testa-ment theme).

Other scholars recall Jesus' removal of clothing in chapter 13 in order to serve his disciples—a service interpreted in light of "the hour" and the cross. Still other (particularly patristic) interpreters think of the "seamless" unity of the church, but this view seems problematic since the garment is taken away from Jesus. A more commonplace view, that this was simply a precious item of clothing (made perhaps by his mother?) may be the best way forward. The reason for seamless tunics was for Jews to be assured that no two fabrics were mixed, a practice prohibited under the law (Deut. 22:11). The tunic pre-sents us with a problem that we will examine further in the Bridging Con-texts section. We must be cautious lest we read more into John's story than he intended.

Jesus' Final Deeds and Death (19:25–30)

IT WAS NOT uncommon for a crucified person to make a pronouncement or to distribute his estate from the cross. Josephus records meeting many of his friends on crosses surrounding Jerusalem while the city was under Titus's siege in A.D. 70. Each of the Gospels records important words of Jesus from the cross, which have gone down in Christian tradition as some of the most sacred, treasured utterances in the Bible.

John records a number of people at the foot of the cross.[9] These include (1) his mother; (2) his aunt [his mother's sister]; (3) Mary "[wife] of Clopas;" (4) Mary [from the village of] Magdala; and (5) the Beloved Disciple. We know nothing about "Mary of Clopas," but Mary of Magdala was from a village just north of Tiberius (on the west side of the Sea of Galilee). Mark and Luke tell us that she had been freed from a number of demons thanks to Jesus' ministry (Mark 16:9; Luke 8:2). John's reference to Jesus' "aunt" is most intriguing. In an impressive study, Brown has analyzed the names of each person at the cross in all four Gospels, showing not only the consistent report of who was there but identifying many of them.[10] The most important feature of the study is his compelling argument that "Jesus' mother's sister" is the same as Matthew's "the mother of the sons of Zebedee" (Matt. 27:56). John and Matthew say that these women are both at the cross and *they may well be the same person, thus making Jesus and the sons of Zebedee cousins.*

If this is true (and I believe it is likely), it explains why the mother of these young men could expect special favors from Jesus (Matt. 20:20; Mark 10:35). It also helps explain why in the present verses (John 19:26–27) Jesus speaks when he sees his mother and the Beloved Disciple standing before him. Jesus now is appealing to a family responsibility that will be a feature of John's own discipleship. His form of address ("Woman!") is respectful (not impolite, see comment on 2:4), and he is pointing Mary to John (the Beloved Disciple), placing her under the protective care of this disciple.

All of this makes sense when we think that Jesus' brothers have abandoned him (7:5), and the absence of Joseph in the story makes us suspect that Mary is alone. She has supported Jesus all along, and now with his death, a woman in her culture would be bereft and at risk. The Beloved Disciple is being called now to take Mary into his family, and he does this obediently (19:27b). This should not surprise us. In Jesus' culture extended families were extremely important and cousin relationships highly treasured. For Jesus to be linked to his extended family would be commonplace.

Jesus' second statement on the cross is a cry of thirst (19:28), which John alone records. Just as the loss of his clothing was a fulfillment of Scripture, John notes that this cry too fulfills Scripture. Jesus is fully aware that the work he has been sent to the world to do is finished. He had revealed the Father's name, gathered those given to him, and exhibited God's love and revealed his word. All is finished. But he also knows that these things are a

---

9. How high was Jesus raised in the air? It is likely that the cross was no higher than six or seven feet, high enough to elevate the victim's feet. This is why victims on a cross were sometimes attacked by wild animals outside the city walls. Jesus can talk with ease to his mother and friends.

10. R. E. Brown, *The Death of the Messiah*, 2:1013–26. See chart, 2:1016.

fulfillment of God's plan; the cross is a portion of the work God has sent him to do. His cry of thirst is not a desperate word from a dying man under a Middle Eastern sun. Jesus speaks in order to fulfill Scripture. "I thirst" recalls Psalm 69:21, "They put gall in my food and gave me vinegar for my thirst" (cf. John 2:17; 15:25, which also quote Ps. 69).

In response, the soldiers provide him with a sponge soaked in vinegar (19:29). This drink (Gk. *oxos*) was a diluted wine drunk by soldiers and peasants. We must not confuse this drink with the offer of wine mixed with drugs extended to him earlier as he walked to Golgotha (Mark 15:23). Jesus refused this earlier narcotic. Now the soldiers put the sponge on a branch of hyssop (a small shrub) and offer it to Jesus. This is possible because the cross was not elevated in the air, but low, no higher than the height of one of the soldiers. The flexible branches of the shrub would barely work for this effort, but a center stalk would.

Mark and Matthew say that the sponge was placed on a stiff branch or stick (Gk. *kalamos*). The detail of hyssop is important here since the plant was used at the Passover to brush lamb's blood on the lintels and door posts of Israelite homes (Ex. 12:22). Is this a direct allusion linking Jesus with Passover, which implies that he is a Passover sacrifice? Since John will continue to allude to the Passover (19:31–37), we need to keep this possibility open.

Mark says that Jesus utters a loud cry just before expiring but he does not tell us what it is (15:37). It is tempting to compare this with John 19:30, "When he had received the drink, Jesus said, "It is finished."" What Jesus knows about the finality of his work (19:28) he now utters aloud (19:30a). This confirms the sense we have seen throughout the Passion story that here Jesus is accomplishing what he intends. He is *not* a victim, but a servant doing God's bidding. This is *not* a cry of desolation ("At last it is over!") but an announcement of triumph ("It is accomplished").

At this moment John says that Jesus bows his head and "handed over the spirit" (NIV "gave up his spirit"). The word "spirit" (*pneuma*) may be anthropomorphic (as in 11:33; 13:21), so that Jesus is here giving up his life. This would then compare with Matthew 27:50 ("he gave up his spirit") and Luke 23:46 ("Father, into your hands I commit my spirit."). This language is customary in Greek to describe death.

But John uses an unusual verb here, which does not mean "give up." The Greek *paradidomi* means to "hand over," and nowhere in Greek literature is *paradidomi to pneuma* used as a reference to death.[11] Note that John does not refer to a recipient for his spirit, such as the Father (as in Luke). This verb

---

11. Porsch, *Pneuma und Wort*, 328; Burge, *The Anointed Community*, 134. In the LXX of Isa. 53:12 the verb is used for death but in a completely different form.

means to hand on something to a successor.[12] The expression may well be John's characteristic double meaning at work, giving the subtle, general impression that the gift of the Spirit (a part of Jesus' promised work) is active at the time of the cross. This coheres with what we learned earlier that the Spirit is linked to "the hour" (7:39; 16:7); indeed it is a fruit of Jesus' death. Thus he bows his head, looking directly at those most loved, those ideal disciples at the foot of the cross—and we recognize them as the recipients of his gift. The Spirit is not actually given (see 20:22), but in a symbolic, pro-leptic fashion—at the shifting of the eras when the moment of sacrifice comes—the movement of God toward humanity is the Spirit."[13]

If it is true that the Spirit is somehow "loosed" at the time of Jesus' death, this symbolism may equally be at work in 19:28 in the images of water and thirst that run through these verses.[14] A cry of thirst is remarkable from the one in whom rivers of living water run (7:37). Jesus had said, "Whoever drinks the water I give him will never thirst" (4:14). *The source of living water now thirsts!* Elsewhere when John uses the language of "thirst" it refers to his work as one who can satisfy all thirst (4:13–15; 6:35; 7:37). As his life escapes, as the Spirit is released (19:30), as this living water is poured out (19:34), Jesus is keenly aware of this emptying, which is felt sharply in his thirst. This imagery will return shortly in 19:34.

The final scene points us once more toward the setting of Passover (19:31–37). John reminds us that it is the "day of Preparation" (19:31), which most naturally refers to Sabbath preparation, not preparation for the Passover (see comments on 13:1; 18:28). The balance of the verse makes this clear in that the Jews, whose concern has been purity all along (11:55; 18:28), now wish to remove the bodies from the crosses because of the onset of dusk and the beginning of the Sabbath. Deuteronomy 21:22–23 gives helpful back-ground, "If a man guilty of a capital offense is put to death and his body is hung on a tree, you must not leave his body on the tree overnight. Be sure to bury him that same day."[15] Thus we can assume that the same group of Jews

---

12. Büchsel, "παραδίδωμι," *TDNT* 2·169–72; BAGD, 614–15.

13. Burge, *Anointed Community,* 135; cf. Hoskyns, *John,* 633; T. Smail, *Reflected Glory· The Spirit in Christ and Christians* (London: Hodder, 1975), 106–7; E. A. Russell, "The Holy Spirit in the Fourth Gospel," *IBS* 2 (1980): 90; Some interpreters (Carson, *John,* 621) believe that 20:22 prohibits any such symbolism as this at 19:30, but this unduly limits John's desire to create theological symbols at critical theological turning points.

14. Brown, *John,* 2:930; Lindars, *John,* 581

15. Josephus tells us the same. He criticizes the impiety of the Idumeans thus: "They pro-ceeded to that degree of impiety, as to cast away their dead bodies without burial, although the Jews used to take so much care of the burial of men, that they took down those that were condemned and crucified, and buried them before the going down of the sun" (*Wars,* 4.5.2 [317]).

who asked for a change to the title on the cross (19:21) now make a second request. In the interest of spiritual devotion to the law, they wish to remove the three men from their crosses.

The Roman practice was to leave crucified bodies on crosses for a long time as a public display of discipline. Some people would last for days on a cross. Outside the city walls, such victims were often attacked by wild animals and carrion, such as vultures. But in order to hasten death, the soldiers would strike the legs with a heavy hammer, accelerating asphyxiation and promoting profuse bleeding as the bones tore through the skin due to body weight. The one crucifixion skeleton discovered in 1968 shows evidence of this: It is a male whose right tibia was completely crushed; his left calf bones (tibia and fibula) were fractured, clear evidence of the Roman mallet.[16] Were the Jewish leaders interested in this practice not only to speed these three deaths but also to further mutilate Jesus and deepen his shame?

But such was not to be. The squad of soldiers break the legs of the two men next to Jesus (19:32), but when they come to Jesus—and here John makes the point with absolute clarity—they do not break his legs since he is already dead (19:33). If they are confident of this, however, it seems odd that one of them takes a lance to test him further. But one does, and when Jesus' side is pierced, blood and water flow from the wound.

Exegetes and physicians have explored this phenomenon of blood and water at length, and we can only provide the barest summary of their work. Few today hold the view that Jesus' heart "bursts," despite the homiletic possibilities this offers.[17] Two solid theories are available. (1) P. Barbet once argued that the spear may have penetrated Jesus' heart, so that the blood from his heart as well as fluid from the pericardial sac were released simultaneously.[18] Today many physician-interpreters favor this view. (2) The surgeon A. F. Sava objected to this theory since Barbet took his evidence from cadavers twenty-four hours old. His own experiments with four- to six-hour cadavers did not produce the same results. However, among victims of traumatic accidents (especially with chest injuries), massive fluids build up between the body lining and the lung, in some instances providing as much as two liters of fluid. When this is tested on cadavers two to four hours after

---

16. N. Haas, "Antropological Observations on the Skeletal Remains from Giv'at ha-Mivtar," *IEJ* 20 (1970): 38–59 (includes numerous sketches and photographs).

17. This view originally came from J. C. Stroud, M.D., *The Physical Cause of the Death of Christ* (London: Hamilton & Adams, 1847, rev. 1871).

18. P. Barbet, *A Doctor at Calvary: The Passion of Our Lord Jesus Christ as Described by a Surgeon*, (New York: Doubleday, 1953); also W. D. Edwards, W. J. Gabel, F. E. Hosmer, "On the Physical Death of Jesus Christ," *Journal of the American Medical Association* 255 (1986): 1455–63.

death, the bloody serum separates into a layer of deep red with a layer of pale straw-colored liquid above it. Therefore, Sava argues that it is the flogging of Jesus that produces a large accumulation in Jesus' torso, and this is then pierced.[19]

No doubt this medical debate will continue. But we can be sure that John's primary intention is to let his readers know that Jesus is most certainly dead. Theologically this is important for a couple of reasons. John is working to affirm the full humanity of Jesus, whose life was dependent on his flesh (1:14). Moreover, already in John's time false teachers were doubting the true incarnation of Christ (1 John 4:1–6), and it is likely that in 1 John 5:6– 9, he may even be alluding to this event.

But just as with the many other events on this day, John no doubt sees symbolism that goes beyond the surface meaning of piercing. Most evangelicals are reluctant to see sacramental symbolism here (such as baptism and the Lord's Supper in the images of water and blood) although this has been a common view from the earliest centuries. More promising is the view that sees Passover symbolism at work. John may be making the point that the crucified Jesus qualifies as a Passover victim. He notes, for instance, that Jesus' legs are not broken, likely because it was illegal for any Passover sacrifice to have broken bones. The lamb must be a perfect sacrifice. In case we miss this subtle point, John even alludes to the Passover requirement in Exodus 12:46 at the end of the paragraph, "Not one of his bones will be broken" (John 19:36; see also Num. 9:12; Ps. 34:20).

But there are more theological allusions to Passover. J. Massyngberde Ford has successfully argued that one of the responsibilities of the temple during Passover sacrifices was to verify that the lamb was not *already* dead as it was brought forward for sacrifice. This was done by watching for the strong flow of blood that would "spurt forth" when the lamb's throat was cut.[20] The blood must flow, the Talmud later argued, *as water (or fluid)*. Thus the *Mishnah* provides guidelines for testing a valid sacrifice, and flowing, fluid blood is prominent (*m. Hullin* 2.6). Again, the image of Jesus on the cross evokes major Passover symbolism. His was a *living* sacrifice, a genuine life that had been taken.

Most interpreters agree that John's symbolism points to a sign that the life and cleansing that come now from Jesus' death have arrived. Christ's death is the basis of eternal life and renewal (6:53–54). According to Hebrews 9:19, Moses inaugurated the first covenant with blood, water, and hyssop;

---

19. A. E. Sava, "The Wound in Christ's Side," *CBQ* 19 (1957): 343–46; for a survey of theories see J. Wilkinson, "The Incident of the Blood and Water in John 19·34," *SJT* 28 (1975): 149–72.

20. J. Massyngberde Ford, "Mingled Blood from the Side of Christ (John XIX.34)," *NTS* 15 (1969): 337–38.

likewise, Jesus is inaugurating another covenant through his death. But we should also note another set of symbols. Water flows from Jesus' body. In John 7:37–39 at the Feast of Tabernacles Jesus gave a specific promise referring to himself and water flowing "from his belly" for any who desired to drink. True, this is a metaphor, and John quickly interprets it to say that this water is the Spirit, which will only come when Jesus is glorified. Water and Spirit have come together frequently in the Gospel of John (3:5; 4:10–24; 7:37–39) and it should come as no surprise. Judaism made the same connection (Ezek. 36:25–32; 47:1–12).

But most remarkably, this union of water and Spirit has been anchored at Tabernacles—the setting of John 7 (which helps us understand 19:34). As we discovered in chapter 7, Tabernacles had a water festival in the late autumn, in which Israel remembered the miracle of water conducted by Moses when he struck the rock at Meribah (Ex. 17:6). This struck rock became a vital part of the Jewish story. It was a rock that gave water and life! In some rabbinic legends this rock followed them in the desert! The rock of water even merged into the promises for the future described by Zechariah (Zech. 13:1; 14:8), becoming a model for the eternal flowing that would spring from Jerusalem. When the rabbis were asked what this eternal water really represented, their answer was simple: It referred to the Holy Spirit.[21]

Early medieval rabbinic commentaries enjoyed expanding this rock/water story, and an extensive tradition must have developed in which speculation analyzed the miracle. Paul even uses it in 1 Corinthians 10:4 to say that the rock of the desert was Christ. In medieval Jewish commentaries, scholars noted that Moses hit the rock twice. The first time it gave blood and only the second time it gave water.[22]

Therefore 19:34 joins 19:30 as one more suggestion that at the death of Christ, not only the life-giving benefits of his death, but likewise the promise of his Spirit are now coming free. John 19:34 is then a symbolic fulfillment of 7:38, which Jesus gave *at the Feast of Tabernacles.* "Out of his heart [or belly] shall flow rivers of living water" (RSV).

Even though 19:35 does not mention the Beloved Disciple, this is an accurate inference since he has already been introduced at the foot of the cross (19:26). This is an unusual verse (cf. also 21:24), where John's authority

---

21. See Burge, *Anointed Community*, 92; Schnackenburg, *John,* 2:156.

22. *Midrash Rabbah Exodus* 3:13 [Ex 4:9], "He smote the rock and it brought forth blood, as it is said, 'Behold, He smote the rock, that waters gushed out' [Ps. 78:20]." "For this reason did he smite the rock twice, because at first he brought forth blood and finally water." Some scholars, however, date this late into the medieval period. For full references to rabbinic sources, see Burge, *The Anointed Community*, 87–99; also L. Ginzberg, *The Legends of the Jews*, 7 vols. (Philadelphia: Jewish Publish Society, 1925, 1953), 2:322; 5.421n.132.

not as a collector of traditions about Jesus but as a personal eyewitness to Jesus stands firm. In its simplest terms it means that the things recorded here are true and reliable. His words in this Gospel become a part of the evidence for Jesus' life, evidence we have been reading and weighing from the beginning. This same confident stance appears in 1 John 1:1–4, showing that in his mind, the foundation of his apostolic ministry is that he was there; his own eyes and hands confirm the reality of what transpired.

John concludes the picture of Jesus on the cross with a scriptural summation (19:36–37). Both the failure to break Jesus' legs and his piercing with a soldier's lance recalled passages that lend meaning to these events. We discovered how Exodus 12:46 helped interpret the failure to break Jesus' legs (see comments on 19:33), and so John here paraphrases the verse. But also John reflects on Zechariah 12:10, where the prophet describes poignantly how Israel will look on the prophet (or God? or the Messiah?) and lament Israel's harmful lack of faith: "They will look on me, the one they have pierced, and they will mourn for him as one mourns for an only child, and grieve bitterly for him as one grieves for a firstborn son." As John stands at the foot of the cross—an eyewitness to Jesus' remarkable work—he contemplates the symbolism of Israel now gazing at the very messenger, God's Son, sent to redeem the world.

Jesus' Burial (19:38–42)

WHILE MOST OF the events recorded by John at the cross are uniquely Johannine, in the burial story he returns to materials shared by the other Gospels (Matt. 27:57–61; Mark 15:42–47; Luke 23:50–56). Each of the evangelists confirms that a man named Joseph asks Pilate for the body of Jesus. Building a composite picture, the Gospels add that he is wealthy (Matt. 27:57) and a member of the Sanhedrin (Mark 15:43; Luke 23:50), which made him a resident of Jerusalem. This explains why he would have a tomb just outside the city.

Originally Joseph was from "Arimathea," but archaeologists have not been successful locating this village. The best suggestions are Ramah (Ramathaim-zophim) or Ramallah in Judea north of Jerusalem.[23] Ramah played an important role in Samuel's life (1 Sam. 1:1, 19; 2:11; 7:17) and therefore was a city of strong Jewish tradition. Luke refers to Arimathea as a "Judean town" (Luke 23:50). He also notes that Joseph was a courageous man who was looking for the kingdom of God and that he did not concur with the prosecution of Jesus (23:51).[24]

John includes few of these details, but adds that Joseph is one of Jesus' disciples (19:38; cf. Matt. 27:57) and that he comes secretly because he fears the

---

23. S. Porter, "Joseph of Arimathea," *ABD* 3:971–72.
24. The *Gospel of Peter* 2:3 notes that Joseph was a friend of Pilate.

Sanhedrin leadership.[25] This may be explained by his disagreement with the Sanhedrin's prosecution of Jesus (Luke 23:51). John's description of him, however, may be critical, given what he says in John 12:42–43 about secret followers of Jesus among these authorities, who out of fear refused to give a public witness, "for they loved praise from men more than praise from God."

Nicodemus (19:39) is another member of the Sanhedrin (7:50; see also 3:1–10), and he joins Joseph. John's portrait may sound critical, but Joseph and Nicodemus redeem their images since in this final deed they make a public gesture that holds risk. The Sanhedrin understood that the bodies had to be buried before sundown (19:31), and they would have put Jesus' body in a common grave outside the city walls (Josephus, *Ant.* 5.1.14[44]). Joseph risks ceremonial uncleanness from touching a dead body (thus prohibiting him from all festival ceremonies), not to mention challenges to his political and religious career. To place Jesus in a tomb of prestige implies some endorsement, some honor to this man the council has deemed a criminal.

Together these men bury Jesus in a garden tomb that has never been used before (19:41), near the site of crucifixion (19:42).[26] John says that this takes place "in accordance with Jewish burial customs" (19:40b). In the first century, bodies were prepared for burial by wrapping them tightly with cloth and spices. The powdered spice would either be fitted among the cloth wrappings or packed beneath the body. Coins were often placed on the eyes and a napkin covered the face (20:7).

Nicodemus brings a considerable number of burial spices. Myrrh was an embalming powder commonly used in Egypt; aloe was a fragrant powdered sandalwood used generally as a perfume. The weight of these two spices is about seventy-five pounds.[27] This is a remarkable amount and is reminiscent of the excessive wine in Cana (2:1–10) that marked Jesus' first public appearance. At

---

25. This is a good place to note John's peculiar use of the phrase "the Jews." John says that Joseph "feared the Jews" (NIV). Joseph himself was a Jew, so how can he fear "the Jews?" John means that Joseph feared "the Jewish leaders."

26. While many visitors to Jerusalem are often confused by "two sites" for the burial place of Jesus, knowledgeable visitors understand that the Protestant "Garden Tomb" is a sixth-century B.C. burial site. For an excellent survey of the evidence, see J. MacRay, *Archaeology and the New Testament* (Grand Rapids: Baker, 1991), 206–17. See also G. Barkay, "The Garden Tomb. Was Jesus Buried Here?" *BAR* 12.2 (1986): 40–53, 56–57; and D. Bahat, "Does the Holy Sepulchre Church Mark the Burial of Jesus?" *BAR* 12.3 (1986): 26–45; both available in *Archaeology and the Bible The Best of B A R Archaeology in the World of Herod, Jesus and Paul* (Washington D.C.: Biblical Archaeology Society, 1990), 226–70. For an excellent argument for the Church of the Holy Sepulchre, see J. Wilkinson, *Jerusalem as Jesus Knew It: Archaeology as Evidence* (London: Thames & Hudson, 1978), 123–59.

27. In the Roman pound the Gk. word used here (*litra*) was about 12 ounces. John says that Nicodemus brought "one hundred *litras*," making this about seventy-five modern pounds (see NIV note).

Herod the Great's death, hundreds of servants carried spices (Josephus, *Ant.* 17:9.8 [199]), and when Gamaliel the Elder died in the first century, eighty pounds of spices were burned.[28] Such spices are a signal of Jesus' honor. We should recall too that Mary has already symbolically anointed Jesus for burial in Bethany (12:1–8). In the Synoptic tradition, the women at the cross come to anoint Jesus on Sunday (Mark 16:1), no doubt not realizing what Josephus and Nicodemus have done.

First-century Jews carved cave tombs in the limestone hills surrounding Jerusalem's walls. The type of tomb described in the Gospels for Jesus was typically characterized by the following elements: (1) *A rolling stone.* The door of the tomb was a heavy, wheel-shaped stone anywhere from four to six feet tall, which was placed in a shallow trough and held upright by a short wall on either side of the tomb opening. Rolling stones could be opened again for ongoing use but required great strength—thus the women's anxiety about finding assistance (Mark 16:3) and about breaking the Roman guard and seal (Matt. 27:65–66). In the Synoptics, an earthquake rolls open Jesus' tomb (Matt. 28:2).[29]

(2) *A burial chamber.* Upon entering the tomb, one entered a square preparation room, encircled by a stone bench running along the room's perimeter. Here the body was laid and prepared for burial. When the Synoptics say that "Jesus was laid in his own new tomb" (Matt. 27:60), they refer to this bench. Note in John 20:5 Jesus' burial clothes are discovered laying here, rolled up on one side.

(3) *Burial niches (or kokhim).* The prepared body was then slipped into a small, six-foot tunnel (height about 24 inches) that was carved in the wall, usually above the bench (or in another chamber where these niches would be cut). Here the body would rest until it decomposed.[30]

(4) *Bone boxes (or ossuaries).* After decomposition, the bones would be gathered into a decorated limestone "bone box" and kept on the tomb floor. These tombs were costly and generally contained numerous niches and ossuaries. "Family tombs" were common. When John notes that Jesus is placed in a "new" tomb, this means that there are no ossuaries and no used burial niches. He is the first laid in a newly cut *kokh*.[31]

---

28. Brown, *John* 2:960.

29. Jesus' burial in a rolling-stone tomb has been recently challenged by A. Kloner, "Did a Rolling Stone Close Jesus' Tomb?" *BAR* 25.5 (1999): 22–29. According to Kloner, of nine hundred second-temple burial tombs found in Judea, only four had rolling stones.

30. An alternate type of tomb, an *arcosolium*, built private shelves with a decorative arch to lay the body rather than *kokhim*.

31. An excellent example of this type of tomb complex is available at the so-called Tomb of the Kings in East Jerusalem. This is actually the first-century tomb of Queen Helena of Adiabene (in N. Mesopotamia), and it displays all of these architectural features On Helena, see Josephus, *Ant* 20:2–4 [17–96].

Bridging Contexts

As an interpreter it is important for me to grasp John's theology of the cross. John is not simply supplementing a larger mosaic begun by the Synoptics. Each of the evangelists is a theologian weaving a tapestry that is very much his own, dependent on the traditional guidelines current in the church but nevertheless bearing marks of its creator's interests and character. If I represent John's story of the cross and lapse inadvertently into a generalized discussion of "Jesus dying on Golgotha," I will miss the unique and unrivaled message John offers. John is asking us to look through his lens. It isn't Luke's lens, nor is it Matthew's. Through John's lens we may gain a new glimpse, a fresh appraisal of an old story.

John and the Synoptics. The first hurdle for any interpreter, therefore, is to make a decision regarding John and the Synoptics. This is the same struggle I described in 18:1–19:16a, since here in the Passion story we have a significant body of material that overlaps the other three Gospels. But in the present section, it is not so much that we have literary sections that are the same between John and perhaps Mark, but that while John is writing with the same backdrop (Jesus on the cross), he records completely *different* episodes. No crowds mock Jesus on the cross. Simon of Cyrene fails to appear. There is no cry of dereliction.

But John does introduce things we have not heard elsewhere. Different prophecies are fulfilled and different words come from Jesus. Jesus speaks to his mother and delivers her into the care of the Beloved Disciple. When Jesus dies, we read about a spear-thrust and blood and water; this is joined with an explanation of why Jesus' legs are left unbroken. Here we even learn that Joseph and Nicodemus anoint Jesus' body for burial, hardly leaving room for the women to come with burial spices on Sunday.

I am strongly tempted to harmonize these details—and to some degree I must, since I am theologically committed to Jesus' death on the cross as the center point of my salvation. But I have an equally strong reflex to leave them alone, to read the Johannine story on its own terms, and to see what his tapestry looks like without unweaving it and intertwining it with the others.

Interpretation and symbolism. The second hurdle—and here I believe we confront a far more difficult challenge—is to place some hermeneutical boundaries on the symbolism of the chapter. It is evident by now that John is a writer who loves wordplay and double meaning. Sometimes he tells us up front what the deeper meaning is (e.g., 2:21; 11:49–53); at other times he is subtle, leaving us to guess (e.g., 3:5; 4:10). But how do we know when John is simply describing events he has witnessed at the cross (19:35) and when is he suggesting that we should look beneath the surface, obtaining meanings that are nuanced and figurative?

There are nine different episodes in the present section, each of which invites some degree of symbolic interpretation: (1) Jesus' title on the cross, written in Greek, Aramaic, and Latin; (2) the seamless garment taken by the soldiers; (3) Jesus' mother and the Beloved Disciple at the foot of the cross; (4) Jesus' words on the cross joined to an apparent giving of the Spirit; (5) breaking the legs of the crucified; (6) blood and water from Jesus' side; (7) burial spices used for Jesus at the tomb; (8) Nicodemus and Joseph of Arimathea; and (9) a newly-built tomb.

In each case interpreters have wondered if in fact there are secondary meanings. For example, the blood and water from Jesus' side (19:34) may simply describe the violence of the scene. But as early as the fourth century exegetes pointed to Genesis 2:21 and the creation of Eve (who came from the side of Adam). For early medieval interpreters, 19:34 is the birth of the church, the "bride" of Christ, now removed from Jesus' side. For Tertullian and Aquinas, the water represents baptism by water while the blood represents baptism by martyrdom. Others have seen in these symbols the establishment of the sacraments of Eucharist and baptism.

Few Protestant exegetes today are inclined to follow this thinking, but similar suggestions circulate today. Take the garden, where the tomb was located. In a couple days Jesus will appear here and meet Mary Magdalene (20:1). Is this a play on the Garden of Eden? Or take the seamless tunic of Christ: Is this the seamless unity of the church? Some have looked at the spices anointing Jesus in 19:40 and said that this points to a "sweet-smelling" sacrifice offered to God. Others, seeing the reference here to Nicodemus, are reminded of chapter 3 and the discussion of water and rebirth, and wonder if this could be another sacramental allusion to baptism.

There *must* be some interpretative control in all of this. We do not have license to free-associate John's imagery. Otherwise the teacher or preacher can suddenly make the Passion story a canvas on which any picture may appear. Some symbolism is simply *not* there. For instance, I seriously doubt whether the seamless tunic conveys any secondary meaning other than to underscore its preciousness. Yet when John gives me a hint, for example, by citing a Scripture reference, or when he has alluded to the events of the cross elsewhere in his Gospel, this gives me license to look beneath the surface of the narrative.

Two hermeneutical principles therefore must control how we work. (1) Symbols must be anchored responsibly in the wider cultural context of first-century Judaism or Hellenism, teasing out, as it were, the background John's audience knows well. This is the case when Jesus is dying on the cross. Passover symbolism abounds, and John is likely assuming that his audience (which knows Passover ritual) will recognize it at once. Like a British poem referring to "the holly and the ivy" at once calls up the season of Christmas, so we must permit John to do the same in *his* culture.

(2) Symbols must also be anchored in the literary clues John has provided elsewhere in his story. This is true, for example, when we link the water and blood description to other references to water in the Gospel, especially to the one that predicts water flowing from Christ himself (7:37–39; cf. 4:15). In this case, I must treat John's Gospel as a literary whole, employing intratextual links as keys to meaning. John wrote chapter 12 knowing what he would write in chapter 19. When he was finished, he perhaps returned to chapter 12 and revised it, fine-tuning allusions and connections. It is no accident that Joseph of Arimathea is described in 19:38 as a secret disciple who feared the temple leaders. One glance at 12:42–43 shows that John has in mind a *type* of disciple, one whose image Joseph matches exactly.

Major ideas. If we try to organize the chief themes at work in 19:16b–42, it becomes apparent that three major ideas are at work. (1) The subject of Jesus' kingship, which played such an important role in 18:28–19:16a, continues here. If Jesus is indeed "the king of the Jews" (18:19), we should expect to see kingship themes at work in the present section. On the cross, he is "lifted up" (not merely crucified), and after he dies he is buried in a manner highly peculiar for a common criminal.

(2) John's theology of the cross incorporates not simply suggestions of glorification, but also the idea that Jesus is a sacrifice dying on the cross, and we must draw our understanding of this imagery from the season in which he dies, namely, Passover. The presence of genuine Passover motifs in chapter 19 has come under debate in recent years, and occasionally commentaries will note it.[32] But we must be clear that it *is* exegetically reasonable and defensible to see that John has a theology of sacrifice and that salvation and eternal life are dependent on Jesus' death, not merely his revelation of God. This means that John's view of Jesus on the cross coheres with the overall New Testament presentation of Christ's death. In John's thinking, there is no doubt that the "blood of Jesus ... purifies us from all sin" (1 John 1:7). Thus, we can look confidently at the cross in chapter 19 as a place of redemptive sacrifice.

(3) John also links the cross and the Spirit. Jesus' death is not merely the culmination of his life, nor is his work simply a sacrifice by which his followers may gain life eternal. Jesus' death also opens up new possibilities for spiritual life and renewal. In short, symbolism of the Spirit is at work in the description of Jesus' death, and these deserve close treatment. Christians are prone to see the work of Christ as limited to atonement, but in fact, another feature of his work, another gift from the cross, is his Spirit given in the epochal "hour" as he begins his glorious return to the Father.

---

32. C. H. Dodd, *Interpretation of the Fourth Gospel*, 424, and many commentaries.

Secondary issues. There are also a number of secondary issues that deserve note. (1) John wants us to see clearly that Jesus is a victor, not a victim. He has placed subtle clues in the story to highlight Jesus' strength and control even at Golgotha.

(2) The appearance of Joseph and Nicodemus at the end of the story is a surprise. Are they "secret disciples" like those mentioned in 12:42–43? If so, what comment is John making? Should they be compared with the other major male antagonists in the story—Pilate, Annas, and Caiaphas?

(3) The tomb is linked not to the resurrection (as in the Synoptics) but to the cross in this Gospel. It serves as a continuation and completion of themes developed on Golgotha, not as a platform for the resurrection of chapter 20. This is not to say that the resurrection is insignificant, and interpreters who say that it is a mere postscript to the story are clearly wrong. But John wants us to see the tomb's relation to the drama that unfolded on Good Friday, not merely let it serve an apologetic that defends the resurrection (as we have, for instance, in Matthew).

THE CROSS OF Christ is *the great sign* we have awaited throughout the entire course of this Gospel. Each of the events recorded in the Book of Signs (chs. 1–12) pointed to another event, a greater event, hallmarked by "the hour." These miracles were "signs" bearing a meaning that exceeded the mere event at hand. Stone pots in Cana, the new temple, living bread in Galilee, Siloam in Jerusalem, Lazarus of Bethany— all were important signs in their own right, but their deeper meaning awaited "the hour," that time when Christ would perform the greatest sign of all, the sign whose historic reality matches its deeper meaning.

In his death, Jesus provides the gift that every other sign promised. The bread of Galilee (ch. 6) pointed to heavenly bread, consumed when Jesus gave his flesh for the life of the world (6:51). The water of Samaria (ch. 4) or Tabernacles (ch. 7) is truly the Holy Spirit (4:24; 7:39), which must look toward the hour (4:23; 7:39) for distribution. The new temple will only discover its true meaning when Christ has died and been raised to life (2:21– 22). The deeper importance of Lazarus's story is not that one man in a village is now alive, but that *the man* is present who reigns over death and life and whose own death will therefore pose to insurmountable difficulty.

The cross is therefore the great sign, the reality from which every other sign becomes like a shadow, outlining that reality but lacking its complete form. Effects of every other sign will fade. Lazarus remained mortal, the crowds in Galilee would hunger again the next day. But this final sign, this great sign, achieved a work that would never be repeated. The hour brings a work that has eternal consequences.

But since it is a sign, it is still possible for those who live in darkness, who belong to the world, to miss its meaning (1:5). Jesus is simply a dying man to the high priests. Pilate senses that something huge and important is going on here, but he lacks the moral courage to act on his instincts. But having said that, we should also note that the reality, the truth of this epochal event is so strong that it forces its way to the surface even in these men's lives. Caiaphas cannot help but describe Jesus' death as salvation for the nation (11:50). Pilate cannot help but describe Jesus as the king of the Jews (18:39). The light is shining and winning despite the darkness, despite every attempt to suppress its truth. Indeed, this is the hour "of glory" when Scripture is fulfilled (19:24, 28, 36–37), Jesus completes what he set out to accomplish (19:30), and he begins his return to the Father.

Jesus the king. We discovered in 18:1–19:16a that Jesus is Israel's king *incognito*. John constructs his story to make the regal glory of Jesus the central motif of his Passion story. In the crucifixion and burial scenes, John returns to this theme. For instance, we already know that Jesus is "lifted up" on the cross, lifted as if elevated in glory (3:14; 8:28; 12:32, 34). Here the title over the cross ("JESUS OF NAZARETH, THE KING OF THE JEWS"), which will *not* be changed, makes the imagery obvious.

It is not that he is merely king over Israel, but John notes that Jesus' title is written for all of the major languages of the Mediterranean: Greek, Latin, and Aramaic. This king is not a provincial ruler, but a supreme monarch, whose authority now sweeps up those people speaking "foreign" tongues. Jesus has "other sheep" not of this fold (10:16), who also will benefit from his heroic deed as a dying shepherd (10:17). These are sheep who do not speak Aramaic, sheep outside the flock of Israel. The title on the cross, therefore, anticipates Peter's gigantic step into Caesarea, where he claims one of Jesus' Latin-speaking sheep (Acts 10:30–48). It also anticipates the Greek-speaking church of Antioch (11:19), whose place in the kingdom was challenged by other Christians in Jerusalem. Jesus is a *global* king, and in God's eye the cross included countless more languages than these three: Russian, Swahili, Swedish, Bemba, Arabic, Spanish; 19:20 suggests that there is no limit.

But if Jesus is a king, he deserves a king's burial. Royal burials were expensive. Herod the Great was despised at the end of his reign, but Josephus records the elaborate effort that went into his funeral. His bier was gold and embroidered with precious stones, his body was covered with purple linens, a gold crown was on his head and a gold scepter in his hand. The funeral party marched from Jerusalem to the Herodium (east of Bethlehem), and the procession alone was eight "stadia" (1500 meters) long. Five hundred slaves carried aromatic oils and spices.[33]

It is no accident, then, that when we read about Jesus' tomb, similar themes prevail. His was no pauper's grave. *At great expense* a wealthy man provided a tomb no doubt among other wealthy family tombs on the fringes of Jerusalem. *At great expense,* a religious leader brought a tremendous amount of burial spice to Jesus' grave. Such cost was customary for Israel's kings. When Jeremiah spoke to Zedekiah and told him that Babylon would take Jerusalem, he assured the king that he would not be killed by the sword, but would die with honor. "And as spices were burned for your ancestors, the earlier kings who preceded you, so they will burn spices for you and lament for you" (Jer. 34:5, NRSV). Jesus was buried in a king's hoard of spices.

Moreover, John tells us that Jesus was buried in a "garden," and it is striking that this was the same setting for the entombment of Israel's kings (2 Kings 21:18, 26). King David's tomb was considered a garden (Neh. 3:16 LXX), and according to Acts 2:29 it was well known in the New Testament period. Thus, such a setting provides a perfect climax to the regal death and burial of Jesus, the King of the Jews. Jerusalem had burial places for criminals and slaves. According to Acts 1, this is the region of Jerusalem where Judas finally found his grave. But Jesus is buried in splendor, in beauty, in an unused tomb, as if it had been carved for him alone.

In the modern world, we are hard pressed to find a corresponding image for "royal burials." In recent memory, no doubt the funeral of England's Diana, Princess of Wales, on September 6, 1997, is our best example. On the morning of her funeral, the coffin and its extensive cortège traveled from Kensington Palace to Westminster Abbey in London. During that procession, the Abbey's tenor bell rang every minute as thirty-one million people in Britain and two billion people around the world looked on.[34] The one-hour ceremony was accompanied by organ music from Mendelssohn, Bach, Dvořák, Vaughan Williams, and Elgar, and virtually every person in the royal family of Great Britain was present. Following the service, Diana's coffin was taken to an island in the center of an ornamental lake at Althorp, her parent's home.[35]

Perhaps one of the best literary images for such a "royal funeral" has been written by J. R. R. Tolkien in his three-volume set, *The Lord of the Rings*. Following the climactic battle that determines the fate of Middle Earth, the great King Thèoden and his valiant lady Eowyn are found dead on the battlefield

---

33. Josephus, *Ant* 17:8.3 [196–99].

34. About 580,000 e-mail messages were sent from around the world to the princess's family.

35. For details about Diana and her funeral, go to the official British web site: http://www.royal.gov.uk/start.htm

of Pelennor. Noble songs are sung, a regal tomb is prepared, and lords and nobles bear their bodies in splendor to their final rest (Book 5, chs. 6–8). We who live in a culture without royalty can barely comprehend this pageantry. This is the picture of Nicodemus and Joseph at work. Jesus is King!

The cross and sacrifice. At the beginning of the Gospel, we were introduced to Jesus by John the Baptist. "Look, the Lamb of God, who takes away the sin of the world!" (1:29). While I mentioned at that verse the difficulty of seeing this reference as the Passover lamb, still the suggestion is clear that Jesus was a *sacrificial* lamb. When we come to the Passion story, John carefully reminds us that it occurred in the season of Passover, when Judaism celebrated its departure from Egypt and its protection through the spilled blood of a lamb. Even though Jesus had already celebrated his Passover meal the night before and even though lambs in Jerusalem had already been slain, the imagery of Jesus as a Passover sacrifice is unmistakable. Jesus' legs were not broken because no lamb could come to the temple as a sacrifice with broken bones. Jesus' wound offered evidence sought by every priest that indeed he was a qualified lamb, an acceptable sacrifice, able to meet the stringent demands of the festival.

There is an unusual connection in this regard with 19:17, where John emphasizes that Jesus carried his *own* cross to Golgotha. This reminded early church fathers such as Chrysostom of Genesis 22:6, where Isaac carried the wood (laid on his back by Abraham) needed for his sacrifice. In first-century Judaism Isaac was held up as a model who accepted voluntary death, and most interesting, his sacrifice was dated on Nisan 15, the date of Passover. Moreover, the phrase "God himself will provide the lamb" (Gen. 22:8) became the basis of lamb sacrifice, generally leading Jewish interpreters in the first century to compare Isaac's near-sacrifice with the lamb of the Passover story.[36] When Jesus bears his wooden cross at Passover—as a lamb whose limbs cannot be broken—Jewish readers may at once have recalled Isaac, the precious son of Abraham, whose story was repeated and cherished at this time of year. Genesis 22 describes Isaac as "the only son," a word translated in the LXX as the "beloved" (Gk. *agapetos*) son.

Viewing Jesus as a sacrifice that covered personal sin was important to John and his followers. Walking in the light means having the blood of Christ as a cleansing for sin (1 John 1:7). Paul presses this application further. Calling his followers to be righteous, he uses Passover terminology: "Get rid of the old yeast that you may be a new batch without yeast—as you really

36. For the history of interpretation, see Brown, *John*, 2:917; see also G. Vermes, "Redemption and Genesis 22: The Binding of Isaac and the Sacrifice of Jesus," in G. Vermes, *Scripture and Tradition in Judaism* (Leiden: Brill, 1961), 192–227.

are. For Christ, our Passover lamb, has been sacrificed" (1 Cor. 5:7). In other words, it was commonplace among the earliest Christians to look at Jesus as a sacrificial lamb, even a Passover lamb, slain for their benefit.

Thus, as we view Christ dying on the cross, we too at once should reflect on the benefits of his death for our lives. As Judaism viewed the lamb whose blood in the Exodus story saved them from certain death and led to freedom from captivity, so too Jesus' death brings protection and freedom and life. In his most explicit teaching on his death, Jesus speaks of this gift of his life as necessary for salvation (John 6:51–58). We cannot simply be enlightened by Jesus; we must see ourselves as *saved*, rescued from a crisis as terrible as slavery to the Egyptians. The pathos of the Passover story—its grim tale of slavery and the thrill of its redemption—must be recreated in our hearts if we are to appreciate the depth of what John saw when he witnessed Jesus dying on the cross that Passover season.

Recreating this story for people today requires that we must both dramatically relive the Passover story and Jesus' participation in it as well as generate modern stories that help us reexperience the meaning of costly sacrifice. Books of sermons have these in abundance, and sometimes I fear that they trivialize the depth of Jesus' sacrifice on Calvary. While many of these stories seem emotionally overcharged, I recently discovered a story that was truly astounding. Albrecht Dürer was the famous artist of the German Renaissance, who lived from 1471–1528 in Nürnberg, Germany. Many Christians will have seen his famous wood cuttings of the horsemen of the Apocalypse. In 1508 Dürer made his famous "Study of Praying Hands," which were modeled on his best friend, Franz Knigstein. These two men were young, poor, aspiring artists who had made a pact. They "drew straws" (or "lots" in that day) and the man who won would go on to art school, supported by the labor of the other. When one artist found fame, he would return and finance the art studies of his friend.

Dürer won. Later when he returned to his friend in Nürnberg, he found him in ill health from hard work, his fingers so disfigured through labor that he could not study art for the rest of his life. His fingers were so twisted and bent he could not even hold a brush. Dürer was filled with sorrow, and once when he saw his friend praying, he was so moved by his sacrifice and piety that he modeled his "Study of Praying Hands" on Franz's hands. The portrait became a testimony to his friend's sacrifice that marked Dürer for the rest of his life.[37]

The cross and the Spirit. One of the most provocative themes in John's story of the cross centers on his many suggestions that at the time of Jesus'

---

37. This story was first introduced to me by Rev. Stephen Campbell, Cambridge Community Church, Cambridge, on Nov. 1, 1998. Many web pages on the Internet repeat the details of this story.

death, the Spirit is at work. In my exegesis I have demonstrated how this motif appears in 19:30 and 34. At the hour of death, Jesus does not "give up" his spirit as much as he "hands over" his Spirit. In the same manner the water that flows from Jesus' side recalls 7:37–39 and the Tabernacles water that Jesus promises will flow from within him. Throughout the Book of Signs water is frequently associated with the gift of the Spirit. In John 1 Jesus' water baptism is supplanted by his being anointed in the Spirit. In Jesus' conversation with Nicodemus, water and Spirit form a unity bringing new life. In chapter 4 Jesus offers living water to the Samaritan woman, which (we learn later) is water that symbolizes the Spirit, offered again as living water at Tabernacles in chapter 7. In fact, throughout the Book of Signs water is generally associated with the messianic gift that is to come, a gift that will generally arrive when Jesus is "lifted up" during "the hour."

In Jesus' Farewell Discourse he makes the explicit promise of the Spirit and links its coming with his death and departure. "But I tell you the truth: It is for your good that I am going away. Unless I go away, the Counselor [the Spirit-Paraclete] will not come to you" (16:7). In other words, the coming of the Spirit is dependent on the departure of Jesus; in some fashion, when Jesus dies, when he begins his departure to the Father, the arrival of the Spirit will be a feature of his gifts. In fact (as we saw in chs. 14 and 16) the identities of Jesus and the Spirit-Paraclete are so closely aligned that they are almost indistinguishable. The promised Spirit will be Jesus' alter-ego, resuming the role of Jesus after his departure.

The result of this connection between Christ and the Spirit—the promises of Christ and the gift of the Spirit—is that, despite our Trinitarian instincts, the Spirit becomes an aspect of the life of Christ in John's Gospel. The Spirit is Christ's Spirit, linked intimately to his life. In John's language, Christians do not receive the Holy Spirit, they have Christ's own Spirit (see 1 John 4:13), given as a gift when his life expires. Thus we see the irony of the source of living water experiencing thirst. Thus we see symbols at work on the cross that at the moment of death, when Jesus expires, the Spirit becomes free. In John's thought Jesus Christ is like a precious vial of perfume, filled with the fragrant Spirit of God. It is a gift he offers throughout his life but cannot genuinely extend until "the hour" when the vial is broken, when the crystal is shattered and the fragrance of its contents fills the world.[38]

The spiritual implications for this are significant. This means that the gift of Christ is not merely a gift of salvation, if by salvation we mean freedom from condemnation and the promise of eternal life. John affirms this and more.

---

38. I provide exhaustive theological support for this view in *The Anointed Community: The Holy Spirit in the Johannine Tradition* (Grand Rapids: Eerdmans, 1987), 49–110.

He understands that the gift of Christ has to do with transformation and renewal. Jesus offers *life*, not mere freedom from eternal judgment. Jesus offers *himself*, and the vehicle of this gift is the Spirit, by which he and the Father will indwell the believer (14:23). Jesus came into the world in order that men and women might become children of God by the power of God (1:12). And this miracle can only take place as a result of the Spirit of God entering and transforming them. The cross and the Spirit are thus an inseparable unity in this Gospel because the Spirit is an integral feature of Jesus' own life.

All of this anticipates the giving of the Spirit in chapter 20, where John's imagery will be complete. On Easter Sunday Jesus does not send a foreign power to indwell his followers, he breathes on them, giving to them personally and filling them with his own Spirit and life (20:22).

Any evangelical theology, therefore, that disparages the Spirit, that is critical of so-called charismatic Christians *on theological grounds*, will find itself in sharp disagreement with John. But any charismatic theology that neglects the cross and only celebrates renewal and infilling will likewise find itself at odds with this apostle. For John, the work of Christ embraces both historic sacrifice and the Spirit.

Three secondary issues. (1) *Jesus as victor.* Throughout the trial sequence in 18:1–19:16a we learned how John portrays Jesus as the victorious king, knowing more than his captors and controlling the progress of events. Jesus is *not* a victim in this story. The same theme appears in the story of the cross. Jesus carries his own cross and requires no help (19:17). His opponents are powerless to alter the regal title of his cross. His final cry is significant as well: "It is finished" (19:30). The word used here can mean "to bring to an end," but it bears the nuance of "to fulfill" or "bring to completion." In 4:34 Jesus described his "food" as doing God's will and *completing* his work. In 17:4 Jesus uses the same verb again: "I have brought you glory on earth by *completing* the work you gave me to do." Now on the cross Jesus is finished as he brings to completion his divine tasks.

Why is this important? "It is finished" is our signal that God has succeeded in accomplishing everything he designed to do in the life of his Son. In Jesus Christ God himself was at work demonstrating his love for us, revealing his will for our lives, and bringing about a reconciliation that needs no supplement. *Jesus' victory is the basis of our security.* My confidence in God and the assurance of my salvation cannot be anchored in my religious performance. "It is finished." What was needed to satisfy God ought to satisfy us as well. This is the good news of the gospel.

(2) *The tomb and the cross.* In the Synoptic Gospels, the tomb of Jesus serves as a prelude from which we await the resurrection. The tomb is shut and sealed, a guard is posted, and everyone awaits as angels arrive and an earth-

quake breaks open this grave that cannot contain its occupant. As Matthew, Mark, and Luke envision the tomb, it is theologically linked to Easter Sunday, becoming a vital part of the early Christian apologetic for Jesus' resurrection.

John, of course, employs the tomb of Jesus in the resurrection story (20:1–10). But there is no account of guards or seals or heavy stones rolled in front. This tomb is the resting place for the great King, the culmination of his work on the cross, the terminus of his journey through the hands of Caiaphas and Pilate. The resurrection for John is not a solution to a problem (Jesus' death and burial), but another step along the way, as Jesus moves from earth to heaven. Therefore the tomb story offers little in the way of apologetic material for Easter, but points us to motifs developed on Golgotha.

The tomb thus is not a place of depressing, exhausted defeat. It too, like the cross, is a place of glory and victory. Its chambers, unspoiled by secular use ("in the garden there was a *new* tomb," italics added), are filled with the fragrance of regal spices as two leading figures of Jerusalem bear Jesus to rest. There is something here for us to consider when we build our Good Friday worship services. When we cloak the altar, when we extinguish the candles and leave in silence, have we in fact commemorated the defeat of Jesus, the martyrdom of our Lord? This is not John's understanding. Jesus has "finished" his work. The hour is nearing its close.

(3) *Joseph and Nicodemus.* It has been the view of a variety of scholars that Joseph of Arimathea and Nicodemus are not merely historical figures but symbols. I agree. In many ways their description in 19:38–39 sounds similar to the severe exhortation John gives in 12:42–43. "Yet at the same time many even among the leaders believed in him. But because of the Pharisees they would not confess their faith for fear they would be put out of the synagogue; for they loved praise from men more than praise from God." Is Joseph one of these? Is Nicodemus? If John is identifying a type of disciple, it seems beyond dispute that these are men who lived two lives: They belonged to the inner circle of Jewish leadership, but they were intrigued with Jesus. Nicodemus even speaks up in his defense in 7:50–51, and in 19:38 John calls Joseph a disciple.

In 12:32 Jesus predicted that when he was lifted up from the earth, he would draw "all men to himself." Now that Jesus has been lifted up on the cross, Joseph and Nicodemus are drawn; they step out from their ambivalent positions at tremendous risk and publicly acknowledge Jesus' honor. Imagine a dialogue between Caiaphas, the high priest, and Joseph, a member of his ruling council. Why does Jesus deserve a burial of honor? Why not bury him with frauds and vagrants? These men risked their personal honor by protecting Jesus' honor. To bury him like this was a statement noted undoubtedly by their peers throughout Jerusalem.

The models of discipleship we witnessed among Andrew, Peter, Philip, and Nathanael (1:35–51) as well as the Samaritan woman (4:27–42), each point to the importance of the public visibility of faith among true disciples. As professionals with considerable social prestige, Joseph and Nicodemus were stepping into the circle of true discipleship, joining the community of the faithful. There is a lot in this that is worthy of notice. Especially among men and women for whom the public visibility of faith comes at some risk, John is setting before us a sterling example of two men who used their considerable resources to glorify Jesus—and in doing so, chose to become genuine followers of Christ.

John 20:1-31

EARLY ON THE first day of the week, while it was still dark, Mary Magdalene went to the tomb and saw that the stone had been removed from the entrance. ²So she came running to Simon Peter and the other disciple, the one Jesus loved, and said, "They have taken the Lord out of the tomb, and we don't know where they have put him!"

³So Peter and the other disciple started for the tomb. ⁴Both were running, but the other disciple outran Peter and reached the tomb first. ⁵He bent over and looked in at the strips of linen lying there but did not go in. ⁶Then Simon Peter, who was behind him, arrived and went into the tomb. He saw the strips of linen lying there, ⁷as well as the burial cloth that had been around Jesus' head. The cloth was folded up by itself, separate from the linen. ⁸Finally the other disciple, who had reached the tomb first, also went inside. He saw and believed. ⁹(They still did not understand from Scripture that Jesus had to rise from the dead.)

¹⁰Then the disciples went back to their homes, ¹¹but Mary stood outside the tomb crying. As she wept, she bent over to look into the tomb ¹²and saw two angels in white, seated where Jesus' body had been, one at the head and the other at the foot.

¹³They asked her, "Woman, why are you crying?"

"They have taken my Lord away," she said, "and I don't know where they have put him." ¹⁴At this, she turned around and saw Jesus standing there, but she did not realize that it was Jesus.

¹⁵"Woman," he said, "why are you crying? Who is it you are looking for?"

Thinking he was the gardener, she said, "Sir, if you have carried him away, tell me where you have put him, and I will get him."

¹⁶Jesus said to her, "Mary."

She turned toward him and cried out in Aramaic, "Rabboni!" (which means Teacher).

¹⁷Jesus said, "Do not hold on to me, for I have not yet returned to the Father. Go instead to my brothers and tell them, 'I am returning to my Father and your Father, to my God and your God.'"

[18]Mary Magdalene went to the disciples with the news: "I have seen the Lord!" And she told them that he had said these things to her.

[19]On the evening of that first day of the week, when the disciples were together, with the doors locked for fear of the Jews, Jesus came and stood among them and said, "Peace be with you!" [20]After he said this, he showed them his hands and side. The disciples were overjoyed when they saw the Lord.

[21]Again Jesus said, "Peace be with you! As the Father has sent me, I am sending you." [22]And with that he breathed on them and said, "Receive the Holy Spirit. [23]If you forgive anyone his sins, they are forgiven; if you do not forgive them, they are not forgiven."

[24] Now Thomas (called Didymus), one of the Twelve, was not with the disciples when Jesus came. [25]So the other disciples told him, "We have seen the Lord!"

But he said to them, "Unless I see the nail marks in his hands and put my finger where the nails were, and put my hand into his side, I will not believe it."

[26]A week later his disciples were in the house again, and Thomas was with them. Though the doors were locked, Jesus came and stood among them and said, "Peace be with you!" [27]Then he said to Thomas, "Put your finger here; see my hands. Reach out your hand and put it into my side. Stop doubting and believe."

[28] Thomas said to him, "My Lord and my God!"

[29]Then Jesus told him, "Because you have seen me, you have believed; blessed are those who have not seen and yet have believed."

[30]Jesus did many other miraculous signs in the presence of his disciples, which are not recorded in this book. [31]But these are written that you may believe that Jesus is the Christ, the Son of God, and that by believing you may have life in his name.

CHAPTER 20 IS perhaps one of the least understood but theologically important chapters in the Fourth Gospel. Its most obvious value is in the record it provides for the resurrection of Jesus. But unlike the Synoptics John takes us far deeper into the details of what transpired on Easter morning. Matthew and Mark provide minimal information

about the resurrection appearances. Matthew reports a meeting of Jesus with Mary Magdalene and "the other Mary" at the tomb (Matt. 28:2) and then tells us how Jesus met the disciples later (28:9), who "clasped his feet and worshiped him." Mark says that the circle of women included Mary Magdalene as well as Mary the mother of James and Salome (Mark 16:1), but his shorter ending (to 16:8) gives no resurrection appearance.[1] Luke refers as well to the visit of the women and adds to Mark's list that Joanna was there too (Luke 24:10). But for Luke, the chief story that conveys the importance of this day comes in 24:13–35, when Jesus appears along the Emmaus road to two disciples.[2]

John's Gospel takes us in new directions. Three sections divide the chapter. (1) John begins by richly supplementing the Synoptic story, telling us about a personal reunion between Jesus and Mary Magdalene (20:1–18). While this story could fit easily into the minimalist tomb stories in the Synoptics, for John it is an important vehicle for telling us things about Jesus and what it means for Christians to have a transformed relationship with the resurrected Lord. Embedded in this account is the most explicit "empty tomb" description in the New Testament. Peter and the Beloved Disciple race to the tomb and become eyewitnesses, pointing to the evidence for Jesus' resurrection.

(2) Jesus appears on Easter Sunday to the circle of apostles in seclusion in Jerusalem (20:19–23). This adds to the strength of the apostolic eyewitness by supplying a record not only of an empty tomb but also giving a personal eyewitness of Jesus alive from the grave. But once again, this is not John's only interest in the story. Jesus' presence conveys something more, a lesson and a description of what it means to experience this Jesus and to become one of his disciples filled with his Spirit. In a passage that has seen lengthy debate among interpreters, Jesus breathes on his disciples, filling them with his Spirit.

(3) The story takes an unexpected turn when we learn that Thomas, one of Jesus' disciples who has appeared twice before in the Gospel (11:16; 14:5), is absent on Easter Sunday. One week later Jesus reappears, providing Thomas with the evidence enjoyed by the others. Again, this episode underscores the significance of solid apostolic eyewitness testimony (now Thomas may join his colleagues). But as in the two previous sections this one goes a step further. Jesus points beyond such evidence and tells Thomas and those who follow

---

1. Mark's longer ending refers to an appearance to Mary Magdalene (16:9) as well as to a variety of other appearances. Mark 16:9–20, however, no doubt did not belong to the original edition of this Gospel.

2. Compare Mark 16.12–13: "Afterward Jesus appeared in a different form to two of them, while they were walking into the country. These returned and reported it the rest, but they did not believe them either."

him (the church) about the value of such evidence and the privilege of possessing it. This final section is followed by summary verses that may have originally ended the Gospel (20:30–31).

John has designed chapter 20 in order to instruct us as readers about two chief themes: the historical evidence for Jesus' resurrection and the nature of what it means to be his disciple in the era of his resurrection. (1) Since the Gospel's earliest chapters we have observed how John compiles evidence for the "trial" of Jesus. As readers we have been jurors, weighing the evidence and making judgments. Now John provides us with the most significant evidence yet—the resurrection—as a final testimony of the divine identity of Jesus.

(2) But another theme threads through the chapter as well. Jesus promised that he would not leave his followers desolate (14:18). He would not abandon them or leave them alone following his death and departure. Rather, in several places in his Farewell Discourse (chs. 14–17) Jesus promised to send the Spirit, the Paraclete, as his departing blessing on his followers. John 20 is theologically linked to those chapters as fulfillment is linked to promise. John's description of the scene and the anointing of the Spirit evoke images set in these earlier chapters.

Mary and the Empty Tomb (20:1–18)

THE NAME "MARY MAGDALENE" refers to Mary who came from the Galilean village of Magdala (located north of Tiberias on the west coast of the Sea of Galilee). She appears in John for the first time at the cross (19:25) and enjoys this lengthy and important episode on Easter Sunday. Elsewhere in the Gospels she is mentioned in Luke 8:1–3 among a list of women in Galilee who followed Jesus devoutly.[3] Jesus had expelled numerous demons from her and, along with other women, she followed Jesus to Jerusalem to care for his needs (Matt. 27:55) and was even so bold as to stand with him on Golgotha (John 19:25).

Mary's return to the tomb (along with other women) indicates that Jesus' burial on Friday was done in some haste or that the women did not know about the preparations completed by Joseph and Nicodemus (19:40). Or perhaps Nicodemus did not have time on Friday to anoint completely Jesus' body because of the vast amount of spices he had provided. The women wish to contribute to Jesus' burial (Mark 16:1) and so bring spices as soon as the Sabbath is over. Mark suggests that when they arrive it is dawn on Sunday, but John tells us that it is so early, the morning is "still dark" (John 20:1).

---

3 Mary should not be confused with the woman in Luke 7:36–50, who is described as a "sinner."

On Friday Jesus was left on the burial preparation bench in the receiving room of the tomb chamber. No doubt the women thought they could return following the Sabbath, roll back the stone, and complete the burial, sliding Jesus' body into one of the tomb's burial niches (on Jewish burial practices, see comments on 19:38–42). Mary's arrival misses the details seen later by Peter and John (20:6–7), no doubt because of the darkness.

Rolling stone tombs were meant to be opened and closed.[4] The wheel-shaped stone door rolled on a stone track for access as other family members might be buried over the years. The Synoptics record the women's anxiety about who will assist them in moving the heavy stone. Mary's discovery that the tomb door has been rolled to one side suggested immediately to her that someone has entered the tomb. Perhaps someone came that night—or was in the tomb at that moment. The Synoptics tell us that the women step inside, and perhaps Mary's flight (20:2) should be keyed to the appearance of an angel inside (see Mark 16:5). While John does not tell us these details, it is not hard to suppose that Mary examines the tomb's interior, sees that Jesus is gone, and flees to find some of the others.

Mary's report to Peter and "the other disciple" (presumably the Beloved Disciple or John, also mentioned in 13:23, 18:15–16; 19:35) conveys something of her dismay and fear. The reference to "they" ("*they* have taken the Lord") likely refers to the temple authorities (cf. chs. 18–19), Jesus' opponents who now (possibly) have done something further to him. Mary's use of the plural for herself ("and *we* don't know where they have put him") suggests that she is not alone but accompanied by other women (listed in the Synoptics). A woman would rarely venture out alone outside the city walls in the dark under such circumstances.[5]

Peter and the Beloved Disciple[6] immediately sprint to the tomb to see what has happened (20:4–5). While Peter departs first, the other disciple *arrives* first. What follows is an unusual description comparing the two men and their examination of the tomb. The Beloved Disciple arrives first, does not enter, and sees the burial clothes. Peter arrives second, steps into the tomb, and sees the burial clothes in greater detail. Then the other disciple enters, and when he sees everything alongside Peter, he "believes." Oddly the story is silent about the faith of Peter.

---

4. I note this because of the common Christian apologetic showing the weight of the tomb door and the impossibility of opening it. On the contrary, tomb doors made opening them difficult but never impossible.

5. Morris, *John*, 734.

6. While the story only refers to this man as "the other disciple," it would not be inappropriate to refer to him either as the Beloved Disciple or even John (presupposing the arguments listed in the Introduction).

John's description of the clothes includes some unexpected details. The wrapping garment (Gk. *othonion*) is the same as that mentioned in 19:40. Likewise the facial cloth (a type of handkerchief) was a detail mentioned in the Lazarus story (11:44).[7] Such small cloths were apparently wrapped under the chin and tied on the top of the head (to keep the mouth from falling open). Hence when John says that the napkin is "rolled up," it is likely in an oval loop, as it was during the burial. These items are "lying there"—implying that they are resting in the location where Jesus has laid. From the description of 20:7 it appears that the clothing is lying flat, in contrast to the facial napkin rolled and set to one side.

The scene, then, is not chaotic or confused. Rather, something purposeful has transpired here. If someone had simply stolen Jesus' body, surely the clothes would be missing, or at least strewn about the floor. But here is a scene in which the body is missing but the clothes appear undisturbed. Jesus' body has simply left them behind. We can also assume that a significant collection of burial spices rests nearby the clothes (see 19:40).

When the Beloved Disciple enters, what does he "believe" (20:8b)? This is difficult on a number of counts. According to verse 9 they do not know the Scripture concerning Jesus' resurrection from death. How then can John believe? If we read this account without reference to the resurrection, the most obvious meaning is that the disciple believes Mary's word in 20:2 that Jesus is missing. But this solution seems far too obvious since throughout the Gospel, this disciple is the one who demonstrates faith not simply in what he sees, but in Jesus and God's power at work in him. Elsewhere in the Gospel any absolute use of the verb "to believe" indicates a robust, complete faith in Christ (cf. 5:44; 6:47). The empty tomb is akin to one of the signs in the Gospel that Jesus calls his followers to believe (4:48). Beneath the surface of what the eye can see is a significance, a meaning that demands faith.

The Beloved Disciple has penetrated the deeper meaning of this empty tomb despite the fact that he does not yet grasp the larger *biblical and theological context* in which these things are taking place (20:9). "They *still* did not understand the Scripture" (italics added) means that eventually all will become clear in their thinking. This insight is similar to the Emmaus story told in Luke 24:13–35. Following the revelation of Jesus' person, the disciples' minds nevertheless need to be opened for them to grasp the larger picture of what this resurrection means. Hence the Beloved Disciple believes that Jesus is now alive—but as yet he does not know the scriptural and theological undergirding that have made this resurrection inevitable.

---

7. In Luke 19:20 the third servant uses a "napkin" to put his money away safely (cf. Acts 19:12).

Luke notes the tragedy that when the women at the tomb report their experiences to the disciples, the men are incredulous ("their words seemed to them like nonsense," Luke 24:11). John notes how Mary alone experiences the first and most profound moment with the resurrected Jesus once the two disciples have departed for home (John 20:11–18). Mary of Magdala is hardly in Jesus' inner circle when compared with the apostles; yet angels who refuse to appear to the two men now unveil themselves to her as she examines the tomb. Each of the Gospels refers to angels present at (or in) the tomb; here Mary's worries are assuaged by their words. They do not solve the riddle of Jesus' disappearance but by their question ("Woman, why are you crying?") they suggest that sorrow is not what the present moment requires.

But it is their presence that is telling. It has *not* been robbers who removed the body. Rather, what has happened here stems from God's power. The scene buttresses once more that the tomb is evidence that Jesus is not dead—but it also interprets it, saying, in effect, that we are seeing divine involvement that validates the truth of Jesus (not unlike Peter's explanation in Acts 2:32: "God has raised this Jesus to life, and we are all witnesses of the fact").

The solution for Mary's deeper grief will only come when she sees Jesus personally. Since she has only stooped in to look at the tomb (20:11b), she hears someone approach from behind and suddenly meets a man, whom she concludes must be the caretaker of the garden surrounding the tomb (20:14). He repeats the angels' words ("Woman, why are you crying?") but deflects the question to a more profound level: "Who is it you are looking for?" Her conclusion that perhaps this man has moved Jesus' body since he is the gardener indicates that she has not heard the man standing before her. Her mind remains on the problem of the tomb, while Jesus is trying to lift her to something else. Jesus' question points her in another direction. The reality of meeting him is more important than the riddle of the tomb. The tomb is now history, it is a cave to be disregarded (as it was among the earliest Christians), and only the living Jesus matters.

When Jesus utters Mary's name (20:16), at once she recognizes him and in her joy she uses the familiar Hebrew title "Rabboni" (which John translates for us as "Teacher"). Jesus' mild rebuke in 20:17 ("Do not hold on to me") implies that Mary has embraced him.[8] But it is Jesus' explanation that has led to enormous confusion among interpreters. Jesus tells Mary not to hold him because he has not yet ascended to the Father (20:17a) but then directs her to go and tell his disciples that he is presently ascending to the Father (20:17b).

---

8. Matt. 28:9 describes how the women see Jesus on Easter day in the garden and "clasp [*ekratesan*] his feet." In John Jesus uses the verb *haptomai*, which is almost synonymous.

This means that the final step of "the hour" is advancing. Jesus' betrayal, trial, crucifixion, and resurrection are complete, and now all that remains is for him to return to the place from which he descended (17:5). But before he does so, Jesus must honor one more promise mentioned throughout his Farewell Discourse. In order that his followers will not be left desolate or orphaned (14:18), he will distribute to them the Holy Spirit as his parting gift.

The crux in the present section centers on Jesus' initial correction to Mary's embrace. Why does Jesus prohibit Mary from touching him? Some commentators offer solutions that are as ingenious as they are hard to believe. (1) Some suggest that Jesus prohibits a *literal* touching. But this can hardly be the case since later Thomas is invited to do this very thing (20:26–29). And it is not convincing to argue that Jesus' wounds are sore or that he is kindly warning her about the ritual defilement that could come to her for touching a dead body. The resurrection itself eliminates such possibilities. Some have suggested that Jesus is ascending as a priest and so must remain "unstained and separated" (Heb. 7:26) for his tasks. But no place in the Gospel does Jesus ever fear such contact.[9]

(2) Other scholars attempt to alter Jesus' words. The Greek phrase "do not hold on to me" is *me mou haptou*. If a scribe misread an original *me ptou*, Jesus would be saying "do not fear." Others wonder if the negative adverb is an addition and Jesus really said, *mou haptou*, "Touch me!" This would make Mary's invitation parallel to that of Thomas in 20:27. But corrections to any text should be made with extreme caution; in this case we have no warrant for it.

(3) Incredibly, Bultmann once argued that John's theological perspective on the resurrection is disguised here. Mary should not touch Jesus because he did not have a resurrection body. Unfortunately this contradicts all the evidence of the chapter.

(4) The best solution is to see the prohibition as a theological or spiritual commentary about Jesus' transformed relationship with Mary. Mary *sees* Jesus, and we are at once reminded of the farewell promise in 14:18–19. Before long, they would *see* him and rejoice. When Mary leaves this scene, she brings this very report back to the disciples, "I have *seen* the Lord!" (20:18). Mary is thinking that the resurrection of Jesus is Jesus' resumption of normal relations with his disciples. Mary's words remind us of what Jesus had said in 16:22, "I will see you again and you will rejoice, and no one will take away your joy." Mary is trying to hold on to the joy she now discovers in her resurrected Lord. In telling her not to hold on, Jesus is saying that his permanent "return" and presence must come in another form. She cannot embrace

---

9. The most bizarre solution is to suggest that since Jesus' grave clothes were left in the grave, such embracing would be inappropriate.

what she finds in the garden. Things are going to change. Jesus' correction is a spiritual redirection away from Jesus' physical presence, a preparation for the Spirit that is about to be given.

We find this same theme in chapter 16. The *coming* of Jesus is on one level discovered within the resurrection—but it will also be discovered in a deeper manner in the coming of the Spirit-Paraclete (which is the coming of Jesus in yet a new form). The "not yet" of 20:17 thus matches the "not yet" of 7:39: "Up to that time the Spirit had not been given, since Jesus had not yet been glorified." The coming of the Spirit is still future (20:22), and this will be the momentous gift that will return Jesus to them permanently. Therefore the story with Mary can be seen as an *interpretative vehicle* to stress the transition now underway in Jesus' life and in his relationship with each of his disciples. Mary is then charged to ready Jesus' disciples for his "coming," namely, his coming both in body (in the Upper Room) but more profoundly, his "coming" in the Holy Spirit.

Jesus underscores this change in relationship by pointing to his departure: "for I have not yet returned to the Father." But it should be read to imply that she is impeding his departure or interfering with his plans by embracing him. The Greek sentence can easily be translated: "Do not cling to me. Since [Gk. *gar*] I have not yet ascended to the Father, go to my brothers and tell them that I am ascending. . . ."[10] Jesus' imminent departure is the basis for the mission to go to the disciples—not merely the reason for her to release Jesus. He wants to see them before he goes. Therefore Mary becomes a courier of news for the second time (20:18). She alone is the bearer of the report not only that the tomb was empty (20:2) but also that the resurrected Jesus has come and she has "seen" him, thus fulfilling Jesus' promise in 16:19–22: "In a little while you will see me no more, and then after a little while *you will see me*" (italics added).

Jesus and the Upper Room (20:19–23)

IN AN IMPORTANT parallel passage, Luke 24:33–43 describes how the followers of Jesus remained in Jerusalem and did not return immediately to Galilee. Here Jesus appeared to them unexpectedly; they were frightened, and their doubts only disappeared when Jesus provided evidence to them by displaying his wounds and eating a meal.

John builds the same scene but with important differences. It is the evening of this Easter Sunday (20:19) and the doors are shut (or as the NIV paraphrases, the doors are "locked"). Fear has gripped their hearts and they

---

10. This reading sees *gar* as anticipatory rather than causal; see J. McGehee, "A Less Theological Reading of John 20:17," *JBL* 105 (1986): 299–302.

no doubt conclude that the tragic fate of Jesus may soon be theirs. The temple authorities (Gk. "the Jews") will find them and arrest them too. But instead Jesus "comes" to them and stands in their midst. No doubt this appearance is miraculous since John has just told us that the doors were shut tight. But we can hardly speculate how he has materialized among them.

His words "peace be with you" (repeated in 20:19 and 21) were a standard Hebrew greeting (Judg. 6:23; 19:20; 1 Sam. 25:6; 3 John 1:15), still used in the Middle East today. But here these words are far more than a greeting. At a profoundly personal level, Jesus is summing up the essence of his work and presence in the world. Peace is the gift of his kingdom. In 14:27 and 16:33 Jesus promised that this peace would be his gift to them; now he has delivered it.

The disciples' response (20:20) to his appearance—after they see the evidence of his wounds—is likewise a fulfillment of what was promised. "I tell you the truth, you will weep and mourn while the world rejoices. You will grieve, *but your grief will turn to joy.* . . . Now is your time of grief, but I will see you again and *you will rejoice*, and no one will take away your joy" (16:20–22, italics added). Once they see Jesus in this room, the disciples are filled with joy.[11]

Throughout this Gospel Jesus has been described as the One who was sent by God (e.g., 4:3; 5:23; 6:38). Now with his work nearly completed, his final task is to commission his followers as he was commissioned by the Father. Thus as Jesus was God's special representative (or agent) in the world, so too his disciples become Jesus' agents, working in the world and witnessing to the reality of God and the truth of Jesus' words.

But in this Gospel one feature of Jesus' commission is his empowering. God not only sent his Son but also empowered him with the Spirit. For example, in Jesus' baptism the central event (from John's view) was not the water baptism itself, but the anointing in the Spirit that came to Jesus. Our first introduction of Jesus came from the prophetic words of John the Baptist, whom God had told, "The man on whom you see the Spirit come down and remain is he who will baptize with the Holy Spirit" (1:33).

This image is reinforced in many ways. In 3:34 Jesus is known as the one person whom God has given the Spirit *without measure* (cf. 6:27). Above all, Jesus is described as the One in whom the Spirit flows like a living spring, a source of life and refreshment and renewal that will be offered following his glorification (4:15; 7:37–39; 19:30, 34). Therefore to be commissioned (20:21), to advance the work of God as God's agent, means being empowered

---

11. In all of these verses, the use of "rejoice" (Gk. *chairo*) provides a direct link between chs. 16 and 20. These links are an important part of the argument for viewing the gift of the Spirit in 20:22 as a fulfillment of the Spirit-Paraclete promises. See further below.

as Jesus was empowered—obtaining the Spirit, just as Jesus was anointed and as Jesus promised.

Thus John 20:22 becomes the climax to the entire Gospel. The Spirit—suggested throughout his public ministry, promised in the Upper Room, and symbolized at the cross—is now given to the disciples in a provocative and personal way. Jesus breathes (on them) and says, "Receive [the] Holy Spirit."[12] John 20:22 fulfills the word given at the Feast of Tabernacles, where Jesus' offer of living water referred to the Holy Spirit, which could not be distributed until Jesus was glorified (7:39). Now the hour of glorification has reached its climax. Jesus is departing, and he places the Spirit that is within him in their lives.

This passage is one of the most controversial in the Gospel.[13] While every interpreter must come to terms with the theological meaning of the Easter anointing for John's narrative, many try to discern the relationship of this anointing to the giving of the Spirit in Acts 2. Three exegetical positions are common.

(1) **A symbol.** For some, the account in John 20 recounts a symbolic gesture much like Jesus' many signs in the Gospel. The disciples did not receive the Spirit, but were offered a symbol of what it would be like. While this provides a convenient harmony with Acts 2 (the only giving of the Spirit then takes place on Pentecost), it fails to permit the anointing to be a determinative event for John. Jesus' breathing recalls the Greek text of Genesis 2:7, when God made Adam (cf. Ezek. 37:5–14).[14] Jesus is recreating what sin had ruined in the Garden of Eden. Moreover, the imperative language ("receive") of John 20:22 points directly to the promise of 14:17 and suggests an experience that will come immediately (as in 19:26–27; 20:27). The world cannot *receive* the Spirit, but Jesus' followers will.[15]

---

12. The definite article "the" is not in the Greek text. Similarly, although most English versions translate, "breathed *on them*," these last two words do not appear. However they may be naturally inferred from the force of the verb. Certainly Jesus does not simply "exhale" or "sigh."

13. Some critical readers will turn immediately to this text to see how I deal with this troublesome passage. I have written an exhaustive treatment of the subject in *The Anointed Community· The Holy Spirit in the Johannine Tradition*, 114–49, another thorough treatment critical of my own can be found in M. Turner, *The Holy Spirit and Spiritual Gifts* (Peabody, Mass.. Hendrickson, 1996), 90–102.

14. In both cases, the Gk. vb. *emphysao* is used.

15. Carson's commentary is no doubt the most exhaustive argument for the symbolic interpretation. A thorough critique and review of his views, however, can be found in T R Hatina, "John 20:22 in Its Eschatological Context: Promise or Fulfillment?" *Bib* 74.2 (1993): 196–219; see also R. W. Lyon, "John 20:22 Once More," *Asbury Theological Journal* 43 1 (1988): 73–85; J. van Rossum, "The 'Johannine Pentecost': John 20:22 in Modern Exegesis and in Orthodox Theology," *Saint Vladimir's Theological Quarterly* 35 (1991): 149–67; J. Swetnam, "Bestowal of the Spirit in the Fourth Gospel," *Bib* 74.4 (1993): 556–76.

(2) **A partial anointing.** In order to reconcile this with Acts 2, others have wondered if the disciples experienced an anointing in the Spirit that prepared them for the fuller gift given seven weeks later. This view has the merit of viewing the anointing of John 20 as a real event. But what sort of event was it? This position argues that the anointing was a partial gift of the Spirit, but not the complete giving of the Spirit-Paraclete promised in the Farewell Discourse. They note that the Paraclete promises are highly personal while this gift of the Spirit seems strangely impersonal.[16] (a) Perhaps this is an "ordination gift," equipping these disciples for the work of ministry. The surrounding verses (20:21, 23) point to the disciples' mission to the world. (b) Perhaps this gift refers to the power of life and conversion. In 6:63 life and Spirit are directly associated and here perhaps we should see this as the conversion of Jesus' followers, where they are "saved" and embrace Jesus in his full messianic identity. (c) Perhaps the physical presence of Jesus disqualifies 20:22 as describing the awaited gift of the Spirit. Jesus' glorification (7:39) and departure (16:7) are prerequisites for this gift. Therefore in John's mind, this is a genuine gift of the Spirit that will be completed at Pentecost later. As one interpreter puts it, this is an embryonic Paraclete, given in advance of Jesus' ascension.

(3) **A genuine anointing.** The crux of the issue is that John does not anticipate another gift of the Spirit. He gives no hint of something to come, and if we did not possess the narrative of Acts, we would easily conclude that John 20 fulfills all of Jesus' promises. At the same time, Luke provides no hint that another giving of the Spirit occurred on Easter. He points forward to one giving on Pentecost, following Jesus' ascension. This has led many scholars to conclude that within John's theological perspective, John 20:22 is indeed the moment when the disciples were anointed with the Spirit. The language of the chapter closely links promises in chapters 14–16 and bears every feature of a genuine event. Moreover, the phrase used by Jesus ("receive Holy Spirit") may well have been an easily recognized formula used by the early Christians for the gift of the Spirit.[17]

This view (which is compelling) urges that John 20 not be held hostage by Acts 2, but that we see this gift of the Spirit as a genuine transforming experience on Easter Sunday. John's Gospel sustains a consistent expectation of fulfillment (eschatological fulfillment), and any interpretation that robs this Gospel of this element seriously misrepresents its theology. The time in

---

16. Some point out that 20:22 omits the definite article: "Receive Holy Spirit" is not quite the same as "receive *the* Holy Spirit." But such an argument is strained. The article is likewise absent in 1:32 at Jesus' baptismal anointing. Luke also omits the article on occasion but refers nevertheless to the full giving of the Spirit (Acts 2:4; 8:7, 15).

17. John 7:39; 14:17; Rom. 8:15; 1 Cor. 2:12; 2 Cor. 11:4; Gal. 3:2, 14 This phrase is particularly common in the book of Acts: 1:8; 2.38; 8:15, 17, 19; 10:47; 19:2.

which the resurrected Jesus lived among his followers was no doubt a period of remarkable spiritual experiences. To be with him and to understand him, to see him as he truly was, required a gift of God's Spirit (as Luke knows well, Luke 24:13–35). I believe the disciples experienced numerous moments of overwhelming glory as the Spirit touched and transformed them—and it all began the moment Jesus returned on Easter. That they would be empowered again, in a different way, on Pentecost does not eliminate the possibility that they were filled earlier.

The gift of the Spirit is framed with two messages outlining aspects of the church's work in the world. In 20:21 we observed how the disciples will enjoy a mission that parallels the mission of Jesus (cf. 17:18a). And in 20:23 Jesus points to their ability to forgive sin (no doubt as a part of that mission). It is inevitable that to understand this verse we should look at the close parallels in Matthew 16:19 and 18:18, where during the course of his ministry, Jesus similarly empowered his followers (cf. Luke 24:47). These verses have led to considerable division in the church. Is Jesus giving all of his followers (surely more than the apostles are present) this power? Or is this an office reserved for the leaders, the apostles—and so the leadership and bishops, the apostolic successors in later centuries? Raymond Brown spells out the tumultuous history of these interpretations, which will sober any eager exegete.[18]

The Protestant view has pointed to the more generic ministry of the church, in particular to the work of baptizing and making disciples (which is also a part of Jesus' resurrection commission, Matt. 28:19; Mark 16:16). When John describes the work of Jesus, he likewise places in tension salvation and judgment. Jesus has entered the world to save humankind (John 3:16–17), but for those who reject this salvation, who spurn his revelation, there remains the prospect of blindness and judgment (9:39).

Thus the death of Jesus spells the salvation of the world, but also the judgment of the world. As the "hour" arrives, the hour that saves the world, Jesus says, "Now is the time for judgment on this world" (12:31). In a similar manner, Christians who bear Christ's Spirit, who continue his efforts in the world, sustain his judging/saving work through their proclamation. Pointing to what God has disclosed in Christ, unveiling divine light in darkness, the prospect of judgment and salvation is suddenly placed before every man and woman. Christians do not distribute forgiveness on a whim (or retain the sins of any). As Jesus' life was a divine response of the Father's prompting (14:31), similarly Christians can do nothing except what Jesus-in-Spirit prompts them to do (15:5). Their life likewise must be a response to what Jesus is prompting through his Spirit in the world.

---

18. Brown, *John*, 2:1039–45.

Thomas and Jesus (20:24–29)

WE MET THOMAS already earlier in the Gospel. In 11:16 he committed himself to following Jesus even though it meant he might die. It was a loyal (though pessimistic) sentiment. In 14:5 he readily admitted his ignorance of Jesus' words as the Lord described his departure. In this final episode Thomas is absent when Jesus reveals himself to his disciples in Jerusalem on Easter Sunday (20:24). Upon hearing their assertion that Jesus has been resurrected ("We have seen the Lord," cf. 20:18, 20) and that he has visited them, Thomas remains skeptical and obstinate. He demands evidence (20:25). This demand reminds us of the Capernaum official in 4:48, "'Unless you people see miraculous signs and wonders,' Jesus told him, 'you will never believe.'" There too we found people who demanded hard proof before they would trust Jesus in faith.

The following account takes pains to show us that Thomas's experience is very much like that of the other disciples. Once again it is the day after the Sabbath (20:26a), that is, Sunday one week later.[19] Again the disciples are in a room with the doors shut, and Jesus appears to them and greets them. All of this carefully duplicates what transpired on Easter Sunday (20:19–23).

Jesus has heard Thomas' challenge in 20:25. The evidence he demands—to see and touch Jesus' wounds—is now provided (20:26).[20] Not only can Thomas see that Jesus is alive, but in addition he can touch the mark of the nails and the wound of the spear. John does not say whether Thomas acts on Jesus' invitation; in 20:29 it is Thomas's seeing that is credited with his faith.[21] John gives no information concerning the nature of Jesus' wounds. Have they healed? Are they painful? To consider that he is still suffering or is in mortal danger is to misunderstand the power and character of his resurrection.

Jesus' exhortation, "Stop doubting and believe," has a fine rhythm in Greek: (lit.) "Do not become unbelieving [*apistos*] but believing [*pistos*]" (20:27). Thomas is being challenged to change, to become like the others

---

19. The Gk. refers to "eight days later," which reflects Jewish custom for counting forward that includes the present day. Both appearances of Jesus thus take place on a Sunday. In the *Epistle of Barnabas* 15:9 Sunday is likewise described as the eighth day.

20. Note the parallel with Luke 24:38–39: "He said to them, 'Why are you troubled, and why do doubts rise in your minds? Look at my hands and my feet It is I myself! Touch me and see; a ghost does not have flesh and bones, as you see I have.'"

21. The Apostolic Father Ignatius was confident that the disciples touched Jesus. Writing to the Smyrnaeans in about A.D. 110 he said, "For I know and believe that he was in the flesh even after the resurrection; and when he came to Peter and those with him, he said to them: 'Take hold of me; handle me and see that I am not a disembodied demon.'" And immediately they touched him and believed, being closely united with his flesh and blood. . . . After his resurrection he ate and drank with them like one who is composed of flesh although spiritually he was united with the Father" (*Smyr.* 3:1–3)

who, upon seeing Jesus, embrace him with faith. His response, "My Lord and my God!" (20:28), is not a word of astonishment or praise to God. It is a confession of Thomas's heartfelt belief in Jesus. Thus we learn that "the most outrageous doubter of the resurrection of Jesus utters the greatest confession of the Lord who rose from the dead."[22]

These words supply the closing frame of the Gospel, matching the high and lofty descriptions of Christ the Word in 1:1–18. As the gospel comes to its close, no more explicit identification of Jesus can be imagined. In Revelation 4:11 the elders fall before the throne of God with a similar word of praise: "You are worthy, our Lord and God, to receive glory and honor and power, for you created all things, and by your will they were created and have their being."[23]

But the climax of the passage comes in 20:29. The first half of the verse is a statement (KJV, NEB, NIV), not a question (RSV, NRSV). Jesus does not disparage the faith of Thomas ("So *now* you believe because you see me?") but simply cites a fact ("Because you have seen me, you have believed"). Thomas's faith is anchored to sight. Then Jesus goes on to utter a blessing not on those who see and believe—which is certainly a virtue paraded throughout the chapters of the Gospel. Rather, he offers a blessing on those who believe but have *not seen*. Here Jesus points forward beyond Thomas, beyond the apostolic circle, to the world of the church, to believers who come to faith through the testimony of the apostles. Juxtaposed in these verses are faith based on sight and faith based on the word of those who testify. Thomas's faith is not necessarily blemished because of his need for sight; it is simply privileged, for few would ever have the gift of what these disciples have experienced.

Jesus has in mind people (such as ourselves) who are now reading this Gospel and have not had Thomas's opportunity to touch Jesus' wounds. There can be no more remarkable privilege. But John has provided us with a record of signs—his Gospel (20:31)—that can serve us in a similar capacity. While not doing what Thomas did, we have his story, and this should give us a reasonable ground for belief.

Conclusion (20:30–31)

FOR MANY SCHOLARS these verses constitute the conclusion of John's Gospel.[24] John acknowledges that Jesus provided many other signs with his disciples and

---

22. Beasley-Murray, *John*, 385.

23. Brown, *John*, 2:1047, notes that the words "Lord and God" were used in Latin for the reigning emperor, Domitian (A.D. 81–96), *"Dominus et Deus noster."*

24. For many scholars, the Gospel originally ended at 20:31, and chapter 21 was added at a later time as an appendix. Perhaps chapter 21 was included following John's death (21:22–23) by his closest followers, who identify themselves in 21:24.

that the selection offered here in his Gospel is a mere collection (20:30). This means that John is aware of a rich source of traditions about Jesus and that he, as an editor, has had to make a careful selection to suit his own literary needs.

In 20:31 John discloses his purpose for writing the Gospel. Belief leads to life, and this life is a gift given through the power of Jesus Christ, God's Son. But in what sense is John hoping to call forward belief? Oddly enough, different manuscripts record two different spellings for "believe," and the difference may be important. (1) The verb may be an "aorist subjunctive" (*pisteusēte*), or (2) it may be a "present subjunctive" (*pisteuēte*); a simple Greek "s" (*sigma*) separates them.

It is amazing how much exegetical energy has been spent divining the difference this makes for the Gospel. The tense of the aorist subjunctive verb suggests that John is writing in order to bring people to faith ("that you come to believe"), while the present subjunctive implies John is taking Christians deeper into their faith ("that you may continue believing"). The first points to evangelism, the second to encouragement. Manuscript evidence cannot decide the issue. While the bulk of the evidence supports the aorist (or first option given), the present tense is attested by important witnesses and cannot be dismissed.[25]

Many scholars doubt if we can press such a fine grammatical distinction on this verb. The purpose of John's Gospel must be studied with a wider view, one that looks at the design of his writing and the assumptions he holds for his readers. If we do this, it appears that John assumes that his readers know at least the rudimentary things of Jesus' life and thought. They may even have read one of the Synoptic Gospels.[26] We see this in our use of John's Gospel today. It is the beloved gospel of Christians; it is "the spiritual gospel," which mature believers can study in order to gain insights into Jesus Christ. A quick glance at John's Farewell Discourse (chs. 14–16) shows us how Jesus prepares his followers for life *as believers* in the world following his death.

But this is hardly to say that it is not a useful or beneficial Gospel for those who possess no belief. Frequently the issues of faith and doubt that trouble the unbeliever are the same as those that burden the Christian. John's Gospel serves both audiences with perhaps the clearest, most poignant explanation of Jesus and his mission in the world. John writes to strengthen faith, and it makes no difference what might be your starting point.

---

25. The translation committee of the United Bible Society's Greek text decided to place the sigma in brackets because of their uncertainty of the readings. See B. Metzger, *A Textual Commentary on the Greek New Testament* (London: UBS, 1971), 256.

26. See R. Bauckham, "John for Readers of Mark," in R. Bauckham, ed., *The Gospels for All Christians: Rethinking the Gospel Audiences* (Grand Rapids: Eerdmans, 1998), 147–71, who suggests that internally John presupposes his readers have read Mark.

Bridging Contexts

THIS CHAPTER CONCENTRATES a number of vital theological themes within its thirty-one short verses, and each deserves careful attention. John has come to the end of the story about Jesus' public ministry. From the day Jesus was baptized by the Baptist, John's perspective on Jesus was not just descriptive. Jesus was the Son of God bearing promises for his followers. This is Jesus, who is not merely baptized but who will baptize his followers in the Holy Spirit (1:33). He will tear down the temple of his body and raise it again (2:19). He will offer rebirth (3:3) and living water (4:10) and even his own flesh for the life of the world (6:51). This is not merely a shepherd who takes care of his sheep; this is a shepherd who lays it down only to take it up again (10:17).

The Gospel's story continually points *forward* to promises described mysteriously in its narrative, awaited as the climactic scenes in Jerusalem unfold. Again and again, we are pointed to "the hour," the culmination of Jesus' mission in the world, when through his death, his resurrection, and his return to the Father, his followers are transformed by all of those promises suggested in virtually every story. Typically the Lazarus story of chapter 11 is about one dead man, surrounded by his grieving friends and family. But the story is more. It is about the Master of life and resurrection, who not only pulls Lazarus from the tomb but foreshadows by this deed his own tomb, his own resurrection, his own shocking recovery from death.

John 20 is thus the *denouement* of John's story to which every other story points. Here the mysteries of plot and promise are unraveled. This is the final resolution of the play, in which the main character, Jesus, steps to the center and discloses all.[27]

Four examples of faith. Not only does Jesus disclose and supply all that the previous chapters have promised, but we observe four examples of faith, four different scenes that offer to us responses to Jesus from his disciples as they experience the reality of their risen Lord.

(1) Peter and the Beloved Disciple race to the tomb. Although the risen Jesus is not seen, they see the evidence of his resurrection and the Beloved Disciple chooses to believe.

(2) Mary meets a man who utters her name, and she recognizes him to be Jesus. "I have seen the Lord" is her report, which echoes promises given by Jesus in his farewell.

---

27. I will suggest that chapter 21 is truly an appendix to the Gospel. This does not mean that it is insignificant, but that it is an "afterword," a closing scene that completes the story following the climactic ch. 20.

(3) The disciples are huddled in the Upper Room. They not only see evidence of the resurrection, they see Jesus, hear him, and receive the Spirit. Episode builds on episode, and we wonder what more could be expected!

(4) In the final scene, we meet Thomas, a man no different from us. He is a man for whom faith will only be a reality when the concrete evidence of resurrection is provided to him. He possesses no experience at an empty tomb, nor has he heard or seen Jesus. Thus, faith seems for him daunting and impossible. Thomas becomes a template for us, who read the story of Jesus *from a distance.* We hear the report, we read John's Gospel, and at once we are challenged to believe. Thomas obtains what he desires and so believes, but he misses the blessing that Jesus pronounces on those who believe even though they cannot touch Jesus' wounds. This is precisely our position as we live out our lives and our faith in the modern world.

Theological building blocks. Together these four stories supply us with the primary theological building blocks that lie at the center of John's thought in this chapter. Discerning these will unlock the theological heart of John's message. Three themes deserve our attention.

(1) John is telling us about the reality of the resurrection. Threaded through each story is some aspect of the power and certainty of Jesus' life from death. This is no illusion, no vision or fantasy that serves to inspire the disciples in the midst of their distress following Good Friday. *The tomb was empty.* Peter and John run to the cave, examine the evidence, and step away stunned and hopeful. Likewise, when Mary meets with Jesus he is no phantom, but a genuine man—truly transformed no doubt—but genuinely a man who speaks and listens and can be embraced. In the Upper Room, when Jesus introduces himself (20:20), he immediately offers proof that he is no ghost but the same man who hung on the cross, a physical man, a man with wounds so real that soon Thomas will be invited to touch them.

For John, the reality of the resurrection plays a critical role in validating the truth of Jesus Christ. The resurrection proves the assertion of 11:25. If Jesus is the resurrection and the life, his own capacity to step from the grave becomes the first evidence that proves him right. When John thinks about the Jesus he proclaims, the Jesus embraced in faith in his churches, he writes with a telling reminder of this reality. Listen to the opening words of his first letter (1 John 1:1–2):

That which was from the beginning, which we have heard, *which we have seen with our eyes, which we have looked at and our hands have touched—* this we proclaim concerning the Word of life. The life appeared; we have seen it and testify to it, and we proclaim to you the eternal life, which was with the Father and has appeared to us. (italics added)

It is likely true that John is not referring to the resurrection visit of Jesus exclusively in these verses. But he is referring to the concrete reality of Jesus that the resurrection could not diminish. The reality of Jesus burned itself into the consciousness of John, and he would never forget it. This reality was no different after Easter. The resurrected Jesus was a historical reality not unlike any other historical datum and needed to be a part of everyone's faith. In a similar manner it is critical for us today in the modern world to probe our own understanding of this resurrection. One of the remarkable developments in so much of modern theology is the attempt to affirm the value of Jesus for Christian faith while all along discarding the historicity of the resurrection. We need to explore this.

(2) John is also telling us about the resurrected Jesus and how disciples should perceive their relationship with him. As I urged in my exegesis, John 20 is a fulfillment of all the promises offered in the Farewell Discourse of chapters 14–16, in which Jesus spoke of his return and his indwelling through the power of the Holy Spirit.

John's endearing story about Mary is a correction to those disciples (like Mary) who think that the resurrection points to a resumption of Jesus' physical presence with them. On the contrary, Jesus is being glorified; his presence with his followers must change. Mary cannot "hold on" to the way Jesus has lived and worked with them but must instead rethink the nature of intimacy with Jesus. It will be a new intimacy, a spiritual intimacy, realized in the coming of the Holy Spirit, which is fulfilled in the next episode in the Upper Room.

The gift given in the Upper Room can be seen as the satisfaction of what Mary longs for in the garden. Jesus desires to enter his disciples' lives, to indwell them completely, to provide them with his Spirit (symbolized through his breath), in order to fulfill the hope he offered three days earlier. In 1 John the author tries to explain that which gives Christians an identity and a power that sets them apart from the world. He writes, "We know that we live in him and he in us, because he has given us of *his Spirit*" (1 John 4:13, italics added). The Holy Spirit is Jesus' Spirit; it is the powerful presence of Christ within his friends. We need to explore what this emphasis means for us and what possibilities it offers for Christian experience today.

(3) John 20 has much to tell us about faith. This should come as no surprise since John tells us at the end of these verses that promoting faith has been his aim from the beginning of the Gospel: "These are written that you may believe that Jesus is the Christ, the Son of God, and that by believing you may have life in his name" (20:31).

In this climactic chapter we have stories of faith and a catalogue of experiences that are each unique. Peter and John possess the evidence of the tomb; Mary enjoys the "evidence" of an encounter. The apostles (along with others) finally experience the Spirit. *But the spotlight is on Thomas.* He refuses to believe (20:25) until his "evidence" matches theirs. When he is given an objective basis for believing (20:27), Jesus recognizes his faith (20:29) but indicates that the demand for such evidence will not be met for everyone. Those who are truly blessed are men and women who believe but are *not* like Thomas in that they do not make faith contingent on such physical demands.

This does not, of course, present an easy assignment for us who live outside the apostolic era. Should faith be based on some objective criteria? If so, where do we go for it? Or is faith an inner experience of hope and resolve unrelated to objective realities? Is faith entirely experiential and affective, an inner-emotional or psychological decision shaping how we live and think, but not anchored to specific events in history (such as a tomb)?

This theme also appears in John's letters, where John gives marked attention to the subject of faith (the "faith" word group appears twenty-one times) and supplies one of the chief themes of his letters. "Everyone who believes that Jesus is the Christ is born of God, and everyone who loves the father loves his child as well" (1 John 5:1). So what is the character of faith? We must explore this theme as well in order to bring John's thoughts into the modern world.

THE RESURRECTION, THE Spirit, and faith! What three themes could be more central to the Christian life? To John's mind the maturing Christian must have a well-reasoned appreciation of what these things mean. Each theme links directly to John's Christology, making Jesus himself the center of our discipleship. The resurrection validates Jesus' identity as the Son of God, the divine messenger bringing us truth and grace from God. The Spirit is the indwelling of Jesus-in-Spirit within his disciples, making them his messengers so that like him they will convey to the world God's grace and truth. They (like Jesus) now echo what they "hear and see" because like Jesus, God's Spirit is in them. Faith defines how we live out our lives in the world under the promises and the empowering of God. It supplies us with confidence and hope so that we will not compromise our commitment to Christ despite what we experience in the world.

The truth of the resurrection. In October 1994 Moody Memorial Church in Chicago hosted a lively and important debate between two scholars with very different views of the resurrection. Moderated by the syndicated columnist William F. Buckley Jr., the debate invited William Lane Craig of Talbot

School of Theology (Los Angeles) and John Dominic Crossan of DePaul University (Chicago) to contend for the historicity of the person of Jesus in the Gospels.

Buckley opened the evening with a citation from that great New Testament scholar (the late) George Ladd and set the agenda:

> The uniqueness of the scandal of the Christian religion rests on the mediation of revelation through historical events. Christianity is not just a code for living or a philosophy of religion. It is rooted in real events of history. To some people this is scandalous because it means that the truth of Christianity is inexplicably bound up with the truth of certain historical facts. And if those facts should be disproved, Christianity would be false. This, however, is what makes Christianity unique because, unlike other world religions, modern man has a means of actually verifying Christianity's truth by historical evidence.[28]

Buckley rightly saw the importance of this quote because it underscores what became the heart of the debate. Are historical events important to Christianity? Can divine events in history be defended? If one of Christianity's chief claims—the resurrection of Jesus—proves to be unhistorical, what happens to our faith?

As the debate unfolded, it is remarkable how quickly the historicity of Jesus turned to the historicity of the *resurrection* of Jesus. For Crossan the resurrection is a metaphor but not an historical fact. Metaphors bear truth, he claimed, but that does not mean that they must be based on real things happening in history. The Christian notion of the resurrection of Jesus may have come from visions or hallucinations or from beliefs springing from reading the Scriptures, but not from evidence in history.[29] Craig's response reconfirmed his interest and expertise in the resurrection as a defensible historical fact.[30] But what Craig effectively uncovered is that for Crossan, the *absence* of an historical resurrection makes no difference to his understanding of Christianity.

---

28. The full transcript of the debate can be found in P. Copan, ed., *Will the Real Jesus Please Stand Up? A Debate Between William Lane Craig and John Dominic Crossan* (Grand Rapids: Baker, 1998). The debate is recorded in about forty-three pages and is followed in the book by a series of articles lining up on both sides of the issues. Buckley's opening citation of Ladd is on p. 24.

29. Crossan has become famous for the wide publicity given to his views. In fact, he personally believes that Jesus was buried in a shallow criminal's grave and his body eaten by wild dogs. Of course there is utterly no evidence for this. See his *Jesus: A Revolutionary Biography* (San Francisco: Harper, 1994), and *The Birth of Christianity: Discovering What Happened in the Years Immediately After the Execution of Jesus* (San Francisco: Harper, 1999).

30. See W. L. Craig, *The Historical Argument for the Resurrection of Jesus* (New York: Edwin Mellen, 1989), and *Assessing the New Testament Evidence for the Historicity of the Resurrection of Jesus* (New York: Edwin Mellen, 1989).

This debate has increased its intensity over the years. A colleague of Crossan, New Testament scholar Marcus Borg, has likewise led a campaign both in writing and in personal appearances, forcing Christians to rethink the historicity of Jesus.[31] For him, the resurrection simply does not matter. The physicality of Jesus' resurrection body is simply a myth conjured up by Jesus' later followers. Opposed to this has stood N. T. Wright, a British New Testament scholar who has engaged Borg in numerous public debates and recently published a volume in which the two scholars confront each other's views blow-by-blow.[32]

Perhaps the chief concern for us is that we understand what is at issue in this debate. Our defense of the historicity of Jesus and his resurrection does not depend in the first instance on our commitment to the reliability of the Bible. Something more fundamental is at stake. For the last three hundred years theologians and philosophers have debated the relationship between history and theology (or revelation).[33] The New Testament story about Jesus, it is claimed, presents us with a mythological portrait that has little to do with genuine fact. Once Jesus was believed to be the Messiah, pious but misdirected devotion created myths and legends about him. As the supernaturalism of the Gospels was expunged, the resurrection fell as one of the first victims.

The scholars who line up here insist that objective historical facts are inaccessible to us (since historical records never give us unvarnished accounts of what happened), but they also claim such facts are theologically unimportant. True faith does not rest on the reliability of events in history. As one scholar put it, "Accidental truths of history can never become the proof of necessary truths of reason."[34] For these scholars, truth is pursued outside the

---

31. With Crossan, Borg is one of the founding members of the well-known "Jesus Seminar." See his popular book, *Meeting Jesus Again for the First Time* (San Francisco: Harper, 1995).

32. M. J. Borg and N. T. Wright, *The Meaning of Jesus. Two Visions* (San Francisco. Harper, 1998). Wright has written numerous books. On the present subject, see *Who Was Jesus?* (Grand Rapids: Eerdmans, 1992) and the more technical *Jesus and the Victory of God* (Minneapolis: Fortress, 1996). See his recent *The Challenge of Jesus: Rediscovering Who Jesus Was and Is* (Downers Grove: InterVarsity, 1999). Wright is Canon Theologian at Westminster Abbey, London.

33. See D. Fuller, *Easter Faith and History* (London. Tyndale, 1965), or more recently, C. Brown, ed., *History, Criticism and Faith* (Downers Grove: InterVarsity, 1977), idem, "Historical Jesus, Quests of," in J. Green, S. McKnight, I. H. Marshall, *Dictionary of Jesus and the Gospels* (Downers Grove: InterVarsity, 1992), 326–41.

34. G. Lessing, cited in Fuller, *Easter Faith and History*, 34. For Lessing, the gap between history and theology became a "broad ugly ditch" he could not get over He went on to write that "revelation gives nothing to the human race which human reason could not arrive at on its own."

arena of history—particularly in the domain of reason or personal experience—and religious research must work at peeling away layers of myth and superstition that have grown up in Christian thought since biblical times. Once this task is done, our job is then to locate the timeless truth that the mythological story was trying to convey. Listen to the words of Marcus Borg:

> I now see Easter very differently. For me it is irrelevant whether or not the tomb was empty. Whether Easter involved something remarkable happening to the physical body of Jesus is irrelevant. My argument is not that we know the tomb was not empty or that nothing happened to his body, but simply that it doesn't matter. The truth of Easter, as I see it, is not at stake in this issue.[35]

The reason that debates about the historicity of Jesus finally focus on his resurrection is that this one event, this one claim to history, becomes the most objectionable. Easter claims that divine events, such as the stupendous event of Jesus' emerging alive from the tomb, happen in history. Easter claims that such events should not only be catalogued and studied as genuine events in history, but they can be viewed as a reliable basis for belief. We believe in a *God who acts in history* and those activities must be taken as serious disclosures of his revelation to humankind.

Increasingly New Testament scholars have conceded that this alleged divorce between theology and history is untenable. Such a belief will lead inevitably to a modern Gnosticism that possesses no objective, historic anchor.[36] Scholars have made a case not only for the absolute necessity for history in Christian theology[37] but for the reliability and surprising trustworthiness of the Gospels themselves.[38] Those who (like Borg and Crossan) call for a Christianity void of history, a Christianity not anchored in divine events, represent an era of skepticism that is being rejected more and more. Their voices, though loud and well-publicized, hark back to an earlier era of skepticism that is at odds with the faith promoted by John.

John's account of the resurrection is nothing if it is not a singular affirmation that true historical events happened on that Easter Sunday. This is the chief reason we are given so many details about the character of the empty

---

35. M. Borg, *The Meaning of Jesus*, 131.

36. I am here thinking of the famous lecture of E. Käsemann, "The Problem of the Historical Jesus," given in 1953. See his *Essays on New Testament Themes* (Naperville, Ill.: Allenson, 1964), 15–47.

37. See C. Stephen Evans, *The Historical Christ and the Jesus of Faith: Incarnational Narrative as History* (Oxford: Oxford Univ. Press, 1996).

38. See C. Blomberg, *The Historical Reliability of the Gospels* (Downers Grove: InterVarsity, 1987).

tomb (the placement of the burial clothes) and the nature of Jesus' resurrection body (his many wounds). John is trying to affirm the very thing Borg and Crossan deny: This Jesus is not a fantasy but a real man, a resurrected man who can talk and be touched despite the fact that he has been transformed by the power of his resurrection. Thomas steps into the drama (perhaps) as an ancient theological skeptic, arguing that divine events do not happen in history and he will not believe until he confirms the reality himself. Hence the Thomas episode is a dramatic gift for modern cynics.

We are invited—no, we are challenged—to believe like Thomas. Yet John understands perfectly well that we do not have the same opportunities. "Blessed are those who have not seen and yet have believed." This is why in the story of John 20 the Beloved Disciple becomes one of the most important figures. He looks into the tomb, sees the evidence, and believes (20:8). While not seeing the resurrected Jesus, he sees what has been left behind; he sees the remnants of divine activity in history in stone and fabric and decides to believe.

This is our situation today. John has provided us with the best evidence he can muster to persuade us that belief is not only a reasonable choice, but a necessary decision if we are going to follow Jesus. Jesus is not an *idea* whose ongoing validity finds a home in our ideas or our ethics. Jesus is a person— he is God incarnate in human history—and in coming into history, he has left marks that we can see and measure and trust. The resurrection is the capstone event in Jesus' career, which demonstrates the reality of what has happened since the moment of his incarnation. Without the resurrection, the infrastructure of Christological thinking falls apart and Jesus becomes merely one more Jewish teacher with a series of good ideas.

Paul makes the same point in 1 Corinthians 15:14: "If Christ has not been raised, our preaching is useless and so is your faith." No less than John Updike echoes the same in his poem "Seven Stanzas at Easter":

Make no mistake: if He rose at all
it was as His body;
if the cells' dissolution did not reverse,
 the molecules reknit, the amino
 acids rekindle,
the church will fall. . . .

Let us not mock God with metaphor,
Analogy, sidestepping transcendence;
Making of the event a parable, a sign
 painted in the faded credulity of
 earlier ages:
Let us walk through the door.

The stone is rolled back, not papier-mâché,
Not a stone in a story,
But the vast rock of materiality that in the slow
  grinding of time will eclipse for each of us
The wide light of day....[39]

The centrality of the Spirit. One of the most famous paintings depicting the dramatic scene of Mary and Jesus in the garden appears on a medieval Italian fresco in Padua, Italy. Giotto di Bondini paints Jesus striding from his tomb, holding his right hand out, prohibiting a kneeling, pleading Mary from coming close. She stretches out both arms, yearning to reach him, but he walks away, keeping her at a distance with one arm and bearing a victor's flag with the other. It is an unfortunate scene, and its influence on the interpretation of John 20 tragic. Jesus is aloof; he is leaving, and he cannot be held back by this woman. "Do not hold me" may well be the words on his lips.[40]

The picture of Mary in the garden is a prominent image in John 20. But its emphasis springs from ideas utterly missed by Bondini. This story works together with the Upper Room account that follows in order to speak to us about the dwelling and fellowship that Jesus is about to establish with his disciples. But other motifs, hidden in the story, prepare the way.

A number of biblical images suggest themselves in the story. People in the New Testament world knew the stories and metaphors of the Bible so well that they became a ready source for rich imagery. Allusions that may seem remote to us today may well have felt comfortable and obvious centuries ago. For instance, John alone tells us that these events took place in a garden—a garden filled with spices (19:39)—and this at once suggests the imagery of the Song of Songs (Song 1:3, 12; 3:6; 4:6, 10; 5:1, 13). Mary is a woman who finds the one she loves amidst a spice-filled garden and yearns to be with him, to embrace him.[41] Therefore the setting points us toward intimacy and union, bliss and renewal.

39. J. Updike, "Seven Stanzas at Easter," from *Telephone Poles and Other Poems* (New York: A. Knopf, 1963).

40. Giotto di Bondoni (1267–1337) was a well-known and highly influential medieval Italian artist. This picture, *Noli me tangere* ("Do Not Hold Me"), is found at the Capella Scrovegni, Padua, and can be seen on the World Wide Web at http://gallery.euroweb.hu/html/g/giotto/padova/3christ/index.html. Find scene 37. See the interpretation of the fresco by Teresa Okure, "The Significance Today of Jesus' Commission to Mary Magdalene," *IRM* 81 (1992): 177–88.

41. See J. D. Derrett, "Miriam and the Resurrection (John 20:16)," *Downside Review* 111 (1993): 174–86. In the Western liturgy, the Feast of St. Mary Magdalene (22 July) makes the connection to the Song of Songs explicit.

Nor has John missed the symbolic importance of Mary's name. Miriam was the most famous sister of Moses, who oversaw her little brother's journey down the Nile. In an ancient Jewish synagogue at Dura Europos on the Euphrates a fresco depicts this scene carefully. The floating bed of Moses becomes a coffin and tomb from which the baby Moses is raised to life (thus avoiding death).[42] Old Testament Miriam even becomes a prophet (Ex. 15:20–21; Num. 12:1–2) who bears a message to Israel. While John refers to Mary in the narrative with the Greek word *Maria*, when Jesus (the new Moses) meets her in 20:16, oddly, he employs the Hebrew form of the name: Miriam (Gk. *Mariam*, Heb. *Miryam*). He names her "Miriam Magdalene"— where Magdalene connotes the Hebrew noun *migdal*, "tower." This caretaker of the new Moses, this intimate helper, is now transformed from a mere "Mary" into a Miriam, into a *migdal* that now bears a prophetic message to the apostles. Women rarely (if ever) enjoyed the status of courier or messenger, much less as legal witness for critical events. Mary's commission to run and speak is a deep honoring that Jesus gives her alone.[43]

Moreover, some interpreters believe that John is consciously sweeping up numerous biblical motifs that connect with the theme of "garden." If so, it is no accident that in 20:15, here in this garden, Mary misunderstands the identity of Jesus and thinks he is the gardener. Nicholas Wyatt, after showing the historical evidence in Judaism that placed the Garden of Eden in the Holy Land, goes on to show how motifs from the Eden story reappear in numerous literatures of the period. If this imagery is at work (and here many would caution us[44]), in this story we are viewing a woman in "Paradise" meeting the ruler of the Garden himself, Jesus.[45]

Therefore the composite that emerges from the story is not that of Giotto di Bondini, where Mary is pushed away. Rather, it is an intimate scene that evokes feelings of personal care and desire. A woman in a garden replete with spices looking for her master is a potent biblical image. *Mary's desires, however, must be suspended.* She cannot "hold on" to the relationship with Jesus that characterized his earlier life. She must be the courier of another message. Jesus

---

42. This fresco is now at the National Gallary, Damascus, but can be viewed at Duke University on the World Wide Web at http://www.duke.edu/~nwb/synagoge/durplan.html#kraelp51. See E. J. Bickerman, "Symbolism in the Dura Synagogue: A Review Article," *TR* 58 (1965): 127–51.

43. G. O'Collins and D. Kendall, "Mary Magdalene as Major Witness to Jesus' Resurrection," *TS* 48 (1987): 631–46. This reluctance to see a woman as primary witness appears even in Paul's list of witnesses in 1 Cor. 15:5–8, where Mary's name (or the name of any woman) is absent!

44. Brown, *John*, 2:990; Barrett, *John*, 560.

45. N. Wyatt, "'Supposing Him to be the Gardener,' (John 20,15): A Study of the Paradise Motif in John," *ZNW* 81 (1990): 21–38.

has not abandoned his friends but is coming to them. When he does, he will show them the sort of interior life he desires to take up with them.

This is why for the present theme Jesus' appearance in the Upper Room takes center stage. His arrival fulfills many of the promises held out in his earlier farewell (see comments in Original Meaning). Above all, his arrival comes with a gift. He breathes on them, giving them "Holy Spirit." This "master of the garden" now breathes into his followers, transforming their lives, and we cannot doubt that John finds echoes here of God's great creative work in Genesis 2. In that ancient story another garden saw divine breath enter a man and life enter the world. Now a new gardener, God's Son, does the same.

In 1 John 4:13 John writes that one feature of our assurance in Christ is in his gift of the Spirit. "By this we know that we abide in him and he in us, because he has given us of *his own Spirit*" (RSV, italics added). This is no impersonal spirit; this is no ambiguous inspiration from God. This is Jesus *himself* indwelling his disciples, taking up the residence promised in 14:23. Jesus desires intimacy with Mary and his followers, but the vehicle of that intimacy will now be experienced through the agency of the Holy Spirit. The reason that the work of the Spirit in John 14–16 is so highly personal is that this Spirit is the Spirit of Jesus—his own Spirit—that is now poured out at the hour of glorification. The intimacy of the garden scene is now satisfied. Mary's yearnings are met. Jesus will be within her in a way she could not formerly comprehend.

This careful union of Christ and Spirit in John makes an important theological point. Discipleship is defined not only by belief in Jesus but by the indwelling of the Son through the Spirit. Some theological traditions separate Jesus and the Spirit, urging that to accept Christ as Savior is one matter and receiving the Holy Spirit is a second, necessary experience. But this is an unacceptable division in John. To receive Christ is to obtain the Spirit; to be filled by the Holy Spirit is to experience the living presence of Jesus Christ within. Christian transformation is Christ at work within us, bringing about his glory in our Spirit-led renewal (Col. 1:27).

Other theological traditions, particularly in the evangelical community, create yet another theological problem by making the Spirit disappear into Christology. For these Christians the chief evidence of the Spirit is found in conversion and sanctification. To believe in Jesus is the hallmark of the disciple, but little is said about the more mysterious and mystical work of the Spirit. Personal conviction is the premier evidence of the presence of God, but little is said of his power. For those in this tradition, John would have us recover something of the depth and the power of God's Spirit today in ways that may even make us uncomfortable. John's own church was certainly "pneumatic" (or what we today might call charismatic). The evidence of his letters (and his emphasis on the Spirit in his Gospel) makes this evident. But those outside this world of experience often fail to see its importance.

Zeb Bradford Long and Douglas McMurry are two Presbyterian (U.S.A.) ministers who have discovered this power. Their recent book *Receiving the Power: Preparing the Way for the Holy Spirit* makes compelling reading as they chronicle momentous workings of the Spirit both in Asia and in the United States.[46] If this is ministry, if this is what it means for Jesus to indwell and empower his disciples, some new and startling directions for ministry seem necessary.

Among John's disciples in the first century, bearing the Spirit was one of a number of markers that distinguished Christian discipleship. Yet this was not simply about power. The chief theme of John 20 is the relationship that Jesus desires to have with his followers. The story of Mary underscores the intimacy that should characterize this relationship. The story of the Upper Room underscores that this is a relationship forged by the work of the Spirit. Christian discipleship is a union with Jesus Christ that empowers and transforms, that is mystical, that exceeds our rational abilities to understand and quantify. To make it less is to miss the work that Jesus tried to accomplish with his first followers on the first Easter.

The necessity of faith. Thus John has finished the main body of his Gospel. The choice is ours. After reading the many episodes from Jesus' life in these twenty chapters, we are summoned to make a judgment. Since chapter 5 we learned that the trial of Jesus was not *really* taking place in a Jerusalem courtroom with Pilate or the high priest. The venue of Jesus' trial was in fact the entire world. Accusations have come and gone—divine acts (signs) with potent meanings have been given—and we have watched as men and women have been divided. *No one remained neutral.* Some found Jesus' personal claims so outrageous that they were filled with rage and worked to sabotage him. Others observed his deeds, listened to his words, and decided to believe that he indeed was God's messenger, his Son, bearing divine truth for the world. The pressing question rests here: How will we stand in this parting of the crowd?

Through his literary expertise John has placed us in the drama by making us view the evidence in the case for and against Jesus. He knows well that his readers—in Jerusalem, Ephesus, Rome, Singapore, Lusaka, Cambridge, and Chicago—will not have the same experience that he or even Thomas had. We look on the evidence from afar. Nevertheless, there is still good evidence to be had—there is an historical story that must be read—and this

---

46. Z. Long and D. McMurry, *Receiving the Power: Preparing the Way for the Holy Spirit* (Grand Rapids: Baker, 1996).

story is sufficient to make belief not only defensible but reasonable. We stand with the Beloved Disciple looking at the emptiness of the tomb (20:8), recognizing that these indeed were Jesus' burial clothes. John invites us to make the same decision uttered in that garden: "The other disciple, who had reached the tomb first, also went inside. He saw *and believed*" (italics added).

Throughout the Gospel faith and seeing are joined (6:36; 11:40; 6:46–47; 20:25–29). But this means more than seeing Jesus and choosing to believe. It is about a different sort of vision altogether. Many saw Jesus and marveled, but it was *seeing through faith* that permitted them to see his glory, to recognize his sonship, to respond to his shepherd's voice. Faith permits a vision, a knowing inaccessible to the person whose sight remains shaped by the world. As C. H. Dodd reminds us, however, "now that He is no longer visible to the bodily eye, faith remains the capacity for seeing His glory."[47] Therefore we are called to read John's story and there discover a vision, a knowledge, that invests everything in the historic person of Jesus Christ.

It is striking that John never uses the noun "faith" (Gk. *pistis*) in his Gospel. Yet the verb "to believe" (Gk. *pisteuo*) appears almost a hundred times. The Synoptic Gospels together use this verb only about thirty-five times, and Paul uses it about a hundred times in all of his writings combined. John's interest is to underscore the act of believing (as opposed to the content of faith). More than anywhere else in the New Testament, John's Gospel follows this verb with a preposition (*eis*, into), which demands not that we simply believe, but that we place our faith into someone; in most instances, it is into Jesus (e.g., 3:16; 4:50; 8:30; 12:11; 14:1).

Faith, then, is more a matter of relationship than of creed.[48] On occasion it means accepting that a message given is true and trustworthy (2:22), but for the most part faith springs from confidence in the works Jesus has done (2:11; 10:38) and results in a desire to invest all hope in him.[49] Faith is personal and transforming since it is dependent on a person who has demonstrated himself powerful and trustworthy. It is the decision whereby a person gains eternal life and the power to become a child of God (1:12; 3:16) and so marks himself or herself as a member of Jesus' community.

---

47. Dodd, *The Interpretation of the Fourth Gospel*, 186.

48. D. Guthrie, *New Testament Theology* (Downers Grove: InterVarsity, 1981), 581.

49. In Bultmann's penetrating study of John's theology, he rightly sees faith as the central experience of the believer, but he denies that Jesus Christ is the object of faith. Rather, faith is an existential decision, an eschatological life, lived against the world and its values (*Theology of the New Testament* [London: SCM, 1955], 2:75–94).

John 21:1–25

❦

AFTERWARD JESUS APPEARED again to his disciples, by the Sea of Tiberias. It happened this way: ²Simon Peter, Thomas (called Didymus), Nathanael from Cana in Galilee, the sons of Zebedee, and two other disciples were together. ³"I'm going out to fish," Simon Peter told them, and they said, "We'll go with you." So they went out and got into the boat, but that night they caught nothing.

⁴Early in the morning, Jesus stood on the shore, but the disciples did not realize that it was Jesus.

⁵He called out to them, "Friends, haven't you any fish?"

"No," they answered.

⁶He said, "Throw your net on the right side of the boat and you will find some." When they did, they were unable to haul the net in because of the large number of fish.

⁷ Then the disciple whom Jesus loved said to Peter, "It is the Lord!" As soon as Simon Peter heard him say, "It is the Lord," he wrapped his outer garment around him (for he had taken it off) and jumped into the water. ⁸The other disciples followed in the boat, towing the net full of fish, for they were not far from shore, about a hundred yards. ⁹When they landed, they saw a fire of burning coals there with fish on it, and some bread.

¹⁰Jesus said to them, "Bring some of the fish you have just caught."

¹¹Simon Peter climbed aboard and dragged the net ashore. It was full of large fish, 153, but even with so many the net was not torn. ¹²Jesus said to them, "Come and have breakfast." None of the disciples dared ask him, "Who are you?" They knew it was the Lord. ¹³Jesus came, took the bread and gave it to them, and did the same with the fish. ¹⁴This was now the third time Jesus appeared to his disciples after he was raised from the dead.

¹⁵When they had finished eating, Jesus said to Simon Peter, "Simon son of John, do you truly love me more than these?"

"Yes, Lord," he said, "you know that I love you."

Jesus said, "Feed my lambs."

¹⁶Again Jesus said, "Simon son of John, do you truly love me?"

He answered, "Yes, Lord, you know that I love you."

Jesus said, "Take care of my sheep."

[17]The third time he said to him, "Simon son of John, do you love me?"

Peter was hurt because Jesus asked him the third time, "Do you love me?" He said, "Lord, you know all things; you know that I love you."

Jesus said, "Feed my sheep. [18]I tell you the truth, when you were younger you dressed yourself and went where you wanted; but when you are old you will stretch out your hands, and someone else will dress you and lead you where you do not want to go." [19]Jesus said this to indicate the kind of death by which Peter would glorify God. Then he said to him, "Follow me!"

[20]Peter turned and saw that the disciple whom Jesus loved was following them. (This was the one who had leaned back against Jesus at the supper and had said, "Lord, who is going to betray you?") [21]When Peter saw him, he asked, "Lord, what about him?"

[22]Jesus answered, "If I want him to remain alive until I return, what is that to you? You must follow me." [23]Because of this, the rumor spread among the brothers that this disciple would not die. But Jesus did not say that he would not die; he only said, "If I want him to remain alive until I return, what is that to you?"

[24]This is the disciple who testifies to these things and who wrote them down. We know that his testimony is true.

[25]Jesus did many other things as well. If every one of them were written down, I suppose that even the whole world would not have room for the books that would be written.

Original Meaning

SCHOLARS ARE DIVIDED over the literary history and role of John 21.[1] Some view it as a vital and necessary conclusion to the Gospel, intimately linked to the previous twenty chapters. Others conclude that this final chapter is a supplement to the Gospel, an addition penned either by the same author who wrote chapters 1–20 or by his disciples

---

1. A current survey of the major interpretative issues can be found in F. Neirynck, "John 21," *NTS* 36 (1990): 321–36; T. Wiarda, "John 21:1–23: Narrative Unity and Its Implication," *JSNT* 46 (1992): 53–71; and W. S. Vorster, "The Growth and Making of John 21,"

(who identify themselves in 21:24). The chief problem is that within the narrative of the Gospel, chapter 21 appears extraneous. Note how 20:29 ends the Easter story with a final benediction and 20:30–31 provides an excellent closing to the book as a whole. Moreover, to some scholars it seems odd that these seven disciples would depart for Galilee, resume their previous occupation, and not recognize Jesus immediately, given the stupendous experiences recorded in chapter 20.

At the same time, however, there is no evidence in the manuscript tradition that this Gospel ever circulated without this final chapter.[2] And even if this Gospel seems to end with chapter 20, it is improper to impose a standard of consistency on John's Gospel that was never intended.[3] Some scholars may be overly confident about their prediction of what John *should* have done.[4] Vocabulary studies of the chapter likewise point to its integrity. There are twenty-eight words in chapter 21 that do not appear in chapters 1–20, yet in chapter 21 we have a new subject (fishing), which alone demands new vocabulary.[5] Today most scholars see the present chapter as fully integrated (by someone) into the earliest stage of the Gospel.

The list of links between these verses and the balance of John is extensive. Note the following: Sea of Tiberias; the names Simon Peter, Thomas the Twin, Nathanael of Cana; the Greek word for "fish" (*opsarion*, 21:6, 9, 11); the contrast of Peter and the Beloved Disciple; Jesus' "charcoal fire"; the distribution of bread and fish (cf. 6:11); the numbering of Jesus' appearances (21:14); Simon's father's named "John"; the sheep metaphor; the double use of *amen*; an emphasis on "true witness" (21:24; cf. 19:35); the triple restoration of Peter (following his triple denial); the parenthesis of 21:19 (cf. 12:33); and the reference to the Beloved Disciple as "the one who had leaned back against Jesus" (cf. 13:25).[6] Each of these words or themes appears elsewhere in the Gospel.

---

in F. Neirynck, ed., *The Four Gospels* (Louvain: Leuven Univ. Press, 1992), 2207–21. See also G. Osborne, "John 21: Test Case for History and Redaction in the Resurrection Narratives," in R. T. France and D. Wenham, ed., *Gospel Perspectives II: Studies of History and Tradition in the Four Gospels* (Sheffield: JSOT Press: 1981), 293–328.

2. There is one fifth- or sixth-century Syriac manuscript that omits this chapter, but this is likely due to the loss of a folio leaf.

3. Morris, *John*, 758.

4. Typically Brown (*John*, 2:1077–82) objects that if chapter 21 was an original part of the Gospel, the author should have moved the closing verses (20:30–31) to the end of chapter 21. Barrett (577) writes, "...it is extremely unlikely that an author, wishing to add fresh material to his own book, would add it in so clumsy a manner. The supplementary material would have been added by him before 20:30, and the impressive conclusion left undisturbed."

5. See the list of Greek terms in Barrett, *John*, 576.

6. For extensive lists of these see Brown, *John*, 2.1077–80; also V. C. Pfitzner, "They Knew It Was the Lord: The Place and Function of John 21:1–14 in the Gospel of John," *Lutheran Theological Journal* 20 (1986): 68–69.

For instance, 18:18 describes a charcoal fire precisely like the one mentioned in 21:9 (Gk. *anthrakia*), and this Greek word appears nowhere else in the entire New Testament. These links are so compelling that either we have a chapter that is intimately a part of John's narrative, or we have a later writer who has consciously imitated John's style and incorporated many of his ideas.

Our dilemma is that while the style and form of the chapter appears Johannine, it seems to interrupt the main force of the Gospel's story. The best explanation is to see these stories as secondary but authentically Johannine. With the exception of 21:24–25 (and also perhaps vv. 20–23), the bulk of John 20 has come from the same pen as John 1–20. Thus, it is not unreasonable to point to the Beloved Disciple (who is likely John, son of Zebedee) as the author.[7]

But now a crisis may have swept John's church. John may have died or been near death (see 21:23), and faithful disciples who identify themselves in 21:24 ("we know that his testimony is true") have collated John's final stories and added them to his Gospel. John 20:31 says that there were many other signs worked by Jesus; these followers have saved one of them, the miraculous catch of fish. These were likely accounts written up by John that are now patched into his Gospel lest they be lost. These editors were skilful and wove the chapter artfully so that its link to the foregoing narrative is unmistakable (cf. 21:14, "this is now the third time Jesus appeared. . ."). They perhaps added the glorious prologue as well (1:1–18), enabling the Gospel to confront those issues the apostle fought toward the end of his life, particularly in his first letter.[8]

If an appendix is defined as an addition that bears no connection to previous material, we should then view chapter 21 as an *epilogue*, which picks up previous themes and develops them, bringing these subjects to a firm conclusion.[9] John is not interested in giving us yet one more proof of Jesus' resurrection. If a reader has not been convinced by the account in chapter 20, these added stories will not help.

John 21 develops two entirely different subjects. (1) The apostolic mission of the church is symbolized not only by the great catch of fish but by Peter's private conversation with Jesus. This is a theme echoed in the Synoptics, wherein no Gospel could be complete without some signal that the work of Jesus' followers must now follow his resurrection and departure (see Matt. 28:16–20; Mark 16:14–20 [though this is an addition]; Luke 24:44–53). The

---

7. See the Introduction for arguments concerning authorship of the Gospel.

8. I have outlined the relationship of John's Gospel to the problems addressed in John's letters in *The Letters of John* (NIVAC; Grand Rapids: Zondervan, 1996), 20–27.

9. P. F. Ellis, "The Authenticity of John 21," *SVTQ* 36 (1992): 17–25; and J. Breck, "John 21, Appendix, Epilogue or Conclusion?" *SVTQ* 36 (1992): 27–49.

fish hauled in from the sea and the sheep Peter is called to love suggest those in the world whom Jesus likewise loves, those who will believe in Christ later through the disciples' words (17:20)—other sheep perhaps not yet in Jesus' fold (10:16).

(2) John concentrates on the character of Peter, whose name threads through the entire chapter. Peter's threefold denial of Christ (18:15–18, 25–27) is matched by his threefold announcement of love. In addition, while the Beloved Disciple is the one who recognizes Jesus from the boat (21:7), Peter rushes to the shore in his zeal to see the Lord and is later invited to haul in the great catch of fish. This is Peter's restoration. Jesus sees in this fallen disciple genuine potential for good and now not only demonstrates marked personal interest in him but predicts that Peter will follow Jesus even in a death that will "glorify God" (21:19).

The Fishing Miracle (21:1–14)

WHILE THE RESURRECTED Jesus appeared to his followers in Jerusalem according to John and Luke (Luke 24; John 20), the other Gospels point to Galilee as the place where they will meet him. Mark 16:7 (cf. Matt. 28:7) records the words of an angel, "But go, tell his disciples and Peter, 'He is going ahead of you into Galilee. There you will see him, just as he told you.'" This suggests no contradiction. The disciples have simply been instructed to return to what had been their "base" throughout Jesus' ministry and there receive further instructions. In John's narrative, Jesus appeared already on Easter Sunday and then eight days later; now he appears a third (and final) time on the shore of Galilee. John 21:14 helpfully numbers these appearances.

The Sea of Tiberias is the Sea of Galilee, about seventy-five miles north of Jerusalem and surrounded by the hills of Galilee and Golan (see comments on 6:1). The fishing villages of Bethsaida and Capernaum are here— both significant residences of leading disciples. Peter is from Bethsaida (Heb. "house of fish," see 1:44), and he decides to return to his long-neglected work of fishing.[10] Other disciples are there too, even though some are not from the region (Nathanael is from Cana); the seven listed in 21:2 decide to join Peter for a night's fishing.

The best fishing can be found in the early hours before sunrise (NIV "night"), and families generally worked together in pairs (cf. Luke 5:2). Two boats generally used compound nets (trammel nets) that would encircle a school of fish by setting them up vertically with cork floaters on one edge and stone or metal sinkers on the other. Once the school was surrounded,

---

10. In the Synoptics Peter is also identified with Capernaum (Mark 1:29–31), which suggests he later moved there.

the net was tightened by the boats and the men would throw "cast nets" (about ten feet across), bearing lead sinkers over the unwary fish. These filled nets would either be emptied by a swimmer or pulled into the boat while many of the other fish would get caught in the net wall surrounding them.[11] Peter's boat is using this method in the shallow water about a hundred yards from shore (21:8), and it is likely that he is diving into the sea checking the cast nets (21:7).[12]

The seven disciples have an unsuccessful morning on the sea and they are frustrated. At sunrise they are finishing up when an unknown voice from shore instructs them to try the opposite side of the boat. "Throw your net on the right side of the boat and you will find some," Jesus called out (21:6). To toss a cast net at random into the sea was virtually futile. Only a school captured by a trammel net could be picked up in this manner. But the stranger may have seen a large school of fish from the shore, and Peter quickly spins the net over his head and lets it sail, like a parachute, dropping onto the sea as he watches the sinkers take it down.

In these shallow waters, the miraculous catch cannot be mistaken. Pinned to the net are over one hundred fish (later counted at 153), and its weight is more than the boat can take. Recently members of Kibbutz Ginosar in Galilee found such a first-century fishing boat (now on display at the Beit Yigal Allon Museum, Ginosar), and its size gives some insight.[13] Its length is 26.5 feet and its width 7.5 feet. If this bears any resemblance to Peter's boat, seven men would have filled it—which lends further support to the notion that these men use two vessels.[14]

Immediately the Beloved Disciple recognizes Jesus on the shore (21:7) and conveys the news to Peter. What Peter does next has invited unnecessary confusion (obscured by a paraphrase in the NIV). Some translations, reflecting the literal Greek, report that when Peter hears that it is the Lord, he "put on his clothes for he was naked." The idea is that Peter is wearing a loin cloth for

---

11. For fishing practices in the Sea of Galilee, see G. Burge, "Fishers of Men: The Maritime Life of Galilee's North Shore," *Christian History* 59 (1998): 36–37; M. Nun, *The Sea of Galilee and Its Fishermen in the New Testament* (Kibbutz Ein Gev, Israel: np, 1989).

12. It is interesting to compare the story of the miraculous catch of fish in Luke 5:1–11. In Luke's story, the men have finished with their compound nets and are on shore, removing caught fish and washing and repairing the nets. Jesus instructs them to return to the sea and let down their great encircling nets (5:6); there they surround a tremendous school of fish. In John's story, Peter is told to cast his net (singular; i.e., his cast net).

13. The Ginosar boat is well known and can be viewed on the internet at http://mahal.zrc.ac.il/ancient-boat/anc-boat.htm or can be visited about two miles north of Tiberius on Hwy 90 (inside Kibbutz Nof Ginosar).

14. John uses two different nouns for the boats in 21:6 and 21:8, the latter being a smaller boat.

diving into he sea (full nudity would be unusual) and now he gets dressed to join Jesus. The problem is that he gets dressed in order to jump *fully clothed* into the sea.

A more plausible translation recognizes that the verb "to dress" (Gk. *dia-zonymmi*) actually refers to wrapping or tucking clothes around oneself (as one would with a robe or toga). In 13:4 Jesus thus "wraps" (*diazonymmi*) a towel around himself at the footwashing. Here Peter is wearing a worker's smock (Gk. *epedytes*) on the boat, but he wants to swim to shore to meet the Lord. Because he is naked (Gk. *gymnos*) *underneath the smock,* when he hears that Jesus is on the shore, he tucks or wraps his smock into his belt to give him a tight fit and leaps into the water.[15]

None of the others respond with Peter's impulsiveness. John tells us that the other men turn their boats toward shore and slowly drag the bursting cast net (21:8). Rather than anchoring at a coastal harbor, they likely drop their stone anchor when the water became shallow, as it does quickly on the northern coasts. Later Peter runs out to the net, frees it from the boat, and pulls it to shore.

In Judaism, an abundant catch was a sign of God's favor and blessing (*T. Zebulon* 6:1–8); this is precisely what Jesus has done. He blesses them further by greeting them with a fire and roasting fish together with fresh bread (the mainstays of a first-century meal in Galilee). Peter is told to haul the 153 netted fish to shore not to supplement Jesus' breakfast, but to preserve the catch as any responsible fisherman would do. Some of the minor harbors in Galilee (such as Kursi) had stone catch-basins where newly caught fish can be kept fresh for later cleaning.[16] Peter either drops the fish into one of these or keeps them in the shallows.

While they are eating, John says that the men know it is Jesus but are also afraid to ask (21:12). This is unusual. In the garden Mary (who knew Jesus intimately) spoke with him and mistook him to be a gardener, only later recognizing him when he said her name (20:16). The disciples now do the same. Jesus' resurrected appearance bears some traits that give everyone pause: He is the same Jesus, but the events of Easter have also made him unmistakably different. Jesus' offer of "bread and fish" precisely parallels what he did at the miraculous feeding in 6:11, and this no doubt serves as a signal that removes any uncertainties (cf. Luke 24:30 for similar recognition at a meal).

Much speculation has surrounded the meaning of the 153 fish. For some, this is merely the count of fish here offered to establish the size of the miracle

---

15. See Brown, *John,* 2:1072; Barrett, *John,* 580–81 for a discussion of the language.
16. See M. Nun, "The Ports of Galilee. Modern Drought Reveals Harbors from Jesus' Time," *BAR* 25 (July/August 1999): 18–31.

(although a parallel miracle in Luke 5 provides no such number). Others see a deeper symbolism. The most popular explanation began with Jerome, who argued that in antiquity mariners understood that there were 153 species of fish. Jesus' miracle is then a symbol of the "many species," the many nations, who now must be netted. Jerome gives his source for this comment (the naturalist writer Oppian), but a quick glance at Oppian's words does not bear this result. Antiquity did *not* believe that there were 153 species of fish. An earlier writer, Pliny, even tells us that according to his research there were seventy-four species in the world (plus thirty crustaceans)! [17]

Since Greek and Hebrew letters had numerical values and this system became a code for symbolic meanings (called *gematria*), some have sought a numerical value in 153 (as many have done with the number 666 in Rev. 13:18). For instance, the Greek words "Simon" and "fish" total 153. The Hebrew phrase "church of love" does as well. One scholar recently argued for the Hebrew word *Pisgah*, the mountain in Moab from which Moses commissioned his followers after viewing the land of Israel before his death (Deut. 3:27; 34:1).[18]

In 1958 a better suggestion was given pointing to Ezekiel.[19] Ezekiel 47 says that at the end of time, a stream will flow from Jerusalem filled with fish from "En-Gedi to En-Egalaim" (47:9–10). En-Gedi is 17 and En-Egalaim represents 153. The number 17 is significant because it is the "triangular number" of 153 $(1+2+3+4\ldots+17 = 153)$, and ancient mathematicians and scholars studied these sequences.[20] Once we see the relation between 153 and 17, speculation becomes endless. Augustine noted the number 17 and thought of 153 believers who were inspired by the "7" gifts of the Spirit to obey the "10" commandments. Origen thought that 153 should be divided to symbolize the trinity: $153 = (50 \times 3) + 3$.

Patristic interpreters give us some clue to how fantastic such interpretations may become, and no doubt they should warn us about doing the same. Cyril of Alexandria thought the number represented 100 pagans, fifty Jews, and the Trinity! If John had a symbolic meaning in mind, we can only guess what it was. As with the other miracles of quantity in the Gospel (the wine in Cana, the food in Galilee), this number may simply represent extreme abundance and blessing from the One who controls good gifts from heaven.

---

17. See his *Nat. Hist.* 9.16 [43].

18. O. T. Owen, "One Hundred and Fifty Three Fishes," *ExpTim* 100 (1988): 52–54. This article inspired numerous responses in the pages of *ExpTim*.

19. J. A. Emerton, *JTS* 9 (1958): 86–89; also 11 (1960): 335–36.

20. Mathematicians would illustrate this by building equilateral triangles. Starting at the corner, dots can be arranged (first one, then two, then three, etc.) until all three sides are equal. In this case, seventeen dots on one side provides a total of 153 dots.

I imagine that Greek mathematicians recognized 153 as numerically important and likely saw it as a symbol of a "perfect and unique catch of fish."[21]

John ends this section (21:14) by reminding us that this appearance was the third time Jesus had revealed himself since his resurrection. No doubt he has in mind the events of Easter, where he appeared to Mary and to the Twelve (20:11–23), and the second revelation in the Upper Room the following week, when he appeared for the benefit of Thomas (20:26–29). This reference closely links 21:1–14 with the stories of chapter 20.

The Restoration of Peter (21:15–17)

FOLLOWING THEIR MEAL as they sit on the beach thinking about their handsome catch of fish, Jesus strikes up a conversation with Peter. The solemn character of the moment is underscored by Jesus' form of address: "Simon son of John." Simon was the apostle's given name but Jesus had renamed him "Peter" (Gk. *petros*, rock, Matt. 16:18). Peter's name occurs frequently in this Gospel[22] but not like this. Each time Jesus questions Peter here, he uses this full and formal form of address.

We should keep in mind that these verses are closely linked with the fishing miracle of 21:1–14. Thus, when Jesus asks Peter, "Do you love me *more than these*," we are forced to examine the context to unravel the meaning of "these." Is Jesus asking, "Do you love me more than you love these boats and fish?" Or, "do you love me more than you love these men with whom you are working?" These two options are relevant since Peter has rejoined his fishing career and now with his friends around him, perhaps Jesus is calling him to make a choice. Does he love his career or is he willing to be Christ's disciple with a thoroughgoing call to ministry?

We must keep in mind that it was Peter who spoke up when Jesus predicted his betrayal. In the Synoptics he said that he alone would continue to be faithful even if the others fell away (Matt. 26:33; Mark 14:29). John describes for us Peter's zeal to follow Jesus despite warnings of death. "Lord, why can't I follow you now? I will lay down my life for you" (13:37; cf. 15:12–13). And, of course, the deepest irony of this story is that once Peter utters this pledge, he denies Christ three times. But in the present setting, Jesus is the One who knows all things (1:42; 2:25; 16:30), and he understands that despite this

---

21. Hoskyns, *John*, 556; Hoskyns refers to A. L. Heath, *A History of Greek Mathematics* (Oxford: Clarendon, 1921), 76 (reprint; New York: Dover, 1981). Another theory argues that there were 154 fish—153 plus one on the fire! And this new number represents the Greek word "day" (*hemera*), since Jesus is the light who makes such a catch possible. K. Candwell, "The Fish on the Fire: John 21:9," *ExpTim* 102 (1990): 12–14.

22. "Peter" occurs thirty-four times, of which fifteen include the name "Simon."

terrible falling, Peter is still a man of faith and commitment. Jesus may then be asking, "Do you [indeed] love me more than these other men love me?" Jesus is asking Peter to examine the strength of his earlier pledges.

The first step in Peter's restoration comes when Jesus asks Peter to bring "the fish" to shore (21:10). Even this mundane task sets him apart, affirming his position as a leader among these men. Jesus may even be remembering his call to make these men "fishers of men" (Matt. 4:19), so that now the "catch" is going to be Peter's responsibility. But fishing will not be the primary metaphor for Peter's future.

Jesus' three queries in 21:15–17 are perhaps the most celebrated exchange of questions and answers in the entire Bible. Three times Jesus asks Peter if he loves him, and three times Peter affirms his love. In each case he is commissioned to tend Jesus' flock. There are nuances of language here, however, that are often identified in the passage, and it may be helpful to outline the exchange in Greek.

> [15] Jesus: Do you love [*agapao*] me?   Peter: I love [*phileo*] you.
> [16] Jesus: Do you love [*agapao*] me?   Peter: I love [*phileo*] you.
> [17] Jesus: Do you love [*phileo*] me?   Peter: I love [*phileo*] you.

Interpreters have to make a decision. Do these two words for love convey some hidden difference of meaning? Some commentators have argued that *phileo* represents an inferior form of love and that Jesus is challenging Peter to elevate his level of commitment. In effect, Jesus asks Peter, "Do you possess a profound love for me?" and Peter responds, "Yes Lord, I am fond of you." In the end (21:17) Jesus reduces his expectation to Peter's humble and limited affections. This nuance is behind the NIV translation of "truly love" and "love" for the two verbs.

One of the problems with this view is that if the conversation took place in Aramaic, such variation in Greek would not have been present—although this explanation fails to recognize that John is using Greek to represent the nuances of the exchange and his choice of words remains important. Another difficulty is that Peter oddly says "yes" to Jesus two times when (according to the view that emphasizes the difference between *agapao* and *phileo*) he should have said "no." The two times Peter is asked, "Do you love [*agapao*] me?" Peter should then say, "No, Lord, I do not love you that deeply." But Peter seems to be acknowledging and accepting that he indeed bears the sort of love Jesus describes, even though he uses *phileo*.

This has led many exegetes to see the variation between *agapao* and *phileo* as insignificant and to understand these two words as synonyms. In the LXX, for instance, Jacob's love for Joseph is expressed with both verbs (Gen. 37:3–4). In Proverbs 8:17 both words are used to represent one

Hebrew verb. This is the view of major lexicons[23] as well as grammarians. N. Turner refers to John's regular use of "needless" synonyms in order to bring variety to his narratives.[24] John has two words each for love, send, heal, ask, speak, do, feed, sheep, and know, and in most cases these variations seem to merely avoid monotony.

Leon Morris echoes this sentiment: "There is no difference on the grounds of Johannine usage, for seeing a difference in meaning between these two verbs."[25] The focus of Peter's conversation with Jesus has to do with his commission to tend the flock of Christ, not the quality of his love for him. Peter is thus upset (21:17) not because Jesus has changed the verb for love, but because Jesus has asked him the same question for the third time.

The same sort of comment can be said for the charges given to Peter following each affirmation of love. Once again there is variation, but these word shifts bear no theological importance. Jesus commissions Peter three times to care for his "flock":

(1) Feed (*basko*) my lambs (*arnion*)
(2) Tend (*poimaino*) my sheep (*probaton*)
(3) Feed (*basko*) my sheep (*probaton*)

Attempts to find deeper meaning in the connections among these words should be viewed with utmost caution.

The Death of Peter and the Beloved Disciple (21:18–23)

DEATH AND GLORIFICATION are united so thoroughly in the Fourth Gospel that John regularly refers to Jesus' death simply as "his glorification" (e.g., 12:23). The same correlation now applies to Peter (21:19). Discipleship for Peter will include not simply a ministry tending the flock of Christ (21:15–17) but also martyrdom that glorifies God. "I tell you the truth" (NIV) reflects the double formula "truly, truly" (see comment on 1:51), an expression reserved for Jesus' most important sayings. Peter's youth was characterized by freedom. He dressed himself and was free to go where he desired. This may be a well-known proverb in Jesus' day.[26] Old age, by contrast, will be characterized by limitations. At this time Peter will have to be dressed and led about.

---

23. See BAGD, 4.

24. N. Turner, *A Grammar of New Testament Greek· Vol. 4 Style* (Edinburgh: T. & T. Clark, 1976), 76–77.

25. Morris, *John*, 770; also Barrett, *John*, 584, Carson, *John*, 676–77, and many more. For a thorough study of countless examples of Johannine variation, see L Morris, "Variation— A Feature of the Johannine Style," in his *Studies in the Fourth Gospel* (Grand Rapids. Eerdmans, 1969), 293–319.

26. Barrett, *John*, 585; Bultmann, *John*, 713.

While some interpreters think that Jesus is simply referring to Peter's dependence, a strong case can be made for typical Johannine double meaning. In another day, someone will "stretch out your hands," Jesus says to Peter. This language points clearly to crucifixion; the Greek word used here was used by many early Christian writers to represent death on the cross.[27] If this is true—and I am convinced it is—then we may also have one more allusion to crucifixion in 21:18. In old age, Peter will not be "dressed" (NIV), but "bound" (Gk. *zonnyo*), as many victims were "fastened" with ropes to the cross. Those who lead him will not be charitable, but will force him to go where he does not want to.

We should no doubt read these verses together with 13:36–38, where Peter makes his bold promise to "lay down his life" for Jesus. Indeed, Jesus promises, while Peter cannot go where Jesus is going now, Peter will "follow later." Jesus is anticipating his own hour of glorification, and both in 13:37 and in 21:18 he is prophesying Peter's fate. Peter *will* lay down his life for Jesus (13:38); he will be crucified too; he will likewise glorify God in the same manner as his Lord— but this must await a time in the future. "Follow me" in 21:19 now takes on a poignant and provocative new meaning. Peter will follow Jesus to the cross.

Interest now shifts to the Beloved Disciple in 21:20–23. This name appeared first in 13:23 (also 19:26; 20:2; 21:7, 20) and may also connect with an unnamed disciple at other key places (1:37; 19:36). Note that the "sons of Zebedee" accompanied Peter fishing (21:2), and this adds plausibility to the suggestion that this Beloved Disciple is John.[28] Throughout the Gospel this disciple is an exemplar of faithfulness and commitment. We are reminded, for instance, that it was he who spoke to Jesus about betrayal at their last meal (21:20b). He was faithful, standing with Jesus at the cross (19:26), and later he was the first to express faith at the empty tomb (20:8). Here at the shore, Peter is charged to "follow" Jesus (21:19), but we learn that John, the disciple whom Jesus loved, is "following" already (21:20). Again he is a model who on one level may be following nearby as Jesus talks privately with Peter, but who (on another level) is found to be the ideal "follower" whom Peter should emulate.

Encouraged perhaps by his own commission and restoration (21:22), Peter asks Jesus pointedly about John's fate, "Lord, what about him?" Will John have a similar commission? Will he share a similar glorious martyrdom? Do we dare sense in Peter's tone a rivalry that echoes the two men's race to the tomb (20:4)? Jesus' answer is nothing if not abrupt: It is not Peter's privilege to know how or

---

27. Barrett, *John*, 585, points to how Isa. 65:2 (LXX, "hands spread out") was used in *Ep. Barnabas* 12:4, Justin (*First Apol.* 35), Irenaeus (*Apost. Preaching*, 79), and Cyprian (*Test.* 2.20) as a foreshadowing of crucifixion.

28. See the Introduction and the explanation of authorship. For a suggestive defense of the Beloved Disciple as John, son of Zebedee, see Brown, *John*, 2:1119–20.

when John will die—or if, for that matter, John will remain alive until Jesus comes back in his powerful return (cf. 14:3; 1 John 2:28). Again, Jesus tells the apostle to *follow*, and this time the form is emphatic (cf. 21:19).[29] To paraphrase: "Peter, this matter is not your concern; it is mine. *You* have one duty: Follow me."

John 21:23 corrects what must have been an unusual misinterpretation of Jesus' words that had circulated for some time in the church. No doubt among John's followers many believed that their beloved leader would not die but would remain until Christ returned. Disciples in the Johannine church could thus keep their hope in the Second Coming alive and then increase their anticipation as John grew in age.

The problem, of course, is that once John died and Christ had not returned, the enemies of the church would have ample opportunity to ridicule Christian believers (2 Peter 3:4; cf. Matt. 16:28; 1 Thess. 4:15). The Gospel repeats Jesus' original words again (21:23b), suggesting that the same exhortation given to Peter perhaps should come to devout Christians. The Gospel uses an emphatic "but" in the second half of the verse (Gk. *alla*) as if to say, "*But* let's be clear—Jesus did *not* say that John would not die." As Peter should not speculate about John, so too should John's followers abandon any eschatology linked to the apostle's fate.

Has John already died? Exegetes are divided. Some believe that John is very old since one can hardly imagine his followers saying, "He will not die," if John is already dead. But others argue convincingly that 21:23 may serve another purpose. Perhaps John's followers once believed he would survive, but now he is dead, and the community has been thrown into disarray. They have built an eschatology hinged to his surviving and now all has collapsed. John's followers venerated his apostleship to such a degree that they now respond to the confusion caused by his death with an editorial explanation. It may also be at this time that they put the finishing touches on his Gospel (adding perhaps John's prologue and chapter 21?) and giving their leader his famous name, "the Beloved Disciple."

Validating John's Testimony (21:24–25)

JOHN'S DISCIPLES NOW explicitly affirm the veracity of their leader's work. When they write, "*We know* that his testimony is true" (italics added), at once we are alerted to their presence in the narrative. Here we have a third party standing between John's reliable testimony and ourselves as readers. With devotion and humility, they now pen the Gospel's closing frame.

This "Beloved Disciple" described in 21:21–23, the man whose intimate relationship with Jesus was a hallmark of his life, is affirmed as the eyewitness

---

29 The second call to follow uses the Greek emphatic pronoun *sy*.

source of the stories recorded in this Gospel. This disciple is no idealized figure of faith promoted in the narrative, but a genuine man whose life built a community of believers and whose death shook their confidence. He was a man who saw the events of Jesus' life (see 19:35) and wrote them down (21:24) so that other generations might benefit. "These things" (21:24) refer not simply to the episodes of chapter 21 but to the great span of the Gospel's larger narrative. Moreover, John is the final witness in a long line of witnesses (such as John the Baptist and a host of signs), who is supplying with his Gospel record the final testimony of evidence for Christ.

Are these writers and editors the elders of the church of Ephesus, as church tradition suggests? According to Clement of Alexandria, John wrote his Gospel only after his disciples and fellow bishops urged him to do so.[30] We cannot be certain of this tradition, but we must take the "we" of 21:24 seriously. John's ministry resulted in the birth of a community committed to the preservation of the apostolic witness. For them the things of Jesus were true because people like John had seen them in history and recorded them accurately. This Gospel is no fanciful speculation, no whimsical, inspired redrawing of Jesus' portrait. It is a record of what happened, given by a man who had seen it.[31]

The Gospel's closing verse may well stem from the hand of John himself (following the quick editorial insertion of 21:24).[32] John reminds us that there is far more to Jesus' life than what is recorded in his Gospel. This suggests again the possibility that John knew of other stories (Synoptic stories?) that he did not record (cf. 20:30). At best we can say that the Fourth Gospel is a partial rendering—but also a sufficient rendering—of a story whose scope surpasses any one effort.

With playful and delightful hyperbole, John says that even all the books of the world could not contain Jesus' story. Such expressions were common in antiquity. Rabbi Johanan ben Zakkai, a first-century teacher, wrote, "If all heaven were a parchment, and all the trees produced pens, and all the waters were ink, they would not suffice to inscribe the wisdom I have received from my teachers: and yet from the wisdom of the wise I have enjoyed only so much as the water a fly which plunges into the sea can remove."[33] John ends his Gospel with similar humility. The story is larger than anything he can imagine. His effort, while glorious for us to read, pales in comparison to the glory of the Person whom his story describes.

---

30. Eusebius, *Church History*, 6.14.7.

31. Morris provides an exhaustive survey of the entire Gospel, noting every evidence that John was an eyewitness to what he records. See "Was the Author of the Fourth Gospel an 'Eyewitness'?" in L. Morris, *Studies in the Fourth Gospel* (Grand Rapids: Eerdmans, 1969), 139–214.

32. Scholars point to a change in style in 21:25; "I suppose . . ." sets this final verse apart from 21:24.

33. Cited in Hoskyns, *John*, 561.

THE WORK OF THE CHURCH. In many respects this chapter-long epilogue serves the Gospel much like the final verses of Matthew, Mark, and Luke. Matthew ends his Gospel with the Great Commission, where Jesus takes his followers to a Galilee mountain and charges them to go into the world and make disciples (Matt. 28:16–20). This charge focuses on the church and its work, empowering and commissioning the disciples to nurture and tend the followers of Jesus. Luke's ending is similar (24:44–53); he shifts the focus to Jerusalem, where Jesus calls them to be his witnesses in the world—men and women empowered by the Holy Spirit, who will testify concerning the events of Jesus' life and bring new followers into discipleship. Again, the topic is the church and its work. Although Mark's longer ending (Mark 16:9–20) is surely inauthentic, a later scribe sensed the need to supplement the dramatic ending of 16:8 by including similar themes. The disciples are commissioned to go to the world as preachers, recreating the powerful signs of Jesus and bringing new believers into the community of faith. Once again, the story of Jesus ends with an emphasis on the church and its work in the world.

This closing frame of the Gospel of John echoes these same interests but supplements them with concerns of its own. These are not stories that affirm the reality of the resurrection or the truth of Jesus' message. The fishing miracle of chapter 21 is *not* a sign for unbelievers, compelling them to believe in the resurrected Christ. Chapter 21 is an epilogue addressed to the church and its responsibilities and work in the world. The principal story in the chapter—the great catch of fish and Jesus' subsequent conversation around the morning fire—reinforces the apostolic commission to take responsibility for those who come into the kingdom of Christ. Peter is to be fisherman and shepherd; some followers even may be called to be martyrs, but each has a task to glorify God by obediently following Jesus.

We have seen secondary, symbolic meanings throughout this Gospel. John delights in using irony and wordplay, but we have also seen that due caution is in order when we look for these meanings. The catch of fish, for instance, likely has little numerical symbolism. This is simply a miracle of abundance not unlike the enormous volume of wine in Cana (ch. 2) or Jesus' distribution of bread (ch. 6). Nevertheless the miraculous sign may symbolize the work of Peter that now Jesus wishes to direct. It is no accident that the Beloved Disciple points us to what is most important in the story. This is his literary role on many occasions. He is the one who recognizes Jesus' identity (21:7) when others cannot; and when Peter races to the shore, he is the one who stays with the fish, bringing them laboriously to land. Peter's zeal is outdone again by John's perception and insight. The fish—as practical gift and symbol of divine work—must not be neglected.

Jesus wants to direct his followers to the tasks that will continue his work in the world. The Spirit, which they now possess (20:22), is not merely a private gift of reassurance and comfort. It is an equipping that should inspire their witness in the world (15:26–27) and strengthen them for the confrontations that will inevitably come (16:7–11). It will mean pastoral work that mediates to the world knowledge of Christ's saving work (20:23), which gathers new believers into a new flock (10:16)—a flock that Christ had not yet gathered, but which he now desires to build. The work of Christ is now the work of the church, his disciples—focused narrowly in this chapter on Peter—who must feed and tend the sheep of Jesus (21:15–17).

Secondary themes. There are also a couple of secondary themes that anticipate this primary message of Jesus' instructions for work in the church. (1) The story of Peter's reconciliation to Jesus is a story of Peter's healing. It is no accident that Peter, the man who denied Jesus three times following a bravado-filled promise of faithfulness, now affirms his love for Christ three times. Much can (and ought) to be said for ministers and laypersons who work for Christ but need to have their own confidence in their relationship with him healed.

(2) The gentle rivalry between Peter and the Beloved Disciple reaches its peak in this chapter. We do not have enough information to probe beneath the surface to learn what transpired between these two men. But in 21:21 Peter finally unmasks his feelings: "Lord, what about him? What about this other man on the margin of our conversation? Will his death rival mine in bringing you glory?" Jesus' rebuke is a rebuke to each of us.

(3) In order to develop John 21 for an audience today, we should also probe the personal issues in Peter's life and make them a paradigm for personal health in ministry today. The work of the church—the gathering of fish, the nurture of sheep—cannot go forward unless its ministers are healed of their histories and renewed by God's Spirit.

 CHAPTER 21 IS about discipleship and leadership. As its story unfolds, Peter remains in the spotlight (along with the Beloved Disciple, John), modeling for us what it means to shepherd the flock of Christ. The disciples have now not only witnessed the resurrection of Jesus, but they have experienced the Spirit. They know the truth and have experienced the Spirit of truth. One question remains: What will they do with

it? Will they simply privatize these spiritual moments with Jesus or will these moments lead them somewhere significant?

The miraculous catch of fish no doubt is *symbol* as well as *surprise*. Jesus is still the disciples' champion, aiding them in the struggle of their labors. But more, he wants to direct their work, and with his help they will find catches beyond their wildest belief. This symbolism can be applied to the church and its work. As Jesus worked through the direction of the Father, so too the disciples must work at the word of Jesus. He is a coworker and with him success is assured.

But with a mix of metaphors, this "catch of fish" now must become a flock that these men learn to nurture and tend. They must look to the model of shepherding given by Jesus, both in his life and in his words (ch. 10). The charge given to Peter must become the charge heard by contemporary church leaders today. Christ's church needs decisive leaders. This has been the case throughout the church's two thousand-year history. But many who would claim to play that role bear the weaknesses and shortcomings shown to us in the life of Peter. In fact, we may well see Peter's literary role in the chapter as a reflection of our own leadership, complete with its personal struggles and wounds. Through Peter's healing we may gain insight into our own.

Peter and Jesus. One of the first pilgrims to visit the Holy Land and record her experiences was a woman named Egeria. Little is known of her except that she traveled from the Atlantic coast of Europe and spent three years in the Holy Land (A.D. 381–384). Fourth-century travel was dangerous and arduous and her courage must have astounded the many bishops who met her. Egeria was eager to visit monasteries as well as holy sites; she also desired to participate in Jerusalem's ceremonies from Lent to Easter, and it is from her pen that we have a record of Jerusalem's most ancient liturgies.[34]

On her visit to Galilee she made a point of locating a site with "Seven Springs" called in Greek "Heptapagon."[35] Her interest here centered on the feeding miracles of Jesus. On Galilee's north shore she was taken to a small Byzantine church. She was escorted to a stone altar and told that this is where Jesus offered his disciples bread and fish in John 21. By the ninth century the site gained the name "The Place of Coals," because Jesus had built a "charcoal fire" there (21:9) and cooked fish on it. This was an important destination for this remarkable woman because it recalled a moment in time that transformed one man's life.

---

34 A comprehensive, annotated edition of Egeria's travels is found in J. Wilkinson, *Egeria's Travels to the Holy Land* (Jerusalem: Ariel Publishing, 1981).

35. Today this site, just west of Capernaum, takes the Arabic title Tabgha, which originated from the Greek word Heptapagon. There are "seven fresh water springs" at this site.

Today Protestants rarely take the time to visit this beautiful Franciscan site with its cultivated grounds and gardens.[36] The church steps seen by Egeria (possibly cut in the second or third century) are still visible as well as the shoreline used by Jesus to call his disciples to breakfast. The Franciscans also commissioned what is arguably the finest statue in Galilee adjacent to the shoreline chapel. It offers a life-size portrayal of Peter, who has now met his Lord on the beach. We also see Jesus, renewing his love for Peter and commissioning him. Jesus towers over Peter, both forgiving and commissioning this great man of God. Christians who visit the site sense what Egeria knew. Something momentous transpired here, and it speaks not just of Peter but of us.

Peter made a terrible mistake. His triple denial at Jesus' interrogation is one of the few stories shared by the four Gospels. Knowledge of it was widespread among the evangelists, and it was deemed to be such an important episode that none chose to omit it. Luke notes not only that Peter denied Jesus, but at the crowing of the cock, Jesus (who must have been in the high priest's courtyard) looked directly at him. Peter immediately remembered his promises of faithfulness as well as Jesus' prediction. He then went out and wept bitterly (Luke 22:62).

True ministry now was impossible for Peter. On the one hand, he could have spent the balance of his life working for the kingdom and promoting faith in Jesus. He could have become one of the most zealous apostles, intolerant of those who might compromise, inflexible with any who didn't take discipleship with utmost seriousness. All of this energy would look excellent on the surface, but it would have been mere compensation—perhaps even overcompensation—for the failings of his earlier life. This sort of Christianity (so familiar to ardent conservatives) is destructive. It produces a spiritual regimen that is merely a Protestant penance. "Because I failed God, because I have failed myself, I have a lot to make up for." Such a ministry knows nothing of the "rejoicing heart" Jesus promised to his followers in John 16:22.

On the other hand, Peter could have become a man filled with despair. Seeing his own weakness so directly, knowing that Jesus had seen it and now even his fellow apostles knew about it, how could he still enjoy anyone's respect? Yes, Peter could have continued in ministry, having packed away the burden of his sin in some of the deepest recesses of his heart. But it would have eroded his soul. Self-criticism, depression, and a spiritual pessimism (disguised as a "theology of the cross") would have characterized his work.

---

36. From the Chapel of the Multiplication of the Loaves and the Fishes (traditional Tabgha) walk out to the main road and turn right, walking five minutes (east). The gated entrance will be on your right.

This burden would have sapped his energy; but because of his fear of disappointing himself and God once more, he could not quit. Without realizing it, the Christianity he promoted would become destructive to himself and to others. Any ministry like this also knows nothing of the "rejoicing heart" Jesus promised in the Upper Room in John 16.

Jesus wanted none of this. His first plan was a gift of such good humor I can just imagine him smiling as he contemplated his friends hauling in a net full of fish. He had done this once before at the lakeshore (see Luke 5:1–11). Early in his ministry he got their attention with a dramatic catch of fish, and this launched their ministries together in Galilee. "I will teach you to catch people," he said. And (Luke notes) they left their boats and followed him. Now Jesus must get their attention again by evoking an old memory. When Peter saw his net filled to capacity, the apostolic squeals from this apostolic boat could likely be heard for miles.

When Peter learned that it was Jesus who had done this—the fishing-miracle-worker Jesus—it is no accident that he ran to the shore. He ran to the only one who could heal his memories, who could rewrite the terrible pictures and sounds of his recent past—the courtyard, the charcoal fire, the young woman. The miracle demonstrated that despite Peter's failings, Jesus was still on his side, cooking a good meal for friends, having fun filling nets with fish. Then the invitation to affirm his love three times drowned out the echoes of his betrayal that haunted him. The last time Peter stood over a *charcoal* fire, he denied Jesus (18:18). Now Jesus makes him stand over another *charcoal* fire (21:9) and with it, review old memories and remove them.

Many pastors and laypersons in ministry need to visit the shores of Tabgha in Galilee and reread John 21. The work of the church can only go forward when we are unburdened of our destructive memories through the gracious forgiveness of God. When this happens, we will be empowered and transformed and made ready to represent Jesus with a rejoicing heart.[37]

Peter and John. We have had a number of occasions to note the not-so-subtle comparison made between Peter and the Beloved Disciple (or John). Throughout the latter parts of the Gospel, John appears as a man of remarkable insight and wisdom. He is the one who enjoys an intimate conversation with Jesus in the Upper Room (13:21–30) while Peter must make his inquiries through him. In chapter 18 he is also known to the high priest, which gains Peter access to the courtyard. And when Jesus is on the cross, John stands faithfully with Jesus' mother, not only lending support but also serving as a

---

37. There is a great deal of literature on the healing of memories. Two excellent sources are D. and M. Linn, *Healing Life's Hurts; Healing Memories Through Five Stages of Forgiveness* (New York: Paulist, 1988), and Francis MacNutt, *Healing* (Anniversary Edition; Notre Dame, Ind. Ave Maria, 1999).

witness to Jesus' suffering and death (19:25–37). While Peter may race first to the empty tomb, John looks in and believes (20:1–10). Now in the present episode, it is John who recognizes Jesus (Peter seems oblivious) and while Peter sprints to shore, John remains behind hauling the fish to shore (20:1–14).

In the history of the interpretation of John, scholars have tried to attach some fairly grand theories to this so-called rivalry. For instance, some have argued that these two characters were merely symbols of two rival churches—one Greek, one Jewish—that struggled for dominance in the first century.[38] The trouble with such theories is not only their speculative nature, but their denial of any historical reminiscence in the Gospel. I prefer to see this as a genuine reflection of Peter and John's relationship. All sources portray Peter as a strong leader, impulsive perhaps, but nevertheless possessing valuable skills. This is possibly why Jesus cultivates him as a leader along with James and John in the Synoptic Gospels. In our present chapter Peter announces, "I'm going out to fish" (21:3), and the others follow. As the story in Acts unfolds, Peter's prominence and strength are underscored so that he becomes a vital and trusted leader in the early church.

The Synoptic picture also places John within this inner circle of disciple-leaders. He is invited to observe some of Jesus' most powerful miracles (Mark 5:37) and even to witness Jesus' transfiguration (9:2). In the early chapters of Acts, John joins Peter as they become articulate defenders of the faith. A casual reading of the letters of John demonstrates that this apostle likewise possessed many leadership traits. Able to confront and decisive in thought, John understands the heresy that has gripped his community and has chosen to fight it.

But John has one characteristic that sets him apart. The style of his Gospel and the form of his letters hint at it. John is a perceptive, abstract thinker. He probes the inner meaning of Jesus, and what he may have lacked in Peter's personal presence, he makes up for in his faith, insight, and intelligence. His Gospel's prologue, for instance, reaches heights of discovery unmatched in any other Gospel.

Two strong men; one Christian movement. Yet John possessed intuitive skills that permitted him to grasp aspects of Christ's personhood in a way that may have eluded others. The leadership of the body of Christ demands a diversity of gifts, and John possessed his own unique set. For this we can be thankful. When in later centuries Christian theologians debated the nature of the Trinity or the character of the Incarnation, they frequently turned to John's writing to help them sort through the issues.

---

38. This was the view of the nineteenth-century Tübingen theologian Ferdinand Christian Baur (1792–1860).

Thus the ministries of John and Peter would be different. Peter would be the shepherd, John the seer; Peter the preacher, John the penman; Peter the foundational witness, John the faithful writer; Peter would die in the agony and passion of martyrdom, John would live on to a great age and pass away in quiet serenity.[39]

Following Jesus' reaffirmation of his commitment to Peter (and Peter's love for Jesus), Jesus discloses that Peter will some day follow him in martyrdom. This will be an opportunity when his courage and strength will glorify God. But rather than thinking about his own discipleship, Peter does something that surprises us: He wants to know how John will fare. Will John likewise have this opportunity? Will this become another moment of one-upmanship for Peter? Jesus' rebuke in 21:22 is firm.

Personal competition and rivalry destroy the work of the church. Men and women with differing gifts frequently find themselves looking over their shoulder at someone else (as Peter noticed John), wondering if another's successes are outpacing their own. This is another good reason for us to visit the shores of Tabgha on Galilee. This is the site not simply of Peter's restoration to Jesus Christ, but the scene of Jesus' exhortation. Peter's healing thus had to move in two directions. Christ's flock has need of many shepherds and (thankfully) each will bring to the community a variety of gifts.[40]

Peter and the church. Peter's restoration to Christ makes possible his service to the church. Jesus' command to feed and tend his sheep becomes Peter's mandate for life. He affirms his love for Jesus, but now he understands that this means a great deal more. Jesus does not come to us as a "single person" (as it were), unattached. He is "married," and the bride whom he loves and for which he sacrifices himself is the church (Eph. 5:25).[41] To be in a relationship with Christ and to love him genuinely means that we must also love the church. For us to disparage the church is no more acceptable to Jesus than for us (in a human context) to disparage our good friend's spouse.

Peter—and each of us—is called to embrace the body of Christ, to love it, to tend it, and to protect it. A quick glimpse at Peter's letters gives some insight into the depth of his commitment to this mission. In later years Peter wrote to later church leaders who were expected to take up the same commission:

---

39. B. Milne, *The Message of John* (Downers Grove: InterVarsity, 1993), 319.

40. An interesting exploration of different personalities and how this relates to spiritual formation can be found in C. P. Michael and M. C. Norrisey, *Prayer and Temperament: Different Prayer Forms for Different Personality Types* (Charlottesville, Va.: Open Door, 1991). The authors use the Myers-Briggs Type Indicator to create paradigms and frequently interpret New Testament characters through them.

41. Milne, *The Message of John*, 318.

To the elders among you, I appeal as a fellow elder, a witness of Christ's sufferings and one who also will share in the glory to be revealed: Be shepherds of God's flock that is under your care, serving as overseers—not because you must, but because you are willing, as God wants you to be; not greedy for money, but eager to serve; not lording it over those entrusted to you, but being examples to the flock. And when the Chief Shepherd appears, you will receive the crown of glory that will never fade away. (1 Peter 5:1–4)

The chief images of John 21 (fish and sheep) both speak to us about the work of the church. We must gather up those to whom Christ directs us and nurture those who live in his flock. This is labor, divinely directed labor that must be inspired by our devotion to Christ.

But note that Jesus participates in these efforts too. We misuse the story of the great catch of fish if we use it to illustrate the work Christ has for us to do. We often view the story as Jesus' exhortation for Peter to give his fishing "one more try." With extra effort, with diligent work, with persistence that goes beyond our fatigue, Jesus can bless because he will join us in fruitful labor, serving the church. But this is not the meaning of the story. To throw a cast net into the ocean, especially after sunup and when no encircling net is present, is an act of desperation. No expert fisherman would assume he could make a significant catch.

Jesus is not calling for renewed skill or renewed energy, but for faith. He has challenged Peter to do what may appear ridiculous or fanciful. But in doing it, Peter discovers unmistakably that the fruit of his labor is a gift from God. No energy or expertise can make a catch like this. Thus Jesus desires to participate in our labors, and at his direction the burden of our work will be lifted.

But how does Jesus continue to participate in the labor of the church? How does he assist his shepherds in their work? This answer is found in the sustained emphasis on the Holy Spirit not only in the pages of John's Gospel, but also in the five short letters penned by Peter and John. Each man understood that the Spirit is not merely an ambiguous spiritual influence, but is rather the Spirit of Jesus himself living in his followers (1 Peter 1:11; 1 John 3:24; cf. John 14:23). The work of the church, therefore, is not religious energy fueled by our sense of commission; it is a call to work, wed to a divine empowering; it is ministering knowing that Christ himself (through the Spirit) is ministering in and through our efforts.

Ministry is thus the service of healed men and women who understand their personal histories (and handicaps) well, who have made their brokenness transparent before God and been forgiven as well as transformed by the Spirit of God. They are fishermen (seeking those Christ calls them to "net") and shepherds (nurturing those who have joined the flock). But above all they are people who love the church *because they love Jesus Christ*. As he was the good Shepherd, so they strive to be good shepherds, serving and leading and in some cases (as with Peter) discovering that sacrifice may be included in their call.

This realization of sacrifice (even to death) remained with Peter throughout his life. In 2 Peter 1:12—15 the apostle wrote about his life and the reality of his death. His ministry always took on a marked degree of intensity since (he writes) "I know that my death will come soon, *as indeed our Lord Jesus Christ has made clear to me*" (2 Peter 1:14 NRSV).

Such good shepherds are not people whose ministry promotes ego and personal glory, who disguise their own ambitions in pursuits of "excellence" in so-called great churches and institutions (ministries, denominations, colleges, or mission agencies). These are not people whose competitiveness harms other shepherds, who always look over their shoulder to see if someone else will enjoy a parallel glory. These are men and women who simply hear Jesus' words, "Follow me," and obey, thinking about their own discipleship more than that of others.

The result is a rich life that glorifies God in humility as it bears witness to Jesus (21:24). Peter understands this lesson given by Jesus on the lakeshore. His pastoral exhortations in his two letters point again and again to the demeanor of the Christian leader: "Therefore, rid yourselves of all malice and all deceit, hypocrisy, envy, and slander of every kind" (1 Peter 2:1). "Now that you have purified yourselves by obeying the truth so that you have sincere love for your brothers, love one another deeply, from the heart" (1:22). Peter is a pastor whose heart has been purged of envy and comparison, which facilitates the great love he has for the sheep he tends.

This profile no doubt describes the life of John as well. He has written his Gospel and supplied us with his testimony. His three letters show that he was a man who loved the church and defended it with all his might. John's disciples knew that he was the "Beloved Disciple" because Jesus held a special affection for him. But this title also has another meaning (have we not seen countless double meanings in this Gospel?). This amazing title also describes one church's love for its own shepherd. John was *likewise* beloved among those he led, and this Gospel, this beloved Gospel now concluded by his devoted disciples, stands as a memorial of John's witness and work for the church.

Scripture Index

Subject Index